American | Government

POWER AND PURPOSE

10TH CORE EDITION

American | Government

POWER AND PURPOSE

THEODORE J. LOWI
CORNELL UNIVERSITY

BENJAMIN GINSBERG
THE JOHN HOPKINS UNIVERSITY

KENNETH A. SHEPSLE
HARVARD UNIVERSITY

W. W. NORTON & COMPANY
NEW YORK · LONDON

W. W. Norton & Company has been independent since its founding in 1923, when William Warder Norton and Mary D. Herter Norton first published lectures delivered at the People's Institute, the adult education division of New York City's Cooper Union. The firm soon expanded its program beyond the Institute, publishing books by celebrated academics from America and abroad. By mid-century, the two major pillars of Norton's publishing program—trade books and college texts—were firmly established. In the 1950s, the Norton family transferred control of the company to its employees, and today—with a staff of four hundred and a comparable number of trade, college, and professional titles published each year—W. W. Norton & Company stands as the largest and oldest publishing house owned wholly by its employees.

Manufacturing by Quebecor World—Taunton Division
Editor: Ann Shin
Manuscript editor: Abigail Winograd
Project editor: Lory A. Frenkel
Electronic media editor: Dan Jost
Graphic artist: John McAusland
Book design by Anna Palchik
Production manager: Jane Searle
Editorial assistant: Mollie Eisenberg

ISBN 978-0-393-11385-3 (pbk.)

W. W. Norton & Company Inc.
500 Fifth Avenue, New York, N.Y. 10110
www.wwnorton.com

W. W. Norton & Company Ltd.
Castle House, 75/76 Wells Street, London W1T 3QT
1 2 3 4 5 6 7 8 9 0

FOR OUR FAMILIES

Angele, Anna, and Jason Lowi
Sandy, Cindy, and Alex Ginsberg
Rise, Nilsa, and Seth Shepsle

CONTENTS

PART 2   INSTITUTIONS   177

PART 3   POLITICS   377

APPENDIX   A1

PREFACE

THIS BOOK WAS WRITTEN for faculty and students who are looking for a little more than just "nuts and bolts" and who are drawn to an analytical perspective. Most Americans are at least somewhat familiar with the politics and government of their own country. No fact about the government is intrinsically difficult to grasp, and in such an open society, facts abound. In the United States information about the government is readily available that would be suppressed elsewhere. The ubiquity of information can be a problem when the sheer quantity of facts and news overwhelms us, but it can be turned into a virtue. Common knowledge about the government gives us a vocabulary that is widely shared, and enables us to communicate effectively at the most basic level of the book, avoiding professional jargon. However, reaching beyond the common knowledge identifies what is, to us, the single most important task of the teacher of political science—confronting the popular ideas and choosing from among them the small number of really significant concepts. This book aims to help instructors and students accomplish that task.

The first of our two prefaces is addressed to students taking the course, and it is designed to appeal to every student's personal self-interest. Students will hear a lot about the "rationality principle" in the assigned chapters; we will apply the same principle in this preface by demonstrating how easy and valuable it will be to gain the essential knowledge of government and politics. Preface II is aimed at the teacher, to provide an awareness of our pedagogy.

PREFACE I—TO THE STUDENT

Let us begin with our pledge to you: We are not here to tell you what to think. We are here to tell you what to think about, and to offer an analytical framework for thinking about it. Our objective is to reveal some of the reasons that it is in your rational self-interest to increase your knowledge of American government by taking this book seriously.

Are you ready? We begin with a pop quiz to test your understanding of American government and politics. Imagine that a new amendment to the Constitution has been adopted, with a new rule that U.S. citizenship will be granted only to residents age 18 and above, native born or immigrant, who correctly answer 12 of the following 16 items. This quiz is entirely confidential. You can keep your own score, and you will have only yourself to praise or blame.

A Citizenship Quiz

Among the various branches and levels of government and, among all our government agencies, where would you go:

1. for a driver's license?
2. for a marriage license?
3. for car registration?
4. for a license to practice law?
5. for a license to practice medicine?
6. to register sale of a piece of property?
7. if arrested for assault?
8. to complain about your child's education?
9. to pass your estate down to your children?
10. to sue Phillip Morris for your cancer?
11. to register to vote?
12. to become a candidate for Congress?
13. to become a candidate for city council?
14. to form a new political party?
15. to lobby members of Congress?
16. to join the National Guard?

Here's how to evaluate the results:

1. If you answered "national government" to any of the items, you're incorrect.

2. If you answered "don't know" or incorrectly to four or more of the items, you flunk.

3. You'll find the correct answers in this book, but you'll also end up with a lot more questions, along with answers to questions that have not yet been asked.

How can there be a civic knowledge gap in a media culture such as ours? It seems virtually impossible for Americans to be unfamiliar with our government and its politics—with the latest developments in the Middle East, in Congress with its Democratic majority versus a Republican president, with budget deficits, international trade, and immigration. But issues change from day to day, new issues replace older ones, and the newer the issue the more prominent the treatment. We become jammed and bored with issues, and to a certain extent we have to forget yesterday's concerns to make room for tomorrow's. We are overwhelmed with *information* but often lacking in *knowledge.* To have knowledge, we must have the concepts and categories to organize information in meaningful ways. We have to classify issues and then provide some kind of context to give them meaning. Bear in mind: a poem is a lot easier to memorize and recite than an equal number of unconnected words and syllables. A good textbook is not poetry but it seeks to provide structure and context for the enormous flow of otherwise unconnected pieces of information about politics.

As we shall see, institutions and policies are the rules, relatively permanent restraints within which politics in all its forms is played. Yes, it's true, politics is something of a game. Whether we're players in the game or treat it as a spectator sport, we have to know the rules. Newcomers from distant cultures who watch our football or baseball for the first time may be totally bewildered. But turn the tables, Americans, and watch the game of cricket. Most of us would be equally bewildered. We don't know the players or their positions, their strange bats and balls, where the bases are set up, what the rules are, what constitutes a score (the hardest part of understanding the game), or what strategies and tactics of play are most effective. The game of American politics is even more complicated than cricket; without knowledge, it is a series of highly confusing movements, events, and issues that have little meaning. Our book guides you through the American game of politics.

PREFACE II—TO THE TEACHER

Preface I concluded with a recognition that politics is, to a great extent, a kind of game. But a book about politics needs an additional metaphor. A good teaching book has to be more like serious fiction, which is written on two levels. One is the level of the narrative: the story line, the characters, the action. The second is the level of character development, the argument, and the moral of the story. This book is full of narrative, with the characters and the complex situations in which the characters find themselves. We are equally determined to keep the second level in sight with an argument about how we can understand the "narrative" developments.

Although we emphasized the knowledge gap in Preface I, our collective experience as teachers has taught us not to underestimate our students. Their raw intelligence cries out for that second level, providing a logic and context linking the disparate parts of what we are treating as a single system of government and politics. These linkages have to be made in ordinary language—which we ardently hope we have maintained in this book.

We have tried to enrich the student-teacher discourse by going beyond the nuts and bolts into a carefully prepared analytical perspective. We provide a distinct pedagogy, which will readily be understood by the teacher as an integration of the historical-institutional perspective with a rational-choice perspective. We help bring the students into the discourse with a set of tools—the "Five Principles of Politics"—that enable them to think analytically about government and politics. We have developed this framework through the two previous editions of the book based on the encouragements and criticisms we received from adopters and reviewers of the text.

This pedagogy is based on the belief that we can transcend the clutter by repeated applications of a small number of the core ideas of our discipline. The book's analytic approach is incorporated through repeated emphasis on these five fundamental principles as tools for analysis throughout each chapter:

1. All political behavior has a purpose.
2. All politics is collective action.
3. Institutions routinely solve collective-action problems.
4. Political outcomes are the products of individual preferences and institutional procedures.
5. History matters.

Numerous pedagogical features apply this framework and the analytical approach to the topic of each chapter:

1. **A "Previewing the Principles" box at the beginning of each chapter** focuses students on the most important ways the principles will help them understand the material in the chapter.

2. **An "analytic narrative" ties the five principles together.** Each time one of the five principles is used in the analysis, a marginal icon appears, reminding students of the core principle. A **"Principles of Politics in Review" box** at the end of the chapter revisits the ways that the principles were used in the chapter.

3. **NEW "Analyzing the Evidence" units in every chapter** take a closer look at the ways political scientists analyze data (both quantitative and qualitative) to understand some political phenomenon discussed in the chapter. These two-page spreads use a highly visual format to help students see *how we know what we know* about a specific topic.

4. **NEW "Applying the Principles: Politics in the News" units in every chapter** present recent articles from the *New York Times* to show students how to use the five principles to understand the political situations reported in the news, ranging from recent decisions about energy policy, to questions about presidential power in the war on terror, to debates about immigration legislation.

5. **Online exercises based on "Applying the Principles" and "Analyzing the Evidence"** help students build their analytical skills through active learning. To preview these exercises, go to wwnorton.com/lowi.

6. **A NEW Online Reader** is closely integrated with the text and includes over 100 of the recent articles and classic works cited in the text. An "online reading" icon next to the citation signals sources that are represented in the online reader. Access to the online reader is free with new copies of the text.

For our 10th edition, we have profited greatly from the guidance of many teachers who have used the 9th or earlier editions, and from the suggestions of numerous thoughtful reviewers. We thank each of them by name in the acknowledgments. We recognize that there is no one-best-way to craft an introductory text, and we are grateful for the advice that we have received.

Theodore J. Lowi
Benjamin Ginsberg
Kenneth A. Shepsle

ACKNOWLEDGMENTS

Our students at Cornell, Johns Hopkins, and Harvard have already been identified as an essential factor in the writing of this book. They have been our most immediate intellectual community, a hospitable one indeed. Another part of our community, perhaps a large suburb, is the discipline of political science itself. Our debt to the scholarship of our colleagues is scientifically measurable, probably to several decimal points, in the footnotes of each chapter. Despite many complaints that the field is too scientific or not scientific enough, political science is alive and well in the United States. It is an aspect of democracy itself, and it has grown and changed in response to the developments in government and politics that we have chronicled in our book. If we created a time line on the history of political science, it would show a close association with developments in "the American state." Sometimes the discipline has been out of phase and critical; at other times, it has been in phase and perhaps apologetic. But political science has never been at a loss for relevant literature, and without that literature, our job would have been impossible.

There have, of course, been individuals on whom we have relied in particular. Of all writers, living and dead, we find ourselves most in debt to two—James Madison and Alexis de Tocqueville. Many other great authors have shaped us as they have shaped all political scientists. But Madison and Tocqueville have stood for us not only as the bridge to all timeless political problems but also as representations of the ideal of political science itself—that political science must be steadfastly scientific in the search for what is, yet must keep alive a strong sense of what ought to be, recognizing that democracy is neither natural nor invariably good, and must be fiercely dedicated to constant critical analysis of all political institutions in order to contribute to the maintenance of a favorable balance between individual freedom and public power.

We are pleased to acknowledge our debt to the many colleagues who had a direct and active role in criticism and preparation of the manuscript. The First Edition was read and reviewed by Gary Bryner, Brigham Young University; James F. Herndon, Virginia Polytechnic Institute and State University; James W. Riddlesperger, Jr., Texas Christian University; John Schwarz, University of Arizona; Toni-Michelle Travis, George Mason University; and Lois Vietri, University of Maryland. We also want to reiterate our thanks to the four colleagues who allowed us the privilege of testing a trial edition of our book by using it as the major text in their introductory American Government courses: Gary Bryner, Brigham Young University; Allan J. Cigler, University of Kansas; Burnet V. Davis, Albion College; and Erwin A. Jaffe, California State University—Stanislaus.

For subsequent editions, we relied heavily on the thoughtful manuscript reviews we received from David Canon, University of Wisconsin; Russell Hanson, Indiana University; William Keech, Carnegie Mellon University; Donald Kettl, University of Wisconsin; Anne Khademian, University of Wisconsin; William McLauchlan, Purdue University; J. Roger Baker, Wittenburg University; James Lennertz, Lafayette College; Allan McBride, Grambling State University; Joseph Peek, Jr., Georgia State University; Grant Neeley, Texas Tech University; Mark Graber, University of Maryland; John Gilmour, College of William and Mary; Victoria Farrar-Myers, University of Texas at Arlington; Timothy Boylan, Winthrop University; Robert Huckfeldt, University of California—Davis; Mark Joslyn, University of Kansas; Beth Leech, Rutgers University; Charles Noble, California State University, Long Beach.

For the Eighth Edition, we benefited from the comments of Scott Ainsworth, University of Georgia; Thomas Brunell, Northern Arizona University; Daniel Carpenter, Harvard University; Brad Gomez, University of South Carolina; Paul Gronke, Reed College; Marc Hetherington, Bowdoin College; Gregory Huber, Yale University; Robert Lowry, Iowa State University; and Anthony Nownes, University of Tennessee; Scott Adler, University of Colorado—Boulder; John Coleman, University of Wisconsin—Madison; Richard Conley, University of Florida; Keith Dougherty, University of Georgia; John Ferejohn, Stanford University; Douglas Harris, Loyola College; Brian Humes, University of Nebraska—Lincoln; Jeffrey Jenkins, Northwestern University; Paul Johnson, University of Kansas; Andrew Polsky, Hunter College—CUNY; Mark Richards, Grand Valley State University; Charles Shipan, University of Iowa; Craig Volden, Ohio State University; and Garry Young, George Washington University.

For the Ninth Edition, we were guided by the comments of John Baughman; Lawrence Baum, Ohio State University; Chris Cooper, Western Carolina State University; Charles Finochiaro, State University of New York—Buffalo; Lisa Garcia-Bellorda, University of California—Irvine; Sandy Gordon, New York University; Steven Greene, North Carolina State University; Richard Herrera, Arizona State University; Ben Highton, University of California—Davis; Trey Hood, University of Georgia; Andy Karch, University of Texas—Austin; Glen Krutz, University of Oklahoma; Paul Labedz, Valencia Community College; Brad Lockerbie, University of Georgia; Wendy Martinek, State University of New York—Binghamton; Nicholas Miller, University of Maryland Baltimore County; Russell Renka, Southeast Missouri State University; Debbie Schildkraut, Tufts University; Charles Shipan, University of Iowa; Chris Shortell, California State University, Northridge; John Sides, University of Texas—Austin; Sean Theriault, University of Texas—Austin; and Lynn Vavreck, University of California, Los Angeles.

Most recently, for the Tenth Edition, we were grateful for the detailed comments of Christian Grose, Vanderbilt University; Kevin Esterling, University of California—Riverside; Martin Johnson, University of California—Riverside; Scott Meinke, Bucknell University; Jason MacDonald, Kent State University; Alan Wiseman, Ohio State University; Michelle Swers, Georgetown University; William Hixon, Lawrence University; Gregory Koger, University of Miami; and Renan Levine, University of Toronto.

We owe thanks to Greg Wawro of Columbia University, who served as an intellectual bridge between the Sixth and Seventh Editions, and helped us set our sights for future editions of the book. We owe a debt to Paul Gronke of Reed College for authoring the "Applying the Principles: Politics in the News" features. We also are grateful for the talents and hard work of several research assistants, most recently Sean Richard Boutin.

Jacqueline Pastore not only typed several drafts of the manuscript, but also helped to hold the project together. We thank her for her hard work and dedication.

An important contribution to the Tenth Edition was made by the authors of the new "Analyzing the Evidence" units. Jamie Carson of the University of Georgia authored the "Analyzing the Evidence" spreads for Chapters 5, 6, 7, 8, 10, and 11. Dan Kapust, also of the University of Georgia, authored the spreads in Chapters 1, 2, 3, and 12. John Sides of George Washington University wrote the "Analyzing the Evidence" units for Chapters 9 and 13. We thank the three of them for their excellent contributions to the book. We also thank Erin Ackerman of John Jay College, who spent many hours helping to assemble and edit the readings included in the accompanying online reader.

Perhaps above all, we wish to thank those who kept the production and all the loose ends of this Tenth Edition coherent and in focus. Ann Shin has been a talented editor, offering numerous suggestions for this edition. Lory Frenkel has been a superb project editor, following in the great tradition of her predecessors. Jane Searle has been an excellent production manager and Mollie Eisenberg has been a helpful assistant editor. Dan Jost brought a vision to the Web site and spent countless hours making it a reality.

We are more than happy, however, to absolve all these contributors from any flaws, errors, and misjudgments that this book contains. We wish it could be free of all production errors, grammatical errors, misspellings, misquotes, missed citations, etc. From that standpoint, a book ought to try to be perfect. But substantively we have not tried to write a flawless book; we have not tried to write a book to please everyone. We have again tried to write an effective book, a book that cannot be taken lightly. Our goal was not to make every reader a political scientist. Our goal was to restore politics as a subject of vigorous and enjoyable discourse, releasing it from the bondage of the thirty-second sound bite and the thirty-page technical briefing. Every person can be knowledgeable because everything about politics is accessible. One does not have to be a television anchorperson to profit from political events. One does not have to be a philosopher to argue about the requisites of democracy, a lawyer to dispute constitutional interpretations, an economist to debate public policy. We will be very proud if our book contributes in a small way to the restoration of the ancient art of political controversy.

Theodore J. Lowi
Benjamin Ginsberg
Kenneth A. Shepsle

American Government

POWER AND PURPOSE

Part One | Foundations

Five Principles of Politics

AMERICAN GOVERNMENT AND POLITICS are extraordinarily complex. The United States has many levels of government: federal, state, county, city, and town—to say nothing of a host of special and regional authorities. Each of these governments operates under its own rules and statutory authority and is related to the others in complex ways. In many nations, regional and local governments are appendages of the national government. This is not true in the United States. America's state and local governments possess a considerable measure of independence and authority. Each level of government, moreover, consists of an array of departments, agencies, offices, and bureaus undertaking a variety of sometimes overlapping tasks. Sometimes this complexity gets in the way of effective governance, as in the case of governmental response to emergencies. America's federal, state, and local public safety agencies seldom share information and frequently use incompatible communications equipment, so they are often not even able to speak to one another. For example, on September 11, 2001, New York City's police and fire departments could not effectively coordinate their actions because their communications systems were not linked.

The complexity of America's government is no accident. Complexity was one element of the founders' grand constitutional design. The framers of the Constitution hoped that an elaborate division of power among institutions and between the states and the federal government would allow a variety of competing groups, forces, interests, and ideas to have a voice in public affairs—while preventing any single group or coalition from monopolizing power. One set of interests might be active and powerful in some states, other forces would be influential in the national legislature, and still other groups might prevail in the executive branch. The overall pattern would disperse power and opportunity, allowing many groups to achieve at least some of their political goals. In this way, America's political tradition associates complexity with liberty and political opportunity.

But while America's institutional complexity creates many avenues and possibilities for political action, its complexity also places a considerable burden on citizens who might wish to achieve something through political participation, for they may not easily discern where particular policies are actually made, who the influential decision makers are, and what forms of political participation are most likely to be effective. This is one of the paradoxes of political life: In a dictatorship, lines of political authority may be simple, but opportunities to influence the use of power are few; in America, political opportunities are plentiful, but how they should be used is far from obvious. Indeed, precisely because America's institutional and political arrangements are so complex, many Americans are mystified by government. As we shall see in Chapter 9, most Americans have difficulty making sense of even the basic features of the Constitution.

If America's government seems complex, its politics can be utterly bewildering. Like the nation's governmental structure, its political processes have numerous components. For most Americans, the focal point of politics is the electoral process. As we shall see in Chapter 10, tens of millions of Americans participate in a host of national, state, and local elections, during which they listen to thousands of candidates debate a perplexing array of issues. Candidates inundate the media with promises, charges, and countercharges while an army of pundits and journalists, whom we discuss in Chapter 13, adds its own clamor to the din.

Politics, however, does not end on Election Day. Indeed, given the growing tendency of losers to challenge election results in the courts, even elections do not end on Election Day. Long after the voters have spoken, political struggles continue in Congress, the executive branch, and the courts and embroil political parties, interest groups, and the mass media. In some instances, the participants in political struggles and their goals seem fairly obvious. For example, it is no secret that business and upper-income wage earners strongly support programs of tax reduction, farmers support maintenance of agricultural price supports, and labor unions oppose "outsourcing" of production. Each of these forces has created or joined organized groups to advance its cause. We examine some of these groups in Chapter 12.

In other instances, though, the participants in political struggles and their goals are not so clear. Sometimes corporate groups hide behind environmental causes to surreptitiously promote their economic interests. Other times groups claiming to want to help the poor and downtrodden seek only to help themselves. And to make matters worse, many of the government's policies are made behind closed doors, away from the light of publicity.

Ordinary citizens can hardly be blamed for failing to understand bureaucratic rule making and other obscure techniques of government. For the most part, these are topics that even experienced journalists have failed to comprehend fully. Take, for example, a presidential office called OIRA (Office of Information and Regulatory Affairs). This office, within the White House Office of Management and Budget (OMB), is responsible for the president's regulatory agenda. OIRA has become an important instrument of presidential power but has gone largely unnoticed by the press. Can you recall reading a story about OIRA? Search online to see how often the media mention OIRA and its mission. Then read Chapters 6 and 7.

MAKING SENSE OF GOVERNMENT AND POLITICS

Can we find order in the apparent chaos of politics? The answer is that we can, and doing so is precisely the purpose of this text. In this chapter, we offer a number of concepts and principles that should clarify the nature of government and the logic of the political process. In later chapters, we apply the principles presented here to the government and politics of the United States.

What Is Government?

government
The institutions and procedures through which a land and its people are ruled.

Government is the term generally used to describe the formal institutions through which a land and its people are ruled. To govern is to rule. Government is composed of institutions and processes that rulers establish to strengthen and perpetuate their power or control over a land and its inhabitants. A government may be as simple as a tribal council that meets occasionally to advise the chief or as complex as our own vast establishment, with its elaborate procedures, laws, and bureaucracies. This more complex government is sometimes called the state, an abstract concept referring to the source of all public authority.

Forms of Government

Governments vary in their institutional structure, in their size, and in their modes of operation. Two questions are of special importance in determining how governments differ from one another: Who governs? How much government control is permitted?

In some nations, governing is done by a single individual—a king or dictator, for example. This state of affairs is called an **autocracy.** When a small group of landowners, military officers, or wealthy merchants controls most of the governing decisions, the government is said to be an **oligarchy.** If more people participate and the populace is deemed to have some influence over decision making, the government is tending toward **democracy.**

Governments also vary considerably in terms of how they govern. In the United States and a small number of other nations, governments are severely limited in terms of *what* they are permitted to control (they are restricted by substantive limits) as well as *how* they go about exercising that control (they are restricted by procedural limits). Governments that are so limited are called **constitutional** (or liberal) governments. In other nations, including many in Europe, South America, Asia, and Africa, although the law imposes few real limits, a government is nevertheless kept in check by other political and social institutions that it is unable to control but must come to terms with, such as autonomous territories, an organized church, organized business groups, or organized labor unions. Such governments are generally called **authoritarian.** In a third group of nations, including the Soviet Union under Joseph Stalin, Nazi Germany, and perhaps pre–World War II Japan and Italy, governments not only are free of legal limits but also seek to eliminate those organized social groupings that might challenge or limit their authority. These governments typically attempt to dominate or control every sphere of political, economic, and social life and, as a result, are called **totalitarian.**

Foundations of Government

Whatever their makeup, governments historically have included two basic components: a means of coercion, such as an army or police force, and a means of collecting revenue.

The Means of Coercion   Government must have the power to get people to obey its laws and punish them if they do not. Coercion takes many forms, and each year millions of Americans are subject to one form of government coercion or another. Table 1.1 is an outline of the uses of coercion by federal and state governments in America.

autocracy A form of government in which a single individual rules.

oligarchy A form of government in which a small group of landowners, military officers, or wealthy merchants controls most of the governing decisions.

democracy A system of rule that permits citizens to play a significant part in the governmental process, usually through the selection of key public officials.

constitutional government A system of rule in which formal and effective limits are placed on the powers of the government.

authoritarian government A system of rule in which the government recognizes no formal limits but may nevertheless be restrained by the power of other social institutions.

totalitarian government A system of rule in which the government recognizes no formal limits on its power and seeks to absorb or eliminate other social institutions that might challenge it.

TABLE 1.1 The Means of Coercion

Form	Instances	Level of Government
Arrests	10,047,300	Federal, state, and local (2004)
Prison inmates	1,496,629	Federal and state (2004)
Jail inmates	713,990	County and municipal (2004)
Executions	60	State (2005)

Source: U.S. Bureau of the Census, *Statistical Abstract of the United States: 2006* (Washington, D.C.: U.S. Department of Commerce, 2006).

One aspect of coercion is *conscription,* whereby a government requires certain involuntary services of its citizens. The best-known example of conscription is military conscription, which is called the draft. Although there has been no draft since 1973, there were drafts during the Civil War, World War I, World War II, and the wars in Korea and Vietnam. With these drafts, our government compelled millions of men to serve in the armed forces; 500,000 of these soldiers made the ultimate contribution by giving their lives in their nation's service. If the need arose, military conscription would probably be reinstituted. All eighteen-year-old men are required to register today, just in case.

However, military conscription is not the only form of involuntary service that a government can compel its citizens to perform. Americans can, by law, be compelled to serve on juries, appear before legal tribunals when summoned, file a great variety of official reports, including income-tax returns, and attend school or send their children to school.

The Means of Collecting Revenue   Each year American governments collect enormous sums from their citizens to support their institutions and programs. Taxation has grown steadily over the years. In 2005, the national government alone collected $1.1 trillion in individual income taxes, $307 billion in corporate income taxes, $771 billion in social insurance taxes, $87 billion in excise, state, and gift taxes, and another $31 billion in customs duties. The grand total amounted to more than $2.3 trillion, or almost $7,500 from every person in the United States. And of course while some groups receive more in benefits from the government than they pay in taxes, others get less for their tax dollar. One of the perennial issues in American politics is the distribution of tax burdens versus the distribution of program benefits. Every group would like more of the benefits while passing more of the burdens of taxation onto others.

conscription Compulsory military service, usually for a prescribed period or for the duration of a war; the draft.

Why Is Government Necessary?

As we have just seen, control is the basis for government. But what forms of government control are justifiable? To answer this question, we begin by examining the ways in which government benefits individuals. The Analyzing the Evidence unit for this chapter explores how our understanding of the purpose of government has evolved over time.

To Maintain Order   Human beings usually do not venture out of their caves (or the modern counterpart) unless there is a reasonable probability that they can return safely. But for people to live together peacefully, law and order are required, the institutionalization of which is called government. From the standpoint of this definition, the primary purpose of government is to maintain order. But order can come about only by controlling a territory and its people. This may sound like a threat to freedom until you ponder the absence of government, or anarchy—the absence of rule. According to Thomas Hobbes (1588–1679), author of the first masterpiece of political philosophy in English, anarchy is even worse than the potential tyranny of government because anarchy, or life outside "the state," is characterized by "continual fear, and danger of violent death . . . [where life is] solitary, poor, nasty, brutish and short."[1] Governmental power can be a threat to freedom, yet we need government to maintain order so that we can enjoy our freedom.

To Protect Property   After safety of persons comes security of a person's labor, which we call property, or private property. Protection of property is almost universally recognized as a justifiable function of government. John Locke (1632–1704), the worthy successor to Hobbes, was the first to assert clearly that whatever we have removed from nature and also mixed our labor with is considered our property. But even Locke recognized that although the right to own what we have produced by our own labor is absolute, it means nothing if someone with greater power than ours decides to take it or trespass on it.

So something we call our own is ours only as long as the laws against trespass improve the probability that we can enjoy it, use it, consume it, trade it, or sell it. In reality, then, property can be defined as all the laws against trespass that permit us not only to call something our own but also to make sure that our claim sticks. In other words, property—that is, private property—is virtually meaningless without a government of laws and policies that makes trespass prohibitive.

To Provide Public Goods   David Hume (1711–76), another worthy successor to Hobbes, observed that although two neighbors may agree voluntarily to cooperate in draining a swampy meadow, the more neighbors there are, the more difficult it will be to cooperate to get the task done. A few neighbors might clear the swamp because they understand the benefits each of them will receive. But as you expand the number of neighbors who benefit from clearing the swamp, many neighbors will realize that all of them can get the same benefit if only a few clear the swamp and the rest do nothing. This is an example of *free riding*. A *public* (or collective) *good* is, therefore, a benefit that neighbors or members of a group cannot be kept from enjoying once any individual or a small minority of members have provided the benefit for themselves—the clearing of the swamp, for example, or national defense, for another example. National

free riding Enjoying the benefits of some good or action while letting others bear the costs.

public good A good that (1) may be enjoyed by anyone if it is provided and (2) may not be denied to anyone once it has been provided.

---

[1]Thomas Hobbes, *Leviathan, or The Matter, Forme, and Power of a Common Wealth, Ecclesiasticall and Civil* (1651; repr., New York: Macmillan, 1947), p. 82.

The Nature and Purpose of Government

One way for political scientists to understand government is to compare how different societies and thinkers have understood government in the past. For example, classical political thinkers such as Plato (429–347 BCE), Aristotle (384–322 BCE), and Cicero (106–43 BCE), differed from modern social contract thinkers in crucial ways.

As Aristotle wrote in *Politics*, "man is by nature a political animal."[1] What he meant is that certain distinctively human attributes can best be achieved within a political association. Many classical political thinkers viewed political associations as natural communities with broad moral purposes, such as fostering unity or promoting virtue through education. The central question of ancient political thought, then, centered on the issue of justice and what kind of state best realized particular human excellences.

By contrast, social contract thinkers such as Thomas Hobbes (1588–1679) and John Locke (1632–1704), approached political association in a very different way. Rather than viewing the state as a natural entity designed to foster virtues or develop particular capacities, social contract theorists saw the state as a human creation designed for more specific purposes. Social contract thinkers typically resorted to the philosophical construct of a state of nature in which human beings lived prior to political associations. In this state of nature, human beings are considered equal and possess certain rights. From this pre-political state of nature, and due to problems associated with it, humans established governments by conscious collective decisions.

Classical Political Thought	Social Contract Theory
POLITICS AS THE REALIZATION OF HUMAN EXCELLENCE	POLITICS AS PROTECTING INDIVIDUAL RIGHTS

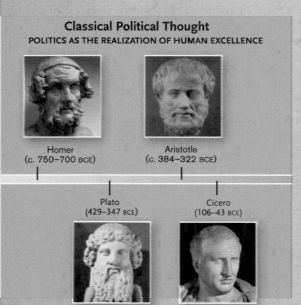

Homer
(c. 750–700 BCE)

Aristotle
(c. 384–322 BCE)

Plato
(429–347 BCE)

Cicero
(106–43 BCE)

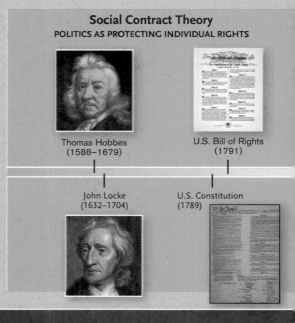

Thomas Hobbes
(1588–1679)

U.S. Bill of Rights
(1791)

John Locke
(1632–1704)

U.S. Constitution
(1789)

Article I

Congress shall make no law respecting an establishment of religion, or prohibiting the free exercise thereof; or abridging the freedom of speech, or of the press; or the right of the people peaceably to assemble, and to petition the Government for a redress of grievances.

Building on the ideas of social contract thinkers, the American founders saw government as having two broad purposes: protecting individual rights and providing avenues for citizens to affect governance. These purposes are evident in the Bill of Rights. For example, the free exercise clause can be seen as an example of *freedom from* government, whereas the right to petition the government for redress of grievances can be seen as *freedom to affect* government.

The social contract understanding of the nature and origins of political association yields two important consequences: (1) because humans are by nature free, legitimate authority derives from those who create governments; and (2) restrictions on human freedom must be (at least in principle) consensual. Such a conception of government, then, views the protection of individuals and their rights—both freedom from government and freedom to affect government—as the paramount concern of government. We will see in subsequent chapters that the protection of individual rights was a key concern for the founders of the United States and affected how they designed the framework for American government.

[1] Aristotle. *Politics.* Translated by C.D.C. Reeve. (Indianapolis: Hackett, 1998), p. 4.

defense is one of the most important public goods—especially when the nation is threatened by war or terrorism. Without government's coercive powers through a policy (backed by taxation) to build a bridge, produce an army, or provide a swamp-free meadow, "legal tender," or uniform standards of weights and measures, there is no incentive—in fact, very often there is a *dis*incentive—for even the richest, most concerned members to provide the benefit.[2]

FIVE PRINCIPLES OF POLITICS

In its broadest sense, the term **politics** refers to conflicts over the character, membership, and policies of any organization to which people belong. As Harold Lasswell, a famous political scientist, once put it, politics is the struggle over "who gets what, when, how."[3] Although politics is a phenomenon that can be found in any organization, in this book politics will refer only to conflicts and struggles over the leadership, structure, and policies of governments. The goal of politics, as we define it, is to have a share or a say in the composition of the government's leadership, how the government is organized, or what its policies are going to be. Most people are eager to have some say in matters affecting them; witness the willingness of so many individuals over the past two centuries to risk their lives for the right to vote and share in representative government. In recent years, Americans have become more skeptical about their actual "say" in government, and many do not bother to vote. This increased skepticism, however, does not mean that Americans no longer want to have a share in the governmental process. Rising levels of skepticism mean, rather, that many Americans doubt the capacity of the political system to provide them with influence.

Politics takes many forms. As they attempt to influence the policies and leadership of the government, individuals may run for office, vote, join political parties and movements, contribute money to candidates, lobby public officials, participate in demonstrations, write letters, talk to their friends and neighbors, go to court, and engage in numerous other activities. Some forms of politics are aimed at gaining power, some at influencing those in power, and others at bringing new people to power and throwing the old rascals out. Those in power use myriad means and strategies to try to achieve their goals. But even though it takes many forms, politics possesses an underlying logic that can be understood in terms of five simple principles:

1. All political behavior has a purpose.
2. All politics is collective action.
3. Institutions routinely solve collective-action problems.
4. Political outcomes are the products of individual preferences and institutional procedures.
5. History matters.

politics The conflicts and struggles over the leadership, structure, and policies of government.

ONLINE READING ○

[2]The most instructive treatment of the phenomenon of public goods and the free rider is Mancur Olson Jr., *The Logic of Collective Action: Public Goods and the Theory of Groups* (1965; repr., Cambridge, Mass.: Harvard University Press, 1971), pp. 33–43, esp. n. 53.

ONLINE READING ○

[3]Harold D. Lasswell, *Politics: Who Gets What, When, How* (1936; repr., New York: Meridian Books, 1958).

Armed with these principles, a student of politics can perceive the order underlying the apparent chaos of political events whenever and wherever they take place.

The Rationality Principle: All Political Behavior Has a Purpose

One compelling reason why governments do what they do is that all people have goals and work to achieve those goals through their political behavior. For many citizens, political behavior is as simple as reading a headline or an editorial in the newspaper while drinking their morning coffee or discussing the latest local political controversy with a neighbor over the back fence. Though political, these actions are basically routines of everyday life. Beyond these almost perfunctory acts, citizens' political behavior broadens to include still relatively modest activities, like watching a political debate on television, arguing about politics with a co-worker, signing a petition, or attending a city-council meeting. These are understood to be explicitly political activities that require some forethought and advanced reflection—these are discretionary choices rather than mechanical acts, like accidentally catching sight of a political headline in the newspaper on your way to the sports section, the comics, or the movie listings. Political behavior requiring even more premeditation—even calculation—includes going to the polls and casting a vote in the November election (having first registered in a timely manner), writing one's legislative representatives about a political issue, contributing time or money to a political campaign, or even running for local office.

Some of these acts require effort, time, financial resources, and courage, whereas others place small, even insignificant demands on a person. Nevertheless, all of them are done for specific reasons. They are not random; they are not entirely automatic or mechanical, even the smallest of them. Sometimes they are engaged in for the sake of entertainment (reading the front page in the morning) or just to be sociable (chatting about politics with a neighbor, co-worker, or family member). At other times, they take on considerable personal importance explicitly because of their political content—because an individual cares about, and wants to influence, an issue, a candidate, a party, or a cause. We will treat all of this political activity as purposeful, as having a goal. Indeed, our attempts to discern the goals of various political activities will help us understand them better.

We've just noted that many of the political activities of ordinary citizens are hard to distinguish from conventional everyday behavior—reading newspapers, watching television news, discussing politics, and so on. For the professional politician, on the other hand—the legislator, executive, judge, party leader, bureau chief, or agency head—nearly every act is political. The legislator's decision to introduce a particular piece of legislation, give a speech in the legislative chamber, move an amendment to a pending bill, vote for or against that bill, or accept a contribution from a PAC[4] requires his or her careful attention. There are pitfalls and dangers, and the slightest miscalculation can have huge consequences. Introduce a bill that appears to be too pro-labor in

Rationality Principle

All political behavior has a purpose.

---

[4]A PAC (political action committee) is a group established by an interest group, labor union, or some other organization to collect donations and distribute them as campaign contributions to candidates and political parties.

the eyes of your constituents, for example, and before you know it you're charged with being in bed with the unions during the next election campaign. Give a speech against job quotas for minorities, and you risk your standing with the minority communities in your state or district. Accept campaign contributions from industries known to pollute, and environmentalists think you are no friend of the earth. Nearly every move a legislator makes is fraught with risks. And because of these risks, legislators think about their moves before they make them—sometimes carefully, sometimes not; sometimes correctly, sometimes not. But whatever actions they take or decide against taking, they make their choices with forethought, with deliberation, with calculation. Their actions are not knee-jerk but are, in a word, ***instrumental.*** Individuals think through the benefits and the costs of a decision, speculate about future effects, and weigh the risks of their decision. Making decisions is all about weighing probabilities of various events and determining the personal value of various outcomes.

As an example of instrumental behavior, consider the electoral politician. Most politicians want to keep their positions or move up the political ladder to even more important positions. They like their jobs for a variety of reasons—salary, privileges, prestige, stepping-stones, and opportunities for accomplishment, to name just a few. So we can go a long way in trying to understand why politicians do what they do by thinking of their behavior as instrumental, as trying to keep their jobs. This is quite straightforward in regard to elected politicians. They often see no further than the next election and think mainly about how to prevail in that contest. To understand their routines and behaviors, it is essential to figure out who can help them win. "Retail" politics involves dealing directly with constituents, as when a politician helps you navigate a federal agency, helps your parent find a misplaced Social Security check, or helps your child apply to a service academy. "Wholesale" politics involves appealing to collections of constituents, as when a legislator introduces a bill that would benefit a group that is active back home (say, veterans), secures money for a bridge or public building in his or her state or district, or intervenes in an official proceeding on behalf of an interest group that will, in turn, contribute to the next campaign. Politicians may do any and all of these things just because it is "right" or makes them feel good. But we institute elections and provide incentives for politicians to do such things as a means of winning those elections just in case their generosity of spirit and sense of doing good are insufficient. Elections and electoral politics are thus premised on instrumental behavior by politicians.

The Collective-Action Principle: All Politics Is Collective Action

Collective-Action Principle

All politics is collective action.

The second factor that helps explain why governments do what they do is that political action is collective, involving the building, combining, mixing, and amalgamating of the individual goals of people. People join together to achieve those goals. But as we shall see, collective action can be very difficult to orchestrate because the individuals involved in the decision-making process often have somewhat different goals and preferences. The result is mixed motives for cooperation. Conflict is inevitable; the question is how it can be resolved. The most typical and widespread means is bargaining among a small number of individuals. But when the number of parties involved is too large to engage in face-to-face bargaining, incentives must be provided to get everyone to act collectively.

instrumental Done with purpose, sometimes with forethought, and even with calculation.

Informal Bargaining Political bargaining is a process that may be highly formal or entirely informal. Relations among neighbors, for example, are usually based on informal give-and-take. To present a personal example, one of this book's authors has a neighbor with whom he shares a privet hedge on their property line. First one takes responsibility for trimming the hedge and then the other, alternating from year to year. This arrangement is merely an understanding, not a legally binding agreement, and it was reached amicably and without much fuss or fanfare after a brief conversation. No organizational effort—like hiring lawyers, drafting an agreement, and having it signed, witnessed, notarized, filed at the county courthouse, and so on—was required.

Bargaining in politics can be similarly informal and unstructured. Whether called horse trading, back-scratching, logrolling, or wheeling and dealing, it has much the same flavor as the casual, over-the-fence negotiation beween neighbors that was just described. Deals will be struck depending on the preferences and beliefs of the participants. If preferences are too incompatible or beliefs too inconsistent with one another, then a deal simply may not be in the cards. On the other hand, if preferences and beliefs are not too far out of line, then there will be a range of possible bargaining outcomes, some of which slightly advantage one party, others of which advantage other parties.

In fact, much of politics *is* informal, unstructured bargaining. First, many disputes subjected to bargaining are of sufficiently low impact that establishing elaborate formal machinery for dealing with them is just not worth the effort. Rules of thumb often develop as a benchmark—such as "split the difference" or "take turns" (the outcome of the hedge-trimming example given earlier). Second, there is repetition. If a small group engages in bargaining today over one matter and tomorrow over another—as neighbors bargain over draining a meadow one day, fixing a fence another, and trimming a hedge on still another occasion—then patterns develop. If one party constantly tries to extract maximal advantage, then the other parties will undoubtedly cease doing business with him. If, on the other hand, each party "gives a little to get a little," reciprocating kindness at one point with kindness at another, then a pattern of cooperation develops over time. It is the repetition of mixed-motive occasions that allows this pattern to emerge without formal trappings. Many political circumstances are either amenable to rules of thumb like those mentioned or are repeated with sufficient frequency so as to allow cooperative patterns to emerge.

Formal Bargaining Formal bargaining entails interactions that are governed by rules. The rules describe such things as who gets to make the first offer, how long the recipient parties have to consider it, whether recipient parties must take it or leave it or can make counteroffers, the method by which they convey their assent or rejection, what happens when all (or some decisive subset) of the others accept or reject it, what transpires next if the proposal is rejected, and so on. One could not imagine two neighbors deciding how to trim their common hedge under procedures as explicit and formal as these. One could, however, imagine a bargaining session over wages and working conditions between labor and management at a manufacturing plant proceeding in just this manner. The distinction suggests that some parties are more appropriately suited to formal proceedings, whereas others get on well enough without them. The same may be said about situations. A husband and wife are likely to divide household chores by informal bargaining, but this same couple would employ a formal procedure if it were household assets they were dividing (in a divorce settlement).

Formal bargaining is often associated with events that take place in official institutions—legislatures, courts, party conventions, administrative and regulatory agencies. These are settings in which mixed-motive situations arise over and over again. Year in and year out, legislatures pass statutes, approve executive budgets, and oversee the administrative branch of government. Courts administer justice, determine guilt or innocence, impose sentences, resolve differences between disputants, and render interpretive opinions about the meaning of the law. Party conventions nominate candidates and approve the platforms on which they base their campaigns. Administrative and regulatory agencies implement policy and make rulings about its applicability. All of these are instances of mixed-motive circumstances in which gains from cooperation are possible but bargaining failures are also a definite possibility. Consequently, the formal bargaining that takes place under the aegis of institutions is governed by rules that regularize proceedings both to maximize the prospects of reaching agreement and to guarantee that procedural wheels don't have to be reinvented each time a similar bargaining problem arises.

Collective Action   The idea of political bargaining suggests an intimate kind of politics, involving face-to-face relations, negotiation, compromise, give-and-take, and so on. Such bargaining results from the combination of mixed motives and small numbers. When the numbers become large, bargaining may no longer be practical. If 100 people own property bordering a swampy meadow or if a privet hedge runs the length of Main Street in a small town, insulating hundreds of households from the street, how do those communities solve the swamp's mosquito problem or resolve to trim the hedge to a consistent height? How do the communities secure the dividends that arise from cooperation?

These are clearly mixed-motive situations. Everyone shares some common values—eliminating the mosquito habitat or giving the hedge a uniform look—but they may disagree on other matters. Some may want to use pesticides in the meadow, while others are concerned about the environmental impact. Some may want the hedge cut very short, allowing it to be maintained easily by each household; others may want it kept tall, to shield homes from street noise. And in both situations, there are bound to be disagreements over how to pay for the project. The collective-action problem arises, as in these examples, when there is something to be gained if the group can cooperate and assure group members that some do not get away with bearing less than their fair share of the effort. Face-to-face bargaining, however, is compromised by sheer numbers. The issue, then, is how to accomplish some common objective when explicit bargaining is not an option.

Groups of individuals intent on ***collective action*** will ordinarily establish some decision-making procedures—relatively formal arrangements by which to resolve differences, coordinate the group to pursue a course of action, and sanction slackers, if necessary. Most groups will also require a leadership structure, which is necessary even if all the members of the group are in agreement about how to proceed. This structure is necessary to deal with a phenomenon we saw in the swamp-draining example: free riding. Each owner of land bordering the swamp wants the area cleared. If one or a few owners were to clear the swamp alone, their actions would benefit all

collective action
The pooling of resources and the coordination of effort and activity by a group of people (often a large one) to achieve common goals.

the other owners as well, without any efforts on the part of the other owners. Those owners would be free riders, enjoying the benefit of others' efforts without contributing themselves. It is this prospect of free riding that risks undermining collective action. A leadership structure will have to be in place to threaten and, if necessary, inflict punishments to discourage individuals from reneging on the individual contributions required to enable the group to pursue its common goals.

Various solutions to the collective-action problem have been proposed. The most famous is Mancur Olson's **by-product theory.**[5] Briefly, Olson's idea is this: The nub of free riding derives from the fact that most individuals in a large group don't make much difference to the final result, and they know it. This is why they may comfortably abstain from participation: They know that in following their inclination to avoid the costs of participation, they do not damage their prospects (or anyone else's) for receiving benefits. The problem is that while no one person's free riding does much harm, if enough people free ride, then the purpose of the collective action will be compromised. What if, however, something of value were at stake that would be lost if the person abstained from participation? What if participants were given something special that non-participants were denied? That is, what if some benefits were contingent on contributing to the group effort? Many organizations use this tactic, giving dues-paying or effort-contributing members special insurance or education benefits, reduced-fare travel, free or subsidized subscriptions to magazines and newsletters, bowling and golf tournaments, soccer leagues, access to members-only social events, and so on. Olson argued that if members were prepared to "pay their dues" to join an organization partially (or even mainly) for these special benefits, of which they would otherwise be deprived—what Olson called **selective benefits**—then the collective cooperation would end up being provided as well, as a by-product, with whatever surplus the dues structure generated. A member's inclination to free ride would be diminished, not because of feelings of obligation to his or her fellow members, not because of a moral imperative to participate, and not even because of a desire for the collective benefit supplied by the group, but rather because of naked self-interest—the desire for selective benefits. Clearly this is an extreme version of the argument; the main point is that the selective benefits available only to participants and contributors—and denied to nonparticipants and noncontributors—are the key to successful collective action. A group that appeals to its members *only* on the basis of its common collective purposes is a group that will have trouble achieving those purposes.[6]

One of the most notorious collective-action problems involves too much of a good thing. Known as the tragedy of the commons, it is an acknowledgment of how

by-product theory
The idea that groups provide members with private benefits to attract membership. The possibility of group collective action emerges as a consequence.

selective benefits
Benefits that do not go to everyone but, rather, are distributed selectively—only to those who contribute to the group enterprise.

○ ONLINE READING

---

[5] On the general subject of collective action, the interested reader should consult Kenneth A. Shepsle and Mark S. Bonchek, *Analyzing Politics: Rationality, Behavior, and Institutions* (New York: Norton, 1997), chap. 9, where Olson's work, among others, is taken up.

[6] Getting such an organizational effort up and running, however, is no small feat. Olson's argument appreciates what is necessary to keep a group going but underestimates what it takes to organize collective action in the first place. Put differently, a prior collective-action problem needs to be solved—and that is an organizational problem. The solution is leadership, and the individuals imaginative enough to see this need are referred to as political entrepreneurs. That is, there must be a selective benefit available to those who bear organizational burdens, thereby facilitating the collective action; the selective benefits of leadership include perquisites of office, financial reward, and honor and status.

unbridled self-interest can have damaging collective consequences, as we shall see in the following section. A party's reputation, for example, is not irreparably harmed if one of its legislators pushes her advantage by getting approval for a minor amendment helpful to a special interest in her district. But if lots of party members do it, the party comes to be known as the champion of special interests, and its reputation is tarnished. A pool of resources is not much depleted if someone takes a little of it. But it does become depleted if lots of people take from it—a forest is lost a pine tree at a time; an oil reserve declines a gallon at a time; the atmosphere is polluted a particle at a time.

To summarize, individuals try to accomplish things not only as individuals but also as members of larger collectivities (families, friendship groups, clubs and associations, and political parties) and even larger categories (like economic class, ethnicity, and nationality). The rationality principle covers individual initiative. The collective action principle describes the paradoxes encountered, the obstacles that must be overcome, and the incentives necessary for individuals to combine with like-minded others to coordinate their energies, accomplish collective purposes, and secure the dividends of cooperation. Much of politics is about doing this or failing to do this. The next principle takes this argument to its logical conclusion, focusing on collective activities that are regularized because they are both important and frequently occurring. Institutions do the public's business while relieving communities of having to reinvent collective action each time it is required. Here we provide a rationale for government.

The Institution Principle: Institutions Routinely Solve Collective-Action Problems

Institution Principle

Institutions routinely solve collective-action problems.

In the last section, we looked at the conditions in which people engage in bargaining, cooperation, and collective action to solve some political problem. Because people, especially elected leaders and other government officials, are repeatedly required to confront recurring problems, they develop routines and standard ways of dealing with things. In a word, responses to regularly recurring problems are institutionalized. Collective action results because standard procedures and rules are established that provide people with appropriate incentives to take the action necessary to solve the problems. Routinized, structured relations are what we call *institutions*. Institutions are the rules and procedures that provide incentives for political behavior, thereby shaping politics. What interests students of politics most is how institutions discourage conflict, enable bargaining, and thus facilitate decision making, cooperation, and collective action.

Consider publicly owned parks and land reserves that are today the object of great passion by those who place significant value on the natural environment. In an earlier time in Europe (and still today in various parts of the world), commons were valued for more practical reasons—notably as places to graze cattle and forage. Today examples of commons include not only public parks, land reserves, and sites for grazing and foraging but also bodies of water used for commercial fishing, irrigation systems, urban water supplies, and, indeed, even the earth's atmosphere.[7]

institutions The rules and procedures that provide incentives for political behavior, thereby shaping politics.

---

[7]A most insightful discussion of "common pool problems," of which these are examples, is Elinor Ostrom, *Governing the Commons: The Evolution of Institutions for Collective Action* (New York: Cambridge University Press, 1990).

A common is, by definition, "owned" by everyone (in common) and therefore is the responsibility of no one individual. On a field owned by a village, each villager gets to graze his or her cattle "for free." If a villager is contemplating adding a head to his herd, he will take into account his personal costs of doing so, but this calculation will *not* include the cost of grazing. If the common is large and the village demands on it minimal, this will not pose serious problems. But even if demands on the common grow, no villager has an incentive to restrict his or her use of this free resource, resulting in "the tragedy of the commons."[8] The common will be overgrazed and ultimately destroyed, inasmuch as its capacity to regenerate itself will have been disabled. As a metaphor, the tragedy of the commons suggests that individual purposes may sometimes clash with collective welfare: A collective reputation is tarnished; a common is overgrazed; a common asset is depleted.

Institutions are part script and part scorecard. As scripts, they choreograph political activity. As scorecards, they list the players, their positions, what they want, what they can do, and when they can do it. While the Constitution sets the broad framework, much adaptation and innovation takes place as the institutions themselves are bent to the various political purposes of strategic political actors who want to win for their side and defeat the other side. Our focus here will be on the authority that institutions provide politicians for the pursuit of public policies. The discussion is divided into four broad subjects: jurisdiction, decisiveness, agenda and veto power, and delegation.

Jurisdiction   A critical feature of an institution is the designation of someone who has the authority to apply the rules or make the decisions; members recognize the jurisdiction of the main players and are quick to impose limits on those players if they feel jurisdictional authority has been exceeded. Political institutions are full of specialized jurisdictions. One of the most unusual features of the U.S. Congress is the existence of the "standing committee," whose jurisdictions are carefully defined by law. Some members of Congress are generalists, but most become specialists in all aspects of the jurisdiction of their committees—and they often seek committee assignments based on the subject in which they want to specialize. Committee members are granted specific authority within their jurisdiction to set the agenda of the larger parent chamber. Thus the legislative institution in the United States is affected by the way its jurisdiction-specific committees are structured.

Decisiveness   Another crucial feature of an institution is its rules for making decisions. It might sound like a straightforward task to lay out the rules for decision making, but it really isn't so easy to do without a raft of conditions and qualifications. Every organization has rules of some sort, and the more an organization values participation by the broadest range of its members, the more it needs those rules: The requirement of participation must be balanced with the need to bring discussion and activity to a close at some point so that a decision can be made. This is why one of the motions that can be made on the floor of a legislature is to move the previous question, a motion to

---

[8]Garrett Hardin, "The Tragedy of the Commons," *Science* 162 (1968): 1243–48. This now-classic essay is must reading for the interested student.

ONLINE READING

close the debate and move immediately to a vote.[9] In some legislatures, though, inaction seems to take precedence over action. In the U.S. House of Representatives, for example, a motion to adjourn takes precedence over a motion to move the question. It is no accident that *House Practice*, a book of rules and interpretations about procedure in the House of Representatives, runs to more than 1,000 pages!

Even juries have rules for decisiveness; if discussion goes on too long among the members, the judge may in fact declare a hung jury, leading to a new trial and another round of discussion (or the dropping of charges). In most organizations, including corporations, the decision to close discussion is left in the hands of the presiding officer, who might simply ask for a motion to vote on the issue in question. But even such a ruling by the chair can be appealed if the participants decide that they have not discussed the matter enough to make a decision.

Agenda Power and Veto Power   If decisiveness characterizes what it takes to win, then ***agenda power*** describes who determines what will be taken up for consideration in the first place. Those who exercise some form of agenda power are said to engage in gatekeeping. They determine which alternatives may pass through the gate onto the agenda and which ones will have the gate slammed in their face. Gatekeeping, in other words, consists of the power to make proposals and the power to block proposals from being made. The ability to keep something off an institution's agenda should not be confused with ***veto power***. The latter is the ability to defeat something even if it does become part of the agenda. In the legislative process, for example, the president has (limited) veto power. And while Congress has agenda power—it cannot be prevented from taking up a particular bill—the president does not have such power in Congress. Congress also cannot be prevented from passing a measure, but the president has no power to block a bill in Congress. And a presidential veto can prevent a measure from becoming the law of the land. We'll examine these processes in more detail in Chapters 5 and 6.

Delegation   Representative democracy is the quintessential instance of ***delegation***, in which citizens, through voting, delegate the authority to make decisions on their behalf to representatives—chiefly legislators and executives—rather than exercising political authority directly. We can think of our political representatives as our agents, just as we may think of professionals and craftspeople whose services we retain—doctors, lawyers, accountants, plumbers, mechanics, and so on—as agents whom we hire to act on our behalf. Now why would those with authority, whom we will call principals, delegate some of their authority to agents? In effect, we are asking about the virtues of decentralization and of division and specialization of labor. The answer is that both principals and agents benefit from it. Principals benefit because they are able to off-load to experts and specialists tasks that they themselves are far less capable of performing. Ordinary citizens, for example, are not as well versed in the tasks of governance as are professional politicians. Thus by delegating, citizens do not have to be specialists and can focus their energies on other things. This is the rationale for representative democracy.

agenda power The control over what a group will consider for discussion.

veto power The ability to defeat something even if it has made it on to the agenda of an institution.

delegation The transmission of authority to some other official or body for the latter's use (though often with the right of review and revision).

---

[9]For a general discussion of motions to close debate and get on with the decision, see Henry M. Robert, *Robert's Rules of Order* (1876), items III. 21 and VI. 38. *Robert's* has achieved the status of an icon and now exists in an enormous variety of forms and shapes.

This same rationale applies to the division and specialization of labor we often observe in specific political institutions. Legislators generally benefit from a decentralized arrangement in which they focus on those aspects of public policy for which they are best equipped—issues of special interest to their constituents or on which their occupational and other experiences have given them familiarity and perspective. In exchange, they are freed from having to be policy generalists and can avoid areas of little interest or relevance to them. The legislative committee system accomplishes this task by partitioning policy into different jurisdictions and allowing legislators to gravitate to those committees that most suit their purposes.

The delegation principle, in which a principal delegates authority to an agent, seems almost too good to be true. But there is a dark side to this ***principal-agent relationship.*** As the eighteenth-century economist Adam Smith noted in his classic, *The Wealth of Nations* (1776), economic agents are not motivated by the welfare of their customers to grow vegetables, make shoes, or weave cloth; rather, they do those things out of their own self-interest. Thus a principal must take care when delegating to agents that those agents are properly motivated to serve the principal's interests, either by sharing his or her interests or by deriving something of value (reputation, compensation, and so on) for acting to advance those interests. Alternatively, the principal will need to have some instruments by which to monitor and validate what his or her agent is doing and then reward or punish the agent accordingly. Nevertheless, a principal will not bother to eliminate entirely the agent's prospective deviations from the principal's interests. The reason is ***transaction costs.*** The organizational effort necessary to negotiate and then police every aspect of a principal-agent relationship becomes, at some point, more costly than it is worth. In sum, the upside of delegation consists of the assignment of activities to precisely those agents who possess a comparative advantage in performing them. (A corollary is that those who are poorly prepared to conduct these activities are relieved of performing them.) The downside is the prospective misalignment of the goals of agents with the goals of principals and thus the possibility of agents marching to the beat of their own drummer.

Characterizing institutions in terms of jurisdiction, decisiveness, agenda power and veto power, and delegation covers an immense amount of ground. Our purpose here has been to introduce the reader to the multiplicity of ways collectivities arrange their business and routinize it, thereby enabling cooperation, facilitating recurring requirements of bargaining, and solving collective-action problems. A second purpose has been to impress on the reader the potential diversity in institutional arrangements—there are so many ways to do things collectively—because this diversity underscores the amazing sophistication and intelligence of the framers of the U.S. Constitution in the institutional choices they made more than two centuries ago. Finally, we want to make clear that institutions not only make rules for governing but also describe strategic opportunities for various political interests. As George Washington Plunkitt, the savvy and candid political boss of Tammany Hall, said of the institutional situations in which he found himself, "I seen my opportunities, and I took 'em."[10]

principal-agent relationship The relationship between a principal and his or her agent. This relationship may be affected by the fact that each is motivated by self-interest, yet their interests may not be well aligned.

transaction costs The cost of clarifying each aspect of a principal-agent relationship and monitoring it to make sure arrangements are complied with.

---

[10]In the nineteenth century and well into the twentieth, Tammany Hall was the club that ran New York City's Democratic party like a machine.

The Policy Principle: Political Outcomes Are the Products of Individual Preferences and Institutional Procedures

At the end of the day, politics leads to collective decisions that emerge from the political process, and these decisions have consequences for individuals. A Nebraska farmer may not be interested in the various facets of the institutions we've just described, even those concerning the House Agriculture Committee. What he does care about is how public laws and rulings affect his welfare and that of his family, friends, and neighbors. He cares about how export policies affect the prices his crops and livestock products earn in international markets and how monetary policy influences inflation and, as a result, the cost of purchasing fuel, feed, seed, and fertilizer; the funding of public and private research and development efforts and their effect on the quality and reliability of the scientific information he obtains; and the affordability of the state university, where he hopes to educate his children. He also cares, eventually, about inheritance laws and their effect on his ability to pass his farm on to his kids without Uncle Sam's taking a huge chunk of it in estate taxes. As students of American politics, we need to consider the link between institutional arrangements and policy outcomes. Do the organizational features of institutions leave their marks on policy? What biases, predilections, and tendencies manifest themselves in policies?

The linchpin connecting institutions to policy is the motivations of political actors. As we saw in our discussion of the rationality principle, their ambitions—ideological, personal, electoral, and institutional—provide politicians with the incentives to craft policies in particular ways. In fact, most policies make sense only as reflections of individual politicians' interests, goals, and beliefs. Examples include

Personal interests:	Congressman X is an enthusiastic supporter of subsidizing home heating oil (but opposes regulation to keep its price down) because some of his friends own heating-oil distributorships.[11]
Electoral ambitions:	Senator Y, a well-known political moderate, has lately been introducing very conservative amendments to bills dealing with the economy to appeal to more conservative financial donors, who might then contribute to her budding presidential campaign.
Institutional ambitions:	Representative Z has promised his vote and given a rousing speech on the House floor supporting a particular amendment because he knows it is near and dear to the Speaker's heart. He hopes his support will earn him the Speaker's endorsement next year for an assignment to the prestigious Appropriations Committee.

These examples illustrate how policies are politically crafted according to institutional procedures and individual aspirations. The procedures, as we saw in a pre-

---

[11]These friends would benefit from people having the financial means to buy home heating oil but would not want the price they charge for the oil restricted.

vious discussion, are a series of chutes and ladders that shape, channel, filter, and prune the alternatives from which ultimate policy choices are made. The politicians who populate these institutions, as we have just noted, are driven both by private objectives and by public purposes, pursuing their own private interests while working on behalf of their conception of the public interest.

Because the institutional features of the American political system are complex and policy change requires success at every step, change is often impossibly difficult, meaning the status quo usually prevails. A long list of players must be satisfied with the change, or it won't happen. Most of these politicians will need some form of "compensation" to provide their endorsement and support.

Majorities are usually built by legislators drafting bills so as to spread the benefits to enough members of the legislature to get the requisite number of votes for that particular bill. Derisively, this is called pork-barrel legislation. It can be better understood by remembering that the overwhelming proportion of pork-barrel projects that are distributed to build policy majorities are justified to voters as valuable additions to the public good of the various districts. What may be pork to the critic is actual bridges, roads, and post offices.

Elaborate institutional arrangements, complicated policy processes, and intricate political motivations make for a highly combustible mixture. The policies that emerge are inevitably lacking in the neatness that citizens desire. But policies in the United States today are sloppy and slapdash for a clear reason: The tendency to spread the benefits broadly results when political ambition comes up against a decentralized political system.

The History Principle: History Matters

There is one more aspect of our analysis that is important: We must ask how we have gotten where we are. By what series of steps? When by choice and when by accident? To what extent was the history of Congress, the parties, and the presidency a fulfillment of constitutional principle, and when were the developments a series of dogged responses to economic necessity? Are the parties a product of democracy, or is democracy a product of the parties? Every question and problem we confront has a history. History will not tell the same story for every institution. Nevertheless, without history, there is neither a sense of causation nor a full sense of how institutions are related to one another. In explaining the answer to why governments do what they do, we must turn to history to see what choices were available to political actors at a given time and what consequences resulted from those choices.

Imagine a tree growing from the bottom of the page. Its trunk grows upward from some root-ball at the bottom, dividing into branches that continue to grow upward, further dividing into smaller branches. Imagine a path through this tree, from its very roots at the bottom of the page to the end of one of the highest branches at the top of the page. There are many such paths, from the one point at the bottom to many possible points at the top. If instead of a tree this were a time diagram, then the root-ball at the bottom would represent some specific beginning point and all of the top-branch endings would represent some terminal time. Each path is now a history,

History Principle

History matters.

the delineation of movement from some specific beginning to some concluding time. Alternative histories, like paths through trees, entail irreversibilities. Once one starts down a historical path (or up a tree), one cannot always retrace one's steps.[12] Once things happen, they cannot always un-happen. Some futures are foreclosed by the choices people have already made or, if not literally foreclosed, then made extremely unlikely.

It is in this sense that we explain a current situation at least in part by describing the historical path by which we arrived at it. Some scholars use the term **path dependency** to suggest that some possibilities are more or less likely because of events that occurred, and choices that were made, earlier in history.

Three factors that help to explain why history commonly matters in political life are rules and procedures, loyalties and alliances, and historically conditioned points of view. As to the first of these factors, rules and procedures, choices made during one point in time continue to have important consequences for years, decades, or even centuries. For example, America's single-member-district plurality voting rules, established in the eighteenth century, continue to shape the nation's party system today. Those voting rules, as we shall see in Chapter 11, help explain why the United States has a two-party system rather than the multiparty systems found in many other Western democracies. Thus a set of choices made 200 years ago affects party politics today.

A second way in which history often matters in politics is through the persistence of loyalties and alliances. Many of the political alliances that are important in American politics today are products of events that took place decades ago. For example, Jewish voters are among the Democratic party's most loyal supporters, consistently giving nearly 90 percent of their votes to Democratic presidential candidates. Yet on the basis of economic interest, Jews, one of the wealthier social groups in America, might be expected to vote for the Republicans. In recent years, moreover, the GOP has been a stronger supporter of Israel than the Democrats. Why, then, do Jews overwhelmingly support the Democrats? Part of the answer has to do with history. In the late nineteenth and early twentieth centuries, Jews suffered considerable discrimination in the United States. In the 1930s, though, under the leadership of Franklin Roosevelt, the Democratic party was one vehicle through which Jews in America began their climb to the success they enjoy today. This historical experience continues to shape Jewish political identity. Similar historical experiences help to explain the political loyalties of African Americans, Cuban Americans, and others.

A third factor explaining why history matters is the fact that past events and experiences shape current viewpoints and perspectives. For example, many Americans now in their fifties and sixties view events in Iraq through the lens of the Vietnam War. Those influenced by the memory of Vietnam often see U.S. military involvement in a third world country as likely to lead to a quagmire of costs and casualties. Interestingly, in the 1960s, many older Americans viewed events in Vietnam through the lens of the 1930s, when the Western democracies were slow to resist Adolf Hitler's Germany. Thus to those influenced by events of the 1930s and World War II, failure to respond to aggression strongly was seen as a form of ap-

path dependency
The idea that certain possibilities are made more or less likely because of the historical path taken.

---

[12]Clearly with tree climbing this is not literally true, or once we started climbing a tree, we would never get down! So the tree analogy is not perfect here.

peasement that would only encourage hostile powers to use force against American interests. Both groups saw the world through perspectives that they had learned from their own histories. Of course, a knowledge of history can be an important guide to action in the present. However, we may sometimes be hampered in our responses to contemporary events by the heavy hand of the past.

THE PRINCIPLES OF POLITICS IN ACTION

In just the first eight years of the twenty-first century, several seismic events have changed many facets of American political life: the terrorist attacks of September 11, 2001, and their still-unfolding consequences, including the war on terrorism; the wars in Afghanistan and Iraq; the devastation caused by Hurricane Katrina; and the elections of 2006 and 2008. These events have affected the objectives and strategies, and the attention, of politicians and citizens (the rationality principle), the deployment of political resources and the mobilization of activities (the collective-action principle), the agendas of our political institutions (the institution principle), the policies of government, the ones pursued and the ones deferred (the policy principle), and the ways in which history has shaped our responses and our responses will shape tomorrow's history (the history principle). In this section, we briefly examine these events and demonstrate how our five principles can help us organize our thinking about them. In a nutshell, this is what political scientists do: look at real events and, using principles, try to explain them.

In early 2003, President George W. Bush began a series of diplomatic and military moves aimed at the regime of Saddam Hussein in Iraq. Hussein and his Baathist party cronies had dominated Iraq for several decades, using oil revenues, police-state tactics, and military incursions against its neighbors (Iran and Kuwait in particular) to quash domestic opposition, enrich themselves financially, and entrench themselves politically. President Bush was intent on diminishing the threat of Hussein in the Middle East. He sought acknowledgment from the Iraqi regime that it possessed weapons of mass destruction (WMDs) and was committed to destroying existing stocks and capabilities and to ending dealings with terrorist elements. Frustrated by a lack of progress in securing these objectives, the administration increasingly focused on removing Hussein and deposing the Baathist regime, by diplomatic or collective military measures if possible and by (essentially) unilateral means if necessary.

Without much enthusiasm, the administration allowed United Nations weapons inspections to run their course over many months without uncovering any WMDs in Iraq. Under pressure from the Democrats and domestic public opinion, President Bush agreed in the first months of 2003 to continue pursuing a diplomatic solution. He sent Secretary of State Colin Powell to the United Nations to lay out the administration's case against the Iraqi regime. But our nominal allies on the UN Security Council, especially France and Russia, refused to sanction military action. So together with a "coalition of the willing" (several dozen countries, including Australia, Great Britain, Spain, and Japan), the United States launched a war against Iraq in March 2003 without UN support.

Military results came quickly. The Iraqi army and police were defeated and disbanded; Hussein's sons, his heirs apparent, were killed; and Hussein was ultimately captured. Indeed, at one point President Bush landed on an aircraft carrier in full flight gear beneath a banner reading "Mission Accomplished." Alas, only the initial *military* mission had been accomplished. The postwar reconstruction of a ravaged Iraqi infrastructure and economy was but the first of many headaches facing the victorious coalition. The task of what had been thought of as neutralizing "pockets of resistance" grew into the much bigger task of defeating a broad military resistance, especially in the Sunni Triangle of north-central Iraq.

As American casualties mounted and the vast scope of what remained to be done to stabilize Iraq and transform it politically and economically became increasingly apparent, political repercussions began to be felt at home. The financial burdens of the war and reconstruction were immense. With domestic tax revenues already reduced by the combination of a shaky economy at home and huge tax cuts engineered by the Bush administration and the Republican Congress, Americans were facing historically unprecedented deficits that promised to burden the economy for years to come.

Nonetheless, in the 2004 national elections, President Bush was able to persuade many Americans that his policies in Iraq and at home were protecting the nation from the continuing threat of terrorism. Bush and the Republicans defeated their Democratic rivals and retained control of the White House and both houses of Congress. By 2006, though, Americans had grown weary of continuing casualties in Iraq and had begun to wonder whether the administration's policies at home were effective. In 2006, the Democrats won majorities in both houses of Congress. By 2008, a serious financial crisis further undermined popular support for Bush's economic policies and the expensive war in Iraq, and the Democrats won the presidency while also increasing their majorities in Congress.

Now that we have reviewed these important events, we can ask ourselves, Why did the people involved make the choices they did, and what were the consequences? Answering these questions becomes much easier using our five principles of politics.

The Rationality Principle

Throughout his first term, President Bush was highly focused on reelection. He was intent on avoiding the fate of his father: being a one-term president. His Republican brethren in the House and the Senate were also keen on staying in office and holding their majorities; they realized that their fates were intertwined with that of the president. Although it is unfair and inaccurate to accuse President Bush of being single-minded in his pursuit of reelection, it is clear that no action was taken without considering its ramifications for reelection and the electoral prospects of Republican members of Congress.

The Collective-Action Principle

To succeed politically, the war on terrorism and the wars in Afghanistan and Iraq needed to produce results through collective action. The commitment of manpower and financial resources was essential. The orchestration of policy—through the Department of Homeland Security and the Department of Justice on the home front and the Department of Defense overseas—was also essential. The need for coordination meant that some players gained strength and others were marginalized. The initial winners were the leaders of the Department of Defense and the Department of Homeland Security, as the focus on the war on terrorism and the war in Iraq increased their importance. The biggest loser was the Department of State and its secretary, Colin Powell (who was replaced after the 2004 elections by Condoleezza Rice). Other domestic agencies were also sidelined by this focus. (The No Child Left Behind education policy, one of President Bush's domestic centerpieces, was significantly underfunded, for example.) The initial bureaucratic sorting that occurred was the product of results-oriented politics taking place against the backdrop of the 2004 election. After continuing casualties in Iraq hurt the GOP in the 2006 election, President Bush fired Defense Secretary Donald Rumsfeld.

In 2005, Hurricane Katrina further highlighted the challenges of collective action in the newly reorganized bureaucracy. Many of the agencies responsible for planning and post-emergency response simply weren't on the same page. At the federal level, many of those agencies had recently been brought under the Department of Homeland Security. Whether because of the newness of the department, the rivalries among some of its parts, or the lack of professional competence of its political appointees, the nation was unprepared for a disaster like the storm that devastated New Orleans and the Mississippi, Alabama, and Louisiana Gulf Coast. The institutional failure of collective action was exacerbated by federal-state miscoordination, state-local miscoordination, and a general sense that there were many chiefs and many followers but no clear lines of command or communication between or across levels of government. Katrina provides an exemplary illustration of the proposition that collective action is often most difficult at exactly the point when it is most needed.

The Institution Principle

The single biggest institutional manifestation of the war policies that were highlighted during George W. Bush's first term was the creation of the Department of Homeland Security (DHS). Coordinated collective action is crucial, of course, to produce major policy results. Wars, whether against amorphous terrorist organizations or concrete nations, are complex undertakings with many different moving parts. A continuing effort cannot depend on ad hoc, one-off arrangements; it needs to be institutionalized. It is still too early to judge whether the new department has successfully synchronized the many agencies that now fall under its control. Several of the DHS's emergency response agencies did not function well in responding to the aftermath of Hurricane Katrina in 2005. And it should be emphasized that institutional arrangements like the DHS are not set in stone. There will be incessant tinkering with their structure, jurisdiction, and budget—all in response to a changing environment, their initial track record, and bureaucratic maneuverings by politicians.

In 2005, President Bush continued reorganizing national-security institutions by creating the Office of the Director of National Intelligence, headed by an official popularly known as the intelligence czar. This position was a response to a proposal of the 9/11 Commission, an expert body formed to investigate the 2001 terrorist attacks and recommend actions to prevent future attacks. The purpose of the new office was to coordinate and oversee the operations of established intelligence agencies and, in particular, to make certain they shared information with one another. The creation of the new office touched off a round of bureaucratic warfare as the Defense Department, the Central Intelligence Agency, and other agencies saw their autonomy threatened. The first intelligence czar, John Negroponte, struggled to assert his authority in the face of resistance from the established bureaucracies.

The Policy Principle

Policies are the result of political ambitions played out in a context of institutional processes. President Bush's seizing of the initiative after the horrors of September 11, first in fighting the Taliban in Afghanistan, then in developing the broader war against terrorism, and finally in destroying Saddam Hussein's regime in Iraq, reflected his ambition for a successful first term and a successful campaign for a second. This is, as noted earlier, an oversimplification; clearly President Bush aspired to accomplish much more. But his first nine months in office were unspectacular, and the challenges following September 11 gave his administration an opportunity to respond forcefully. Bush's ambitions, together with the powers of a chief executive faced with a security threat, were translated into policies as diverse as congressional authorization to use force in Afghanistan and Iraq, the budgetary means to fight those wars, and legislation (for example, the USA Patriot Act, which empowered executive agencies to prosecute a domestic war against terrorism). Bush's political ambitions were a necessary ingredient, but so too was his effective mobilization of the political power of institutions to produce the desired policies. During this period, the Bush administration transformed small majorities in each legislative chamber into winning coalitions on policies that enabled his ambitions to be realized.

Another illustration of the ambition-institutions nexus (ambition + institutions = policy) relates to a piece of domestic legislation that Congress passed in late 2004— a major farm bill. The Democratic minority in the Senate was unhappy with various aspects of its provisions and was prepared to filibuster the bill (that is, engage in delaying tactics that would prevent it from coming to a vote). To do this, the bill's opponents needed nearly all Democrats to participate in the tactic. Of all people, however, the Democratic leader in the Senate, Tom Daschle of South Dakota, announced he would support the bill and oppose any delaying tactic. The reason? Daschle was engaged in a tough reelection contest (one he ultimately lost by a slim margin). Agriculture is the major industry in South Dakota, and South Dakota farmers generally favored the farm bill's generous subsidies for the crops they grew as well as the financial backing for converting corn into ethanol. (See the Applying the Principles: Politics in the News box at the end of this chapter.) So Daschle's political ambitions, though they ran counter to the preferences of the party of which he was the Senate leader, led him to play a pivotal institutional role in defeating the delaying tactics and, in the end, allowing passage of legislation that his constituents expected to be a boon to his state.

The History Principle

History mattered a lot to President Bush. As is true of any president, he looked to his reputation and historical legacy. And he had the experience of his father's failed reelection bid as a burr under his saddle. When Bush addressed firefighters, police, and rescue workers at ground zero just after September 11, 2001, and spoke to Congress and the American people shortly after that, he surely had in mind the image of Franklin Roosevelt the day after the attack on Pearl Harbor in 1941. It was his opportunity to come across as a decisive leader, rescue his faltering administration, reinvigorate his reelection prospects, and strike a pose for the history books.

It was a heroic moment in which he not only made history but also drew on history. Bush's decisive leadership after September 11 and his bold initiatives in Afghanistan and Iraq transformed him into a "war president" and put him in the same category, at least initially, as previous war presidents. Historically, being in this category is a double-edged sword. On the one hand, it contrasts favorably with instances of presidential weakness in times of war (such as his father's decision not to take the fighting all the way to Baghdad in the 1991 Persian Gulf War or Jimmy Carter's ineffectual handling of the Iranian hostage crisis in 1979–80) and creates positive associations with instances of presidential strength (such as Roosevelt after Pearl Harbor). On the other hand, it risks having one's actions compared to instances of presidential failure (Harry Truman in Korea, Lyndon Johnson and Richard Nixon in Vietnam). History worked against Bush as voters remembered previous instances, such as Korea and Vietnam, in which American forces seemed involved in costly conflicts with no clear end in sight. In November 2006, President Bush made an official visit to Vietnam and spoke on the war in Iraq while standing in front of a bust of the late Vietnamese leader Ho Chi Minh, whose forces had battled Americans some thirty years earlier. Bush said the lesson of the Vietnam War was that America would succeed unless it quit. The president's critics said the lesson of Vietnam was that America should not get bogged down in third world countries for unclear objectives.

Putting It All Together

This introductory chapter has asked much of the reader. We have set the stage for an analytical treatment of the variety of phenomena that constitutes American politics. This analytical approach requires attention to *argument* and *evidence*. To construct an argument about some facet of American politics—Why were voters attracted to Barack Obama in 2008? How does the goal of reelection affect politicians' decisions? Why is it so hard to coordinate an effective response to a major disaster like Hurricane Katrina?—we provide a set of five principles. The linchpin is the Rationality Principle, emphasizing individual goal-seeking as a key explanation for behavioral patterns. But politics is a collective undertaking, and it is often structured by political arrangements, so we also focus on collective action and the institutions in which collective action takes place (Collective Action Principle, Institution Principle). The combination of goal-seeking individuals engaging in collective activity in institutional contexts provides leverage for understanding why governments govern as they do—making laws, passing budgets, implementing policies, rendering judicial judgments (Policy Principle). But we could not make complete sense of these activities without an appreciation of the broader historical landscape (History Principle). These five principles, then, are tools of analysis. They are also tools of discovery, permitting the interested observer to uncover new ideas about why politics works as it does.

Rationality Principle	Collective-Action Principle	Institution Principle	Policy Principle	History Principle
All political behavior has a purpose.	All politics is collective action.	Institutions routinely solve collective-action problems.	Political outcomes are the products of individual preferences and institutional procedures.	History matters.

Arguments may be tight or loose, compelling or questionable, persuasive or dubious. To know if an argument has anything to contribute to understanding what's going on in the real world around us, we need to sift through evidence. In the study of American politics, much of this evidence is quantitative and much of it is easily accessible on significant Web sites. Making sense of such evidence is what political scientists do in their workaday world. We provide some examples of how to go about this task with the "Analyzing the Evidence" units in each chapter of this book. We hope these explorations of "how political scientists know what we know" prove helpful in allowing *you* to analyze evidence as we move through the empirical chapters of the book.

Drawing on the lesson of the History Principle, we begin in the remaining chapters of Part One by setting the historical stage. With analytical principles and strategies for analyzing evidence in hand, we are in a position to understand what influenced and inspired the founding generation more than two centuries ago to create a national government and a federal political system, while preserving individual rights and liberties.

SUMMARY

Government is composed of institutions and processes that rulers establish to strengthen and perpetuate their power or control over a land and its inhabitants. Politics refers to the conflicts and struggles over the character, leadership, and policies of government. American government and politics are extraordinarily complex. Understanding the complexities of government and politics might seem like an overwhelming task, but this chapter proposes five basic principles to help understand the apparent chaos.

The five principles of politics introduced in this chapter are employed throughout this book. Each time one of the principles is referred to in the text, an icon appears in the margin to highlight the principle involved and how it applies to the discussion. As you read—in fact, even when you encounter politics outside the classroom—keep this framework in mind. If you find yourself wondering why collective action on environmental problems is so difficult or why immigration policy has been so controversial, think about these principles. Consider the rationality principle: What are the goals of the individuals involved? Consider the collective-action principle: What are the challenges to forming effective coalitions in this situation? Consider the institution principle: What institutional rules are in place that shape the debate? Consider the policy principle: What consequences are likely to result, considering the people involved and the rules they are working under? And consider the history principle: How has this issue been shaped by past events? These are the questions that you (thinking like a political scientist) can ask and, using our five principles of politics, begin to answer.

FOR FURTHER READING

Bianco, William T. *American Politics: Strategy and Choice.* New York: Norton, 2001.

Dahl, Robert A. *Who Governs? Democracy and Power in an American City.* New Haven, Conn.: Yale University Press, 1961.

Downs, Anthony. *An Economic Theory of Democracy.* New York: Harper & Row, 1957.

Hindmoor, Andrew. *Rational Choice.* New York: Palgrave-Macmillan, 2006.

ONLINE READING Lupia, Arthur, and Mathew D. McCubbins. *The Democratic Dilemma: Can Citizens Learn What They Need to Know?* New York: Cambridge University Press, 1998.

Mueller, Dennis. *Public Choice III.* New York: Cambridge, 2003.

ONLINE READING Olson, Mancur, Jr. *The Logic of Collective Action: Public Goods and the Theory of Groups.* 1965. Reprinted with new preface and appendix. Cambridge, Mass.: Harvard University Press, 1971.

Putnam, Robert D. *Making Democracy Work: Civic Traditions in Modern Italy.* Princeton, N.J.: Princeton University Press, 1993.

Riker, William H. *Liberalism against Populism: A Confrontation between the Theory of Democracy and the Theory of Social Choice.* San Francisco: Freeman, 1982.

Shepsle, Kenneth A. "Rational Choice Institutionalism," in R.A.W. Rhodes, Sarah A. Binder, and Bert A. Rockman, eds. *The Oxford Handbook of Political Institutions.* New York: Oxford, 2006, pp. 23–39.

ONLINE READING ———, and Mark S. Bonchek. *Analyzing Politics: Rationality, Behavior, and Institutions.* New York: Norton, 1997.

Federal energy policy is now firmly in favor of corn-based ethanol as opposed to ethanol from other sources that may ultimately be more efficient. This policy stance seems counter to the broader interests of consumers and contrary to the opinions of the scientific community. The principles of politics help us understand why this outcome was reached.

Corn-based ethanol has always had allies in Congress due to an institutional feature of the American political system: Every state, regardless of population, is represented by two senators, which means that less populous rural states have a higher ratio of senators to constituents—giving them proportionately more power. Senators from corn-producing states—where ethanol producer Archer Daniels Midland was a powerful influence—had a political self-interest in promoting ethanol use.

Now, with fuel prices rising and increased attention to the threat of global warming, politicians across the political spectrum—national security advocates, farm state supporters, members of Congress from oil producing states, and left-leaning environmentalists—find it in their political self-interest to promote corn-based ethanol. This is the rationality principle in action.

However, diversion of corn for ethanol production may increase food prices both domestically and worldwide, and could hurt the trade deficit. More worrisome, perhaps, are indications that corn-based ethanol does not save petroleum, since it takes a lot of energy to grow corn. But that may not matter, since the political and economic forces are now lined up behind ethanol, and it may take another energy crisis to push us along a different policy path.

The New York Times, January 23, 2007

Springtime for Ethanol

BY ALEXEI BARRIONUEVO

The Renewable Fuels Association, the ethanol industry's major lobbyist, works out of cramped offices that it shares with a lawyer near Capitol Hill. Pictures of ethanol plants from its 61 board members hang everywhere. "We're about to run out of wall space," said Bob Dinneen, the association's president.

The association may only have six staff members but it is now bursting with energy, a far cry from the early days when its founder, a South Dakota farm boy who was convinced America needed to break the stranglehold of foreign oil,

quit in frustration after four years.

After three decades of surviving mostly on tax subsidies, the industry is poised tonight to get its biggest endorsement from on high that it has a long-term future as a home-grown alternative to gasoline.

In his State of the Union address, President Bush is expected to call for a huge increase in the amount of ethanol that refiners mix with gasoline, probably double the current goal of 7.5 billion gallons by 2012. * * * 15 billion gallons of ethanol would work out to more than 10 percent of the country's current gasoline consumption, and is far beyond the current capacity of about 5.4 billion gallons.

At least half of the new ethanol would come from corn, signaling the administration's support to the Midwest farm states that have benefited the most from the recent ethanol boom.

For an industry once dominated by the will of a single powerful producer, Archer Daniels Midland, ethanol has come a long way, joining the oil industry and producers of major agricultural commodities as an entrenched political force in Washington. And it now enjoys a powerful role in presidential politics because of Iowa's status as one of the first states to select delegates to the parties' nominating conventions.

But with dozens of new ethanol plants coming online this year, the ethanol lobby is facing a critical point. The political reality is that corn's days as the chief crop for making the fuel may be numbered.

Corn-based ethanol can only marginally reduce America's dependence on foreign oil. But it does little, if anything, to improve energy efficiency, and the mounting concern of some politicians is that relying on corn is leading to collateral damage in other parts of the agricultural economy and threatening the nation's status as the leading corn exporter. The big increase in the works may mean consumers would end up paying more at the supermarket.

So the ethanol lobby and its political supporters now face the challenge of trying to maintain the momentum of ethanol's feel-good story before the potential negative consequences of the rapid ramp-up become all too apparent. * * *

Today, to keep the ethanol train moving, ethanol makers are cozying up to the oil industry * * * as they race to make a quicker transition to cellulosic ethanol made from nonfood crops, like switchgrass. * * *

Some analysts, though, believe that politics has already trumped economics. "Once we have a corn-based technology up and running the political system will protect it," said Lawrence J. Goldstein, a board member at the Energy Policy Research Foundation. "We cannot afford to have 15 billion gallons of corn-based ethanol in 2015, and that's exactly where we are headed."

Mr. Goldstein said that rather than speed up the process of producing more ethanol, Congress should "step back and reflect on the damage we have already done."

By contrast, ethanol advocates in Congress are pushing to accelerate research into cellulosic sources with the stated goal of speeding the timetable for when corn can be supplemented—or supplanted—as the chief ethanol crop.

"We need additional funds for transitioning to making more energy crops for our national security," Senator Tom Harkin, an Iowa Democrat and the new chairman of the Senate Agriculture Committee, said in an interview earlier this month.

The agriculture secretary, Mike Johanns, said there will be an "adjustment period" for ethanol that will last a few years. But he is confident that more corn will emerge to ease the pain of higher grain prices. * * *

With the influence of Dwayne O. Andreas, A.D.M.'s longtime chief executive and now chairman emeritus, Congress passed the federal excise tax in 1978 that gave ethanol its primary subsidy, a credit worth 51 cents per gallon of ethanol, or $21 per barrel of oil. Mr. Andreas had powerful friends in Congress, including Senator Robert J. Dole, a Republican from Kansas who rose to majority leader

History Principle

By creating incentives for a particular economic activity, such as using corn-based ethanol, the government can cement into place powerful political alliances which can make it difficult to pursue an alternative energy path in the future.

Rationality Principle

It's easy for rational politicians to support corn-based ethanol: the presidential aspirant needs support in the farm states, the Midwestern politician wants to support the rural economy, the environmentalist turns to ethanol as a cleaner alternative, and everyone supports a fuel that is domestically produced.

and who pushed consistently over the years to retain the ethanol subsidy.

In those early days the influence of Mr. Andreas and A.D.M.'s generous contributions to both Republicans and Democrats kept ethanol alive. The company also held greater sway within the organization because of its great weight as an ethanol producer. Even today, at around 25 percent of total ethanol capacity, A.D.M. remains the largest maker.

At first, the ethanol producers had few allies. The National Corn Growers Association was agnostic about ethanol at best, and the American Farm Bureau opposed ethanol, worrying that it could raise the price of livestock feed and cut into exports. * * *

That began to change in the late 1980s when the groups began to work together to supply ethanol to some 30 cities as a gasoline additive in the winter months. Those months were also when A.D.M.'s wet mill corn processing plants made more ethanol.

While the ethanol and corn forces preferred their wintertime plan, they later threw their support behind a federal proposal to implement a reformulated gasoline with an "oxygenate"—either ethanol or methyl tertiary-butyl ether—in nine of the country's smoggiest cities. The program took effect in 1995.

Ethanol's big breakthrough came over the battle to ban M.T.B.E. After gasoline spills in California revealed that M.T.B.E. could corrode groundwater, the Renewable Fuels Association and the corn growers were among those pushing ethanol as an environmentally safer alternative.

California banned M.T.B.E. in 1999 and requested a waiver from the federal oxygenate standard, arguing it could make a cleaner-burning gasoline without ethanol. President Bush rejected the waiver, spurring an ethanol construction miniboom.

In 2001, Mr. Dinneen took over as president, focused on reaching détente with the oil industry. To win approval for the renewable fuels standard, he eventually cobbled together an unlikely coalition of consumer groups, the American Petroleum Institute and environmentalists like the Natural Resources Defense Council.

The fuel standard Congress approved in 2005, which called for a ramp-up of ethanol use to 7.5 billion gallons by 2012, ended up lighting a fire under the industry. When oil prices shot over $50 a barrel, ethanol became profitable, and then President Bush set off an industry building boom when he said last January that "America is addicted to oil."

It helped that the mix of ethanol's advocates had been changing. About a decade ago farmers began investing in ethanol plants; today more than half of the 110 ethanol plants in production are at least partly owned by farmers. The ownership by farmers brought home the rural benefits of the ethanol industry more directly.

The association's expanding board, which is 10 times the size it was some 20 years ago, has also become more diverse and less beholden to the business agendas of its biggest members.

As ethanol expands, Mr. Dinneen dismissed the concerns of some economists that its explosive growth could threaten exports and livestock prices, and that a potential investment bubble could burst before cellulosic ethanol has a chance to hit the market.

"I don't get all that worried that we are building too fast," he said. "I am not bright enough or foolish enough to try to control the market."

Institution Principle

When the Bush administration rejected California's proposal, it meant that petroleum companies and ethanol companies were no longer in competition—they had to cooperate to combine gasoline and ethanol as a cleaner burning fuel.

Rationality Principle

Political support for corn-based ethanol is much stronger now that politicians can argue that ethanol supports the interests of family farmers and not just a few large producers.

2

Constructing a Government: The Founding and the Constitution

"NO TAXATION WITHOUT REPRESENTATION" were words that stirred a generation of Americans long before they even dreamed of calling themselves Americans rather than Englishmen. In reaction to English attempts to extract tax revenues to pay for the troops that were being sent to defend the colonial frontier, protests erupted throughout the colonies against the infamous Stamp Act of 1765. This act required that all printed and legal documents, including newspapers, pamphlets, advertisements, notes and bonds, leases, deeds, and licenses, be printed on official paper stamped and sold by English officials. To show their displeasure with the act, the colonists held mass meetings, participated in parades, lit bonfires, and conducted other demonstrations throughout the spring and summer of 1765. In Boston, for example, a stamp agent was hanged and burned in effigy. Later the home of the lieutenant governor was sacked, leading to his resignation and that of his colonial commission and stamp agents. By November 1765, business was proceeding and newspapers were being published without the stamp; in March 1766, Parliament repealed the detested law. Through their protest, the nonimportation agreements that the colonists subsequently adopted, and the Stamp Act Congress that met in October 1765, the colonists took the first steps down a path that ultimately would lead to war and the establishment of a new nation.

The people of every nation tend to glorify their own history and especially their nation's creation. Generally, through such devices as public-school textbooks and national holidays, governments encourage a heroic view of the nation's past as a way of promoting national pride and unity. Great myths are part of the process of nation building and citizenship training in every nation, and the United States is no exception. To most contemporary Americans, the Revolutionary period represents a brave struggle by a determined and united group of colonists against British oppression. The Boston Tea Party, the battles of Lexington and Concord, the winter at Valley

Forge—these are the events that we emphasize in our history.

To really understand the character of the American founding and the meaning of the American Constitution, however, it is essential to look beyond the myths and the rhetoric. The first principle of politics is that all political behavior has a purpose. The men and women who became revolutionaries were guided by a number of purposes. Most of the nation's founders were not political theorists. They were, rather, hardheaded and pragmatic in their commitments and activities. Although their interests were not identical, they did agree that a relationship of political and economic dependence on a colonial power, one that did not treat them as full-fledged citizens of the empire, was intolerable. In the end, the decision to break away and, over the succeeding decade, fashion institutions of self-governance was the consequence.

Many of those most active in the initial days of the Revolution felt backed into a corner, their decisions forced. For years, the imperial center in London, preoccupied by a war with France that had spread across several continents, had left the colonists to their own devices. These were years in which the colonists enjoyed an immense amount

All five principles of politics come into play in this chapter. The framers of the Constitution, in addition to being guided by underlying values, also had conflicting interests, which were ultimately settled through the rules and procedures set forth in the Constitution. The Constitution not only provides a framework for government but also often guides the policy process—even to this day.

of local control and home rule. But suddenly, as the war with France drew to a close in the 1760s, the British presence became more onerous and more intrusive. This historical experience incited the initial reactions to taxation. As we saw in Chapter 1, history matters. Nearly a century of relatively light-handed colonial administration by London had produced a set of expectations among the colonists that later British actions unmistakably violated.

This is where we begin our story in the present chapter. We first assess the political backdrop of the American Revolution. Then we examine the Constitution that ultimately emerged—after a rather bumpy experience in self-government just after the Revolution—as the basis for America's government. We conclude with a reflection on the founding period by emphasizing a lesson to be learned from the founding that continues to be important throughout American history. The lesson is that politics, as James Madison said in *The Federalist,* generally involves struggles among conflicting interests. In 1776, the conflict was between pro-Revolutionary and anti-Revolutionary forces. In 1787, the struggle was between the Federalists and the Antifederalists. Today the struggle is between the Democrats and the Republicans, each representing competing economic, social, and sectional interests. Often political ideas are the weapons developed by competing interests to further their own causes. The New England merchants who cried "no taxation without representation" cared more about lower taxes than expanded representation. Yet today representation is one of the foundations of American democracy.

The policy principle tells us that institutional procedures help shape political outcomes. And in the United States, no set of institutional procedures is more important than the Constitution, which was drafted during our founding period. What are the basic rules embodied in the Constitution? What significance have constitutional precepts had for American life? These are the important questions addressed in this chapter.

THE FIRST FOUNDING: INTERESTS AND CONFLICTS

Competing ideals often reflect competing interests, and so it was in Revolutionary America. The American Revolution and the Constitution were outgrowths and expressions of a struggle among economic and political forces within the colonies.

Five sectors of society had interests that were important in colonial politics: (1) the New England merchants; (2) the southern planters; (3) the "royalists"—holders of royal lands, offices, and patents (licenses to engage in a profession or business activity); (4) shopkeepers, artisans, and laborers; and (5) small farmers. Throughout the eighteenth century, these groups were in conflict over issues of taxation, trade, and commerce. For the most part, however, the southern planters, the New England merchants, and the royal officeholders and patent holders—groups that together made up the colonial elite—were able to maintain a political alliance that held in check the more radical forces representing shopkeepers, laborers, and small farmers. After 1750, however, by seriously threatening the interests of New England merchants and southern planters, British tax and trade policies split the colonial elite, permitting radical forces to expand their political influence, and set into motion a chain of events that culminated in the American Revolution.[1]

British Taxes and Colonial Interests

Beginning in the 1750s, the debts and other financial problems faced by the British government forced it to search for new revenue sources. This search rather quickly led to the Crown's North American colonies, which on the whole paid remarkably little in taxes to the mother country. The British government reasoned that a sizable fraction of its debt was, in fact, attributable to the expenses it had incurred in defense of the colonies during the recent French and Indian Wars, as well as to the continuing protection from Indian attacks that British forces were giving the colonists and to the protection that the British navy was providing for colonial shipping. Thus during the 1760s, England sought to impose new, though relatively modest taxes on the colonists.

Like most governments of the period, the British regime had at its disposal only limited ways to collect revenues. The income tax, which in the twentieth century became the single most important source of government revenue, had not yet been developed. For the most part in the mid-eighteenth century, governments relied on tariffs, duties, and other taxes on commerce, and it was to such taxes, including the Stamp Act, that the British turned during the 1760s.

The Stamp Act and other taxes on commerce, such as the Sugar Act of 1764, which taxed sugar, molasses, and other commodities, most heavily affected the two groups in colonial society whose commercial interests and activities were most extensive: the New England merchants and southern planters. Under the famous slogan "no taxation without representation," the merchants and planters together sought to organize opposition to the new taxes. In the course of the struggle against British tax measures, the planters and merchants broke with their Royalist allies and turned to their former adversaries—the shopkeepers, small farmers, laborers, and artisans—for help. With the assistance of these groups, the merchants and planters organized demonstrations and a boycott of British goods that ultimately forced the Crown to rescind most of

History Principle

The American colonists, who had become used to self-governance, believed that the Stamp Act of 1765 threatened their autonomy.

---

[1]The social makeup of colonial America and some of the social conflicts that divided colonial society are discussed in Jackson Turner Main, *The Social Structure of Revolutionary America* (Princeton, N.J.: Princeton University Press, 1965).

its new taxes. It was in the context of this unrest that a confrontation between colonists and British soldiers in front of the Boston customhouse on the night of March 5, 1770, resulted in what came to be known as the Boston Massacre. Nervous British soldiers opened fire on the mob surrounding them, killing five colonists and wounding eight others. News of this event quickly spread throughout the colonies and was used by radicals to fan anti-British sentiment.

From the perspective of the merchants and planters, however, the British government's decision to eliminate most of the hated taxes represented a victorious end to their struggle with the mother country. They were eager to end the unrest they had helped arouse, and they supported the British government's efforts to restore order. Indeed, most respectable Bostonians supported the actions of the British soldiers involved in the Boston Massacre. In their subsequent trial, the soldiers were defended by John Adams, a pillar of Boston society and a future president of the United States. Adams asserted that the soldiers' actions were entirely justified, provoked by a "motley rabble of saucy boys, negroes and mulattoes, Irish teagues and outlandish Jack tars." All but two of the soldiers were acquitted.[2]

Despite the efforts of the British government and the better-to-do strata of colonial society, it proved difficult to bring an end to the political strife. The more radical forces representing shopkeepers, artisans, laborers, and small farmers, who had been mobilized and energized by the struggle over taxes, continued to agitate for political and social change within the colonies. These radicals, led by individuals like Samuel Adams, cousin of John Adams, asserted that British power supported an unjust political and social structure within the colonies, and they began to advocate an end to British rule.[3]

Organizing resistance to the British authorities required widespread support, however. Collective action, as we saw in the previous chapter, may emerge spontaneously in certain circumstances, but the colonists' campaign against the British imperial power in late-eighteenth-century America was a series of encounters, maneuvers, and ultimately, confrontations that required planning, coalition building, bargaining, compromising, and coordinating—all elements of the give-and-take of politics. Conflicts among the colonists had to be resolved by bargaining, persuasion, and even force. Cooperation needed cultivation and encouragement. Leadership was clearly a necessary ingredient.

Collective-Action Principle

The colonists required strong leaders to resolve differences and organize resistance to British authority.

Political Strife and the Radicalizing of the Colonists

The political strife within the colonies was the background for the events of 1773–74. In 1773, the British government granted the politically powerful East India Company a monopoly on the export of tea from Britain, eliminating a lucrative form of trade for colonial merchants. To add to the injury, the East India Company sought to sell the tea directly in the colonies instead of working through the colonial mer-

---

[2]Quoted in George B. Tindall and David E. Shi, *America: A Narrative History,* 6th ed. (New York: Norton, 2004), p. 199.

[3]For a discussion of events leading up to the Revolution, see Charles M. Andrews, *The Colonial Background of the American Revolution: Four Essays in American Colonial History* (New Haven, Conn.: Yale University Press, 1924).

chants. Tea was an extremely important commodity in the 1770s, and these British actions posed a mortal threat to the New England merchants. The merchants once again called on their radical adversaries for support. The most dramatic result was the Boston Tea Party of 1773, led by Samuel Adams.

This event was of decisive importance in American history. The merchants had hoped to force the British government to rescind the Tea Act, but they did not support any demands beyond this one. They certainly did not seek independence from Britain. Samuel Adams and the other radicals, however, hoped to provoke the British government to take actions that would alienate its colonial supporters and pave the way for a rebellion. This was precisely the purpose of the Boston Tea Party, and it succeeded. By dumping the East India Company's tea into Boston Harbor, Adams and his followers goaded the British into enacting a number of harsh reprisals. Within five months of the incident in Boston, the House of Commons had passed a series of acts that closed the port of Boston to commerce, changed the provincial government of Massachusetts, provided for the removal of accused persons to England for trial, and most important, restricted movement to the West—further alienating the southern planters who depended on access to new western lands. These acts of retaliation confirmed the worst criticisms of England and helped radicalize Americans and move them toward collective resistance to British rule.

The choice of this course of action by English politicians looks puzzling in retrospect, but at the time it appeared reasonable to those who prevailed in Parliament that a show of force was required. The toleration of lawlessness and the making of concessions, they felt, would only egg on the more radical elements in the colonies to take further liberties and demand further concessions. The English, in effect, drew a line in the sand. Their repressive reactions served as a clear point around which dissatisfied colonists could rally. Radicals like Samuel Adams had been agitating for more violent measures to deal with England. But ultimately they needed Britain's political repression to create widespread support for independence.

Thus the Boston Tea Party set into motion a cycle of provocations and retaliations that in 1774 resulted in the convening of the First Continental Congress, an assembly consisting of delegates from all parts of the colonies, which called for a total boycott of British goods and, under the prodding of the radicals, began to consider the possibility of independence from British rule. The eventual result was the Declaration of Independence.

The Declaration of Independence

In 1776, the Second Continental Congress appointed a committee consisting of Thomas Jefferson of Virginia, Benjamin Franklin of Pennsylvania, Roger Sherman of Connecticut, John Adams of Massachusetts, and Robert Livingston of New York to draft a statement of American independence from British rule. The Declaration of Independence, written by Jefferson and adopted by the Second Continental Congress, was an extraordinary document in both philosophical and political terms. Philosophically, the Declaration was remarkable for its assertion that certain rights, called "unalienable rights"—including life, liberty, and the pursuit of happiness—could not be abridged by governments. In the world of 1776, a world in which some kings still claimed to rule by divine right, this was a dramatic statement. Politically, the Declaration was remarkable because, despite the differences of interest that divided the colonists along economic, regional, and philosophical lines, it identified and focused on problems, grievances, aspirations, and principles that might unify the various colonial groups. The Declaration was an attempt to identify and articulate a history and a set of principles that might help to forge national unity.[4]

The Articles of Confederation

Having declared their independence, the colonies needed to establish a governmental structure. In November of 1777, the Continental Congress adopted the *Articles of Confederation and Perpetual Union*—the United States' first written constitution. Although it was not ratified by all the states until 1781, it was the country's operative constitution for almost twelve years, until March 1789.

The Articles of Confederation formed a constitution concerned primarily with limiting the powers of the central government. The central government, first of all, was based entirely in Congress. Because it was not intended to be a powerful government, it was given no executive branch. Execution of its laws was to be left to the individual states. Second, Congress had little power. Its members were not much more than delegates or messengers from the state legislatures. They were chosen by the state legislatures, their salaries were paid out of the state treasuries, and they were subject to immediate recall by state authorities. In addition, each state, regardless of its size, had only a single vote.

Congress was given the power to declare war and make peace, to make treaties and alliances, to coin or borrow money, and to regulate trade with Native Americans. It could also appoint the senior officers of the U.S. Army. But it could not levy taxes or regulate commerce among the states. Moreover, the army officers it appointed had no army to serve in because the nation's armed forces were composed of the state militias. Probably the most unfortunate aspect of the Articles of Confederation was that the central government could not prevent one state from discriminating against other states in the quest for foreign commerce.

In brief, the relationship between Congress and the states under the Articles of Confederation was much like the contemporary relationship between the United Nations and its member states, a relationship in which virtually all governmental powers are retained by the states. It was properly called a confederation because, as provided under Article II, "each state retains its sovereignty, freedom, and independence, and every power, jurisdiction, and right, which is not by this Confederation expressly delegated to the United States, in Congress assembled." Not only was there no executive, but there was also no judicial authority and no other means of enforcing Congress's will. If there were to be any enforcement at all, it would be done for Congress by the states.[5] All told, the Articles of Confederation were an inadequate institutional basis for collective action.

Articles of Confederation and Perpetual Union America's first written constitution. Adopted by the Continental Congress in 1777, the Articles of Confederation and Perpetual Union were the formal basis for America's national government until 1789, when they were supplanted by the Constitution.

---

[4]See Carl L. Becker, *The Declaration of Independence: A Study in the History of Political Ideas* (New York: Vintage, 1942).

[5]See Merrill Jensen, *The Articles of Confederation* (Madison: University of Wisconsin Press, 1963).

THE SECOND FOUNDING: FROM COMPROMISE TO CONSTITUTION

The Declaration of Independence and the Articles of Confederation were not sufficient to hold the nation together as an independent and effective nation-state. Almost from the moment of armistice with the British in 1783, moves were afoot to reform and strengthen the Articles of Confederation.

International Standing and Balance of Power

There was a special concern for the country's international position. Competition among the states for foreign commerce allowed the European powers to play the states against one another, creating confusion on both sides of the Atlantic. At one point during the winter of 1786–87, John Adams, a leader in the struggle for independence, was sent to negotiate a new treaty with the British, one that would cover disputes left over from the war. The British government responded that because the United States under the Articles of Confederation was unable to enforce existing treaties, it would negotiate with each of the thirteen states separately.

At the same time, well-to-do Americans—in particular the New England merchants and southern planters—were troubled by the influence that "radical" forces exercised in the Continental Congress and in the governments of several of the states. The colonists' victory in the Revolutionary War not only had meant the end of British rule but also had significantly changed the balance of political power within the new states. As a result of the Revolution, one key segment of the colonial elite—the royal land, office, and patent holders—was stripped of its economic and political privileges. In fact, many of these individuals, along with tens of thousands of other colonists who considered themselves loyal British subjects, had left for Canada after the British surrender. And while the pre-Revolutionary elite was weakened, the pre-Revolutionary radicals were now better organized than ever before and were the controlling forces in such states as Pennsylvania and Rhode Island, where they pursued economic and political policies that struck terror in the hearts of the pre-Revolutionary political establishment. In Rhode Island, for example, between 1783 and 1785 a legislature dominated by representatives of small farmers, artisans, and shopkeepers had instituted economic policies, including drastic currency inflation, that frightened businessmen and property owners throughout the country. Of course, the central government under the Articles of Confederation was powerless to intervene.

Institution Principle

Institutional arrangements, such as the Articles of Confederation, can be flawed.

The Annapolis Convention

The continuation of international weakness and domestic economic turmoil led many Americans to consider whether their newly adopted form of government might not already require revision. Institutional arrangements are experiments in governance, and they don't always work out. Nearly a decade under the Articles had made amply clear the flaws it contained. In the fall of 1786, many state leaders accepted an invitation from the Virginia legislature to attend a conference of representatives of all the states. Delegates from five states actually attended. This conference, held in Annapolis, Maryland, was the first step toward the second founding. The one positive thing that came out of the Annapolis Convention was a carefully worded resolution calling on Congress to send commissioners to Philadelphia at a later time "to devise such further provisions as shall appear to them necessary to render the Constitution of the Federal Government adequate to the exigencies of the Union."[6] This resolution was drafted by Alexander Hamilton, a thirty-four-year-old New York lawyer who had played a significant role in the Revolution as George Washington's secretary and would play a still more significant role in framing the Constitution and forming the new government in the 1790s. But the resolution did not necessarily imply any desire to do more than improve and reform the Articles of Confederation.

Shays's Rebellion

It is possible that the Constitutional Convention of 1787 in Philadelphia would never have taken place at all except for a single event that occurred soon after the Annapolis Convention: Shays's Rebellion. Like the Boston Tea Party, this was a focal event. It concentrated attention, coordinated beliefs, produced widespread fear and apprehension, and thus convinced waverers that something was broke and needed fixing. In short, it prompted collective action by providing politicians who had long been convinced that the Articles were flawed and insufficient with just the ammunition they needed to convince a much broader public of these facts.[7]

Daniel Shays, a former army captain, led a mob of farmers in a rebellion against the government of Massachusetts. The purpose of the rebellion was to prevent foreclosures on their debt-ridden land by keeping the county courts of western Massachusetts from sitting until after the next election. The state militia dispersed the mob, but for several days Shays and his followers terrified the state government by attempting to capture the federal arsenal at Springfield, provoking an appeal to Congress to help restore order. Within a few days, the state government regained control and captured fourteen of the rebels (all were eventually pardoned). In 1787, a newly elected Massachusetts legislature granted some of the farmers' demands.

Although the incident ended peacefully, its effects lingered and spread. George Washington summed it up:

> I am mortified beyond expression that in the moment of our acknowledged independence we should by our conduct verify the predictions of our transatlantic foe, and render ourselves ridiculous and contemptible in the eyes of all Europe.[8]

Congress under the Confederation had been unable to act decisively in a time of crisis. This inadequacy provided critics of the Articles of Confederation with precisely the evidence they needed to push Hamilton's Annapolis resolution through the Con-

History Principle

Shays's Rebellion focused attention on the flaws of the Articles of Confederation, leading to the Constitutional Convention.

---

[6]Quoted in Samuel Eliot Morison, Henry Steele Commager, and William E. Leuchtenburg, *The Growth of the American Republic*, 6th ed., 2 vols. (New York: Oxford University Press, 1969), I, p. 244.

[7]For an easy-to-read argument that supports this view, see Keith L. Dougherty, *Collective Action under the Articles of Confederation* (New York: Cambridge University Press, 2001).

[8]Quoted in Morison et al., *The Growth of the American Republic*, I, p. 242.

gress. Thus the states were asked to send representatives to Philadelphia to discuss constitutional revision. Delegates were eventually sent by every state except Rhode Island.

The Constitutional Convention

Twenty-nine of a total of seventy-three delegates selected by the state governments convened in Philadelphia in May 1787, with political strife, international embarrassment, national weakness, and local rebellion fixed in their minds. Recognizing that these issues were symptoms of fundamental flaws in the Articles of Confederation, the delegates soon abandoned the plan to revise the Articles and committed themselves to a second founding—a second and ultimately successful attempt to create a legitimate and effective national system. This effort occupied the convention for the next five months.

A Marriage of Interest and Ideals   For years, scholars have disagreed about the motives of the founders in Philadelphia. Among the most controversial views of the framers' motives is the "economic" interpretation put forward by the historian Charles Beard and his disciples.[9] According to Beard's account, America's founders were a collection of securities speculators and property owners whose only aim was personal enrichment. From this perspective, the Constitution's lofty principles were little more than sophisticated masks behind which the most venal interests sought to enrich themselves.

Contrary to Beard's approach is the view that the framers of the Constitution were concerned with philosophical and ethical ideas. Indeed, the framers sought to devise a system of government consistent with the dominant philosophical and moral values of the day. But in fact, these two views belong together: The founders' interests were reinforced by their principles. The convention that drafted the U.S. Constitution was chiefly organized by the New England merchants and southern planters. Although the delegates representing these groups did not all hope to profit personally from an increase in the value of their securities, as Beard would have it, they did hope to benefit in the broadest political and economic sense by breaking the power of their radical foes and establishing a system of government more compatible with their long-term economic and political interests. Thus the framers sought to create a new government capable of promoting commerce and protecting property from radical state legislatures. They also sought to liberate the national government from the power of individual states and their sometimes venal and corrupt local politicians. At the same time, they hoped to fashion a government less susceptible than the existing state and national regimes to populist forces hostile to the interests of the commercial and propertied classes.

The Great Compromise   The proponents of a new government fired their opening shot on May 29, 1787, when Edmund Randolph of Virginia offered a resolution that proposed corrections and enlargements in the Articles of Confederation. The proposal, which showed the strong influence of James Madison, was not a simple motion. It provided for virtually every aspect of a new government. Randolph later admitted it was intended to be an alternative draft constitution, and it did in fact serve as the framework for what ultimately became the Constitution. (There is no

---

[9]Charles A. Beard, *An Economic Interpretation of the Constitution of the United States* (New York: Macmillan, 1913).

verbatim record of the debates, but Madison was present during virtually all of the deliberations and kept full notes on them.)[10]

This proposal, known as the Virginia Plan, provided for a system of representation in the national legislature based on the population of each state, the proportion of each state's revenue contribution, or both. (Randolph also proposed a second branch of the legislature, but it was to be elected by the members of the first branch.) Because the states varied enormously in size and wealth, the Virginia Plan was thought to be heavily biased in favor of the large states.

While the convention was debating the Virginia Plan, additional delegates arriving in Philadelphia were beginning to mount opposition to it. Their resolution, introduced by William Paterson of New Jersey and known as the New Jersey Plan, did not oppose the Virginia Plan point for point. Instead, it concentrated on specific weaknesses in the Articles of Confederation, in the spirit of revision rather than radical replacement of that document. Supporters of the New Jersey Plan did not seriously question the convention's commitment to replacing the Articles. But their opposition to the Virginia Plan's scheme of representation was sufficient to send its proposals back to committee to be worked into a common document. In particular, delegates from the less populous states, which included Delaware, New Jersey, Connecticut, and New York, asserted that the more populous states, such as Virginia, Pennsylvania, North Carolina, Massachusetts, and Georgia, would dominate the new government if representation were to be determined by population. The smaller states argued that each state should be equally represented in the new regime regardless of its population.

The issue of representation was one that threatened to wreck the entire constitutional enterprise. Delegates conferred, factions maneuvered, and tempers flared. James Wilson of Pennsylvania told the small-state delegates that if they wanted to disrupt the Union they should go ahead. The separation could, he said, "never happen on better grounds." Small-state delegates were equally blunt. Gunning Bedford of Delaware declared that the small states might look elsewhere for friends if they were forced. "The large states," he said, "dare not dissolve the confederation. If they do the small ones will find some foreign ally of more honor and good faith, who will take them by the hand and do them justice." These sentiments were widely shared. The Union, as Oliver Ellsworth of Connecticut put it, was "on the verge of dissolution, scarcely held together by the strength of a hair."

The outcome of this debate was the Connecticut Compromise, also known as the ***Great Compromise.*** Under the terms of this compromise, in the first branch of Congress—the House of Representatives—the representatives would be apportioned according to the number of inhabitants in each state. This, of course, was what delegates from the large states had sought. But in the second branch—the Senate—each state would have an equal vote regardless of its size; this was to deal with the concerns of the small states. This compromise was not immediately satisfactory to all the delegates. Indeed, two of the most vocal members of the small-state faction, John Lansing and Robert Yates of New York, were so incensed by the concession that their colleagues had made to the large-state forces that they stormed out of the convention.

Great Compromise An agreement reached at the Constitutional Convention of 1787 that gave each state an equal number of senators regardless of its population but linked representation in the House of Representatives to population.

---

[10]Madison's notes, along with the somewhat less complete records kept by several other participants in the convention, are available in a four-volume set. See Max Farrand, ed., *The Records of the Federal Convention of 1787*, rev. ed., 4 vols. (New Haven, Conn.: Yale University Press, 1966).

In the end, however, both sets of forces preferred compromise to the breakup of the Union, and the plan was accepted.

The Question of Slavery: The Three-fifths Compromise

Many of the conflicts that emerged during the Constitutional Convention were reflections of the fundamental differences between the slave and nonslave states, differences that pitted the southern planters and New England merchants against each other. This was the first premonition of a conflict that would almost destroy the Republic in later years. In the midst of debate over large versus small states, Madison observed:

> The great danger to our general government is the great southern and northern interests of the continent, being opposed to each other. Look to the votes in Congress, and most of them stand divided by the geography of the country, not according to the size of the states.[11]

Over 90 percent of all slaves resided in five states—Georgia, Maryland, North Carolina, South Carolina, and Virginia—where they accounted for 30 percent of the total population. In some places, slaves outnumbered nonslaves by as much as 10 to 1. If the Constitution were to embody any principle of national supremacy, some basic decisions would have to be made about the place of slavery in the general scheme. Madison hit on this point on several occasions as different aspects of the Constitution were being discussed. For example, he observed:

> It seemed now to be pretty well understood that the real difference of interests lay, not between the large and small but between the northern and southern states. The institution of slavery and its consequences formed the line of discrimination. There were five states on the South, eight on the northern side of this line. Should a proportional representation take place it was true, the northern side would still outnumber the other: but not in the same degree, at this time; and every day would tend towards an equilibrium.[12]

Northerners and southerners eventually reached agreement through the **Three-fifths Compromise.** The seats in the House of Representatives would be apportioned according to a "population" in which five slaves would count as three people. The slaves would not be allowed to vote, of course, but the number of representatives would be apportioned accordingly. This arrangement was supported by the slave states, which included some of the biggest and some of the smallest states at that time. It was also accepted by many delegates from nonslave states who strongly supported the principle of property representation, whether that property were expressed in slaves or in land, money, or stocks. The concern exhibited by most delegates was over how much slaves would count toward a state's representation rather than whether the institution of slavery would continue. The Three-fifths Compromise, in the words of the political scientist Donald Robinson,

> gave Constitutional sanction to the fact that the United States was composed of some persons who were "free" and others who were not, and it established the principle, new in republican theory, that a man who lives among slaves had a greater share in

Three-fifths Compromise An agreement reached at the Constitutional Convention of 1787 stipulating that for purposes of the apportionment of congressional seats, every slave would be counted as three fifths of a person.

---

[11]Ibid., I, p. 476.

[12]Ibid., II, p. 10.

the election of representatives than the man who did not. Although the Three-fifths Compromise acknowledged slavery and rewarded slave owners, nonetheless, it probably kept the South from unanimously rejecting the Constitution.[13]

The issue of slavery was the most difficult one faced by the framers, and it nearly destroyed the Union. Although some delegates believed slavery to be morally wrong, an evil and oppressive institution that made a mockery of the ideals and values espoused in the Constitution, morality was not the issue that caused the framers to support or oppose the Three-fifths Compromise. Whatever they thought of the institution of slavery, most delegates from the northern states opposed counting slaves in the distribution of congressional seats. Wilson of Pennsylvania, for example, argued that if slaves were citizens, they should be treated and counted like other citizens. If, on the other hand, they were property, then why should not other forms of property be counted toward the apportionment of Congress? But southern delegates made it clear that if the northerners refused to give in, they would never agree to the new government. William Davie of North Carolina heatedly said that it was time "to speak out." He asserted that the people of North Carolina would never enter the Union if slaves were not counted as part of the basis for representation. Without such agreement, he asserted ominously, "the business was at an end." Even southerners like Edmund Randolph of Virginia, who conceded that slavery was immoral, insisted on including slaves in the allocation of congressional seats. This conflict between the southern and northern delegates was so divisive that many came to question the possibility of creating and maintaining a union of the two. Pierce Butler of South Carolina declared that the North and the South were as different as Russia and Turkey. Eventually the North and the South compromised on the issue of slavery and representation. Indeed, northerners even agreed to permit a continuation of the odious slave trade to keep the South in the Union. But in due course, Butler proved to be correct, and a bloody war was fought when the disparate interests of the North and the South could no longer be reconciled.

Collective-Action Principle

The framers preferred compromise to the breakup of the Union and thus accepted the Great Compromise and the Three-fifths Compromise.

THE CONSTITUTION

The political significance of the Great Compromise and the Three-fifths Compromise was to reinforce the unity of the mercantile and planter forces that sought to create a new government. The Great Compromise reassured those who feared that the importance of their own local or regional influence would be reduced by the new governmental framework. The Three-fifths Compromise temporarily defused the rivalry between the merchants and the planters. Their unity secured, members of the alliance supporting the establishment of a new government moved to fashion a constitutional framework consistent with their economic and political interests.

The framers of the Constitution understood that well-designed institutions make it easier to achieve collective goals. They understood also that the institutions they built could affect political outcomes for decades, if not centuries, to come. Ac-

---

[13]Donald L. Robinson, *Slavery in the Structure of American Politics, 1765–1820* (New York: Harcourt Brace Jovanovich, 1971), p. 201.

cordingly, the framers took great care to construct institutions that over time would help the nation accomplish what they viewed as important political purposes.

In particular, the framers sought first a new government that would be strong enough to promote commerce and protect property from radical state legislatures such as Rhode Island's. This goal became the basis for national control over commerce and finance, as well as for both the establishment of national judicial supremacy and the effort to construct a strong presidency. Second, the framers sought to prevent what they saw as the threat posed by the "excessive democracy" of the state and national governments under the Articles of Confederation. Here again the framers' historical experience mattered. This goal led to such constitutional principles as *bicameralism* (division of the Congress into two chambers), checks and balances, staggered terms in office, and indirect election (selection of the president by an electoral college rather than directly by the voters). Third, the framers, lacking the power to force the states or the public at large to accept the new form of government, sought to identify principles that would help secure support. This goal became the basis for the constitutional provision for direct popular election of representatives and, subsequently, the basis for the addition of the Bill of Rights to the Constitution. Finally, the framers wanted to be certain that the government they created did not use its power to pose even more of a threat to its citizens' liberties and property rights than did the radical state legislatures they feared and despised. To prevent the new government from abusing its power, the framers incorporated into the Constitution such principles as the separation of powers and federalism.

The framers provided us with a grand lesson in instrumental behavior. They came to Philadelphia united by a common distaste for government under the Articles and animated by the agitation following Shays's Rebellion. They didn't always agree on what it was they disliked about the Articles. They certainly didn't agree on how to proceed—hence the necessity for the historic compromises we have just described. But they did believe that the acts of fostering commerce and protecting property could better be served by a set of institutional arrangements other than that provided by the Articles. They agreed that the institutional arrangements of government mattered for their lives and for those of their fellow citizens. They believed that both too much democracy and too much governmental power were threats to the common good, and they felt compelled to find instruments and principles that weighed against them. Let us assess the major provisions of the Constitution's seven articles to see how each relates to these objectives.

The Legislative Branch

The first seven sections of Article I of the Constitution provide for a Congress consisting of two chambers—a House of Representatives and a Senate. Members of the House of Representatives are given two-year terms in office and are to be elected directly by the people. Members of the Senate are to be appointed by the state legislatures (this provision was changed in 1913 by the Seventeenth Amendment, which instituted direct election of senators) for six-year terms. These terms, moreover, are staggered so that the appointments of one third of the senators expire every two years. The Constitution assigns somewhat different tasks to the House and the Senate. Though the approval of each body is required for the enactment of a law, the Senate alone is given the power to ratify treaties and approve presidential appointments. The House, on the other hand, is given the sole power to originate revenue bills.

Rationality Principle

The framers of the Constitution were guided by ideals, but they were also influenced by their interests.

Institution Principle

The constitutional framework promoted commerce, protected property, prevented "excessive democracy," and limited the power of the national government.

bicameralism The division of a legislative assembly into two chambers, or houses.

The character of the legislative branch is directly related to the framers' major goals. The House of Representatives was designed to be directly responsible to the people, to encourage popular consent for the new Constitution and to help enhance the power of the new government. At the same time, to guard against "excessive democracy," the power of the House of Representatives is checked by the Senate, whose members are to be appointed rather than elected directly by the people and are to serve long (six-year) terms. The purpose of this provision, according to Alexander Hamilton, was to avoid "an unqualified complaisance to every sudden breeze of passion, or to every transient impulse which the people may receive."[14] Staggered terms of service in the Senate, moreover, were intended to make that body even more resistant to popular pressure. Because only one third of the senators would be selected at any given time, the composition of the institution would be protected from changes in popular preferences transmitted by the state legislatures. This would prevent what James Madison called "mutability in the public councils arising from a rapid succession of new members."[15] Thus the structure of the legislative branch was designed to contribute to governmental power, promote popular consent for the new government, and at the same time place limits on the popular political currents that many of the framers saw as a radical threat to the economic and social order.

The issues of power and consent are important throughout the Constitution. Section 8 of Article I lists the specific powers of Congress, which include the authority to collect taxes, borrow money, regulate commerce, declare war, and maintain an army and navy. By granting it these powers, the framers indicated clearly that they intended the new government to be far more influential than its predecessor. At the same time, by defining the new government's most important powers as belonging to Congress, the framers sought to promote popular acceptance of this critical change by reassuring citizens that their views would be fully represented whenever the government exercised its new powers.

As a further guarantee to the people that the new government would pose no threat to them, the Constitution implies that any powers not listed are not granted at all. This is the doctrine of **expressed power.** The Constitution grants only those powers specifically expressed in its text. But the framers intended to create an active and powerful government, and so they included the **necessary and proper clause,** sometimes known as the elastic clause, which signifies that the enumerated powers are meant to be a source of strength to the national government, not a limitation on it. No new powers can be seized on by the national government without a constitutional amendment. In the absence of such an amendment, any power not enumerated is conceived to be "reserved" to the states (or the people). The framers' views on governmental power are discussed further in the Analyzing the Evidence unit for this chapter.

The Executive Branch

The Constitution provides for the establishment of the presidency in Article II. As Alexander Hamilton commented, the presidential article was aimed toward creating

expressed power
The notion that the Constitution grants to the federal government only those powers specifically named in its text.

necessary and proper clause
Article I, Section 8, of the Constitution, which enumerates the powers of Congress and provides Congress with the authority to make all laws "necessary and proper" to carry them out; also referred to as the elastic clause.

ONLINE READING

---

[14]Alexander Hamilton, James Madison, and John Jay, *The Federalist,* ed. E. M. Earle (New York: Modern Library, 1937), no. 71.

[15]Ibid., no. 62.

"energy in the Executive." It did so in an effort to overcome the natural stalemate that was built into both the bicameral legislature and the separation of powers among the legislative, executive, and judicial branches. The Constitution afforded the president a measure of independence from the people and from the other branches of government, particularly the Congress.

In line with the framers' goal of increased power in the national government, the president is granted the unconditional power to accept ambassadors from other countries; this provision amounts to the power to "recognize" other countries. The president is also given the power to negotiate treaties, although their acceptance requires the approval of the Senate. The president is given the unconditional right to grant reprieves and pardons, except in cases of impeachment. And the president is provided with the power to appoint major departmental personnel, convene Congress in a special session, and veto congressional enactments. (The veto power is formidable, but it is not absolute because Congress can override it by a two-thirds vote.)

The framers hoped to create a presidency that would make the federal government, rather than the states, the agency capable of timely and decisive action to deal with public issues and problems. This goal is the meaning of the "energy" that Hamilton hoped to impart to the executive branch.[16] At the same time, however, the framers sought to help the president withstand (excessively) democratic pressures by making the office subject to indirect rather than direct election (through selection by a separate electoral college). The extent to which the framers' hopes were realized is the topic of Chapter 6.

The Judicial Branch

In establishing the judicial branch in Article III, the Constitution reflects the framers' preoccupations with enhancing the power of the national government and checking radical democratic impulses while guarding against potential interference with liberty and property from the new national government itself.

Under the provisions of Article III, the framers created a court that was to be literally a supreme court of the United States and not merely the highest court of the national government. The most important expression of this intention was granting the Supreme Court the power to resolve any conflicts that might emerge between federal and state laws. In particular, the Supreme Court was given the right to determine whether a power was exclusive to the federal government, concurrent with the states, or exclusive to the states. The significance of this was noted by Justice Oliver Wendell Holmes Jr., who observed, "I do not think the United States would come to an end if we lost our power to declare an act of Congress void. I do think the union would be imperilled if we could not make that declaration as to the laws of the several states."[17]

In addition, the Supreme Court was assigned jurisdiction over controversies between citizens of different states. The long-term significance of this provision was that as the country developed a national economy, it came to rely increasingly on the federal judiciary, rather than the state courts, for the resolution of disputes.

---

[16]Ibid., no. 70.

[17]Oliver Wendell Holmes Jr., *Collected Legal Papers* (New York: Harcourt, Brace, 1920), pp. 295–96.

Sources and Concepts of the Framers

One way to understand the American Revolution and the Constitution is to explore their intellecutal background, which has been debated among political scientists and historians. Some scholars have focused on the importance of *liberalism* in the founding period, while others have stressed the importance of *republicanism*. What do these terms mean, and how does examining the founding period in light of these concepts help us to understand it?

The term *liberalism* can be confusing because in the contemporary United States it implies the preference for *greater* government involvement in people's lives, whereas historically and in most of the world, liberalism implies *less* government involvement. It is important to note that in this discussion, we are referring to *classical* liberalism, which emphasizes individual freedom. Scholars who focus on the liberalism of colonial political thought point to the value placed on individual rights and freedom, including freedom from government—which is often termed a negative conception of liberty. This focus on the individual is evident in the conflict over representation and taxation. John Locke, a British thinker who influenced the American founders, argued that because government is formed to protect one's person, goods, and liberty, it "cannot take from any man any part of his property without his own consent."[1] Locke's influence is clear in the words of James Otis, a Massachusetts lawyer who wrote in a 1764 essay that Parliament "cannot take from any man any part of his property, without his consent . . .."[2] Similarly, in the Declaration of Independence, Thomas Jefferson noted the "imposing (of) taxes on us without our consent" as evidence of George III's tyranny.

liberalism	republicanism
negative liberty	positive liberty
government protects individual	government serves common good
securing individual rights	promoting virtue and checking corruption

Other scholars have emphasized the republican character of colonial thought. As with liberalism, we should clarify and note that in this context *republican* does not refer to the Republican party. Here, republicanism refers to a system that depends on the consent of the governed and emphasizes civic virtue. We can see these ideas in the framers' approach to government, as well as a connection between collective self-government and liberty—a conception of liberty that is often termed positive. Rather than viewing the Revolution as the product of Lockean liberalism, these writers see it as an effort to check British corruption and protect American virtue and liberty through the creation of a republican government. We can see such a conception in Article I, Section 8 of the Constitution, and its provision of many powers to secure the common good.

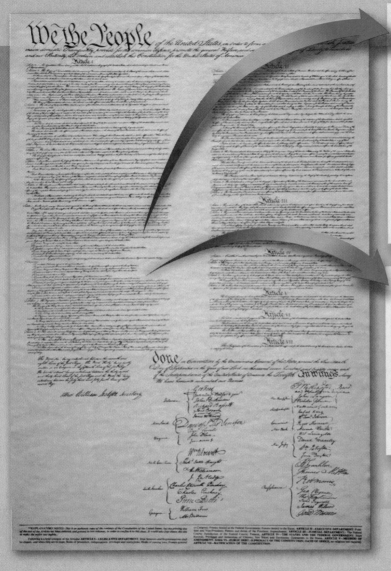

From Article I, Section 8 (republicanism)

"To make all Laws which shall be necessary and proper for carrying into Execution the foregoing Powers and all other Powers vested by this Constitution in the Government of the United States, or in any Department or Officer thereof."

From Article I, Section 9 (liberalism)

"The Privilege of the Writ of Habeas Corpus shall not be suspended, unless when in Cases or Rebellion or Invasion the public Safety may require it."

More recently, scholars have argued that the political thought of the founding period is best understood as a mixture of liberalism and republicanism. For instance, while Article I, Section 8 of the Constitution grants broad powers to the national government for securing the common good (republicanism), Article I, Section 9 provides for individual protections from the national government (liberalism).

[1] John Locke. *Second Treatise on Government.* C.B. MacPherson, ed. (Indianapolis: Hackett, 1980), p. 73.

[2] James Otis, "The Rights of the Colonies Asserted and Proved," in *Tracts of the American Revolution, 1763–1776,* ed. Merrill Jensen (Indianapolis: Hackett, 2003), p. 26.

Judges were given lifetime appointments to protect them from popular politics and interference by the other branches. This did not mean, however, that the judiciary would remain totally impartial to political considerations or to the other branches, for the president is to appoint the judges and the Senate is to approve the appointments. Congress also has the power to create inferior (lower) courts, change the jurisdiction of the federal courts, add or subtract federal judges, and even change the size of the Supreme Court.

No direct mention is made of *judicial review*—the power of the courts to render the final decision when a conflict of interpretation of the Constitution or of laws arises between the courts and Congress, the courts and the executive branch, or the courts and the states. Scholars generally feel that judicial review is implicit in the very existence of a written constitution and in the power given directly to the federal courts over "all Cases . . . arising under this Constitution, the Laws of the United States, and Treaties made, or which shall be made, under their Authority" (Article III, Section 2). The Supreme Court eventually assumed the power of judicial review. Its assumption of this power, as we shall see in Chapter 8, was based not on the Constitution itself but on the politics of later decades and the membership of the Court.

National Unity and Power

Various provisions in the Constitution address the framers' concern with national unity and power, including Article IV's provisions for comity (reciprocity) among states and among the citizens of all states.

Each state is prohibited from discriminating against the citizens of other states in favor of its own citizens, with the Supreme Court charged with deciding in each case whether a state has discriminated against goods or people from another state. The Constitution restricts the power of the states in favor of ensuring that the national government holds enough power to give the country a free-flowing national economy.

The framers' concern with national supremacy was also expressed in Article VI, in the *supremacy clause,* which provides that national laws and treaties "shall be the supreme Law of the Land." This means that all laws made under the "Authority of the United States" are superior to all laws adopted by any state or any other subdivision, and the states are expected to respect all treaties made under that authority. This provision was a direct effort to keep the states from dealing separately with foreign nations or businesses. The supremacy clause also binds the officials of all state and local, as well as federal, governments to take an oath of office to support the national Constitution. This means that every action taken by the U.S. Congress must be applied within each state as though the action were in fact state law.

Amending the Constitution

The Constitution establishes procedures for its own revision in Article V. Its provisions are so difficult that Americans have availed themselves of the amending process only seventeen times since 1791, when the first ten amendments were adopted. Many other amendments have been proposed in Congress, but fewer than forty of them have come even close to fulfilling the Constitution's requirement of a two-thirds vote in Congress, and only a fraction have gotten anywhere near adoption by three fourths of the states. The Constitution can also be amended by a constitutional convention.

judicial review The power of the courts to declare actions of the legislative and executive branches invalid or unconstitutional. The Supreme Court asserted this power in *Marbury v. Madison* (1803).

supremacy clause A clause of Article VI of the Constitution, that states that all laws passed by the national government and all treaties are the supreme laws of the land and superior to all laws adopted by any state or any subdivision.

Occasionally proponents of particular measures, such as a balanced-budget amendment, have called for a constitutional convention to consider their proposals. Whatever the purpose for which it was called, however, such a convention would presumably have the authority to revise America's entire system of government.

It should be noted that any body of rules, including a national constitution, must balance the need to respond flexibly to changes on the one hand with the caution not to be too flexible on the other. An inflexible body of rules is one that cannot accommodate major change. It risks being rebelled against, a circumstance in which the slate is wiped clean and new rules are designed—or ignored altogether. Too much flexibility, however, is disastrous. It invites those who lose in normal everyday politics to replay battles at the constitutional level. If institutional change is too easy to accomplish, the stability of the political system becomes threatened.

Ratifying the Constitution

The rules for ratification of the Constitution of 1787 are set forth in Article VII of the Constitution. This provision actually violated the amendment provisions of the Articles of Confederation. For one thing, it adopts a nine-state rule in place of the unanimity required by the Articles. For another, it provides for ratification to occur in special state conventions called for that purpose rather than in the state legislatures. All the states except Rhode Island eventually did set up state conventions to ratify the Constitution.

Constitutional Limits on the National Government's Power

As we have indicated, although the framers sought to create a powerful national government, they also wanted to guard against possible misuse of that power. To that end, the framers incorporated two key principles into the Constitution: the *separation of powers* and *federalism* (see Chapter 3). A third set of limitations, in the form of the *Bill of Rights,* was added to the Constitution to help secure its ratification when opponents of the document charged that it paid insufficient attention to citizens' rights.

The Separation of Powers   No political belief was more widely shared at the time of the founding than the idea that power must be used to balance power. The French political theorist Baron de Montesquieu (1689–1755) believed that this balance was an indispensable defense against tyranny, and his writings, especially his major work, *The Spirit of the Laws,* "were taken as political gospel" at the Philadelphia convention.[18] The idea of the separation of powers is nowhere to be found explicitly in the Constitution, but it is clearly built on Articles I, II, and III, which provide for the following:

1. Three separate and distinct branches of government (Figure 2.1).

2. Different methods of selecting the top personnel, so that each branch is responsible to a different constituency. This arrangement is supposed to produce a "mixed regime," in which the personnel of each department will develop

separation of powers The division of governmental power among several institutions that must cooperate in decision making.

federalism The system of government in which a constitution divides power between a central government and regional governments.

Bill of Rights The first ten amendments to the U.S. Constitution, adopted in 1791. The Bill of Rights ensures certain rights and liberties to the people.

---

[18]Max Farrand, *The Framing of the Constitution of the United States* (New Haven, Conn.: Yale University Press, 1962), p. 49.

FIGURE 2.1 The Separation of Powers

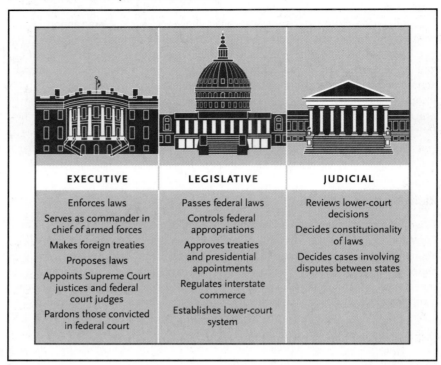

EXECUTIVE	LEGISLATIVE	JUDICIAL
Enforces laws	Passes federal laws	Reviews lower-court decisions
Serves as commander in chief of armed forces	Controls federal appropriations	Decides constitutionality of laws
Makes foreign treaties	Approves treaties and presidential appointments	Decides cases involving disputes between states
Proposes laws		
Appoints Supreme Court justices and federal court judges	Regulates interstate commerce	
Pardons those convicted in federal court	Establishes lower-court system	

different interests and outlooks on how to govern and different groups in society will be assured some access to governmental decision making.

3. **Checks and balances**—a system in which each of the branches is given some power over the others. Familiar examples are the power of the president to veto legislation, the power of the Senate to approve presidential appointments, and the power of the Supreme Court to review acts of Congress (see Figure 3.4).

One clever formulation of the separation of powers is that of a system not of separated powers but of "separated institutions sharing power"—and thus diminishing the chance that power will be misused.[19]

Federalism   Compared with the confederation principle of the Articles of Confederation, federalism was a step toward greater centralization of power. The delegates agreed that they needed to place more power at the national level, without completely undermining the power of the state governments. Thus they devised a system of two sovereigns—the states and the nation—with the hope that competition between the two would be an effective limitation on the power of both.

checks and balances The mechanisms through which each branch of government is able to participate in and influence the activities of the other branches.

---

[19]Richard E. Neustadt, *Presidential Power and the Modern Presidents: The Politics of Leadership from Roosevelt to Reagan* (1960; rev. ed., New York: Free Press, 1990), p. 33.

The Bill of Rights   Late in the Philadelphia convention, a motion was made to include a bill of rights in the Constitution. After a brief debate, in which hardly a word was said in its favor and only one speech was made against it, the motion to include it was almost unanimously turned down. Most delegates sincerely believed that because the federal government was already limited to its expressed powers, any further protection of citizens was not needed. The delegates argued that the states should adopt bills of rights because their greater powers needed greater limitations. But almost immediately after the Constitution was ratified, there was a movement to adopt a national bill of rights. This is why the Bill of Rights, adopted in 1791, makes up the first ten amendments to the Constitution and is not incorporated into the body of it. We shall have a good deal more to say about the Bill of Rights in Chapter 4.

THE FIGHT FOR RATIFICATION: FEDERALISTS VERSUS ANTIFEDERALISTS

The first hurdle faced by the new Constitution was ratification by state conventions of delegates elected by the people of each state. This struggle for ratification was carried out in thirteen separate campaigns. Each involved different men, moved at a different pace, and was influenced by local as well as national considerations. Two sides faced off throughout the states, however, calling themselves Federalists and Antifederalists (Table 2.1).[20] The Federalists (who ought to have called themselves Nationalists but took their name to appear to follow in the Revolutionary tradition) supported the Constitution and preferred a strong national government. The Antifederalists opposed the Constitution and preferred a decentralized federal government; they took their name by default, in reaction to their better-organized opponents. The Federalists were united in their support of the Constitution, while the Antifederalists were divided in what they believed the alternative to the Constitution should be.

During the struggle over ratification of the proposed Constitution, Americans argued about great political issues and ideals. How much power should the national government be given? What safeguards were most likely to prevent the abuse of power? What institutional arrangements could best ensure adequate representation for all Americans? Was tyranny to be feared more from the many or from the few?

In political life, of course, ideals—and values—are seldom completely divorced from some set of interests. In 1787, Americans were divided along economic, regional, and political lines. These divisions inevitably influenced their attitudes toward the profound political questions of the day. Many well-to-do merchants and planters, as we saw earlier, favored the creation of a stronger central government that would have the capacity to protect property, promote commerce, and keep some of the more radical state legislatures in check. At the same time, many powerful

Rationality Principle

The debate over ratification revealed the conflicting interests of the Federalists and the Antifederalists.

---

[20]An excellent analysis of the ratification campaigns—based on a quantitative assessment of the campaigners' own words as found in campaign documents, pamphlets, tracts, public letters, and the eighteenth-century equivalent of op-ed pieces (like the individual essays that make up the *Federalist Papers*)—is William H. Riker, *The Strategy of Rhetoric: Campaigning for the American Constitution* (New Haven, Conn.: Yale University Press, 1996).

TABLE 2.1 Federalists vs. Antifederalists

	Federalists	Antifederalists
Who were they?	Were property owners, creditors, merchants	Were small farmers, frontiersmen, debtors, shopkeepers
What did they believe?	Believed that elites are best fit to govern and that "excessive democracy" is dangerous	Believed that government should be close to the people and that the concentration of power in the hands of the elites is dangerous
What system of government did they favor?	Favored strong national government; believed in "filtration" so that only elites would obtain governmental power	Favored retention of power by state governments and protection of individual rights
Who were their leaders?	Were led by Alexander Hamilton, James Madison, George Washington	Were led by Patrick Henry, George Mason, Elbridge Gerry, George Clinton

state leaders, like Governor George Clinton of New York, feared that strengthening the national government would reduce their own influence and status. Each of these interests, of course, justified its position with an appeal to basic values.

Ideas are often important weapons in political warfare, and seeing how and by whom they are wielded can illuminate their otherwise obscure implications. In our own time, dry academic discussions of topics such as free trade become easier to grasp once it is noted that free trade and open markets are generally favored by low-cost producers, whereas protectionism is the goal of firms whose costs of production are higher than the international norm.

Even if an idea is invented and initially brandished to serve an interest, however, once it has been articulated, it can take on a life of its own and prove to have implications that transcend the narrow interests it was created to serve. For example, some opponents of the Constitution who criticized the absence of a bill of rights in the initial document did so simply with the hope of blocking the document's ratification. Yet the bill of rights that was added to the Constitution has proved for two centuries to be a bulwark of civil liberty in the United States.

Similarly, during the 1960s support for the extension of voting rights and massive legislative redistricting under the rubric of "one man, one vote" came mainly from liberal Democrats who were hoping to strengthen their own political base because the groups that would benefit most from these initiatives were overwhelmingly Democratic. The principles of equal access to the ballot and one man, one vote have a moral and political validity, however, that is independent of the political interests that propelled them into the political arena.

These examples show us that truly great political ideas surmount the interests that initially set them forth. The first step in understanding a political value is understanding why and by whom it is espoused. The second step is understanding the full implications of the idea itself—implications that may go far beyond the interests that launched it. Thus even though the great political values about which Americans argued in 1787 *did* reflect competing interests, they also represented views of society, government, and politics that surmount interest and so must be understood in their own terms. Whatever the underlying clash of interests that may have guided them, the Federalists and the Antifederalists presented important alternative visions of America.

During the ratification struggle, thousands of essays, speeches, pamphlets, and letters were presented in support of and in opposition to the proposed Constitution. The best-known pieces supporting ratification of the Constitution were the eighty-five essays written under the name Publius by Alexander Hamilton, James Madison, and John Jay between the fall of 1787 and the spring of 1788. These *Federalist Papers,* as they are collectively known today, defended the principles of the Constitution and sought to dispel fears of a national authority. The Antifederalists published essays of their own, arguing that the new Constitution betrayed the Revolution and was a step toward monarchy. Among the best of the Antifederalist works were the essays, usually attributed to the New York Supreme Court justice Robert Yates, that were written under the name Brutus and published in the *New York Journal* at the same time the *Federalist Papers* appeared. The Antifederalist view was also ably presented in pamphlets and letters written by a former delegate to the Continental Congress and future U.S. senator, Richard Henry Lee of Virginia, using the pen name the Federal Farmer. These essays highlight the major differences of opinion between Federalists and Antifederalists. Federalists appealed to basic principles of government in support of their nationalist vision. Antifederalists cited equally fundamental precepts to support their vision of a looser confederacy of small republics.

The two sides engaged in what was almost certainly the very first nationwide political campaign in the history of the world. Though each side was itself only loosely organized, a rudimentary form of coordination and cooperation was manifest—especially in the division of labor among Hamilton, Madison, and Jay as they alternately wrote under the Publius pseudonym on different aspects of the newly drafted Constitution in an effort to effect its ratification in the state of New York.

Representation

One major area of contention between the two sides was the question of representation. The Antifederalists asserted that representatives must be "a true picture of the people, . . . [possessing] the knowledge of their circumstances and their wants."[21] This could be achieved, argued the Antifederalists, only in small, relatively homogeneous republics such as the existing states. In their view, the size and extent of the entire nation precluded the construction of a truly representative form of government.

The absence of true representation, moreover, would mean that the people would lack confidence in and attachment to the national government and would

---

[21]Melancton Smith, quoted in Herbert J. Storing, *What the Anti-Federalists Were For: The Political Thought of the Opponents of the Constitution* (Chicago: University of Chicago Press, 1981), p. 17.

refuse to obey its laws voluntarily. As a result, according to the Antifederalists, the national government described by the Constitution would be compelled to resort to force to secure popular compliance. The Federal Farmer averred that laws of the remote federal government could be "in many cases disregarded, unless a multitude of officers and military force be continually kept in view, and employed to enforce the execution of the laws, and to make the government feared and respected."[22]

Federalists, for their part, did not long for pure democracy and saw no reason why representatives should be precisely like those they represented. In their view, government must be representative *of* the people but must also have a measure of autonomy *from* the people. Their ideal government was to be constructed such that it would be capable of serving the long-term public interest even if doing so conflicted with the public's current preference.

Federalists also dismissed the Antifederalist claim that the distance between representatives and constituents in the proposed national government would lead to popular disaffection and compel the government to use force to secure obedience. Federalists replied that the system of representation they proposed was more likely to produce effective government. In Hamilton's words, there would be "a probability that the general government will be better administered than the particular governments."[23] Competent government, in turn, should inspire popular trust and confidence more effectively than simple social proximity between rulers and ruled.

The Threats Posed by the Majority

A second important issue dividing Federalists and Antifederalists was the threat of **tyranny**—unjust rule by the group in power. Both opponents and defenders of the Constitution frequently affirmed their fear of tyrannical rule. Each side, however, had a different view of the most likely source of tyranny and, hence, of the way in which the threat was to be forestalled.

From the Antifederalist perspective, the great danger was the tendency of all governments—including republican governments—to become gradually more and more "aristocratic" in character, with the small number of individuals in positions of authority using their stations to gain more and more power over the general citizenry. In essence, the few would use their power to tyrannize the many. For this reason, Antifederalists were sharply critical of those features of the Constitution that divorced governmental institutions from direct responsibility to the people—institutions such as the Senate, the executive, and the federal judiciary. The latter, appointed for life, presented a particular threat: "I wonder if the world ever saw . . . a court of justice invested with such immense powers, and yet placed in a situation so little responsible," protested Brutus.[24]

The Federalists, too, recognized the threat of tyranny. They were not naive about the motives and purposes of individuals and took them to be no less opportunistic and self-interested than the Antifederalists did. But the Federalists believed that the

tyranny Oppressive government that employs the cruel and unjust use of power and authority.

ONLINE READING ○

ONLINE READING ○

---

[22]"Letters from the Federal Farmer," no. 2, in *The Complete Anti-Federalist*, ed. Herbert J. Storing, 7 vols. (Chicago: University of Chicago Press, 1981).

[23]*The Federalist*, no. 27.

[24]"Essays of Brutus," no. 15, in *The Complete Anti-Federalist*.

danger particularly associated with republican governments was not aristocracy but, instead, majority tyranny. The Federalists were concerned that a popular majority, "united and actuated by some common impulse of passion, or of interest, adverse to the rights of other citizens," would endeavor to "trample on the rules of justice."[25] From the Federalist perspective, it was precisely those features of the Constitution attacked as potential sources of tyranny by the Antifederalists that offered the best hope of averting the threat of oppression. The size and extent of the nation, for instance, were for the Federalists a bulwark against tyranny. In Madison's famous formulation,

> The smaller the society, the fewer probably will be the distinct parties and interests . . . the more frequently will a majority be found of the same party; and the smaller the number of individuals composing a majority, and the smaller the compass within which they are placed, the more easily will they concert and execute their plans of oppression. Extend the sphere, and you take in a greater variety of parties and interests; you make it less probable that a majority of the whole will have a common motive to invade the rights of other citizens; or if such a common motive exists, it will be more difficult for all who feel it to discover their own strength, and to act in unison with each other.[26]

The Federalists understood that in a democracy, temporary majorities could abuse their power. The Federalists' misgivings about majority rule were reflected in the constitutional structure. The indirect election of senators, the indirect election of the president, the judicial branch's insulation from the people, the separation of powers, the president's veto power, the bicameral design of Congress, and the federal system were all means to curb majority tyranny. These features of the Constitution suggest the framers' awareness of the problems of majority rule and the need for institutional safeguards. Except for the indirect election of senators (which was changed in 1913), these aspects of the constitutional structure remain in place today.[27]

To some extent, the Federalists were influenced by an understanding of history that differed from that of the Antifederalists. Federalists believed that colonial history, to say nothing of the history of the Greeks, showed that republican governments were often endangered by mob rule. The Antifederalists, by contrast, thought that history revealed the dangers of aristocratic conspiracies against popular liberties. History matters, but it is always subject to interpretation.

History Principle

The Federalists and Antifederalists were influenced by different understandings of history.

Governmental Power

A third major difference between Federalists and Antifederalists was the issue of governmental power. Both the opponents and the proponents of the Constitution agreed on the principle of limited government. They differed, however, on the fundamentally important question of how to place limits on governmental action.

○ ONLINE READING

---

[25] *The Federalist*, no. 10.

[26] Ibid.

[27] A classic development of this theme is found in James M. Buchanan and Gordon Tullock, *The Calculus of Consent: Logical Foundations of Constitutional Democracy* (Ann Arbor: University of Michigan Press, 1962). For a review of the voting paradox and a case study of how it applies today, see Kenneth A. Shepsle and Mark S. Bonchek, *Analyzing Politics: Rationality, Behavior, and Institutions* (New York: Norton, 1997), pp. 49–81.

Antifederalists favored limiting and enumerating the powers granted to the national government in relation to both the states and the people at large. To them, the powers given the national government ought to be "confined to certain defined national objects."[28] Otherwise, the national government would "swallow up all the power of the state governments."[29] Antifederalists bitterly attacked the supremacy clause and the necessary and proper clause of the Constitution as unlimited and dangerous grants of power to the national government.[30]

Antifederalists also demanded that a bill of rights be added to the Constitution to place limits on the government's exercise of power over the citizenry. "There are certain things," wrote Brutus, "which rulers should be absolutely prohibited from doing, because if they should do them, they would work an injury, not a benefit to the people."[31] Similarly, the Federal Farmer maintained that "there are certain unalienable and fundamental rights, which in forming the social compact . . . ought to be explicitly ascertained and fixed."[32]

Federalists favored the construction of a government with broad powers. They wanted a government that had the capacity to defend the nation against foreign foes, guard against domestic strife and insurrection, promote commerce, and expand the nation's economy. Antifederalists shared some of these goals but still feared governmental power. Hamilton pointed out, however, that these goals could not be achieved without allowing the government to exercise the necessary power. Federalists acknowledged, of course, that every power could be abused but argued that the way to prevent misuse of power was not by depriving the government of the powers needed to achieve national goals. Instead, they argued that the threat of abuse of power would be mitigated by the Constitution's internal checks and controls. As Madison put it,

> The power surrendered by the people is first divided between two distinct governments, and then the portion allotted to each subdivided among distinct and separate departments. Hence a double security arises to the rights of the people. The different governments will control each other, at the same time that each will be controlled by itself.[33]

The Federalists' concern with avoiding unwarranted limits on governmental power led them to oppose a bill of rights, which they saw as nothing more than a set of unnecessary restrictions on the government.

The Federalists acknowledged that abuse of power remained a possibility but felt that the risk had to be taken because of the goals to be achieved. "The very idea of power included a possibility of doing harm," said the Federalist John Rutledge during South Carolina's ratification debates. "If the gentleman would show the power that could do no harm," Rutledge continued, "he would at once discover it to be a power that could do no good."[34]

ONLINE READING   [28]"Essays of Brutus," no. 7.

ONLINE READING   [29]"Essays of Brutus," no. 6.

[30]Storing, *What the Anti-Federalists Were For,* p. 28.

ONLINE READING   [31]"Essays of Brutus," no. 9.

ONLINE READING   [32]"Letters from the Federal Farmer," no. 2.

ONLINE READING   [33]*The Federalist,* no. 51.

[34]Quoted in Storing, *What the Anti-Federalists Were For,* p. 30.

CHANGING THE INSTITUTIONAL FRAMEWORK: CONSTITUTIONAL AMENDMENT

The Constitution has endured for more than two centuries as the framework of government. But it has not endured without change. Without change, the Constitution might have become merely a sacred relic, stored under glass.

Amendments: Many Are Called, Few Are Chosen

The need for change was recognized by the framers of the Constitution, and the provisions for amendment incorporated into Article V were thought to be "an easy, regular and Constitutional way" to make changes that would occasionally be necessary because members of Congress "may abuse their power and refuse their consent on the very account . . . to admit to amendments to correct the source of the abuse."[35] Madison made a more balanced defense of the amendment procedure in Article V: "It guards equally against that extreme facility, which would render the Constitution too mutable; and that extreme difficulty, which might perpetuate its discovered faults."[36]

Experience since 1789 raises questions about even Madison's more modest claims. Between 1789 and 1993, 9,746 amendments were formally offered in Congress. Of those, Congress officially proposed only 29, and 27 of them were eventually ratified by the states. But the record is even more severe than that. Since 1791, when the first 10 amendments, the Bill of Rights, were added, only 17 amendments have been adopted. And two of them—Prohibition and its repeal—cancel each other out, so that for all practical purposes only 15 amendments have been added to the Constitution since 1791. Despite vast changes in American society and its economy, only 12 amendments have been adopted since the Civil War amendments in 1868.

Four methods of amendment are provided for in Article V:

1. Passage in House and Senate by two-thirds vote; then ratification by majority vote of the legislatures of three fourths (now thirty-eight) of the states.

2. Passage in House and Senate by two-thirds vote; then ratification by conventions called for that purpose in three fourths of the states.

3. Passage in a national convention called by Congress in response to petitions by two thirds (now thirty-four) of the states; ratification by majority vote of the legislatures of three fourths of the states.

4. Passage in a national convention, as in method 3; then ratification by conventions called for that purpose in three fourths of the states.

(Figure 2.2 illustrates each of these methods.) Because no amendment has ever been proposed by national convention, however, routes 3 and 4 have never been employed. And route 2 has been employed only once (for the Twenty-first Amendment,

Institution Principle

The procedures for amending the Constitution are difficult. As a result, the amendment route to political change is extremely limited.

---

[35]Observation by George Mason, delegate from Virginia, early in the convention period; quoted in Farrand, *The Records of the Federal Convention of 1787*, I, pp. 202–3.

[36]Alexander Hamilton, James Madison, and John Jay, *The Federalist Papers*, ed. Clinton L. Rossiter (New York: New American Library, 1961), no. 43, p. 278.

ONLINE READING

FIGURE 2.2 Routes of Amendment

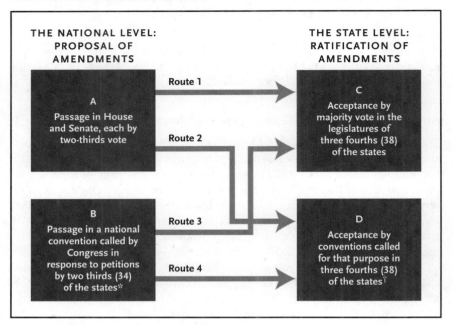

THE NATIONAL LEVEL:
PROPOSAL OF
AMENDMENTS

THE STATE LEVEL:
RATIFICATION OF
AMENDMENTS

A
Passage in House
and Senate, each by
two-thirds vote

Route 1

Route 2

C
Acceptance by
majority vote in the
legislatures of
three fourths (38)
of the states

B
Passage in a national
convention called by
Congress in
response to petitions
by two thirds (34)
of the states*

Route 3

Route 4

D
Acceptance by
conventions called
for that purpose in
three fourths (38)
of the states†

*This method of proposal has never been employed. Thus amendment routes 3 and 4 have
never been attempted.

†In each amendment proposal, Congress has the power to choose the method of ratification, the time limit for consideration by the states, and other conditions of ratification.

which repealed the Eighteenth, or Prohibition, Amendment). Thus method 1 has
been used for all the others.

Now we should be better able to explain why it has been so difficult to amend
the Constitution. The main reason is the requirement of a two-thirds vote in the
House and the Senate, which means that any proposal for an amendment in Congress can be killed by only 34 senators *or* 146 members of the House. What is more,
if the necessary two-thirds vote is obtained, the amendment can still be killed by the
refusal or inability of only thirteen state legislatures to ratify it. Because each state
has an equal vote regardless of its population, the thirteen holdout states may represent a very small fraction of the total American population.

The Twenty-seven Amendments

Despite difficulties in the process, the Constitution has been amended twenty-seven
times since the framers completed their work. The first ten of these amendments,
known as the Bill of Rights, were added to the Constitution shortly after its ratification.
As we saw, Federalists feared that a bill of rights would weaken the new government,
but they were forced to commit themselves to the principle of an enumeration of rights
when the Antifederalists charged that the proposed Constitution was a threat to liberty.

Most of the Constitution's twenty-seven amendments share a common characteristic: All but two are concerned with the structure or composition of government. This is consistent with the dictionary, which defines *constitution* as the "makeup or composition of a thing"—anything. And it is consistent with the concept of a constitution as higher law because the whole point and purpose of a higher law is to establish a framework within which government and the process of making ordinary law can take place. Even those who would have preferred more changes in the Constitution would have had to agree that there is great wisdom in this principle. A constitution ought to enable legislation and public policies to take place, but it should not determine what that legislation or those public policies ought to be.

The purpose of the ten amendments in the Bill of Rights was basically structural: to give each of the three branches clearer and more restricted boundaries. The First Amendment clarifies the jurisdiction of Congress. Although the powers of Congress under Article I, Section 8, do not justify laws regulating religion, speech, and the like, the First Amendment makes this limitation explicit: "Congress shall make no law . . ." The Second, Third, and Fourth Amendments similarly spell out limits on the executive branch. Such limits were seen as a necessity given the abuses of executive power Americans had endured under British rule.

The Fifth, Sixth, Seventh, and Eighth Amendments contain some of the most important safeguards for individual citizens against the arbitrary exercise of governmental power. And these amendments sought to accomplish their goal by defining the judicial branch more concretely and clearly than had been done in Article III of the Constitution. Table 2.2 analyzes the ten amendments included in the Bill of Rights.

Five of the seventeen amendments adopted since 1791 are directly concerned with expansion of the electorate (Table 2.3). These occasional efforts to expand the electorate were made necessary by the fact that the founders were unable to establish a national electorate with uniform voting qualifications. Stalemated on that issue, the delegates decided to evade it by providing in the final draft of Article I, Section 2, that eligibility to vote in a national election would be the same as "the Qualifications requisite for Electors of the most numerous Branch of the State Legislature." Article I, Section 4, added that Congress could alter state regulations as to the "Times, Places and Manner of holding Elections for Senators and Representatives." Nevertheless, this meant that any important expansion of the American electorate would almost certainly require a constitutional amendment.

Six more amendments are also electoral in nature, although not concerned directly with voting rights and the expansion of the electorate (Table 2.4). These six amendments are concerned with the elective offices themselves (the Twentieth, Twenty-second, and Twenty-fifth) or with the relationship between elective offices and the electorate (the Twelfth, Fourteenth, and Seventeenth).

Another five amendments have sought to expand or limit the powers of the national and state governments (Table 2.5).[37] The Eleventh Amendment protects the

---

[37]The Fourteenth Amendment is included in this table as well as in Table 2.3 because it not only seeks to define citizenship but also *seems* to intend that this definition of citizenship include, along with the right to vote, all the rights of the Bill of Rights, regardless of the state in which the citizen resides. A great deal more will be said about this in Chapter 4.

TABLE 2.2 The Bill of Rights: Analysis of Its Provisions

Amendment	Purpose
I	Limits on Congress: Congress is not to make any law establishing a religion or abridging the freedom of speech, press, or assembly or the right to petition the government.
II, III, IV	Limits on the executive: The executive branch is not to infringe on the right of people to keep arms (II), is not to arbitrarily take houses for use by a militia (III), and is not to engage in the search or seizure of evidence without a court warrant swearing to a belief in the probable existence of a crime (IV).
V, VI, VII, VIII	Limits on the courts: The courts are not to hold trials for serious offenses without provision for a grand jury (V), a petit (trial) jury (VII), a speedy trial (VI), presentation of charges, and confrontation of hostile witnesses (VI). Individuals may not be compelled to testify against themselves (V) and are immune from trial more than once for the same offense (V). Neither bail nor punishment can be excessive (VIII), and no property can be taken without just compensation (V).
IX, X	Limits on the national government: All rights not enumerated are reserved to the states or the people.

states from suits by private individuals and takes away from the federal courts any power to hear suits by private individuals of one state (or a foreign country) against another state. Three other amendments in Table 2.5 are obviously designed to reduce state power (the Thirteenth), reduce state power and expand national power (the Fourteenth), and expand national power (the Sixteenth). The Twenty-seventh puts a limit on Congress's ability to raise its own salary.

The two missing amendments underscore the meaning of the rest: the Eighteenth, or Prohibition, Amendment and the Twenty-first, its repeal. They represent the only instance in which the country tried to *legislate* by constitutional amendment. In other words, the Eighteenth is the only amendment that was designed to deal directly with some substantive social problem. And it was the only amendment ever to have been repealed. Two other amendments—the Thirteenth, which abolished slavery, and the Sixteenth, which established the power to levy an income tax—can be said to have had the effect of legislation. But the purpose of the Thirteenth Amendment was to restrict the power of the states by forever forbidding them to treat any human being as property. As for the Sixteenth Amendment, it is certainly true that income-tax legislation followed immediately; nevertheless, the amendment concerns itself strictly with establishing the power of Congress to enact such legislation. The legislation came later; and if down the line a majority in Congress had wanted to abolish the income tax, they could also have done so by legislation rather than through the arduous path of a constitutional amendment repealing the income tax.

For those whose hopes for change center on the Constitution, it must be emphasized that the amendment route to social change is, and always will be, extremely lim-

TABLE 2.3 Amending the Constitution to Expand the Electorate

Amendment	Purpose	Year Proposed	Year Adopted
XIV	Provided, in Section 1, a national definition of citizenship*	1866	1868
XV	Extended voting rights to all races	1869	1870
XIX	Extended voting rights to women	1919	1920
XXIII	Extended voting rights to residents of the District of Columbia	1960	1961
XXIV	Extended voting rights to all classes by abolition of poll taxes	1962	1964
XXVI	Extended voting rights to citizens aged 18 and over	1971	1971

*In defining citizenship, the Fourteenth Amendment actually provided the constitutional basis for expanding the electorate to include all races, women, and residents of the District of Columbia. Only the "eighteen-year-olds' amendment" should have been necessary because it changed the definition of citizenship. The fact that additional amendments were required after the Fourteenth suggests that voting is not considered an inherent right of U.S. citizenship. Instead, it is viewed as a privilege.

ited. Through a constitution it is possible to establish a working structure of government, and through a constitution it is possible to establish basic rights of citizens by placing limitations and obligations on the powers of that government. Once these things have been accomplished, the real problem is how to extend rights to those people who do not already enjoy them. Of course, the Constitution cannot enforce itself. But it can and does have a real influence on everyday life because a right or an obligation set forth in it can become a cause of action in the hands of an otherwise powerless person.

Private property is an excellent example. Property is one of the most fundamental and well-established rights in the United States, but it is well established not because it is recognized in so many words in the Constitution but because legislatures and courts have made it a crime for anyone, including the government, to trespass or to take away property without compensation.

REFLECTIONS ON THE FOUNDING: IDEALS OR INTERESTS?

The final product of the Constitutional Convention has to be considered an extraordinary victory for the groups that had most forcefully called for the creation of a new system of government to replace the Articles of Confederation. Antifederalist criticisms forced the Constitution's proponents to accept the addition of a bill of rights

TABLE 2.4 Amending the Constitution to Change the Relationship between the Elected Offices and the Electorate

Amendment	Purpose	Year Proposed	Year Adopted
XII	Provided a separate ballot for the vice president in the electoral college	1803	1804
XIV	Eliminated, in Section 2 , the counting of slaves in the apportionment of House seats	1866	1868
XVII	Provided for the direct election of senators	1912	1913
XX	Eliminated "lame duck" sessions of Congress	1932	1933
XXII	Limited the presidential term	1947	1951
XXV	Provided for presidential succession in case of disability	1965	1967

designed to limit the powers of the national government. In general, however, it was the Federalist vision of America that triumphed. The Constitution adopted in 1789 created the framework for a powerful national government that for more than two centuries has defended the nation's interests, promoted its commerce, and maintained national unity. In one notable instance, the national government fought and won a bloody war to prevent the nation from breaking apart. To interpret this history in light of our five principles of politics, we can say that the framers strove collectively to achieve a common purpose: the creation of a set of institutions that would, on a permanent basis, help Americans work together to achieve what the framers themselves viewed as important political goals. The framers' ideas were shaped by their historical experiences and, in turn, shaped history.

Though the Constitution was the product of a particular set of political forces, the form of government it established has a significance that goes far beyond the interests of its authors. As we have observed, political ideals often take on lives of their own. The great political values incorporated into the Constitution continue, more than two centuries later, to shape our political lives in ways that the framers may not have anticipated. For example, when they empowered Congress to regulate commerce among the states in Article I, Section 8, of the Constitution, they could hardly have anticipated that this provision would become the basis for many of the federal government's regulatory activities in areas as diverse as the environment and civil rights.

Two great constitutional notions, federalism and civil liberties, will be discussed in Chapters 3 and 4. A third important constitutional principle that has affected America's government for the past two centuries is the principle of checks and balances. As we saw earlier, the framers gave each of the three branches of government a means of intervening in, and blocking, the actions of the others. Often checks and balances have seemed to prevent the government from getting much done. During the 1960s, for ex-

TABLE 2.5 Amending the Constitution to Expand or Limit the Power of Government

Amendment	Purpose	Year Proposed	Year Adopted
XI	Limited the jurisdiction of federal courts over suits involving the states	1794	1798
XIII	Eliminated slavery and the rights of states to allow property in the form of persons	1865*	1865
XIV	In Section 2, applied due process of the Bill of Rights to the states	1866	1868
XVI	Established the national power to tax income	1909	1913
XXVII	Limited Congress's power to raise its own salary	1789	1992

*The Thirteenth Amendment was proposed on January 31, 1865, and adopted less than a year later, on December 6, 1865.

ample, liberals were often infuriated as they watched Congress stall presidential initiatives in the area of civil rights. Later, conservatives were outraged when President Bill Clinton thwarted congressional efforts to enact legislation promised by the Republicans. Still later, Republicans were angered as a Democratic Congress castigated President George W. Bush. At various times, all sides have vilified the judiciary for invalidating legislation enacted by Congress and signed by the president.

Over time, checks and balances have acted as brakes on the governmental process. Groups hoping to bring about changes in policy or in governmental institutions have seldom been able to bring about decisive and dramatic transformations in a short time. Instead, checks and balances have slowed the pace of change and increased the need for compromise and accommodation.

Groups able to take control of the White House, for example, must bargain with rivals who remain entrenched on Capitol Hill. New forces in Congress must reckon with the influence of other forces in the executive branch and in the courts. Checks and balances inevitably frustrate those who desire change, but they also function as a safeguard against rash action. During the 1950s, for example, Congress was caught up in a quasi-hysterical effort to unmask subversive activities in the United States, an effort that might have led to a serious erosion of American liberties if not for the checks and balances provided by the executive and the courts. Thus a governmental principle that serves as a frustrating limitation one day may become a vitally important safeguard the next.

As we close our discussion of the founding, it is worth reflecting on the Antifederalists. Although they were defeated in 1789, the Antifederalists present us with an important picture of a road not taken, an America that might have been.

Policy Principle

The constitutional framework, with its principle of checks and balances, can act as a brake on the policy process.

Rationality Principle	Collective-Action Principle	Institution Principle	Policy Principle	History Principle
The framers of the Constitution were guided by ideals, but they were also influenced by their interests. The debate over ratification revealed the conflicting interests of the Federalists and the Antifederalists.	The colonists required strong leaders to resolve differences and organize resistance to British authority. The framers preferred compromise to the breakup of the Union and thus accepted the Great Compromise and the Three-fifths Compromise.	Institutional arrangements, such as the Articles of Confederation, can be flawed. The constitutional framework promoted commerce, protected property, prevented "excessive democracy," and limited the power of the national government. The procedures for amending the Constitution are difficult. As a result, the amendment route to political change is extremely limited.	The constitutional framework, with its principle of checks and balances, can act as a brake on the policy process.	The American colonists, used to self-governance, believed that the Stamp Act of 1765 threatened their autonomy. Shays's Rebellion focused attention on the flaws of the Articles of Confederation, leading to the Constitutional Convention. The Federalists and Antifederalists were influenced by different understandings of history.

Would we have been worse off as a people if we had been governed by a confederacy of small republics linked by a national administration with severely limited powers? Were the Antifederalists correct in predicting that a government given great power in the hope that it might do good would, through "insensible progress," inevitably turn to evil purposes? More than two centuries of government under the federal Constitution are not necessarily enough to definitively answer these questions. Only time will tell.

SUMMARY

Political conflicts between the colonies and England and among competing groups within the colonies led to the first founding as expressed by the Declaration of Independence. The first constitution, the Articles of Confederation, was adopted one year later (1777). Under this document, the states retained their sovereignty. The central government, composed solely of Congress, had few powers and no means of enforcing its will. The national government's weakness soon led to the creation of the Constitution of 1787, the second founding.

In this second founding, the framers sought first to fashion a new government sufficiently powerful to promote commerce and protect property from radical state legislatures. Second, the framers sought to bring an end to the "excessive democracy" of the state and national governments under the Articles of Confederation. Third, the framers introduced mechanisms that helped secure popular consent for the new government. Finally, the framers made certain that their new government would not itself pose a threat to liberty and property.

The Constitution consists of seven articles. In part, Article I provides for a Congress of two chambers (Sections 1–7), defines the powers of the national government (Section 8), and interprets the national government's powers as a source of strength rather than a limitation (the necessary and proper clause). Article II describes the presidency and establishes it as a separate branch of government. Article III deals with the judiciary. Although there is no direct mention of judicial review in this article, the Supreme Court eventually assumed that power. Article IV addresses reciprocity among states and their citizens. Article V describes the procedures for amending the Constitution. Thousands of amendments have been offered, but only twenty-seven have been adopted. With the exception of the two Prohibition amendments, all amendments are oriented toward some change in the framework or structure of government. Article VI establishes that national laws and treaties are "the supreme Law of the Land." Finally, Article VII specifies the procedure for ratifying the Constitution of 1787.

The struggle for the ratification of the Constitution pitted the Antifederalists against the Federalists. The Antifederalists thought the proposed new government would be too powerful, and they fought against the ratification of the Constitution. The Federalists supported the Constitution and were able to secure its ratification after a nationwide political debate.

FOR FURTHER READING

Amar, Akhil Reed. *America's Constitution: A Biography*. New York: Random House, 2005.

Bailyn, Bernard. *The Ideological Origins of the American Revolution*. Cambridge, Mass.: Harvard University Press, 1967.

Beard, Charles A. *An Economic Interpretation of the Constitution of the United States*. New York: Macmillan, 1913.

Breyer, Stephen. *Active Liberty: Interpreting Our Democratic Constitution*. New York: Knopf, 2005.

Chernow, Ron. *Alexander Hamilton*. New York: Penguin, 2004.

Ellis, Joseph. *Founding Brothers: The Revolutionary Generation*. New York: Knopf, 2000.

———. *His Excellency, George Washington*. New York: Knopf, 2004.

Farrand, Max, ed. *The Records of the Federal Convention of 1787*. Rev. ed. 4 vols. New Haven, Conn.: Yale University Press, 1966.

ONLINE READING ○   Hamilton, Alexander, James Madison, and John Jay. *The Federalist Papers*. Ed. Isaac Kramnick. New York: Viking Press, 1987.

Riker, William H. *The Strategy of Rhetoric: Campaigning for the American Constitution*. New Haven, Conn.: Yale University Press, 1996.

ONLINE READING ○   Storing, Herbert J., ed. *The Complete Anti-Federalist*. 7 vols. Chicago: University of Chicago Press, 1981.

Recent years have seen an explosion of proposed constitutional amendments, dealing with issues as varied as a balanced budget, campaign finance, gay marriage, term limits, and flag burning. Why has proposing a constitutional amendment become a popular avenue to address various social and political problems that normally might be addressed through legislation? The principles of politics can help us identify some of the reasons.

First, as the two political parties have become more polarized, forging successful legislation has become more difficult and is much more likely to be a product of collective action within one party than across parties. As a result, frustrated members of Congress may turn to other institutional avenues, such as constitutional amendments, to satisfy their political desires. Second, because many of the proposed amendments deal with issues that constituents are passionate about, rational, self-interested politicians can gain electoral advantage by supporting an amendment even when it has no chance of passing. The long-simmering debate over a flag-burning amendment illustrates these points.

The New York Times, June 28, 2006

Flag Amendment Narrowly Fails in Senate Vote

By Carl Hulse

A proposed Constitutional amendment to allow Congress to prohibit desecration of the flag fell a single vote short of approval by the Senate on Tuesday, an excruciatingly close vote that left unresolved a long-running debate over whether the flag is a unique national symbol deserving of special legal standing.

The 66-to-34 vote on the amendment was one vote short of the 67 required to send the amendment to the states for potential ratification as the 28th Amendment. It was the closest proponents of the initiative have come in four Senate votes since the Supreme Court first ruled in 1989 that flag burning was a protected form of free speech.

The opponents—30 Democrats, 3 Republicans and an independent—asserted that the amendment would amount to tampering with the Bill of Rights in an effort to eliminate relatively rare incidents of burning the flag. They said it violated the very freedoms guaranteed by the symbolism of the flag.

"This objectionable expression is obscene, it is painful, it is unpatriotic," said Senator Daniel Inouye, a Hawaii Democrat who won the Medal of Honor for his service in World War II. "But I believe Americans gave their lives in many wars to make certain all Americans have a right to express themselves, even those who harbor hateful thoughts."

Proponents of the amendment, which was backed by 52 Republicans and 14 Democrats, disputed the assertion that burning the flag was a form of speech. They said the amendment was simply an effort to reassert Congressional authority after a misguided court

Policy Principle

Because the Supreme Court has ruled multiple times that state and federal laws against flag burning are unconstitutional, the only avenue left to establish such a policy is a constitutional amendment.

ruling. They said it was particularly appropriate to act now when American troops are at risk.

"Old Glory lost today," said Senator Bill Frist, the majority leader, who scheduled the debate and vote in the week before Congress broke for its Fourth of July recess.

The full text of the proposed amendment is, "The Congress shall have power to prohibit the physical desecration of the flag of the United States."

The vote is likely to be an issue in the Congressional elections in November, and Senator Orrin G. Hatch, the Utah Republican who was the chief sponsor of the amendment, predicted the minority who opposed it would be held accountable by the voters. * * *

Eleven senators facing re-election this year opposed the amendment and several are facing potentially difficult races. * * *

The leader of the Citizens Flag Alliance, which had been running newspaper advertisements on the issue in selected states, said it would continue to press the issue and make sure voters know where their senators stand on the amendment. * * *

Prior to the vote on the amendment itself, the Senate voted 64 to 36 against a proposed bill that would have criminalized flag desecration. Senator Richard J. Durbin of Illinois * * * said his plan had been written to avoid Supreme Court objections, but backers of the constitutional approach dismissed that idea.

President Bush, whose father was president when the flag fight initially erupted in the aftermath of two high court rulings, said he was disappointed in the outcome. "I commend the senators from both parties who voted to allow the amendment ratification process to protect our flag to go forward, and continue to believe that the American people deserve the opportunity to express their views on this important issue."

The House has routinely approved the flag amendment on bipartisan votes and did so last year. Had the Senate passed the amendment, it would have been likely to win ratification from the required 38 states since, supporters say, all states have endorsed the amendment in some form.

While the amendment gained three votes since it was last considered in 2000, its future prospects are uncertain. Senator Mitch McConnell, Republican of Kentucky, is in line to become the Republican leader in the next Congress, and he opposes the initiative on free speech grounds. In addition, most analysts expect Republicans to lose Senate seats in the November election. * * *

The vote, which came after the Senate earlier this month defeated a proposed constitutional amendment to ban same-sex marriage, will not be the last ideologically charged vote in the run-up to the midterm elections. The House Republican leadership announced Tuesday that it plans votes this summer on social issues, including a same-sex marriage amendment, abortion rights, Internet gambling, property rights and the Pledge of Allegiance.

"The American Values Agenda will defend America's founding principles," Speaker J. Dennis Hastert said. "Through this agenda, we will work to protect the faith of our people, the sanctity of life and freedoms outlined by our founding fathers."

And the House on Tuesday approved on a voice vote a proposal that

Institution Principle

An amendment must pass in both the House and the Senate. In recent years, many amendments have passed in the House with relative ease because House members knew that the amendments would never make it out of the Senate, where individual members can stop them much more easily.

would prohibit condominium associations and other homeowner groups from preventing residents from displaying the flag.

The American Civil Liberties Union, which has been deeply involved in opposing the amendment for years, credited the senators who took a potentially politically tough vote to block it.

"The Senate came close to torching our Constitution, but luckily it came through unscathed," said Caroline Fredrickson, director of the organization's Washington legislative office. * * *

Besides senators up for re-election, the issue also divided lawmakers considered possible presidential candidates in 2008. Those voting yes included Mr. Frist, George Allen of Virginia, John McCain of Arizona, Sam Brownback of Kansas and Chuck Hagel of Nebraska, all Republicans, and Evan Bayh of Indiana, a Democrat. Voting no on the Democratic side were Christopher J. Dodd of Connecticut, Hillary Rodham Clinton of New York, Joseph R. Biden Jr. of Delaware, Russell D. Feingold of Wisconsin and John Kerry of Massachusetts.

 Rationality Principle

Members of Congress are guided by political concerns as well as their personal views on the matter. Some may be worried about reelection. Those with presidential ambitions have to consider that their vote on this matter could come up in the future.

Federalism and the Separation of Powers

TWO OF THE MOST IMPORTANT ELEMENTS of the American Constitution are federalism and the separation of powers. Federalism seeks to limit government by dividing it into two levels, national and state, each with sufficient independence to compete with the other, thereby restraining the power of both.[1] The separation of powers seeks to limit the power of the national government by dividing government against itself—by giving the legislative, executive, and judicial branches separate functions, thus forcing them to share power.

Consistent with one of our key principles—that institutions matter—these two features of America's institutional structure have important consequences for politics and policy in the United States. Federalism means that the national government is not the only significant decision-making body in America. The fifty individual states are not agencies of the national government but instead have a good deal of power in their own rights. The separation of powers means that within the national government there is no neat decision-making hierarchy. Each of the three branches of government exercises power over the other two. Both federalism and the separation of powers complicate policy making in the United States. If governmental power were arranged neatly and simply in a single hierarchy, decisions could certainly be made more easily and more efficiently. But would they be better decisions? The framers thought that complexity, multiple checks, and institutionalized second-

ONLINE READING

[1]The notion that federalism requires separate spheres or jurisdictions in which lower and higher levels of government are uniquely decisive is developed fully in William H. Riker, *Federalism: Origin, Operation, Significance* (Boston: Little, Brown, 1964). This American version of federalism is applied to the emerging federal arrangements in the People's Republic of China during the 1990s in a paper by Barry R. Weingast, "The Economic Role of Political Institutions: Market-Preserving Federalism and Economic Development," *Journal of Law, Economics, and Organization* 11 (1995): 1–32.

guessing, while messy, would allow more interests to have a voice and would eventually produce better results. And along the way, complex decision processes might preserve liberty and prevent tyranny. Let us see how federalism and the separation of powers matter in the United States.

The Dynamics of the Framework: A Case Study

In 1994, the voters of the state of Oregon approved a ballot measure authorizing physicians to assist terminally ill patients who wish to commit suicide. Under this state law, which survived a 1997 repeal effort, a physician may prescribe a lethal dose of medication for a patient requesting it if two doctors agree that the individual is within six months of dying from an incurable disease. More than 200 patients have made use of the law to end their lives.

In 2001, U.S. Attorney General John Ashcroft declared that physician-assisted suicide was not a legitimate medical procedure and that any physician administering federally controlled drugs for such a purpose would be in violation of the federal Controlled Substances Act and would be prosecuted by the federal government. The Controlled

Although this chapter refers to all five principles of politics, the most salient principle is that institutions matter—that is, rules and procedures shape politics. As we learned in Chapter 1, institutions are part script and part scorecard. Throughout American political history, the institutional script has determined whether states or the national government would exercise influence in a given policy area. Similarly, at the national level the separation-of-powers system that delineates the role and authority of members of Congress, the president, and the courts provides the scorecard that allows political actors to predict who will be influential on a given political issue. And in that they are consequential, these institutional structures channel and constrain the actions of political actors as they pursue their different goals.

Substances Act, enacted by Congress in 1970, gives the federal government the authority to regulate the manufacture, possession, and distribution of a variety of drugs. The drugs used for assisted suicide were among those falling under federal regulation.

The state of Oregon quickly announced its intention to oppose Attorney General Ashcroft's order. The state, joined by several physicians, pharmacists, and terminally ill patients, brought suit in U.S. District Court. The court ruled in favor of the state and declared that the attorney general had no authority under the Controlled Substances Act to prohibit doctors from prescribing drugs for use in assisted suicides. The district court's opinion was affirmed by the U.S. Court of Appeals for the Ninth Circuit and, in 2006, by the U.S. Supreme Court.[2] The Supreme Court ruled that the federal government had the power to regulate drugs but not the power to overrule state laws determining how those drugs could be used, so long as the drugs were not prohibited by federal law.

This case illustrates both federalism and the separation of powers in action. An executive official of the federal government—the attorney general of the United States—told the state of Oregon that its law was inconsistent with federal statute and that physicians who followed the state law would be prosecuted by the federal government. In most countries, regional governments are simply administrative units of the national government, and a decision by the equivalent of the attorney general would end the matter. In the United States, though, states have a considerable measure of sovereign power. The state of Oregon chose to oppose the federal government and defend its policy against the attorney general's ruling.

To defend itself, the state made use of the separation of powers. The federal courts have the power to examine acts of Congress and decisions by the executive and decide whether they are consistent with law and the Constitution. Oregon appealed for help to the federal judiciary, and eventually the federal courts ruled

---

[2]*Gonzales v. Oregon,* 546 U.S. (2006).

against the federal government's executive branch and in favor of the state. The U.S. Supreme Court ruled that while Congress does have the power to regulate the use of drugs, states also have the power to decide how those drugs will be used within their jurisdiction. Thus in the *Gonzales* case, the institutions of federalism and the separation of powers interacted to produce a particular outcome that probably would not have occurred anywhere else in the world.

FEDERALISM AND THE SEPARATION OF POWERS AS POLITICAL INSTITUTIONS

The great achievement of American politics is the fashioning of an effective constitutional structure of political institutions. Although it is an imperfect and continuously evolving work in progress, this structure of law and political practice has served its people well for more than two centuries by managing conflict, providing inducements for bargaining and cooperation, and facilitating collective action. There has been one enormous failure: the cruel practice of slavery, which ended only after a destructive civil war. But the basic configuration of institutions first formulated in Philadelphia in 1787 survived that debacle, although it was severely scarred by it, and has otherwise stood the test of time.

As we mentioned in Chapter 1, institutional arrangements like federalism and the separation of powers are part script and part scorecard. As two of the most important features of the constitutional structure, federalism and the separation of powers serve to channel and constrain political agents, first by limiting their jurisdictional authority and then by pitting them against each other as political competitors.

One of the ingenious features of the constitutional design adopted by the framers is the principle of dividing and separating. Leaving political authority unobstructed and undivided, it was thought, would invite intense competition of a winner-take-all variety. In such a situation, the winners would be in a position to tyrannize, while the losers would either submit or, with nothing else to lose, be tempted to mount violent opposition. By adopting the divide-and-separate principle—implemented as federalism and the separation of powers and consisting of checks and balances—the framers of the Constitution created jurisdictional arrangements. The Constitution reflects these arrangements in two distinct ways. First, it encourages diversity in the political actors occupying the various institutions of government by requiring that they be selected at different times, from different constituencies, and by different modes (chiefly various forms of election and appointment). This diversity, it was believed, would prevent a clique or narrow slice of the political elite from dominating all the institutions of government at the same time. Second, the Constitution allocates the consideration of different aspects of policy to different institutional arenas. Some explicitly mentioned activities, like the coinage of money or the declaration of war, are assigned to Congress. Matters relating to the execution and implementation of the law are delegated to the president and the executive bureaucracy. Other activities, like adjudicating disputes between states, were made the preserve of the

 Institution Principle

The Constitution created jurisdictional arrangements by encouraging diversity in the elected leaders and allocating the consideration of different aspects of policy to different institutional arenas.

judicial branch. Those activities not explicitly mentioned in the Constitution and reserved to the states. In short, through a jurisdictional arrangement the framers of the Constitution sought a balance in which there is the capacity for action but power is not so concentrated as to make tyranny likely.

The amazing thing about these American political institutions is that they are not carved in granite (even if the official buildings that house them are!). While the Constitution initially set a broad framework for the division of authority between the national government and the states and the division of labor among the branches of the national government, much adaptation and innovation took place as these institutions themselves were bent to the purposes of various political players. Politicians, remember, are goal oriented and constantly exploring the possibilities provided them by their institutional positions and political situations. Another political player that has helped shape the current jurisdictional arrangements and sharing of power is worth remembering as well. This is the U.S. Supreme Court. As the former Supreme Court justice Charles Evans Hughes once remarked, "We are under a Constitution, but the Constitution is what the judges say it is."[3] As we shall see in this chapter, the Court has been a central player in settling the ongoing debate over how power should be divided between the national government and the states and between Congress and the president.

WHO DOES WHAT? STABILITY AND CHANGE IN THE FEDERAL FRAMEWORK

Federalism can be defined with misleading ease and simplicity as the division of powers and functions between the national government and the state governments. Federalism limits national and state power by creating two levels of government—the national government and the state governments, each with a large measure of ***sovereignty*** and thus the ability to restrain the power of the other. As we saw in Chapter 2, the states existed as former colonies before independence, and for nearly thirteen years they were virtually autonomous units under the Articles of Confederation. In effect, the states had retained too much power under the Articles, a problem that led directly to the Annapolis Convention in 1786 and to the Constitutional Convention in 1787. Under the Articles, disorder within states was beyond the reach of the national government (see Shays's Rebellion, discussed in Chapter 2), and conflicts of interest between states were not manageable. For example, states were making their own trade agreements with foreign countries and companies, which might then play off one state against another for special advantages. Some states adopted trade tariffs and further barriers to foreign commerce that were contrary to the interests of other states.[4] Tax and other barriers were also being erected between the states.[5] But even

Rationality Principle

As political institutions, federalism and the separation of powers have adapted to the purposes of various political players.

History Principle

Since the time of the founding, federalism has been shaped strongly by the Supreme Court.

federalism The system of government in which a constitution divides power between a central government and regional government.

sovereignty Supreme and independent political authority

---

[3]Charles Evans Hughes, speech at Elmira, N.Y., 3 May 1907.

[4]For a good treatment of these conflicts of interest between states, see Forrest McDonald, *E Pluribus Unum: The Formation of the American Republic, 1776–1790* (Boston: Houghton Mifflin, 1965), chap. 7, esp. pp. 319–38.

[5]See David M. O'Brien, *Constitutional Law and Politics*, 3rd ed., 2 vols. (New York: Norton, 1997), I, pp. 602–3.

after the ratification of the Constitution, the states continued to be more important than the national government. For nearly a century and a half, virtually all of the fundamental policies governing the lives of Americans were made by the state legislatures, not by Congress.

Federalism in the Constitution

The United States was the first nation to adopt federalism as its governing framework. With federalism, the framers sought to limit the national government by creating a second layer of government in the states. American federalism recognized two sovereigns in the original Constitution and reinforced the principle in the Bill of Rights by granting a few *expressed powers* to the national government and reserving the rest to the states.

The Powers of the National Government   As we saw in Chapter 2, the expressed powers granted to the national government are found in Article I, Section 8, of the Constitution. These seventeen powers include the powers to collect taxes, coin money, declare war, and regulate commerce (which, as we shall see, became a very important power for the national government). Article I, Section 8, also contains an important source of power for the national government: the *implied powers* that enable Congress "to make all Laws which shall be necessary and proper for carrying into Execution the foregoing Powers." Not until several decades after the founding did the Supreme Court allow Congress to exercise the power granted in this *necessary and proper clause,* but as we shall see later in this chapter, this doctrine allowed the national government to expand considerably the scope of its authority, although the process was a slow one. In addition to these expressed and implied powers, the Constitution affirms the power of the national government in the supremacy clause (Article VI), which makes all national laws and treaties "the supreme Law of the Land."

The Powers of State Government   One way in which the framers sought to preserve a strong role for the states was through the Tenth Amendment to the Constitution. The Tenth Amendment states that the powers the Constitution does not delegate to the national government or deny to the states are "reserved to the States respectively, or to the people." The Antifederalists, who feared that a strong central government would encroach on individual liberty, repeatedly pressed for such an amendment as a way of limiting national power. Federalists agreed to the amendment because they did not think it would do much harm, given the powers the Constitution already granted to the national government. The Tenth Amendment is also called the *reserved powers* amendment because it aims to reserve powers to the states.

The most fundamental power retained by the states is that of coercion—the power to develop and enforce criminal codes, administer health and safety rules, and regulate the family via marriage and divorce laws. The states have the power to regulate individuals' livelihoods: If you're a doctor or a lawyer or a plumber or a barber, you must be licensed by the state. Even more fundamental, the states had the power to define private property: Private property exists because state laws against trespass define who is and who is not entitled to use a piece of property. If you own

expressed powers The notion that the Constitution grants to the federal government only those powers specifically named in its text.

implied powers Powers derived from the necessary and proper clause (Article I, Section 8) of the Constitution. Such powers are not specifically expressed but are implied through the expansive interpretation of delegated powers.

necessary and proper clause Article I, Section 8, of the Constitution, which enumerates the powers of Congress and provides Congress with the authority to make all laws "necessary and proper" to carry them out; also referred to as the elastic clause.

reserved powers Powers, derived from the Tenth Amendment to the Constitution, that are not specifically delegated to the national government or denied to the states.

a car, your ownership isn't worth much unless the state is willing to enforce your right to possession by making it a crime for anyone else to drive your car without your permission. These are fundamental matters, and the powers of the states regarding such domestic issues are much greater than the powers of the national government, even today.

A state's authority to regulate these fundamental matters is commonly referred to as the ***police power*** of the state and encompasses the state's power to regulate the health, safety, welfare, and morals of its citizens. Policing is what states do—they coerce you in the name of the community in order to maintain public order. And this was exactly the type of power the founders intended the states to exercise.

In some areas, the states share ***concurrent powers*** with the national government: They retain and share some power to regulate commerce and affect the currency—for example, by chartering banks, granting or denying corporate charters, granting or denying licenses to engage in a business or practice a trade, and regulating the quality of products or the conditions of labor. This issue of concurrent versus exclusive power has come up from time to time in our history, but wherever there has been a direct conflict of laws between the federal and the state levels, the issue has most often been resolved in favor of national supremacy.

States' Obligations to One Another   The Constitution also creates obligations among the states. These obligations, spelled out in Article IV, were intended to promote national unity. By requiring the states to recognize actions and decisions taken in other states as legal and proper, the framers aimed to make the states less like independent countries and more like parts of a single nation.

Article IV, Section 1, calls for "Full Faith and Credit" among states, meaning that each state is normally expected to honor the "public Acts, Records, and Proceedings" that take place in any other state. So, for example, if two people are married in Texas—marriage being regulated by state law—Missouri must recognize that marriage even though the couple was not married under Missouri state law.

This ***full faith and credit clause*** has recently become embroiled in the controversy over same-sex marriage. In 1993, the Hawaii Supreme Court prohibited discrimination against such marriage except in very limited circumstances. Many observers believed that Hawaii would eventually fully legalize gay marriage. In fact, after a long political battle Hawaii passed a constitutional amendment in 1998 outlawing gay marriage. In December 1999, however, the Vermont Supreme Court ruled that same-sex couples should have the same rights as heterosexuals. The Vermont legislature responded with a new law that allowed gay men and lesbians to form "civil unions." Although not considered legal marriages, such unions allow same-sex couples to recieve most of the benefits of marriage, such as eligibility for a partner's health insurance, the right to inherit from his or her estate, and the right to transfer property. The Vermont statute could have broad implications for other states. More than thirty states have passed "defense of marriage acts," which define marriage as a union between a man and a woman only. Eager to show its disapproval of gay marriage, Congress passed the Defense of Marriage Act in 1996, which declared that states will *not* have to recognize a same-sex marriage even if it is legal in another state. The act also says that the federal government will not recognize gay marriage—even if it is legal under state law—and that gay marriage partners will

police power The power reserved to the government to regulate the health, safety, and morals of its citizens.

concurrent powers The authority possessed by *both* state and national governments, such as the power to levy taxes.

full faith and credit clause The provision in Article IV, Section 1, of the Constitution requiring that the states normally honor the public acts and judicial decisions that take place in another state.

not be eligible for the federal benefits, such as Medicare and Social Security, normally available to spouses.[6]

In 2004, a presidential election year, Alabama, Georgia, Kentucky, Michigan, Montana, North Dakota, Ohio, Oklahoma, and Utah approved state constitutional amendments strictly defining marriage as between a man and a woman. The large-scale approval of such amendments was probably prompted by a Massachusetts court decision permitting gay men and lesbians to wed, which was to go into effect in May 2004. These developments put fire back into President George W. Bush's pledge to support a constitutional amendment banning same-sex marriage, even though polls had shown that substantial majorities favored some form of same-sex union, whether marriage or "civil union." Although opponents of gay marriage could not find enough support to pass an amendment to the U.S. Constitution, in 2008 several additional states had propositions to ban gay marriage on the ballot. In 2008, high courts in California and Connecticut ruled that same-sex couples should be allowed to marry. However, the California ruling was quickly overturned in November 2008, when voters passed an amendment to the state constitution banning same-sex marriage. In effect, although a great many state laws are observed in a normal, routine way in sister states, laws that affect what have come to be called values may be exempt from comity—or taken off the table altogether by an amendment to that effect in the U.S. Constitution.

Because of this controversy, the extent and meaning of the full faith and credit clause is likely to be considered by the Supreme Court. In fact, it is not clear that the clause requires states to recognize gay marriage because the Court's past interpretation of the clause has provided exceptions for "public policy" reasons: If states have strong objections to a law, they do not have to honor it. In 1997, the Court took up a case involving the full faith and credit clause. A Michigan court order had prevented a former engineer for General Motors from testifying against the company. The engineer, who left the company on bad terms, later testified in a Missouri court about a car accident in which a woman died when her Chevrolet Blazer caught fire. General Motors challenged his right to testify, arguing that Missouri should give "full faith and credit" to the Michigan ruling. The Supreme Court ruled that the engineer could testify and that the court system in one state cannot hinder other state courts in their "search for the truth."[7]

Article IV, Section 2, known as the comity clause, also seeks to promote national unity. It provides that citizens enjoying the ***privileges and immunities*** of one state should be entitled to similar treatment in other states. What this clause has come to mean is that a state cannot discriminate against someone from another state or give special privileges to its own residents. For example, in the 1970s, when Alaska passed a law that gave residents preference over nonresidents in obtaining work on the state's oil and gas pipelines, the Supreme Court ruled the

privileges and immunities The provision from Article IV, Section 2, of the Constitution stating that a state cannot discriminate against someone from another state or give its own residents special privileges.

---

[6]Ken I. Kersch, "Full Faith and Credit for Same-Sex Marriages?" *Political Science Quarterly* 112 (Spring 1997): 117–36; Joan Biskupic, "Once Unthinkable, Now under Debate," *Washington Post*, 3 September 1996, p. A1.

[7]Linda Greenhouse, "Supreme Court Weaves Legal Principles from a Tangle of Legislation," *New York Times*, 30 June 1988, p. A20.

law illegal because it discriminated against citizens of other states.[8] This clause also regulates criminal justice among the states by requiring states to return fugitives to the states from which they have fled. Thus in 1952, when an inmate escaped from an Alabama prison and sought to avoid being returned to Alabama on the grounds that he was being subjected to "cruel and unusual punishment" there, the Supreme Court ruled that he must be returned, according to Article IV, Section 2.[9] This example highlights the difference between the obligations among states and those among different countries. In the late 1990s, France refused to return an American fugitive because he might be subject to the death penalty, which does not exist in France.[10] The Constitution clearly forbids states from doing something similar.

Limitations on the States   Although most of the truly coercive powers of government are reserved to the states, the Constitution does impose some significant limitations. One example was given in the discussion of the privileges and immunities clause: that one state cannot discriminate against a person residing in another state. But the most prominent application of this clause is extradition; any person in any state "who shall flee from Justice . . . [to] another State, shall on Demand . . . be delivered up . . . to the State having Jurisdiction" (Article IV, Section 2). In the last section, we gave the example of the case of an Alabama inmate.

Another limitation on states that occasionally becomes significant is in a clause in Article I, Section 10, that provides that "no State shall, without the Consent of Congress, . . . enter into any Agreement or Compact with another State." Compacts are a way for two or more states to reach a legally binding agreement about how to solve a problem that crosses state lines. In the early years of the Republic, states turned to compacts primarily to settle border disputes. Today they are used for a wide range of issues but are especially important in regulating the distribution of river water, addressing environmental concerns, and operating transportation systems that cross state lines.[11] The most famous contemporary example is the Port of New York Authority, a compact formed between New York and New Jersey in 1921. Without it, such public works as the bridge connecting Brooklyn and Staten Island, the bridges connecting New Jersey and Staten Island, the Lincoln Tunnel, the George Washington Bridge, the expansion and integration of the New York port area, and the expansion and integration of the three major airports and countless approaches and transfer facilities could not have been financed or completed.[12] In 1972, the name of the agency was appropriately changed to the Port Authority of New York and New Jersey.

---

[8] *Hicklin v. Orbeck*, 437 U.S. 518 (1978).

[9] *Sweeney v. Woodall*, 344 U.S. 86 (1953).

[10] Marlise Simons, "France Won't Extradite American Convicted of Murder," *New York Times*, 5 December 1997, p. A9.

[11] Patricia S. Florestano, "Past and Present Utilization of Interstate Compacts in the United States" *Publius* (Fall 1994): 13–26.

[12] A good discussion of the status of the New York Port Authority in politics is found in Wallace Sayre and Herbert Kaufman, *Governing New York City—Politics in the Metropolis* (New York: Russell Sage Foundation, 1960), chap. 9.

Local Government and the Constitution   Local government occupies a peculiar but very important place in the American system. In fact, the status of American local government is probably unique in world experience. First, it must be pointed out that local government has no status in the American Constitution. *State* legislatures created local governments, and *state* constitutions and laws permit local governments to take on some of the responsibilities of the state governments. Most states amended their own constitutions to give their larger cities *home rule*—a guarantee of noninterference in various areas of local affairs. But local governments enjoy no such recognition in the Constitution. Local governments have always been mere conveniences of the states.[13]

Local governments became administratively important in the early years of the Republic because the states possessed little administrative capability. They relied on local governments—cities and counties—to implement the laws of the state. Local government was an alternative to a statewide bureaucracy.

The Slow Growth of the National Government's Power

Before the 1930s, America's federal system could have been characterized as one of *dual federalism,* a two-layered system—national and state—in which the states and their local principalities do most of the governing. The structure of dual federalism is demonstrated in Table 3.1. The items in each column (disregarding the local-level functions discussed in the previous section) are the important types of public policies that governed America for the first century and a half under the Constitution. We refer to it here as the traditional system precisely because almost nothing about our pattern of government changed during two thirds of our history. That is, of course, with the exception of the four years of the Civil War, after which we returned to the traditional system.

But there was more to dual federalism than merely the existence of two tiers. The two tiers were functionally quite different from each other. There have been debates every generation over how to divide responsibilities between the two tiers. As we have seen in this chapter, the Constitution delegated a list of specific powers to the national government and reserved all the rest to the states. That left a lot of room for interpretation, however, because of the final "elastic" clause of Article I, Section 8. The three formal words *necessary and proper* amounted to an invitation to struggle over the distribution of powers between national and state governments. We shall confront this struggle throughout the book. However, the most remarkable thing about the history of American federalism is that federalism remained dual for nearly two thirds of that history, with the national government remaining steadfastly within a "strict construction" of Article I, Section 8. The results are clear in Table 3.1.

 Institution Principle

In answering the question, Who does what? federalism determines the flow of governmental functions and, through that, the political development of the country.

home rule The power delegated by the state to a local unit of government to manage its own affairs.

dual federalism The system of government that prevailed in the United States from 1789 to 1937, in which most fundamental governmental powers were shared between the federal and state governments.

---

[13]A good discussion of the constitutional position of local governments is in York Y. Willbern, *The Withering Away of the City* (Bloomington: Indiana University Press, 1971). For more on the structure and theory of federalism, see Thomas R. Dye, *American Federalism: Competition among Governments* (Lexington, Mass.: Lexington Books, 1990), chap. 1; and Martha Derthick, "Up-to-Date in Kansas City: Reflections on American Federalism," *PS: Political Science and Politics* 25 (December 1992): 671–75.

TABLE 3.1 The Federal System: Specialization of Governmental Functions in the Traditional System, 1789–1937

National Government Policies (Domestic)	State Government Policies	Local Government Policies
Internal improvements	Property laws (including slavery)	Adaptation of state laws to local conditions (variances)
Subsidies	Estate and inheritance laws	Public works
Tariffs	Commerce laws	Contracts for public works
Public lands disposal	Banking and credit laws	Licensing of public accommodations
Patents	Corporate laws	Assessable improvements
Currency	Insurance laws	Basic public services
	Family laws	
	Morality laws	
	Public health laws	
	Education laws	
	General penal laws	
	Eminent domain laws	
	Construction codes	
	Land-use laws	
	Water and mineral laws	
	Criminal procedure laws	
	Electoral and political party laws	
	Local government laws	
	Civil service laws	
	Occupations and professions laws	

commerce clause Article I, Section 8, of the Constitution, which delegates to Congress the power "to regulate Commerce with foreign Nations, and among the several States, and with the Indian Tribes." This clause was interpreted by the Supreme Court to favor national power over the economy.

The best example of the potential elasticity in Article I, Section 8, is in the **commerce clause**, which delegates to Congress the power "to regulate Commerce with foreign Nations, and *among the several States* and with the Indian Tribes" [emphasis added]. It is obvious that this clause can be interpreted broadly or narrowly, and in fact the Supreme Court embraced the broad interpretation throughout most of the nineteenth century. Yet Congress chose not to take the Court's invitation to be expansive. The first and most important case favoring national power was *McCulloch v.*

Maryland.[14] The issue was whether Congress had the power to charter a bank, in particular the Bank of the United States (created by Congress in 1791 over Thomas Jefferson's constitutional opposition), because no power to create banks was found anywhere in Article I, Section 8. Chief Justice John Marshall, speaking for the Supreme Court, answered that such a power could be "implied" from the other specific powers in Article I, Section 8, plus the final clause enabling Congress "to make all Laws which shall be necessary and proper for carrying into Execution the foregoing Powers." Thus the Court created the potential for significant increases in national governmental power.

A second question of national power arose in *McCulloch v. Maryland:* the question of whether Maryland's attempt to tax the bank was constitutional. Once again Marshall and the Supreme Court took the side of the national government, arguing that a legislature representing all the people (Congress) could not be taxed out of business by a state legislature (Maryland) representing only a small portion of the American people. This opinion was accompanied by Marshall's immortal dictum that "the power to tax is the power to destroy." It was also in this case that the Supreme Court recognized and reinforced the supremacy clause: Whenever a state law conflicts with a federal law, the state law should be deemed invalid because "the Laws of the United States . . . shall be the supreme Law of the Land." (This concept was introduced in Chapter 2 and will come up again in Chapter 8.)

This nationalistic interpretation of the Constitution was reinforced by another major case, that of *Gibbons v. Ogden* in 1824. The important but relatively narrow issue was whether the state of New York could grant a monopoly to Robert Fulton's steamboat company to operate an exclusive service between New York and New Jersey. Aaron Ogden had secured his license from Fulton's company, while Thomas Gibbons, a former partner of Ogden's, secured a competing license from the U.S. government. Chief Justice Marshall argued that Gibbons could not be kept from competing because the state of New York did not have the power to grant this particular monopoly. To reach his decision, it was necessary for Marshall to define what Article I, Section 8, meant by "Commerce . . . among the several States." Marshall insisted that the definition was "comprehensive" but added that the comprehensiveness was limited "to that commerce which concerns more states than one." This opinion gave rise to what later came to be called interstate commerce.[15]

Although *Gibbons* was an important case, the precise meaning of interstate commerce would remain uncertain for several decades of constitutional discourse. However, one thing was certain: "Interstate commerce" was a source of power for the national government as long as Congress sought to improve commerce through subsidies, services, and land grants (Table 3.1, col. 1). Later in the nineteenth century, when the national government sought to use its power to *regulate* the economy rather than merely promote economic development, the concept of interstate commerce began to operate as a restraint rather than as a source of national power. Any effort by the federal government to regulate commerce in such areas as fraud, the production of impure goods, the use of child labor, or the

---

[14]*McCulloch v. Maryland,* 4 Wheaton 316 (1819).

[15]*Gibbons v. Ogden,* 9 Wheaton 1 (1824).

ONLINE READING

ONLINE READING

existence of dangerous working conditions or long hours was declared unconstitutional by the Supreme Court as a violation of the concept of interstate commerce. Regulation in these areas would mean the federal government was entering the factory and the workplace, areas inherently local because the goods produced there had not yet passed into commerce and crossed state lines. Any effort to enter these local workplaces was an exercise of police power, a power reserved to the states. No one questioned the power of the national government to regulate certain kinds of businesses, such as railroads, gas pipelines, and waterway transportation, because they intrinsically involved interstate commerce.[16] But well into the twentieth century, most other efforts by Congress to regulate commerce were blocked by the Supreme Court's interpretation of federalism, with the concept of interstate commerce as the primary barrier.

After 1937, the Supreme Court threw out the old distinction between interstate and intrastate commerce, converting the commerce clause from a barrier to a source of power. The Court began to refuse even to review appeals challenging acts of Congress that protected the rights of employees to organize and engage in collective bargaining, regulated the amount of farmland in cultivation, extended low-interest credit to small businesses and farmers, and restricted the activities of corporations dealing in the stock market, as well as many other laws that contributed to the construction of the "regulatory state" and the "welfare state."

Cooperative Federalism and Grants-in-Aid

If the traditional system of two sovereigns performing highly different functions can be called dual federalism, the system since the 1930s can be called *cooperative federalism,* which generally refers to supportive relations, sometimes partnerships, between the national government and the state and local governments. It comes in the form of federal subsidization of special state and local activities; these subsidies are called *grants-in-aid.* But make no mistake about it: Although many of these state and local programs would not exist without the federal grant-in-aid, the grant-in-aid is also an important form of federal influence. (Another form of federal influence, the mandate, is covered in the next section.)

A grant-in-aid is really a kind of bribe, or a "carrot," whereby Congress appropriates money for state and local governments with the condition that the money be spent for a particular purpose as defined by Congress. Congress uses grants-in-aid because it does not have the political or constitutional power to command local governments to do its bidding. When you can't command, a monetary inducement becomes a viable alternative. Grants-in-aid are also mechanisms that help coordinate the separate activities of all those state and local governments with a common set of standards or policy principles in circumstances when a multiplicity of these things would undermine the purposes of the policy.

History Principle

In 1937, the Supreme Court converted the commerce clause from a source of limitations to a source of power for the national government. This precedent guided subsequent court decisions, legislation, and political action.

cooperative federalism A type of federalism existing since the New Deal era, in which grants-in-aid have been used strategically to encourage states and localities (without commanding them) to pursue nationally defined goals. Also known as intergovernmental cooperation.

grants-in-aid A general term for funds given by Congress to state and local governments.

---

[16]In *Wabash, St. Louis, and Pacific Railway Company v. Illinois,* 118 U.S. 557 (1886), the Supreme Court struck down a state law prohibiting rate discrimination by a railroad; in response, Congress passed the Interstate Commerce Act of 1887, creating the Interstate Commerce Commission (ICC), the first federal regulatory agency.

FIGURE 3.1 The Historical Trend of Federal Grants-in-Aid

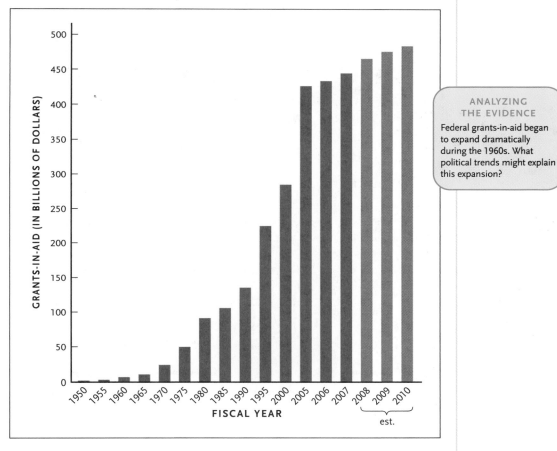

SOURCE: Office of Management and Budget, *Budget of the U.S. Government, Fiscal Year 2008, Analytical Perspectives* (Washington, D.C.: Government Printing Office, 2007).

NOTE: Excludes outlays for national defense, international affairs, and net interest.

ANALYZING THE EVIDENCE

Federal grants-in-aid began to expand dramatically during the 1960s. What political trends might explain this expansion?

Beginning in the late 1930s, this approach was applied to cities. Congress set national goals, such as public housing and assistance to the unemployed, and provided grants-in-aid to meet them. World War II temporarily stopped the distribution of these grants. But after the war, Congress resumed the provision of grants for urban development and school lunches. The value of such ***categorical grants-in-aid*** increased from $2.3 billion in 1950 to $434 billion in 2006 (Figure 3.1). Sometimes Congress requires the state or local government to match the national contribution dollar for dollar, but for some programs, such as the interstate highway system, the congressional grant-in-aid provides a significant percentage of the cost. The nationwide speed limit of fifty-five miles per hour was not imposed on individual drivers by an act of Congress. Instead, Congress

categorical grants-in-aid Funds given by Congress to states and localities that are earmarked by law for specific categories, such as education or crime prevention.

FIGURE 3.2 Two Views of Federalism

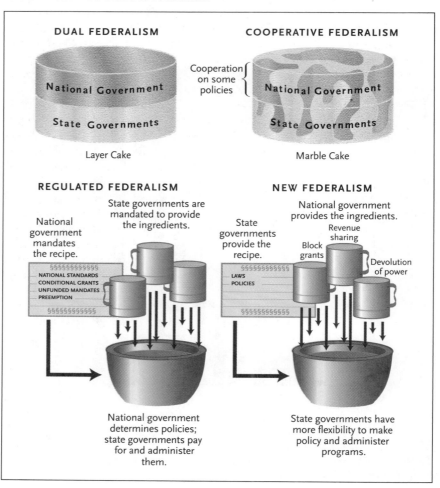

bribed the state legislatures by threatening to withdraw the federal highway grants-in-aid if the states did not set that speed limit. In the early 1990s, Congress began to ease up on the states, permitting them, under certain conditions, to go back to the sixty-five-mile-per-hour (or higher) limit without losing their highway grants.

For the most part, the categorical grants created before the 1960s simply helped the states perform their traditional functions, such as educating and policing.[17] In the 1960s, however, the national role expanded, and the number of categorical

Collective-Action Principle

Grants-in-aid allow the national government to coordinate state and local policies with a common set of national standards.

---

[17]Kenneth T. Palmer, "The Evolution of Grant Policies," in *The Changing Politics of Federal Grants,* ed. Lawrence D. Brown, James W. Fossett, and Kenneth T. Palmer (Washington, D.C.: Brookings Institution, 1984), p. 15.

grants increased dramatically. For example, during the Eighty-ninth Congress (1965–66) alone, the number of categorical grant-in-aid programs grew from 221 to 379.[18] The grants authorized during the 1960s announced national purposes much more strongly than did earlier grants. Central to that national purpose was the need to provide opportunities to the poor.

Many of the categorical grants enacted during the 1960s were *project grants,* which require state and local governments to submit proposals to federal agencies. In contrast to the older *formula grants,* which used a formula (composed of such elements as need and state and local capacities) to distribute funds, the new project grants made funding available on a competitive basis. Federal agencies would give grants to the proposals they judged to be the best. In this way, the national government acquired substantial control over which state and local governments got money, how much they got, and how they spent it.

One of the most important scholars of the history of federalism, Morton Grodzins, characterized the shift to post–New Deal cooperative federalism as a move from "layer cake federalism" to "marble cake federalism,"[19] in which the line distinguishing intergovernmental cooperation and sharing has blurred, making it difficult to say where the national government ends and the state and local governments begin. Figure 3.2 demonstrates the financial basis of the marble cake idea. At the high point of grant-in-aid policies, in the late 1970s, federal aid contributed 25 to 30 percent of the operating budgets of all the state and local governments in the country (Figure 3.3). Table 3.2 represents federal aid to America's ten largest cities, which was significantly lower by 2004.

TABLE 3.2 Federal Aid to Cities

Federal aid as a percentage of general annual revenue in the nation's 10 largest cities, 2004			
New York	5.2	Phoenix	17.4
Los Angeles	4.6	San Antonio	3.1
Chicago	8.5	San Diego	10.5
Houston	6.6	Dallas	3.0
Philadelphia	14.7	San Jose	2.5

Source: Statistical Abstract of the United States.

project grants Grant programs in which state and local governments submit proposals to federal agencies and for which funding is provided on a competitive basis.

formula grants Grants-in-aid in which a formula is used to determine the amount of federal funds a state or local government will receive.

---

[18]Ibid., p. 6.

[19]Morton Grodzins, "The Federal System," in *Goals for Americans,* ed. President's Commission on National Goals (Englewood Cliffs, N.J.: Prentice-Hall, 1960), p. 265. In a marble cake, the white cake is distinguishable from the chocolate cake, but the two are streaked rather than arranged in distinct layers.

FIGURE 3.3 The Rise, Decline, and Recovery of Federal Aid

ANALYZING
THE EVIDENCE

The extent to which state and local governments rely upon federal funding has varied a great deal over time. What difference does it make if the states are fiscally dependent upon the federal government?

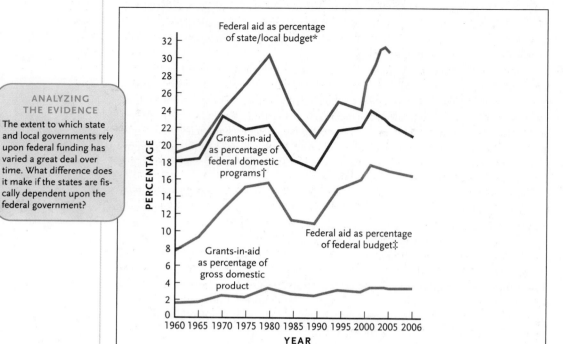

SOURCES: Office of Management and Budget, *Budget of the U.S. Government, Fiscal Year 2006, Analytical Perspectives* (Washington, D.C.: Government Printing Office, 2005), table 8.3, p. 131; U.S. Bureau of the Census, *Statistical Abstract of the United States, 2007* (Washington, D.C.: Government Printing Office, 2007), table 421.

*Federal aid as a percentage of state and local expenditures after transfers.

†Federal aid as a percentage of federal expenditures from the federal government's own funds.

‡Excludes outlays for national defense, international affairs, and net interest.

Regulated Federalism and National Standards

Developments from the 1960s to the present have moved well beyond cooperative federalism to what might be called regulated federalism.[20] In some areas, the national government actually regulates the states by threatening to withhold grant money unless state and local governments conform to national standards. The most notable instances of this kind of regulated federalism are in the areas of civil rights, poverty programs, and environmental protection. This focus reflects a general shift in federal regulation away from the oversight and control of strictly economic activities toward "social regulation"—intervention on behalf of individual rights and lib-

ONLINE READING

[20] The concept and the best discussion of this modern phenomenon are found in Donald F. Kettl, *The Regulation of American Federalism* (1983; repr., Baltimore: Johns Hopkins University Press, 1987), esp. pp. 33–41.

erties, environmental protection, workplace safety, and so on. In these instances, the national government provides grant-in-aid financing but sets conditions the states must meet to keep the grants. The national government refers to these policies as "setting national standards." Important examples include the Asbestos Hazard Emergency Act of 1986, which requires school districts to inspect for asbestos hazards and remove them from school buildings when necessary, and the Americans with Disabilities Act of 1990, which requires all state and local governments to promote access for the handicapped to all government buildings. The net effect of these national standards is that state and local policies are more uniform from coast to coast. As we noted earlier about grants-in-aid, national regulations and standards provide coordination across states and localities and solve collective-action problems. However, there are a number of other programs in which the national government engages in regulated federalism by imposing national standards on the states without providing any funding at all. These have come to be called **unfunded mandates.** They came about in response to states' complaints that mandates took up so much of their budgets they were not able to set their own priorities.[21]

These burdens became a major part of the rallying cry that produced the famous Republican Congress elected in 1994 and its Contract with America. One of the first measures adopted by the Republican 104th Congress in 1995 was an act to limit unfunded mandates: the Unfunded Mandates Reform Act (UMRA). UMRA was considered a triumph of lobbying efforts by state and local governments, and it was "hailed as both symbol and substance of a renewed congressional commitment to federalism."[22] Under this law, any mandate with an uncompensated state and local cost estimated at greater than $50 million a year, as determined by the Congressional Budget Office, can be stopped by a point of order raised on the House or Senate floor. This so-called stop, look, and listen requirement forced Congress to take positive action to own up to a mandate and its potential costs. During 1996, the first full year in which UMRA was in effect, only eleven bills included mandates that exceeded the $50 million threshold. Examples included a minimum wage increase, parity for mental health and health insurance, mandated use of Social Security numbers on driver's licenses, and extension of the federal Occupation Safety and Health Administration's standards to state and local employees. Most of these bills were modified in the House to reduce their costs. However, as one expert put it, "the primary impact of UMRA came not from the affirmative blockage of [mandate] legislation, but rather from its effect as a deterrent to mandates in the drafting and early consideration of legislation."[23]

As indicated by the first year of its operation, the effect of UMRA has not been revolutionary. UMRA does not prevent members of Congress from passing unfunded

---

[21]John J. DiIulio and Donald F. Kettl report that in 1980 there were thirty-six laws that could be categorized as unfunded mandates. And despite the concerted opposition of the administrations of Ronald Reagan and George H. W. Bush, another twenty-seven laws qualifying as unfunded mandates were adopted between 1982 and 1991. See John DiIulio Jr., and Donald F. Kettl, *Fine Print: The Contract with America, Devolution, and the Administrative Realities of American Federalism* (Washington, D.C.: Brookings Institution, 1995), p. 41.

[22]Paul Posner, "Unfunded Mandate Reform: How Is It Working?" *Rockefeller Institute Bulletin* (1998): 35.

[23]Ibid., 36.

unfunded mandates
National standards or programs imposed on state and local governments by the federal government without accompanying funding or reimbursement.

mandates; it only makes them think twice before they do. Moreover, the act exempts several areas from coverage. And states must still enforce antidiscrimination laws and meet other requirements in order to receive federal assistance. On the other hand, UMRA does represent a serious effort to move the national-state relationship a bit further toward the state side.

President George W. Bush made this shift in focus a key feature of his electoral campaign of 2000 and his legislative agenda of 2001. Yet the most heralded item in his domestic policy agenda, the No Child Left Behind (NCLB) Act, a concept going back to his successful program as governor of Texas, *is a very expensive unfunded mandate!* Signed into law in January 2002, NCLB set a national standard for steady improvement in students' performance on standardized tests and punishes schools whose students fail to improve. It also set rules for educating disabled students and presents detailed requirements that, as lobbyists for the states put it, "fail to recognize the tapestry of educational challenges faced by teachers in the nation's 15,000 school districts."[24] President Bush's promise that NCLB would provide the money for compliance brought him support from his leading Democratic voice of opposition in the Senate, Senator Edward Kennedy, but so far the cost of NCLB has been borne mainly by the states.

Opposition lobbying of Congress and the president by state government representatives became so intense that in 2004 the National Conference of State Legislatures (NCSL) began publishing *Mandate Monitor,* which itemizes the "gap" in funding it claims is directly attributable to Congress's failure to appropriate the support necessary to comply with unfunded mandates. The first results of this analysis produced a list of fifteen major federal programs, the largest being education (NCLB and Americans with Disabilities), state drug costs, and the Department of Homeland Security. These programs have contributed to a total "cost shift" from the federal government to the states. According to the NCSL, the cost shift in federal funding to the states for fiscal years 2004 and 2005 collectively was $51 billion and $30 billion for 2006 alone. However, the NCSL insists that these are estimates and that "additional research . . . strongly suggests the cost shift to the states is double these amounts."[25] Although the measurement of these gaps can be criticized, the scale of unfunded and underfunded mandates is undeniable. Note also that the responsibility for this enormous shortfall is not attributable only to the party in power.

New Federalism and the National-State Tug-of-War

Federalism in the United States can best be understood today as a tug-of-war between those seeking more uniform national standards and those seeking more room for variability from state to state. This is a struggle over federalism's script and scorecard—over who does what and how the various activities are structured and sequenced. Presidents Richard Nixon and Ronald Reagan called their efforts to reverse the trend toward national standards and reestablish traditional policy making and implementation the new federalism. They helped craft national policies whose purpose was to return more dis-

---

[24] Sam Dillon, "Report from States Faults Bush's Education Initiative," *New York Times,* 24 February 2005, p. A18.

[25] *Mandate Monitor,* 2, no. 1 (March 2005).

cretion to the states. Examples of these policies include Nixon's revenue sharing and Reagan's ***block grants,*** which consolidated a number of categorical grants into one larger category, leaving the state (or local) government more discretion to decide how to use the money. Presidents Nixon and Reagan, as well as former president George H. W. Bush, were sincere in wanting to return somewhat to a traditional notion of freedom of action for the states. They called it new federalism, but their concepts and their goals were really much closer to the older traditional federalism that predated the 1930s.

In effect, President Bill Clinton adopted the new federalism of Nixon and Reagan even while expanding federal grant activity: He signed the UMRA of 1995 and the Personal Responsibility and Work Opportunity Reconciliation Act of 1996, which goes further than any other act of Congress in the past sixty years to relieve the states of national mandates, funded or unfunded. This new law replaced the sixty-one-year-old program of Aid to Families with Dependent Children (AFDC) and its education, work, and training program with block grants to states for Temporary Assistance for Needy Families (TANF). Although some national standards remain, the place of the states in the national welfare system has been virtually revolutionized through ***devolution,*** the strategy of delegating to the states more and more authority over a range of policies that had until then been under national government authority, plus providing the states with a substantial portion of the cost of these programs. Since the mid-1990s, devolution has been quite consequential for the national-state tug-of-war.

By changing welfare from a combined federal-state program into a block grant to the states, Congress gave the states more responsibility for programs that serve the poor. One argument in favor of devolution is that states can act as "laboratories of democracy" by experimenting with many approaches and thus find one that best meets the needs of their citizens.[26] As states have altered their welfare programs in the wake of the new law, they have indeed designed diverse approaches. For example, Minnesota has adopted an incentive-based approach that offers extra assistance to families that take low-wage jobs. Other states, such as California, have more sticks than carrots in their new welfare programs.[27]

President George W. Bush, though sometimes compared with Ronald Reagan, was not an unwavering supporter of smaller national government, new federalism, and states' rights. On a number of very important matters, Bush was closer to the spirit of the New Deal and "regulated federalism" in terms of both direct expansion of the national government and increasing imposition of national standards on the states. The former has gone by the name compassionate conservatism, and it was not altogether popular among Bush's own partisan supporters. The latter takes the form of unfunded mandates, which not only rankled Bush's supporters but also went against strict rules established by his administration. Some of the expansions of national government under George W. Bush were clearly attributable to September 11 and the gigantic reaction to world terrorism, the creation of the Department of Homeland Security, the war in Iraq, and the cost of Hurricane Katrina, all complicated by

---

[26]The phrase *laboratories of democracy* was coined by Supreme Court Justice Louis Brandeis in his dissenting opinion in *New State Ice Company v. Liebman,* 285 U.S. 262 (1932).

[27]For assessments of welfare grants to states, see both Frances Fox Piven, "Welfare and Work," and Dorothy Roberts, "Welfare's Ban on Poor Motherhood," in *Whose Welfare?,* ed. Gwendolyn Mink (Ithaca, N.Y.: Cornell University Press, 1999), pp. 83–99 and 152–67.

Policy Principle

Devolution has had an important influence on policy outcomes, particularly in the realm of welfare.

Collective-Action Principle

States compete with one another not only to attract new business but also to appear less attractive to welfare recipients.

block grants Federal funds given to state governments to pay for goods, services, or programs, with relatively few restrictions on how the funds may be spent.

devolution The policy of removing a program from one level of government by deregulating it or passing it down to a lower level, such as from the national government to the state and local governments.

failed implementation. But President Bush had other plans for the national government that he brought with him from his experience as a governor. His No Child Left Behind Act increased by 51 percent the budget of the Department of Education, a department that conservatives had vowed since the Reagan administration to abolish. Agriculture subsidies were increased by 40 percent. The 2005 Public Transportation Act included a commitment of $286 billion, of which $24 billion was for pork-barrel projects for favorite congressional districts. The prescription drug benefit that he added to Medicare was another enormous national government commitment; its estimated cost is $534 billion, the largest expansion of the welfare state since Lyndon Johnson.[28] Bush's 2008 budget called for a 4 percent spending increase for the Department of Justice and another 5 percent increase for the Medicare program.

The Supreme Court as Referee   For much of the nineteenth century, federal power remained limited. The Tenth Amendment was used to bolster arguments about ***states' rights***, which in their extreme version claimed that the states did not have to submit to national laws when they believed the national government had exceeded its authority. Arguments in favor of states' rights were voiced less often after the Civil War. But the Supreme Court continued to use the Tenth Amendment to strike down laws that it thought exceeded national power, including the Civil Rights Act passed in 1875.

In the early twentieth century, however, the Tenth Amendment appeared to lose its force. Reformers began to press for national regulations to limit the power of large corporations and to preserve the health and welfare of citizens. The Supreme Court approved of some of these laws, but it struck down others, including a law combating child labor. The Court stated that the law violated the Tenth Amendment because only states should have the power to regulate conditions of employment. By the late 1930s, however, the Supreme Court had approved such an expansion of federal power that the Tenth Amendment appeared irrelevant. In fact, in 1941, Justice Harlan Fiske Stone declared that the Tenth Amendment was simply a "truism," that it had no real meaning.[29]

Recent years have seen a revival of interest in the Tenth Amendment and important Supreme Court decisions limiting federal power. Much of the renewed interest stems from conservatives who believe that a strong federal government encroaches on individual liberties. They believe freedom is better protected by returning more power to the states through the process of devolution. In 1996, the Republican presidential candidate, Bob Dole, carried a copy of the Tenth Amendment in his pocket as he campaigned, pulling it out to read at rallies.[30] Around the same time, the Eleventh Amendment concept of ***state sovereign immunity*** was revived by the Court. This legal doctrine holds that states are immune from lawsuits by private individuals or groups claiming that the state violated a statute enacted by Congress.

The Supreme Court's ruling in *United States v. Lopez* in 1995 fueled further interest in the Tenth Amendment. In that case, the Court, stating that Congress had exceeded its authority under the commerce clause, struck down a federal law that barred

states' rights The principle that states should oppose increases in the authority of the national government. This view was most popular before the Civil War.

state sovereign immunity A legal doctrine holding that states cannot be sued for violating an act of Congress.

---

[28]The figures and judgments in this paragraph, excluding the final sentence, are provided by George F. Will, one of America's most distinguished conservative columnists and philosophers, in "The Last Word," *Newsweek*, 27 October 2005, p. 78.

[29]*United States v. Darby*, 312 U.S. 100 (1941).

[30]W. John Moore, "Pleading the 10th," *National Journal*, 29 July 1995, p. 1940.

handguns near schools.[31] It was the first time since the New Deal that the Court had limited congressional powers in this way. The Court further limited the power of the federal government over the states in a 1996 ruling based on the Eleventh Amendment. That ruling prevented Seminole Indians from suing the state of Florida in federal court. A 1988 law had given Indian tribes the right to sue a state in federal court if the state did not negotiate in good faith issues related to gambling casinos on tribal land. The Supreme Court's ruling appeared to signal a much broader limitation on national power by raising new questions about whether individuals can sue a state if it fails to uphold federal law.[32]

Another significant decision involving the relationship between the federal government and state governments was the 1997 case of *Printz v. United States,* in which the Court struck down a key provision of the Brady bill, enacted by Congress in 1993 to regulate gun sales. Under the terms of the act, state and local law enforcement officers were required to conduct background checks on prospective gun purchasers. The Court held that the federal government cannot require states to administer or enforce federal regulatory programs.[33] Because the states bear administrative responsibility for a variety of other federal programs, this decision could have far-reaching consequences. Finally, in another major ruling from the 1996–97 term, in *City of Boerne v. Flores,* the Court ruled that Congress had gone too far in restricting the power of the states to enact regulations they deemed necessary for the protection of public health, safety, or welfare (see Chapter 4).[34] These rulings signal a move toward a much more restricted federal government.

In 1999, the Court's ruling on another Eleventh Amendment case further strengthened the doctrine of state sovereign immunity by finding that "the federal system established by our Constitution preserves the sovereign status of the States. ... The generation that designed and adopted our federal system considered immunity from private suits central to sovereign dignity."[35] In 2000, in *United States v. Morrison,* the Supreme Court invalidated an important provision of the 1994 Violence against Women Act, which permitted women to bring private damage suits if their victimization was "gender-motivated." Although the 1994 act did not add any new national laws imposing liability or obligations on the states, the Supreme Court still held the act to be "an unconstitutional exercise" of Congress's power.[36] And although *Morrison* is a quite narrow decision on federalism, when it is coupled with *United States v. Lopez,* there is a definite trend toward questioning the need for federal intervention in American sociey. This trend has continued with the 2006 *Gonzales v. Oregon* case, examined earlier in this chapter.

These developments put federalism and the Court directly in the line of fire. But there is nothing new in this. The Court under John Marshall was, in essence, a nationalizing court. Marshall's successor, Chief Justice Roger Taney, gave us the

---

[31] *United States v. Lopez,* 514 U.S. 549 (1995).

[32] *Seminole Tribe v. Florida,* 517 U.S. 44 (1996).

[33] *Printz v. United States,* 521 U.S. 898 (1997).

[34] *City of Boerne v. Flores,* 521 U.S. 507 (1997).

[35] *Alden v. Maine,* 527 U.S. 706 (1999).

[36] *United States v. Morrison,* 529 U.S. 598 (2000).

ONLINE READING

most extreme denationalizing period, virtually inventing the concept of states' rights, as slavery and its extension were endangering the Union. The Court in place when Franklin Roosevelt was first elected was extremely anti-national; it declared virtually all the novel New Deal programs unconstitutional. And most notoriously, that same Court, after Roosevelt's landslide 1936 reelection, followed public opinion into the longest and most profound pro-nationalizing era. (It should be explained once again that the national government was permitted to expand, but not at the expense of the states.) The only remarkable thing about the current era has been the moderation and patience of the Burger and Rehnquist Courts in turning the tendency back toward the states.

This tug-of-war between state and national levels of government will almost certainly continue. The Roberts Court will surely take us further back toward the state level, but how far back will depend on new judicial appointments as presidents and parties change and vacancies on the Court arise.

THE SEPARATION OF POWERS

In his discussion of the separation of powers, James Madison quoted the originator of the idea, the French political thinker Baron de Montesquieu: "There can be no liberty where the legislative and executive powers are united in the same person . . . [or] if the power of judging be not separated from the legislative and executive powers."[37] Using this same reasoning, many of Madison's contemporaries argued that there was not *enough* separation among the three branches, and Madison had to backtrack to insist that complete separation was not required:

> Unless these departments [branches] be so far connected and blended as to give to each a constitutional control over the others, the degree of separation which the maxim requires, as essential to a free government, can never in practice be duly maintained.[38]

This is the secret of how Americans have made the separation of powers effective: They have made it self-enforcing by giving each branch of government the means to participate in, and partially or temporarily obstruct, the workings of the other branches. The Analyzing the Evidence unit for this chapter explores this concept in more detail.

Checks and Balances

The means by which each branch of government interacts with the others is known informally as ***checks and balances.*** The best-known examples are the presidential power to veto legislation passed by Congress; the power of Congress to override the

checks and balances The mechanisms through which each branch of government is able to participate in and influence the activities of the other branches.

---

[37]Alexander Hamilton, James Madison, and John Jay, *The Federalist Papers*, ed. Clinton L. Rossiter (New York: New American Library, 1961), no. 47, p. 302.

[38]Ibid., no. 48, p. 308.

veto by a two-thirds majority vote, the power of Congress to impeach the president, and the power of the Senate to approve presidential appointments; the power of the president to appoint the members of the Supreme Court and the other federal judges with Senate approval; and the power of the Supreme Court to engage in judicial review (discussed below). These and other examples are shown in Figure 3.4. The framers sought to guarantee that the three branches would in fact use the checks and balances as weapons against one another by giving each branch a different political constituency: direct, popular election of the members of the House and indirect election of senators (until the Seventeenth Amendment, adopted in 1913); indirect election of the president (which still exists, at least formally); and appointment of federal judges for life. All things considered, the best characterization of the separation-of-powers principle in action is, as we said in Chapter 2, "separated institutions sharing power."[39]

Institution Principle

Checks and balances are a system of separated institutions sharing power.

Legislative Supremacy

Although each branch was to be given adequate means to compete with the other branches, it is also clear that within the system of separated powers the framers provided for **legislative supremacy** by making Congress the preeminent branch. Legislative supremacy made the provision of checks and balances in the other two branches all the more important.

Institution Principle

The framers provided for legislative supremacy by making Congress the preeminent branch.

The most important indication of the intention of legislative supremacy was made by the framers when they decided to place the provisions for national powers in Article I, the legislative article, and to treat the powers of the national government as powers of Congress. In a system based on the "rule of law," the power to make the laws is the supreme power. Section 8 provides in part that "*Congress shall have Power To lay and collect Taxes . . . ; To borrow Money . . . ; To regulate Commerce*" [emphasis added]. The founders also provided for legislative supremacy in their decision to give Congress the sole power over appropriations and to give the House of Representatives the power to initiate all revenue bills. Madison recognized legislative supremacy as part and parcel of the separation of powers:

> It is not possible to give to each department an equal power of self-defense. In republican government, the legislative authority necessarily predominates. The remedy for this inconveniency is to divide the legislature into different branches; and to render them, by different modes of election and different principles of action, as little connected with each other as the nature of their common functions and their common dependence on the society will admit.[40]

In other words, Congress was so likely to dominate the other branches that it would have to be divided against itself, into House and Senate. One could say that the Constitution provided for four branches, not three.

legislative supremacy The preeminent position assigned to Congress by the Constitution.

ONLINE READING

---

[39]Richard E. Neustadt, *Presidential Power and the Modern Presidents: The Politics of Leadership from Roosevelt to Reagan* (1960; rev. ed., New York: Free Press, 1990), p. 33.

[40]*The Federalist Papers*, no. 51, p. 322.

Individual Interests and the Separation of Powers

In this chapter, we see how the different branches of government check and balance each other. James Madison feared the excessive concentration of power in government; part of the solution to this danger that he proposes in *Federalist* 51 is the separation of powers and federalism. But his solution did not rely on institutional checks alone; Madison also argued that "The interest of the man must be connected with the constitutional rights of the place." Why is it important that the interests of individual political actors be connected with the constitutional rights of their offices? Let us take a closer look at *Federalist* 51.

For Madison, human beings are "not angels" and political actors are no different. Recognizing that political actors are generally ambitious, Madison believed that this natural human tendency could be used to help thwart the ambitions of others. In addition to the presence of institutional checks and balances, then, we can also rely on human ambition to prevent the excessive accumulation of power in any single branch of government.

Federalist 51

"...the great security against a gradual concentration of the several powers in the same department, consists in giving to those who administer each department the necessary constitutional means and personal motives to resist encroachments of the others. ...Ambition must be made to counteract ambition. **The interest of the man must be connected with the constitutional rights of the place.** It may be a reflection on human nature, that such devices should be necessary to control the abuses of government. But what is government itself, but the greatest of all reflections on human nature? If men were angels, no government would be necessary. If angels were to govern men, neither external nor internal controls on government would be necessary."

How does this work in practice? A threat to the power or prestige of the institution of the presidency, for example, is also a threat to the individual president's power and prestige. We can rely on the president's personal ambition to provide an incentive to resist efforts by the legislative or judicial branch to diminish or infringe on the rights of his office. Similarly, we can rely on the ambition of justices, judges, and members of Congress to link their individual interests to the constitutional rights of their offices.

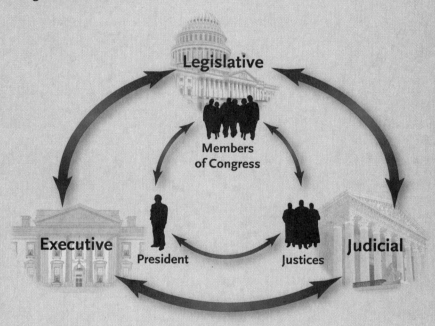

Recent events provide an illustration of Madison's idea in action. In May 2006, Louisiana congressman William J. Jefferson's office was searched by agents of the Justice Department (part of the executive branch) as part of a corruption probe. Although Jefferson was a Democrat seeking reelection at the time of the raid, the Republican Speaker of the House, J. Dennis Hastert, joined Democratic Minority Leader Nancy Pelosi and other Democrats in protesting the raid. In defending the institution of Congress from what they saw as unlawful interference by the executive branch, Hastert and Pelosi issued a joint statement, saying that "The Justice Department was wrong to seize records from Congressman Jefferson's office in violation of the constitutional principle of separation of powers."[1] Hastert's response can be seen as the product of his personal interests being linked to the interests of his office (Speaker of the House), with the goal of preventing the executive branch from overstepping its powers and infringing on the powers and prerogatives of Congress.

[1]Carl Hulse, "House Leaders Demand Return of Seized Files," *New York Times*, 25 May, 2006.

FIGURE 3.4 Checks and Balances

Executive over Legislative
- President can veto acts of Congress.
- President can call a special session of Congress.
- President carries out, and thereby interprets, laws passed by Congress.
- Vice president casts tie-breaking vote in the Senate.

Legislative over Judicial
- Congress can change size of federal court system and number of Supreme Court justices.
- Congress can propose constitutional amendments.
- Congress can reject Supreme Court nominees.
- Congress can impeach and remove federal judges.
- Congress can amend court jurisdictions.
- Congress controls appropriations.

LEGISLATIVE

Legislative over Executive
- Congress can override presidential veto.
- Congress can impeach and remove president.
- Senate can reject president's appointments and refuse to ratify treaties.
- Congress can conduct investigations into president's actions.
- Congress can refuse to pass laws or provide funding that president requests.

Judicial over Legislative
- Court can declare laws unconstitutional.
- Chief Justice presides over Senate during hearing to impeach the president.

JUDICIAL

Executive over Judicial
- President nominates Supreme Court justices.
- President nominates federal judges.
- President can pardon those convicted in federal court.
- President can refuse to enforce the court's decisions.

EXECUTIVE

Judicial over Executive
- Court can declare executive actions unconstitutional.
- Court has the power to issue warrants.
- Chief Justice presides over impeachment of president.

Although "presidential government" seemed to supplant legislative supremacy after 1937, the relative power position of the executive and legislative branches since that time has varied. The degree of conflict between the president and Congress has changed with the rise and fall of political parties, and it has been especially tense during periods of ***divided government,*** when one party controls the White House and another controls the Congress, as has been the case almost solidly since 1969.

The Role of the Supreme Court

The role of the judicial branch in the separation of powers has depended on the power of judicial review (see Chapter 8), a power not provided for in the Constitution but asserted by Chief Justice Marshall in 1803:

> If a law be in opposition to the Constitution; if both the law and the Constitution apply to a particular case, so that the Court must either decide that case conformable to the law, disregarding the Constitution, or conformable to the Constitution, disregarding the law; the Court must determine which of these conflicting rules governs the case: This is of the very essence of judicial duty.[41]

Review of the constitutionality of acts of the president or Congress is relatively rare.[42] For example, there were no Supreme Court reviews of congressional acts in the fifty plus years between *Marbury v. Madison* (1803) and *Dred Scott v. Sandford* (1857). In the century or so between the Civil War and 1970, eighty-four acts of Congress were held unconstitutional (in whole or in part), but there were long periods of complete Supreme Court deference to the Congress, punctuated by flurries of judicial review during times of social upheaval. The most significant of these was 1935–36, when twelve acts of Congress were invalidated, blocking virtually the entire New Deal program.[43] Then, after 1935, when the Court made its great reversals, no significant acts were voided until 1983, when the Court declared unconstitutional the legislative veto, a practice in which Congress authorized the president to take action but reserved the right to rescind presidential actions with which it disagreed.[44] Another decision, in 1986, struck down the Gramm-Rudman Act of 1985, which mandated a balanced budget. That act, the Court held, delegated too much power to the comptroller general, a congressional official, to direct the president to reduce the budget.[45] The Supreme Court became much more activist (that is, less deferential to Congress) after the elevation of Justice William H. Rehnquist to the position of chief justice (in 1986).[46] All of the cases in Table 3.3 altered some aspect of federalism by declaring unconstitutional all or an important portion of an act of Congress, and the end of this episode of judicial activism against Congress is not over. Between 1995 and 2002, at least twenty-six acts or parts of acts of Congress were struck down on constitutional grounds.[47]

Since the New Deal period, the Court has been far more deferential toward the president, with only five significant confrontations. One was the so-called steel

---

[41] *Marbury v. Madison,* 1 Cranch 137 (1803).

[42] C. Herman Pritchett, *The American Constitution* (New York: McGraw-Hill, 1959), pp. 180–86.

[43] The Supreme Court struck down eight out of ten New Deal statutes. For example, in *Panama Refining Company v. Ryan,* 293 U.S. 388 (1935), the Court ruled that a section of the National Industrial Recovery Act of 1933 was an invalid delegation of legislative power to the executive branch. And in *Schechter Poultry Corporation v. United States,* 295 U.S. 495 (1935), the Court found the National Industrial Recovery Act itself to be invalid for the same reason.

[44] *Immigration and Naturalization Service v. Chadha,* 462 U.S. 919 (1983).

[45] *Bowsher v. Synar,* 478 U.S. 714 (1986).

[46] Cass R. Sunstein, "Taking Over the Courts," *New York Times,* 9 November 2002, p. A19.

[47] Ibid.

TABLE 3.3 A New Federal System? The Case Record, 1995–2006

Case	Date	Court Holding
United States v. Lopez, 514 U.S. 549	1995	Voids federal law barring handguns near schools: It is beyond Congress's power to regulate commerce.
Seminole Tribe v. Florida, 517 U.S. 44	1996	Voids federal law giving tribes the right to sue a state in federal court: "Sovereign immunity" requires a state's permission to be sued.
Printz v. United States, 521 U.S. 898	1997	Voids key provision of Brady law requiring states to make background checks on gun purchases: As "unfunded mandate," it violated state sovereignty under the Tenth Amendment.
City of Boerne v. Flores, 521 U.S. 507	1997	Restricts Congress's power under the Fourteenth Amendment to regulate city zoning and health and welfare policies to "remedy" rights: Congress may not expand those rights.
Alden v. Maine, 527 U.S. 706	1999	Declares states "immune" from suits by their *own* employees for overtime pay under the Fair Labor Standards Act of 1938. (See also the *Seminole* case.)
United States v. Morrison, 529 U.S. 598	2000	Extends *Seminole* case by invalidating Violence against Women Act: States may not be sued by individuals for failing to enforce federal laws.
Gonzales v. Oregon, 546 U.S.	2006	Upholds state assisted-suicide law over attorney general's objection.

seizure case of 1952, in which the Court refused to permit President Harry Truman to use "emergency powers" to force workers back into the steel mills during the Korean War.[48] A second case was *United States v. Nixon,* in which the Court declared unconstitutional President Nixon's refusal to respond to a subpoena to make available the infamous White House tapes as evidence in a criminal prose-

---

[48] *Youngstown Sheet and Tube Company v. Sawyer,* 343 U.S. 579 (1952).

cution. The Court argued that although *executive privilege* did protect confidentiality of communications to and from the president, this protection did not extend to data in presidential files or tapes linked to criminal prosecutions.[49] During the heat of the Clinton scandal, the Supreme Court rejected the claim that the pressures and obligations of the office of president were so demanding that all litigation "but the most exceptional cases" should be deferred until the end of the president's term.[50] But of far greater importance, the Supreme Court struck down the Line Item Veto Act of 1996 on the grounds that it violated Article I, Section 7, which prescribes procedures for congressional enactment, and presidential acceptance or veto, of statutes. The Court held that any such change in the procedures of adopting laws would have to be made by amendment to the Constitution, not by legislation.[51]

The fifth confrontation came after the September 11, 2001, terrorist attacks. But because of the terrorism scare, it was the least restrictive of the five. In *Rasul v. Bush,* the Court held that the estimated 650 "enemy combatants" detained without formal charges at the U.S. Naval Station at Guantánamo Bay, Cuba, had the right to seek release through a *writ of* habeas corpus.[52] However, the *Rasul* decision left a very large escape hatch by relegating to the lower district courts the decision, case by case, of whether to actually grant the writ. The first application came in early 2005, when a federal district judge in Washington, D.C., denied *habeas corpus* to seven detainees. Essential to the judge's reasoning was the resolution that Congress adopted on September 18, 2001, authorizing President Bush to use "all necessary and appropriate force" and that "unless Congress adopts legislation limiting the president's powers, there is nothing the courts can do."[53] One glint of hope for the detainees had come in a Supreme Court case handed down earlier in 2004, in which Justice Sandra Day O'Connor (in one of the several opinions in a disjointed Court) asserted that the requirements of due process could be met in a military tribunal. The Pentagon quickly embraced her invitation.[54]

Like federalism, the separation of powers is an ongoing struggle. Deference to the president is not necessarily a permanent condition. However, more and more activities of the executive branch are being put beyond the reach of the courts, and if the more conservative justices display the same deference as the liberal justices, discretionary executive power will be increasingly difficult to harness as a constructive participant in the separation of powers. Eventually such deference will unbalance the checks and balances.

---

[49] *United States v. Nixon,* 418 U.S. 683 (1974).

[50] *Clinton v. Jones,* 520 U.S. 681 (1997).

[51] *Clinton v. City of New York,* 524 U.S. 417 (1998).

[52] *Rasul v. Bush,* 542 U.S. 466 (2004).

[53] Reported in Charles Lane and John Mintz, "Detainees Lose Bid for Release," *Washington Post,* 20 January 2005, p. A03.

[54] Reported in David B. Rivkin and Lee A. Casey, "Bush's Good Day in Court," *Washington Post,* 4 August 2004, p. A19. Although a military tribunal does not favor the defendant with a presumption of innocence, it is far better than no trial at all.

executive privilege The claim that confidential communications between the president and the president's close advisers should not be revealed without the consent of the president.

writ of *habeas corpus* A court order demanding that an individual in custody be brought into court and shown the cause for detention. *Habeas corpus* is guaranteed by the Constitution and can be suspended only in cases of rebellion or invasion.

ALTERING THE BALANCE OF POWER: WHAT ARE THE CONSEQUENCES?

Federalism and the separation of powers are two of the three fundamental constitutional principles on which the American system of limited government is based (the third is individual rights). By its very existence, the first of these principles, federalism, recognizes the idea of two sovereigns: the national government and the state government (hence the term *dual federalism*). In addition, the Constitution specifically restrained the power of the national government to regulate the economy. As a result, the states were free to do most of the fundamental governing for the first century and a half of American government. This began to change during and after the New Deal as the national government began to exert more influence over the states through grants-in-aid and mandates. In the last decade, however, we have noticed a countertrend to the growth of national power as Congress has opted to devolve some of its powers to the states. The most recent notable instance of devolution was the welfare reform plan of 1996.

But the problem that arises with devolution is that programs that were once uniform across the country (because they were the national government's responsibility) can become highly variable, with some states providing benefits not available in other states. To a point, variation can be considered one of the virtues of federalism. But there are dangers inherent in large variations and inequalities in the provision of services and benefits in a democracy. Take, for example, the Food and Drug Administration, which has been under attack in recent years. Could its problems be solved by devolving its regulatory tasks to the states? Would people care if drugs required caution labels in some states but not in others? Would Americans want each state to set its own policies for air- and water-pollution control without regard to the fact that pollution crosses state boundaries? Devolution, as attractive as it may be, is not an approach that can be applied across the board without analyzing carefully the nature of the program it is being applied to and the problems it is designed to solve. Even the capacity of states to handle "devolved" programs would vary. According to the Brookings Institution, a Washington, D.C., research organization, the level of state and local government employment varies from state to state, from a low of 400 per 10,000 residents in some states to a high of 700 per 10,000 in others. Thus, it has been pointed out, "such administrative diversity is bound to mediate the course and consequences of any substantial devolution of federal responsibility; no one-size-fits-all devolution [from federal to state and local government] can work."[55]

Moreover, the temptation is ever present for federal politicians to limit state discretion to achieve their own policy objectives. Indeed, the "devolution revolution" promised by congressional Republicans created much more rhetoric than action. Despite the complaints of Republican governors, Congress has continued to use its power to preempt state action and impose mandates on states. The No Child Left Behind Act sets some exacting national standards, and Bush's prescription drug program and welfare reform plans are strong additions to the national safety net. One of the

History Principle

The legacy of cooperative federalism and national standards has raised some doubts about devolution.

---

[55]Eliza Newlin Carney, "Power Grab," *National Journal*, 11 April 1998, p. 798.

most ominous dangers in devolution is what has come to be called the race to the bottom, in which states in this age of globalization are free to compete with one another in giving concessions to foreign and interstate companies to attract new industry.

The second feature of limited government, the separation of powers, is manifested in our system of checks and balances, whereby separate institutions of government share power with one another. Even though the Constitution clearly provides for legislative supremacy, checks and balances have functioned well. Some would say they have worked too well. The last fifty years have witnessed long periods of divided government, when one party has controlled the White House and the other has controlled Congress. During these periods, the level of conflict between the executive and legislative branches has been particularly divisive, resulting in what some analysts derisively call gridlock.

In 2008, the Democrats elected a new president and won large majorities in both houses of Congress. In the final days of the campaign, when it seemed clear that Barack Obama would defeat Republican presidential candidate John McCain, Republicans urged voters to support GOP Senate and House candidates in order to safeguard the system of checks and balances. This argument seemed not to sway many voters, and, for the time being at least, Congress seemed likely to follow the president's lead on legislation.

SUMMARY

In this chapter, we have traced the development of two of the three basic principles of the U.S. Constitution: federalism and the separation of powers. Federalism involves a division between two layers of government: national and state. The separation of powers involves the division of the national government into three branches. These principles serve as limitations on the powers of government; Americans agreed to them as a condition for giving their consent to be governed. And they became the framework within which the government operates. The persistence of local government and the reliance of the national government on grants-in-aid to coerce local governments to follow national goals were used as case studies to demonstrate the continuing vitality of the federal framework. Examples also demonstrated the intense competition among the president, Congress, and the courts to dramatize the continuing vitality of the separation of powers.

The purpose of a constitution is to organize the makeup, or the composition, of the government, the framework within which government and politics, including actual legislation, can take place. A country does not require federalism and the separation of powers in order to have a real constitutional government. And a country does not have to approach individual rights in the manner that the American Constitution does. But to be a true constitutional government, a government must have a few limits so that it cannot be manipulated by people in power merely for their own convenience. This is the essence of constitutional government: Limits on power are above the reach of everyday legislators, executives, bureaucrats, and politicians yet are not so far above their reach that they cannot be adapted to changing times.

 Rationality Principle	 Collective-Action Principle	 Institution Principle	 Policy Principle	 History Principle
As political institutions, federalism and the separation of powers have adapted to the purposes of various political players.	Grants-in-aid allow the national government to coordinate state and local policies with a common set of national standards. States compete with one another not only to attract new business but also to appear less attractive to welfare recipients.	The Constitution created jurisdictional arrangements by encouraging diversity in the elected leaders and allocating the consideration of different aspects of policy to different institutional arenas. The national-state tug-of-war is an institutional feature of the federal system. In answering the question, Who does what? federalism determines the flow of governmental functions and, through that, the political development of the country. Checks and balances are a system of separated institutions sharing power. The framers provided for legislative supremacy by making Congress the pre-eminent branch.	Devolution has had an important influence on policy outcomes, particularly in the realm of welfare.	Since the time of the founding, federalism has been shaped strongly by the Supreme Court. In 1937, the Supreme Court converted the commerce clause from a source of limitations to a source of power for the national government. This precedent guided subsequent court decisions, legislation, and political action. The legacy of cooperative federalism and national standards has raised some doubts about devolution.

FOR FURTHER READING

Bernstein, Richard B., with Jerome Agel. *Amending America—If We Love the Constitution So Much, Why Do We Keep Trying to Change It?* (Lawrence: University Press of Kansas, 1993).

ONLINE READING ○   Campbell, Tom. *Separation of Powers in Practice.* Palo Alto, Calif.: Stanford University Press, 2004.

ONLINE READING ○   Crenson, Matthew, and Benjamin Ginsberg. *Presidential Power: Unchecked and Unbalanced.* New York: Norton, 2007.

Ferejohn, John A., and Barry R. Weingast, eds. *The New Federalism: Can the States Be Trusted?* Stanford, Calif.: Hoover Institution Press, 1997.

Fisher, Louis. *Congressional Abdication on War and Spending.* College Station: Texas A&M University Press, 2000.

Karmis, Dimitrios, and Wayne Norman. *Theories of Federalism: A Reader.* New York: Palgrave, Macmillan, 2005.

Nagel, Robert. *The Implosion of American Federalism.* New York: Oxford University Press, 2001.

Noonan, John T. *Narrowing the Nation's Power: The Supreme Court Sides with the States.* Berkeley: University of California Press, 2002.

Peterson, Paul E. *The Price of Federalism.* Washington, D.C.: Brookings Institution, 1995.

Posner, Richard. *Not a Suicide Pact: The Constitution in a Time of National Emergency.* New York: Oxford University Press, 2006.

Smith, Rogers M. *Civic Ideals: Conflicting Visions of Citizenship in U.S. History.* New Haven, Conn.: Yale University Press, 1997.

Winston, Pamela. *Welfare Policymaking in the States: The Devil in Devolution.* Washington, D.C.: Georgetown University Press, 2002.

○ ONLINE READING

○ ONLINE READING

*Illegal immigration has become a flash point of conflict between the federal govern-
ment and the states. Immigration policy is made by Congress, and border enforcement is the job of Customs and Border Protection, now part of the Department of
Homeland Security. Many state and local officials complain that the federal government is shirking its responsibilities and allowing unchecked movement across the border, dumping the problem—and the financial burden—on the states. Others,
however, argue that federal, state, and local cooperation is essential if immigration
laws are to be fully enforced.*

*The five principles of politics help us to analyze the political dynamics of the im-
migration issue. Most important, the institutional basis of American government—
specifically, federalism as defined in the U.S. Constitution—gives federal, state, and
local governments different responsibilities that bear on laws and public policies related to immigration. For example, Congress has complete authority over immigration. The courts have rarely intruded, except with regard to constitutional protections
for aliens. The executive branch is responsible for implementing immigration laws and
securing the border. However, states and localities are given many responsibilities for
maintaining the health and welfare of their residents—often regardless of their legal
status. Not surprisingly, then, as illegal immigration has increased in recent years,
states and localities have found it in their self-interest to act collectively to press for
reforms in immigration policy. Ultimately, U.S. immigration policy—the political
outcome—is a patchwork of federal, state, and local laws, reflecting the complex
patchwork of responsibilities in the American federal system.*

The New York Times, November 12, 2006

Immigrant Protection Rules Draw Fire

BY JESSE McKINLEY

Dr. Stephen B. Turner built a prof-
itable business here by providing
low-cost "immigrant medical
exams," including immunizations and
blood tests, to hundreds of newcomers
to America. Many of his clients did not
speak English, but they paid in cash,
spending a total of nearly $250,000 at
Dr. Turner's practice from 2003 to 2005.

It was only later, after a tip from a
suspicious client, that the San Francisco
police and the district attorney's office
learned the truth: Dr. Turner had been
throwing out his clients' blood samples
and injecting them with "inoculations"
of saline.

Kamala D. Harris, the San Francisco
district attorney, said the case, which led
to a seven-year prison term for Dr.
Turner, was one of many her office had
been able to pursue under San Francisco's so-called sanctuary policy, which
forbids police and city officials from asking people they encounter in the course
of an investigation about their immigration status. It is a protection Ms. Harris

says has made immigrants—legal and illegal—more willing to come forward about crimes.

With immigration continuing to flare and frustrate as a national political issue, sanctuary cities like San Francisco may soon be the next battlefront. Critics argue that sanctuary policies discourage the police from enforcing laws, though about 50 cities and counties have enacted variations on sanctuary. * * * They include Detroit, Los Angeles, New York and Washington. A handful of states have similar policies, including Alaska, Maine and Oregon.

Conservative legal groups and politicians have begun to challenge such policies. Yet on the other side, cities like Chicago have announced they will avoid involving their police in * * * federal immigration enforcement. And while a federal proposal to punish sanctuary cities recently failed to become law, some states have passed laws discouraging sanctuary policies.

"To say to a law enforcement official, if you encounter a foreign national who is in this country illegally and you believe that information would be of use and benefit to federal authorities, that you can't call them, that's just wrong," said Representative John Campbell, Republican of California, who authored a provision in the federal Homeland Security bill that would have denied federal antiterrorism money to cities with sanctuary policies. The provision passed the House, but was not part of the bill eventually signed by President Bush.

But even with Democrats in control of Congress, immigration hard-liners say the issue is here to stay.

"It's mind-blowing for us to see taxpayer dollars spent to subsidize criminal activity * * * ," said Christopher J.

Farrell, director of research for Judicial Watch, a conservative legal group that is suing the Los Angeles Police Department over its sanctuary rule.

Some states have also taken up the issue. In Colorado, a law signed by the governor in May prevents localities from passing ordinances that stop officials or police from communicating or cooperating with federal officials on immigration.

Other states have taken up larger immigration issues involving local cooperation with the federal authorities. A Georgia law enacted in April authorizes the state to enter into an agreement with federal officials to train and certify state law enforcement officials to enforce immigration. The Georgia law also requires the police to make a "reasonable effort" to determine the legal status of those they arrest for felonies or drunk driving.

Both the Colorado and Georgia laws include some protections against and stiffer penalties for exploitation of illegal immigrants.

* * *

An organization of police chiefs, the Major Cities Chiefs Association, said that requiring the local police to enforce immigration policy did not "take into full account the realities of local law enforcement dealing with this issue on the ground." The association said its concerns included a lack of authority, training, and resources, as well as risks of liability.

Advocates for illegal immigrants, meanwhile, said they feared that getting rid of sanctuary rules would encourage immigrant communities not to report crime, including human and drug trafficking, prostitution, domestic violence, and even terrorism.

* * *

History Principle

Police power—maintaining basic public order—has been traditionally reserved to state and local officials. Local officials argue that if their police are now called upon to enforce federal immigration law, their ability to pursue crimes will be hindered.

Institution Principle

Collective action is not always voluntary. Some state legislatures are using their institutional position to force localities to cooperate with the federal government.

Rationality Principle

Members of Congress often use the power of the purse as a way to compel action by state and local officials. In this case, Congress is saying, "Cooperate with us, or else we'll deny you valuable funds used to train your public safety officers."

Civil Liberties and Civil Rights

4

WHEN THE FIRST CONGRESS under the new Constitution met in late April of 1789 (having been delayed since March 4 by the lack of a quorum because of bad winter roads), the most important item of business was consideration of a proposal to add a bill of rights to the Constitution. Such a proposal by the Virginia delegate George Mason had been turned down with little debate in the waning days of the Philadelphia Constitutional Convention in September 1787, not because the delegates were too tired or too hot or against rights but because of arguments by Alexander Hamilton and other Federalists that a bill of rights was irrelevant in a constitution providing the national government with only delegated powers. How could the national government abuse powers not given to it in the first place? But when the Constitution was submitted to the states for ratification, Antifederalists, most of whom had *not* been delegates in Philadelphia, picked up on the argument of Thomas Jefferson (who also had not been a delegate) that the omission of a bill of rights was a major imperfection of the new Constitution. Whatever the merits of Hamilton's or Jefferson's positions, to gain ratification, the Federalists in Massachusetts, South Carolina, New Hampshire, Virginia, and New York made an "unwritten but unequivocal pledge" to add a bill of rights and a promise to confirm (in what became the Tenth Amendment) the understanding that all powers not delegated to the national government or explicitly prohibited to the states were reserved to the states.[1]

James Madison, who had been a delegate to the Philadelphia convention and later became a member of Congress, may still have believed privately that a bill of rights was not needed. But in 1789, recognizing the urgency of obtaining the Antifederalists' support for the Constitution and the new government, he fought for the bill

---

[1]Clinton L. Rossiter, *1787: The Grand Convention* (New York: Norton, 1987), p. 302.

of rights, arguing that the ideals it embodied would acquire "the character of fundamental maxims of free Government, and as they become incorporated with the national sentiment, counteract the impulses of interest and passion."[2] Madison and his fellow Virginia delegates were, if nothing else, practical individuals. They may have conceded in the abstract Hamilton's argument against the need for a bill of rights. They understood, however, that as a practical political matter it was essential to put to rest the fears of the less than enthusiastic supporters of the Constitution. It was also thought prudent to take off the table, so to speak, a possible issue—the absence of the explicit protections a bill of rights would provide—that could be brandished by opponents of the new regime the first time a crisis occurred. In this instance, as in so many others, the actions of the Constitution's framers illustrate the first principle of politics: All political behavior has a purpose. The framers were interested in abstract ideas. Their actions, though, were usually calculated to achieve practical political purposes.

---

[2]Quoted in Milton Konvitz, "The Bill of Rights: Amendments I–X," in *An American Primer,* 2 vols., ed. Daniel J. Boorstin (Chicago: University of Chicago Press, 1966), I, p. 159.

We can conceive of both civil liberties and civil rights as the rules that govern governmental action and the responsibilities the government has to protect citizens from one another. History matters as well. The rules and procedures that are adopted in one era live on and shape the political reasoning, goals, and actions of political actors in subsequent eras. In many ways, debates over civil liberties and civil rights today are shaped by the historical development of these concepts and their interpretation by key political actors, most notably the members of the Supreme Court.

Rationality Principle

Madison believed a bill of rights would remove a potential source of opposition to the new government.

Madison fought for a bill of rights because he recognized that it would increase the likelihood that the proposed new Constitution would be adopted.

"After much discussion and manipulation . . . at the delicate prompting of Washington and under the masterful prodding of Madison," the House adopted seventeen amendments; the Senate adopted twelve of these. Ten of the amendments were ratified by the necessary three-fourths of the states, making them part of the Constitution on December 15, 1791—from the start, these ten were called the Bill of Rights.[3]

The Bill of Rights—its history and the controversy of interpretation surrounding it—can be usefully subdivided into two categories: civil liberties and civil rights. This chapter is divided accordingly. *Civil liberties* are defined as protections of citizens from improper governmental action. When adopted in 1791, the Bill of Rights was seen as guaranteeing a private sphere of personal liberty free of governmental restrictions. As Jefferson had put it, a bill of rights "is what people are entitled to against every government on earth." In this sense, we could call the Bill of Rights a bill of liberties because the amendments focus on what government must *not* do. For example (with emphasis added),

1. "Congress shall make *no* law . . ." (I)

2. "The right . . . to . . . bear Arms, shall *not* be infringed." (II)

3. "*No* Soldier shall . . . be quartered . . ." (III)

4. "*No* Warrants shall issue, but upon probable cause . . ." (IV)

5. "*No* person shall be held to answer . . . unless on a presentment or indictment of a Grand Jury . . ." (V)

6. "Excessive bail shall *not* be required . . . *nor* cruel and unusual punishments inflicted." (VIII)

Thus the Bill of Rights is a series of thou shalt nots—restraints addressed to governments. Some of these restraints are *substantive,* putting limits on *what* the government

civil liberties The protections of citizens from improper governmental action.

---

[3]Rossiter, *1787,* p. 303, where he also reports that "in 1941 the States of Connecticut, Massachusetts, and Georgia celebrated the sesquicentennial of the Bill of Rights by giving their hitherto withheld and unneeded assent."

shall and shall not have the power to do, such as establishing a religion, quartering troops in private homes without consent, or seizing private property without just compensation. Other restraints are *procedural,* dealing with *how* the government is supposed to act. For example, even though the government has the substantive power to declare certain acts to be crimes and to arrest and imprison persons who violate its criminal laws, it may not do so except by fairly meticulous observation of procedures designed to protect the accused. The best-known procedural rule is that a person is presumed innocent until proven guilty. This rule does not question the government's power to punish someone for committing a crime; it questions only the way the government determines *who* committed the crime. Substantive and procedural restraints together identify the realm of civil liberties.

We define *civil rights* as obligations imposed on government to guarantee equal citizenship and protect citizens from discrimination by other private citizens and other government agencies. Civil rights did not become part of the Constitution until 1868, with the adoption of the Fourteenth Amendment, which addresses the issue of who is a citizen and provides for each citizen "the equal protection of the laws." From that point on, we can see more clearly the distinction between civil liberties and civil rights, because civil liberties issues arise under the "due process of law" clause and civil rights issues arise under the "equal protection of the laws" clause.

We turn first to civil liberties and the long history of the effort to make personal liberty a reality for every citizen in America. The struggle for freedom against arbitrary and discriminatory actions by governments continues to this day. And inevitably it is tied to the continuing struggle for civil rights, to persuade those same governments to take positive action. We deal with that in the second section of this chapter.

CIVIL LIBERTIES: NATIONALIZING THE BILL OF RIGHTS

The First Amendment provides that "Congress shall make no law respecting an establishment of religion . . . or abridging the freedom of speech, or of the press; or the right of . . . [assembly and petition]." But this is the only amendment in the Bill of Rights that addresses itself exclusively to the national government. For example, the Second Amendment provides that "the right of the people to keep and bear Arms, shall not be infringed." The Fifth Amendment says, among other things, that *no person* "shall . . . be twice put in jeopardy of life or limb" for the same crime, that *no person* "shall be compelled in any criminal case to be a witness against himself," that *no person* shall "be deprived of life, liberty, or property, without due process of law," and that private property cannot be taken "without just compensation."[4] Because the First Amendment is the only part of the Bill of Rights that is explicit in its intention to put

---

[4]It would be useful at this point to review all the provisions of the Bill of Rights to confirm this distinction between the wording of the First Amendment and the wording of the rest (see the Appendix). The emphasis in the examples is not in the original. For a spirited and enlightening essay on the extent to which the entire Bill of Rights is about equality, see Martha Minow, "Equality and the Bill of Rights," in *The Constitution of Rights: Human Dignity and American Values,* ed. Michael J. Meyer and William A. Parent (Ithaca, N.Y.: Cornell University Press, 1992), pp. 118–28.

civil rights The legal or moral claims that citizens are entitled to make on the government.

limits on the national government, a fundamental question inevitably arises: Do the remaining amendments of the Bill of Rights put limits on state governments, or do they put them only on the national government?

Dual Citizenship

The question of whether the Bill of Rights also limits state governments was settled in 1833 in a way that seems odd to Americans today. The 1833 case was *Barron v. Baltimore,* and the facts were simple. In paving its streets, the city of Baltimore had disposed of so much sand and gravel in the water near John Barron's wharf that the value of the wharf for commercial purposes was virtually destroyed. Barron brought the city into court on the grounds that it had, under the Fifth Amendment, unconstitutionally deprived him of his property. Barron had to take his case all the way to the Supreme Court, despite the fact that the argument made by his attorney seemed airtight. This is Chief Justice John Marshall's characterization of Barron's argument:

> The plaintiff [Barron] . . . contends that it comes within that clause in the Fifth Amendment of the Constitution which inhibits the taking of private property for public use without just compensation. He insists that this amendment, being in favor of the liberty of the citizen, ought to be so construed as to restrain the legislative power of a state, as well as that of the United States.[5]

Then Marshall, in one of the most significant Supreme Court decisions ever handed down, disagreed:

> The Constitution was ordained and established by the people of the United States for themselves, for their own government, and not for the government of individual States. Each State established a constitution for itself, and in that constitution provided such limitations and restrictions on the powers of its particular government as its judgment dictated. . . . If these propositions be correct, *the fifth amendment must be understood as restraining the power of the General Government, not as applicable to the States.*[6]

In other words, if an agency of the *national* government had deprived Barron of his property, there would have been little doubt about Barron's winning his case. But if the constitution of the state of Maryland contained no such provision protecting citizens of Maryland from such action, then Barron had no legal leg to stand on against Baltimore, an agency of the state of Maryland.

Barron v. Baltimore confirmed "dual citizenship"—that is, that each American was a citizen of the national government and separately a citizen of one of the states. This meant that the Bill of Rights did not apply to decisions or procedures of state (or local) governments. Even slavery could continue because the Bill of Rights could not protect anyone from state laws treating people as property. In fact, the Bill of Rights did not become a vital instrument for the extension of civil liberties for anyone until after a bloody civil war and the revolutionary Fourteenth Amendment intervened. And even so, as we shall see, nearly another century would pass before the

Institution Principle

Dual citizenship meant that the Bill of Rights did not apply to decisions or procedures of state governments.

---

[5] *Barron v. Mayor and City of Baltimore,* 32 U.S. 243 (1833).

[6] Ibid. [emphasis added].

Bill of Rights would truly come into its own. This is a case where America's history has truly mattered. America's states predated the creation of the federal government. The states joined the Union voluntarily, retaining many of their sovereign powers. In many other nations, subnational governments were created by and for the administrative convenience of the central government. In the United States, the nationalization of governmental powers has proceeded slowly and in fits and starts.

The Fourteenth Amendment

From a constitutional standpoint, the defeat of the South in the Civil War settled one question and raised another. It probably settled forever the question of whether secession was an option for any state. After 1865, there was to be more "united" than "states" to the United States. But this left unanswered just how much the states were obliged to obey the Constitution and, in particular, the Bill of Rights. Just reading the words of the Fourteenth Amendment, anyone might think it was almost perfectly designed to impose the Bill of Rights on the states and thereby reverse *Barron v. Baltimore*. The very first words of the Fourteenth Amendment point in that direction:

> All persons born or naturalized in the United States, and subject to the jurisdiction thereof, are citizens of the United States and of the State wherein they reside.

This provides for a single national citizenship, and at a minimum that means civil liberties should not vary drastically from state to state. That would seem to be the spirit of the Fourteenth Amendment: to nationalize the Bill of Rights by nationalizing the definition of citizenship.

This interpretation of the Fourteenth Amendment is reinforced by the next clause of the Amendment:

> No State shall make or enforce any law which shall abridge the privileges or immunities of citizens of the United States; nor shall any State deprive any person of life, liberty, or property, without due process of law.

All of this sounds like an effort to extend the Bill of Rights in its entirety to citizens wherever they might reside. But this was not to be the Supreme Court's interpretation for nearly a century. Within five years of ratification of the Fourteenth Amendment, the Court was making decisions as though the amendment had never been adopted. The shadow of *Barron* grew longer and longer. In an important 1873 decision known as *The Slaughter-House Cases,* the Supreme Court determined that the federal government was under no obligation to protect the "privileges and immunities" of citizens of a particular state against arbitrary actions by that state's government. The case had its origins in 1867, when a corrupt Louisiana legislature conferred upon a single corporation a monopoly on the slaughterhouse business in the city of New Orleans. The other slaughterhouses, facing bankruptcy, brought suits claiming, like John Barron, that this was a seizure of their property in violation of Fifth Amendment rights. But unlike Barron, they believed that they were protected now because, they argued, the Fourteenth Amendment incorporated the Fifth Amendment, applying it to the states. The suits were all rejected. The Supreme Court argued, first, that the primary purpose of the Fourteenth Amendment was to protect "Negroes as a class." Second, and more to the point here, the Court argued, without trying to prove it, that the framers of the Fourteenth Amendment could not have intended to incorporate the entire Bill of Rights.[7] Yet when the Civil Rights Act of 1875 attempted to protect blacks from discriminatory treatment by proprietors of hotels, theaters, and other public accommodations, the Supreme Court disregarded its own primary argument in the previous case and held the act unconstitutional, declaring that the Fourteenth Amendment applied only to discriminatory actions by state officials, "operating under cover of law," and not to discrimination against blacks by private individuals, even though these private individuals were companies offering services to the public.[8] Such narrow interpretations raised the inevitable question of whether the Fourteenth Amendment had incorporated *any* of the Bill of Rights. The Fourteenth Amendment remained shadowy until the mid-twentieth century. The shadow was *Barron v. Baltimore* and the Court's unwillingness to "nationalize" civil liberties—that is, to interpret the civil liberties expressed in the Bill of Rights as imposing limitations not only on the federal government but also on the states.

It was not until the very end of the nineteenth century that the Supreme Court began to nationalize the Bill of Rights by incorporating its civil liberties provisions into the Fourteenth Amendment. Table 4.1 outlines the major steps in this process. The only change in civil liberties during the first sixty years after the adoption of the Fourteenth Amendment came in 1897, when the Supreme Court held that the due process clause of the Fourteenth Amendment did in fact prohibit states from taking property for a public use without just compensation.[9] This effectively overruled *Barron* because it meant that the citizen of Maryland, or any state, was henceforth protected from a "public taking" of property even if the state constitution did not provide such protection. The power of public agencies to seize private property is called eminent domain. According to the Fifth Amendment, private owners must be paid "just compensation" by the government if it decides that it needs their property. In a broader sense, however, *Barron* still cast a shadow because the Supreme Court had "incorporated" into the Fourteenth Amendment only the property protection provision of the Fifth Amendment and no other clause, let alone the other amendments of the Bill of Rights. In other words, although due process applied to the taking of life and liberty as well as property, only property was incorporated into the Fourteenth Amendment as a limitation on state power.

No further expansion of civil liberties through incorporation occurred until 1925, when the Supreme Court held that freedom of speech is "among the fundamental personal rights and 'liberties' protected by the due process clause of the Fourteenth Amendment from impairment by the states."[10] In 1931, the Court added freedom of the press to that short list of civil rights protected by the Bill of Rights from state action; in 1934, it added freedom of religion; and in 1939, it added freedom of assembly.[11] But that was as far as the Court was willing to go. This one-

History Principle

Dual citizenship was upheld by the Supreme Court for nearly a century after *Barron v. Baltimore* (1833).

---

[7] *The Slaughter-House Cases,* 83 U.S. 36 (1873).

[8] *The Civil Rights Cases,* 109 U.S. 3 (1883).

[9] *Chicago, Burlington, and Quincy Railroad Company v. Chicago,* 166 U.S. 226 (1897).

[10] *Gitlow v. New York,* 268 U.S. 652 (1925).

[11] *Near v. Minnesota ex rel. Olson,* 283 U.S. 697 (1931); *Hague v. Committee for Industrial Organization,* 307 U.S. 496 (1939).

TABLE 4.1 Incorporation of the Bill of Rights into the Fourteenth Amendment

Selected Provisions and Amendments	Date "Incorporated"	Key Cases
Eminent domain (V)	1897	*Chicago, Burlington, and Quincy Railroad v. Chicago*
Freedom of speech (I)	1925	*Gitlow v. New York*
Freedom of the press (I)	1931	*Near v. Minnesota ex rel. Olson*
Free exercise of religion (I)	1934	*Hamilton v. Regents of the University of California*
Freedom of assembly (I)	1939	*Hague v. Committee for Industrial Organization*
Freedom from unnecessary search and seizure (IV)	1949	*Wolf v. Colorado*
Freedom from warrantless search and seizure ("exclusionary rule") (IV)	1961	*Mapp v. Ohio*
Freedom from cruel and unusual punishment (VIII)	1962	*Robinson v. California*
Right to counsel in any criminal trial (VI)	1963	*Gideon v. Wainwright*
Right against self-incrimination and forced confessions (V)	1964	*Mallory v. Hogan Escobedo v. Illinois*
Right to privacy (III, IV, and V)	1965	*Griswold v. Connecticut*
Right to remain silent (V)	1966	*Miranda v. Arizona*
Right against double jeopardy (V)	1969	*Benton v. Maryland*

by-one application of the provisions of the Bill of Rights is known as selective incorporation. As late as 1937, the Supreme Court was still loath to nationalize civil liberties beyond the First Amendment. In fact, the Court in that year took one of its most extreme turns backward toward *Barron v. Baltimore.*

The state of Connecticut had indicted a man named Frank Palko for first-degree murder, but a lower court found him guilty of only second-degree murder and sentenced him to life in prison. Unhappy with the verdict, the state of Connecticut appealed the conviction to its highest court, won the appeal, got a new trial, and succeeded in getting Palko convicted of first-degree murder. Palko appealed to the Supreme Court on what seemed an open-and-shut case of double jeopardy—being tried twice for the same crime. Yet though a majority of the Court agreed that this could indeed be considered a case of double jeopardy, the justices decided that double jeopardy was *not* one of the provisions of the Bill of Rights incorporated into the Fourteenth Amendment as a restriction on the powers of the states. Justice Benjamin Cardozo, considered one of the most able Supreme Court justices of the twentieth century, rejected the argument made by Palko's lawyer that "whatever is forbidden by the Fifth Amendment is forbidden by the Fourteenth also." Cardozo responded tersely, "There is no such general rule." As far as Cardozo and the majority were concerned, the only rights from the Bill of Rights that ought to be incorporated into the Fourteenth Amendment as applying to the states as well as to the national government were those that were "implicit in the concept of ordered liberty." He asked the questions, Does double jeopardy subject Palko to a "hardship so acute and shocking that our polity will not endure it? Does it violate those 'fundamental principles of liberty and justice which lie at the base of all our civil and political institutions?' . . . The answer must surely be 'no.'"[12] Palko was eventually executed for the crime—because he lived in the state of Connecticut rather than in a state whose constitution included a guarantee against double jeopardy.

Cases like *Palko* extended the shadow of *Barron* into its second century, despite adoption of the Fourteenth Amendment. The Constitution, as interpreted by the Supreme Court, left standing the framework in which the states had the power to determine their own law on a number of fundamental issues. It left states with the power to pass laws segregating the races—and thirteen states chose to exercise that power. The constitutional framework also left states with the power to engage in searches and seizures without a warrant, indict accused persons without benefit of a grand jury, deprive persons of trial by jury, force persons to testify against themselves, deprive accused persons of their right to confront adverse witnesses, and as we have seen, prosecute accused persons more than once for the same crime.[13] All of these were implicitly identified in the *Palko* case as "not incorporated" into the Fourteenth Amendment as limitations on the powers of the states. Few states chose the option to use those kinds of powers, but some states did, and the authority to do so was there for any state whose legislative majority so chose.

History Principle

Once a case is decided by the Supreme Court, its implications persist for decades.

The Constitutional Revolution in Civil Liberties

For more than thirty years after the *Palko* case, the nineteenth-century framework was sustained, but signs of change came after 1954, in *Brown v. Board of Education,* when the Supreme Court overturned the infamous *Plessy v. Ferguson.*[14] *Plessy* was a civil rights case involving the "equal protection" clause of the Fourteenth Amendment but was not an issue of applying the Bill of Rights to the states. (We will discuss *Plessy*'s significance

---

[12] *Palko v. Connecticut,* 302 U.S. 319 (1937).

[13] *Palko* was explicitly reversed in *Benton v. Maryland,* 395 U.S. 784 (1969), in which the Court said that double jeopardy was in fact incorporated into the Fourteenth Amendment as a restriction on the states.

ONLINE READING ○ [14] *Brown v. Board of Education,* 347 U.S. 483; *Plessy v. Ferguson,* 163 U.S. 537 (1896).

for civil rights later in this chapter.) Nevertheless, *Brown* indicated clearly that the Supreme Court was going to be expansive about civil liberties because in that case the Court effectively promised that it was actively going to subject the states and all actions affecting civil rights and civil liberties to *strict scrutiny*. In retrospect, one could say that this constitutional revolution was given a jump start by the *Brown* decision,[15] even though the results were not apparent until after 1961, when the number of incorporated civil liberties increased (Table 4.1).

Nationalizing the Bill of Rights As with the federalism revolution, the constitutional revolution in civil liberties was a movement toward nationalization. But the two revolutions required opposite motions on the part of the Supreme Court. In the area of commerce (the first revolution), the Court had to decide to assume a *passive* role by not interfering as Congress expanded the meaning of the commerce clause of Article I, Section 8. This expansion has been so extensive that the national government can now constitutionally reach a single farmer growing twenty acres of wheat or a small restaurant selling barbecues to local "whites only" without the farmer or the restaurant being anywhere near interstate commerce routes. In the second revolution, involving the Bill of Rights and the Fourteenth Amendment rather than the commerce clause, the Court had to assume an *active* role, which required close review not of Congress but of the laws of state legislatures and the decisions of state courts to apply a single national Fourteenth Amendment standard to the rights and liberties of all citizens.

Table 4.1 shows that until 1961, only the First Amendment had been fully and clearly incorporated into the Fourteenth Amendment.[16] After 1961, several other important provisions of the Bill of Rights were incorporated. Of the cases that expanded the Fourteenth Amendment's reach, among the most famous (partly because it became the subject of a best-selling book and a popular movie) is *Gideon v. Wainwright,* which established the right to counsel in a criminal trial.[17] In *Mapp v. Ohio,* the Court held that evidence obtained in violation of the Fourth Amendment ban on unreasonable searches and seizures would be excluded from trial.[18] This "exclusionary rule" was particularly irksome to police and prosecutors because it meant that patently guilty defendants sometimes got to go free because the evidence that clearly damned them could not be used. In *Miranda,* the Court's ruling required that arrested persons be informed of the rights to remain silent and have counsel present during interrogation.[19] This is the basis of the **Miranda rule** of

> **Miranda rule** The convention derived from the Supreme Court's 1966 ruling in the case of *Miranda v. Arizona* whereby persons under arrest must be informed of their legal rights, including their right to counsel, before undergoing police interrogation.

---

[15] The first constitutional revolution began with *National Labor Relations Board v. Jones and Laughlin Steel Corporation,* 301 U.S. 1 (1937).

[16] The one exception was the right to a public trial (the Sixth Amendment), but the 1948 case did not mention the right to a public trial as such; it was cited in a 1968 case as establishing the right to a public trial as part of the Fourteenth Amendment. The 1948 case was *In re Oliver,* 333 U.S. 257, where the issue was put more generally as "due process," and public trial itself was not mentioned. Later opinions, such as *Duncan v. Louisiana,* 391 U.S. 145 (1968), cited the *Oliver* case as the precedent for incorporating public trials as part of the Fourteenth Amendment.

[17] Anthony Lewis, *Gideon's Trumpet* (New York: Random House, 1964); *Gideon v. Wainwright,* 372 U.S. 335 (1963).

[18] *Mapp v. Ohio,* 367 U.S. 643 (1961).

[19] *Miranda v. Arizona,* 384 U.S. 436 (1966).

○ ONLINE READING

○ ONLINE READING

reading persons their rights, which is familiar to most Americans from movies and TV police shows. By 1969, in *Benton v. Maryland,* the Supreme Court had come full circle regarding the rights of the criminally accused, explicitly reversing the *Palko* ruling and thereby incorporating double jeopardy.

During the 1960s and early 1970s, the Court expanded another important area of civil liberties: rights to privacy. When the Court began to take a more activist role in the mid-1950s and the 1960s, the idea of a right to privacy was revived. In 1958, the Supreme Court recognized "privacy in one's association" in its decision to prevent the state of Alabama from using the membership list of the National Association for the Advancement of Colored People (NAACP) in its investigations.[20] As we shall see later in this chapter, legal questions about the right to privacy have come to the fore in more recent cases concerning birth control, abortion, homosexuality, and assisted suicide.

Institution Principle

Most of the important provisions of the Bill of Rights were nationalized by the Supreme Court during the 1960s.

THE BILL OF RIGHTS TODAY

Since liberty requires restraining the power of government, the general status of civil liberties can never be considered fixed and permanent.[21] Every provision in the Bill of Rights is subject to interpretation, and in any dispute involving a clause of the Bill of Rights, interpretations will always be shaped by the interpreter's interest in the outcome. As we have seen, the Court continuously reminds everyone that if it has the power to expand the Bill of Rights, it also has the power to contract it.[22]

The best way to examine the Bill of Rights today is the simplest way: to take the provisions one at a time. Some of these provisions are settled areas of law, and some are not. Any one of them can be reinterpreted by the Court at any time.

The First Amendment and Freedom of Religion

> Congress shall make no law respecting an establishment of religion, or prohibiting the free exercise thereof; or abridging the freedom of speech, or of the press; or the right of the people peaceably to assemble, and to petition the Government for a redress of grievances.

The Bill of Rights begins by guaranteeing freedom, and the First Amendment provides for that freedom in two distinct clauses: "Congress shall make no law [1] respecting an establishment of religion, or [2] prohibiting the free exercise thereof." The first clause is called the establishment clause, and the second is called the free exercise clause.

Separation between Church and State The ***establishment clause*** has been interpreted quite strictly to mean that a virtual wall of separation exists between church

establishment clause The First Amendment clause that says, "Congress shall make no law respecting an establishment of religion." This law means that a wall of separation exists between church and state.

[20] *NAACP v. Alabama,* 357 U.S. 449 (1958).

[21] This section is taken from Benjamin Ginsberg, Theodore J. Lowi, and Margaret Weir, *We the People: An Introduction to American Politics,* 6th ed. (New York: Norton, 2006).

[22] For a lively and readable treatment of the possibilities of restricting provisions of the Bill of Rights without actually reversing prior decisions, see David G. Savage, *Turning Right: The Making of the Rehnquist Supreme Court* (New York: Wiley, 1992).

and state. The separation of church and state was especially important to the great number of American colonists who had sought refuge from persecution for having rejected membership in state-sponsored churches. The concept of a wall of separation was Jefferson's own formulation, and it has figured in all of the modern Supreme Court cases arising under the establishment clause. For two centuries, Jefferson's words have had a powerful impact on our understanding of the proper relationship between church and state in America.

Despite the absolute sound of the phrase *wall of separation,* there is ample room to disagree on how high the wall is or of what materials it is composed. For example, the Court has been consistently strict in cases of school prayer, striking down such practices as Bible reading,[23] nondenominational prayer,[24] a moment of silence for meditation, and pre-game prayer at public sporting events.[25] In each of these cases, the Court reasoned that school-sponsored observations, even of an apparently nondenominational character, are highly suggestive of school sponsorship and therefore violate the prohibition against establishment of religion. On the other hand, the Court has been quite permissive (and some would say inconsistent) about the public display of religious symbols, such as city-sponsored Nativity scenes in commercial or municipal areas.[26] And although the Court has consistently disapproved of government-financed support for religious schools, even when the purpose has been purely educational and secular, it has permitted certain direct aid to students of such schools in the form of busing, for example. In 1971, after thirty years of cases involving religious schools, the Court attempted to specify some criteria to guide its decisions and those of lower courts, indicating, for example, in a decision invalidating state payments for the teaching of secular subjects in parochial schools, circumstances under which the Court might allow certain financial assistance. The case was *Lemon v. Kurtzman;* in its decision, the Supreme Court established three criteria to guide future cases, in what came to be called the **Lemon *test.*** The Court held that government aid to religious schools would be accepted as constitutional if (1) it had a secular purpose, (2) its effect was neither to advance nor to inhibit religion, and (3) it did not entangle government and religious institutions in each other's affairs.[27]

Although these restrictions make the *Lemon* test a hard test to pass, imaginative authorities are finding ways to do so, and the Supreme Court has demonstrated a willingness to let them. In 1995, for example, the Court narrowly ruled that a student religious group at the University of Virginia could not be denied student-activities funds merely because it was a religious group espousing a particular viewpoint about a deity. The Court called the denial "viewpoint discrimination" and declared that it violated the free speech rights of the group.[28] This led two years

---

[23] *Abington School District v. Schempp,* 374 U.S. 203 (1963).

[24] *Engel v. Vitale,* 370 U.S. 421 (1962).

[25] *Wallace v. Jaffree,* 472 U.S. 38 (1985).

[26] *Lynch v. Donnelly,* 465 U.S. 668 (1984).

[27] *Lemon v. Kurtzman,* 403 U.S. 602 (1971). The *Lemon* test is still good law, but as recently as the 1994 Court term, four justices urged that it be abandoned. Here is a settled area of law that may become unsettled.

[28] *Rosenberger v. University of Virginia,* 515 U.S. 819 (1995).

Lemon test Rule articulated in *Lemon v. Kurtzman* according to which governmental action in respect to religion is permissible if it is secular in purpose, does not lead to "excessive entanglement" with religion, and neither promotes nor inhibits the practice of religion.

Racial Equality

As we discuss in this chapter, civil rights is a major political issue in the United States. Especially since the 1960s, most forms of racial discrimination have been prohibited by law, and a large number of government programs have been designed to promote greater political, social, and economic equality between black and white Americans. Despite these efforts, progress in the direction of racial equality has been uneven. As we can see in the following figures and tables, some data suggest that the United States has made great strides toward the color-blind society envisioned by the early leaders of the civil rights movement. Other data, though, indicate that we have a long way to go.

In assessing racial equality in the United States, we could also consider numerous other statistics and other racial and ethnic groups. Depending upon which evidence is selected, one might argue that racial equality in the United States has increased substantially in recent years or that it has not.

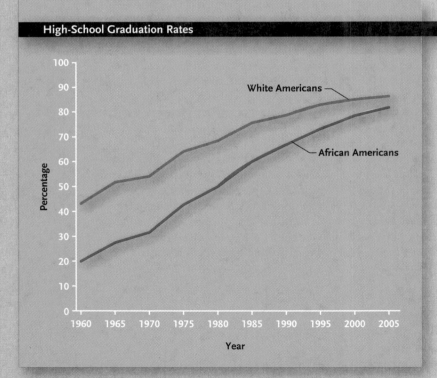

High-School Graduation Rates

One encouraging statistic is the change in black versus white levels of educational attainment over the past 45 years. In 1960, black Americans were less than half as likely to finish high school or graduate from college as whites. Today, the percentage of blacks graduating from high school is nearly identical to the percentage of whites who earn diplomas.

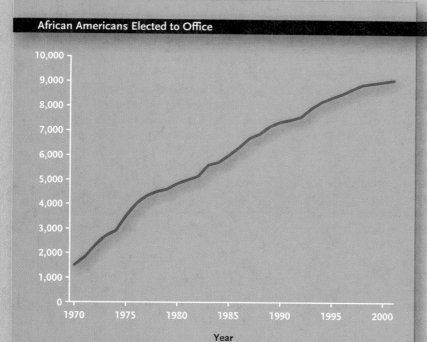

African Americans Elected to Office

Year

Progress has also been made in the political arena. As recently as 1970, only 1,469 African Americans held elected office in the United States—out of approximately half a million federal, state, and local offices. By 2001, the last year the government collected data, there were more than 9,000 black elected officials, an increase of more than 600 percent.

In the economic realm the gap between blacks and whites has decreased more slowly. In 2004, the average income of black men was only 67 percent of the average for white men. This represented only a slight increase since 1990. During the same period, the average income of black women actually fell relative to that of white women.

Median Income (2004 Dollars)

	Men			Women		
	1990	2000	2004	1990	2000	2004
White	29,668	32,684	31,335	14,459	17,637	17,648
Black	18,034	23,411	22,714	11,671	17,420	17,383

later to a new, more conservative approach to the separation of church and state. In 1997, the Court accepted the practice of sending public-school teachers into parochial schools to provide remedial education to disadvantaged children.[29]

More recently, the establishment clause has been put under pressure by the school-voucher and charter-school movements. Vouchers financed by public revenues are supporting tuition to religious schools, where common prayer and religious instruction are known parts of the curriculum. In addition, many financially needy church schools are actively recruiting students with tax-supported vouchers, considering them an essential source of revenue if they are to keep their schools operating. In both these respects, vouchers and charter schools are creating the impression that public support is aiding the establishment of religion.[30] Yet the Supreme Court has refused to rule on the constitutionality of these programs.

In 2004, the question of whether the phrase "under God" in the Pledge of Allegiance violates the establishment clause was brought before the Court. Written in 1892, the Pledge had been used in schools without any religious references. But in 1954, in the midst of the cold war, Congress voted to change the Pledge, in response to the "godless Communism" of the Soviet Union. The conversion was made by adding two key words, so that the revised version read, "I pledge allegiance to the flag of the United States of America and to the Republic for which it stands, one nation *under God,* indivisible, with liberty and justice for all" [emphasis added].

Ever since the change was made, there has been a constant murmuring of discontent from those who object to an officially sanctioned profession of belief in a deity as a violation of the religious freedom clause of the First Amendment. When saying the Pledge, those who object to the phrase have often simply stayed silent during the recitation of the two key words. In 2003, Michael Newdow, the father of a kindergarten student in a California elementary school, forced the issue to the surface when he brought suit against the local school district. Newdow, an atheist, argued that the reference to God turned the daily recitation of the Pledge into a religious exercise. A federal court ruled that although students were not required to recite the Pledge at all, having to stand and listen to others say "under God" still violated the First Amendment's establishment clause. The case was appealed to the Supreme Court, and on June 14, 2004—fifty years to the day after the adoption of "under God" in the Pledge—the Court ruled that Newdow lacked a sufficient personal stake in the case to bring the complaint.[31] This inconclusive decision by the Court left "under God" in the Pledge while keeping the issue alive for possible resolution in a future case.

Free Exercise of Religion   The ***free exercise clause*** protects the right to believe and practice whatever religion one chooses; it also protects the right to be a nonbeliever. The precedent-setting case involving free exercise was *West Virginia State Board of Education v. Barnette* (1943), which involved the children of a family of Jehovah's

free exercise clause
The First Amendment clause that protects a citizen's right to believe and practice whatever religion he or she chooses.

[29]*Agostini v. Felton,* 521 U.S. 203 (1997). The case being overruled was *Aguilar v. Felton,* 473 U.S. 402 (1985).

[30]For good coverage of voucher and charter-school experiments, see Peter Schrag, "The Voucher Seduction," *American Prospect,* 23 November 1999, pp. 46–52.

[31]*Elk Grove Unified School District v. Newdow,* 542 U.S. 1 (2004).

Witnesses who refused to salute and pledge allegiance to the American flag on the grounds that their religious faith did not permit it. Three years earlier, the Court had upheld such a requirement and had permitted schools to expel students for refusing to salute the flag. But the entry of the United States into a war to defend democracy coupled with the ugly treatment to which the Jehovah's Witnesses' children had been subjected induced the Court to reverse itself and endorse the free exercise of religion even when it may be offensive to the beliefs of the majority.[32]

Although the Supreme Court has been fairly consistent and strict in protecting the free exercise of religious belief, it has taken pains to distinguish between religious beliefs and *actions* based on those beliefs. In one case, for example, two Native Americans had been fired from their jobs for smoking peyote, an illegal drug. They claimed they had been fired from their jobs illegally because smoking peyote was a religious sacrament protected by the free exercise clause. The Court disagreed with their claim in an important 1990 decision,[33] but Congress supported the claim and went on to engage in an unusual controversy with the Court, involving the separation of powers as well as the proper application of the separation of church and state. Congress literally reversed the Court's 1990 decision with the enactment of the Religious Freedom Restoration Act (RFRA) of 1993, which forbids any federal agency or state government to restrict a person's free exercise of religion unless the federal agency or state government demonstrates that its action "furthers a compelling government interest" and "is the least restrictive means of furthering that compelling governmental interest." One of the first applications of the RFRA was to a case brought by St. Peter's Catholic Church against the city of Boerne, Texas, which had denied permission to the church to enlarge its building because the building had been declared a historic landmark. The case went to federal court on the argument that the city had violated the church's religious freedom as guaranteed by Congress in the RFRA. The Supreme Court declared the RFRA unconstitutional, but on grounds rarely utilized, if not unique to this case: Congress had violated the separation-of-powers principle, infringing on the powers of the judiciary by going so far beyond its law-making powers that it ended up actually expanding the scope of religious rights rather than just enforcing them. The Court thereby implied that questions requiring a balancing of religious claims against public policy claims were reserved strictly to the judiciary.[34]

The *City of Boerne* case did settle some matters of constitutional controversy over the religious exercise and the establishment clauses of the First Amendment, but it left a lot more unsettled. What about polygamy, a practice allowed by some factions in the Mormon faith? Or the refusal of Amish parents to send their children to school beyond eighth grade because of their belief that exposing their children to "modern values" undermines their religious commitment? In this last example, the Court decided in favor of the Amish and endorsed a very strong interpretation of the protection of free exercise.[35]

 Institution Principle

Constitutional checks and balances give Congress the power to override Supreme Court decisions.

---

[32] *West Virginia State Board of Education v. Barnette*, 319 U.S. 624 (1943). The case it reversed was *Minersville School District v. Gobitis*, 310 U.S. 586 (1940).

[33] *Employment Division v. Smith*, 494 U.S. 872 (1990).

[34] *City of Boerne v. Flores*, 521 U.S. 507 (1997).

[35] *Wisconsin v. Yoder*, 406 U.S. 205 (1972).

The First Amendment and Freedom of Speech and the Press

Congress shall make no law . . . abridging the freedom of speech, or of the press.

Because democracy depends on an open political process and politics is basically talk, freedom of speech and freedom of the press are considered critical. For this reason, they were given a prominence in the Bill of Rights equal to that of freedom of religion. In 1938, freedom of speech (which in all important respects includes freedom of the press) was given extraordinary constitutional status when the Supreme Court established that any legislation that attempts to restrict these fundamental freedoms "is to be subjected to a more exacting judicial scrutiny . . . than are most other types of legislation."[36]

The Court was saying that the democratic political process must be protected at almost any cost. This higher standard of judicial review came to be called **strict scrutiny.** Strict scrutiny implies that speech—at least some kinds of speech—will be protected almost absolutely. But as it turns out, only some types of speech are fully protected against restrictions (Figure 4.1). As we shall see, many forms of speech are less than absolutely protected—even though they are entitled to strict scrutiny. This section will look at these two categories of speech: absolutely protected speech and conditionally protected speech.

Absolutely Protected Speech   There is one and only one absolute defense against efforts to place limitations on speech, oral or in print: the truth. The truth is protected even when its expression damages the person to whom it applies. And of all forms of speech, political speech is the most consistently protected.

POLITICAL SPEECH   Political speech was the activity of greatest concern to the framers of the Constitution, even though they found it most difficult provision to observe. Within seven years of the ratification of the Bill of Rights, Congress adopted the infamous Alien and Sedition Acts, which, among other things, made it a crime to say or publish anything that might tend to defame or bring into disrepute the government of the United States. Quite clearly, the acts' intentions were to criminalize the very conduct given absolute protection by the First Amendment. Fifteen violators, including several newspaper editors, were indicted, and a few were convicted before the relevant portions of the acts were allowed to expire.

The first modern free speech case arose immediately after World War I. It involved persons who had been convicted under the federal Espionage Acts of 1917 for opposing American involvement in the war. The Supreme Court upheld the act and refused to protect the speech rights of the defendants on the grounds that their activities—appeals to draftees to resist the draft—constituted a *"clear and present danger"* to security.[37] This is the first and most famous "test" of when government intervention or censorship can be permitted.

It was only after the 1920s that real progress toward a genuinely effective First Amendment was made. Since then, political speech has been consistently protected

[36] *United States v. Carolene Products Company,* 304 U.S. 144 (1938), 384. This footnote is one of the Court's most important doctrines. See Alfred H. Kelly, Winfred A. Harbison, and Herman Belz, *The American Constitution: Its Origins and Development,* 7th ed., 2 vols. (New York: Norton, 1991), II, pp. 519–23.

[37] *Schenck v. United States,* 249 U.S. 47 (1919).

strict scrutiny The crtiteria used by the Supreme Court in racial discrimination cases and other cases involving civil liberties and civil rights. Strict scrutiny places the burden of proof on the government, rather than on the challengers, to show that the law in question is constitutional.

clear and present danger The criterion used to determine whether speech is protected or unprotected, based on its capacity to present a "clear and present danger" to society.

FIGURE 4.1 The Protection of Free Speech by the First Amendment

	PROTECTED SPEECH	UNPROTECTED SPEECH
If content is true:	All speech is protected by the First Amendment when it is the truth.	"True" speech can be regulated *only* if: • it fails the clear and present danger test, or • it falls below community standards of obscenity or pornography.
If content is false:	Defamatory speech is protected when: • it is spoken or written by a public official in the course of official business, or • it is spoken or written by a citizen or the press against someone in the public eye.	"False" speech can be regulated or punished *only* when it can be demonstrated that there was a reckless disregard for the truth (as in libel or slander).

by the courts even when it has been deemed "insulting" or "outrageous." Here is the way the Supreme Court put it in one of its most important statements on the subject:

> The constitutional guarantees of free speech and free press do not permit a State to forbid or proscribe advocacy of the use of force or of law violation *except where such advocacy is directed to inciting or producing imminent lawless action and is likely to incite or produce such action.*[38] [Emphasis added]

This statement was made in the case of a Ku Klux Klan leader, Charles Brandenburg, who had been arrested and convicted of advocating "revengent" action against the president, Congress, and the Supreme Court, among others, if they continued "to suppress the white, Caucasian race." Although Brandenburg was not carrying a weapon, some members of his audience were. Nevertheless, the Supreme Court reversed the state courts and freed Brandenburg while declaring Ohio's Criminal Syndicalism Act unconstitutional because it punished persons who "advocate, or teach the duty, necessity, or propriety [of violence] as a means of accomplishing industrial or political reform" or who publish materials or "voluntarily assemble . . . to teach or advocate the doctrines of criminal syndicalism." The Supreme Court argued that the statute did not distinguish "mere advocacy" from "incitement to imminent lawless action." It would be difficult to go much further in protecting freedom of speech.

Another area of recent expansion of political speech—the participation of wealthy persons and corporations in political campaigns—was opened up in 1976 with the Supreme Court's decision in *Buckley v. Valeo*.[39] Campaign finance reform laws of the early 1970s, arising out of the Watergate scandal, sought to put severe

Collective-Action Principle

The courts recognize the importance of collective action and have developed rules to protect speech that promotes collective political action.

---

[38] *Brandenburg v. Ohio*, 395 U.S. 444 (1969).

[39] *Buckley v. Valeo*, 424 U.S. 1 (1976).

limits on campaign spending, and a number of important provisions were declared unconstitutional on the basis of a new principle that spending money by or on behalf of candidates is a form of speech protected by the First Amendment. The issue came up again in 2003, after passage of a new and still more severe campaign finance law, the Bipartisan Campaign Reform Act (2002). In *McConnell* v. *Federal Election Commission,* the majority seriously reduced the area of speech protected by the *Buckley v. Valeo* decision by holding that Congress was well within its power to put limits on the amounts individuals could spend, plus severe limits on the amounts of "soft money" that could be spent by corporations and their PACs. The Court argued that "the selling of access . . . has given rise to the appearance of undue influence [that justifies] regulations impinging on First Amendment rights . . . in order to curb corruption or the appearance of corruption."[40]

SYMBOLIC SPEECH, SPEECH PLUS, AND THE RIGHTS OF ASSEMBLY AND PETITION   The First Amendment treats the freedoms of assembly and petition as equal to the freedoms of religion and political speech. Freedom of assembly and freedom of petition are closely associated with speech but go beyond it to speech associated with action. Since at least 1931, the Supreme Court has sought to protect actions that are designed to send a political message. (Usually the purpose of a symbolic act is not only to send a direct message but also to draw a crowd—to do something spectacular in order to draw spectators to the action and thus strengthen the message.) Thus the Court held unconstitutional a California statute making it a felony to display a red flag "as a sign, symbol or emblem of opposition to organized government."[41] Although today there are limits on how far one can go with actions that symbolically convey a message, the protection of such action is very broad. Thus although the Court upheld a federal statute making it a crime to burn draft cards to protest the Vietnam War on the grounds that the government had a compelling interest in preserving draft cards as part of the conduct of the war itself, it considered the wearing of black armbands to school a protected form of assembly.

Another example is the burning of the American flag as a symbol of protest. In 1984, at a political rally held during the Republican National Convention in Dallas, a political protester burned an American flag in violation of a Texas statute that prohibited desecration of a venerated object. In a 5–4 decision, the Supreme Court declared the Texas law unconstitutional on the grounds that flag burning is expressive conduct protected by the First Amendment.[42] Congress reacted immediately with a proposal for a constitutional amendment reversing the Court's decision, and when the amendment failed to receive the necessary two-thirds majority in the Senate, Congress passed the Flag Protection Act of 1989. Protesters promptly violated this act, and their prosecution moved quickly into the federal district court, which declared the new law unconstitutional. The Supreme Court, in another 5–4 decision, affirmed the lower court's decision.[43] A renewed effort began in Congress to propose a constitutional

---

[40] *McConnell v. Federal Election Commission,* 540 U.S. 93 (2003).

[41] *Stromberg v. California,* 283 U.S. 359 (1931).

[42] *Texas v. Johnson,* 491 U.S. 397 (1989).

[43] *United States v. Eichman,* 496 U.S. 310 (1990).

amendment that would reverse the Supreme Court and place this form of expressive conduct outside the realm of protected speech or assembly. Since 1995, the House of Representatives has six times passed a resolution for a constitutional amendment to ban flag burning, but each time the Senate has failed to go along.[44] In 2003, the Supreme Court struck down a Virginia cross-burning statute, ruling that states could make cross burning a crime as long as the statute required prosecutors to prove that the act of setting fire to the cross was intended to intimidate. Justice Sandra Day O'Connor wrote for the majority that the First Amendment permits the government to forbid cross burning as a "particularly virulent form of intimidation" but not when the act was "a form of symbolic expression."[45] This decision will almost inevitably become a more generalized First Amendment protection of any conduct, including flag burning, that can be shown to be a form of symbolic expression.

Closer to the original intent of the assembly and petition clause is the category of ***speech plus***—following speech with physical activity such as picketing, distributing leaflets, and other forms of peaceful demonstration or assembly. Such assemblies are consistently protected by courts under the First Amendment; state and local laws regulating such activities are closely scrutinized and frequently overturned. But the same assembly on private property is quite another matter and can in many circumstances be regulated. For example, the directors of a shopping center can lawfully prohibit an assembly protesting a war or supporting a ban on abortion. Assemblies in public areas can also be restricted under some circumstances, especially when the assembly or demonstration jeopardizes the health, safety, or rights of others. This condition was the basis of the Supreme Court's decision to uphold a lower-court order restricting the access that abortion protesters had to the entrances of abortion clinics.[46]

Freedom of the Press   For all practical purposes, freedom of speech implies and includes freedom of the press. With the exception of the broadcast media, which are subject to federal regulation, the press is protected under the doctrine prohibiting ***prior restraint.*** Beginning with the landmark 1931 case of *Near v. Minnesota,*[47] the Supreme Court has held that except under the most extraordinary circumstances, the First Amendment prohibits government agencies from seeking to prevent newspapers or magazines from publishing whatever they wish. Indeed, in the case of *New York Times v. United States,* the so-called Pentagon Papers case, the Supreme Court ruled that the government could not even block publication of secret Defense Department documents furnished to *The New York Times* by an opponent of the Vietnam War who had obtained the documents illegally.[48] In a

speech plus Speech accompanied by activities such as sit-ins, picketing, and demonstrations. Protection of this form of speech under the First Amendment is conditional, and restrictions imposed by state or local authorities are acceptable if properly balanced by considerations of public order.

prior restraint An effort by a government agency to block the publication of material it deems libelous or harmful in some other way; censorship. In the United States, the courts forbid prior restraint except under the most extraordinary circumstances.

---

[44]Carl Hulse, "Flag Amendment Narrowly Fails in Senate Vote," *New York Times,* 28 June, 2006. This article is included at the end of Chapter 2.

[45]*Virginia v. Black,* 538 U.S. 343 (2003).

[46]For a good general discussion of "speech plus," see Louis Fisher, *American Constitutional Law* (New York: McGraw-Hill, 1990), pp. 544–46. The case upholding the buffer zone against the abortion protesters is *Madsen v. Women's Health Center,* 512 U.S. 753 (1994).

[47]*Near v. Minnesota ex rel. Olson,* 283 U.S. 697 (1931).

[48]*New York Times v. United States,* 403 U.S. 713 (1971).

1990 case, however, the Supreme Court upheld a lower-court order restraining the Cable News Network (CNN) from broadcasting tapes of conversations between the former Panamanian dictator Manuel Noriega and his lawyer, supposedly recorded by the American government. By a vote of 7–2, the Court held that CNN could be restrained from broadcasting the tapes until the trial court in the Noriega case had listened to the tapes and decided whether their broadcast would violate Noriega's right to a fair trial.[49]

Conditionally Protected Speech   At least four forms of speech fall outside the absolute guarantees of the First Amendment and therefore outside the realm of absolute protection. Since they do enjoy some protection, they qualify as conditionally protected types of speech: libel and slander, obscenity and pornography, fighting words, and commercial speech. It should be emphasized once again that these four types of speech still enjoy considerable protection by the courts.

LIBEL AND SLANDER   Some speech is not protected at all. If a written statement is made in "reckless disregard of the truth" and is considered damaging to the victim because it is "malicious, scandalous, and defamatory," it can be punished as **libel**. If an oral statement of such nature is made, it can be punished as **slander.**

Today most libel suits involve freedom of the press, and the realm of free press is enormous. Historically, newspapers were subject to the law of libel, which provided that newspapers that printed false and malicious stories could be compelled to pay damages to those they defamed. In recent years, however, American courts have greatly narrowed the meaning of libel and made it extremely difficult, particularly for politicians or other public figures, to win a libel case against a newspaper. In the important case of *New York Times v. Sullivan,* the Court held that to be deemed libelous a story about a public official not only had to be untrue but also had to result from "actual malice" or "reckless disregard" for the truth.[50] In other words, the newspaper had to *deliberately* print false and malicious material. In practice, it is nearly impossible to prove that a paper deliberately printed maliciously false information, and it is especially difficult for a politician or other public figure to win a libel case. Essentially, the print media have been able to publish anything they want about a public figure.

In at least one recent case, however, the Court has opened up the possibility of public officials' filing libel suits against the press. In 1985, the Court held that the press was immune from libel only when the printed material was "a matter of public concern." In other words, in future cases a newspaper would have to show that the public official was engaged in activities that were indeed *public.* This new principle has made the press more vulnerable to libel suits, but it still leaves an enormous realm of freedom for the press. For example, the Reverend Jerry Falwell, a cofounder of the Moral Majority, lost his libel suit against *Hustler* magazine even though the magazine had published a cartoon depicting Falwell having drunken intercourse with his mother in an outhouse. A unanimous Supreme Court rejected a

libel A written statement made in "reckless disregard of the truth" and considered damaging to a victim because it is "malicious, scandalous, and defamatory."

slander An oral statement made in "reckless disregard of the truth" and considered damaging to a victim because it is "malicious, scandalous, and defamatory."

---

[49] *Cable News Network v. Noriega,* 111 S.Ct. 451 (1990).

[50] *New York Times v. Sullivan,* 376 U.S. 254 (1964).

jury verdict in favor of damages for "emotional distress" on the grounds that parodies, no matter how outrageous, are protected because "outrageousness" is too subjective a test and thus would interfere with the free flow of ideas protected by the First Amendment.[51]

OBSCENITY AND PORNOGRAPHY   If libel and slander cases can be difficult because of the problem of determining the truth of statements and whether those statements are malicious and damaging, cases involving pornography and obscenity can be even more sticky. It is easy to say that pornography and obscenity fall outside the realm of protected speech, but it is impossible to draw a clear line defining where protection ends and unprotected speech begins. Not until 1957 did the Supreme Court confront this problem, and it did so with a definition of obscenity that may have caused more confusion than it cleared up. Justice William Brennan, in writing the Court's opinion, defined obscenity as speech or writing that appeals to the "prurient interest"—that is, books, magazines, films, and other material whose purpose is to excite lust as this appears "to the average person, applying contemporary community standards." Even so, Brennan added, the work should be judged obscene only when it is "utterly without redeeming social importance."[52] Brennan's definition, instead of clarifying the Court's view, caused more confusion. In 1964, Justice Potter Stewart confessed that although he found pornography impossible to define, "I know it when I see it."[53]

All attempts by the courts to define pornography and obscenity have proved impractical because each instance required courts to screen thousands of pages of print material or feet of film alleged to be pornographic. The vague and impractical standards that had been developed meant ultimately that almost nothing could be banned on the grounds that it was pornographic and obscene. An effort was made to strengthen the restrictions in 1973, when the Supreme Court expressed its willingness to define pornography as a work that as a whole is deemed prurient by the "average person" according to "community standards," depicts sexual conduct "in a patently offensive way," and lacks "serious literary, artistic, political, or scientific value." This definition meant that pornography would be determined by local rather than national standards. Thus a local bookseller might be prosecuted for selling a volume that was a best seller nationally but was deemed pornographic locally.[54] This new definition of standards did not help much either, and not long after 1973 the Court again began to review all such community anti-pornography laws, reversing most of them. Consequently, today there is a widespread fear that Americans are free to publish any and all variety of intellectual expression, whether there is any "redeeming social value" or not. Yet this area of free speech is far from settled.

In recent years, the battle against obscene speech has focused on pornography on the Internet. Opponents of this form of expression argue that it should be

---

[51] *Hustler Magazine v. Falwell*, 485 U.S. 46 (1988).

[52] *Roth v. United States*, 354 U.S. 476 (1957).

[53] Concurring opinion in *Jacobellis v. Ohio*, 378 U.S. 184 (1964).

[54] *Miller v. California*, 413 U.S. 15 (1973).

banned because of the easy access children have to the Internet. The first major effort to regulate the content of the Internet occurred on February 1, 1996, when the 104th Congress passed major telecommunications legislation. Attached to the Telecommunications Act was an amendment, called the Communications Decency Act (CDA), that was designed to regulate the online transmission of obscene material. The constitutionality of the CDA was immediately challenged in court by a coalition of interests led by the American Civil Liberties Union (ACLU). In the 1997 Supreme Court case of *Reno v. ACLU,* the Court struck down the CDA, ruling that it suppressed speech that "adults have a constitutional right to receive" and that governments may not limit the adult population to messages that are fit for children. Supreme Court Justice John Paul Stevens described the Internet as the "town crier" of the modern age and said that it was entitled to the greatest degree of First Amendment protection possible.[55] Congress again tried limiting children's access to Internet pornography with the 2001 Children's Internet Protection Act, which required public libraries to install anti-pornography filters on all library computers with Internet access. Though the act made cooperation a condition for receiving federal subsidies, it did permit librarians to unblock a site at the request of an adult patron. The law was challenged, and in 2003 the Court upheld it, asserting that its provisions did not violate library patrons' First Amendment rights.[56]

In 2000, the Supreme Court also extended the highest degree of First Amendment protection to cable (not broadcast) television. In *United States. v. Playboy Entertainment Group,* the Court struck down a portion of the Telecommunications Act of 1996 that required cable TV companies to limit the broadcast of sexually explicit programming to late-night hours. In its decision, the Court noted that the law already provided parents with the means to restrict access to sexually explicit cable channels through various blocking devices. Moreover, such programming could come into the home only if parents decided to purchase such channels in the first place.[57]

FIGHTING WORDS   Speech can also lose its protected position when it moves toward the sphere of action. "Expressive speech," for example, is protected until it moves from the symbolic realm to the realm of actual conduct—to direct incitement of damaging conduct with the use of so-called *fighting words.* In 1942, the Supreme Court upheld the arrest and conviction of a man who had violated a state law forbidding the use of offensive language in public. He had called the arresting officer a "goddamned racketeer" and "a damn Fascist." When his case reached the Supreme Court, the arrest was upheld on the grounds that the First Amendment provides no protection for such offensive language because such words "are no essential part of any exposition of ideas."[58] This case was reaffirmed in a much more famous and more important case decided at the height of the cold war, when the Supreme Court held that

---

[55] *Reno v. ACLU,* 521 U.S. 844 (1997).

[56] *United States v. American Library Association,* 539 U.S. 194 (2003).

[57] *United States v. Playboy Entertainment Group, Inc.,* 529 U.S. 803 (2000).

[58] *Chaplinsky v. State of New Hampshire,* 315 U.S. 568 (1942).

fighting words
Speech that directly incites damaging conduct.

there is no substantial public interest in permitting certain kinds of utterances: the lewd and obscene, the profane, the libelous, and the insulting or "fighting" words—those which by their very utterance inflict injury or tend to incite an immediate breach of the peace.[59]

Since that time, however, the Supreme Court has reversed almost every conviction based on arguments that the speaker had used "fighting words." But again, does not mean this is an absolutely settled area. In recent years, the increased activism of minority and women's groups has prompted a movement against words that might be construed as offensive to members of a particular group. This movement has come to be called, derisively, political correctness, or PC. In response to this movement, many organizations have attempted to impose codes of etiquette that acknowledge these enhanced sensitivities. These efforts to formalize the restraints on the use of certain words in public are causing great concern over their possible infringement on freedom of speech. But how should we determine what words are "fighting words" and therefore fall outside the protections of the freedom of speech?

One category of conditionally protected speech is the free speech of high-school students in public schools. In 1986, the Supreme Court backed away from a broad protection of student free speech rights by upholding the punishment of a high-school student for making a sexually suggestive speech. The Court opinion held that such speech interfered with the school's goal of teaching students the limits of socially acceptable behavior.[60] Two years later the Supreme Court took another conservative step by restricting students' speech and press rights even further, defining them as part of the educational process and not to be treated with the same standard as adult speech in a regular public forum.[61]

In addition, scores of universities have attempted to develop speech codes to suppress utterances deemed to be racial or ethnic slurs. What these universities find, however, is that the codes often produce more problems than they solve. Speech codes at some universities have been struck down by federal judges as unconstitutional infringements of speech. Such concerns are not limited to universities, although universities have probably moved furthest toward efforts to formalize "politically correct" speech guidelines. Similar developments have taken place in large corporations, both public and private, in which many successful complaints and lawsuits have been brought, alleging that the words of employers or their supervisors create a "hostile or abusive working environment." The Supreme Court has held that "sexual harassment" that creates a "hostile working environment" includes "unwelcome sexual advances, requests for sexual favors, and other *verbal* or physical conduct of a sexual nature"[62] [emphasis added]. A fundamental free speech issue is involved in these regulations of hostile speech. So far, the assumption favoring the regulation of hostile

---

[59] *Dennis v. United States*, 341 U.S. 494 (1951), which upheld the infamous Smith Act of 1940, which provided criminal penalties for those who "willfully and knowingly conspire to teach and advocate the forceful and violent overthrow and destruction of the government."

[60] *Bethel School District No. 403 v. Fraser*, 478 U.S. 675 (1986).

[61] *Hazelwood School District v. Kuhlmeier*, 484 U.S. 260 (1988).

[62] *Meritor Savings Bank v. Vinson*, 477 U.S. 57 (1986).

speech in universities and other workplaces is that "some speech must be shut down in the name of free speech because it tends to silence those disparaged by it"[63] even though a threat of hostile action (usually embodied in "fighting words") is not present. However, the courts have been reluctant to draw a precise line between the right to express hostile views and the protection of the sensitivities of minorities and women.

COMMERCIAL SPEECH   Commercial speech, such as newspaper or television advertising, does not have full First Amendment protection because it cannot be considered political speech. Initially considered to be entirely outside the protection of the First Amendment, commercial speech has made gains during the twentieth century. Some commercial speech is still unprotected and therefore regulated. For example, the regulation of false and misleading advertising by the Federal Trade Commission is an old and well-established power of the federal government. The Supreme Court long ago approved the constitutionality of laws prohibiting the electronic media from carrying cigarette advertising.[64] The Court has upheld a state-university ban on Tupperware parties in college dormitories.[65] It has upheld city ordinances prohibiting the posting of all signs on public property (as long as the ban is total, so that there is no hint of censorship).[66] And the Supreme Court, in a heated 5–4 decision written by Chief Justice William Rehnquist, upheld Puerto Rico's statute restricting gambling advertising aimed at residents of Puerto Rico.[67]

However, the gains far outweigh the losses in the effort to expand the protection commercial speech enjoys under the First Amendment. As the scholar Louis Fisher explains, "In part, this reflects the growing appreciation that commercial speech is part of the free flow of information necessary for informed choice and democratic participation."[68] For example, the Court in 1975 struck down a state statute making it a misdemeanor to sell or circulate newspapers encouraging abortions; the Court ruled that the statute infringed on constitutionally protected speech and the right of the reader to make informed choices.[69] On a similar basis, the Court reversed its own earlier decisions upholding laws that prohibited dentists and other professionals from advertising their services. For the Court, medical-service advertising was a matter of health that could be advanced by the free flow of information.[70] In a 1983 case, the Supreme Court struck down a congressional statute that prohibited the unsolicited mailing of advertisements for contraceptives. In 1996, the

---

[63]Charles Fried, "The New First Amendment Jurisprudence: A Threat to Liberty," in *The Bill of Rights and the Modern State*, ed. Geoffrey R. Stone, Richard A. Epstein, and Cass R. Sunstein, (Chicago: University of Chicago Press, 1992) p. 249.

[64]*Capital Broadcasting Company v. Acting Attorney General*, 405 U.S. 1000 (1972).

[65]*Board of Trustees, State University of New York v. Fox*, 492 U.S. 469 (1989).

[66]*City Council v. Taxpayers for Vincent*, 466 U.S. 789 (1984).

[67]*Posadas de Puerto Rico Associates v. Tourism Company of Puerto Rico*, 478 U.S. 328 (1986).

[68]Fisher, *American Constitutional Law*, p. 546.

[69]*Bigelow v. Virginia*, 421 U.S. 809 (1975).

[70]*Virginia State Board of Pharmacy v. Virginia Citizens Consumer Council*, 425 U.S. 748 (1976). Later cases restored the rights of lawyers to advertise their services.

Court struck down Rhode Island laws and regulations banning the advertisement of liquor prices as a violation of the First Amendment.[71] And in a 2001 case, the Court ruled that a Massachusetts ban on all cigarette advertising violated the First Amendment right of the tobacco industry to advertise its products to adult consumers.[72] These instances of commercial speech are significant in themselves, but they are all the more significant because they indicate the breadth and depth of the freedom existing today to direct appeals broadly to a large public, not only to sell goods and services but also to mobilize people for political purposes.

The Second Amendment and the Right to Bear Arms

A well regulated Militia, being necessary to the security of a free State, the right of the people to keep and bear Arms, shall not be infringed.

The point and purpose of the Second Amendment is the provision for militias; they were to be the backing of the government for the maintenance of local public order. *Militia* was understood at the time of the founding to be a military or police resource for state governments, and militias were specifically distinguished from armies and troops, which came within the sole constitutional jurisdiction of Congress.

Thus the right of the people "to keep and bear Arms" is based on and associated with participation in state militias. The reference to citizens' keeping arms underscored the fact that in the 1700s, state governments could not be relied on to provide firearms to militia members, so citizens eligible to serve in militias (white males between the ages of eighteen and forty-five) were expected to keep their own firearms at the ready.

Recent controversy has arisen concerning some citizens who have sought to form *private* militias, unconnected with the government. Yet the Supreme Court made clear that the Second Amendment does not allow citizens to form their own militias free from government control. When a private militia tried to assert such a right, the Supreme Court denied it.[73]

In the 2008 case of *District of Columbia v. Heller,* the U.S. Supreme Court struck down a District of Columbia law that banned handgun possession by private citizens in the District. The Court said that the Second Amendment protected the individual right to "keep and bear arms." The District of Columbia, however, is an agency of the federal government, and the Court specifically neglected to apply the *Heller* decision to the states. Hence, gun ordinances in such cities as New York and Chicago are not affected by the Court's decision. With the election of Barack Obama in November 2008, many opponents of gun control feared new regulations that would limit Americans' right to bear arms, and the debate over whether and to what extent the Second Amendment protects this right seemed certain to continue.

Rights of the Criminally Accused

Except for the First Amendment, most of the battle to apply the Bill of Rights to the states was fought over the various protections granted to individuals who are accused

---

[71] *44 Liquormart, Inc., and Peoples Super Liquor Stores, Inc., Petitioners v. Rhode Island and Rhode Island Liquor Stores Association,* 517 U.S. 484 (1996).

[72] *Lorillard Tobacco v. Reilly,* 533 U.S. 525 (2001).

[73] *Presser v. Illinois,* 116 U.S. 252 (1886).

[74] *Quilici v. Village of Morton Grove,* 695 F.2d 261 (7th Cir. 1982); *cert denied,* 464 U.S. 863 (1983).

of a crime, who are suspects in the commission of a crime, or who are brought before the court as a witness to a crime. The Fourth, Fifth, Sixth, and Eighth Amendments, taken together, are the essence of the due process of law, even though this fundamental concept does not appear until the very last words of the Fifth Amendment. In the next sections, we shall look at specific cases that illuminate the dynamics of this important constitutional issue. The procedural safeguards that we shall discuss may seem remote to most law-abiding citizens, but they help define the limits of governmental action against the personal liberty of every citizen. Many Americans believe that "legal technicalities" are responsible for setting many criminals free. In many cases, that is absolutely true. In fact, setting defendants free is the very purpose of the requirements that constitute due process. One of America's traditional and most strongly held juridical values is that "it is far worse to convict an innocent man than to let a guilty man go free."[75] In civil suits, verdicts rest on "the preponderance of the evidence"; in criminal cases, guilt has to be proved "beyond a reasonable doubt"—a far higher standard. The provisions for due process in the Bill of Rights were added in order to improve the probability that the standard of reasonable doubt will be respected.

The Fourth Amendment and Searches and Seizures

> The right of the people to be secure in their persons, houses, papers, and effects, against unreasonable searches and seizures, shall not be violated, and no Warrants shall issue, but upon probable cause, supported by Oath or affirmation, and particularly describing the place to be searched, and the persons or things to be seized.

The purpose of the Fourth Amendment is to guarantee the security of citizens against unreasonable (that is, improper) searches and seizures. In 1990, the Supreme Court summarized its understanding of the Fourth Amendment brilliantly and succinctly: "A search compromises the individual interest in privacy; a seizure deprives the individual of dominion over his or her person or property."[76] But how are we to define what is reasonable and what is unreasonable?

The 1961 case of *Mapp v. Ohio* illustrates the beauty and the agony of one of the most important of the procedures that have grown out of the Fourth Amendment—the **exclusionary rule,** which prohibits evidence obtained during an illegal search from being introduced in a trial. Dollree (Dolly) Mapp was "a Cleveland woman of questionable reputation" (by some accounts), the ex-wife of one prominent boxer, and the fiancée of an even more famous one. Acting on a tip that Dolly Mapp was harboring a suspect in a bombing incident, several policemen forcibly entered her house, claiming they had a warrant to look for the suspect. The police did not find the suspect but did find some materials connected to the local numbers racket (an illegal gambling operation) and a quantity of "obscene materials," which were in violation of an Ohio law banning possession of such materials. Although the warrant was never produced, the evidence that had been seized was admitted by a court, and Mapp was charged and convicted for illegal possession of obscene materials.

exclusionary rule
The ability of courts to exclude evidence obtained in violation of the Fourth Amendment.

---

[75] *In re Winship,* 397 U.S. 358 (1970). An outstanding treatment of due process in issues involving the Fourth through Seventh Amendments is found in Fisher, *American Constitutional Law,* chap. 13.

[76] *Horton v. California,* 496 U.S. 128 (1990).

By the time Mapp's appeal reached the Supreme Court, the issue of obscene materials had faded into obscurity, and the question before the Court was whether any evidence produced under the circumstances of the search of her home was admissible. The Court's opinion affirmed the exclusionary rule: Under the Fourth Amendment (applied to the states through the Fourteenth Amendment), "all evidence obtained by searches and seizures in violation of the Constitution . . . is inadmissible." This means that even people who are clearly guilty of the crime of which they are accused must not be convicted if the only evidence for their conviction was obtained illegally. This idea was expressed by Supreme Court Justice Benjamin Cardozo nearly a century ago when he wrote that "the criminal is to go free because the constable has blundered."

The exclusionary rule is the most severe restraint ever imposed by the Constitution and the courts on the behavior of the police. The exclusionary rule is a dramatic restriction because it rules out precisely the evidence that produces a conviction; it frees those people who are *known* to have committed the crime of which they have been accused. Because it works so dramatically in favor of persons known to have committed a crime, the Court has since softened the application of the rule. In recent years, the federal courts have relied on a discretionary use of the exclusionary rule, whereby they make a judgment as to the "nature and quality of the intrusion." It is thus difficult to know ahead of time whether a defendant will or will not be protected from an illegal search under the Fourth Amendment.[77]

Another recent issue involving the Fourth Amendment is the controversy over mandatory drug testing. Such testing is most widely used on public employees, and in an important case the Supreme Court upheld the U.S. Customs Service's drug-testing program for its employees.[78] That same year the Court approved drug and alcohol tests for railroad workers if the workers were involved in a serious accident.[79] After Court approvals of those two cases in 1989, more than forty federal agencies initiated mandatory employee drug tests. The practice of drug testing was reinforced by a presidential executive order widely touted as the "campaign for a drug-free federal workplace." These growing practices gave rise to public appeals against the general practice of "suspicionless testing" of employees. Regardless of any need to limit the spread of drug abuse, doing so in this manner, by testing public employees, seemed patently unconstitutional, in violation of the Fourth Amendment. A 1995 case, in which the Court upheld a public school district's policy requiring that all students participating in interscholastic sports submit to random drug tests, surely contributed to the efforts of federal, state, and local agencies to initiate random and suspicionless drug and alcohol testing.[80] The most recent cases suggest, however, that the Court is beginning to consider limits on the "war" against drugs. In a decisive 8–1 decision, the Court applied the Fourth Amendment as a shield against "state action that diminishes personal privacy" when the officials in question are not performing high-risk or

---

[77] For a good discussion of the issue, see Fisher, *American Constitutional Law*, pp. 884–89.

[78] *National Treasury Employees Union v. Von Raab*, 489 U.S. 656 (1989).

[79] *Skinner v. Railroad Labor Executives Association*, 489 U.S. 602 (1989).

[80] *Vernonia School District v. Acton*, 515 U.S. 646 (1995).

safety-sensitive tasks.[81] Using random and suspicionless drug testing as a symbol to fight drug use was, in the Court's opinion, carrying the exceptions to the Fourth Amendment too far.

More recently, the Court found it unconstitutional for police to use trained dogs in roadblocks set up to look for drugs in cars. Unlike drunk-driving roadblocks, where public safety is directly involved, narcotics roadblocks "cannot escape the Fourth Amendment's requirement that searches be based on suspicion of individual wrongdoing."[82] The Court also ruled that a public hospital cannot constitutionally test maternity patients for illegal drug use without their consent.[83] Finally, the Court found that the police may not use thermal-imaging devices to detect suspicious patterns of heat emerging from private homes without obtaining the usual search warrant.[84]

The Fifth Amendment

No person shall be held to answer for a capital, or otherwise infamous crime, unless on a presentment or indictment of a Grand Jury, except in cases arising in the land or naval forces, or in the Militia, when in actual service in time of War or public danger; nor shall any person be subject for the same offense to be twice put in jeopardy of life or limb; nor shall be compelled in any criminal case to be a witness against himself, nor be deprived of life, liberty, or property, without due process of law; nor shall private property be taken for public use, without just compensation.

GRAND JURIES   The first clause of the Fifth Amendment, the right to have a **grand jury** determine whether a trial is warranted, is considered "the oldest institution known to the Constitution."[85] Grand juries play an important role in federal criminal cases. However, the provision for a grand jury is the one important civil liberties provision of the Bill of Rights that was not incorporated by the Fourteenth Amendment to apply to state criminal prosecutions. Thus some states operate without grand juries. In such states, the prosecuting attorney simply files a "bill of information" affirming that there is sufficient evidence available to justify a trial. If the accused person is to be held in custody, the prosecutor must take the available information before a judge to determine whether the evidence shows probable cause.

DOUBLE JEOPARDY   "Nor shall any person be subject for the same offense to be twice put in jeopardy of life or limb" is the constitutional protection from **double jeopardy,** or being tried more than once for the same crime. The protection from double jeopardy was at the heart of the *Palko* case in 1937, which, as we saw earlier in this chapter, also established the principle of selective incorporation of the Bill of Rights. It took more than thirty years for the Court to nationalize the constitutional protection against double jeopardy.

grand jury A jury that determines whether sufficient evidence is available to justify a trial. Grand juries do not rule on the accused's guilt or innocence.

double jeopardy The Fifth Amendment right providing that a person cannot be tried twice for the same crime.

---

[81]*Chandler et al. v. Miller, Governor of Georgia et al.,* 520 U.S. 305 (1997).

[82]*Indianapolis v. Edmund,* 531 U.S. 32 (2000).

[83]*Ferguson v. City of Charleston,* 532 U.S. 67 (2001).

[84]*Kyllo v. United States,* 533 U.S. 27 (2001).

[85]E. S. Corwin and Jack Peltason, *Understanding the Constitution,* p. 286.

SELF-INCRIMINATION   Perhaps the most significant liberty found in the Fifth Amendment, and the one most familiar to many Americans who watch television crime shows, is the guarantee that no citizen "shall be compelled in any criminal case to be a witness against himself." The most famous case concerning self-incrimination is one of such importance that Chief Justice Earl Warren assessed its results as going "to the very root of our concepts of American criminal jurisprudence." Twenty-three-year-old Ernesto Miranda was sentenced to between twenty and thirty years in prison for the kidnapping and rape of an eighteen-year-old woman. The woman had identified him in a police lineup, and, after two hours of questioning Miranda confessed, subsequently signing a statement that his confession had been made voluntarily, without threats or promises of immunity. These confessions were admitted into evidence, served as the basis for Miranda's conviction, and also served as the basis of the appeal of his conviction all the way to the Supreme Court. In one of the most intensely and widely criticized decisions ever handed down by the Supreme Court, Ernesto Miranda's case produced the rules the police must follow before questioning an arrested criminal suspect. The reading of a person's "Miranda rights" has become a standard scene in every police station and on virtually every dramatization of police action on television and in the movies. *Miranda* advanced the civil liberties of accused persons not only by expanding the scope of the Fifth Amendment clause covering coerced confessions and self-incrimination but also by confirming the right to counsel. The Supreme Court under Warren Burger and William Rehnquist considerably softened the *Miranda* restrictions, making the job of the police a little easier, but the Miranda rule still stands as a protection against egregious police abuses of arrested persons. The Supreme Court reaffirmed *Miranda* in *Dickerson v. United States.*[86]

EMINENT DOMAIN   Another fundamental clause of the Fifth Amendment is the "takings clause," which extends to each citizen a protection against the taking of private property "without just compensation." Although this part of the amendment is not specifically concerned with protecting persons accused of crimes, it is nevertheless a fundamentally important instance where the government and the citizen are adversaries. As discussed earlier in this chapter, the power of any government to take private property for a public use is called **eminent domain.** This power is essential to the very concept of sovereignty. The Fifth Amendment neither invented eminent domain nor took it away; its purpose was to put limits on that inherent power through procedures that require a demonstration of a public purpose and the provision of fair payment for the seizure of someone's property. This provision is now universally observed in all American principalities, but it has not always been meticulously observed.

   The first modern case confronting the issue of public use involved a mom-and-pop grocery store in a rundown neighborhood on the southwest side of the District of Columbia. In carrying out a vast urban-redevelopment program in the 1950s, the city government of Washington, D.C., took the property as one of a large number of

eminent domain
The right of the government to take private property for public use, with reasonable compensation awarded for the property.

○   ONLINE READING

---

[86] *Dickerson v. United States*, 530 U.S. 428 (2000).

privately owned lots to be cleared for new housing and business construction. The owner of the grocery store and his successors after his death, took the government to court on the grounds that taking property from one private owner and eventually turning that property back, in altered form, to another private owner was an unconstitutional use of eminent domain. The store owners lost their case. The Supreme Court's argument was a curious but very important one: The "public interest" can mean virtually anything a legislature says it means. In other words, since the overall slum clearance and redevelopment project was in the public interest, according to the legislature, the eventual transfers of property that were going to take place were justified.[87] In 1984 and again in 2005 the Supreme Court reaffirmed that decision.[88]

The Sixth Amendment and the Right to Counsel

> In all criminal prosecutions, the accused shall enjoy the right to a speedy and public trial, by an impartial jury of the State and district wherein the crime shall have been committed, which district shall have been previously ascertained by law, and to be informed of the nature and cause of the accusation; to be confronted with the witnesses against him; to have compulsory process for obtaining witnesses in his favor, and to have the Assistance of Counsel for his defense.

Like the exclusionary rule of the Fourth Amendment and the self-incrimination clause of the Fifth Amendment, the "right to counsel" provision of the Sixth Amendment is notable for freeing defendants who seem to the public to be patently guilty as charged. Other provisions of the Sixth Amendment, such as the right to a speedy trial and the right to confront witnesses before an impartial jury, are less controversial in nature.

Gideon v. Wainwright is the perfect case study because it involved a disreputable person who seemed patently guilty of the crime for which he was convicted. In and out of jails for most of his fifty-one years, Clarence Earl Gideon received a five-year sentence for breaking into and entering a poolroom in Panama City, Florida. While serving time in jail, Gideon became a fairly well qualified "jailhouse lawyer," made his own appeal on a handwritten petition, and eventually won the landmark ruling on the right to counsel in all felony cases.[89]

The right to counsel has been expanded rather than restricted during the past few decades, when the courts have become more conservative. For example, although at first the right to counsel was met by judges assigning lawyers from the community as a formal public obligation, most states and cities have now created an office of public defender whose state-employed professional defense lawyers typically provide poor defendants with much better legal representation. And although these defendants cannot choose their private defense attorney, they do have the right to appeal a conviction on the grounds that the counsel provided by the state was

---

[87] *Berman v. Parker,* 348 U.S. 26 (1954). For a thorough analysis of the case, see Benjamin Ginsberg, "*Berman v. Parker:* Congress, the Court, and the Public Purpose," *Polity* 4 (1971): 48–75.

[88] *Hawaii Housing Authority v. Midkiff,* 469 U.S. 2321 (1984) and *Kelo v. City of New London,* 545 U.S. (2005).

[89] For a full account of the story of the trial and release of Clarence Earl Gideon, see Lewis, *Gideon's Trumpet.* See also David M. O'Brien, *Storm Center,* 2nd ed. (New York: Norton, 1990).

deficient. For example, in 2003 the Supreme Court overturned the death sentence of a Maryland death-row inmate, holding that the defense lawyer had failed to fully inform the jury of the defendant's history of "horrendous childhood abuse."[90] Moreover, the right to counsel extends beyond serious crimes to any trial, with or without a jury, that holds the possibility of imprisonment.[91]

The Eighth Amendment and Cruel and Unusual Punishment   The Eighth Amendment prohibits "excessive bail," "excessive fines," and "cruel and unusual punishment." Virtually all the debate over Eighth Amendment issues focuses on the last clause of the amendment: the protection from "cruel and unusual punishment." One of the greatest challenges in interpreting this provision consistently is that what is considered "cruel and unusual" varies from culture to culture and from generation to generation. And unfortunately, it also varies by class and race.

By far the biggest issue in the inconsistency of class and race as constituting cruel and unusual punishment arises over the death penalty. In 1972, the Supreme Court overturned several state death-penalty laws not because they were cruel and unusual but because they were being applied in a capricious manner—that is, blacks were much more likely than whites to be sentenced to death, the poor more likely than the rich, and men more likely than women.[92] Very soon after that decision, a majority of states revised their capital-punishment provisions to meet the Court's standards.[93] Since 1976, the Court has consistently upheld state laws providing for capital punishment, although it also continues to review numerous death-penalty appeals each year.

Between 1976 and 2000, states executed 683 people. Most of those executions occurred in southern states, with Texas leading the way at 239. As of 2002, thirty-eight states had adopted some form of capital punishment, a move approved of by about three quarters of all Americans.

Although virtually all criminal conduct is regulated by the states, Congress has also jumped on the bandwagon, imposing capital punishment for more than fifty federal crimes. Despite the seeming popularity of the death penalty, the debate has become, if anything, more intense. In 1997, for example, the American Bar Association passed a resolution calling for a halt to the death penalty until concerns about its fairness—that is, whether its application violates the principle of equality—and concerns about ensuring due process are addressed. In 2000, the governor of Illinois imposed a moratorium on the death penalty and created a commission to review the capital-punishment system. After a two-year study by the commission, Illinois adopted a number of reforms, including a ban on executions of the mentally retarded. In June 2002, the Supreme Court banned all executions of mentally retarded defendants, a decision that could move 200 or more people off death row.

---

[90] *Wiggins v. Smith*, 539 U.S. 510 (2003).

[91] For further discussion of these issues, see Corwin and Peltason, *Understanding the Constitution*, pp. 319–23.

[92] *Furman v. Georgia*, 408 U.S. 238 (1972).

[93] *Gregg v. Georgia*, 428 U.S. 153 (1976).

Many death-penalty supporters trumpet its deterrent effects on other would-be criminals. Although studies of capital crimes usually fail to demonstrate any direct deterrent effect, the punishment's failure to act as a deterrent may be due to the lengthy delays—typically years and even decades—between convictions and executions. A system that eliminates undue delays would surely enhance deterrence. And deterring even one murder or other heinous crime, proponents argue, is more than ample justification for such laws. Beyond that argument, the death penalty is seen as a proper expression of retribution, echoed in the biblical phrase "an eye for an eye." People who commit vicious crimes deserve to forfeit their lives in exchange for the suffering they have inflicted. If the world applauded the execution of Nazis after World War II, for example, how could it deny the right of society to execute a serial killer?

Constitutional objections to the death penalty often invoke the Eighth Amendment's protection against punishments that are "cruel and unusual." Yet the death penalty can hardly be considered a violation of this protection, say supporters, since it was commonly used in the eighteenth century and was supported by most early-American leaders. And while the poor, men, and blacks and Latinos are more likely than others to find themselves sitting on death row, this fact reflects the painful reality that these categories of individuals are more likely to commit crimes.

Death-penalty opponents are quick to point out that the death penalty has not been proved to deter crime, either in the United States or abroad. In fact, America is the only Western nation that still executes criminals. The fact that American states execute criminals debases, rather than elevates, society, by extolling vengeance. If the government is to serve as an example of proper behavior, say foes, it has no business sanctioning killing when incarceration will similarly protect society. As for the Constitution, most of the founders surely supported the death penalty. But, foes note, they also countenanced slavery and lived at a time when society was both less informed about, and more indifferent to, the human condition. Modern Americans' greater civility should be reflected in how the society defines individual rights.

Furthermore, according to death-penalty foes, execution is expensive—more expensive than life imprisonment—precisely because the government must make every effort to ensure that it is not executing an innocent person. Curtailing legal appeals would make the possibility of a mistake too great. And although most Americans do support the death penalty, people also support life without the possibility of parole as an alternative. Race also intrudes in death-penalty cases: People of color (who are more likely to face economic deprivation) are disproportionately more likely to be sentenced to death, whereas whites charged with identical crimes are less likely to be given the ultimate punishment. Such disparity of treatment violates the principle of equal protection. Finally, according to opponents, a life sentence may be a worse punishment than the death penalty.

The Right to Privacy

Some of the people all of the time and all of the people some of the time would just like to be left alone, to have their own private domain into which no one—friends, family, government, church, or employer—has the right to enter without permission.

Many Jehovah's Witnesses felt that way in the 1930s. They risked serious punishment in 1940 by telling their children not to salute the flag or say the Pledge of Allegiance in school because of their understanding of the first commandment's prohibition of the worship of "graven images." As noted in our discussion of the free exercise of religion, they lost their appeal, the children were expelled, and the parents were punished. However, the Supreme Court concluded that the 1940 decision had been "wrongly decided." These two cases arose under the freedom of religion provisions of the First Amendment, but they were also the first cases to confront the possibility of another right that is not mentioned anywhere in the Constitution or the Bill of Rights: the right to be left alone. When the Court began to take a more activist role in the mid-1950s and 1960s, the idea of a **right to privacy** was revived. In 1958, the Supreme Court recognized "privacy in one's association" in its decision to prevent the state of Alabama from using the membership list of the NAACP in the state's investigations.

BIRTH CONTROL   The sphere of privacy was drawn in earnest in 1965, when the Court ruled that a Connecticut statute forbidding the use of contraceptives violated the right of marital privacy. Estelle Griswold, the executive director of the Planned Parenthood League of Connecticut, was arrested by the state of Connecticut for providing information, instruction, and medical advice about contraception to married couples. She and her associates were found guilty as accessories to the crime and fined $100 each. The Supreme Court reversed the lower court's decisions and declared the Connecticut law unconstitutional because it violated "a right of privacy older than the Bill of Rights—older than our political parties, older than our school system." Justice William O. Douglas, author of the majority decision in the *Griswold* case, argued that this right of privacy is also grounded in the Constitution because it fits into a "zone of privacy" created by a combination of the Third, Fourth, and Fifth Amendments. A concurring opinion, written by Justice Arthur Goldberg, attempted to strengthen Douglas's argument by adding that "the concept of liberty . . . embraces the right of marital privacy though that right is not mentioned explicitly in the Constitution [and] is supported by numerous decisions of this Court . . . and *by the language and history of the Ninth Amendment*" [emphasis added].[94]

ABORTION   The right to privacy was confirmed and extended in 1973 in the most important of all privacy decisions and one of the most important Supreme Court decisions in American history: *Roe v. Wade*. This decision established a woman's right to seek an abortion and prohibited states from making abortion a criminal act.[95] The Burger Court's decision in *Roe* took a revolutionary step toward establishing the right to privacy. It is important to emphasize that the preference for privacy rights and for their extension to include the rights of women to control their own bodies was not something invented by the Supreme Court in a vacuum. Most states did not

right to privacy The right to be let alone, which has been interpreted by the Supreme Court to entail free access to birth control and abortions.

---

[94] *Griswold v. Connecticut*, 381 U.S. 479 (1965) and *Griswold v. Connecticut*, concurring opinion. In 1972, in *Eisenstadt v. Baird*, 405 U.S. 438 (1972), the Court extended the privacy right to unmarried women.

[95] *Roe v. Wade*, 410 U.S. 113 (1973).

○ ONLINE READING

regulate abortions in any fashion until the 1840s, at which time only six of the twenty-six states had any regulations governing abortion at all. In addition, many states had begun to ease their abortion restrictions well before the 1973 *Roe* decision, although in recent years a number of states have reinstated some restrictions on the procedure.

By extending the umbrella of privacy, this sweeping ruling dramatically changed abortion practices in America. In addition, it galvanized and nationalized the abortion debate. Groups opposed to abortion, such as the National Right to Life Committee, organized to fight the new liberal standard, while abortion rights groups sought to maintain that protection. In recent years, the legal standard shifted against abortion rights supporters in two key Supreme Court cases.

In *Webster v. Reproductive Health Services*, the Court narrowly upheld (by a 5–4 majority) the constitutionality of restrictions on the use of public medical facilities for abortion.[96] And in the 1992 case of *Planned Parenthood v. Casey*, another 5–4 majority of the Court upheld *Roe* but narrowed its scope, refusing to invalidate a Pennsylvania law that significantly limits freedom of choice. The Court's decision defined the right to an abortion as a "limited or qualified" right subject to regulation by the states as long as the regulation does not constitute an "undue burden."[97] More recently, the Court had another opportunity to rule on what constitutes an undue burden. In the 2000 case of *Stenberg v. Carhart*, the Court, by a vote of 5–4, struck down Nebraska's ban on partial-birth abortions because the law had the "effect of placing a substantial obstacle in the path of a woman seeking an abortion."[98]

HOMOSEXUALITY   In the last two decades, the right to be left alone began to include the privacy rights of homosexuals. One morning in Atlanta in the mid-1980s, Michael Hardwick was arrested by a police officer who discovered him in bed with another man. The officer had come to serve a warrant for Hardwick's arrest for failure to appear in court to answer charges of drinking in public. One of Hardwick's unknowing housemates invited the officer to look in Hardwick's room, where he found Hardwick and another man engaging in "consensual sexual behavior." Hardwick was then arrested under Georgia's laws against heterosexual and homosexual sodomy. Hardwick filed a lawsuit against the state, challenging the constitutionality of the Georgia law, and won his case in the federal court of appeals. The state of Georgia, in an unusual move, appealed the court's decision to the Supreme Court. The majority of the Court reversed the lower-court decision, holding against Hardwick on the grounds that "the federal Constitution confers [no] fundamental right upon homosexuals to engage in sodomy" and that there was therefore no basis to invalidate "the laws of the many states that still make such conduct illegal and have done so for a very long time." The Court majority concluded its opinion with a warning that it ought not and would not use its power to "discover new fundamental rights embed-

---

[96] *Webster v. Reproductive Health Services*, 492 U.S. 490 (1989), which upheld a Missouri law that restricted the use of public medical facilities for abortion. The decision opened the way for other states to limit the availability of abortion.

[97] *Planned Parenthood v. Casey*, 505 U.S. 833 (1992).

[98] *Stenberg v. Carhart*, 530 U.S. 914 (2000).

ded in the Due Process Clause." In other words, the Court under Chief Justice Rehnquist was expressing its determination to restrict quite severely the expansion of the Ninth Amendment and the development of new substantive rights. The four dissenters argued that the case was not about a fundamental right to engage in homosexual sodomy but was in fact about "the most comprehensive of rights and the right most valued by civilized men, [namely,] the right to be let alone."[99]

Seventeen years later, and to most everyone's surprise, the Court overturned *Bowers v. Hardwick* with a dramatic pronouncement that gays are "entitled to respect for their private lives" as a matter of constitutional due process. With *Lawrence v. Texas*, state legislatures no longer had the authority to make private sexual behavior a crime.[100] Drawing from the tradition of negative liberty, the Court maintained, "In our tradition the State is not omnipresent in the home. And there are other spheres of our lives and existence outside the home, where the State should not be a dominant presence." Explicitly encompassing lesbians and gay men within the umbrella of privacy, the Court concluded that the "petitioners are entitled to respect for their private lives. The State cannot demean their existence or control their destiny by making their private sexual conduct a crime." This decision added substance to the Ninth Amendment "right of privacy."

THE RIGHT TO DIE   Another area ripe for litigation and public discourse is the so-called right to die. A number of highly publicized physician-assisted suicides in the 1990s focused attention on whether people have a right to choose their own death and receive assistance in carrying it out. Can this become part of the privacy right, or is it a new substantive right? A tentative answer came in 1997, when the Court ruled that a Washington State law establishing a ban on "causing" or "aiding" a suicide did not violate the Fourteenth Amendment or any clauses of the Bill of Rights incorporated into the Fourteenth Amendment. Thus if a state can constitutionally adopt such a prohibition, there is no constitutional right to suicide or assisted suicide. However, the Court left open the narrower question of "whether a mentally competent person who is experiencing great suffering has a constitutionally cognizable interest in controlling the circumstances of his or her imminent death." "Americans are engaged in an earnest and profound debate about the morality, legality, and practicality of physician-assisted suicide. Our holding permits this debate to continue, as it should in a democratic society."[101] Never before has the Supreme Court more openly invited further litigation on a point.

The War on Terrorism   In response to the September 11, 2001, terrorist attacks on the United States, Congress enacted new legislation—the Patriot Act—designed to make it easier for federal law enforcement agencies to investigate and prosecute suspected terrorists. In addition, the president issued a series of orders allowing the

---

[99] *Bowers v. Hardwick*, 478 U.S. 186 (1986). The dissenters were quoting an earlier case, *Olmstead v. United States*, 277 U.S. 438 (1928), to emphasize the nature of their disagreement with the majority in the *Bowers* case.

[100] *Lawrence and Garner v. Texas*, 539 U.S. 558 (2003).

[101] *Washington v. Glucksberg*, 521 U.S. 702 (1997).

ONLINE READING

National Security Agency to eavesdrop on domestic communications and the military to detain and try terrorism suspects. Civil libertarians have argued that the government's new surveillance and eavesdropping authority poses a threat to free speech and privacy. Critics have also declared that the open-ended military detention of terrorism suspects, along with the special military tribunals and procedures established by the president to try such suspects, violates many of the fundamental constitutional protections provided to those accused of criminal actions.

Some of these questions have been raised in the federal courts. In June 2004, the Supreme Court ruled in three cases involving the president's antiterrorism initiatives and claims of executive power and in two of those cases appeared to place some limit on presidential authority. Indeed, the justices were clearly influenced by revelations that U.S. troops abused prisoners in Iraq, and they sought in those cases to make a statement against the absolute denial of procedural rights to individuals in the custody of U.S. military authorities.[102]

In its June 2004 rulings, the Supreme Court did assert that presidential actions were subject to judicial scrutiny and placed some constraints on the president's unfettered power. At the same time, the Court affirmed the president's single most important claim: the unilateral power to declare individuals, including U.S. citizens, "enemy combatants," who can be detained by federal authorities under adverse legal circumstances. Future presidents are likely to cite the Court's decisions as precedents for, rather than limits on, the exercise of executive power.

The same is likely to be true of the Court's June 2006 decision in the case of *Hamdan v. Rumsfeld*.[103] Salim Ahmed Hamdan, a Taliban fighter captured in Afghanistan in 2001 and held at Guantánamo since 2002, was slated for trial by a special military tribunal. Such tribunals, operating outside both the civilian and the military court systems, were created by the Bush administration to deal with suspected terrorists in the wake of the September 11 attacks and the U.S. invasion of Afghanistan. Hamdan challenged the propriety of the tribunals. In its decision, the Supreme Court held that tribunals must either be authorized by statute or follow rules and procedures consistent with the Uniform Code of Military Justice (UCMJ) and the Geneva Conventions. The Court found that President Bush's tribunals were not authorized by statute and were operating under procedures that provided defendants with fewer rights and safeguards than they would receive under the UCMJ. Hence, the tribunals were declared invalid.

But while invalidating these particular tribunals, the Supreme Court accepted the principle that the president could order persons he deemed unlawful combatants to be tried by military tribunals so long as the tribunals were lawfully constituted. Accordingly, President Bush asked Congress to authorize the creation of special tribunals that would operate under the same rules and procedures as those declared unconstitutional by the Supreme Court, a request to which Congress acceded. It seems likely that future presidents may point to the *Hamdan* decision as validating the power of the president to order those they deem dangerous to be tried outside the normal legal framework.

---

[102] *Hamdi v. Rumsfeld*, 542 U.S. 507 (2004); *Rasul v. Bush*, 542 U.S. 466 (2004); *Rumsfeld v. Padilla*, 542 U.S. 426 (2004).

[103] *Hamdan v. Rumsfeld*, 548 U.S. (2006).

With the adoption of the Fourteenth Amendment in 1868, civil rights became part of the Constitution, guaranteed to each citizen through "equal protection of the laws." These words launched a century of political movements and legal efforts to press for racial equality. African Americans' quest for civil rights in turn inspired many other groups—including members of other racial and ethnic groups, women, people with disabilities, and gay men and lesbians—to seek new laws and constitutional guarantees of their civil rights.

Congress passed the Fourteenth Amendment and the states ratified it in the aftermath of the Civil War. Together with the Thirteenth Amendment, which abolished slavery, and the Fifteenth Amendment, which guaranteed voting rights to black men, it seemed to provide a guarantee of civil rights for the newly freed enslaved blacks. But the general language of the Fourteenth Amendment meant that its support for civil rights could be far reaching. The very simplicity of the **equal protection clause** of the Fourteenth Amendment left it open to interpretation:

> No State shall make or enforce any law which shall . . . deny to any person within its jurisdiction the equal protection of the laws.

Plessy v. Ferguson: "Separate but Equal"

The Supreme Court was no more ready to enforce the civil rights aspects of the Fourteenth Amendment than it was to enforce the civil liberties provisions. The Court declared the Civil Rights Act of 1875 unconstitutional on the grounds that it sought to protect blacks from discrimination by *private* businesses, while the Fourteenth Amendment, according to the Court's interpretation, was intended to protect individuals from discrimination only in the case of actions by *public* officials of state and local governments.

In 1896, the Court went still further, in the infamous case of *Plessy v. Ferguson,* by upholding a Louisiana statute that *required* segregation of the races on trolleys and other public carriers (and, by implication, in all public facilities, including schools). Homer Plessy, a man defined as "one-eighth black," had violated a Louisiana law that provided for "equal but separate accommodations" on trains and a $25 fine for any white passenger who sat in a car reserved for blacks or any black passenger who sat in a car reserved for whites. The Supreme Court held that the Fourteenth Amendment's "equal protection of the laws" was not violated by racial distinction as long as the facilities were equal. People generally pretended they were equal as long as some accommodation existed. The Court said that although

> the object of the [Fourteenth] Amendment was undoubtedly to enforce the absolute equality of the two races before the law, . . . it could not have intended to abolish distinctions based on color, or to enforce social, as distinguished from political, equality, or a commingling of the two races upon terms unsatisfactory to either.[104]

equal protection clause The provision of the Fourteenth Amendment guaranteeing citizens "the equal protection of the laws." This clause has served as the basis for the civil rights of African Americans, women, and other groups.

---

[104] *Plessy v. Ferguson,* 163 U.S. 537 (1896).

○ ONLINE READING

What the Court was saying in effect was that the use of race as a criterion of exclusion in public matters was not unreasonable. This was the origin of the *"separate but equal" rule,* which was not reversed until 1954.

Racial Discrimination after World War II

The Supreme Court had begun to change its position on racial discrimination before World War II by defining more strictly the criterion of equal facilities in the "separate but equal" rule. In 1938, the Court rejected Missouri's policy of paying qualified blacks' tuition to out-of-state law schools rather than admitting them to the University of Missouri Law School.[105]

After the war, modest progress resumed. In 1950, the Court rejected Texas's claim that its new "law school for Negroes" afforded education equal to that of the all-white University of Texas Law School; without confronting the "separate but equal" principle itself, the Court's decision anticipated *Brown v. Board of Education* by opening the question of whether *any* segregated facility could be truly equal.[106] The same was true in 1944, when the Supreme Court struck down the southern practice of "white primaries," which legally excluded blacks from participation in the process of nominating candidates. Here the Court simply recognized that primaries could no longer be regarded as the private affairs of the parties but were an integral aspect of the electoral process. This decision made parties "an agency of the State," and any practice of discrimination against blacks was therefore "state action within the meaning of the Fifteenth Amendment."[107] The most important pre-1954 decision was probably *Shelley v. Kraemer,*[108] in which the Court ruled against the widespread practice of "restrictive covenants," whereby the seller of a home added a clause to the sales contract requiring the buyers to agree not to sell their home to any nonwhite, non-Christian, and so on. The Court ruled that although private persons could sign such restrictive covenants, they could not be judicially enforced because the Fourteenth Amendment prohibits any organ of the state, including the courts, from denying equal protection of its laws.

However, none of these pre-1954 cases confronted head-on the principle of "separate but equal" as such and its legal and constitutional support for racial discrimination. Each victory by the Legal Defense Fund of the NAACP was celebrated for itself and was seen, it was hoped, as a trend, but each was still a small victory, not a leading case. The massive effort by the southern states to resist direct desegregation and to prevent further legal actions against it by making a show of equalizing the quality of white and black schools convinced the NAACP that the Supreme Court was unready for a full confrontation with the constitutional principle sustaining segregation. But the continued unwillingness of Congress after 1948 to consider fair employment legislation seemed to convince the NAACP that the courts were their only hope. Thus by 1951, the NAACP had de-

---

"separate but equal" rule The doctrine that public accommodations could be segregated by race but still be equal.

[105] *Missouri ex rel. Gaines v. Canada,* 305 U.S. 337 (1938).

[106] *Sweatt v. Painter,* 339 U.S. 629 (1950).

[107] *Smith v. Allwright,* 321 U.S. 649 (1944).

[108] *Shelley v. Kraemer,* 334 U.S. 1 (1948).

cided to attack the principle of segregation itself as unconstitutional and, in 1952, instituted cases in South Carolina, Virginia, Kansas, Delaware, and the District of Columbia. The strategy was to file suits simultaneously in different federal districts so that inconsistent results between any two states would more quickly lead to Supreme Court acceptance of at least one appeal.[109] Of these suits, the Kansas case became the chosen one. It seemed to be ahead of the pack in its district court, and it had the special advantage of being located in a state outside the Deep South.[110]

Oliver Brown, the father of three girls, lived "across the tracks" in a low-income, racially mixed Topeka neighborhood. Every school-day morning, Linda Brown took a school bus to the Monroe School for black children, about a mile away. In September 1950, Oliver Brown took Linda to the all-white Sumner School, which was closer to home, to enter her in the third grade, in defiance of state law and local segregation rules. When they were refused, Brown took his case to the NAACP, and soon thereafter *Brown v. Board of Education* was born. In mid-1953, the Court announced that the several cases on their way up would be re-argued within the context of a set of questions having to do with the intent of the Fourteenth Amendment. Almost exactly a year later, the Court responded to those questions in one of the most important decisions in its history.

In deciding the case, the Court, to the surprise of many, basically rejected as inconclusive all the learned arguments about the intent and the history of the Fourteenth Amendment and committed itself to considering only the consequences of segregation:

> Does segregation of children in public schools solely on the basis of race, even though the physical facilities and other "tangible" factors may be equal, deprive the children of the minority group of equal educational opportunities? We believe that it does. . . . We conclude that, in the field of public education, the doctrine of "separate but equal" has no place. Separate educational facilities are inherently unequal.[111]

The *Brown* decision altered the constitutional framework in two fundamental respects. First, after *Brown,* the states would no longer have the power to use race as a criterion of discrimination in law. Second, the national government would from then on have the constitutional basis for extending its power (hitherto in doubt, as we saw earlier) to intervene with strict regulatory policies against the discriminatory actions of state or local governments, school boards, employers, and many others in the private sector.

Institution Principle

The 1954 *Brown* decision altered the constitutional framework by giving the national government the power to intervene to prevent discriminatory actions by state and local governments and some aspects of the private sector.

---

[109] The best reviews of strategies, tactics, and goals is found in John Hope Franklin, *From Slavery to Freedom: A History of Negro Americans,* 4th ed. (New York: Knopf, 1974), chap. 22; and Richard Kluger, *Simple Justice: The History of* Brown v. Board of Education *and Black America's Struggle for Equality* (New York: Vintage, 1977), chaps. 21 and 22.

[110] The District of Columbia case came up too, but because the District of Columbia is not a state, the case did not directly involve the Fourteenth Amendment and its "equal protection" clause. It confronted the Court on the same grounds, however: that segregation is inherently unequal. Its victory in effect was "incorporation in reverse," with equal protection moving from the Fourteenth Amendment to become part of the Bill of Rights. See *Bolling v. Sharpe,* 347 U.S. 497 (1954).

[111] *Brown v. Board of Education,* 347 U.S. 483 (1954).

○ ONLINE READING

Civil Rights after *Brown v. Board of Education*

History Principle

The precedent established in *Brown* has shaped and guided court decisions, legislation, and other political action related to civil rights since 1954.

Although *Brown v. Board of Education* withdrew all constitutional authority to use race as a criterion of exclusion, this historic decision was merely a small opening move. First, most states refused to cooperate until sued, and many ingenious schemes were employed to delay obedience (such as paying the tuition of white students to attend newly created "private" academies). Second, even as southern school boards began to cooperate by eliminating their legally enforced (**de jure**) segregation, there remained extensive actual (**de facto**) school segregation in the North and the South as a consequence of racially segregated housing, which could not be affected by the 1954 *Brown* principles. Third, discrimination in employment, public accommodations, juries, voting, and other areas of social and economic activity was not directly touched by *Brown*.

A decade of frustration following *Brown* made it fairly obvious that adjudication alone would not succeed. The goal of equal protection required positive, or affirmative, action by Congress and administrative agencies. And given massive southern resistance and generally negative national public opinion toward racial integration, progress would not be made through courts, Congress, *or* agencies without intense, well-organized support. The number of peaceful civil rights demonstrations for voting rights and public accommodations increased greatly during the fourteen years following *Brown*.[112]

Collective-Action Principle

Given the massive resistance to the 1954 *Brown* decision, the civil rights movement required large, well-organized protests.

Organized civil rights demonstrations began to mount slowly but surely after *Brown v. Board of Education*. By the 1960s, the many organizations that made up the civil rights movement had accumulated experience and built networks capable of launching massive direct-action campaigns against southern segregationists. The Southern Christian Leadership Conference, the Student Nonviolent Coordinating Committee, and many other organizations had built a movement that stretched across the South. That movement used the media to attract nationwide attention and support. In the massive March on Washington in 1963, the Reverend Martin Luther King Jr. staked out the movement's moral claims in his "I Have a Dream" speech. Also in the 1960s, images of protesters being beaten, attacked by police dogs, and set upon with fire hoses did much to win broad sympathy for the cause of black civil rights and discredit state and local governments in the South. In this way, the movement created intense pressure for a reluctant federal government to take more assertive steps to defend black civil rights.

de jure segregation Racial segregation that is a direct result of law or official policy.

de facto segregation Racial segregation that is not a direct result of law or government policy but is, instead, a reflection of residential patterns, income distributions, or other social factors.

One of the tenets of our five principles of politics from Chapter 1 is that individuals have little incentive to participate in mass-action politics. After all, what possible difference could one person make by taking part in a civil rights protest? Participation was costly in terms of time, and in the case of civil rights marchers even one's health or life was endangered. The risks outweighed the potential benefits, yet hundreds of thousands of people *did* participate. Why?

Even though little scholarly attention has been paid by those who apply this perspective to the civil rights movements,[113] a general answer is available. Most rational

---

[112]Jonathan D. Casper, *The Politics of Civil Liberties* (New York: Harper & Row, 1972), p. 90.

[113]One notable exception is Dennis Chong, *Collective Action and the Civil Rights Movement* (Chicago: University of Chicago Press, 1991).

analysis takes behavior to be *instrumental*—motivated by and directed toward some purpose or objective. But behavior may also be *experiential*. People do things, on this account, because they like doing them—they feel good inside, they feel free of guilt, they take pleasure in the activity for its own sake. We maintain that this second view of behavior is entirely compatible with rational accounts. Instrumental behavior may be thought of as *investment activity*, whereas experiential behavior may be thought of as *consumption activity*. It is the behavior itself that generates utility, rather than the consequences produced by the behavior. To take a specific illustration of collective action, many people certainly attended the 1963 March on Washington because they cared about civil rights. But it is unlikely that many deluded themselves into thinking their individual participation made a large difference to the fate of the civil rights legislation in support of which the march was organized. Rather, they attended because they wanted to be part of a social movement, hear Martin Luther King speak, and identify with the hundreds of thousands of others who felt the same way. Also—and this should not be minimized—they participated because they anticipated that the march would be fun, an adventure of sorts.

So, experiential behavior is consumption-oriented activity predicated on the belief that the activity in question is fulfilling, apart from its consequences. Individuals, complicated things that they are, are bound to be animated both by the consumption value of a particular behavior *and* by its instrumental value, the rational (investment) explanation that we have used throughout this book. To insist on only one of these complementary forms of rationality while excluding the other is to provide but a partial explanation.

Collective-Action Principle

People participated in the civil rights movement for experiential as well as instrumental purposes.

School Desegregation, Phase One   Although the District of Columbia and some of the school districts in the border states began to respond almost immediately to court-ordered desegregation, the states of the Deep South responded with a carefully planned delaying tactic known as massive resistance. Southern politicians stood shoulder to shoulder to declare that the Supreme Court's decisions and orders were without effect. The legislatures in these states enacted statutes ordering school districts to maintain segregated schools and state superintendents to terminate state funding wherever there was racial mixing in the classroom. Some southern states violated their own long traditions of local school autonomy by centralizing public-school authority under the governor or the state board of education and giving states the power to close schools and provide alternative private schooling wherever local school boards might be tending to obey the Supreme Court.

Most of these plans of massive resistance were tested in the federal courts and struck down as unconstitutional.[114] But southern resistance was not confined to legislation. In 1957, for example, Governor Orval Faubus mobilized the Arkansas National Guard to intercede against enforcement of a federal court order to integrate Little Rock's Central High School, and President Dwight D. Eisenhower was forced to deploy U.S. troops and place the city under martial law. The Supreme

---

[114]The two most important cases were *Cooper v. Aaron*, 358 U.S. 1 (1958), which required Little Rock, Arkansas, to desegregate, and *Griffin v. Prince Edward County School Board*, 377 U.S. 218 (1964), which forced all the schools of that Virginia county to reopen after they had been closed for five years to avoid desegregation.

TIME LINE OF CAUSE AND EFFECT IN THE CIVIL RIGHTS MOVEMENT

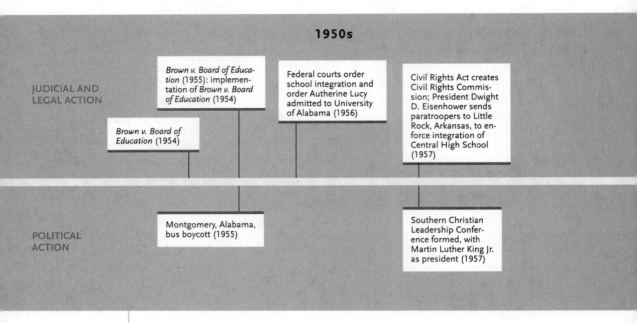

1950s

JUDICIAL AND LEGAL ACTION

Brown v. Board of Education (1955): implementation of *Brown v. Board of Education* (1954)

Brown v. Board of Education (1954)

Federal courts order school integration and order Autherine Lucy admitted to University of Alabama (1956)

Civil Rights Act creates Civil Rights Commission; President Dwight D. Eisenhower sends paratroopers to Little Rock, Arkansas, to enforce integration of Central High School (1957)

POLITICAL ACTION

Montgomery, Alabama, bus boycott (1955)

Southern Christian Leadership Conference formed, with Martin Luther King Jr. as president (1957)

Court considered the Little Rock confrontation so historically important that the opinion it rendered in that case not only was agreed to unanimously but also and unprecedentedly was signed personally by every one of the justices. The end of massive resistance, however, became the beginning of still another southern strategy, "pupil placement" laws, which authorized school districts to place each pupil in a school according to a variety of academic, personal, and psychological considerations, never mentioning race at all. These laws put the burden of transferring to an all-white school on the nonwhite children and their parents, making it almost impossible for a single court order to cover a whole district, let alone a whole state. The effect was to delay desegregation a while longer.[115]

As new devices were invented by the southern states to avoid desegregation, the federal courts followed with cases and decisions quashing them. Ten years after *Brown*, less than 1 percent of black school-age children in the Deep South were attending schools with whites. It had become unmistakably clear well before that time that the federal courts could not do the job alone. The first modern effort to legislate

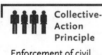

Collective-Action Principle

Enforcement of civil rights law required courts and legislatures to work together.

---

[115] *Shuttlesworth v. Birmingham Board of Education*, 358 U.S. 101 (1958), upheld a pupil placement plan purporting to assign pupils on various bases, with no mention of race. This case interpreted *Brown* to mean that school districts must stop explicit racial discrimination but were under no obligation to take positive steps to desegregate. For a while, black parents were doomed to case-by-case approaches.

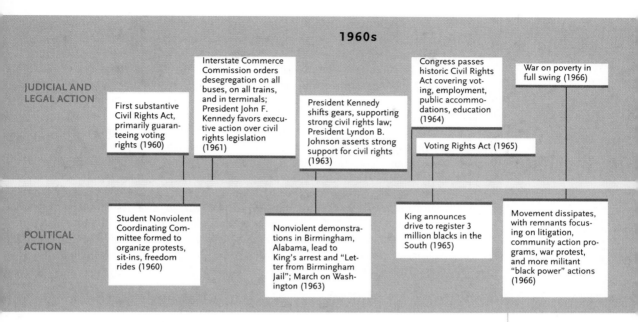

1960s

JUDICIAL AND LEGAL ACTION

First substantive Civil Rights Act, primarily guaranteeing voting rights (1960)

Interstate Commerce Commission orders desegregation on all buses, on all trains, and in terminals; President John F. Kennedy favors executive action over civil rights legislation (1961)

President Kennedy shifts gears, supporting strong civil rights law; President Lyndon B. Johnson asserts strong support for civil rights (1963)

Congress passes historic Civil Rights Act covering voting, employment, public accommodations, education (1964)

War on poverty in full swing (1966)

Voting Rights Act (1965)

POLITICAL ACTION

Student Nonviolent Coordinating Committee formed to organize protests, sit-ins, freedom rides (1960)

Nonviolent demonstrations in Birmingham, Alabama, lead to King's arrest and "Letter from Birmingham Jail"; March on Washington (1963)

King announces drive to register 3 million blacks in the South (1965)

Movement dissipates, with remnants focusing on litigation, community action programs, war protest, and more militant "black power" actions (1966)

---

in the field of civil rights was made in 1957, but the law contained only a federal guarantee of voting rights, without any powers of enforcement, although it did create the Civil Rights Commission to study abuses. Much more important legislation for civil rights followed, especially the Civil Rights Act of 1964. It is important to observe here the mutual dependence of the courts and the legislatures—not only do the legislatures need constitutional authority to act, but the courts also need legislative and political assistance, through the power of the purse, the power to organize administrative agencies to implement court orders, and the ability to focus political support. Consequently, even as Congress finally moved into the field of school desegregation (and other areas of equal protection), the courts continued to exercise their powers, not only by issuing court orders against recalcitrant school districts but also by extending and reinterpreting aspects of the equal protection clause to support legislative and administrative actions.

School Desegregation: Busing and Beyond   The most important judicial extension of civil rights in education after 1954 was probably the *Swann* decision of 1971, which held that state-imposed desegregation could be brought about by busing children across school districts even where relatively long distances were involved. But the decision went beyond that, adding that under certain limited circumstances even racial quotas could be used as the "starting point in shaping a remedy to correct past constitutional violations" and that the pairing or grouping of schools and the reorganizing of school attendance zones would also be acceptable (Figure 4.2).[116]

Three years later, however, the *Swann* case was severely restricted when the Supreme Court determined that only cities found guilty of deliberate and *de jure* racial segregation (segregation in law) would have to desegregate their schools. This decision was handed down in the 1974 case of *Milliken v. Bradley*, involving the city of Detroit and its suburbs.[117] The *Milliken* ruling had the effect of exempting most northern states and cities from busing because school segregation in northern cities is generally *de facto* (segregation in fact), following from segregated housing and thousands of acts of private discrimination against blacks and other minorities.

Additional progress in the desegregation of schools is likely to be extremely slow unless the Supreme Court decides to permit federal action against *de facto* segregation and the various kinds of private schools and academies that have sprung up for the purpose of avoiding integration. The prospects for further school integration diminished with a series of more recent Supreme Court decisions. In 1995, in *Missouri v. Jenkins*, the Court signaled to the lower courts that they should "disengage from desegregation efforts."[118] In 2007, the Supreme Court invalidated programs in Seattle, Washington, and Louisville, Kentucky, that sought to promote racial diversity in schools by assigning students to schools on the basis of race. The Court declared that these plans constituted racial discrimination even if intended for a good purpose.

The Rise of the Politics of Rights

Despite the agonizingly slow progress of school desegregation, there was some progress in other areas of civil rights during the 1960s and 1970s. Voting rights were established and fairly quickly began to revolutionize southern politics, and service on juries was no longer denied to minorities. But progress in securing the right to participate in politics and government dramatized the relative lack of progress in the economic domain, and it was in this area that battles over civil rights were increasingly fought.

Outlawing Discrimination in Employment The federal courts and the Justice Department entered this area through Title VII of the Civil Rights Act of 1964, which outlaws job discrimination by all private and public employers, including government agencies (such as fire and police departments), that employ more than fifteen workers. We have already seen that the Supreme Court gave "interstate commerce" such a broad definition that Congress had the constitutional authority to ban discrimination by virtually any local employers.[119] Title VII makes it unlawful to discriminate in employment on the basis of color, religion, sex, or national origin, as well as race.

The first problem with Title VII is that the complaining party has to show that deliberate discrimination was the cause of the failure to get a job or a training opportunity. Rarely does an employer explicitly admit discrimination on the basis of race,

---

[116] *Swann v. Charlotte-Mecklenburg Board of Education*, 402 U.S. 1 (1971).

[117] *Milliken v. Bradley*, 418 U.S. 717 (1974).

[118] *Missouri v. Jenkins*, 515 U.S. 70 (1995). The quotation is from David M. O'Brien, *Supreme Court Watch 1996* (New York: Norton, 1996), p. 220.

[119] See especially *Katzenbach v. McClung*, 379 U.S. 294 (1964).

FIGURE 4.2 The Percentage of Southern Black Schoolchildren Attending School with Whites, 1955–73

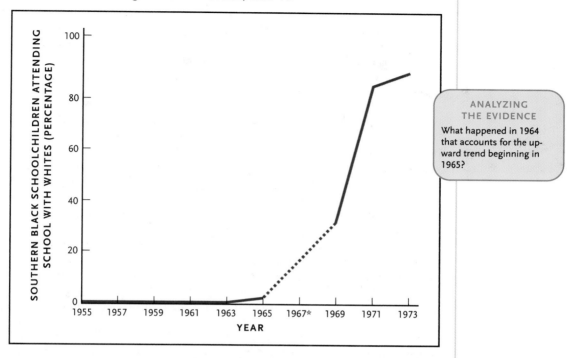

ANALYZING THE EVIDENCE

What happened in 1964 that accounts for the upward trend beginning in 1965?

SOURCE: Gerald N. Rosenberg, *Hollow Hope: Can Courts Bring About Social Change?* (Chicago: University of Chicago Press, 1991), pp. 50–51.

NOTE: Dashed line indicates missing data.

sex, or any other illegal reason. Recognizing the rarity of such an admission, the courts have allowed aggrieved parties (the plaintiffs) to make their case if they can show that an employer's hiring practices had the *effect* of exclusion. A leading case in 1971 involved a "class action" by several black employees in North Carolina attempting to show with statistical evidence that blacks had been relegated to one department of the Duke Power Company, which involved the least desirable of manual-labor jobs, and that they had been kept out of contention for the better jobs because the employer had added high-school education and passing grades on specially prepared aptitude tests as qualifications for those jobs. The Supreme Court held that although the statistical evidence did not prove intentional discrimination and the requirements were race neutral in appearance, their effects were sufficient to shift the burden of justification to the employer to show that the requirements were a "business necessity" that bore "a demonstrable relationship to successful performance."[120] The ruling in this case was subsequently applied to other hiring,

---

[120]*Griggs v. Duke Power Company*, 401 U.S. 424 (1971). See also Allan P. Sindler, *Bakke, DeFunis, and Minority Admissions: The Quest for Equal Opportunity* (New York: Longman, 1978), pp. 180–89.

promotion, and training programs.[121] In recent years, though, the Supreme Court has placed a number of limits on employment discrimination suits. In 2007, for example, in the case of *Ledbetter v. Goodyear Tire and Rubber Co.* the Court said that a complaint of gender discrimination must be brought within 180 days of the time the discrimination was alleged to have occurred.[122] This blocks suits based on events that might have taken place in the past.

Gender Discrimination   Title VII provided a valuable tool for the growing women's movement in the 1960s and 1970s.[123] In fact, in many ways the law fostered the growth of the women's movement. The first major campaign of the National Organization for Women (NOW) involved picketing the Equal Employment Opportunity Commission (EEOC) for its refusal to ban sex-segregated employment advertisements. NOW also sued *The New York Times* for continuing to publish such ads after the passage of Title VII. Another organization, the Women's Equity Action League (WEAL), pursued legal action on a wide range of sex discrimination issues, filing lawsuits against law schools and medical schools for their discriminatory admission policies, for example.

Building on these victories and the growth of the women's movement, feminist activists sought an equal rights amendment (ERA) to the Constitution. The proposed amendment was short: Its substantive passage stated that "equality of rights under the law shall not be denied or abridged by the United States or by any State on account of sex." The amendment's supporters believed that such a sweeping guarantee of equal rights was a necessary tool for ending all discrimination against women and for making gender roles more equal. Opponents charged that it would be socially disruptive and would introduce changes—such as coed restrooms—that most Americans did not want. The amendment easily passed Congress in 1972 and won quick approval in many state legislatures but fell three states short of the thirty-eight needed to ratify the amendment by the 1982 deadline for its ratification.[124]

Despite the failure of the ERA, gender discrimination expanded dramatically as an area of civil rights law. In the 1970s, the conservative Burger Court helped to establish gender discrimination as a major and highly visible civil rights issue. Although the Burger Court refused to treat gender discrimination as the equivalent of racial discrimination,[125] it did make it easier for plaintiffs to file and win suits on the basis of gender discrimination by applying an "intermediate" level of review to these cases.[126] This **intermediate scrutiny** is midway between traditional rules of evidence, which put the burden of proof on the plaintiff, and the doctrine of strict scrutiny, which requires the defendant to show not only that a particular classification is reasonable but also that there is a need or compelling interest for it. Intermediate

intermediate scrutiny The test used by the Supreme Court in gender discrimination cases. Intermediate scrutiny places the burden of proof partially on the government and partially on the challengers to show that the law in question is constitutional.

---

[121] For a good treatment of these issues, see Charles O. Gregory and Harold A. Katz, *Labor and the Law*, 3rd ed. (New York: Norton, 1979), chap. 17.

[122] *Ledbetter v. Goodyear Tire and Rubber Co.*, 05-1074 (2007).

[123] This and the next five sections are from Ginsberg et al., *We the People*.

[124] See Jane J. Mansbridge, *Why We Lost the ERA* (Chicago: University of Chicago Press, 1986); and Gilbert Steiner, *Constitutional Inequality* (Washington, D.C.: Brookings Institution, 1985).

[125] See *Frontiero v. Richardson*, 411 U.S. 677 (1973).

[126] See *Craig v. Boren*, 423 U.S. 1047 (1976).

scrutiny shifts the burden of proof partially onto the defendant, rather than leaving it entirely on the plaintiff.

One major step was taken in 1992, when the Court decided in *Franklin v. Gwinnett County Public Schools* that violations of Title IX of the 1972 Education Act could be remedied with monetary damages.[127] Title IX forbids gender discrimination in education, but it initially sparked little litigation because of its weak enforcement provisions. The Court's 1992 ruling opened the door for more legal action in the area of education. The greatest impact has been in the areas of sexual harassment—the subject of the *Franklin* case—and in equal treatment of women's athletic programs. The potential for monetary damages has made universities and public schools take the problem of sexual harassment more seriously. Colleges and universities have also started to pay more attention to women's athletic programs. In the two years after the *Franklin* case, complaints to the Education Department's Office for Civil Rights about unequal treatment of women's athletic programs nearly tripled. In several high-profile legal cases, some prominent universities have been ordered to create more women's sports programs; many other colleges and universities have begun to add more women's programs in order to avoid potential litigation.[128] In 1997, the Supreme Court refused to hear a petition by Brown University challenging a lower-court ruling that the university establish strict sex equity in its athletic programs. The Court's decision meant that in colleges and universities across the country, varsity athletic positions for men and women must reflect their overall enrollment numbers.[129]

In 1996, the Supreme Court made another important decision about gender and education by putting an end to all-male schools supported by public funds. It ruled that the Virginia Military Institute's policy of not admitting women was unconstitutional.[130] Along with the Citadel, an all-male military college in South Carolina, Virginia Military Institute (VMI) had never admitted women. It argued that the unique educational experience it offered, including intense physical training and the harsh treatment of freshmen, would be destroyed if women were admitted. The Court, however, ruled that the male-only policy denied "substantial equality" to women. Two days after the Court's ruling, the Citadel announced that it would accept women. VMI considered becoming a private institution in order to remain all-male, but in September 1996 the school board finally voted to admit women. The legal decisions may have removed formal barriers to entry, but the experience of the female cadets at these schools has not been easy. The first female cadet at the Citadel, Shannon Faulkner, won admission in 1995 under a federal court order but quit after four days. Although four women were admitted to the Citadel after the Supreme Court decision, two of them quit several months later. They charged harassment by male students, including attempts to set the female cadets on fire.[131]

---

[127] *Franklin v. Gwinnett County Public Schools*, 503 U.S. 60 (1992).

[128] Jennifer Halperin, "Women Step Up to Bat," *Illinois Issues* 21 (September 1995): 11–14.

[129] Joan Biskupic and David Nakamura, "Court Won't Review Sports Equity Ruling," *Washington Post*, 22 April 1997, p. A1.

[130] *United States v. Virginia*, 518 U.S. 515 (1996).

[131] Judith Havemann, "Two Women Quit Citadel over Alleged Harassment," *Washington Post*, 13 January 1997, p. A1.

Courts began to find sexual harassment a form of sex discrimination during the late 1970s. Although sexual harassment law applies to education, most of the law of sexual harassment has been developed by courts through interpretation of Title VII of the Civil Rights Act of 1964. In 1986, the Supreme Court recognized two forms of sexual harassment—the quid pro quo type, which involves sexual extortion, and the hostile-environment type, which involves sexual intimidation.[132] Employers and many employees have worried that hostile-environment sexual harassment is too ambiguous. When can an employee bring charges? When is the employer liable? In 1986, the Court said that sexual harassment may be legally actionable even if the employee did not suffer tangible economic or job-related losses in relation to it. And in 1993, the Court said that sexual harassment may be legally actionable even if the employee did not suffer tangible psychological costs as a result of it.[133] In two 1998 cases, the Court further strengthened the law when it said that whether or not sexual harassment results in economic harm to the employee, an employer is liable for the harassment if it was committed by someone with authority over the employee—by a supervisor, for example. But the Court also said that an employer may defend itself by showing that it had a sexual harassment prevention and grievance policy in effect.[134]

The development of gender discrimination as an important part of the civil rights struggle has coincided with the rise of women's politics as a discrete movement in American politics. As with the struggle for racial equality, the relationship between changes in government policies and political action suggests that changes in government policies to a great degree produce political action. Today the existence of a powerful women's movement derives in large measure from the enactment of Title VII of the Civil Rights Act of 1964 and from the Burger Court's vital steps in applying that law to the protection of women. The recognition of women's civil rights has become an issue that in many ways transcends the usual distinctions of American political debate. In the heavily partisan debate over the federal crime bill enacted in 1994, for instance, the section of the bill that enjoyed the widest support was the Violence against Women Act, whose most important feature was that it defined gender-biased violent crimes as a matter of civil rights and created a civil rights remedy for women who have been the victims of such crimes. But since the act was ruled unconstitutional by the Supreme Court in 2000, the struggle for women's rights will likely remain part of the political debate.

Latinos and Asian Americans The labels "Latino" or "Hispanic" and "Asian American" encompass a wide range of groups with diverse national origins, distinctive cultural identities, and particular experiences. For example, the early political experiences of Mexican Americans were shaped by race and region. In 1898, Mexican Americans were given formal political rights, including the right to vote. In many places, however, and especially in Texas, Mexican Americans were segregated and

---

[132] *Meritor Savings Bank v. Vinson* (1986).

[133] *Harris v. Forklift Systems*, 510 U.S. 17 (1993).

[134] *Burlington Industries v. Ellerth*, 524 U.S. 742 (1998); *Faragher v. City of Boca Raton*, 524 U.S. 775 (1998).

prevented from voting by such means as the white primary and the poll tax.[135] Region made a difference too. In contrast to the northeastern and midwestern cities in which most European immigrants settled, the Southwest did not have a tradition of ethnic mobilization associated with machine politics. Particularly after the political reforms enacted in the first decade of the twentieth century, city politics in the Southwest was dominated by a small group of white elites. In the countryside, when Mexican Americans participated in politics, it was often as part of a political organization dominated by a large white landowner, or *patron*.

The earliest independent Mexican American political organizations, the League of United Latin American Citizens (LULAC) and the American GI Forum, worked to stem discrimination against Mexican Americans in the years after World War II. By the late 1950s, the first Mexican American had been elected to Congress, and four others followed in the 1960s. In the late 1960s, a new kind of Mexican American political movement was born. Inspired by the black civil rights movement, Mexican American students launched boycotts of high-school classes in Los Angeles, Denver, and San Antonio. Students in colleges and universities across California joined in as well. Among their demands were bilingual education, an end to discrimination, and greater cultural recognition. In Crystal City, Texas, which had been dominated by Anglo politicians despite a population that was overwhelmingly Mexican American, the newly formed La Raza Unida party took over the city government.[136]

Since that time, Mexican American political strategy has developed along two tracks. One is a traditional ethnic-group path of voter registration and voting along ethnic lines. The second is a legal strategy using the various civil rights laws designed to ensure fair access to the political system. The Mexican American Legal Defense and Education Fund (MALDEF) has played a key role in designing and pursuing the latter strategy.

The early Asian experience in the United States was shaped by a series of naturalization laws dating back to 1790, the first of which declared that only white aliens were eligible for citizenship. Chinese immigrants had begun arriving in California in the 1850s, drawn by the boom of the gold rush. They were immediately met with hostility. The virulent antagonism toward Chinese immigrants in California led Congress in 1870 to declare Chinese immigrants ineligible for citizenship. In 1882, the first Chinese Exclusion Act suspended the entry of Chinese laborers.

At the time of the Exclusion Act, the Chinese community was composed predominantly of single male laborers, with few women and children. The few Chinese children in San Francisco were initially denied entry to the public schools; only after parents of American-born Chinese children pressed legal action were the children allowed to attend public school. Even then, however, they were made to attend a separate Chinese school. American-born Chinese children could not be

---

[135]New Mexico had a different history because not many Anglos settled there initially. (*Anglo* is the term for a non-Hispanic white of European background.) Mexican Americans had considerable power in territorial legislatures between 1865 and 1912. See Lawrence H. Fuchs, *The American Kaleidoscope* (Hanover, N.H.: University Press of New England, 1990), pp. 239–40.

[136]On the La Raza Unida party, see Carlos Muñoz Jr. and Mario Barrera, "La Raza Unida Party and the Chicano Student Movement in California," in *Latinos and the Political System*, ed. F. Chris Garcia (Notre Dame, Ind.: University of Notre Dame Press, 1988), pp. 213–35.

denied citizenship, however; this right was confirmed by the Supreme Court in 1898, when it ruled in *United States v. Wong Kim Ark* that anyone born in the United States was entitled to full citizenship.[137] Still, new Chinese immigrants were barred from the United States until 1943; China by then had become a key wartime ally, and Congress repealed the Chinese Exclusion Act and permitted Chinese residents to become citizens.

Immigration climbed rapidly after the 1965 Immigration and Nationality Services Act, which lifted discriminatory quotas. In spite of this and other developments, limited English proficiency barred many Asian Americans and Latinos from full participation in American life. Two developments in the 1970s, however, established rights for language minorities. In 1974, the Supreme Court ruled in *Lau v. Nichols,* a suit filed on behalf of Chinese students in San Francisco, that school districts have to provide education for students whose English is limited.[138] It did not mandate bilingual education, but it established a duty to provide instruction that students could understand. The 1970 amendments to the Voting Rights Act of 1965 permanently outlawed literacy tests in all fifty states and mandated bilingual ballots or oral assistance for those who speak Spanish, Chinese, Japanese, Korean, Native American languages, or Eskimo languages.

Asian Americans and Latinos have also been concerned about the impact of immigration laws on their civil rights. Many Asian American and Latino organizations opposed the Immigration Reform and Control Act of 1986 because it imposes sanctions on employers who hire undocumented workers. Such sanctions, they feared, would lead employers to discriminate against Latinos and Asian Americans. These suspicions were confirmed in a 1990 report by the General Accounting Office that found employer sanctions had created a "widespread pattern of discrimination" against Latinos and others who appear foreign.[139] Organizations such as MALDEF and the Asian Law Caucus monitor and challenge such discrimination. These groups have turned their attention to the rights of legal and illegal immigrants as anti-immigrant sentiment has grown in recent years.

The Supreme Court has ruled that illegal immigrants are eligible for education and medical care but can be denied other social benefits; legal immigrants are to be treated much the same as citizens. But growing immigration—including an estimated 300,000 illegal immigrants per year—and mounting economic insecurity have undermined these practices. Groups of voters across the country now strongly support drawing a sharper line between immigrants and citizens. Not surprisingly, the movement to deny benefits to noncitizens began in California, which experienced sharp economic distress in the early 1990s and has the highest levels of immigration of any state. In 1994, Californians voted in favor of Proposition 187, which denied illegal immigrants all services except emergency medical care. Supporters of the measure hoped to discourage illegal immigration and pressure illegal immigrants already in the country to leave. Opponents contended that denying basic services to illegal immigrants risked creating a subclass of residents in the United States whose lack of

---

[137] *United States v. Wong Kim Ark,* 169 U.S. 649 (1898).

[138] *Lau v. Nichols,* 414 U.S. 563 (1974).

[139] Dick Kirschten, "Not Black and White," *National Journal,* 2 March 1991, p. 497.

education and poor health would threaten all Americans. In 1994 and 1997, a federal court declared most of Proposition 187 unconstitutional, affirming previous rulings that illegal immigrants should be granted public education.

The question of the rights of legal immigrants points to an even tougher problem. Congress has the power to deny public benefits to this group, but doing so would go against long-standing traditions in American political culture. Legal immigrants have traditionally enjoyed most of the rights and obligations of citizens (such as paying taxes). As the constitutional scholar Alexander Bickel points out, the Constitution begins with "We the People of the United States"; likewise the Bill of Rights refers to the rights of *people*, not the rights of citizens. These issues were at the fore in 2007 when Congress debated comprehensive new immigration laws that promised to legalize the status of some illegal immigrants. These proposals ultimately failed to be enacted by the Congress when opponents argued that they rewarded illegal immigrants for breaking the law.

Native Americans   The political status of Native Americans was left unclear in the Constitution. But by the early 1800s, the courts had defined each of the Indian tribes as a nation. As members of an Indian nation, Native Americans were noncitizens of the United States until 1924, when congressional legislation granted citizenship to those who were born in the United States. A variety of changes in federal policy toward Native Americans during the 1930s paved the way for a later resurgence of their political power. Most important was the federal decision to encourage Native Americans on reservations to establish local self-government.[140]

The Native American political movement gathered force in the 1960s as Indians began to use protest, litigation, and assertion of tribal rights to improve their situation. In 1968, Dennis Banks co-founded the American Indian Movement (AIM), the most prominent Native American protest organization. AIM won national attention in 1969 when 200 of its members, representing twenty tribes, took over the famous prison island of Alcatraz in San Francisco Bay, claiming it for Native Americans. In 1973, AIM members took over the town of Wounded Knee, South Dakota, the site of the massacre of over 200 Sioux men, women, and children by the U.S. Army in December 1890. The federal government responded with the Indian Self-determination and Education Assistance Act (1975), which began to give Indians more control over their own land.[141]

As a language minority, Native Americans were also affected by the 1975 amendments to the Voting Rights Act and the *Lau* decision, which established the right of Native Americans to be taught in their own languages. This ruling marked quite a change from the boarding schools once run by the Bureau of Indian Affairs, at which members of Indian tribes were forbidden to speak their own languages. Native Americans have also sought to expand their rights on the basis of

---

[140]Not all Indian tribes agreed with this, including the Navajos. See Ronald Takaki, *A Different Mirror: A History of Multicultural America* (Boston: Little, Brown, 1993), pp. 238–48.

[141]On the resurgence of Indian political activity, see Stephen Cornell, *The Return of the Native: American Indian Political Resurgence* (New York: Oxford University Press, 1990); and Dee Brown, *Bury My Heart at Wounded Knee* (New York: Holt, 1971).

their sovereign status. Since the 1920s and 1930s, Native American tribes have sued the federal government for illegally seizing land, seeking monetary reparations and land as damages. Both types of damages have been awarded in such suits, but only in small amounts. Native American tribes have been more successful in winning federal recognition of their sovereignty. Sovereign status has, in turn, allowed them to exercise greater self-determination. Most significant economically was a 1987 Supreme Court decision that freed Native American tribes from most state regulations prohibiting gambling.[142] The establishment of casino gambling on Native American lands has brought a substantial flow of new income into desperately poor reservations.

Americans with Disabilities   The concept of rights for people with disabilities began to emerge in the 1970s as the civil rights model spread to other groups. The seed was planted in a little-noticed provision of the 1973 Rehabilitation Act that outlawed discrimination against individuals on the basis of disabilities. As in many other cases, the law itself helped give rise to the movement demanding rights.[143] Modeling itself on the NAACP's Legal Defense Fund, the disability movement founded a Disability Rights Education and Defense Fund to press its legal claims. The movement achieved its greatest success with the passage of the Americans with Disabilities Act (ADA) of 1990, which guarantees the disabled equal employment rights and access to public businesses. Claims of discrimination in violation of this act are considered by the EEOC. The impact of the law has been far-reaching as businesses and public facilities have installed ramps, elevators, and other devices to meet its requirements.[144]

In 1998, the Supreme Court interpreted the ADA to apply to people with HIV. Until then, ADA was interpreted as applying to people with AIDS but not people with HIV. The case arose when a dentist was asked to fill a cavity for a woman with HIV; he would do it only if the procedure was done in a hospital setting. The woman sued, and her complaint was that HIV had already disabled her because it was discouraging her from having children. (The act prohibits discrimination in employment, housing, and health care.) Although there have been widespread concerns that the ADA was being expanded too broadly and the costs were becoming too burdensome, corporate America did not seem to be disturbed by the Court's ruling. Stephen Bokat, general counsel of the U.S. Chamber of Commerce, said businesses in general had already been accommodating people with HIV as well as those with AIDS and the case presented no serious problem.[145]

---

[142]*California v. Cabazon Band of Mission Indians*, 480 U.S. 202 (1987).

[143]See the discussion in Robert A. Katzmann, *Institutional Disability: The Saga of Transportation Policy for the Disabled* (Washington, D.C.: Brookings Institution, 1986).

[144]For example, after pressure from the Justice Department, one of the nation's largest rental-car companies agreed to make special hand controls available to any customer requesting them. See "Avis Agrees to Equip Cars for Disabled," *Los Angeles Times*, 2 September 1994, p. D1.

[145]The case and the interview with Stephen Bokat were reported in Margaret Warner, "Expanding Coverage: Defining Disability," *Online NewsHour*, 30 June 1998 (www.pbs.org/newshour/bb/law/jan-june98/hiv_6-30.html).

The Aged   The 1967 federal Age Discrimination in Employment Act (ADEA) makes age discrimination illegal when practiced by employers with at least twenty employees. Many states have added to the federal provisions with their own age discrimination laws, and some of the state laws are stronger than the federal provisions. The major lobbyist for seniors, AARP (formerly the American Association of Retired Persons), with its claim to more than 30 million members, has been active in keeping these laws on the books and making sure they are vigorously implemented.

Gays and Lesbians   In less than thirty years, the gay movement has become one of the largest civil rights movements in contemporary America. Beginning with street protests in the 1960s, it has grown into a well-financed and sophisticated lobby. The Human Rights Campaign is the primary national PAC focused on gay rights; it provides campaign financing and volunteers to work for candidates endorsed by the group. The movement has also formed legal rights organizations, including the Lambda Legal Defense and Education Fund.

Gay rights drew national attention in 1993, when President Bill Clinton confronted the question of whether gays should be allowed to serve in the military. As a candidate, Clinton had said he favored lifting the ban on homosexuals in the military. The issue set off a huge controversy in the first months of his presidency. After nearly a year of deliberation, the administration enunciated a compromise: its "don't ask, don't tell" policy, which allows gays and lesbians to serve in the military as long as they do not openly proclaim their sexual orientation or engage in homosexual activity. The administration maintained that the ruling would protect gay men and lesbians from witch-hunting investigations, but many gay advocates expressed disappointment, charging the president with reneging on his campaign promise.

But until 1996, there was no Supreme Court ruling or national legislation explicitly protecting gays and lesbians from discrimination. The first gay rights case that the Court decided, *Bowers v. Hardwick* (1986), ruled against a right to privacy that would protect consensual homosexual activity. After the *Bowers* decision, the gay rights movement sought suitable legal cases to test the constitutionality of discrimination against gays and lesbians, much as the civil rights movement had done in the late 1940s and 1950s. As one advocate put it, "lesbians and gay men are looking for their *Brown v. Board of Education*."[146] Among the cases tested were those stemming from local ordinances restricting gay rights (including the right to marry), job discrimination, and family-law issues such as adoption and parental rights. In 1996, in *Romer v. Evans*, the Supreme Court explicitly extended fundamental civil rights protections to gays and lesbians by declaring unconstitutional a 1992 amendment to the Colorado state constitution that prohibited local governments from passing ordinances to protect gay rights.[147] The decision's forceful language highlighted the connection between gay rights and civil rights as it declared discrimination against gay people unconstitutional.

---

[146]Quoted in Joan Biskupic, "Gay Rights Activists Seek a Supreme Court Test Case," *Washington Post*, 19 December 1993, p. A1.

[147]*Romer v. Evans*, 517 U.S. 620 (1996).

In *Lawrence v. Texas* (2003), the Court overturned *Bowers* and struck down a Texas statute criminalizing certain intimate sexual conduct between consenting partners of the same sex.[148] A victory for lesbians and gay men every bit as significant as *Roe v. Wade* was for women, *Lawrence v. Texas* extends at least one aspect of civil liberties to sexual minorities: the right to privacy. However, this decision by itself does not undo the various exclusions that deprive lesbians and gay men of full civil rights, including the right to marry, which became a hot-button issue.

Early in 2004, the Supreme Judicial Court of Massachusetts ruled that under that state's constitution same-sex couples were entitled to marry. The state senate then requested the court to rule on whether a civil-union statute (avoiding the word *marriage*) would, as it did in Vermont, satisfy the court's ruling, in response to which the court ruled negatively, asserting that civil unions are too much like the "separate but equal" doctrine that maintained legalized racial segregation from 1896 to 1954. In San Francisco, meanwhile, hundreds of gay men and lesbians responded to the opportunity provided by the mayor, who had directed the city clerk to issue marriage licenses to same-sex couples in defiance of California law. At the same time, signs indicated that Massachusetts might move toward a state constitutional amendment that would ban gay unions by whatever name. Voters in Missouri and Louisiana approved a ban on same-sex marriages, joining Alaska, Hawaii, Nebraska, and Nevada in implementing such a ban. Voters in eleven other states approved similar bans in the November 2004 elections.

Affirmative Action

The politics of rights not only spread to increasing numbers of groups in the society but also expanded its goal. The relatively narrow goal of equalizing opportunity by eliminating discriminatory barriers had been developing toward the far broader goal of *affirmative action*—compensatory action to overcome the consequences of past discrimination and encourage greater diversity. An affirmative action policy tends to involve two novel approaches: (1) positive or benign discrimination in which race or some other status is taken into account, but for compensatory action rather than mistreatment, and (2) compensatory action to favor members of the disadvantaged group who themselves may never have been the victims of discrimination. Quotas may be—but are not necessarily—involved in affirmative action policies.

In 1965, President Lyndon Johnson attempted to inaugurate affirmative action by executive orders directing agency heads and personnel officers to pursue vigorously a policy of minority employment in the federal civil service and in companies doing business with the national government. But affirmative action did not become a prominent goal until the 1970s.

The Supreme Court and the Burden of Proof As this movement spread, it began to divide civil rights activists and their supporters. The whole issue of qualification versus minority preference was addressed in the case of Allan Bakke. Bakke, a

affirmative action A policy or program designed to redress historic injustices committed against specific groups by making special efforts to provide members of these groups with access to educational and employment opportunities.

ONLINE READING

---

[148] *Lawrence and Garner v. Texas*, 539 U.S. 558 (2003).

white man with no minority affiliation, brought suit against the University of California Medical School at Davis on the grounds that in denying him admission the school had discriminated against him on the basis of his race (that year the school had reserved 16 of 100 available slots for minority applicants). He argued that his grades and test scores had ranked him well above many students who had been accepted at the school and that the only possible explanation for his rejection was that the others were black or Hispanic and he was white. In 1978, Bakke won his case before the Supreme Court and was admitted to the medical school, but he did not succeed in getting affirmative action declared unconstitutional. The Court rejected the procedures at the University of California because its medical school had used both a quota *and* a separate admissions system for minorities. The Court agreed with Bakke's argument that racial categorizations are suspect categories that place a severe burden of proof on those using them to show a "compelling public purpose." The Court went on to say that achieving "a diverse student body" was such a public purpose, but the method of a rigid quota of student slots assigned on the basis of race was incompatible with the equal protection clause. Thus the Court permitted universities (and other schools, training programs, and hiring authorities) to continue to take minority status into consideration but limited severely the use of quotas to situations in which previous discrimination had been shown and the quotas were used more as a guideline for social diversity than as a mathematically defined ratio.[149]

For nearly a decade after *Bakke,* the Supreme Court was tentative and permissive about efforts by corporations and governments to experiment with affirmative action programs in employment.[150] But in 1989, the Court returned to the *Bakke* position, ruling that any "rigid numerical quota" is suspect. In *Wards Cove v. Atonio,* the Court further weakened affirmative action by easing the way for employers to prefer white men, holding that the burden of proof of unlawful discrimination should be shifted from the defendant (the employer) to the plaintiff (the person claiming to be the victim of discrimination).[151] This decision virtually overruled the Court's prior holding.[152] That same year, the Court ruled that any affirmative action program already approved by federal courts could be challenged by white men who alleged that the program discriminated against them.[153]

In 1995, the Supreme Court's ruling in *Adarand Constructors v. Pena* further weakened affirmative action. This decision stated that race-based policies, such as preferences given by the government to minority contractors, must survive strict scrutiny, placing the burden on the government to show that such affirmative action programs serve a compelling government interest and are narrowly tailored to address identifiable past discrimination.[154] President Clinton responded to the *Adarand*

[149] *Regents of the University of California v. Bakke,* 438 U.S. 265 (1978).

[150] *United Steelworkers of America v. Weber,* 443 U.S. 193 (1979), and *Fullilove v. Klutznick,* 448 U.S. 448 (1980).

[151] *Wards Cove Packing Company v. Atonio,* 490 U.S. 642 (1989).

[152] *Griggs v. Duke Power Company* (1971).

[153] *Martin v. Wilks,* 490 U.S. 755 (1989).

[154] *Adarand Constructors v. Pena,* 515 U.S. 200 (1995).

decision by ordering a review of all government affirmative action policies and practices. Although many observers suspected that the president would use the review as an opportunity to back away from affirmative action, the conclusions of the task force largely defended existing policies. Reflecting the influence of the Supreme Court's decision in *Adarand*, President Clinton acknowledged that some government policies would need to change. But on the whole, the review found that most affirmative action policies were fair and did not "unduly burden nonbeneficiaries."[155]

Although Clinton sought to "mend, not end" affirmative action, developments in the courts and the states continued to restrict it in important ways. One of the most significant was the *Hopwood* case, in which white students challenged admissions practices at the University of Texas Law School, charging that the school's affirmative action program discriminated against whites. In 1996, a federal court ruling on the case (the U.S. Court of Appeals for the Fifth Circuit) stated that race could never be considered in granting admissions and scholarships at state colleges and universities.[156] This decision effectively rolled back the use of affirmative action permitted by the 1978 *Bakke* case. In *Bakke,* as noted earlier, the Supreme Court had outlawed quotas but said that race could be used as one factor among many in admissions decisions. Many universities and colleges have since justified affirmative action as a way of promoting racial diversity among their student bodies. What was new in the *Hopwood* decision was the ruling that race could *never* be used as a factor in admissions decisions, even to promote diversity.

In 1996, the Supreme Court refused to hear a challenge to the *Hopwood* case. This meant that its ruling remains in effect in the states covered by the Fifth Circuit— Texas, Louisiana, and Mississippi—but does not apply to the rest of the country. The impact of the *Hopwood* ruling is greatest in Texas because Louisiana and Mississippi are under conflicting court orders to desegregate their universities. In Texas in the year after the *Hopwood* case, minority applications to state universities declined. Concerned about the ability of Texas public universities to serve the state's minority students, the Texas legislature quickly passed a new law granting students who graduate in the top 10 percent of their class automatic admission to the state's public universities. State officials hoped that this measure would ensure a racially diverse student body.[157]

The weakening of affirmative action in the courts was underscored in a case the Supreme Court agreed to hear in 1998. A white schoolteacher in New Jersey who had lost her job had sued her school district, charging that her layoff was racially motivated: A black colleague hired on the same day was not laid off. Under former president George H. W. Bush, the Justice Department had filed a brief on her behalf in 1989, but in 1994 the Clinton administration formally reversed course in a new brief supporting the school district's right to make distinctions based on race as long as they did not involve the use of quotas. Three years later, the adminis-

---

[155] Ann Devroy, "Clinton Study Backs Affirmative Action," *Washington Post,* 19 July 1995, p. A1.

[156] *Hopwood v. State of Texas,* 78 F. 3d 932 (Fifth Cir., 1996).

[157] See Lydia Lum, "Applications by Minorities Down Sharply," *Houston Chronicle,* 8 April 1997, p. A1; R. G. Ratcliffe, "Senate Approves Bill Designed to Boost Minority Enrollments," *Houston Chronicle,* 8 May 1997, p. A1.

tration, worried that the case was weak and could result in a broad decision against affirmative action, reversed course again and filed a brief with the Court urging a narrow ruling in favor of the dismissed worker. Because the school board had justified its actions on the grounds of preserving diversity, the administration feared that a broad ruling by the Supreme Court could totally prohibit the use of race in employment decisions, even as one factor among many designed to achieve diversity. But before the Court could issue a ruling, a coalition of civil rights groups brokered and arranged to pay for a settlement. This unusual move reflected the widespread fear of a sweeping negative decision. Cases involving dismissals, as the New Jersey case did, are generally viewed as much more difficult to defend than cases that concern hiring. In addition, the particular facts of the New Jersey case—two equally qualified teachers hired on the same day—were seen as unusual and unfavorable to affirmative action.[158]

This betwixt and between status of affirmative action was where things stood in 2003, when the Supreme Court took two cases against the University of Michigan that were virtually certain to clarify, if not put closure on, affirmative action. The first suit, *Gratz v. Bollinger,* alleged that by using a point-based ranking system that automatically awarded 20 points (out of 150) to African American, Latino, and Native American applicants, the university's undergraduate admissions policy discriminated unconstitutionally against white students with otherwise equal or superior academic qualifications. The Supreme Court agreed, 6–3, arguing that something tantamount to a quota was involved because undergraduate admissions lacked the necessary "individualized consideration," employing instead a "mechanical one," based too much on the favorable minority points.[159] The Court's ruling in *Gratz v. Bollinger* was not surprising, given *Bakke's* holding against quotas and recent decisions calling for strict scrutiny of all racial classifications, even those that are intended to remedy past discrimination or promote future equality.

The second case, *Grutter v. Bollinger,* broke new ground. Barbara Grutter sued the University of Michigan Law School on the grounds that it had discriminated in a race-conscious way against white applicants with grades and law boards equal or superior to those of minority applicants. A precarious vote of 5–4 aligned the majority of the Supreme Court with Justice Lewis Powell's opinion in *Bakke* for the first time. In *Bakke,* Powell had argued that diversity in education is a compelling state interest and that constitutionally race could be considered a positive factor in admissions decisions. In *Grutter,* the Court reiterated Powell's holding and, applying strict scrutiny to the law school's policy, found that its admissions process was narrowly tailored to the school's compelling state interest in diversity because it gave a "highly individualized, holistic review of each applicant's file," in which race counted but was not used in a "mechanical way."[160]

---

[158]Linda Greenhouse, "Settlement Ends High Court Case on Preferences," *New York Times,* 22 November 1997, p. A1; Barry Bearak, "Rights Groups Ducked a Fight, Opponents Say," *New York Times,* 22 November 1997, p. A1.

[159]*Gratz v. Bollinger,* 539 U.S. 244 (2003).

[160]*Grutter v. Bollinger,* 539 U.S. 306 (2003).

ONLINE READING

Throughout the 1990s, federal courts, including the Supreme Court, had subjected public affirmative action programs to strict scrutiny to invalidate them. *Adarand Constructors v. Pena* (1995) definitively established the Supreme Court's view that constitutionally permissible use of race must serve a compelling state interest. Between *Korematsu v. United States* (1944)[161] and *Grutter*, no consideration of race had survived strict scrutiny. Such affirmative action plans that had survived constitutional review did so before 1995, under a lower standard of review, one reserved for policies intended to remedy racial injustice. For affirmative action to survive under the post-1995 judicial paradigm, the Court needed to find that sometimes racial categories can be deployed to serve a compelling state interest. That the Court found exactly this in *Grutter* puts affirmative action on stronger ground—at least if its specific procedures pass the Supreme Court's muster and until the Court's majority changes.

Policy Principle

Individual challenges in the courts as well as several state and local referenda have weakened affirmative action.

Referendums on Affirmative Action   The courts have not been the only center of action: Challenges to affirmative action have also emerged in state and local politics, in the form of ballot initiatives or referendums that ask voters to decide the issue. One of the most significant state actions was the passage of the California Civil Rights Initiative, also known as Proposition 209, in 1996. Proposition 209 outlawed affirmative action programs in the state and local governments of California, thus prohibiting state and local governments from using race or gender preferences in their decisions about hiring, contracting, and university admissions. The political battle over Proposition 209 was heated, and supporters and defenders took to the streets and airwaves to make their case. When the referendum was held, the measure passed with 54 percent of the vote, including 27 percent of the black vote, 30 percent of the Latino vote, and 45 percent of the Asian American vote.[162] In 1997, the Supreme Court refused to hear a challenge to the new law.

Many observers predicted that the success of California's ban on affirmative action would provoke similar movements in states and localities across the country. But the political factors that contributed to the success of Proposition 209 in California may not exist in many other states. Winning a controversial state referendum takes leadership and lots of money. The popular California Republican governor Pete Wilson led with a strong anti–affirmative action stand (favoring Proposition 209), and his campaign had a lot of money for advertising. But similar conditions did not exist elsewhere. Few prominent Republican leaders in other states were willing to come forward to lead the anti–affirmative action campaign. Moreover, the outcome of any referendum, especially a complicated and controversial one, depends greatly on how the issue is drafted and placed on the ballot. California's Proposition 209 was framed as a civil rights initiative: "The state shall not discriminate against, or grant preferential treatment to, any individual or group on the basis of race, sex, color, ethnicity, or national origin." Different wording can produce quite different outcomes, as a 1997 vote on affirmative action in Houston revealed. There the ballot

---

[161] *Korematsu v. United States*, 323 U.S. 214 (1944).

[162] Michael A. Fletcher, "Opponents of Affirmative Action Heartened by Court Decision," *Washington Post*, 13 April 1997, p. A21.

initiative asked voters whether they wanted to ban affirmative action in city contracting and hiring, not whether they wanted to end preferential treatment. In that city, 55 percent of voters decided in favor of affirmative action.[163]

SUMMARY

Civil liberties and *civil rights* are different phenomena and have to be treated legally and constitutionally in different ways. We have defined *civil liberties* as that sphere of individual freedom of choice created by restraints on governmental power. When the Constitution was ratified, it was already seen as inadequate in the provision of protections of individual freedom and required the addition of the Bill of Rights. The Bill of Rights explicitly placed a whole series of restraints on government. Some of these were *substantive*, regarding *what* government could do, and some were *procedural*, regarding *how* the government was permitted to act. We call the rights in the Bill of Rights civil liberties because they are rights to be free from arbitrary government interference.

But *which* government? This question was settled in the *Barron* case in 1833, when the Supreme Court held that the restraints in the Bill of Rights were applicable only to the national government and not to the states. The Court was recognizing "dual citizenship." At the time of its adoption, in 1868, the Fourteenth Amendment was considered by many a deliberate effort to reverse *Barron*, put an end to dual citizenship, and nationalize the Bill of Rights, applying its restrictions to state governments as well as the national government. But the post–Civil War Supreme Court interpreted the Fourteenth Amendment otherwise. Dual citizenship remained almost as it had been before the war, and the shadow of *Barron* extended across the rest of the nineteenth century and well into the twentieth. The slow process of nationalizing the Bill of Rights began in the 1920s, when the Supreme Court recognized that at least the restraints of the First Amendment had been "incorporated" into the Fourteenth Amendment as restraints on the state governments. But it was not until the 1960s that most of the civil liberties in the Bill of Rights were incorporated into the Fourteenth Amendment. Almost exactly a century after the adoption of that amendment, the Bill of Rights was nationalized. All citizens now enjoy close to the same civil liberties regardless of the state in which they reside.

As for the second aspect of protection of the individual, *civil rights*, stress has been put on the expansion of governmental power rather than restraints on it. If the constitutional base of civil liberties is the due process clause of the Fourteenth Amendment, the constitutional base of civil rights is the equal protection clause. This clause imposes a positive obligation on government to advance civil rights, and its original motivation seems to have been to eliminate the gross injustices suffered by African Americans. But as with civil liberties, there was little advancement in the

---

[163]See Sam Howe Verhovek, "Houston Vote Underlined Complexity of Rights Issue," *New York Times*, 6 November 1997, p. A1.

 Rationality Principle	 Collective-Action Principle	 Institution Principle	 Policy Principle	 History Principle
Madison believed a bill of rights would remove a potential source of opposition to the new government.	The courts recognize the importance of collective action and have developed rules to protect speech that promotes collective political action. Given the massive resistance to the 1954 *Brown* decision, the civil rights movement required large, well-organized protests. People participated in the civil rights movement for experiential as well as instrumental purposes. Enforcement of civil rights law required courts and legislatures to work together.	Dual citizenship meant that the Bill of Rights did not apply to decisions or procedures of state governments. Most of the important provisions of the Bill of Rights were nationalized by the Supreme Court during the 1960s. Constitutional checks and balances give Congress the power to override Supreme Court decisions. The 1954 *Brown* decision altered the constitutional framework by giving the national government the power to intervene to prevent discriminatory actions by state and local governments and some aspects of the private sector.	Individual challenges in the courts as well as several state and local referenda have weakened affirmative action.	Dual citizenship was upheld by the Supreme Court for nearly a century after *Barron v. Baltimore* (1833). Once a case is decided by the Supreme Court, its implications persist for decades. The precedent established in *Brown* has shaped and guided court decisions, legislation, and other political action related to civil rights since 1954.

interpretation or application of the equal protection clause until after World War II. The major breakthrough came in 1954, with *Brown v. Board of Education,* and advancements came in fits and starts during the succeeding ten years.

After 1964, Congress finally supported the federal courts with effective civil rights legislation that outlawed a number of discriminatory practices in the private sector and provided for the withholding of federal grants-in-aid to any local government, school, or private employer as a sanction to help enforce the civil rights laws. From that point, civil rights developed in two ways. First, the definition of civil rights was expanded to include victims of discrimination other than African Americans. Second, the definition of civil rights became increasingly positive; affirmative action has become an official term. Judicial decisions, congressional statutes, and actions of administrative agencies all have moved beyond the original goal of eliminating discrimination toward the creation of new opportunities for minorities and, in some areas, the compensation of today's minorities for the consequences of discriminatory actions against members of their group in the past. Because compensatory civil rights action has sometimes relied on quotas, there has been intense debate over the constitutionality, as well as the desirability, of affirmative action.

The story has not ended and is not likely to end. The politics of rights will remain an important part of American political discourse.

FOR FURTHER READING

Ackerman, Bruce. *Before the Next Attack: Preserving Civil Liberties in an Age of Terrorism*. New Haven, Conn.: Yale University Press, 2006.

Baer, Judith, and Leslie Goldstein. *The Constitutional and Legal Rights of Women*. Los Angeles: Roxbury, 2006.

Drake, W. Avon, and Robert D. Holsworth. *Affirmative Action and the Stalled Quest for Black Progress*. Urbana: University of Illinois Press, 1996.

Dworkin, Ronald. *Justice in Robes*. Cambridge, Mass.: Belknap Press, 2006.

Garrow, David J. *Bearing the Cross: Martin Luther King, Jr., and the Southern Christian Leadership Conference: A Personal Portrait*. New York: Morrow, 1986.

Gerstmann, Evan. *Same-Sex Marriage and the Constitution*. New York: Cambridge University Press, 2004.

Glendon, Mary Ann. *Rights Talk: The Impoverishment of Political Discourse*. New York: Free Press, 1991.

Greenberg, Jack. *Crusaders in the Courts: How a Dedicated Band of Lawyers Fought for the Civil Rights Revolution*. New York: Basic Books, 1994.

Jackson, Thomas. *From Civil Rights to Human Rights*. Philadelphia: University of Pennsylvania Press, 2006.

Klarman, Michael. *From Jim Crow to Civil Rights: The Supreme Court and the Struggle for Racial Equality*. New York: Oxford University Press, 2004.

Levy, Leonard W. *Freedom of Speech and Press in Early America: Legacy of Suppression*. New York: Harper & Row, 1963.

Lewis, Anthony. *Gideon's Trumpet*. New York: Random House, 1964.

Meltsner, Michael. *The Making of a Civil Rights Lawyer*. Charlottesville: University of Virginia Press, 2006.

ONLINE READING ○ Posner, Richard. *Not a Suicide Pact: The Constitution in a Time of National Emergency*. New York: Oxford University Press, 2006.

Rosenberg, Gerald N. *The Hollow Hope: Can Courts Bring About Social Change?* Chicago: University of Chicago Press, 1991.

Thernstrom, Abigail M. *Whose Votes Count? Affirmative Action and Minority Voting Rights*. Cambridge, Mass.: Harvard University Press, 1987.

ONLINE READING ○ Tushnet, Mark, and Michael Olivas. *Colored Men and Hombres Aqui: Hernandez v. Texas and the Emergence of Mexican American Lawyering*. Houston: Arte Publico Press, 2006.

What are the limits of our freedoms and civil liberties in a time of war? Since September 11, this has been a crucial issue animating debates between the Bush administration, members of Congress, civil libertarians, and the courts.

In the case of domestic surveillance, the Bush administration argues that the demands of national security require that all records of the program—even the computers used by defense counsel—must be in the control of the executive branch. This means that in lawsuits involving wiretapping the Justice Department controls certain procedures, overriding traditional legal rights. But the rationality principle reminds us that those arguing for and against the administration's position may be doing so for reasons other than high-minded constitutional and national security concerns.

Conservatives have long argued that the courts have leaned too far in the direction of the rights of defendants. By stating that the Justice Department should have exclusive control of domestic surveillance records, the administration's position strengthens the hand of the executive branch relative to judges and defense lawyers. On the other side, the ACLU (among others) argues that the administration's position violates citizens' rights. The ACLU has emphasized the independence of the judicial branch in this case—a legitimate constitutional concern, but the ACLU also stands to benefit by establishing a common interest with judges.

The fight over the domestic surveillance program and similar programs instituted after September 11 is essentially a dispute over the history principle. What guides our current understanding of individual freedoms? Is it the path of an increasingly open government that we have followed over the past fifty years? Or has the war on terror moved us onto a completely new historical path, where freedom must be tempered by a concern for security and safety?

The New York Times, January 26, 2007

Secrecy Is at Issue in Suits Opposing Spy Program

By Adam Liptak

The Bush administration has employed extraordinary secrecy in defending the National Security Agency's highly classified domestic surveillance program from civil lawsuits. Plaintiffs and judges' clerks cannot see its secret filings. Judges have to make appointments to review them and are not allowed to keep copies.

Judges have even been instructed to use computers provided by the Justice Department to compose their decisions.

But now the procedures have started to meet resistance. At a private meeting with the lawyers in one of the cases this month, the judges who will hear the first appeal next week expressed uneasiness about the procedures, said a lawyer who attended, Ann Beeson of the American Civil Liberties Union.

Lawyers suing the government and some legal scholars say the procedures threaten the separation of powers, the adversary system and the lawyer-client privilege.

Justice Department officials say the circumstances of the cases, involving a highly classified program, require extraordinary measures. The officials say they have used similar procedures in other cases involving classified materials.

In ordinary civil suits, the parties' submissions are sent to their adversaries and are available to the public in open court files. But in several cases challenging the eavesdropping, Justice Department lawyers have been submitting legal papers not by filing them in court but by placing them in a room at the department. They have filed papers, in other words, with themselves.

At the meeting this month, judges on the United States Court of Appeals for the Sixth Circuit asked how the procedures might affect the integrity of the files and the appellate records.

In response, * * * a Justice Department official submitted * * * a * * * statement last Friday defending the practices.

"The documents reviewed by the court have not been altered and will not be altered," she wrote, and they "will be preserved securely as part of the record of this case."

Some cases challenging the program, which monitored international communications of people in the United States without court approval, have also involved atypical maneuvering. Soon after one suit challenging the program was filed last year in Oregon, Justice Department lawyers threatened to seize an exhibit from the court file.

This month, in the same case, the department sought to inspect and delete files from the computers on which lawyers for the plaintiffs had prepared their legal filings.

The tactics, said a lawyer in the Oregon case, prompted him to conduct unusual research.

"Sometime during all of this," he said, "I went on Amazon and ordered a copy of Kafka's 'The Trial,' because I needed a refresher course in bizarre legal procedures."

A federal district judge in the case invoked another book after a government lawyer refused to disclose whether he had a certain security clearance, saying information about the clearance was itself classified.

"Frankly, your response," the judge said, "is kind of an Alice in Wonderland response."

Questions about the secret filings may figure in the first appellate argument in the challenges. The judges who will hear the appeal met with lawyers for the Justice Department and the American Civil Liberties Union.

"The court raised questions about the procedures the government had used to file classified submissions in the case and the propriety and integrity of those procedures," said Ms. Beeson, associate legal director of the A.C.L.U. * * *

"They were also concerned about the independence of the judiciary," given that "the Justice Department retains custody and total control over the court filings." Ms. Beeson said.

Nancy S. Marder, * * * an authority on secrecy in litigation, said the tactics were really extreme and deeply, deeply troubling.

"These are the basics that we take for granted in our court system," Professor Marder said. "You have two parties. You

Institution Principle

The right to independent counsel is a fundamental part of our justice system. The Bush Administration argued that the interests of national security can override these rights.

Collective-Action Principle

The interests of the ACLU and the courts align nicely. Whether or not they support domestic surveillance in principle, both can agree that it is important to maintain an independent judiciary.

exchange documents. The documents you've seen don't disappear."

A spokesman for the Justice Department * * * said employees involved in storing the classified documents were independent of the litigators and provided "neutral assistance" to courts in handling sensitive information. The documents, Mr. Boyd said, are "stored securely and without alteration."

The appellate argument in Cincinnati will almost certainly also concern the effects of the administration announcement last week that it would submit the program to a secret court, ending its eavesdropping without warrants.

In a brief filed on Thursday, the government said the move made the case against the program moot.

Ms. Beeson of the A.C.L.U. said the government was wrong.

At least one case, the one in Oregon, is probably not moot. It goes beyond the other cases in seeking damages from the government, because the plaintiffs say they have seen proof that they were wiretapped without a warrant.

In August 2004, the Treasury Department's Office of Foreign Assets Control, which was investigating an Oregon charity, al-Haramain Islamic Foundation, inadvertently provided a copy of a classified document to a foundation lawyer, Lynne Bernabei.

That document indicated, according to court filings, that the government monitored communications between officers of the charity and two of its lawyers without a warrant in spring 2004.

"If I gave you this document today and you put it on the front page of The New York Times, it would not threaten national security," Mr. Eisenberg, a lawyer for the foundation, said. "There is only one thing about it that's explosive, and that's the fact that our clients were wiretapped."

* * *

In February 2006, the charity and the two lawyers who say they were wiretapped sued to stop the program, requesting financial damages. They attached a copy of the classified document, filing it under seal. They have not said how they came to have a copy.

Three weeks later, the lawyers for the foundation received a call from two Justice Department lawyers. The classified document "had not been properly secured," the lawyers said, according to a letter from the plaintiffs' lawyers to the judge.

As Mr. Eisenberg recalled it, the government lawyers said, "The F.B.I. is on its way to the courthouse to take possession of the document from the judge."

But Judge King, at a hurriedly convened hearing, would not yield it, and asked, "What if I say I will not deliver it to the F.B.I.?"

A Justice Department lawyer, Anthony J. Coppolino, gave a measured response, saying: "Your Honor, we obviously don't want to have any kind of a confrontation with you. But it has to be secured in a proper fashion."

The document was ultimately deposited in a "secure compartmented information facility" at the bureau office in Portland.

* * *

Policy Principle

The Justice Department believed that they had crafted a policy that satisfied the preferences of all the players. Their program honored a defendant's right to counsel and maintained separation of powers, yet still protected secret documents.

Part Two | Institutions

5

Congress: The First Branch

THE U.S. CONGRESS is the "first branch" of government under Article I of our Constitution and is also among the world's most important representative bodies. Congress is the only national representative assembly that can be said to govern. Many of the world's representative bodies only represent—that is, their governmental functions consist mainly of affirming and legitimating the national leadership's decisions. The only national representative body that actually possesses powers of governance is the U.S. Congress. For example, while the U.S. Congress never accedes to the president's budget proposals without making major changes, both the British House of Commons and the Japanese Diet always accept the budget exactly as proposed by the government. This follows from the institution principle. In the separation-of-powers regime institutionalized by the U.S. Constitution, the American executive cannot govern alone. The legislature, in particular, actively participates. In Richard Neustadt's memorable phrase, the executive and the legislature in the United States are "separated institutions sharing power."[1] In parliamentary regimes, in contrast, the executive controls its majority in parliament.

In this chapter, we shall try to understand how Congress is able to serve simultaneously as a representative assembly and a powerful agency of government. Congress controls a formidable battery of powers that it uses to shape policies and, when necessary, defend its prerogatives against the executive branch.

Congress has vast authority over the two most important powers given to any government: the power of force (control over the nation's military forces) and the power over money. Specifically, according to Article I, Section 8, Congress can "lay and collect Taxes," deal with indebtedness and bankruptcy, impose duties, borrow and coin money,

---

[1]Richard E. Neustadt, *Presidential Power: The Politics of Leadership* (New York: Wiley, 1960), p. 42.

and generally control the nation's purse strings. It also may "provide for the common Defence and general Welfare," regulate interstate commerce, undertake public works, acquire and control federal lands, promote science and "useful Arts" (pertaining mostly to patents and copyrights), and regulate the militia.

In the realm of foreign policy, Congress has the power to declare war, deal with piracy, regulate foreign commerce, and raise and regulate the armed forces and military installations. These powers over war and the military are supreme— even the president, as commander in chief of the military, must obey the laws and orders of Congress *if* Congress chooses to assert its constitutional authority. (In the past century, Congress has usually surrendered this authority to the president.) Further, the Senate has the power to approve treaties (by a two-thirds vote) and the appointment of ambassadors. Capping these powers, Congress is charged to make laws "which shall be necessary and proper for carrying into Execution the foregoing Powers, and all other Powers vested by this Constitution in the Government of the United States, or in any Department or Officer thereof."

All five principles of politics are important to our understanding of Congress. Members of Congress, like all politicians, are ambitious and thus eager to serve the interests of their constituents to improve their own chances of reelection. In many ways, Congress works because its system of representation harnesses individual legislators' goals and puts them to use. Because the policy goals of members of Congress are many and varied, cooperation among members can be difficult to achieve. The internal organization of Congress seeks to remedy the problems of collective action by regularizing patterns of cooperation and creating a division of labor among members. Similarly, the legislative process and the legislative parties try to provide coordination to a diverse institution, and in the legislative process it is clear that rules matter. The legislative process also reveals that political outcomes result from preferences and procedures. Finally, in the discussion of the evolution of the committee system and the influence of political parties in Congress, we see that history matters. In fact, the ebb and flow of Congress's power in the political system can be evaluated only in the context of history.

If it seems to the reader that many of these powers, especially those having to do with war and spending, belong to the president, that is because modern presidents do exercise great authority in these areas. The modern presidency is a more powerful institution than it was two centuries ago, and much of that power has come from Congress, either because Congress has delegated the power to the president by law or because Congress has simply allowed, or even urged, presidents to be more active in these areas.[2] This also helps explain why today the executive branch seems like a more important branch of government than Congress. Still, the constitutional powers of Congress remain intact in the document. As we shall see, congressional power cannot be separated from congressional representation. Indeed, there is a reciprocal relationship between the two. Without its array of powers, Congress could do little to represent effectively the views and interests of its constituents. At the same time, the power of Congress is ultimately a function of its capacity to represent important groups and forces in American society effectively.

We begin our discussion with a brief consideration of representation. Then we examine the institutional structure of the contemporary Congress and the manner in which congressional powers are organized and employed. Throughout, we point out the connections between these two aspects—the ways in which representation affects

---

[2]On the issue of congressional delegation to the executive, two valuable sources are D. Roderick Kiewiet and Mathew D. McCubbins, *The Logic of Delegation: Congressional Parties and the Appropriations Process* (Chicago: University of Chicago Press, 1991); and David Epstein and Sharyn O'Halloran, *Delegating Powers: A Transaction Cost Politics Approach to Policy Making under Separate Powers* (New York: Cambridge University Press, 1999).

congressional operations (especially through "the electoral connection") and the ways in which congressional institutions enhance or diminish representation (especially Congress's division-of-labor and specialization-of-labor committee system).

REPRESENTATION

Congress is the most important representative institution in American government. Each member's primary responsibility is to the district, to his or her **constituency,** not to the congressional leadership, a party, or even Congress itself. Yet the task of representation is not a simple one. Views about what constitutes fair and effective representation differ, and constituents can make very different kinds of demands on their representatives. Members of Congress must consider these diverse views and demands as they represent their districts (Figure 5.1).

Legislators generally vary in the weight they give to personal priorities and the things their campaign contributors and past supporters desire. Some see themselves as perfect agents of others: They have been elected to do the bidding of those who sent them to the legislature, and they act as **delegates.** Others see themselves as having been selected by their fellow citizens to do what they think is "right," and they act as **trustees.** Most legislators are a mix of these two types.

As we discussed in Chapter 1, one person might be trusted to speak for another if the two are formally bound together so that the representative is in some way accountable to those he or she purports to represent. If representatives can somehow be punished or held to account for failing to speak properly for their constituents, then we know they have an incentive to provide good representation even if their own background, views, and interests differ from those they represent. This idea is called **agency representation**—the sort of representation that takes place when constituents have the power to hire and fire their representatives (who act as their agents). Frequent competitive elections constitute an important means by which constituents hold their representatives to account and keep them responsive to their own views and preferences. The idea of a representative as agent is similar to the relationship of lawyer and client. True, the relationship between the member of Congress and as many as 630,000 "clients" in the district or that between the senator and millions of clients in the state is very different from that of the lawyer and client. But the criteria of performance are comparable.

One expects at the very least that each representative will constantly be seeking to discover the interests of the constituency and will be speaking for those interests in Congress and other centers of government.[3] We expect this because we believe that members of Congress, like politicians everywhere, are ambitious. For many, this ambition is satisfied simply by maintaining a hold on their present office and advancing up the rungs of power in that body. Some may be looking ahead to the next level—to higher legislative office, as when a representative seeks a Senate seat, or to an executive

 Institution Principle

According to the idea of agency representation, elections induce a member of Congress to act according to the preferences of his or her constituency.

constituency The district making up the area from which an official is elected.

delegate A representative who votes according to the preferences of his or her constituency.

trustee A representative who votes based on what he or she thinks is best for his or her constituency.

agency representation The type of representation according to which representatives are held accountable to their constituents if they fail to represent them properly. That is, constituents have the power to hire and fire their representatives.

---

[3]The classic description of interactions between politicians and "the folks back home" is given by Richard F. Fenno Jr., *Home Style: House Members in Their Districts* (Boston: Little, Brown, 1978). Essays elaborating on Fenno's classic are found in Morris P. Fiorina and David W. Rohde, eds., *Home Style and Washington Work* (Ann Arbor: University of Michigan Press, 1989).

FIGURE 5.1 How Members of Congress Represent Their Districts

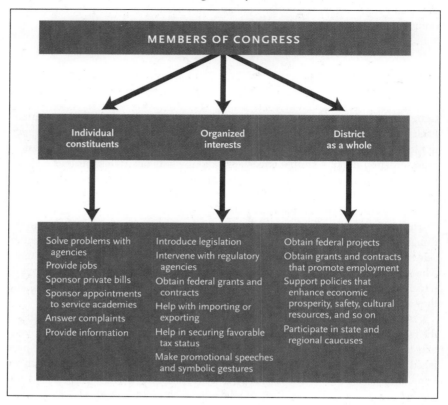

office, as when a legislator returns home to run for the state's governorship, or at the highest level, when a legislator seeks the presidency.[4] We shall return to this topic shortly, in a discussion of elections. But we can say here that in each of these cases the legislator is eager to serve the interests of constituents, either to enhance his or her prospects of contract renewal at the next election or to improve the chances of moving to another level. In short, the agency conception of representation works in proportion to the ambition of politicians (as "agents") and the capacity of constituents (as "principals") to reward or punish on the basis of the legislator's performance and reputation.[5]

Rationality Principle

Members of Congress, like all politicians, are ambitious and thus eager to serve the interests of constituents to improve their chances of reelection.

ONLINE READING

---

[4]For more on political careers generally, see John R. Hibbing, "Lesiglative Careers: Why and How We Should Study Them," *Legislative Studies Quarterly* 24 (1999): 149–71. See also Cherie D. Maestas, Sarah Lutton, L. Sandy Maisel, and Walter J. Stone, "When to Risk It? Institutions, Ambitions, and the Decision to Run for the U.S. House," *American Political Science Review* 100, no. 2 (May 2006): 195–208.

[5]Constituents aren't a legislative agent's only principals. He or she may also be beholden to party leaders and special interests, as well as to members and committees in the chamber. See Forrest Maltzman, *Competing Principals* (Ann Arbor: University of Michigan Press, 1997).

This latter capacity depends on, among other things, the quality of political competition, which in turn is a product of the electoral and campaign finance systems.

House and Senate: Differences in Representation

The framers of the Constitution provided for a *bicameral legislature*—a legislative body consisting of two chambers. As we saw in Chapter 2, the framers intended each of these chambers, the House and the Senate, to represent a different constituency. Members of the House were to be "close to the people," elected popularly every two years. Members of the the Senate, on the other hand, were appointed by state legislatures for six-year terms, were to represent the elite members of society, and were to be attuned more to the interests of property than to those of the population. Today members of both the House and the Senate are elected directly by the people. The 435 members of the House are elected from districts apportioned according to the population; the 100 members of the Senate are elected by state, with two senators from each. Senators continue to have longer terms in office and usually represent much larger and more diverse constituencies than do their counterparts in the House of Representatives (Table 5.1).

The House and the Senate play different roles in the legislative process. In essence, the Senate is the more deliberative of the two bodies: It is the forum in which any and all ideas can receive a thorough public airing. The House is the more centralized and the more organized of the two bodies: It is better equipped to play a routine role in the governmental process. In part, this difference stems from the different rules governing the two bodies. These rules give House leaders more control over the legislative process and provide for House members to specialize in certain legislative areas. The rules of the much smaller Senate give its leadership relatively little power and discourage specialization. This is the institution principle at work. The two legislative chambers are organized in very different ways, reflecting not only their differences in size but also their differences in electoral rhythm, constituencies, and roles. House members specialize, their specialized activities take place mainly in committees, and deliberations by the full House take place mainly in response to committee proposals. The institution is organized to facilitate expeditious consideration of committee bills. The Senate does many of the same things. But senators are less specialized, partly because of their more heterogeneous constituencies, and therefore involve themselves in many more areas of policy. Senate proceedings permit wider participation and more open-ended deliberation.

Both formal and informal factors also contribute to the differences between the two chambers of Congress. Differences in the length of terms and the requirements for holding office specified by the Constitution generate differences in how the members of each body develop their constituencies and exercise their powers of office. The result is that members of the House more effectively and more frequently serve as the agents of well-organized local interests with specific legislative agendas—for instance, used-car dealers seeking relief from regulation, labor unions seeking more favorable legislation, or farmers looking for higher subsidies. The small size and relative homogeneity of their constituencies and the frequency with which they must seek reelection make House members more attuned than senators to the legislative needs of local interest groups. This is what the framers intended when they drafted the Constitution—namely,

bicameral legislature A legislative assembly composed of two chambers, or houses.

TABLE 5.1 Differences between the House and the Senate

	House	**Senate**
Minimum age of member	25 years	30 years
Length of U.S. citizenship	At least 7 years	At least 9 years
Length of term	2 years	6 years
Number per state	Depends on population: 1 per 30,000 in 1789; 1 per 630,000 today	2 per state
Constituency	Tends to be local	Is both local and national

that the House of Representatives would be "the people's house" and that its members would reflect and represent public opinion in a timely manner.

Senators, on the other hand, serve larger and more heterogeneous constituencies. As a result, they are somewhat better able than members of the House to serve as the agents of groups and interests organized on a statewide or national basis. Moreover, with longer terms in office, senators have the luxury of considering "new ideas" or seeking to bring together new coalitions of interests, rather than simply serving existing ones. This, too, was the intent of the Constitution's drafters—that the Senate should provide a balance to the more responsive House, with its narrower and more homogenous constituencies. The Senate was said to be the saucer that cools the tea, bringing deliberation, debate, inclusiveness, calm, and caution to policy formulation.

In recent years, the House has exhibited considerably more intense partisanship and ideological division than the Senate. Because of their diverse constituencies, senators are more inclined to seek compromise positions that will offend as few voters and interest groups as possible. Members of the House, in contrast, with their party's domination in more homogeneous districts, are less inclined to seek compromises and more willing to stick to their partisan and ideological guns. For instance, the House divided almost exactly along partisan lines on the 1998 vote to impeach President Bill Clinton. In the Senate, by contrast, ten Republicans joined Democrats to acquit Clinton of obstruction of justice charges, and in a separate vote five Republicans joined Democrats to acquit Clinton of perjury.[6] In October 2001, the Senate passed an airport security bill unanimously. The House, however, divided along partisan lines over whether new security personnel should be federal employees or private contractors. During the presidency of George W. Bush, even the Senate has grown more partisan and polarized—especially on social issues and the war in Iraq.[7]

---

[6]Eric Pianin and Guy Gugliotta, "The Bipartisan Challenge: Senate's Search for Accord Marks Contrast to House," *Washington Post*, 8 January 1999, p. 1.

[7]However, on the confirmation of Supreme Court nominations, even in an atmosphere of elevated partisanship moderates from both parties in the Senate have prevented partisan extremism from dominating. Chief Justice John Roberts was easily confirmed in 2005, and Justice Samuel Alito, though given a rougher ride during confirmation hearings, was approved with support from both parties in 2006.

The Electoral System

In light of their role as agents of various constituencies in their states and districts and the importance of elections as a mechanism by which principals (constituents) reward and punish their agents, representatives are very much influenced by electoral considerations. Three factors related to the American electoral system affect who gets elected and what he or she does once in office. The first set of issues concerns who decides to run for office and which candidates have an edge over others. The second issue is that of the incumbency advantage. Finally, the way congressional district lines are drawn can greatly affect the outcome of an election. Let us examine more closely the impact of these considerations on who serves in Congress.

Running for Office   Voters' choices are restricted from the start by who decides to run for office. In the past, decisions about who would run for a particular elected office were made by local party officials. A person who had a record of service to the party, or who was owed a favor, or whose "turn" had come up might be nominated by party leaders for an office.[8] Today few party organizations have the power to slate candidates in that way. Instead, the decision to run for Congress is a more personal choice. One of the most important factors determining who runs for office is a candidate's ambition.[9] A potential candidate may also assess whether he or she can attract enough money to mount a credible campaign. The ability to raise money depends on connections to other politicians, interest groups, and the national party organization. Wealthy individuals may finance their own races. In 2000, for example, the New Jersey Democrat and former investment banker Jon Corzine spent more than $60 million of his own money to win a U.S. Senate seat. (In 2005, he spent a similar amount of money to win the governorship of New Jersey.)

In the past, the difficulty of raising campaign funds posed a disadvantage to female candidates. Since the 1980s, however, a number of PACs and other organizations have emerged to recruit women and fund their campaigns. The largest of them, EMILY's List, has become one of the most powerful fund-raisers in the nation. Recent research shows that money is no longer the barrier it once was to women running for office.[10]

Rationality Principle

One of the most important factors determining who runs for office is a candidate's ambition. Access to money doesn't hurt either.

---

[8]In the nineteenth century, it was often an *obligation*, not an honor, to serve in Congress. The real political action was back home in the state capital or a big city, not in Washington. So the practice of "rotation" was devised, according to which a promising local politician was to do a tour of duty in Washington before being slated for an important local office. This is not to say that electoral incentives—the so-called electoral connection in which a legislator's behavior was motivated by the desire to retain the seat for himself or his party—was absent in nineteenth-century America. See, for example, Jamie L. Carson and Erik J. Engstrom, "Assessing the Electoral Connection Evidence from the Early United States," *American Journal of Political Science* 49 (2005): 746–57. See also William T. Bianco, David B. Spence, and John D. Wilkerson, "The Electoral Connection in the Early Congress: The Case of the Compensation Act of 1816," *American Journal of Political Science* 40 (1996): 145–71.

[9]See Linda L. Fowler and Robert D. McClure, *Political Ambition: Who Decides to Run for Congress* (New Haven, Conn.: Yale University Press, 1989); and Alan Ehrenhalt, *The United States of Ambition: Politicians, Power, and the Pursuit of Office* (New York: Times Books, 1991).

[10]See Barbara C. Burrell, *A Woman's Place Is in the House: Campaigning for Congress in the Feminist Era* (Ann Arbor: University of Michigan Press, 1994), chap. 6; and the essays in Elizabeth Adell Cook, Sue Thomas, and Clyde Wilcox, eds., *The Year of the Woman: Myths and Realities* (Boulder, Colo.: Westview Press, 1994).

○ ONLINE READING

Features distinctive to each congressional district also affect the field of candidates. Among them are the range of other political opportunities that may lure potential candidates away. In addition, the way the congressional district overlaps state legislative boundaries may affect a candidate's decision to run. A state-level representative or senator who is considering a run for the U.S. Congress is more likely to assess his or her prospects favorably if the state district coincides with the congressional district (because the voters will already know him or her). For similar reasons, U.S. representatives from small states, whose congressional districts overlap a large portion of the state, are far more likely to run for statewide office than members of Congress from large states. For example, John Thune was elected as the lone representative from South Dakota in 1996. His constituency thus completely overlapped those of Senators Tim Johnson and Tom Daschle. In 2002, Thune challenged Johnson, losing by barely 500 votes. In 2004, he defeated Daschle, then the Democratic leader in the Senate. For any candidate, decisions about running must be made early because once money has been committed to declared candidates, it is harder for new candidates to break into a race. Thus the outcome of a November election is partially determined many months earlier, when decisions to run are finalized.[11]

Incumbency   ***Incumbency*** plays a very important role in the American electoral system and in the kind of representation citizens get in Washington. Once in office, members of Congress are typically eager to remain in office and make politics a career. Throughout the twentieth century, Congress developed into a ***professional legislature,*** a legislature whose members serve full-time for multiple terms (Figure 5.2).[12] The career ambitions of members of Congress are helped by an array of tools that they can use to stack the deck in favor of their reelection. Through effective use of this arsenal of weapons, an incumbent establishes a reputation for competence, imagination, and responsiveness—the attributes most principals look for in an agent. One well-known tool of incumbency is the franking privilege. Under a law enacted by the First Congress in 1789, members of Congress may send mail to their constituents free of charge to keep them informed of governmental business and public affairs. Under current law, members receive an average of about $100,000 in free postage for mailings to their constituents. There is a great variety of franked mail. Some targets special groups on issues of direct interest to them—for example, news about minimum wage legislation sent to union households in the district. Most common of all are "your congressman at work" newsletters, which are sent to households in an entire district on a regular basis.

Members may not use these funds to send mail outside their districts, however, or to send mass mailings within ninety days of a primary or general election. De-

---

incumbency Holding a political office for which one is running.

professional legislature A legislature whose members serve full-time for multiple terms.

[11]Thus the timing of Hurricane Katrina was especially propitious for the Democrats and unfortunate for the Republicans. Occurring in September 2005, the hurricane gave the Democrats a long lead time in which to recruit high-quality candidates to contest the November 2006 congressional elections while discouraging high-quality Republican candidates. Had the tragedy occurred in September 2006, it would not have had consequential effects on recruitment. The disparity in the quality of candidates enabled by events a year or more earlier surely helped the Democrats win House and Senate seats in November 2006. On the thesis of "strategic candidacy," see Gary C. Jacobson, *The Politics of Congressional Elections,* 6th ed. (New York: Pearson Longman, 2004).

[12]Nelson W. Polsby, "The Institutionalization of the U.S. House of Representatives," *American Political Science Review* 62, no. 1 (March 1968): 144–68.

FIGURE 5.2 Turnover in the House of Representatives

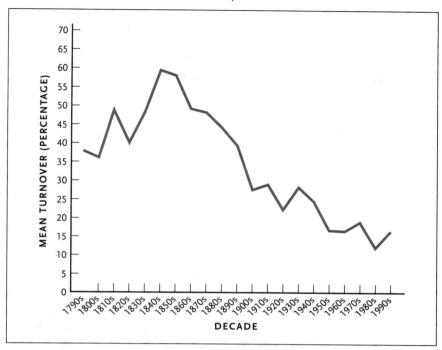

SOURCE: Based on John Swain, Stephen A. Borelli, Brian C. Reed, and Sean F. Evans, "A New Look at Turnover in the U.S. House of Representatives, 1789–1998," *American Politics Quarterly* 28 (2000): 435–57.

NOTE: Overall for this period, the mean turnover was 30.7 percent.

spite the restrictions, the franking privilege provides incumbents with a valuable resource for publicizing their activities and making themselves visible to voters.

A particularly important tool is the incumbent's reputation for constituency service: taking care of the problems and requests of individual voters. Through such services and their advertisement by word of mouth, the incumbent seeks to establish an attractive political reputation and a "personal" relationship with his or her constituents. Well over a quarter of the representatives' time and nearly two thirds of the time of their staff members is devoted to constituency service (termed ***casework***). This service is not merely a matter of writing and mailing letters. It includes talking to constituents, providing them with minor services, presenting special bills for them, and attempting to influence decisions by regulatory commissions on their behalf. Indeed, one might think of the member's legislative staff and office operation as a congressional enterprise, much like a firm, with the member himself or herself as the chief executive officer.[13]

casework An effort by members of Congress to gain the trust and support of constituents by providing personal service. One important type of casework consists of helping constituents obtain favorable treatment from the federal bureaucracy.

---

[13]For more on the congressional office as an enterprise that processes the casework demands of constituents, see Robert H. Salisbury and Kenneth A. Shepsle, "Congressman as Enterprise," *Legislative Studies Quarterly* 6 (1981): 559–76.

One very direct way in which incumbent members of Congress serve as the agents of their constituencies is through the venerable institution of **patronage.** Patronage refers to a variety of forms of direct services and benefits that members provide for their districts. One of the most important forms of patronage is **pork-barrel legislation.** Through pork-barrel legislation, representatives seek to capture federal projects and federal funds for their districts (or states in the case of senators) and thus "bring home the bacon."

A common form of pork barreling is the earmark, the practice through which members of Congress insert into otherwise pork-free bills language that provides special benefits for their own constituents.[14] For example, among the more outrageous earmarks in a 2005 transportation bill was a bridge in Alaska that cost more than $10 million and connected the mainland to an island on which no one lives (the so-called bridge to nowhere). This earmark proved so embarrassing to the Republicans once they began receiving adverse publicity that they rescinded the appropriation.

So why do legislators continue this exasperating practice? One answer is that each legislator can credibly and visibly claim personal responsibility, and thus take personal credit, for earmarked programs and special highway projects. This credit enhances the legislator's reputation back home as a Washington mover and shaker while enhancing his or her reelection prospects. If the same money came to the states or districts through an existing program, like the Highway Trust Fund, the individual legislator would get little credit for it. (As with the bridge to nowhere, however, sometimes this practice can backfire.)

Pork-barrel activities by incumbent legislators bring a number of our principles into play. Incumbent legislators engage in the practice because it furthers their electoral objectives (the rationality principle). They succeed to the degree that they are able to join with fellow legislators in exchanging support for one another's projects (the collective-action principle). These efforts are facilitated by institutional procedures: amendments to appropriations bills, omnibus legislation, opportunities to insert special provisions into bills (the institution principle). And they decidedly influence the mix and location of spending by the federal government (the policy principle). From time to time, as in the example of the bridge to nowhere, the practice becomes so egregious that future Congresses install procedures to restrict the activity (the history principle). Contemporary excesses have led many in Congress to begin considering ways to limit earmarks. The power of the rationality principle, however, poses a high hurdle for reform: Incumbents currently benefit from their ability to target their states and districts for federal spending.

The incumbency advantage is evident in the high rates of reelection among congressional incumbents: over 95 percent for House members and nearly 90 per-

---

[14]For a study of academic earmarking, see James D. Savage, *Funding Science in America: Congress, Universities, and the Politics of the Academic Pork Barrel* (New York: Cambridge University Press, 1999). For a general study of pork-barrel activity, see the excellent book by Diana Evans, *Greasing the Wheels: Using Pork Barrel Projects to Build Majority Coalitions in Congress* (New York: Cambridge University Press, 2004).

FIGURE 5.3 The Power of Incumbency

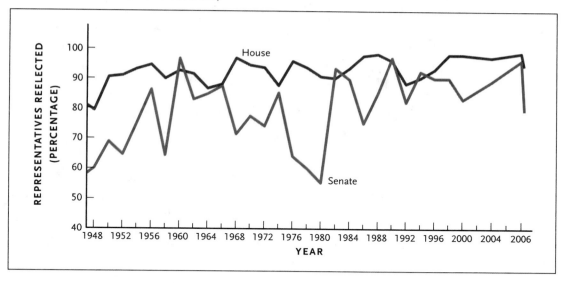

SOURCE: Norman J. Ornstein, Thomas E. Mann, and Michael J. Malbin, *Vital Statistics on Congress, 1995–1996* (Washington, D.C.: Congressional Quarterly Press, 1996), pp. 60–61, and authors' update.

cent for members of the Senate in recent years (Figure 5.3).[15] In 2004, 98 percent of House incumbents running in the general election were successful, and of the handful who were defeated, most lost because redistricting placed them in new and unfriendly districts. Only one incumbent senator was defeated: The Democratic Senate minority leader, Tom Daschle, lost his bid for reelection in South Dakota. In 2006, 93 percent of House incumbents won reelection: an amazing 100 percent of the Democratic incumbents and 87 percent of the Republicans. Moreover, of the House seats held by Republicans who were retiring rather than seeking reelection, the party held fewer than 80 percent; the comparable number for Democrats was nearly 90 percent. In the Senate in 2006, the Democrats retained all the seats held by incumbents who ran, kept two of the three seats held by incumbents who were retiring, and picked up six seats by defeating Republican incumbents.

The incumbency advantage is also evident in what is called sophomore surge—the tendency for candidates to win a higher percentage of the vote when seeking their second term in office than they won in their initial election victory. Once in office, members of Congress find it much easier to raise campaign funds

---

[15]Norman J. Ornstein, Thomas E. Mann, and Michael J. Malbin, *Vital Statistics on Congress, 1995–1996* (Washington, D.C.: Congressional Quarterly Press, 1996), pp. 60–61 (see also subsequent editions); Robert S. Erickson and Gerald C. Wright, "Voters, Candidates, and Issues in Congressional Elections," in *Congress Reconsidered*, 8th ed. Lawrence C. Dodd and Bruce I. Oppenheimer, ed., (Washington, D.C.: Congressional Quarterly Press, 2005), pp. 77–106; and John R. Alford and David W. Brady, "Personal and Partisan Advantage in U.S. Congressional Elections, 1846–1990," ibid., pp. 141–57.

FIGURE 5.4 House and Senate Campaign Expenditures

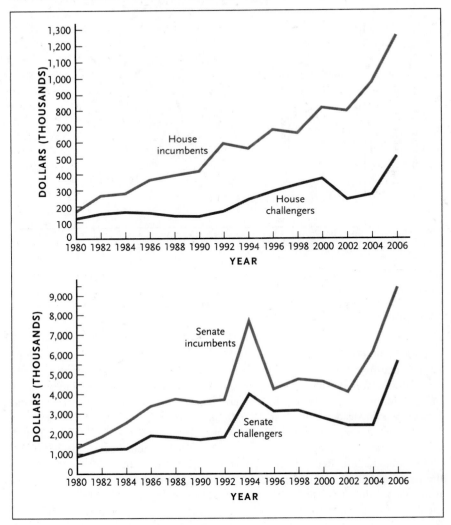

SOURCE: Norman J. Ornstein, Thomas E. Mann, and Michael J. Malbin, *Vital Statistics on Congress, 2001–2002* (Washington, D.C.: American Enterprise Institute, 2002), pp. 87, 93, and Campaign Finance Institute (www.cfinst.org).

and are thus able to outspend their challengers (Figure 5.4).[16] Over the past quarter century, and despite many campaign finance regulations that were meant to level the playing field, the gap between incumbent and challenger spending has grown (in the House) or held steady (in the Senate). Members of the majority party in the

---

[16]Stephen Ansolabehere and James Snyder, "Campaign War Chests and Congressional Elections," *Business and Politics* 2 (2000): 9–34.

House and Senate are particularly attractive to donors who want access to those in power.[17]

Incumbency can help a candidate by scaring off potential challengers. In many races, potential candidates may decide not to run because they fear that the incumbent has simply brought too many benefits to the district, has too much money, or is too well liked or too well-known.[18] Potentially strong challengers may also decide that a district's partisan leanings are too unfavorable. When Republican representative Dan Miller first ran in Florida in 1992, he faced five opponents in the primary and a bruising campaign against his Democratic opponent in the general election. In the 1994 election, by contrast, Miller faced only nominal opposition in the Republican primary, and in the general election, the strongest potential challenger from the Democratic party decided not to run; the combination of the incumbency advantage and the strongly Republican leanings of the district gave the Democrats little chance of winning. Miller was reelected without a challenge.[19]

This story may be repeated for many members in nearly every Congress. The eighth district of Massachusetts is a famous example. Represented by, among others, John F. Kennedy (1947–52) and Tip O'Neill (1953–86), who became president and Speaker of the House, respectively, this seat became vacant when the incumbent Joseph Patrick Kennedy (1987–98) left office. A wide-open Democratic primary, attracting more than a dozen candidates, selected the mayor of Somerville, Mike Capuano, who went on to win the general election. Capuano has remained in this seat ever since, facing only token opposition and rolling up huge majorities.

The advantage of incumbency thus tends to preserve the status quo in Congress by discouraging potentially strong challengers from running. When incumbents do face strong challengers, they are often defeated.[20] The reason is that strong challengers are willing to throw their hat into the ring only when they believe the incumbent is weak, out of touch, too preoccupied with national affairs, or plagued by scandal or declining capabilities. In 2006, for example, Senator Lincoln Chafee (R-R.I.), despite a popularity rating of 62 percent in the polls, was defeated as many Rhode Islanders signaled their displeasure with the Bush administration and the Republican Congress. In 2008, Republican senators John Sununu of New Hampshire and Elizabeth Dole of North Carolina were defeated by Democratic challengers.

The role of incumbency also has implications for the social composition of Congress. For example, the incumbency advantage makes it harder for women to increase their numbers in Congress because most incumbents are men. Female candidates who run for open seats (for which there are no incumbents) are just as likely to win as male candidates.[21] Supporters of term limits argue that such limits

---

[17] Gary W. Cox and Eric Magar, "How Much Is Majority Status in the U.S. Congress Worth?" *American Political Science Review* 93, no. 2 (June 1999): 299–309.

[18] Kenneth Bickers and Robert Stein, "The Electoral Dynamics of the Federal Pork Barrel," *American Journal of Political Science* 40 (1996): 1300–26.

[19] Kevin Merida, "The 2nd Time Is Easy: Many House Freshmen Have Secured Seats," *Washington Post,* 18 October 1994, p. A1.

[20] Jacobson, *The Politics of Congressional Elections.*

[21] See Burrell, *A Woman's Place Is in the House,* and David Broder, "Key to Women's Political Parity: Running," *Washington Post,* 8 September 1994, p. A17.

are the only way to get new faces into Congress. They believe that the incumbency advantage means that very little turnover will occur in Congress unless limits are imposed on the number of terms a legislator can serve.

But the tendency toward the status quo is not absolute. In recent years, political observers have suggested that the incumbency advantage may be declining. In the 1992 and 1994 elections, for example, voters expressed considerable anger and dissatisfaction with incumbents, producing a 25 percent turnover in the House in 1992 and a 20 percent turnover in 1994. Yet the defeat of incumbents was not the main factor at work in either of these elections; 88.3 percent of House incumbents who sought reelection were reelected in 1992, and 90.2 percent won reelection in 1994. In 1992, it was an exceptionally high retirement rate among members of Congress that created more open seats and brought new faces into Congress.[22] In 1994, a large number of open seats combined with an unprecedented mobilization of Republican voters to shift control of Congress to the Republican party. In 2006, the reverse happened. The Democrats needed to gain fifteen seats to capture the House, and they won double that number; in the Senate, they captured the six Republican seats they needed to win control of that chamber. In 2008, the Democrats increased their majorities in both houses.

Congressional Districts The final factor that affects who wins a seat in Congress is the way congressional districts are drawn. Every ten years, state legislatures must redraw congressional districts to reflect population changes. In 1929, Congress enacted a law fixing the total number of congressional seats at 435. As a result, when states with growing populations gain districts, they do so at the expense of states whose population has remained stagnant or declined. In recent decades, this has meant that the nation's growth areas in the South and West have gained congressional seats at the expense of the Northeast and the Midwest (Figure 5.5). After the 2000 census, for example, Arizona, Texas, Florida, and Georgia each gained two seats while New York and Pennsylvania each lost two seats. Redrawing congressional districts is a highly political process: Districts are shaped to create an advantage for the majority party in the state legislature, which controls the redistricting process. In this complex process, those charged with drawing districts use sophisticated computer technologies to come up with the most favorable district boundaries. Redistricting can create open seats and may pit incumbents of the same party against each other, ensuring that one of them will lose. Redistricting can also give an advantage to one party by clustering voters with some ideological or sociological characteristics in a single district or by separating those voters into two or more districts. *Gerrymandering* can have a major effect on the outcome of congressional elections. Before 1980, for example, California's House seats had been almost evenly divided between the two parties. After the 1980 census, a redistricting effort controlled by the Democrats, who held both houses of the state legislature as well as the governorship, resulted in Democrats' taking control of two thirds of the state's

gerrymandering
The apportionment of voters in districts in such a way as to give unfair advantage to one political party.

---

[22]The reason for the high voluntary retirement rate that year is interesting. Congress had passed a reform making it impossible for members to pocket money left in their office accounts when they retired. The last year in which pocketing this money was permitted was 1992, and a number of members took that opportunity to retire, some enriching themselves by hundreds of thousands of dollars.

FIGURE 5.5 Apportionment of House Seats by Region, 1910 and 2000

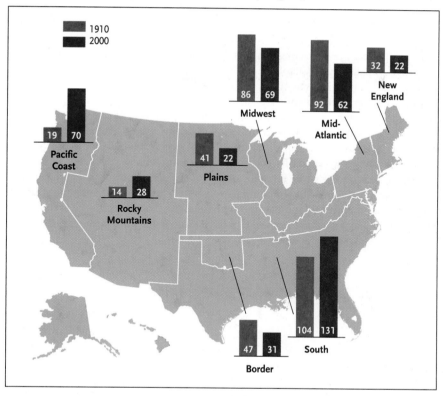

SOURCE: Norman J. Ornstein, Thomas E. Mann, and Michael J. Malbin, *Vital Statistics on Congress, 2001–2002* (Washington, D.C.: American Enterprise Institute, 2002), p. 59.

seats in the U.S. House of Representatives.[23] Another more recent case benefited the Republicans. The 2002 congressional election was the first one under the redistricting required by the 2000 census. In 2003, the Texas legislature, controlled by the Republicans, set to work drawing up a *new* set of congressional districts. Ordinarily this exercise is done once per decade, after the constitutionally required census. But, argued the Texas Republicans, nothing prohibits a state from doing it more frequently. Democrats in the Texas state legislature were furious and twice staged walkouts, even fleeing across the border to Oklahoma to avoid a posse of Texas Rangers sent to retrieve them. These walkouts delayed proceedings by making it difficult to assemble enough legislators to meet the minimum requirements to do legislative business. Finally, however, the Republicans prevailed, redrawing the federal districts

---

[23]David Butler and Bruce Cain, *Congressional Redistricting: Comparative and Theoretical Perspectives* (New York: Macmillan, 1992).

in a way that was very favorable to them. In 2004, the Republicans gained five seats in Texas, defeating four Democratic incumbents, in part as a result of their redistricting maneuver.[24] Examples like these explain why the two parties invest substantial resources in state legislative and gubernatorial contests during the electoral cycle that precedes the year in which congressional district boundaries will be redrawn.

As we shall see in Chapter 10, since the passage of the 1982 amendments to the 1965 Voting Rights Act, race has become a major—and controversial—consideration in drawing voting districts. These amendments, which encouraged the creation of districts in which members of racial minorities have decisive majorities, have greatly increased the number of minority representatives in Congress. After the 1991–92 redistricting, the number of predominantly minority districts doubled, from twenty-six to fifty-two. Among the most fervent supporters of the new minority districts were white Republicans, who used the opportunity to create more districts dominated by white Republican voters.[25] These developments raise thorny questions about representation. Some analysts argue that although the system may grant minorities greater sociological representation, it has made it more difficult for them to win substantive policy goals.[26]

PROBLEMS OF LEGISLATIVE ORGANIZATION

The U.S. Congress is not only a representative assembly. It is also a legislative body. For Americans, representation and legislation go hand in hand. Many parliamentary bodies, however, are representative yet lack the power to legislate. It is no small achievement that the U.S. Congress both represents *and* governs.

Governing is a challenge. It is extraordinarily difficult for a large, representative assembly to formulate, enact, and implement laws. Just the internal complexities of conducting business within Congress—the legislative process—are daunting. In addition, there are many individuals and institutions that have the capacity to influence the legislative process. Because successful legislation requires the confluence of so many distinct factors, it is little wonder that most of the thousands of bills considered by Congress each year are defeated long before they reach the president.

The supporters of legislative proposals often feel that the formal rules of the congressional process are deliberately designed to prevent their own deserving proposals from ever seeing the light of day. But these rules allow Congress to play an important

---

[24]In late 2004, the U.S. Supreme Court ordered a lower federal court to reconsider the "extra" Texas redistricting plan. This case worked its way back to the Supreme Court. In June 2006, the Court ruled that the Texas legislature was within its rights to redistrict more than once per decade; however, it also ruled that some of the particular decisions about district boundaries violated the rights of Latino voters.

[25]David Lublin, *The Paradox of Representation: Racial Gerrymandering and Minority Interests in Congress* (Princeton, N.J.: Princeton University Press, 1997).

[26]Lani Guinier, *The Tyranny of the Majority: Fundamental Fairness in Representative Democracy* (New York: Free Press, 1995). See also David Epstein and Sharyn O'Halloran, "Measuring the Electoral and Policy Impact of Majority-Minority Voting Districts," *American Journal of Political Science* 42 (1999): 367–95.

role in lawmaking. If it wants to be more than a rubber stamp for the executive branch, like so many other representative assemblies around the world, a national legislature like the Congress must develop a division of labor, set an agenda, maintain order through rules and procedures, and place limits on discussion. If it wants to accomplish these things in a representative setting in which a veritable diversity of political preferences exists, then it must find the ways and means to enable cooperation despite the variety of interests and coalitions and to make compromises despite conflicts. We will first take up the general issues that face any legislature or decision-making group possessing diverse preferences: the problems of cooperation, coalitions, and compromises.

Cooperation in Congress

A popularly elected legislative assembly—the Boston City Council, the Kansas state legislature, the U.S. Congress, the French National Assembly, or the European Parliament—consists of politicians who harbor a variety of political objectives. Because they got where they are by winning an election and many hope to stay where they are or possibly advance their political careers, these politicians are intimately aware of whom they must please to do so:

- Because campaigns are expensive propositions, most politicians are eager to please those who can supply resources for the next campaign—campaign donors, PACs, important endorsers, party officials, volunteer activists.

- The most recent campaign—one that the politicians won—provides them with information about just why their victory was secured. It is sometimes quite difficult to sort out the myriad factors, but at the very least the politicians have a good sense of what categories of voters supported them and may be prepared to support them again if performance is adequate.

- Many politicians not only aim to please campaign contributors and voters but also have an agenda of their own. Whether for private gain or public good, politicians come to the legislature with policy goals of personal importance.

Congress consists of a heterogeneous group of legislators, and the specific public policies that they want to pursue are thus many and varied. They may be considered from two perspectives. First, owing to their different constituencies, legislators will give priority to different realms of public policy. A Cape Cod congressman will be interested in shipping, fishing, coastal preservation, harbor development, tourism, and shipbuilding. An inner-city Philadelphia congresswoman may not care much at all about those issues, focusing instead on welfare reform, civil rights policy, aid to inner-city school systems, and job-retraining programs. Montana's sole member of Congress is probably not interested in coastal preservation or inner-city schools but, rather, in ranching, agriculture, mining, and public land use. Evidently, Congress encompasses a mélange of legislative priorities.

Second, the opinions its members hold on any given issue are diverse. While interest in environmental protection, for example, ranges from high priority among those who count many Sierra Club members among their constituents to low priority among those who have other fish to fry, once environmental protection is on the agenda there is a broad range of preferences for specific initiatives. Some want

 Rationality Principle

The political opinions and policy goals of members of Congress are many and varied.

pollution discharges carefully monitored and regulated by a relatively powerful watchdog agency. Others believe that more decentralized and less intrusive means, such as marketable pollution permits, are the way to go. Still others think the entire issue is overblown, that any proposed cure is worse than the disease, and that the Republic would be best served by leaving well enough alone.

Diversity in both priorities and preferences among legislators is sufficiently abundant that the view of no group of legislators predominates. Legislative consensus must be built—this is what legislative politics is all about. Each legislator clamors to get his or her priority issue the attention he or she believes it deserves or to make sure his or her position on a given issue prevails. But neither effort is likely to succeed on its own merits. Support must be assembled, deals consummated, and promises and threats used. In short, legislators intent on achieving their objectives must cooperate, coalesce, and compromise. And these activities are facilitated by rules and procedures. This system leads to the division and specialization of legislative work, the regularization of procedures, and the creation of agenda power. All of these organizational features of Congress arise as part of a governance structure to allow for cooperation and coalition building, activities that yield compromise policies.

Collective-Action Principle

Cooperation on recurring matters like congressional votes is facilitated by the institutionalization of legislative structures and procedures.

Underlying Problems and Challenges

Before we can understand why Congress selects particular ways to institutionalize its practices, we need a finer appreciation of other underlying problems with which legislators must grapple. Then we can consider how the U.S. Congress deals with these problems.

Matching Influence and Interest   Legislatures are highly egalitarian institutions. Each legislator has one vote on any issue coming before the body. Whereas a consumer has a cash budget that she may allocate in any way she wishes to categories of consumer goods, a legislator is not given a vote budget in quite the same sense. Instead, his budget of votes is "earmarked"—one vote for each motion before the assembly. He cannot aggregate the votes in his possession and cast all or some large fraction of them for a motion on a subject near and dear to his heart (or the hearts of his constituents). This is a source of frustration because, as we have noted, the premise of instrumental behavior dictates that legislators would, if they could, concentrate whatever resources they commanded on those subjects of highest priority to them. The egalitarian arrangement thus forces legislators to make deals with one another—"I'll support you on the motion before the legislature if you support me on a future motion."

Information   Legislators do not vote for outcomes directly but, rather, for instruments (or policies) whose effects produce outcomes. Thus legislators, to vote intelligently, must know the connection between the instruments they vote for and the effects they desire. In short, they must have information and knowledge about how the world works.

Few legislators—indeed, few people in general—know how the world works in very many policy domains except in the most superficial of ways. Nearly everyone in the legislature would benefit from the production of valuable information, at the very least information that would allow all of them to eliminate policy instruments that make very little difference in solving social problems or even make matters worse. Producing such information, however, is not a trivial matter. Simply to digest the knowledge that is being produced outside the legislature by knowledge-industry specialists (academics, scientists, journalists, interest groups) is a taxing task. Clearly institutional arrangements that provide incentives to some legislators to produce, evaluate, and disseminate this knowledge for others will permit public resources to be used more effectively. Because legislatures are in competition with other branches of government—particularly the executive—informational requirements must be met just to keep up with the competition.

Compliance   The legislature is not the only game in town. The promulgation of public policies is a joint undertaking in which judges, executives, bureaucrats, and others participate alongside legislators. If the legislature develops no means with which to monitor what happens after a bill becomes law, then it risks seeing public policies implemented in ways other than those intended when the law was passed. Cooperation does not end with the successful passage of a law. If legislators wish to have an impact on the world around them, especially on those matters to which their constituents give priority, then it is necessary to attend to policy implementation, not just policy formulation. But it is just not practical for all 435 representatives and all 100 senators to march down to this or that agency on Pennsylvania Avenue to ensure appropriate implementation by the executive bureaucracy. Compliance will not just happen, and like the production and dissemination of reliable information at the policy-formulation stage, the need for oversight of the executive bureaucracy is but an extension of the cooperation that produced legislation in the first place. It, too, must be institutionalized.

What we have suggested in this abstract discussion about legislative institutions and practices is that Congress is a place in which different kinds of representatives congregate and try to accomplish things so that they may reap the support of their respective constituents back home. This very diversity is problematic—it requires cooperation, coalitions, and compromise. In addition, there is a mismatch of influence and interest (owing to one person, one vote), information about the effectiveness of alternative policies is in short supply, and the legislature must worry about how its product—public laws—gets treated by the other branches of government. These are the problems that legislatures, of which the U.S. Congress is the preeminent example, devise institutional arrangements to mitigate, if not solve altogether.

THE ORGANIZATION OF CONGRESS

We shall now examine the organization of Congress and the legislative process, particularly the basic building blocks of congressional organization: political parties, the committee system, congressional staff, the caucuses, and the parliamentary rules of the House and Senate. Each of these factors plays a key role in the organization of Congress and in the process through which Congress formulates and enacts laws. We will also look at powers Congress has in addition to lawmaking and explore the future role of Congress in relation to the powers of the executive.

Party Leadership and Organization in the House and the Senate

Collective-Action Principle

Political parties in the legislature foster cooperation, coalitions, and compromise.

party caucus, or **party conference** A normally closed meeting of a political or legislative group to select candidates, plan strategy, or make decisions regarding legislative matters.

Speaker of the House The chief presiding officer of the House of Representatives. The Speaker is elected at the beginning of every Congress on a straight party vote. He or she is the most important party and House leader.

majority leader The elected leader of the party holding a majority of the seats in the House of Representatives or the Senate. In the House, the majority leader is subordinate in the party hierarchy to the Speaker.

minority leader The elected leader of the party holding less than a majority of the seats in the House or Senate.

One significant aspect of legislative life is not even part of the *official* organization: political parties. The legislative parties—primarily Democratic and Republican in modern times but numerous others over the course of American history—are organizations that foster cooperation, coalitions, and compromise. They are the vehicles of collective action, both for legislators sharing common policy objectives inside the legislature and for those very same legislators as candidates in periodic election contests back home.[27] In short, political parties in Congress are the fundamental building blocks from which policy coalitions are fashioned to pass legislation and monitor its implementation, thereby providing a track record on which members build electoral support.

Every two years at the beginning of a new Congress, the members of each party gather to elect their House leaders. This gathering is called the **party caucus** by the Democrats and the **party conference** by the Republicans. The elected leader of the majority party is later proposed to the whole House and is automatically elected to the position of **Speaker of the House,** with voting along straight party lines. The House majority caucus (or conference) also elects a **majority leader.** The minority party goes through the same process and selects the **minority leader.** Both parties also elect "whips," who line up party members on important votes and relay voting information to the party leaders.

In December 2006, in the wake of the November elections, the Democrats become the majority party in both chambers. In the House, they selected Nancy Pelosi of California as Speaker, Steny Hoyer of Maryland as majority leader, and James Clyburn of South Carolina as whip. The Republicans, who had in the previous Congress made John Boehner of Ohio their majority leader, kept him on as minority leader, as well as Roy Blunt of Missouri as minority whip.

At one time, party leaders strictly controlled committee assignments, using them to enforce party discipline. Today representatives expect to receive the assignments they want and resent leadership efforts to control assignments. For example, during the 104th Congress (1995–96), the chairman of the powerful Appropriations Committee, Robert Livingston (R-La.), sought to remove freshman Mark Neumann (R-Wisc.) from the committee because of his lack of party loyalty. The entire Republican freshman class angrily opposed this move and forced the leadership to back down. Not only did Neumann keep his seat on the Appropriations Committee, but he was also given a seat on the Budget Committee to placate the freshmen.[28] The

ONLINE READING

---

[27] For a historically grounded analysis of the development of political parties as well as a treatment of their general contemporary significance, see John H. Aldrich, *Why Parties? The Origin and Transformation of Political Parties in America* (Chicago: University of Chicago Press, 1995). For an analysis of the parties in the legislative process, see Gary W. Cox and Mathew D. McCubbins, *Legislative Leviathan: Party Government in the House,* 2nd ed. (Berkeley: University of California Press, 2006). See also their *Setting the Agenda: Responsible Party Government in the U.S. House of Representatives* (New York: Cambridge University Press, 2005). A provocative essay questioning the role of parties is Keith Krehbiel, "Where's the Party?" *British Journal of Political Science* 23 (1993): 235–66.

[28] Linda Killian, *The Freshmen: What Happened to the Republican Revolution?* (Boulder, Colo.: Westview Press, 1998). A recent example went the other way. In December 2004, Speaker J. Dennis Hastert allowed a Colorado Republican to step down from the House Committee on Standards of Official Conduct (the Ethics Committee), in part because of the committee member's role in investigating ethical breaches of the majority leader, Tom DeLay. The member had hoped to remain on the committee.

leadership's best opportunities to use committee assignments as rewards and punishments come when a seat on a committee is sought by more than one member.

Generally representatives seek assignments that will allow them to influence decisions of special importance to their district. Representatives from farm districts, for example, may request seats on the Agriculture Committee.[29] This is one method by which the egalitarian allocation of power in the legislature is overcome. Even though each legislator has just one vote on each issue in the full chamber, he or she, by serving on the right committees, is able to acquire extra influence in areas important to his or her constituents. Seats on powerful committees such as Ways and Means, which is responsible for tax legislation, and Appropriations are especially popular.

Turning to the Senate, the president pro tempore, a position designated in the Constitution, exercises mainly ceremonial leadership. Usually the majority party designates the member with the greatest seniority to serve in this capacity. Real power is in the hands of the majority and minority leaders, each elected by party caucus. Together they control the Senate's calendar, or agenda for legislation. In addition, the senators from each party elect a whip.

The 2002 elections gave the Republican party a one-seat majority in the Senate. In the 2004 election, they gained an additional four seats, for a 55–45 majority. Republicans reelected Bill Frist of Tennessee as majority leader, while Democrats replaced the recently defeated Tom Daschle of South Dakota with Harry Reid of Nevada as the minority leader. After their six-seat gain in the 2006 election, the Democrats named Reid majority leader. With former leader Frist retiring, the Republicans elevated his assistant, Mitch McConnell of Kentucky, to the post of minority leader.

In recent years, party leaders have sought to augment their formal powers by reaching outside Congress for resources that might enhance their influence within the institution. One aspect of this strategy is the increased use of national communications media, including televised speeches and talk-show appearances, by party leaders. The former Republican House Speaker Newt Gingrich, for example, used television extensively to generate support for his programs among Republican loyalists.[30] As long as it lasted, Gingrich's support among the Republican rank and file gave him an added measure of influence over Republican members of Congress. No longer in the House, Gingrich has become a power inside the Beltway as the head of a very influential Republican consulting company.

A second external strategy involves fund-raising. In recent years, congressional leaders have frequently established their own political action committees. Interest groups are usually eager to contribute to these "leadership PACs" in order to curry favor with powerful members of Congress. The leaders, in turn, use the funds to support the various campaigns of their party's candidates and thereby create a sense of obligation. In the 1998 congressional election, for example, the House majority

Rationality Principle

Generally members of Congress seek committee assignments that allow them to acquire more influence in areas important to their constituents.

---

[29]Fenno, *Home Style.* For an extensive discussion of the committee-assignment process in the U.S. House, see Kenneth A. Shepsle, *The Giant Jigsaw Puzzle: Democratic Committee Assignments in the Modern House* (Chicago: University of Chicago Press, 1978); and Scott A. Frisch and Sean Q. Kelly, *Committee Assignment Politics in the U.S. House of Representatives* (Norman: University of Oklahoma Press, 2006). See also E. Scott Adler, *Why Congressional Reforms Fail: Reelection and the House Committee System* (Chicago: University of Chicago Press, 2002).

[30]Douglas Harris, "The Public Speaker" (Ph.D. diss., Johns Hopkins University, 1998).

ONLINE READING

Parties and Agenda Control in Congress

In assessing the influence of political parties on legislative politics, political scientists often ask how parties affect outcomes in Congress. One approach might be to look for evidence of arm twisting or promised favors by party leaders, both of which can be used to influence members' roll-call vote choices. Yet, increasingly, scholars have responded to this question by looking for evidence of agenda manipulation by the majority party. If the majority party can control *what* gets voted on—through its control of committees, including the Rules Committee, and the party leaders' scheduling power—then it can affect outcomes even when the party leaders cannot effectively twist arms or promise favors. Thus, a question that has taken center stage in congressional research is, Who controls the agenda in Congress?

REPUBLICAN AGENDA (104th Congress)	DEMOCRATIC AGENDA (110th Congress)
Balanced budget amendment	Budget reform
Welfare reform	Abortion, family planning
Tax cuts for families	Health care reform
Strong national defense	Homeland security enhancements
Strengthening families	Immigration
Rolling back government regulations	Iraq troop withdrawal
Legal reforms	Minimum wage increase
Congressional term limits	Retirement security

Sources: *Contract with America: The Bold Plan by Representative Newt Gingrich, Representative Dick Armey, and the House Republicans to Change the Nation* © 1994; Marilyn Werber Serafini, "Legislative Priorities: An issue-by-issue rundown on what's on the Democrats' wish list for the new Congress," *National Journal*, Nov. 11, 2006.

Why is agenda control so important in Congress? Whichever party controls a greater number of seats in either the House or the Senate decides which issues will come to the floor for consideration. To illustrate this point, consider the two most recent instances when majority control of Congress changed—in 1994, when Republicans assumed control of both chambers, and in 2006, when Democrats won control of both the House and the Senate. In addition to all the perks that come with majority control, each party was able to push items on it specific agenda. As we see from the table above, there are clear differences between Republicans and Democrats in terms of the legislative policies they chose to pursue.

Congress	Majority Party	Total Final Passage Votes	Majority Rolls	Majority Roll Rate (%)	Minority Rolls	Minority Roll Rate (%)
99th	Democrats	89	1	1.1	35	39.3
100th	Democrats	116	2	1.7	40	34.5
101th	Democrats	108	1	0.93	39	36.1
102th	Democrats	142	0	0	39	27.5
103th	Democrats	160	1	0.63	56	35
104th	Republicans	136	1	0.74	63	46.3
105th	Republicans	133	3	2.3	51	38.4
106th	Republicans	136	4	2.9	51	37.5
107th	Republicans	93	1	1.1	31	33.3
108th	Republicans	119	1	0.84	46	38.7

Source: Gary W. Cox and Mathew D. McCubbins
Setting the Agenda: Responsible Party Government in the U.S. House of Representatives © 2005, Cambridge University Press; calculated by author.

One specific way to think about agenda control in Congress is in terms of the winners and losers on particular pieces of legislation, because this may tell us how much influence the majority party actually has. The most prominent example of this approach has been to look at partisan roll rates. A party (or group of members) is "rolled" when it winds up on the losing side of a vote that passes. In focusing specifically on final passage votes in the U.S. House, political scientists Gary Cox and Mathew McCubbins have found that at the aggregate level, the majority party is essentially never rolled. In contrast, and as we see from the table above, the minority party is significantly more likely to be on the losing side of final-passage votes. This suggests that the majority party controls the agenda and prevents legislation that they oppose (and are likely to lose on) from coming to a vote.

leader, Dick Armey, who was running unopposed, raised more than $6 million, which he distributed to less-well-heeled Republican candidates. Armey's generosity served him well in the leadership struggle that erupted after the election. Likewise, in the 2008 electoral cycle, Nancy Pelosi contributed extensively to the campaigns of fellow Democrats.[31]

In addition to the tasks of organizing Congress, congressional party leaders set the legislative agenda. Not only do the party leaders have considerable sway over Congress's agenda in the large, but they also regulate the fine-grained deliberation over specific items on the agenda. This aspect of agenda setting is multifaceted. At the outset, for example, when a bill is initially dropped in the hopper as a legislative proposal, the Speaker of the House determines which committee has jurisdiction over it. Indeed, since the mid-1970s, the Speaker has been given additional bill-assignment powers, known as multiple referral, permitting him or her to assign different parts of a bill to different committees or the same parts sequentially or simultaneously to several committees.[32] The steering and agenda setting by party leaders work, however, within an institutional framework consisting of structures and procedures. The Analyzing the Evidence unit for this chapter takes a closer look at parties and agenda control.

Having described some of the powers of party leaders, we might pause and ask an even more basic question: Why do members allow themselves to be governed by powerful party leaders? Leaders, after all, are elected by their rank-and-file members, and in their respective party caucuses the rank and file determine how powerful they will permit their leaders to be. Indeed, the power of party leaders has ebbed and flowed over time. From the end of World War II until as late as the 1970s, for example, when the Democrats were the majority party most of the time, party leaders were relatively weak. Speaker of the House Sam Rayburn (D-Tex.), to give one example, was beloved by his followers and was quite successful at persuading members to tow the party line during the 1940s and 1950s. But persuasion was just about the only tool at his disposal. Later party leaders possessed more potent tools. Jim Wright (D-Tex.), for example, who served as Speaker in the 1980s, was provided with considerable power over committee assignments and chaired most of the party committees that formulated policy objectives for the Democrats. Why?

The political scientists John Aldrich and David Rohde have sought to understand these ebbs and flows in the power of a party over its members, or what they call "conditional party government." They suggest that the institutional strength of party leaders is conditional; it depends on particular circumstances. The cir-

---

[31] Rank-and-file members, especially those from safe districts who face limited electoral challenges, have also begun to create their own PACs, which enable them to contribute to their party and its candidates. See Eric S. Heberlig, "Congressional Parties, Fundraising, and Committee Ambition," *Political Research Quarterly* 56 (2003): 151–61.

[32] For a historical look, see David W. Rohde and Kenneth A. Shepsle, "Leaders and Followers in the House of Representatives: Reflections on Woodrow Wilson's *Congressional Government*," *Congress and the Presidency* 14 (1987): 111–33. A recent analysis of the House leadership is Eric Schickler and Kathryn Pearson, "The House Leadership in an Era of Partisan Warfare," in *Congress Reconsidered*, 8th ed., ed. Dodd and Oppenheimer, pp. 207–26. A companion piece on the Senate is C. Lawrence Evans and Daniel Lipinski, "Obstruction and Leadership in the U.S. Senate," ibid., pp. 227–48.

cumstance they emphasize is the degree to which party members share policy goals. If the rank and file are relatively homogeneous in this respect, they will endow their leaders with considerable power to prosecute the shared agenda. If, on the other hand, party members are heterogeneous in their goals, they will be less disposed to empower a leader (indeed, they will be suspicious of any exercise of power by a leader). Thus the Democratic party of the 1940s and 1950s, with its northern liberal wing and its southern conservative wing, was heterogeneous in the extreme and provided its leaders with few power resources. The effects of the Voting Rights Act of 1965, one of which was that formerly Democratic constituencies in the South started electing Republicans, began to be felt in the 1970s, reducing the diversity in the Democratic ranks and thus rendering the party more homogeneous. Under this changed circumstance, Democratic party legislators, who were more focused than before on moderate and liberal goals, were prepared to empower their leaders.[33] Let us now turn to the committee system—the backbone of Congress—and the role of the party leadership in guiding it.

The Committee System: The Core of Congress

If the system of leadership in each party and chamber constitutes the first set of organizational arrangements in the U.S. Congress, then the committee system provides it with a second set of organizational structures. But these are more a division-of-labor and specialization-of-labor system than the hierarchy-of-power system that determines leadership arrangements.

Congress began as a relatively unspecialized assembly, with each legislator participating equally in every step of the legislative process in all realms of policy. By the time of the War of 1812, if not earlier, Congress had begun employing a system of specialists, the committee system, because members with different interests and talents wished to play disproportionate roles in some areas of policy making while ceding influence in areas in which they were less interested.[34] If, Rip van Winkle–like, a congressman had fallen asleep in 1805 and woke up in 1825, he

History
Principle

The committee system evolved during the early nineteenth century as a means of allowing legislators disproportionate influence in areas of policy most important to them.

---

[33] A now-classic treatment of the ebbs and flows of parties and their leaders in the modern era is David W. Rohde, *Parties and Leaders in the Post-reform House* (Chicago: University of Chicago Press, 1991). For a more historical perspective, see David W. Rohde, John H. Aldrich, and Mark M. Berger, "The Historical Variability in Conditional Party Government, 1877–1986," in *Party, Process, and Political Change in Congress: New Perspectives on the History of Congress,* ed. David W. Brady and Mathew D. McCubbins (Palo Alto, Calif.: Stanford University Press, 2002), pp. 17–35. For a development of the analytical argument, see David W. Rohde and John H. Aldrich, "The Logic of Conditional Party Government: Revisiting the Electoral Connection," in *Congress Reconsidered,* 7th ed., ed. Lawrence C. Dodd and Bruce I. Oppenheimer (Washington, D.C.: Congressional Quarterly Press, 2001), pp. 265–92. A complementary theoretical perspective is offered by the political scientists Gary Cox and Mathew McCubbins in both *Legislative Leviathan* and *Setting the Agenda*. Finally, for a recent assessment of the party in light of the 2006 election results, see David W. Rohde, "Political Command and Control," *New York Times,* 18 November 2006, p. A24.

[34] The story of the evolution of the standing committee system in the House and the Senate in the early part of the nineteenth century is told in Gerald Gamm and Kenneth A. Shepsle, "Emergence of Legislative Institutions: Standing Committees in the House and Senate, 1810–1825," *Legislative Studies Quarterly* 14 (1989): 39–66.

ONLINE READING

would have found himself in an entirely transformed legislative world. The legislative chambers in the beginning of that period consisted of bodies of generalists. By the end of the period, in policy area after policy area, the legislative agenda was dominated by groups of specialists serving on standing committees. If, on the other hand, our legislator had fallen asleep in 1825 and awoke a *century* later, the legislature would not seem so very different. In short, organizational decisions in the first quarter of the nineteenth century affected legislative activity over a long horizon. This is the history principle at work.

The congressional committee system consists of a set of standing committees, each with its own jurisdiction, membership, and authority to act. Each **standing committee** is given a permanent status by the official rules, with a fixed membership, officers, rules, a staff, offices, and above all, a jurisdiction that is recognized by all other committees and, usually, the leadership as well (Table 5.2). The jurisdiction of each standing committee is defined by the subject matter of legislation. Except for the Rules Committee in the House and the Rules and Administration Committee in the Senate, all the important committees receive proposals for legislation and process them into official bills. The House Rules Committee decides the order in which bills come up for a vote and determines the rules that govern the length of debate and opportunity for amendments. The jurisdictions of the standing committees usually parallel those of the major departments or agencies in the executive branch. There are important exceptions—Appropriations and Rules in both chambers, for example—but by and large the division of labor is self-consciously designed to parallel executive-branch organization.

Jurisdiction The world of policy is partitioned into policy jurisdictions, which become the responsibility of committees. The members of the Armed Services Committee, for example, become specialists in all aspects of military affairs, the subject matter defining their committee's jurisdiction. Legislators tend to have disproportionate influence in their respective committee jurisdictions, not only because they have become the most knowledgeable members of the legislature in that area of policy but also because they are given the opportunity to exercise various forms of agenda power, a subject we develop further in the next section.

Dividing up institutional activities among jurisdictions, thereby encouraging participants to specialize, has its advantages. But it has its costs, too. If the Armed Services Committee of the House of Representatives had no restraints, its members would undoubtedly shower their districts with military facilities and contracts. In short, the delegation of authority and resources to specialist subunits exploits the advantages of the division and specialization of labor but risks jeopardizing the collective objectives of the group as a whole. The monitoring of committee activities thus goes hand in hand with delegation.

Sometimes new issues arise that fit neatly into no jurisdiction. Some, like the issue of energy supplies that emerged during the 1970s, are so multifaceted that bits and pieces of them are spread across many committee jurisdictions. Other issues, like that of regulating tobacco products, fall into the gray area claimed by several committees—in this case in the House, the Energy and Commerce Committee, with its traditional claim on health-related issues, fought with the Agriculture Com-

TABLE 5.2 Standing Committees of Congress, 2007

House Committees

Agriculture	Natural Resources
Appropriations	Oversight and Government Reform
Armed Services	Rules
Budget	Science and Technology
Education and Labor	Small Business
Energy and Commerce	Standards of Official Conduct (Ethics)
Financial Services	Transportation and Infrastructure
Foreign Affairs Homeland Security	Veterans' Affairs
House Administration	Ways and Means
Judiciary	

Senate Committees

Agriculture, Nutrition, and Forestry	Foreign Relations
Appropriations	Health, Education, Labor, and Pensions
Armed Services	Homeland Security and Governmental Affairs
Banking, Housing, and Urban Affairs	
Budget	Judiciary
Commerce, Science, and Transportation	Rules and Administration
Energy and Natural Resources	Small Business and Entrepreneurship
Environment and Public Works	Veterans' Affairs
Finance	

mittee, whose traditional domain includes crops like tobacco, for jurisdiction over this issue. Turf battles between committees of Congress are notorious.[35] These battles involve committee chairs, the Office of the Parliamentarian, the political leadership of the chamber, and from time to time, select committees appointed to realign committee jurisdictions.

---

[35] An outstanding description and analysis of these battles is found in David C. King, "The Nature of Congressional Committee Jurisdictions," *American Political Science Review* 88, no. 1 (March 1994): 48–63. See also King's *Turf Wars: How Congressional Committees Claim Jurisdiction* (Chicago: University of Chicago Press, 1997).

Authority   Committees may be thought of as agents of the parent body to which jurisdiction-specific authority is provisionally delegated. In this section, we describe committee authority in terms of gatekeeping and after-the-fact authority.

Normally any member of the legislature can submit a bill calling for changes in some policy area. Almost automatically this bill is assigned to the committee of jurisdiction, and very nearly always, there it languishes. In a typical session in the House of Representatives, about 8,000 bills are submitted, fewer than 1,000 of which are acted on by the appropriate committee of jurisdiction. In effect, then, although any member is entitled to make proposals, committees get to decide whether to open the gates and allow the bill to be voted on by the full chamber. Related to *gatekeeping authority* is a committee's *proposal power.* After a bill is referred to a committee, the committee may take no further action on it, amend the legislation in any way, or even write its own legislation before bringing the bill to the floor for a vote. Committees, then, are lords of their jurisdictional domains, setting the table, so to speak, for their parent chamber.[36]

A committee also has responsibilities for bargaining with the other chamber and for conducting oversight, or *after-the-fact authority.* Because the U.S. Congress is bicameral, once one chamber passes a bill, the bill must be considered by the other chamber. If the other chamber passes a bill different from the one passed in the first chamber and the first chamber refuses to accept the changes made, then the two chambers ordinarily meet in a *conference committee,* in which representatives from each chamber hammer out a compromise. In the great majority of cases, conferees are drawn from the committees that had original jurisdiction over the bill. For example, in a sample of Congresses in the 1980s, of the 1,388 House members who served as conferees for various bills during a three-year period, only 7 were not on the committee of original jurisdiction; similarly, in the Senate on only 7 of 1,180 occasions were conferees not drawn from the "right" committee.[37] The committee's effective authority to represent its chamber in conference-committee proceedings constitutes the first manifestation of after-the-fact power that complements its before-the-fact gatekeeping and proposal powers.

A second manifestation of after-the-fact committee authority consists of the committee's primacy in legislative *oversight* of policy implementation by the executive bureaucracy. Even after a bill becomes a law, it is not always (indeed, it is rarely) self-implementing. Executive agents—bureaucrats in the career civil service, commissioners in regulatory agencies, political appointees in the executive branch—march to their own drummers. Unless legislative actors hold their feet to the fire, they may not do precisely what the law requires (especially in light of the fact that

---

Institution Principle

Committees have gatekeeping authority, the right to bargain with the other chamber, and the power of oversight, among other powers.

gatekeeping authority The right and power to decide if a change in policy will be considered.

proposal power The capacity to bring a proposal before the full legislature.

after-the-fact authority The authority to follow up on the fate of a proposal once it has been approved by the full chamber.

conference committee A joint committee created to work out a compromise for House and Senate versions of a piece of legislation.

oversight The effort by Congress, through hearings, investigations, and other techniques, to exercise control over the activities of executive agencies.

---

[36]This setup clearly gives committee members extraordinary power in their respective jurisdictions, allowing them to push policy into line with their own preferences—but only up to a point. If the abuse of their agenda power becomes excessive, the parent body has structural and procedural remedies available to counteract the committee's actions—like stacking the committee with more compliant members, deposing a particularly obstreperous committee chair, or removing policies from a committee's jurisdiction. These are the clubs behind the door that only rarely have to be employed; their mere presence suffices to keep committees from the more outrageous forms of advantage taking.

[37]See Kenneth A. Shepsle and Barry R. Weingast, "The Institutional Foundations of Committee Power," *American Political Science Review* 81, no. 1 (March 1987), pp. 85–104.

statutes are often vague and ambiguous). Congressional committees are continuously watchful of the manner in which legislation is implemented and administered. They play this after-the-fact role by allocating staff and resources to track what the executive branch is doing and, from time to time, holding oversight hearings in which particular policies and programs are given intense scrutiny. This, in turn, gives congressional committees an additional source of leverage over policy in their jurisdictions.

Subcommittees The standing committees of the U.S. House are divided into about 100 even more specialized subcommittees. These subcommittees serve their full committees in precisely the same manner the full committees serve the parent chamber. Thus, in their narrow jurisdictions they have gatekeeping, proposal, interchambers-bargaining, and oversight powers. For a bill on wheat to be taken up by the full Agriculture Committee, for example, it first has to clear the Subcommittee on General Farm Commodities. All of the issues involving assignments, jurisdictions, amendment control, and monitoring that we discussed earlier regarding full committees apply at the subcommittee level as well.

Hierarchy At the committee level, the mantle of leadership falls on the committee chair. He or she, together with the party leaders, determines the committee's agenda and then coordinates the committee's staff, investigatory resources, and subcommittee structure.[38] This coordination includes scheduling hearings, "marking up" bills—that is, transforming legislative drafts into final versions—and scripting the process by which a bill goes from committee to floor proceedings to final passage. For many years, the Congress followed a rigid *seniority* rule for the selection of committee chairs. The benefits of this rule are twofold. First, the chair will be occupied by someone knowledgeable in the committee's jurisdiction, familiar with interest-group and executive-branch players, and politically experienced. Second, the larger institution will be spared divisive leadership contests that reduce the legislative process to efforts in vote grubbing. There are costs, however: Senior individuals may be unenergetic, out of touch, even senile.

The U.S. House operated according to a strict seniority principle from about 1910 (and, informally, even earlier) until the mid-1970s, when most members felt that the burdens of this arrangement were beginning to outweigh its advantages. Committee chairs are now elected by the majority-party members of the full legislature, though there remains a presumption (which may be rebutted) that the most senior committee member will normally assume the chair.[39]

Monitoring Committees If unchecked, committees might easily take advantage of their authority. Indeed, what prevents committees from exploiting their before-the-fact proposal power and their after-the-fact bargaining and oversight authority? As we

---

[38]Because subcommittee chairs do essentially the same things in their narrower jurisdictions, we won't provide a separate discussion of them.

[39]Beginning with the Republican takeover of the House in 1995, committee chairs have been term limited. After three terms, a chair must step down.

seniority The priority or status ranking given to an individual on the basis of length of continuous service on a congressional committee.

saw in Chapter 1, in our discussion of the principal-agent problem, principals must be certain that agents are properly motivated to serve the principal's interests, either by actually sharing the principal's interests themselves or by deriving something of value (reputation, compensation, and so on) for acting to advance those interests. Alternatively, the principal will need to have some instruments by which to monitor and validate what his or her agent is doing, rewarding or punishing the agent accordingly.

Consider again the example of congressional committees. The House or Senate delegates responsibility to its Committee on Agriculture to recommend legislative policy in the field of agriculture. Not surprisingly, legislators from farm districts are most eager to get onto this committee, and for the most part their wishes are accommodated. The Committee on Agriculture, consequently, is composed mainly of farm legislators. And nonfarm legislators are relieved at not having to spend their time on issues of little material interest to them or their constituents. In effecting this delegation, however, the parent legislature is putting itself in the hands of its farm colleagues, benefiting from their expertise on farm-related matters, to be sure, but laying itself open to the danger of planting the fox squarely in the henhouse. The Committee on Agriculture becomes not only a collection of specialists but also a collection of advocates for farm interests. How can the parent body know for certain, therefore, that a recommendation from that committee is not more a reflection of its advocacy than a reflection of its expertise? This is the risk inherent in delegation in principal-agent relationships.

And it is for this reason that the parent legislature maintains a variety of tools and instruments to protect itself from being exploited by its agents. First, it does not allow committees to make final decisions on policy; it allows only recommendations, which the parent legislature retains the authority to accept, amend, or reject. A committee has agenda power, but it is not by itself decisive. Second, the parent body relies on the committee's concern for its own reputation. Making a recommendation on a piece of legislation is not a one-shot action; the committee knows it will return to the parent body time and time again with legislative recommendations, and it will not want to tarnish its reputation for expertise by too much advocacy. Third, the parent body relies on competing agents—interest groups, expert members not on the committee, legislative specialists in the other chamber of the legislature, executive-branch specialists, and even academics—to keep its own agents honest. Finally, in the House there is an institutional club behind the door—the discharge petition. A committee that is sitting on a bill, not permitting it to be taken up by the full chamber, can be discharged of responsibility for the bill if a petition to that effect is signed by a majority of the chamber.

Nevertheless, a principal will not bother to eliminate *entirely* these prospective deviations from his or her interests by agents who have interests of their own. A principal will suffer some *agency loss* from having delegated authority to a "hired hand"; therefore, nearly all principal-agent relationships will be imperfect in some respects from the principal's perspective. Agents will be in a position to extract some advantage from the privileged relationship they have with their principal—not too much, or it will undermine the relationship altogether, but enough to diminish the benefits of the relationship a bit from the principal's point of view. The Committee on Agriculture, for example, cannot get away with spending huge proportions of the federal budget on agricultural subsidies to farmers. But it can insert small items into agriculture bills from time to time—an experimental grain-to-fuel conversion project in an important legislator's state or district, for example, or special funds to the U.S. trade representative to give priority to agriculture-related trade issues. The parent body, as we suggested, will find it worth its while to keep an eye on the Agriculture Committee, but it won't be worth its while to take action on every instance of indulgence by the committee. The cost of doing that—the transaction cost of monitoring and overseeing committee performance—gets excessive if perfection is the objective.

Thus we see the institution principle providing some guidance on how a group of legislators organize themselves for business. They take advantage of the division and specialization of labor, dividing themselves into specialized subgroups (committees and subcommittees) thus enjoying the benefits of expertise from these subunits. But they also guard against the subunits' going off half-cocked in pursuit of their own narrower interests. The parent legislature in effect uses institutional arrangements to regulate and oversee its subunits' activities.

Committee Reform   Over the years, Congress has reformed its organizational structure and operating procedures. Most changes have been made to improve efficiency, but some reforms have also represented a response to political considerations. In the 1970s, a series of reforms substantially altered the organization of power in Congress. Among the most important changes put into place at that time were an increase in the number of subcommittees, greater autonomy for subcommittee chairs, the opening of most committee deliberations to the public, and a system of multiple referral of bills that allowed several committees to consider one bill at the same time. One of the driving impulses behind these reforms was an effort to reduce the power of committee chairs.

As a consequence of those reforms, power became more fragmented, making it harder to reach agreement on legislation. In 1995, the Republican leadership of the 104th Congress sought to concentrate more authority in the party leadership. One of the ways the House achieved this was by abandoning the principle of seniority in the selection of a number of committee chairs, appointing them instead according to their loyalty to the party. This move tied committee chairs more closely to the leadership. In addition, the Republican leadership eliminated 25 of the House's 115 subcommittees and gave committee chairs more power over their subcommittees. The result was an unusually cohesive congressional majority, which pushed forward a common agenda. House Republicans also agreed to impose a three-term limit on committee and subcommittee heads. As a result, all the chairs were replaced in 2001, when the 107th Congress convened. In many instances, chairs were replaced by the most senior Republican committee member, but the net result was a redistribution of power in the House of Representatives.

The Staff System: Staffers and Agencies

A congressional institution ranking just below committees and parties in importance is the staff system. Every member of Congress employs a large number of staff members, whose tasks include handling constituency requests and, to a large and growing extent, dealing with legislative details and the activities of administrative agencies. Increasingly, staffers bear the primary responsibility for formulating and drafting proposals, organizing hearings, dealing with administrative agencies, and negotiating with lobbyists. Indeed, legislators typically deal with one another through staff members rather than through direct, personal contact. Representatives and senators together employ nearly 11,000 staffers in their Washington and home offices. In addition to the personal staffs of individual senators and representatives, Congress also employs roughly 2,000 committee staffers. These individuals make up the permanent staff, who often stay regardless of turnover in Congress and are attached to every House and Senate committee. They are responsible for organizing and administering the committee's work, doing research, scheduling, organizing hearings, and drafting legislation.

Not only does Congress employ personal and committee staffs, but it has also established three **staff agencies** designed to provide the legislative branch with resources and expertise independent of the executive branch. These agencies enhance Congress's capacity to oversee administrative agencies and evaluate presidential programs and proposals. They are the Congressional Research Service, which performs research for legislators who wish to know the facts and competing arguments relevant to policy proposals or other legislative business; the Government Accountability Office, through which Congress can investigate the financial and administrative affairs of any government agency or program; and the Congressional Budget Office, which assesses the economic implications and likely costs of proposed federal programs, such as President George W. Bush's proposed revisions of the Social Security system in 2005.

Informal Organization: The Caucuses

In addition to the official organization of Congress, there also exists an unofficial organizational structure: the caucuses, formally known as legislative service organizations (LSOs). A **congressional caucus** is a group of senators or representatives who share certain opinions, interests, or social characteristics. There are ideological caucuses such as the liberal Democratic Study Group and the conservative Democratic Forum. There are also a large number of caucuses composed of legislators representing particular economic or policy interests, such as the Travel and Tourism Caucus, the Steel Caucus, the Mushroom Caucus, and the Concerned Senators for the Arts. Legislators who share common backgrounds or social characteristics have organized such caucuses as the Congressional Black Caucus, the Congressional Caucus for Women's Issues, and the Hispanic Caucus. All these caucuses seek to advance the interests of the groups they represent by promoting legislation, encouraging Congress to hold hearings, and pressing administrative agencies for favorable treatment.

staff agencies The agencies responsible for providing Congress with independent expertise, administration, and oversight capability.

congressional caucus An association of members of Congress based on party, interest, or social characteristics such as gender or race.

RULES OF LAWMAKING: HOW A BILL BECOMES A LAW

The institutional structure of Congress is one key factor that helps shape the legislative process. A second and equally important set of factors is made up of the rules of congressional procedure. These rules govern all the procedures from introducing a bill through submitting it to the president for signing. Not only do these regulations influence the fate of every bill, but they also help determine the distribution of power in Congress.[40]

Committee Deliberation

Even if a member of Congress, the White House, or a federal agency has spent months developing and drafting a piece of legislation, it does not become a bill until a senator or a representative officially submits it to the clerk of the House or Senate and it is referred to the appropriate committee for deliberation. No floor action on any bill can take place until the committee with jurisdiction over it has taken all the time it needs to deliberate.[41] During the course of its deliberations, the committee typically refers the bill to one of its subcommittees, which may hold hearings, listen to expert testimony, and amend the proposed legislation before referring it to the full committee for its consideration. The full committee may accept the recommendation of the subcommittee or hold its own hearings and prepare its own amendments. Even more frequently, the committee and subcommittee may do little or nothing with a bill and simply allow it to die in committee. In a typical congressional session, roughly 8,000 bills are introduced, and 85 to 90 percent of them die in committee—an indication of the power of the congressional committee system.

Once a bill's assigned committee or committees in the House of Representatives have acted affirmatively, the whole bill or various parts of it are transmitted to the Rules Committee, which determines the specific rules under which the legislation will be considered by the full House. Together with the Speaker, it influences when debate will be scheduled, for how long, what amendments will be in order, and the order in which they will be considered. The Speaker also rules on all procedural points of order and points of information raised during the debate. A bill's supporters generally prefer what is called a *closed rule*, which puts severe limits on floor debate and amendments. Opponents of a bill usually prefer an *open rule*, which permits potentially damaging floor debate and makes it easier to add amendments that may cripple the bill or weaken its chances of passing.

Debate

Party control of the agenda is reinforced by the rule giving the Speaker of the House and the majority leader of the Senate the power of recognition during debate on a bill. Usually the chair knows the purpose for which a member intends to speak well in advance of the occasion. Spontaneous efforts to gain recognition are often foiled. For example, the Speaker may ask, "For what purpose does the member rise?" before

 Institution Principle

The Rules Committee's decision about whether to adopt a closed or open rule for floor debate greatly influences a bill's chances of passing.

closed rule The provision by the House Rules Committee that prohibits the introduction of amendments during debate.

open rule The provision by the House Rules Committee that permits floor debate and the addition of amendments to a bill.

---

[40]We should emphasize, although we don't mean to confuse the reader, that a legislature "suspends" its rules as often as it follows them. There are unorthodox ways to proceed in order to avoid procedural logjams, and the House and, especially, the Senate frequently resort to these unorthodox ways. See Barbara Sinclair, *Unorthodox Lawmaking: New Legislative Processes in the U.S. Congress,* 3rd ed. (Washington, D.C.: Congressional Quarterly Press, 2007).

[41]A bill can be pulled from a committee by a discharge petition, but this is an extreme measure and is resorted to only rarely. There are other parliamentary tricks that may also be attempted, but it is fair to say that most of the time at least it is the committee of jurisdiction that influences the course of a bill.

deciding whether to grant recognition. In general, the party leadership in the House has total control over debate. In the Senate, each member has substantial power to block the close of debate. A House majority can override opposition, while it takes an extraordinary majority (a three-fifths vote) to close debate in the Senate; thus the Senate tends to be far more tolerant in debate, far more accommodating of various views, and far less partisan. In recent years, however, partisanship in both chambers has been on the rise.

In the House, virtually all of the time allotted by the Rules Committee for debate on a given bill is controlled by the bill's sponsor and its leading opponent. These two participants are, by rule and tradition, granted the power to allocate most of the debate time in small amounts to members who are seeking to speak for or against the measure.

In the Senate, other than the power of recognition, the leadership has much less control over floor debate. Indeed, the Senate is unique among the world's legislative bodies for its commitment to unlimited debate. Once given the floor, a senator may speak for as long as he or she wishes unless an extraordinary majority votes to end debate. On a number of memorable occasions, senators have used this right to prevent action on legislation they opposed. Through this tactic, called the *filibuster,* small minorities or even one individual in the Senate can force the majority to give in to his or her demands. During the 1950s and 1960s, for example, opponents of civil rights legislation often sought to block its passage by adopting the filibuster. A vote of three fifths of the Senate, or sixty votes, is needed to end a filibuster. This procedure is called *cloture.*

Although it is the best known, the filibuster is not the only technique used to block Senate action. Under Senate rules, members have a virtually unlimited ability to propose amendments to a pending bill. Each amendment must be voted on before the bill can come to a final vote. The introduction of new amendments can be stopped only by unanimous consent. This, in effect, can permit a determined minority to filibuster by amendment, indefinitely delaying the passage of a bill.

Senators can also place "holds," or stalling devices, on bills to delay debate. Senators place holds on bills when they fear that openly opposing them will be unpopular. Because holds are kept secret, the senators placing the holds do not have to take public responsibility for their actions.

Once a bill is debated on the floor of the House and the Senate, the leaders schedule it for a vote on the floor of each chamber. By then, congressional leaders know what the vote will be; leaders do not bring legislation to the floor unless they are fairly certain it is going to pass. As a consequence, it is unusual for the leadership to lose a bill on the floor. On rare occasions, however, the last moments of the floor vote can be dramatic, as each party's leadership puts its whip organization into action to make sure wavering members vote with the party.

Conference Committee: Reconciling House and Senate Versions of a Bill

Getting a bill out of committee and through one of the houses of Congress is no guarantee that it will be enacted. Frequently bills that began with similar provisions in both chambers emerge with little resemblance to each other. Alternatively, a bill

filibuster A tactic used by members of the Senate to prevent action on legislation they oppose by continuously holding the floor and speaking until the majority backs down. Once given the floor, senators have unlimited time to speak, and it requires a cloture vote of three fifths of the Senate to end a filibuster.

cloture A rule allowing a supermajority of the members of a legislative body to set a time limit on debate over a given bill.

may be passed by one chamber but undergo substantial revision in the other chamber. In such cases, a conference committee composed of the senior members of the committees or subcommittees that initiated the bills may be required to iron out differences between the two pieces of legislation. Sometimes members or leaders will let objectionable provisions pass on the floor with the idea that they will be eliminated in conference. Conference agreement requires a majority of each of the two delegations. Legislation that emerges successfully from a conference committee is more often a compromise than a clear victory of one set of forces over another.

When a bill comes out of conference, it faces one more hurdle. Before it can be sent to the president for signing, the House-Senate conference report must be approved on the floor of each chamber. Usually such approval is given quickly. Occasionally, however, a bill's opponents use the report as one last opportunity to defeat a piece of legislation.

Presidential Action

Once adopted by the House and the Senate, a bill goes to the president, who may choose to sign the bill into law or *veto* it (Figure 5.6). The veto is the president's constitutional power to reject a piece of legislation. To veto a bill, the president returns it within ten days to the house of Congress in which it originated, along with objections to it. If Congress adjourns during the ten-day period and the president has taken no action, the bill is also considered to have been vetoed—by means of the *pocket veto.* The possibility of a presidential veto affects the willingness of members of Congress to push for different pieces of legislation at different times. If they think a proposal is likely to be vetoed, they might shelve it for a later time. Alternatively, the sponsors of a popular bill opposed by the president might push for passage to force the president to pay the political costs of vetoing it.[42] During the entire first term of President George W. Bush (2001–5), not one bill was vetoed. In the next two years, the president vetoed a single bill, the Stem Cell Research Enhancement Act, on July 19, 2006. This unusual record of veto inactivity reflects the fact that the Republicans controlled both legislative chambers throughout the period and thus were able to work hand in glove with a Republican president. The 110th Congress (2007–8) stimulated a higher rate of veto activity as the Republican president faced a Congress controlled by the Democrats.

A presidential veto may be overridden by a two-thirds vote in both the House and the Senate. A veto override says much about the support that a president can expect from Congress, and it can deliver a stinging blow to the executive branch. Presidents will often back down from their threat to veto a bill if they believe Congress will override the veto. These strategic interactions between the legislature and the executive branch are taken up in the next chapter.

Normal and Abnormal Procedures in Congress

We have noted that although there is a "normal" procedure in each chamber, it is often the case that the normal is abandoned and an abnormal, or unorthodox,

Collective-Action Principle

A bill often passes the House and Senate in different forms. Sponsors from both houses then meet in a conference committee to iron out the differences.

veto The president's constitutional power to turn down acts of Congress within ten days of their passage while Congress is in session. A presidential veto may be overridden by a two-thirds vote of each house of Congress.

pocket veto A veto that is effected when Congress adjourns during the time a president has to approve a bill and the president takes no action on it.

---

[42]John B. Gilmour, *Strategic Disagreement: Stalemate in American Politics* (Pittsburgh: University of Pittsburgh Press, 1995).

FIGURE 5.6 How a Bill Becomes a Law

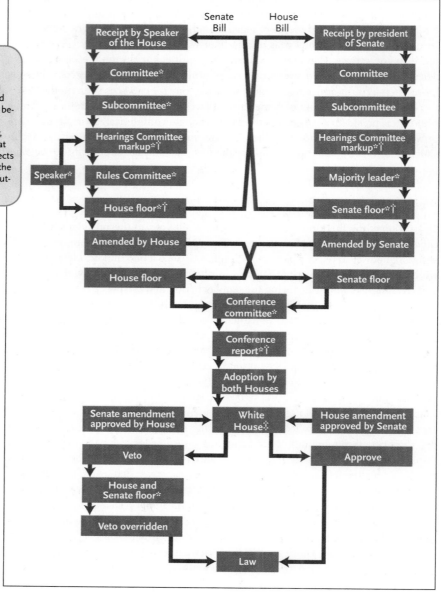

*Points at which the bill can be amended.

†Points at which the bill can die.

‡If the president neither signs nor vetoes the bill within ten days, it automatically becomes law.

procedure is devised. The treatment of appropriations bills in the period leading up to the November 2004 election provides an excellent example.

"Normally" the House passes thirteen separate appropriations bills after each one has passed through an appropriations process, beginning with a subcommittee hearing, followed by full Appropriations Committee deliberations, and concluding with passage by the full House. These thirteen measures are then transmitted to the Senate, which subjects each of them to its own "regular" appropriations process. Each of the bills (thirteen in all) now has a House version and a Senate version. Thirteen separate conference committees are set up to compromise on the differences between each pair. The thirteen compromised versions are then sent back to each chamber for final approval. And in principle, though rarely in practice, this entire process is completed before October 1, the day on which the new fiscal year begins.

But 2004 was an election year, and members up for reelection really did not want to remind the voters that the appropriations bills they were passing were growing to produce the largest deficit in history. So an unorthodox procedure was invented. One of the thirteen appropriations bills passed the House and the Senate through the normal process and was sent to conference. During the conference, the other twelve bills were tacked on, making a single appropriations bill. This omnibus bill was sent to each chamber for a single up-or-down vote. In voting for the omnibus measure, a member was "innoculated" against local objections from constituents. He or she could respond, "I know, I know. The omnibus bill is not ideal. But what was I to do? Defeating it would have shut the government down."

Before leaving this topic, it is worth noting that normal and abnormal procedures involve either the conventional or the creative application of existing rules. Each chamber, however, is granted by the Constitution the privilege of formulating its own rules of procedure. So from time to time, the House or the Senate will change its rules of procedure. At other times, a dominant coalition in a chamber will threaten to do this unless it is allowed its way under the existing rules. Here we see the confluence of the rationality principle and the institution principle as rational legislators seek to (re)arrange their chamber's institutional procedures in order to accomplish particular purposes or realize particular goals.

This phenomenon was dramatically illustrated in May 2005 when President Bush's judicial nominations were threatened by a filibuster by Democratic senators. In the face of nominations whose approval looked vulnerable to a blocking action by the minority party, Bill Frist, the Senate majority leader, unveiled what came to be known as the nuclear option. It entailed a clever parliamentary maneuver in which debate could be brought to a close not by securing the sixty votes normally required (which the Republicans did not control) but by a simple majority. This would be executed by formally requesting the president of the Senate (Vice President Dick Cheney) to end debate without a cloture vote because the issue before the Senate was the constitutional one of "advising and consenting" on a presidential judicial nomination. It was expected that any such move on the part of the Republicans would be followed by the Democrats' appealing any ruling by the Senate president to end debate. But that ruling required only a majority vote to be sustained. In this manner, the Republicans could end-run the practice of unlimited debate that normally prevails in the Senate, on constitutional issues at least. The nuclear option was never implemented, however. The very threat of it induced a number of moderate senators to agree to support a motion to end debate (thereby producing the sixty needed votes) and bring a presidential nominee forward for a final vote. These senators were willing to accommodate a vote so long as the president and the Republican majority did not abuse this concession by bring forward "extremist" nominees.

The Distributive Tendency in Congress

To pass a policy, it is necessary to authorize the policy—that is, to provide statutory authority to a government agency to implement the legislation—and then provide appropriations to fund the implementation. The list of politicians whose consent is required in these processes is extraordinarily long. At a minimum, it includes majorities of the relevant committee and subcommittee of each chamber (almost certainly including their chairs), the Appropriations Committee and the appropriate subcommittee in each chamber (including their chairs), the House Rules Committee, chamber majorities (including leaders of the majority party), and the president. Some of the legislators may go along without requiring much for their states or districts on the assumption that their turn will come on another bill. But most of these politicians will need some form of "compensation" in order to provide their endorsement and support.

With so many hurdles to clear before a legislative initiative can become a law, the benefits must be spread broadly. It is as though a bill had to travel on a toll road past a number of tollbooths, each one housing a collector with his or her hand out for payment. On rare occasions, the required toll takes the form of a personal bribe—a contract to a firm run by a congressman's brother, a job for a senator's daughter, a boondoggle "military inspection" trip to a Pacific isle for a legislator and his or her companion. Occasionally there is a-wink-and-a-nod understanding, usually given by the majority leader or committee chair, that support from a legislator today will result in reciprocal support for legislation of interest to him or her down the road. Most frequently features of the bill are drafted initially or revised so as to be more inclusive, spreading the benefits widely among beneficiaries. This is the *distributive tendency.*

The distributive tendency is part of the American system of representative democracy. Legislators, in advocating the interests of their constituents, are eager to advertise their ability to deliver for their state or district. They maneuver to put themselves in a position to claim credit for good things that happen there and duck blame for bad things. This is the way they earn trust back home, deter strong challengers in upcoming elections, and defeat those who do run against them. It means that legislators must take advantage of every opportunity that presents itself. In some instances, the results may seem bizarre. In April 2003, for example, Senator Thad Cochran (R-Miss.) was able to insert into the bill funding the war in Iraq language that provided $250 million for "disaster relief" for southern catfish farmers.[43] Most Americans would never have guessed that driving Saddam Hussein from power would have an effect on catfish farming in Mississippi.

Policy Principle

The distributive tendency in Congress results from the need for a broad base of support in order for a bill to be passed.

distributive tendency The tendency of Congress to spread the benefits of a policy over a wide range of members' districts.

ONLINE READING

---

[43]Dan Morgan, "War Funding Bill's Extra Riders," *Washington Post*, 8 April 2003, p. A4.

This system, which is practiced in Washington and most state capitals, means that political pork gets spread around; it is not controlled by a small clique of politicians or concentrated in a small number of states or districts. But it also means that public authority and appropriations do not go where they are most needed. The most impoverished cities do not get as much money as is appropriate because some of the available money must be diverted to buy political support. The most needy individuals often do not get tax relief, health care, or occupational subsidies for reasons unrelated to philosophy or policy grounds. It is the distributive tendency at work. And it is one of the unintended consequences of the separation of powers and multiple veto points.[44]

HOW CONGRESS DECIDES

What determines the kinds of legislation that Congress ultimately produces? According to the simplest theories of representation, members of Congress respond to the views of their constituents. In fact, the process of creating a legislative agenda, drawing up a list of possible measures, and deciding among them is very complex, one in which a variety of influences from inside and outside government play important roles. External influences include a legislator's constituency and various interest groups. Influences from inside government include party leadership, congressional colleagues, and the president. Let us examine each of these influences individually and then consider how they interact to produce congressional policy decisions.

Policy Principle

Multiple factors influence how a member of Congress votes on legislation. These include constituency, interest groups, party leaders, congressional colleagues, and the president.

Constituency

Because members of Congress, for the most part, want to be reelected, we would expect the views of their constituents to have a key influence on the decisions legislators make. Yet constituency influence is not so straightforward as we might think. In fact, most constituents do not even know what policies their representatives support. The number of citizens who *do* pay attention to such matters—the attentive public—is usually very small. Nonetheless, members of Congress spend a lot of time worrying about what their constituents think because these representatives realize that their choices may be scrutinized in a future election and used as ammunition by an opposing candidate. Because of this possibility, members of Congress will try to anticipate their constituents' policy views.[45] Legislators are more likely to act in accordance with those views if they think voters will take them into account during elections. In this way, constituents may affect

[44] See George Tsebelis, *Veto Players: How Political Institutions Work* (Princeton, N.J.: Princeton University Press, 2002).

[45] See John W. Kingdon, *Congressmen's Voting Decisions* (New York: Harper & Row, 1973), chap. 3, and R. Douglas Arnold, *The Logic of Congressional Action* (New Haven, Conn.: Yale University Press, 1990). See also Joshua Clinton, "Representation in Congress: Constituents and Roll Calls in the 106th House," *Journal of Politics* 68 (2006): 397–409.

ONLINE READING

congressional policy choices even when there is little direct evidence of their awareness of them.[46]

Interest Groups

Interest groups are another important external influence on the policies that Congress produces. When members of Congress are making voting decisions, interest groups that have some connection to constituents in the districts of particular members are most likely to be influential. For this reason, interest groups with the ability to mobilize followers in many congressional districts may be especially influential in Congress. The small-business lobby, for example, played an important role in defeating President Clinton's proposal for comprehensive health-care reform in 1993–94. The mobilization of networks of small businesses across the country meant that virtually every member of Congress had to take their views into account.

In the 2008 electoral cycle, many millions of dollars in campaign contributions were given by interest groups and PACs to incumbent legislators and challengers. What does this money buy? A popular conception is that campaign contributions buy legislative votes. In this view, legislators vote for whichever proposal favors the bulk of their contributors. Although the vote-buying hypothesis makes for good campaign rhetoric, it has little factual support. Empirical studies by political scientists show little evidence that contributions from large PACs influence legislative voting patterns.[47]

If contributions don't buy votes, what do they buy? Our claim is that campaign contributions influence legislative behavior in ways that are difficult for the public to observe and political scientists to measure. The institutional structure of Congress provides opportunities for interest groups to influence legislation outside the public eye, which legislators and contributors prefer.

Committee proposal power enables legislators, if they are on the relevant committee, to introduce legislation that favors contributing groups. Gatekeeping power enables committee members to block legislation that harms contributing groups. The fact that certain provisions are *excluded* from a bill is as much an indicator of PAC influence as the fact that certain provisions are *included*. The difference is that it is hard to measure what you don't see. Committee oversight powers enable members to intervene in bureaucratic decision making on behalf of contributing groups.

The point here is that voting on the floor, the alleged object of campaign contributions according to the vote-buying hypothesis, is a highly visible, highly public

---

[46]Interest groups from the state or district (which we discuss below) can be useful to legislators in this respect when they provide information concerning the significance of particular issues for various constituency groups. In effect, they provide legislators with heads-up signals and wake-up calls. See Kenneth W. Kollman, *Outside Lobbying: Public Opinion and Interest Group Strategies* (Princeton, N.J.: Princeton University Press, 1998).

ONLINE READING
[47]See Janet M. Grenke, "PACs and the Congressional Supermarket: The Currency Is Complex," *American Journal of Political Science* 33, no. 1 (February 1989): 1–24. More generally, see Jacobson, *The Politics of Congressional Elections*. For a view that too little, not too much, money is spent by interest groups, see Stephen Ansolabehere, John de Figueiredo, and James Snyder, "Why Is There So Little Money in U.S. Politics?" *Journal of Economic Perspectives* 17 (2003): 105–30.

act, one that could get a legislator in trouble with his or her broader electoral constituency. The committee system, on the other hand, provides loads of opportunities for legislators to deliver "services" to PAC contributors and other donors that are more subtle and better hidden from public view. Thus we suggest that the most appropriate places to look for traces of campaign-contribution influence on the legislative process are in the manner in which committees deliberate, mark up proposals, and block legislation from the floor; outside public view, these are the primary arenas for interest-group influence.

Party Discipline

In both the House and the Senate, party leaders have a good deal of influence over the behavior of their party members. This influence, sometimes called party discipline, was once so powerful that it dominated the lawmaking process. Let us define as a *party vote* a vote for which 50 percent or more of the members of one party take one position while at least 50 percent of the members of the other party take the opposing position. At the beginning of the twentieth century, most *roll-call votes* in the House of Representatives were party votes. The frequency of party votes declined through most of the twentieth century as legislative parties grew more ideologically diverse. Democrats included liberals from the big cities and conservatives from the South. Republicans included conservatives from the Midwest and West and moderates from the Northeast. The tail end of this decline in party voting can be observed in Figure 5.7 more between 1955 and 1970. Beginning in the 1970s, however, legislative parties grew more homogeneous and more polarized. Conservative southern districts began electing Republicans and liberal northeastern districts began sending Democrats to Congress. The data shown in the figure reflect this, with party votes ticking upward from the 1970s onward. Some of this change is the result of the intense partisan struggles that began during the administrations of Ronald Reagan and George H. W. Bush. Straight party-line voting was also seen briefly in the 103rd Congress (1993–94) after Bill Clinton's election in 1992. The situation soon gave way, however, to the many long-term factors working against party discipline in Congress, as seen in the decline in party voting over the most recent decade.[48]

In 2001, the newly elected president, George W. Bush, called for an end to partisan squabbling in Congress. During the 2000 campaign, Bush had claimed that as governor of Texas he had been able to build effective bipartisan coalitions, which, he said, should serve as a model for the conduct of the nation's business as well. September 11, 2001, prompted almost every member of Congress to rally behind President Bush's military response. But Democrats and Republicans in the House almost immediately divided sharply over the issue of airport security. Over the next several years, partisan differences emerged on a variety of issues, including taxation and foreign policy. On the issue of taxation, President Bush had sought to slash federal taxes by as much as $700 billion over several years. Many Democrats, on the other hand, opposed most or all of Bush's tax-cut proposals and called for increased federal

party vote A roll-call vote in the House or Senate in which at least 50 percent of the members of one party take a particular position and are opposed by at least 50 percent of the members of the other party. Party votes are less common today than they were in the nineteenth century.

roll-call votes Votes in which each legislator's yes or no vote is recorded.

---

[48]There have been fluctuations during George W. Bush's presidency—declines in party voting following September 11 and then surges and declines in subsequent years (Figure 5.7).

FIGURE 5.7 Party Unity Scores by Chamber

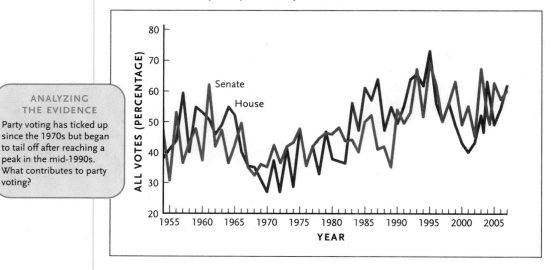

SOURCE: *Congressional Quarterly Weekly Report.*

NOTE: The percentage refers to recorded votes on which the majority of one party voted against the majority of the other party.

spending on social programs, especially health care. On issues of foreign policy, many Democrats were deeply troubled by the president's willingness to use military force on a unilateral basis when he deemed it necessary. Before the war in Iraq, Democratic leaders argued for giving UN weapons inspectors and diplomacy more time. Even after the quick conclusion of the active first phase of the war, some Democrats accused the president of undermining America's relations with its allies. The war in Iraq, as well as the resumption of fighting in Afghanistan, posed policy difficulties for the Bush administration and its congressional allies. Most Republicans stuck with President Bush, although they distanced themselves somewhat from the administration's Iraq policy in the run-up to the 2006 and 2008 elections. Most Democrats, even those who were supportive in the post–September 11 environment, have moved into opposition.

To some extent, party divisions are based on ideology and background. Republican members of Congress are more likely than Democrats to be drawn from rural or suburban areas. Democrats are likely to be more liberal on economic and social questions than their Republican colleagues. This ideological gap has been especially pronounced since 1980 (Figure 5.8). Ideological differences certainly help explain roll-call divisions between the two parties.[49] Ideology and background, however, are only part of the explanation of party unity. The other part has to do with party organization and leadership. Although party organization has weakened since the beginning of the twentieth century, today's party leaders still have some resources at their disposal: (1) committee as-

---

[49] Keith T. Poole and Howard Rosenthal, *Congress: A Political-Economic History of Roll Call Voting* (New York: Oxford University Press, 1997).

FIGURE 5.8 The Widening Ideological Gap between the Parties

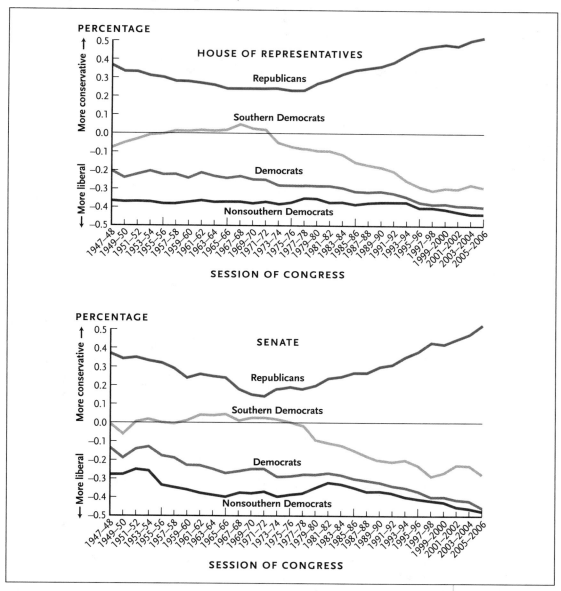

SOURCE: Data from Keith T. Poole and Howard Rosenthal, computed by Gary C. Jacobson, and reprinted in Poole and Rosenthal's *Congress: A Political-Economic History of Roll Call Voting* (New York: Oxford University Press, 1997); updates by Poole.

signments, (2) access to the floor, (3) the whip system, (4) logrolling, and (5) the presidency. These resources are regularly used and are often effective in securing the support of party members.[50]

Committee Assignments Leaders can create debts among members by helping them get favorable committee assignments. These assignments are made early in the congressional careers of most members and ordinarily cannot be taken from them if they later balk at party discipline. Nevertheless, if the leadership goes out of its way to get the right assignment for a member, the effort is likely to create a bond of obligation that can be called on without any other payments or favors.

In 2005, the Republicans removed several members from the House Ethics Committee because of their participation, in the previous Congress, in investigating the House Republican leader, Tom DeLay. Inasmuch as the Ethics Committee is seen as a bipartisan watchdog, these actions were seen as muscle-flexing responses by the Republican leadership. Bipartisan or not, the leadership seemed to be saying, as noted above, there are some lines that should not be crossed.

Access to the Floor The most important everyday resource available to the parties is control over access to the floor. With thousands of bills awaiting passage and most members clamoring for access to influence a bill or publicize themselves, floor time is precious. In the Senate, the leadership allows ranking committee members to influence the allocation of floor time—who will speak for how long; in the House, the Speaker, as head of the majority party (in consultation with the minority leader), allocates large blocks of floor time. Thus floor time is allocated in both houses of Congress by the majority and minority leaders. More important, the Speaker of the House and the majority leader in the Senate possess the power of recognition. Although this power may not appear to be substantial, it is a formidable authority and can be used to stymie a piece of legislation completely or to frustrate a member's attempts to speak on a particular issue. Be-

---

[50]Legislative leaders may behave in ways that embellish their reputation for being willing to punish party members who stray from the party line. The problem of developing such a credible reputation is analyzed in Randall Calvert, "Reputation and Legislative Leadership," *Public Choice* 55 (1987): 81–120, and is summarized in Kenneth A. Shepsle and Mark S. Boncheck, *Analyzing Politics: Rationality, Behavior, Institutions* (New York: Norton, 1997), pp. 397–403. The classic example of such punishment occurred after the 1964 election, in which two prominent House Democrats, John Bell Williams of Mississippi and Albert Watson of South Carolina, were disciplined for having supported the Republican presidential nominee, Barry Goldwater. The party leaders pushed for, and the Democratic caucus supported, a punishment in which each was demoted to the bottom of the seniority roster on the committees of which they were members. In Williams's case, the punishment was serious because he was the second-highest-ranking Democrat on the House Energy and Commerce Committee. Each resigned from the House in the wake of this punishment and ran for elective office (both successfully) as Republicans. The message was clear: There are some partisan lines that party members cross at their peril! Put slightly differently, the famous mid-twentieth-century House Speaker Sam Rayburn is known to have believed that deviation from the party position would be tolerated for "reasons of conscience or constituency." Of one wayward Democrat, he is alleged to have said that the departure from the party line "better be a matter of conscience, because it damn sight isn't because of his constituency." In short, there would be hell to pay!

cause the power is significant, members of Congress usually attempt to stay on good terms with the Speaker and the majority leader to ensure that they will continue to be recognized.[51]

The Whip System   Some influence accrues to party leaders through the **whip system,** which is primarily a communications network. Between twelve and twenty assistant and regional whips are selected by geographic zones to operate at the direction of the majority or minority leader and the whip. They take polls of all the members to learn their intentions on specific bills. This information enables the leaders to know if they have enough support to allow a vote and whether the vote is so close that they need to put pressure on a few swing votes. Leaders also use the whip system to convey their wishes and plans to the members, but only in very close votes do they exert pressure on a member. In those instances, the Speaker or a lieutenant will go to a few party members who have indicated they will switch if their vote is essential. The whip system helps the leaders limit the practice of pressuring members to a few times per session. It helps maintain party unity in both houses of Congress, but it is particularly critical in the House of Representatives because of the large number of legislators whose positions and votes must always be accounted for.

Logrolling   An agreement between two or more members of Congress who have nothing in common except the need for mutual support is called **logrolling**. The agreement states, in effect, "You support me on bill X, and I'll support you on a bill of your choice." Because party leaders are the center of the communications networks in the two chambers, they can help members create large logrolling coalitions. Hundreds of logrolling deals are made each year, and while there are no official records, it would be a poor party leader whose whips did not know who owed what to whom.[52] In some instances, logrolling produces strange alliances. A seemingly unlikely alliance emerged in Congress in June 1994, when 119 mainly conservative senators and representatives from oil-producing states met with President Clinton to suggest that they might be willing to support the president's health-care proposals in exchange for his support for a number of tax breaks for the oil industry. Senator J. Bennett Johnston of Louisiana, a leader of the oil-state representatives, contended that the issues of health care and oil production were closely related because both "affected the long-term economic security of the nation." Ironically, the oil-producing groups that promoted this alliance are generally among the most conservative forces

Collective-Action Principle

The whip system helps maintain party unity in Congress.

Collective-Action Principle

Logrolling is an informal means of facilitating cooperation in Congress.

whip system A communications network in each house of Congress. Whips poll the membership to learn their intentions on specific legislative issues and assist the majority and minority leaders in various tasks.

logrolling A legislative practice wherein reciprocal agreements are made between legislators, usually in voting for or against a bill. In contrast to bargaining, logrolling unites parties that have nothing in common but their desire to exchange support.

---

[51]A recent analysis of how floor time is allocated is found in Cox and McCubbins, *Setting the Agenda*.

[52]For an analysis of the formal problems that logrolling (or vote trading) both solves and creates, see Shepsle and Bonchek, *Analyzing Politics*, pp. 317–19. They argue that logrolling cannot be the entire solution to the problem of assembling majority coalitions out of the diverse preferences found in any political party. The reason is that while party leaders can try to keep track of who owes what to whom, the bookkeeping is imperfect and highly complex at best. Nevertheless, if anyone is positioned to orchestrate a system of logrolling, it is the party leaders. And of all those who have tried to facilitate such "cooperation," Robert Byrd (D-W.Va.), who served as both majority whip and majority leader in the Senate, has been the acknowledged master. For an insightful analysis of the ways party leaders build majority coalitions through the strategic use of pork-barrel projects, see Diana Evans, *Greasing the Wheels*.

in the nation. When asked what he thought of the president's health-care proposal, George Alcorn, a leading industry lobbyist involved in the logrolling effort, dismissed Clinton's plan as "socialized medicine." Another alliance of strange bedfellows was the 1994 "corn for porn" logroll in which liberal urbanites supported farm programs in exchange for rural support for National Endowment for the Arts funding (at a time when many conservatives thought that the art produced by some NEA grantees bordered on the pornographic). Good logrolling, it would seem, is not hampered by minor ideological concerns.[53] In this case, the rationality principle (exemplified by a willingness to support a policy to which one is opposed in exchange for reciprocal support for a policy one cares passionately about) and the institution principle (in which the separation of powers allows the president and legislators to cut deals) work in unusual ways to produce policy outcomes.

The Presidency   Of all the influences that maintain the clarity of party lines in Congress, the influence of the presidency is probably the most important. Indeed, it is a touchstone of party discipline in Congress. Since the late 1940s, under President Harry Truman, presidents each year have identified a number of bills to be considered part of their administration's program. By the mid-1950s, both parties in Congress began to look to the president for these proposals, which became the most significant part of Congress's agenda. The president's support is a criterion for party loyalty, and party leaders are able to use it to rally some members.

Weighing Diverse Influences

Clearly many factors affect congressional decisions. But at various points in the decision-making process, some are likely to be more influential than others. For example, interest groups may be more effective at the committee stage, when their expertise is especially valued and their visibility is less obvious. Because committees play a key role in deciding what legislation reaches the floor of the House or the Senate, interest groups can often put a halt to bills they dislike, or they can ensure that the options that do reach the floor are those that the group's members support.

Once legislation reaches the floor and members of Congress are deciding among alternatives, constituent opinion will become more important. Legislators are also influenced very much by other legislators: Many of their assessments about the substance and politics of legislation come from fellow members of Congress.

The influence of the external and internal forces described in the preceding section also varies according to the kind of issue being considered. On policies of great importance to powerful interest groups—farm subsidies, for example—those groups are likely to have considerable influence. On other issues, members of Congress may be less attentive to narrow interest groups and more willing to consider what they see as the general interest.

Finally, the mix of influences varies according to the historical moment. The Republicans' 1994 electoral victory allowed their party to control both houses of Congress

---

[53]Allen R. Meyerson, "Oil-Patch Congressmen Seek Deal with Clinton," *New York Times*, 14 June 1994, p. D2.

for the first time in forty years. That fact, combined with an unusually assertive Republican leadership, meant that party leaders became especially important in decision making. The willingness of moderate Republicans to support measures they had once opposed indicated the unusual importance of party leadership in this period. As the House minority leader, Richard Gephardt, put it, "When you've been in the desert forty years, your instinct is to help Moses."[54] The Democrats bounced back in 2006, winning majorities in both houses of Congress. In 2008, the Democrats won control of the White House and larger majorities in Congress and pledged to work with the Republicans to bring about needed changes in the nation's foreign and domestic policies.

BEYOND LEGISLATION: ADDITIONAL CONGRESSIONAL POWERS

In addition to the power to make the law, Congress has at its disposal an array of other instruments through which it can influence the process of government.

Advice and Consent: Special Senate Powers

The Constitution has given the Senate a special power, one that is not based on lawmaking: The president has the power to make treaties and appoint top executive officers, ambassadors, and federal judges—but only "with the Advice and Consent of the Senate" (Article II, Section 2). For treaties, two thirds of those senators present must concur; for appointments, a majority is required.

The power to approve or reject presidential requests also involves the power to set conditions. The Senate only occasionally exercises its power to reject treaties and appointments. Only nine Supreme Court nominees have been rejected by the Senate during the past century, while many times that number have been approved.[55]

More common than the Senate rejection of presidential appointees is a senatorial "hold" on an appointment. By Senate tradition, any member may place an indefinite hold on the confirmation of a mid- or lower-level presidential appointment. The hold may be a signal of a senator's willingness to filibuster a nomination, but it is typically used by senators trying to wring concessions from the White House on matters having nothing to do with the appointment in question. With Bush in power, the Democrats in the Senate actively scrutinized judicial nominations. Senate Democrats prevented final confirmation votes on a dozen especially conservative nominees, about which President Bush frequently complained during the 2004 reelection campaign.

Judicial nomination politics loomed large during Bush's second term. In May of 2005, Senate majority leader Frist, responding to the obstructionist tactics by the minority Democrats, threatened the "nuclear option," as we reported

---

[54]Quoted in David Broder, "At 6 Months, House GOP Juggernaut Still Cohesive," *Washington Post*, 17 July 1995, p. A1.

[55]Of President George W. Bush's three nominees, however, while two were confirmed, one was withdrawn because of a concern that it could not succeed.

earlier. Had the option been exercised, it is believed it would have constituted a procedural watershed in the Senate, making this chamber much more similar to the more majoritarian House. In yielding to the nuclear-option threat, the Democrats permitted a number of previously controversial federal court nominees to be confirmed.

Into this highly charged environment, in the summer of 2005, came a number of bolts from the blue. Bush, who had not had a single opportunity to name a Supreme Court justice in his first term, was confronted with a flurry of opportunities during a few short months in his second term. During the summer, Justice Sandra Day O'Connor (the first woman to serve on the Court) announced her retirement. Bush nominated John Roberts, a sitting federal judge, as her replacement. But before he could be confirmed, Chief Justice William Rehnquist died. President Bush withdrew Roberts's nomination and then renominated him to replace Rehnquist as chief justice. Roberts was confirmed in time for the opening of the Court's term in October. After unsuccessfully nominating White House Counsel Harriet Miers, Bush nominated Samuel Alito, a sitting federal judge with a substantial conservative track record, who joined the Court in February 2006. The matter of judicial appointments also became an issue in the 2008 election. It seemed likely that the next president would appoint at least two Supreme Court justices and would certainly appoint many federal district and appeals court judges. Democrats charged that a Republican president would appoint judges who would overturn abortion rights and set back the clock on civil rights. Republicans, for their part, declared that Democratic judges would expand access to abortions and promote same-sex marriage.

Senatorial advice and consent is also required on treaties. Most presidents make every effort to take potential Senate opposition into account in treaty negotiations and will frequently resort to ***executive agreements*** with foreign powers instead of treaties. The Supreme Court has held that such agreements are equivalent to treaties, but they do not need Senate approval.[56] In the past, presidents sometimes concluded secret agreements without informing Congress of the agreements' contents or even their existence. For example, American involvement in the Vietnam War grew in part out of a series of secret arrangements made between American presidents and the South Vietnamese during the 1950s and 1960s. Congress did not even learn of the existence of these agreements until 1969. In 1972, Congress passed the Case Act, which requires that the president inform Congress of any executive agreement within sixty days of its having been reached. This provides Congress with the opportunity to cancel agreements that it opposes. In addition, Congress can limit the president's ability to conduct foreign policy through executive agreement by refusing to appropriate the funds needed to implement an agreement. In this way, for example, executive agreements to provide economic or military assistance to foreign governments can be modified or even canceled by Congress.

executive agreement An agreement between the president and another country that has the force of a treaty but does not require the Senate's "advice and consent."

---

[56] *United States v. Pink*, 315 U.S. 203 (1942). For a good discussion of the problem, see James W. Davis, *The American Presidency: A New Perspective* (New York: Harper & Row, 1987), chap. 8. A recent analysis is found in William G. Howell, *Power without Persuasion: The Politics of Direct Presidential Action* (Princeton, N.J.: Princeton University Press, 2003).

Impeachment

The Constitution, in Article II, Section 4, also grants Congress the power of ***impeachment*** over the president, vice president, and other executive officials. Impeachment means charging a government official (president or otherwise) with "Treason, Bribery, or other high Crimes and Misdemeanors" and bringing him or her before Congress to determine guilt. Impeachment is thus like a criminal indictment, in which the House of Representatives acts like a grand jury, voting (by simple majority) on whether the accused ought to be impeached. If a majority of the House votes to impeach, the impeachment trial is held in the Senate, which acts like a trial jury by voting whether to convict and forcibly remove the person from office (this vote requires a two-thirds majority).

Controversy over Congress's impeachment power has arisen over the grounds for impeachment, especially the meaning of "high Crimes and Misdemeanors." A strict reading of the Constitution suggests that the only impeachable offense is an actual crime. But a more commonly agreed on definition is that "an impeachable offense is whatever the majority of the House of Representatives considers it to be at a given moment in history."[57] In other words, impeachment, especially impeachment of a president, is a political decision.

The United States came closest to impeaching and convicting a president in 1867. Andrew Johnson, a southern Democrat who had battled a congressional Republican majority over Reconstruction, was impeached by the House but saved from conviction by one vote in the Senate. At the height of the Watergate scandal in 1974, the House started impeachment proceedings against President Richard Nixon, but Nixon resigned before the House could proceed. The possibility of impeachment arose again in 1998, when President Clinton was accused of lying under oath and obstructing justice in the investigation into his sexual affair with the White House intern Monica Lewinsky. In October 1998, the House voted to impeach the president. At the conclusion of the Senate trial in 1999, Democrats, joined by a handful of Republicans, acquitted the president of both charges.

The impeachment power is a considerable one; its very existence in the hands of Congress is a highly effective safeguard against the executive tyranny so greatly feared by the framers of the Constitution.

POWER AND REPRESENTATION

Because they feared both executive and legislative tyranny, the framers of the Constitution pitted Congress and the president against each other. And as the history principle suggests, this has provided us with a legacy of interbranch competition. During the first century of American government, Congress was the dominant institution. American foreign and domestic policy was formulated and implemented by Congress, and generally the most powerful figures in American government were the

impeachment The charging of a government official (president or otherwise) with "Treason, Bribery, or other high Crimes and Misdemeanors" and bringing him or her before Congress to determine guilt.

---

[57]Carroll J. Doherty, "Impeachment: How It Would Work," *Congressional Quarterly Weekly Report*, 31 January 1998, p. 222.

Speaker of the House and the leaders of the Senate—not the president. During the nineteenth century, Congress—not the president—dominated press coverage on "the affairs of government."[58] The War of 1812 was planned and fought by Congress. The great sectional compromises before the Civil War were formulated in Congress without much intervention from the executive branch. Even during the Civil War, a period of extraordinary presidential leadership, a joint congressional committee on the conduct of the war played a role in formulating war plans and campaign tactics—and even had a hand in the promotion of officers. After the Civil War, when President Andrew Johnson sought to interfere with congressional plans for Reconstruction, he was summarily impeached, saved from conviction by only one vote. Subsequent presidents understood the moral and did not attempt to thwart Congress.

This congressional preeminence began to diminish at the beginning of the twentieth century, so that by the 1960s the executive had become, at least temporarily, the dominant branch of American government. The major domestic policy initiatives of the twentieth century—Franklin Roosevelt's New Deal, Harry Truman's Fair Deal, John F. Kennedy's New Frontier, and Lyndon Johnson's Great Society—all included some congressional involvement but were essentially developed, introduced, and implemented by the executive. In the area of foreign policy, although Congress continued to be influential during the twentieth century, the focus of decision-making power clearly moved into the executive branch. The War of 1812 may have been a congressional war, but in the twentieth century American entry into World War I, World War II, Korea, Vietnam, Iraq, and a host of lesser conflicts was essentially a presidential—not a congressional—decision. In the last forty years, there has been a good deal of resurgence of congressional power vis-à-vis the executive. This has occurred mainly because Congress has sought to represent many important political forces, such as the civil rights, women's, environmental, consumer, and peace movements, which in turn became constituencies for congressional power. During the mid-1990s, Congress became more receptive to a variety of new conservative political forces, including groups on the social and religious right as well as more traditional economic conservatives. After Republicans won control of both houses in the 1994 elections, Congress took the lead in developing programs and policies supported by these groups. These efforts won Congress the support of conservative forces in its battles for power against a Democratic White House.

To herald the new accessibility of Congress, Republican leaders instituted a number of reforms designed to eliminate many of the practices that they had long criticized as examples of Democratic arrogance. Republican leaders reduced the number of committees and subcommittees, eliminated funding of the various unofficial caucuses, imposed term limits on committee chairs, eliminated the practice of proxy voting, reduced committee staffs by one third, ended Congress's exemption from the labor, health, and civil rights laws that it imposed on the rest of the nation, and prohibited members from receiving most gifts. With these reforms, Republicans hoped to make Congress both more effective and more representative. Term limits and bans on gifts were seen as increasing the responsiveness of Congress to new political forces and to the American people in general. Simplification of the

[58]Samuel Kernell and Gary C. Jacobson, "Congress and the Presidency as News in the Nineteenth Century," *Journal of Politics* 49 (1987): 1016–35.

History Principle

During the first century of American government, Congress was the dominant institution. In recent decades, members of Congress have sought to restore that dominance.

committee structure was seen as making Congress more efficient and thus potentially more effective and more powerful. To some extent, unfortunately, the various reforms worked at cross-purposes. Simplification of the committee structure and elimination of funding for the caucuses increased the power of the leadership, thereby muting the effectiveness of more representative elements. To take another instance, when term limits for committee and subcommittee chairs were finally imposed in 2001, the result was confusion because experienced leaders were forced to step down, spreading power around in a more representative manner but diminishing committee effectiveness. This is the dilemma of congressional reform. Efficiency and representation are often competing principles in our system of government, and we must be wary of gaining one at the expense of the other. In the next chapter, we turn to the second branch of American government, the presidency, to view this dilemma from a somewhat different angle.

SUMMARY

The U.S. Congress is one of the few national representative assemblies that govern. Members of Congress take their representative function seriously. They devote a significant portion of their time to constituent contact and service. Representation and power go hand in hand in congressional history.

The legislative process provides the order necessary for legislation to take place amid competing interests. It depends on a hierarchical organizational structure within Congress. Six basic dimensions affect the legislative process: (1) the parties, (2) the committees, (3) the staff, (4) the caucuses (or conferences), (5) the rules, and (6) the presidency.

Because the Constitution provides only for a presiding officer in each house, methods for conducting business had to be devised. Parties quickly assumed the responsibility for this task. In the House, the majority party elects a leader every two years. This individual becomes Speaker. In addition, a majority leader, a minority leader, and party whips are elected. Each party has a committee whose job is to make committee assignments.

The committee system surpassed the party system in its importance in Congress during much of the twentieth century, although there has been a resurgence of the party system in the last two decades. Nonetheless, standing committees have always been a fundamental aspect of Congress. They have, for the most part, evolved to correspond to executive-branch departments or programs and thus reflect and maintain the separation of powers.

The Senate has a tradition of unlimited debate, on which the various cloture rules it has passed have had little effect. Filibusters still occur. And the mere possibility of one deters the introduction of some pieces of legislation and alters the shape of others. The rules of the House, on the other hand, restrict talk and support committees; deliberation is recognized as committee business. The House Rules Committee has the power to control debate and floor amendments. The rules prescribe the formal procedure through which bills become law. Generally, the parties control scheduling and agenda, but the committees determine action on the floor.

Rationality Principle	Collective-Action Principle	Institution Principle	Policy Principle	History Principle
Members of Congress, like all politicians, are ambitious and thus eager to serve the interests of constituents to improve their chances of reelection.	Cooperation on recurring matters like congressional votes is facilitated by the institutionalization of legislative structures and procedures.	According to the idea of agency representation, elections induce a member of Congress to act according to the preferences of his or her constituency.	The distributive tendency in Congress results from the need for a broad base of support in order for a bill to be passed.	The committee system evolved during the early nineteenth century as a means of allowing legislators disproportionate influence in areas of policy most important to them.
One of the most important factors determining who runs for office is a candidate's ambition. Access to money doesn't hurt either.	Political parties in legislature foster cooperation, coalitions, and compromise.	Party leaders have considerable agenda-setting powers.	Multiple factors influence how a member of Congress votes on legislation. These include constituency, interest groups, party leaders, congressional colleagues, and the president.	During the first century of American government, Congress was the dominant institution. In recent decades, members of Congress have sought to restore that dominance.
The opportunity to run for higher office is often more attractive to a small-state politician, whose constituency significantly overlaps the one for higher office, than it is to a large-state politician.	A bill often passes the House and the Senate in different forms. Sponsors from both houses then meet in a conference committee to iron out the differences.	The committee system is a means of dividing labor and allowing members of Congress to specialize in certain policy areas.		
The political opinions and policy goals of members of Congress are many and varied.	Interest groups with the ability to mobilize followers in many congressional districts are especially influential in Congress.	Committees have gatekeeping authority, the right to bargain with the other chamber, and the power of oversight, among other powers.		
Generally members of Congress seek committee assignments that allow them to acquire more influence in areas important to their constituents.	The whip system helps maintain party unity in Congress.	The House and the Senate have methods of keeping committees in check.		
	Logrolling is an informal means of facilitating cooperation in Congress.	The Rules Committee's decision about whether to adopt a closed or open rule for floor debate greatly influences a bill's chances of passing.		

Committees, seniority, and rules all limit the ability of members to represent their constituents. Yet these factors enable Congress to maintain its role as a major participant in government.

While voting along party lines remains strong, party discipline has declined. Still, parties do have several means of maintaining discipline. In most cases, party leaders accept constituency obligations as a valid reason for voting against the party position.

The power of the post–New Deal presidency does not necessarily signify the decline of Congress and representative government. During the 1970s, Congress again became the "first" branch of government. During the early years of the Reagan administration, some of the congressional gains of the previous decade were diminished, but in the last two years of Reagan's second term and in President George H. W. Bush's term, Congress reasserted its role. At the start of the Clinton administration, congressional leaders promised to cooperate with the White House rather than confront it. But only two years later, confrontation was once again the order of the day. George W. Bush's presidency was marked by close collaboration between the White House and Capitol Hill when the GOP controlled Congress and by frequent confrontations after 2006, when the Democrats won majorities in both houses of Congress. After 2008, when Democrats controlled both houses of Congress *and* the White House, a pattern of collaboration seemed likely to be reestablished.

FOR FURTHER READING

Adler, E. Scott. *Why Congressional Reforms Fail: Reelection and the House Committee System.* Chicago: University of Chicago Press, 2002. ○ ONLINE READING

Arnold, R. Douglas. *The Logic of Congressional Action.* New Haven, Conn.: Yale University Press, 1990. ○ ONLINE READING

Baker, Ross K. *House and Senate.* 3rd ed. New York: Norton, 2001.

Binder, Sarah. *Stalemate: Causes and Consequences of Legislative Gridlock.* Washington, D.C.: Brookings Institution, 2003.

———— and Paul Quirk, eds. *Institutions of Democracy: The Legislative Branch.* New York: Oxford University Press, 2004.

Brady, David, and Mathew D. McCubbins, eds. *Party, Process, and Political Change in Congress: New Perspectives on the History of Congress.* Palo Alto, Calif.: Stanford University Press, 2002.

Cox, Gary C., and Jonathon Katz, *Elbridge Gerry's Salamander: The Electoral Consequences of the Reapportionment Revolution.* Cambridge, England: Cambridge University Press, 2002. ○ ONLINE READING

————, and Mathew D. McCubbins. *Setting the Agenda: Responsible Party Government in the U.S. House of Representatives.* New York: Cambridge University Press, 2005. ○ ONLINE READING

————. *Legislative Leviathan: Party Government in the House.* 2nd ed. Berkeley: University of California Press, 2006.

Dodd, Lawrence C., and Bruce I. Oppenheimer, eds. *Congress Reconsidered.* 8th ed. Washington, D.C.: Congressional Quarterly Press, 2005.

Fenno, Richard F., Jr. *Home Style: House Members in Their Districts.* Boston: Little, Brown, 1978.

————. *The United States: A Bicameral Perspective.* Washington, D.C.: American Enterprise Institute, 1982. ○ ONLINE READING

Fiorina, Morris P. *Congress: Keystone of the Washington Establishment.* 2nd ed. New Haven, Conn.: Yale University Press, 1989.

Frisch, Scott A., and Sean Q. Kelly. *Committee Assignment Politics in the U.S. House of Representatives.* Norman: University of Oklahoma Press, 2006.

ONLINE READING ○ Krehbiel, Keith. *Pivotal Politics: A Theory of U.S. Lawmaking.* Chicago: University of Chicago Press, 1998.

ONLINE READING ○ Mayhew, David R. *Congress: The Electoral Connection.* New Haven, Conn.: Yale University Press, 1974.

Polsby, Nelson W. *How Congress Evolves.* New York: Oxford University Press, 2004.

Rohde, David W. *Parties and Leaders in the Post-reform House.* Chicago: University of Chicago Press, 1991.

Schickler, Eric. *Disjointed Pluralism.* Princeton, N.J.: Princeton University Press, 2001.

Sinclair, Barbara. *The Transformation of the U.S. Senate.* Baltimore: Johns Hopkins University Press, 1989.

Smith, Steven S., and Christopher J. Deering. *Committees in Congress.* 3rd ed. Washington, D.C.: Congressional Quarterly Press, 1997.

Stewart, Charles H. *Analyzing Congress.* New York: Norton, 2001.

Sundquist, James L. *The Decline and Resurgence of Congress.* Washington, D.C.: Brookings Institution, 1981.

The principles of politics are especially useful in helping us understand Congress, where members are motivated by electoral considerations and policy preferences, where the policy positions of their fellow members are well known through their speeches and roll-call votes, and where many institutional rules and procedures help channel the flow of legislation.

The principles also help us understand why the Senate operates so differently from the House. There are three basic differences. First, senators have to worry about reelection, to be sure, but they have a six-year window in which they can work on policy before facing the voters, unlike the two-year terms of the House members. Second, because the Senate is so much smaller, each member has relatively more influence, and there are fewer committees that manage the workload. The U.S. Senate often cultivates presidential ambitions (even though governors have been more successful presidential candidates over the past half-century), so individual senators have a strong incentive to get involved in national and international issues. Finally, because there are fewer rules governing floor activity in the Senate, any individual senator can stall legislative activity by holding the floor indefinitely (unless there is a vote of cloture).

The New York Times, September 17, 2006

How 3 G.O.P. Veterans Stalled Bush Detainee Bill

By Carl Hulse, Kate Zernike and Sheryl Gay Stolberg

Senators John McCain and Lindsey Graham cornered their partner, Senator John W. Warner, on the Senate floor late Wednesday afternoon.

Mr. Warner, the courtly Virginian who is chairman of the Armed Services Committee, had been trying for weeks to quietly work out the three Republicans' differences with the Bush administration's proposal to bring terrorism suspects to trial. But Senators McCain, of Arizona, and Graham, of South Carolina, who are on the committee with Mr. Warner, convinced him that the time for negotiation was over.

The three senators, all military veterans, marched off to an impromptu news conference to lay out their deep objections to the Bush legislation. Mr. Warner then personally broke the news to Senator Bill Frist of Tennessee, the majority leader, and the next day the Armed Services Committee voted to approve a firm legislative rebuke to the president's plan to reinterpret the Geneva Conventions.

It was a stinging defeat for the White House, not least because the views of Mr. Warner, a former Navy secretary, carry particular weight. With a long history of ties to the military, Mr. Warner, 79, has a reputation as an accurate gauge to views that senior officers are reluctant to express in public. Notably, in breaking ranks with the White House, Mr. Warner was joined by Colin L. Powell, the former chairman of the Joint Chiefs of Staff, in a rare public breach with the administration he served as secretary of state.

As Mr. Warner left his Senate office on Friday afternoon, he carried a briefcase of material to prepare for a potential legislative showdown in the coming days. At stake, he said, was more than the fate of "these 20-odd individuals," a reference to the high-level terrorism suspects awaiting possible trial at Guantánamo Bay, Cuba.

"It's how America's going to be perceived in the world, how we're going to continue the war against terror," Mr. Warner said.

Then he showed off the motto on his necktie: "Democracy is not a spectator sport." Ronald Reagan had a similar tie, Mr. Warner said, and had given him a copy.

Democrats and Republicans alike had assumed that Mr. Warner, a smooth negotiator not given to public confrontation, would relent to the administration, especially considering the importance Republicans had placed on passing the legislation as midterm elections approached.

The thinking was that Mr. McCain, who was tortured as a Vietnam prisoner of war, would not budge, nor would Mr. Graham, a military lawyer and zealous guardian of military standards. That left Mr. Warner as the best potential target for the White House. * * *

"He is a man of the Senate," said Mr. Graham, arguing that Mr. Warner's stance spoke volumes because it went against his nature to have so visible a conflict. "He is also a military man and has thought long and hard about this."

Mr. Bush seems equally determined to win provisions he says are needed to interrogate and prosecute terrorism suspects. He and his allies are ratcheting up pressure on Senate Republicans who support alternate rules. * * * Mr. Warner, like his two colleagues, has a

network of high-ranking current and retired military officers who provide regular guidance and support. While he has been consulting them privately, some are expected to weigh in publicly in the days ahead. One aide said on Saturday that the number of Senate Republicans behind the three senators was widening beyond the 8 or 10 they had anticipated, with lawmakers—heavily influenced by Mr. Powell's stance—preparing to soon go public with their views.

In interviews, two senior Bush administration officials acknowledged that the White House had underestimated the depth of opposition. * * * They also said they had focused mostly on gaining Mr. Graham's support and mistakenly believed they had it, based on statements he made about the Geneva Conventions in Senate hearings. A Republican senator separately described the clash between the White House and Mr. Warner's group as "a train wreck." * * *

Mr. Warner's convictions about how military trials should proceed appear to stem largely from his personal experience, beginning with his Navy service in World War II. Hanging with the photographs on his office wall is a worn, small placard that his mother displayed on the door of their Washington home from 1944 to 1946: "There's a Man from this family in the Navy."

"I'm a man that's been through a lot," Mr. Warner said, recounting his days as secretary of the Navy in the early 1970's when he was personally confronted with issues of military prisoners. * * *

Mr. Graham has similarly drawn on his legal and military background in challenging the White House. "The Geneva Convention means more to me than the average person," he said. He said "some people" considered the conventions "a waste of time, but I know they have been helpful."

Mr. Graham acknowledged that the political battle was bruising, but said he could not tolerate a change in the American interpretation of the conventions if it meant short-term benefits at long-term costs.

"President Bush is very sincere in wanting the tools he needs to fight the war on terror," Mr. Graham said in an interview. "I don't want the tools they are given to become clubs to be used against our people." * * *

The bonds between Mr. Warner, Mr. McCain and Mr. Graham were forged in difficult times. Mr. Warner and Mr. McCain first met when Mr. Warner was the Navy secretary and Mr. McCain was returning to his Navy career after his captivity. Mr. McCain and Mr. Graham became close during the 2000 primaries in South Carolina, when Mr. McCain came under attack from Bush Republicans. They teamed up last year in forcing the White House to accept a ban on torture.

After the Supreme Court struck down the administration's earlier plan for military tribunals in June, they joined with top military lawyers to form the chief bulwark against what they said were efforts to undermine military law and the 60-year-old protections of the Geneva Conventions.

"It's not a question of defiance or intransigence, it's the way we've worked," Mr. Warner said. "We've continued to indicate a willingness to look at situations—is there a bridge that we can build between certain provisions? And our core principles are very rooted in the three of us."

Mr. Graham added, "There are three branches of government, not one."

Mr. Warner sought to serve as a counterbalance to the occasionally combative Mr. McCain and Mr. Graham during a turbulent week that fractured the Republican majority on its signature issue, national security. It saw Mr. Powell enlisting with the three Republicans against Mr. Bush, and left Mr. Graham chewing out General Michael V. Hayden, the C.I.A. director, in a closed meeting.

In the Senate, Mr. Warner is known for hearing out colleagues and trying to find consensus.

"John Warner is always very gracious," said Senator Susan Collins, Republican of Maine, who is also on the Armed Services Committee and sided with Senators Warner, McCain and Graham. "He is patient and he is thoughtful. And people sometimes mistake that for uncertainty about his position."

Administration officials said they had focused on Mr. Warner as the key to overcoming Republican opposition in the Senate. When he raised a question with General Hayden about the State Department's view on the matter, Mr. Warner received a phone call within hours from * * * [Condoleezza] Rice. * * *

But once it became clear that Mr. Warner was dug in, the administration began setting its sights on other senators, inviting them to the White House.

* * *

As the fight swirled around him last week, Mr. Warner got a call from his grandson, Nicholas, a boarding school student who was an intern in his office this summer, asking what all the fuss on television was about.

"I took the time to try to explain it to him," Mr. Warner said. "That's one of the jobs we have to do, explain to the American people." He added: "Neither McCain nor Graham nor I nor anybody wants to tie the hands of the intelligence community."

 Rationality Principle

The three senators may have their own reasons for opposing this bill, but they also share a political interest in keeping the Senate powerful. This shared interest allows them to bridge their other differences.

CHAPTER 6

The Presidency as an Institution

ALTHOUGH THE FIRST DOMESTIC EFFECT OF WAR is often a restriction on civil liberties, war has ramifications for all governmental and political institutions as well as for public policies. For example, President Abraham Lincoln's 1862 declaration of martial law and Congress's 1863 legislation giving the president the power to use military tribunals to make arrests and imprison the convicted amounted to a constitutional dictatorship, which lasted through the war and Lincoln's reelection in 1864. But these measures were viewed as emergency powers that could be taken back once the crisis of union was resolved. In less than a year after Lincoln's death, Congress reasserted its power, leaving the presidency in many respects the same as, if not weaker than, it had been before.

During World War II, Franklin Roosevelt, like Lincoln, did not bother to wait for Congress but took executive action first and expected Congress to follow. Roosevelt brought the United States into an undeclared naval war against Germany a year before Pearl Harbor, and he ordered the unauthorized use of wiretaps and other surveillance as well as the investigation of suspicious persons for reasons not clearly specified. The most egregious (and revealing) of these presidential initiatives was his segregation and eventual confinement of 120,000 individuals of Japanese descent, many of whom were American citizens. Even worse, the Supreme Court validated Roosevelt's treatment of the Japanese on the flimsy grounds of military necessity. One dissenter on the Court called the president's assumption of emergency powers "a loaded weapon ready for the hand of any authority that can bring forward a plausible claim of an urgent need."[1]

---

[1]Quoted from the dissenting opinion of Justice Robert Jackson in *Korematsu v. United States*, 323 U.S. 214 (1944).

The "loaded weapon" was seized again on September 14, 2001, when Congress defined the World Trade Center and Pentagon attacks as acts of war and proceeded to adopt a joint resolution authorizing the president

> to use all necessary and appropriate force against those nations, organizations, or persons he determines planned, authorized, committed, or aided the terrorist attacks that occurred on September 11, 2001, or harbored such organizations or persons.[2]

Congress did attach a sunset provision to the authorization resolution and planned for congressional oversight during the war.

September 11 and its aftermath immensely accentuated President George W. Bush's role and place in foreign policy. By 2002, foreign policy was the centerpiece of the Bush administration's agenda. In a June 1 speech at West Point, the "Bush doctrine" of preemptive war was announced. Bush argued that "our security will

---

[2]*Authorization for Use of Military Force*, Public Law 107-40, *U.S. Statutes at Large* 115 (2001): 224.

All presidents have goals and want to be influential, but presidential power is constrained by the constitutional and structural contours of the institution of the presidency. The Constitution endows the president with only a small number of expressed powers, so the presidency is an office whose powers are primarily delegated to it by Congress. Presidents have sought to broaden their inherent powers by their successful execution of the law. Presidential power can be enhanced through strategic interactions that a president has with other political actors and through a president's ability to build and sustain popular support. Historic events requiring bold action and leadership by the president, such as the Great Depression, can also contribute to the president's power. The institution of the presidency has accumulated more and more power over time, but a president's ultimate success is based on the skillful use of those powers.

require all Americans . . . to be ready for preemptive action when necessary to defend our liberty and to defend our lives." His statement was clearly intended to justify his administration's plans to invade Iraq, but it had much wider implications, including the increasing power of the American president in guiding foreign policy.

National emergencies provide presidents with a source of power, and the way presidents exercise that power has profound consequences for the country. As we have seen, civil liberties in particular are threatened by what presidents do during times of war. In this chapter, we go beyond that issue and look at the long-term consequences of national emergencies on presidential power. What circumstances explain why some emergencies produced new and long-lasting powers for the president while others did not? In the instances in which new powers were institutionalized, what was the long-term effect? The central task of this chapter is to explain why the American system of government could be described as presidential government and how it got to be that way. In doing so, we shall see that it's the office that wields great power, not necessarily the person.

The power of the office has gradually developed over time. The framers, wanting "energy in the Executive," provided for a single-headed office with an electoral base independent of Congress. But by giving the presidency no explicit powers independent of Congress, the Constitution set the stage for each president to provide that energy by asserting the inherent powers of the office.

A tug-of-war between formal constitutional provisions for a president who is nominally rather weak and a theory of necessity favoring a strong executive has persisted for over two centuries. It was not until Franklin Delano Roosevelt's election in 1932 that the tug-of-war seems to have been won by the strong executive presidency. After FDR, as we shall see, every president has been strong, whether he was committed to a strong presidency or not.

Thus a strong executive, a genuine chief executive, was institutionalized in the twentieth century. But the office continues to operate in a contradictory environment: As the power of the presidency has increased, popular expectations of presidential performance have increased at an even faster rate, requiring more leadership than was ever exercised by any but the greatest presidents in the past.

Our focus in this chapter is on the development of the institutional character of the presidency, the power of the presidency, and the relationship between the two. The chapter concerns itself with three major topics. First, we review the constitutional origins and powers of the presidency. In particular, we examine the constitutional basis for the president's foreign and domestic roles. Second, we review the history of the American presidency to see how the office has evolved from its original status under the Constitution. We look in particular at the ways in which Congress has augmented the president's constitutional powers by deliberately delegating to the presidency many of its own responsibilities. Third, we assess the means by which presidents can enhance their own ability to govern.

THE CONSTITUTIONAL BASIS OF THE PRESIDENCY

The presidency was established by Article II of the Constitution. Article II begins by asserting, "The executive Power shall be vested in a President of the United States of America." It goes on to describe the qualifications for the office (one must be a natural-born citizen, at least thirty-five years of age, and a resident of the United States for at least fourteen years), the manner in which the president is to be chosen, and the basic powers of the presidency. By vesting the executive power in a single president, the framers were emphatically rejecting proposals for various forms of collective leadership. Some delegates to the Constitutional Convention had argued in favor of a multiheaded executive or an "executive council" to avoid undue concentration of power in the hands of one individual. Most of the framers, however, hoped the president would be capable of taking quick and aggressive action. The framers thought a unitary executive would be more energetic than some form of collective leadership. They believed that a powerful executive would help protect the nation's interests vis-à-vis other nations and promote the federal government's interests relative to the states.

Immediately following the first sentence of Article II, Section 1, of the Constitution, the manner in which the president is to be chosen is defined. This is an odd sequence, and it says something about the struggle the delegates were having over how to provide great power of action to the executive and at the same time balance that power with limitations. The struggle was between those delegates who wanted the president to be selected by, and thus responsible to, Congress and those delegates who preferred that the president be elected directly by the people. Direct popular election would create a more independent and more powerful presidency. With the adoption of a scheme of indirect election through an electoral college, in which the electors would be selected by the state legislatures (and close elections would be resolved in the House of Representatives), the framers hoped to achieve a "republican" solution: a strong president responsible to state and national legislators rather than directly responsible to the electorate. This indirect method of electing the president dampened the power of most presidents in the nineteenth century.

History
Principle

The framers created a unitary executive; they wanted an energetic president but also one whose powers were limited.

Institution
Principle

By structuring the election of the president to be not by the people directly but by the electoral college, the framers sought to downplay presidential power.

The presidency was strengthened somewhat in the 1830s with the introduction of the national convention system of nominating presidential candidates. Until then, candidates had been nominated by their party's congressional delegates. That was the *caucus system* of nominating candidates, and it was derisively called King Caucus because any candidate for president had to be beholden to the party's leaders in Congress to get the party's nomination and the support of the party's congressional delegation in the presidential election. The convention system quickly became the most popular method of nominating candidates for all elective offices and remained so until well into the twentieth century, when it succumbed to the criticism that it was a nondemocratic method dominated by a few leaders in a "smoke-filled room." But in the nineteenth century, it was seen as a victory for democracy over the congressional elite. And the national convention gave the presidency a base of power independent of Congress.

This additional independence did not immediately transform the presidency into the office we recognize today, but the national convention did begin to open the presidency to larger social forces and newly organized interests in society. In other words, it gave the presidency a mass popular base that would eventually support and demand increased presidential power. Improvements in the telephone, the telegraph, and other forms of communication allowed individuals to share their complaints and allowed national leaders—especially presidential candidates and presidents—to reach out directly to people and ally themselves with, and sometimes even create, popular groups and forces. Eventually, though more slowly, the presidential selection process began to be further democratized, with the adoption of primary elections, through which millions of ordinary citizens were given an opportunity to take part in the nominating process by popular selection of convention delegates.

But despite political and social conditions favoring the enhancement of the presidency, the development of presidential government as we know it today did not mature until the middle of the twentieth century. For a long period, even as the national government began to grow, Congress was careful to keep tight reins on the president's power. The real turning point in the history of American national government came during the administration of Franklin Roosevelt.

THE CONSTITUTIONAL POWERS OF THE PRESIDENCY

caucus system A normally closed meeting of a political or legislative group to select candidates, plan strategy, or make decisions regarding legislative matters.

expressed powers Specific powers granted to the president under Article II, Sections 2 and 3, of the Constitution.

Whereas Article II, Section 1, explains how the president is to be chosen, Sections 2 and 3 outline the powers and duties of the president. These two sections identify two sources of presidential power. One source is the specific language of the Constitution. For example, the president is specifically authorized to make treaties, grant pardons, and nominate judges and other public officials. These clearly defined powers are called the *expressed powers* of the office and cannot be revoked by the Congress or any other agency without an amendment to the Constitution. Other expressed powers include the power to receive ambassadors and to command the military forces of the United States.

The second source of presidential power lies in the declaration in Article II that the president "shall take Care that the Laws be faithfully executed." Because the laws are enacted by Congress, this language implies that Congress is to delegate to the president the power to implement or execute its will. Powers given to the president by Congress are called ***delegated powers.*** In principle, Congress delegates to the president only the power to identify or develop the means through which to carry out its decisions. So, for example, if Congress determines that air quality should be improved, it might delegate to a bureaucratic agency in the executive branch the power to identify the best means of bringing about such an improvement, as well as the power to implement the cleanup process. In practice, of course, decisions about how to clean the air are likely to have an enormous effect on businesses, organizations, and individuals throughout the nation. As it delegates power to the executive, Congress substantially enhances the importance of the presidency and the executive branch. In most cases, Congress delegates power to bureaucratic agencies in the executive branch rather than to the president. As we shall see, however, contemporary presidents have found ways to capture a good deal of this delegated power for themselves.

Presidents have claimed a third source of power beyond expressed and delegated powers. These are powers that are not specified in the Constitution or the law but are said to stem from "the rights, duties and obligations of the presidency."[3] They are referred to as the ***inherent powers*** of the presidency and are most often asserted by presidents in times of war or national emergency. For example, after the fall of Fort Sumter and the outbreak of the Civil War, President Lincoln issued a series of executive orders although he had no clear legal basis for doing so. Without even calling Congress into session, Lincoln combined the state militias into a ninety-day national volunteer force, called for 40,000 new volunteers, enlarged the regular army and navy, diverted $2 million in unspent appropriations to military needs, instituted censorship of the U.S. mails, ordered a blockade of southern ports, suspended the writ of *habeas corpus* in the border states, and ordered military police to arrest individuals whom he deemed to be guilty of engaging in or even contemplating treasonous actions.[4] Lincoln asserted that these extraordinary measures were justified by the president's inherent power to protect the nation.[5] Subsequent presidents, including Franklin Roosevelt and George W. Bush, have had similar views.

Expressed Powers

The president's expressed powers, as defined by Article II, Sections 2 and 3, fall into several categories:

Institution Principle

The Constitution has established a presidency of expressed and delegated powers.

delegated powers Constitutional powers that are assigned to one government agency but exercised by another agency with the express permission of the first.

inherent powers Powers claimed by a president that are not expressed in the Constitution but are inferred from it.

---

[3]In the case of *In re Neagle*, 135 U.S. 1 (1890), David Neagle, a deputy U.S. marshal, had been authorized by the president to protect a Supreme Court justice whose life had been threatened by an angry litigant. When the litigant attempted to carry out his threat, Neagle shot and killed him. Neagle was then arrested by local authorities and tried for murder. His defense was that his act was "done in pursuance of a law of the United States." Although the law was not an act of Congress, the Supreme Court declared that it was an executive order of the president and that the protection of a federal judge was a reasonable extension of the president's power to "take Care that the Laws be faithfully executed."

[4]James G. Randall, *Constitutional Problems under Lincoln* (New York: Appleton, 1926), chap. 1.

[5]E. S. Corwin, *The President: Office and Powers*, 4th. ed. (New York: New York University Press, 1957), p. 229.

1. *Military.* Article II, Section 2, provides for the power as "Commander in Chief of the Army and Navy of the United States, and of the Militia of the several States, when called into the actual Service of the United States."

2. *Judicial.* Article II, Section 2, provides the "Power to grant Reprieves and Pardons for Offences against the United States, except in Cases of Impeachment."

3. *Diplomatic.* Article II, Section 2, provides the "Power, by and with the Advice and Consent of the Senate, to make Treaties." Article II, Section 3, provides the power to "receive Ambassadors and other public Ministers."

4. *Executive.* Article II, Section 3, authorizes the president to see to it that all the laws are faithfully executed. Section 2 gives the chief executive power to appoint, remove, and supervise all executive officers and appoint all federal judges.

5. *Legislative.* Article I, Section 7, and Article II, Section 3, give the president the power to participate authoritatively in the legislative process.

Military Power The president's military powers are among the most important of the powers exercised by the chief executive. The position of **commander in chief** makes the president the highest military authority in the United States, with control of the entire defense establishment. The president is also head of the nation's intelligence network, which includes not only the Central Intelligence Agency (CIA) but also the National Security Council (NSC), the National Security Agency (NSA), the Federal Bureau of Investigation (FBI), and a host of less well known but very powerful international and domestic security agencies.

WAR AND INHERENT PRESIDENTIAL POWER   The Constitution, of course, gives Congress the power to declare war. Presidents, however, have gone a long way toward capturing this power for themselves. Congress has not declared war since December 1941, and yet since then American military forces have engaged in numerous campaigns throughout the world under orders of the president. When North Korean forces invaded South Korea in June 1950, Congress was prepared to declare war, but President Harry S. Truman decided not to ask for congressional action. Instead, Truman asserted the principle that the president, and not Congress, could decide when and where to deploy America's military might. Truman dispatched U.S. forces to Korea without a congressional declaration, and in the face of the emergency Congress felt it had to acquiesce. It passed a resolution approving the president's actions, and this sequence of events became the pattern for future congressional-executive relations in the military realm. The wars in Vietnam, Bosnia, Afghanistan, and Iraq, as well as a host of lesser conflicts, were all fought without declarations of war.

In 1973, Congress responded to presidential unilateralism by passing the **War Powers Resolution**—over President Richard Nixon's veto. This resolution reasserted the principle of Congress's power to declare war, required the president to inform Congress of any planned military campaign, and stipulated that forces must be withdrawn within sixty days in the absence of a specific congressional authorization for their continued deployment. Presidents have generally ignored the War Powers Resolution, however, claiming inherent executive power to defend the nation. Thus, for example, in 1989 President George H. W. Bush ordered an invasion of Panama

commander in chief The power of the president as commander of the national military and the state national guard units (when called into service).

War Powers Resolution A resolution of Congress declaring that the president can send troops into action abroad only by authorization of Congress or if U.S. troops are already under attack or seriously threatened.

without consulting Congress. In 1990, the same President Bush received congressional authorization to attack Iraq but had already made it clear that he was prepared to go to war with or without congressional assent. In 1995, President Bill Clinton ordered a massive bombing campaign against Serbian forces in the former nation of Yugoslavia without congressional authorization. And of course President George W. Bush responded to the 2001 attacks by Islamic terrorists by organizing a major military campaign to overthrow the Taliban regime in Afghanistan, which had sheltered the terrorists. In 2002, Bush ordered a major U.S. campaign against Iraq, which he accused of posing a threat to the United States. American forces overthrew the government of Iraqi dictator Saddam Hussein and occupied the country. In both of these most recent instances, Congress passed resolutions approving the president's actions, but President Bush was careful to assert that he did not need congressional authorization. The War Powers Resolution was barely mentioned on Capitol Hill and was ignored by the White House.

However, the fact that presidents since 1974 have ignored the War Powers Resolution, with virtually no objection from Congress, does not mean that tensions stemming from the separation of powers between the president and Congress have ceased. The relationship between the branches is encased in layers of institutional fabric, and as our institution principle suggests, tensions emerge within this complex institutional arrangement. The powers of the purse and of investigation give Congress levers with which to constrain even the most freewheeling executive.

Institution Principle

There is tension in the separation of powers between the president and Congress over policy related to making war.

MILITARY SOURCES OF DOMESTIC POWER   The president's military powers extend into the domestic sphere. Article IV, Section 4, provides that "the United States shall . . . [protect] every State . . . against Invasion . . . and . . . domestic Violence." Congress has made this an explicit presidential power through statutes directing the president as commander in chief to discharge these obligations.[6] The Constitution restrains the president's use of domestic force by providing that a state legislature (or governor when the legislature is not in session) must request federal troops before the president can send them into the state to provide public order. Yet this proviso is not absolute. First, presidents are not obligated to deploy national troops merely because a state legislature or governor makes such a request. And more important, the president may deploy troops in a state or city without a specific request from a state legislature or governor if the president considers it necessary to maintain an essential national service during an emergency, enforce a federal judicial order, or protect federally guaranteed civil rights.

One historic example of the unilateral use of presidential emergency power to protect the states against domestic disorder, even when the states do not request it, is the decision by President Dwight Eisenhower in 1957 to send troops into Little Rock, Arkansas, against the wishes of the state of Arkansas in order to enforce court orders to integrate Little Rock's Central High School. As we saw in Chapter 4, the governor, Orval Faubus, had posted the Arkansas National Guard at the entrance of the school to prevent the court-ordered admission of nine black students. After an effort to negotiate with the governor failed, President Eisenhower

---

[6]These statutes are contained mainly in Title 10 of the United States Code, Sections 331, 332, and 333.

reluctantly sent 1,000 paratroopers to Little Rock; they stood watch while the black students took their places in the all-white classrooms. This case makes quite clear that the president does not have to wait for a request by a state legislature or a governor before acting as a domestic commander in chief.[7] More recently, President George W. Bush sent various military units to the Gulf Coast in response to Hurricanes Katrina and Rita in 2005. In most instances of domestic disorder—whether a result of human or natural events—presidents tend to exercise unilateral power by declaring a "state of emergency," thereby making available federal grants, insurance, and direct assistance.

Military emergencies have typically also led to expansion of the domestic powers of the executive branch. This was true during World Wars I and II and has been the case during the "war on terrorism" as well. Within a month of the September 11 attacks, the White House had drafted, and Congress had enacted, the USA Patriot Act, expanding the power of government agencies to engage in domestic surveillance, including electronic surveillance, and restricting judicial review of such efforts. The following year Congress created the Department of Homeland Security, combining offices of twenty-two federal agencies into one huge new cabinet department that would be responsible for protecting the nation from attack.

Judicial Power   The presidential power to grant reprieves, pardons, and amnesties involves the power of life and death over all individuals who may be a threat to the security of the United States. Presidents may use this power on behalf of a particular individual, as did Gerald Ford when he pardoned Richard Nixon in 1974 "for all offenses against the United States which he . . . has committed or may have committed." Or they may use it on a large scale, as Andrew Johnson did in 1868 when he gave full amnesty to all southerners who had participated in the "Late Rebellion" and as Jimmy Carter did in 1977 when he declared an amnesty for all Vietnam War draft evaders. President Clinton issued a number of controversial pardons during his last weeks in office. This power of life and death over others helped elevate the president to the level of earlier conquerors and kings, by establishing him as the person before whom supplicants might come to make their pleas for mercy.

Diplomatic Power   The president is America's "head of state," its chief representative in dealings with other nations. As head of state, the president has the power to make treaties for the United States (with the advice and consent of the Senate). When President George Washington received Edmond Genet ("Citizen Genet") as the formal emissary of the revolutionary government of France in 1793 and had his cabinet officers and Congress back his decision, he established a greatly expanded interpretation of the power to "receive Ambassadors and other public Ministers," extending it to the power to "recognize" other countries. That power gives the president the almost unconditional authority to review the claims of any new ruling

---

[7]The best study covering all aspects of the domestic use of the military is that of Adam Yarmolinsky, *The Military Establishment* (New York: Harper & Row, 1971). Probably the most famous instance of a president's unilateral use of the power to protect a state "against domestic violence" is President Grover Cleveland's response to the Pullman strike of 1894. The famous Supreme Court case that ensued was *In re Debs*, 158 U.S. 564 (1895).

group to determine whether it indeed controls the territory and population of its country and therefore can, in the president's opinion, legitimately commit it to treaties and other agreements.

In recent years, presidents have expanded the practice of using executive agreements instead of treaties to establish relations with other countries.[8] An *executive agreement* is like a treaty because it is a contract between two countries, but an executive agreement does not require a two-thirds vote of approval by the Senate. Ordinarily executive agreements are used to carry out commitments already made in treaties or to arrange for matters well below the level of policy. But when presidents have found it expedient to use an executive agreement in place of a treaty, Congress has typically acquiesced.

Executive Power The most important basis of the president's power as chief executive is found in Article II, Section 3, which stipulates that the president must see that all the laws are faithfully executed, and Section 2, which provides that the president will appoint, remove, and supervise all executive officers and appoint all federal judges (with Senate approval). The power to appoint the principal executive officers and to require each of them to report to the president on subjects relating to the duties of their departments makes the president the true chief executive officer (CEO) of the nation. In this manner, the Constitution focuses executive power and legal responsibility on the president. The famous sign on President Truman's desk, "The buck stops here," was not merely an assertion of Truman's personal sense of responsibility but was in fact evidence of his recognition of the legal and constitutional responsibility of the president. The president is subject to some limitations because the appointment of all such officers, including ambassadors, ministers, and federal judges, is subject to majority approval by the Senate. But these appointments are at the discretion of the president, and the loyalty and the responsibility of each appointee are presumed to be directed toward the president.

Another component of the president's power as chief executive is *executive privilege.* Executive privilege is the claim that confidential communications between a president and close advisers should not be revealed without the consent of the president. Presidents have made this claim ever since George Washington refused a request from the House of Representatives to deliver documents concerning negotiations of an important treaty. Washington refused (successfully) on the grounds that, first, the House was not constitutionally part of the treaty-making process and, second, that diplomatic negotiations required secrecy.

Executive privilege became a popular part of the checks-and-balances counterpoint between president and Congress, and presidents have usually had the upper hand when invoking it. Although many presidents have claimed executive privilege, the concept was not tested in the courts until the 1971 Watergate affair, during which President Nixon refused congressional demands that he turn over secret

---

[8]In *United States v. Pink*, 315 U.S. 203 (1942), the Supreme Court confirmed that an executive agreement is the legal equivalent of a treaty despite the absence of Senate approval. This case approved the executive agreement that was used to establish diplomatic relations with the Soviet Union in 1933. An executive agreement, not a treaty, was used in 1940 to exchange "fifty over-age destroyers" for ninety-nine-year leases on some important military bases.

executive agreement An agreement between the president and another country that has the force of a treaty but does not require the Senate's "advice and consent."

executive privilege The claim that confidential communications between the president and the president's close advisers should not be revealed without the consent of the president.

White House tapes that congressional investigators thought would establish Nixon's complicity in illegal activities. In *United States v. Nixon*, the Supreme Court ordered Nixon to turn over the tapes.[9] The president complied with the order and was forced to resign from office. *United States v. Nixon* is often seen as a blow to presidential power, but in actuality the Court's ruling recognized for the first time the validity of a claim of executive privilege, although holding that it did not apply in this instance. Subsequent presidents have cited *United States v. Nixon* in support of their claims of executive privilege. For example, the administration of George W. Bush successfully invoked executive privilege when it refused congressional demands for records of Vice President Dick Cheney's 2001 energy task force meetings. The exercise of presidential power through the executive-privilege doctrine has been all the more frequent in the past twenty years, when we have been living nearly 90 percent of the time under conditions of "divided government"; that is, the party that is not in control of the White House is in control of one or both chambers of Congress.[10]

The President's Legislative Power   The president plays a role not only in the administration of government but also in the legislative process. Two constitutional provisions are the primary sources of the president's power in the legislative arena. The first of these is the provision in Article II, Section 3, providing that the president "shall from time to time give to the Congress Information of the State of the Union, and recommend to their Consideration such Measures as he shall judge necessary and expedient." The second of the president's legislative powers is of course the veto power assigned by Article I, Section 7.[11]

Delivering a "State of the Union" address might not appear to be of any great import. It is a mere obligation on the part of the president to make recommendations for Congress's consideration. But as political and social conditions favored an increasingly prominent role for presidents, each president, especially since Franklin

Rationality Principle

Under conditions of divided government, presidents may rationally want the protection of executive privilege from the partisan scrutiny of elements of Congress, and Congress may well suspect a president of hiding questionable activity behind a veil of executive privilege.

Institution Principle

The president's constitutional role provides an opportunity for significant agenda setting by the executive for the Congress.

ONLINE READING ○

---

[9] *United States v. Nixon*, 418 U.S. 683 (1974).

[10] A recent extension of executive power by President George W. Bush is the "signing statement." During each ceremony in which he signs a bill into law, President Bush has claimed the prerogative not to enforce those portions of the bill he believes to be unconstitutional. Thus he has asserted "the power to set aside any statute passed by Congress when it conflicts with his interpretation of the Constitution." This highly controversial assertion remains unsettled as a constitutional matter and surely will reach the Supreme Court in the near future. See Charlie Savage, "Bush Challenges Hundreds of Laws: President Cites Powers of His Office," *Boston Globe*, 30 April 2006.

[11] There is a third source of presidential power implied in the provision for faithful execution of the laws. This is the president's power to impound funds—that is, to refuse to spend money Congress has appropriated for certain purposes. One author referred to this as a "retroactive veto power" (Robert E. Goosetree, "The Power of the President to Impound Appropriated Funds," *American University Law Review*, January 1962). This impoundment power was used freely and to considerable effect by many modern presidents, and Congress occasionally delegated such power to the president by statute. But in reaction to the Watergate scandal, Congress adopted the Budget and Impoundment Control Act of 1974, which was designed to circumscribe the president's ability to impound funds by requiring the president to spend all appropriated funds unless both houses of Congress consent to an impoundment within forty-five days of a presidential request. Since 1974, therefore, the use of impoundment has declined significantly. Presidents have had to bite their tongues and accept unwanted appropriations or revert to the older and more dependable but politically limited method of vetoing an entire bill.

FIGURE 6.1 The Veto Process

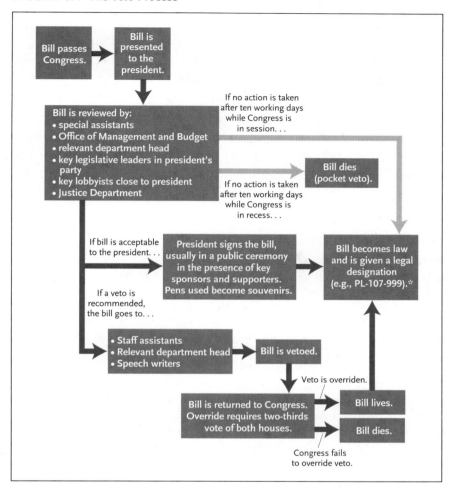

*PL stands for "public law"; 107 is the Congress (e.g., the 107th Congress was in session in 2001–2); 999 is the number of the law.

Roosevelt, has relied on this provision to become the primary initiator of proposals for legislative action in Congress and the principal source for public awareness of national issues, as well as the most important single individual participant in legislative decisions. Few today doubt that the president, together with the executive branch as a whole, is the primary source of many important congressional actions.[12]

The **veto** is the president's constitutional power to turn down acts of Congress (Figure 6.1). It alone makes the president the most important single legisla-

[12]For a different perspective, see William F. Grover, *The President as Prisoner: A Structural Critique of the Carter and Reagan Years* (Albany: State University of New York Press, 1989).

veto The president's constitutional power to turn down acts of Congress within ten days of their passage while Congress is in session. A presidential veto may be overridden by a two-thirds vote of each house of Congress.

tive leader.[13] No bill vetoed by the president can become law unless both the House and Senate override the veto by a two-thirds vote. In the case of a **pocket veto,** Congress does not have the option of overriding the veto but must reintroduce the bill in the next session. A pocket veto can occur when the president is presented with a bill during the last ten days of a legislative session. Usually if a president does not sign a bill within ten days, it automatically becomes law. But if a president chooses not to sign a bill presented within the last ten days that Congress is in session, then the ten-day limit expires while Congress is out of session, and instead of becoming law, the bill is considered vetoed. In 1996, a new power was added to the president's lineup—the **line-item veto**—giving the president power to strike specific spending items from appropriations bills passed by Congress unless they are reenacted by a two-thirds vote of both the House and the Senate. In 1997, President Clinton used this power eleven times to strike eighty-two items from the federal budget. But in 1998 the Supreme Court ruled that the Constitution does not authorize the line-item veto.[14] Only a constitutional amendment would restore this power to the president.

The Games Presidents Play: The Veto   Use of the veto varies according to the political situation that each president confronts. During Bill Clinton's first two years in office, when Democrats controlled both houses of Congress, the president vetoed no bills. After the congressional elections of 1994, however, Clinton confronted a Republican-controlled Congress with a definite agenda, and he began to use his veto power vigorously. Likewise, George W. Bush vetoed no bill during his first term, and only one bill during the first two years of his second term, a period during which Congress was controlled by his party.[15] During the last two years of his second term, however, with Congress controlled by the Democrats, Bush vetoed eleven pieces of legislation. In general, presidents have used the veto to equalize or perhaps upset the balance of power with Congress. While the simple power to reject or accept legislation in its entirety might seem like a crude tool for making sure that legislation adheres to a president's preferences, the politics surrounding the veto is complicated, and it is rare that vetoes are used simply as

Institution Principle

The veto power makes the president the most important single legislative leader.

---

pocket veto A veto that is effected when Congress adjourns during the time a president has to approve a bill and the president takes no action on it.

line-item veto The power of the executive to veto specific provisions (lines) of a bill passed by the legislature.

ONLINE READING

[13]Although the veto power is the most important legislative resource in the hands of the president, it can often end in frustration, especially when the presidency and Congress are held by opposing parties. George H. W. Bush vetoed forty-six congressional enactments during his four years, and only one was overridden. Ronald Reagan vetoed thirty-nine bills in his eight years, and nine were overridden. These numbers compare to thirty-one vetoes during Jimmy Carter's four years, with two overridden. In 1993–94, Bill Clinton did not veto a single bill, a record unmatched since the days of President Millard Fillmore (1850–53); both, of course, were working with Congresses controlled by their own political party. President George W. Bush had not vetoed a single bill in more than five years thus topping Clinton's record, when he vetoed a bill on stem-cell research. For more on the veto, see Chapter 5 and Robert J. Spitzer, *The Presidential Veto: Touchstone of the American Presidency* (Albany: State University of New York Press, 1988).

[14]*Clinton v. City of New York*, 524 U.S. 417 (1998).

[15]A caveat: President George W. Bush, as observed in an earlier footnote, has relied on signing statements as something of a substitute for the veto. Were the Supreme Court to declare the maneuver unconstitutional, the president would be forced to face squarely the decision to use the power of the veto.

bullets to kill legislation. Instead, vetoes are usually part of an intricate bargaining process between the president and Congress, involving threats of vetoes, the repassage of legislation, and second vetoes.[16]

The fact that presidents rarely veto legislation does not mean that vetoes and veto bargaining have an insignificant influence over the policy process. The fact that presidents vetoed only several hundred of the 17,000 public bills that Congress sent to them between 1945 and 1992 belies the centrality of the veto to presidential power. Many of these bills were insignificant and not worth the veto effort. Thus it is important to separate "significant" legislation, for which vetoes frequently occur, from insignificant legislation.[17] Vetoes can also be effective—even though they are rarely employed—because individuals will condition their actions based on how they think others will respond.[18] With respect to vetoes, this means that members of Congress will alter the content of a bill to make it more to a president's liking in order to preempt a veto. Thus the veto power can be influential even when the veto pen rests in its inkwell.[19]

Rhetoric and reputation take on particular importance when vetoes become part of a bargaining process. The key to veto bargaining is uncertainty. Members of Congress are often unsure about the president's policy preferences and therefore don't know which bills the president is willing to sign. When the policy preferences of the president and Congress diverge, as they typically do in a divided government, the president tries to convince Congress that his preferences are more extreme than they really are in order to get Congress to enact legislation that is closer to what he really wants. If members of Congress knew the president's preferences ahead of time, they would pass a bill that was close to what *they* wanted, subject to minimally satisfying the president. Through strategic use of the veto and veto threats, a president tries to shape Congress's beliefs about his policy preferences in order to gain greater concessions from Congress. Reputation is central to presidential effectiveness in this process.[20] By influencing congressional beliefs, the president is building a policy reputation that will affect future congressional behavior. The Analyzing the Evidence unit on page 252 takes a closer look at veto politics.

Back-and-forth negotiating between the president and Congress was especially evident in the events surrounding the creation of a cabinet-level Department of Homeland Security in 2002–3. As part of his decisive leadership in the wake of the terrorist attacks of September 11, 2001, President George W. Bush established the Office of Homeland Security. The president believed that his "terrorism czar," Tom Ridge, had ample authority to coordinate national policy in the fight against terrorism. Critics on Capitol Hill felt that a cabinet-level department should be created,

 Collective-Action Principle

Vetoes are usually part of an intricate bargaining process involving the president and Congress.

 Policy Principle

Because of the president's veto power, Congress will alter the content of a bill to make it more to a president's liking.

Rationality Principle

Bargaining between Congress and the president is strategic: The president tries to influence legislators' beliefs about what they must do to keep the president from using the veto power.

---

[16]Charles M. Cameron, *Veto Bargaining: Presidents and the Politics of Negative Power* (New York: Cambridge University Press, 2000). See also David W. Rohde and Dennis Simon, "Presidential Vetoes and Congressional Response: A Study of Institutional Conflict," *American Journal of Political Science* 29 (1985): 397–427.

[17]David R. Mayhew, *Divided We Govern: Party Control, Lawmaking, and Investigations, 1946–1990* (New Haven, Conn.: Yale University Press, 1991).

[18]Jack H. Nagel, *The Descriptive Analysis of Power* (New Haven, Conn.: Yale University Press, 1975).

[19]See Rohde and Simon, "Presidential Vetoes and Congressional Response."

[20]Richard E. Neustadt, *Presidential Power and the Modern Presidents: The Politics of Leadership from Roosevelt to Reagan* (1960; rev. ed., New York: Free Press, 1990).

○ ONLINE READING

○ ONLINE READING
○ ONLINE READING

partly because they believed Ridge lacked the necessary resources and authority to do the job and partly because they thought it would give the House and the Senate a more explicit role (through the appropriations process). Ultimately President Bush relented, but the conflict between president and Congress continued as the executive and the legislature negotiated, threatened, promised, and eventually settled on the details of the new department. President Bush had veto power as his club behind the door, while Senate Democrats (Bush's main opponents), even though they were in the minority, could threaten delay through dilatory tactics and the filibuster (see Chapter 5). Both sides went public in an effort to sway public opinion and brandished "blame" in attempts to weaken the credibility of the other side. Such public, high-visibility squabbling is unusual, but on matters of salient national policy that pit the two parties against each other, it occasionally emerges, giving us a picture of the full array of powers possessed by executive and legislature.

What about the relationship between mass public support for the president and the use of the veto? At least for the modern presidency, a crucial resource for the president in negotiating with Congress has been his public approval as measured by opinion polls.[21] In some situations, members of Congress pass a bill not because they want to change policy but because they want to force the president to veto a popular bill that he disagrees with in order to hurt his approval ratings.[22] The key is that the public, uncertain of the president's policy preferences, uses information conveyed by vetoes to reassess what it knows about his preferences. As a result, vetoes may come at a price to the president. A president must, according to the rationality principle, weigh the advantages of using the veto or threatening to do so—to gain concessions from Congress—against the hit he may take in his popularity. The president may be reluctant to use the veto or the threat of a veto to gain concessions from Congress if it will hurt him in the polls. But in some cases, the president will take a hit in his approval ratings by vetoing a bill if it is drastically inconsistent with his policies.

⊙ Rationality Principle

A president must weigh the advantages of vetoing legislation against the possible drop in his public approval.

Legislative Initiative   Although not explicitly stated, the Constitution provides the president with the power of *legislative initiative*. To initiate means to originate, and in government that can mean power. The framers of the Constitution clearly saw legislative initiative as one of the keys to executive power. Initiative obviously implies the ability to formulate proposals for important policies, and the president, as an individual with a great deal of staff assistance, is able to initiate decisive action more frequently than Congress, with its large assemblies that have to deliberate and debate before taking action. With some important exceptions, Congress banks on the president to set the agenda of public policy. And quite clearly there is power in initiative: There is power in being able to set the terms of discourse in the making of public policy.

For example, during the weeks immediately following September 11, 2001, Bush took many presidential initiatives to Congress, and each was given almost

legislative initiative The president's inherent power to bring a legislative agenda before Congress.

ONLINE READING ○

---

[21]Theodore J. Lowi, *The Personal President: Power Invested, Promise Unfulfilled* (Ithaca, N.Y.: Cornell University Press, 1985).

[22]Timothy Groseclose and Nolan McCarty, "The Politics of Blame: Bargaining before an Audience," *American Journal of Political Science* 45 (2001): 100–119.

unanimous support: from commitments to pursue al Qaeda, remove the Taliban, and reconstitute the Afghanistan regime all the way to almost unlimited approval for mobilization of both military power and power over the regulation of American civil liberties. After winning reelection in 2004, Bush sought to push forward his domestic legislative agenda, which included making changes in the nation's Social Security system and reforming the tax structure. Bush also called on Congress to act quickly to limit lawsuit awards in medical malpractice cases and to push for tougher educational standards for high schools. Bush said, "I earned capital in this campaign, political capital, and now I intend to spend it. . . . There is a feeling that the people have spoken and embraced your point of view, and that's what I intend to tell the Congress."[23] The first two years of Bush's second term, however, were difficult. Growing problems (and casualties) in Iraq, administrative scandals, and charges of incompetence in responding to the aftermath of Hurricanes Katrina and Rita plagued the president during 2005. A shift in momentum saw Congress taking back some of the initiative in dealing with the president. As presidential popularity ebbed in the polls in 2005, so, too, did Bush's agenda power. Two thousand six was more of the same, with troubles in Iraq, Iran, Israel, and North Korea dominating the public agenda, preoccupying the president, and diminishing his popularity in the polls. The run-up to the midterm elections in November 2006 and a spate of Republican scandals further distracted the president from pursuing his policy agenda. After Democrats won control of Congress in 2006, Bush pursued few new initiatives.

The president's initiative does not end with policy making involving Congress and the making of laws in the ordinary sense of the term. The president has still another legislative role (in all but name) within the executive branch. This is designated as the power to issue **executive orders.** The executive order is foremost a normal tool of management, a power possessed by virtually any CEO to make company policy—rules setting procedures, etiquette, chains of command, functional responsibilities, and so on. But evolving from this normal management practice is a recognized presidential power to promulgate rules that have the effect and formal status of legislation. Most of the executive orders of the president provide for the reorganization of structures and procedures or otherwise direct the affairs of the executive branch—either to be applied across the board to all agencies or to be applied in some important respect to a single agency or department.

The power to issue executive orders illustrates that although reputation and persuasion are typically required in presidential policy making, the practice of issuing executive orders, within limits, allows a president to govern without the necessity to persuade.[24] One of the most important examples is Executive Order No. 8248 of 1939, which established the divisions of the Executive Office of the President. Of equal importance is President Nixon's executive order establishing the Environmental Protection Agency (EPA) in 1971, which included establishment of the Environmental

executive orders
The rules or regulations issued by the president that have the effect and formal status of legislation.

○ ONLINE READING

---

[23]Quoted in Richard W. Stevenson, "Focus on Social Security and the Tax Code," *New York Times,* 5 November 2004, p. A1.

[24]This point is developed in both Kenneth R. Mayer, *With the Stroke of a Pen: Executive Orders and Presidential Power* (Princeton, N.J.: Princeton University Press, 2001), and William G. Howell, *Power without Persuasion: The Politics of Direct Presidential Action* (Princeton, N.J.: Princeton University Press, 2003).

Veto Politics

Although vetoes are relatively rare in the legislative process, scholars are drawn to study them because vetoes carry clear policy implications. Indeed, a president's use of the veto is an ideal example of negative agenda control—it creates an opportunity to block legislative action, but does not give the executive the power to alter proposed legislation after the fact. Nonetheless, chief executives regularly use the threat of a veto in their attempts to shape legislative outcomes.[1] In many cases, a credible veto threat may be sufficient to force compliance on the part of reluctant legislators who would like to avoid a prolonged legislative battle over a controversial bill or resolution, especially near the end of a legislative session. Instead of "losing" to the president, one or both chambers of the legislature may be willing to make concessions if the price of passage necessitates it.

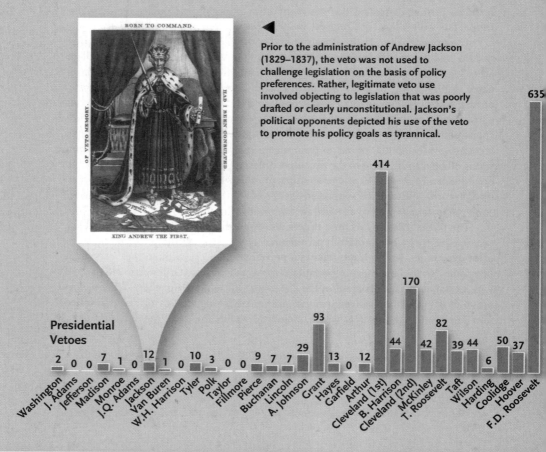

BORN TO COMMAND.

OF VETO MEMORY.

HAD I BEEN CONSULTED.

KING ANDREW THE FIRST.

◀

Prior to the administration of Andrew Jackson (1829–1837), the veto was not used to challenge legislation on the basis of policy preferences. Rather, legitimate veto use involved objecting to legislation that was poorly drafted or clearly unconstitutional. Jackson's political opponents depicted his use of the veto to promote his policy goals as tyrannical.

Presidential Vetoes

President	Vetoes
Washington	2
J. Adams	0
Jefferson	0
Madison	7
Monroe	1
J.Q. Adams	0
Jackson	12
Van Buren	1
W.H. Harrison	0
Tyler	10
Polk	3
Taylor	0
Fillmore	0
Pierce	9
Buchanan	7
Lincoln	7
A. Johnson	29
Grant	93
Hayes	13
Garfield	0
Arthur	12
Cleveland (1st)	414
B. Harrison	44
Cleveland (2nd)	170
McKinley	42
T. Roosevelt	82
Taft	39
Wilson	44
Harding	6
Coolidge	50
Hoover	37
F.D. Roosevelt	635

Veto power is by no means absolute. Consistent with the Madisonian notion of checks and balances, the legislature has the opportunity to override a veto if legislators can muster the necessary votes. In the U.S. Congress, two thirds of both chambers must successfully vote to override a presidential veto. While many override attempts fail as a result of this supermajority requirement, the risk of a successful override attempt provides an important check on unilateral executive power.[2]

PRESIDENTIAL VETOES AND CONGRESSIONAL OVERRIDES, 1945–2007

	Years in Office	Vetoes	Divided Government	Override Attempts		Successes	
Truman	1945–1953	250	1947–1949	22	8.8%	12	54.5%
Eisenhower	1953–1961	181	1955–1961	11	6.1%	2	18.2%
Kennedy	1961–1963	21		0	0.0%	0	0.0%
Johnson	1963–1969	30		0	0.0%	0	0.0%
Nixon	1969–1974	43	1969–1974	21	48.8%	7	33.3%
Ford	1974–1977	66	1974–1977	28	42.4%	12	42.9%
Carter	1977–1981	31		4	12.9%	2	50.0%
Reagan	1981–1989	78	1981–1989	15	19.2%	9	60.0%
G.H.W. Bush	1989–1993	44	1989–1993	21	47.7%	1	4.8%
Clinton	1993–2001	38	1995–2001	14	36.8%	2	14.3%
G.W. Bush	2001–	3	2007–	3	100.0%	0	0.0%

Sources: "Congressional Bills Vetoed: 1789–2001." Contributed by John P. McIver. *Historical Statistics of the United States*, Millennial Edition On Line, edited by Susan B. Carter, Scott S. Gartner, Michael R. Haines, Alan L. Olmstead, Richard Sutch, and Gavin Wright. © Cambridge University Press, 2006; calculated by author.

Veto override attempts and success are more likely to occur under divided government than unified government, which is most likely a function of divergent preferences across the institutions. Note that few or no overrides were attempted during presidencies that enjoyed unified government, with the president's party controlling at least one chamber of Congress.

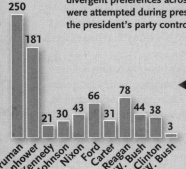

◄ Since Jackson left office in 1837, presidents have routinely vetoed legislation for political reasons. During the twentieth century, for instance, the incidence of presidential vetoes was almost always greater under divided government, in which the executive is controlled by one political party and at least one chamber of Congress by the other.

[1]Charles M. Cameron, *Veto Bargaining: Presidents and the Politics of Negative Power*. (New York: Cambridge University Press, 2000).
[2]David W. Rohde and Dennis M. Simon. 1985. "Presidential Vetoes and Congressional Response: A Study of Institutional Conflict." *American Journal of Political Science* 29: 397–427.

Impact Statement. President Reagan's Executive Order No. 12291 of 1981 provided a regulatory reform process that has been responsible for more deregulation in the past twenty-five years than was accomplished by any acts of congressional legislation.

Delegated Powers

Many of the powers exercised by the president and the executive branch are not found in the Constitution but are the products of congressional statutes and resolutions. Over the past three quarters of a century, Congress has voluntarily delegated a great deal of its own legislative authority to the executive branch. To some extent, this delegation of power has been an almost inescapable consequence of the expansion of governmental activity in the United States since the New Deal. Given the vast range of the federal government's responsibilities, Congress cannot execute and administer all the programs it creates and the laws it enacts. Inevitably Congress must turn to the hundreds of departments and agencies in the executive branch or, when necessary, create new agencies to implement its goals. Thus, for example, in 2002, when Congress sought to protect America from terrorist attacks, it established the Department of Homeland Security and gave it broad powers in the realms of law enforcement, public health, and immigration. Similarly, in 1970, when Congress enacted legislation designed to improve the nation's air and water quality, it assigned the task of implementing its goals to the new Environmental Protection Agency created by Nixon's executive order. Congress gave the EPA substantial power to set and enforce air- and water-quality standards.

As they implement congressional legislation, federal agencies collectively develop thousands of rules and regulations and issue thousands of orders and findings every year. Agencies interpret Congress's intent, promulgate rules aimed at implementing that intent, and issue orders to individuals, firms, and organizations throughout the nation designed to impel them to conform to the law. When it establishes an agency, Congress sometimes grants it only limited discretionary authority, providing very specific guidelines and standards that must be followed by the administrators charged with the program's implementation. Take the Internal Revenue Service (IRS), for example. Most Americans view the IRS as a powerful agency whose dictates can have an immediate and sometimes unpleasant effect on their lives. Yet congressional tax legislation is specific and detailed and leaves little to the discretion of IRS administrators.[25] The agency certainly develops numerous rules and procedures to enhance tax collection. It is Congress, however, that establishes the structure of the tax liabilities, tax exemptions, and tax deductions that determine each taxpayer's burdens and responsibilities.

In most instances, however, congressional legislation is not very detailed. Often Congress defines a broad goal or objective and delegates enormous discretionary power to administrators to determine how that goal is to be achieved. For example, the 1970 act creating the Occupational Safety and Health Administration (OSHA) states that Congress's purpose is "to assure so far as is possible every working man and woman in the nation safe and healthful working conditions." The act, however,

---

[25]Kenneth F. Warren, *Administrative Law*, 3rd ed. (Upper Saddle River, N.J.: Prentice-Hall, 1996), p. 250.

neither defines such conditions nor suggests how they might be achieved.[26] The result is that agency administrators have enormous discretionary power to draft rules and regulations that have the effect of law. Indeed, the courts treat these administrative rules like congressional statutes. For all intents and purposes, when Congress creates an agency like OSHA or the EPA, giving it a broad mandate to achieve some desirable outcome, it transfers its own legislative power to the executive branch.

In the nineteenth and early twentieth centuries, Congress typically wrote laws that provided fairly clear principles and standards to guide executive implementation. For example, the 1922 Tariff Act empowered the president to increase or decrease duties on certain manufactured goods in order to reduce the difference in cost between products produced domestically and those manufactured abroad. The act authorized the president to make the final determination, but his discretionary authority was quite constrained. The statute listed the criteria the president was to consider, fixed the permissible range of tariff changes, and outlined the procedures to be used to calculate the cost differences between foreign and domestic goods. When an importer challenged a particular executive decision as an abuse of delegated power, the Supreme Court had no difficulty finding that the president was merely acting in accordance with Congress's directives.[27]

At least since the New Deal, however, Congress has tended to give executive agencies broad mandates and draft legislation that offers few clear standards or guidelines for implementation by the executive. For example, the 1933 National Industrial Recovery Act gave the president the authority to set rules to bring about fair competition in key sectors of the economy without ever defining what the term meant or how it was to be achieved. Similarly, the 1938 Agricultural Adjustment Act, which led to a system of commodity price supports and agricultural production restrictions, authorized the secretary of agriculture to make agricultural marketing "orderly" without offering any guidance regarding the commodities to be affected, how markets were to be organized, or how prices should be determined. All these decisions were left to the discretion of the secretary and his or her agents.[28] This pattern of broad delegation became typical in the ensuing decades. The 1972 Consumer Product Safety Act, for example, authorizes the Consumer Product Safety Commission to reduce unreasonable risk of injury from household products but offers no suggestions to guide the commission's determination of what constitutes reasonable and unreasonable risks or how these are to be reduced.[29]

This shift from the nineteenth-century pattern of issuing relatively well defined congressional guidelines to administrators to the more contemporary pattern of broadly delegating congressional power to the executive branch is, to be sure, partially a consequence of the great scope and complexity of the tasks that America's contemporary government has undertaken. During much of the nineteenth century,

Policy Principle

The outcome of congressional policy making depends greatly on the amount of leeway executive agencies have to interpret policies.

---

[26]Theodore J. Lowi, *The End of Liberalism: The Second Republic of the United States*, 2nd ed. (New York: Norton, 1979), pp. 117–18.

[27]*J. W. Hampton & Company. v. United States*, 276 U.S. 394 (1928).

[28]David Schoenbrod, *Power without Responsibility: How Congress Abuses the People through Delegation* (New Haven, Conn.: Yale University Press, 1993), pp. 49–50.

[29]Lowi, *The End of Liberalism*, p. 117.

the federal government had relatively few domestic responsibilities, and Congress could pay close attention to details. Today the operation of an enormous executive establishment and thousands of programs under varied and changing circumstances requires that administrators be allowed some considerable measure of discretion to carry out their jobs. Nevertheless, the result is to shift power from Congress to the executive branch.

THE RISE OF PRESIDENTIAL GOVERNMENT

Most of the real influence of the modern presidency derives from the powers granted by the Constitution and the laws made by Congress. Thus any person properly elected and sworn in as president will possess almost all the power held by the strongest presidents in American history. Even when they are lame ducks, presidents still possess all the power of the office. For example, in the weeks after the election of 2000, lame-duck president Clinton took the opportunity to continue major diplomatic efforts to bring peace to the Middle East and to become the first U.S. president to visit a united Vietnam.

What variables account for a president's success in exercising these powers? Why are some presidents considered great successes and others colossal failures? These questions relate broadly to the very concept of presidential power. Is it a reflection of the attributes of the person, or is it more characteristic of the political situations that a president encounters? The personal view of presidential power dominated political scientists' thinking for several decades,[30] but recently scholars have argued that presidential power should be analyzed in terms of the strategic interactions that a president has with other political actors.[31] With the occasional exception, however, it took more than a century, perhaps as much as a century and a half, before presidents came to be seen as consequential players in these strategic encounters. A bit of historical review will be helpful in understanding how the presidency has risen to its current level of influence.

The Legislative Epoch, 1800–1933

In 1885, a then-obscure political science professor named Woodrow Wilson titled his general textbook *Congressional Government* because American government was just that, congressional government. There is ample evidence that Wilson's description of the national government was consistent not only with nineteenth-century reality but also with the intentions of the framers. Within the system of three separate and competing powers, the clear intent of the Constitution was for legislative supremacy. In the

ONLINE READING

[30]Neustadt, *Presidential Power and the Modern Presidents.*

ONLINE READING

[31]Charles M. Cameron, "Bargaining and Presidential Power," in *Presidential Power: Forging the Presidency for the Twenty-first Century,* ed. Robert Y. Shapiro, Martha Joynt Kumar, and Lawrence R. Jacobs (New York: Columbia University Press, 2000) See also Samuel Kernell, *Going Public: New Strategies of Presidential Leadership,* 3rd ed. (Washington, D.C.: Congressional Quarterly Press, 1998).

early nineteenth century, the president was seen by some observers as little more than America's chief clerk. Indeed, most historians agree that after Thomas Jefferson and until the beginning of the twentieth century Presidents Andrew Jackson and Abraham Lincoln were the only exceptions to a succession of weak presidents. Both Jackson and Lincoln are considered great presidents because they used their great power wisely. But it is important in the history of the presidency that neither of them left his powers as an institutional legacy to his successors. That is to say, once Jackson and Lincoln left office, the presidency went back to the subordinate role that it played during the nineteenth century.

One of the reasons that so few great men became president in the nineteenth century is that there was only occasional room for greatness.[32] As Chapter 3 indicated, the national government of that period was not a particularly powerful entity. The presidency of the nineteenth century was also weak because during this period the presidency was not closely linked to major national political and social forces. Indeed, there were few important *national* political or social forces to which presidents could have linked themselves even if they had wanted to. Federalism had taken very good care of this by fragmenting political interests and diverting the energies of interest groups toward the state and local levels of government, where most key decisions were being made.

As discussed earlier in the chapter, the presidency was strengthened in the 1830s when the national convention system of nominating presidential candidates was introduced. However, this additional independence did not change the presidency into the office we see today because the parties disappeared, returning to their states and Congress once the national election was over. In addition, as the national government grew, Congress kept a tight rein on the president's power. For example, when Congress began to make its first efforts to exert power over the economy (beginning in 1887 with the adoption of the Interstate Commerce Act and in 1890 with the adoption of the Sherman Antitrust Act), it sought to keep this power away from the president and the executive branch by placing the new regulatory policies in "independent regulatory commissions" responsible to Congress rather than to the president (see also Chapter 7).

History
Principle

The presidency was strengthened somewhat in the 1830s with the introduction of a national convention system of nominating presidential candidates.

The New Deal and the Presidency

As discussed earlier, the key moment in the history of American national government came during Franklin Roosevelt's administration. The Hundred Days at the outset of the Roosevelt administration in 1933 had no parallel in U.S. history. But it was only the beginning. The policies proposed by President Roosevelt and adopted by Congress during the first 1,000 days of his administration so changed the size and character of the national government that they constitute a moment in American history equivalent to the founding or the Civil War. The president's constitutional obligation

---

[32]For related appraisals, see Jeffrey Tulis, *The Rhetorical Presidency* (Princeton, N.J.: Princeton University Press, 1987); Stephen Skowronek, *The Politics Presidents Make: Leadership from John Adams to Bill Clinton* (Cambridge, Mass.: Harvard University Press, 1997); and Robert J. Spitzer, *President and Congress: Executive Hegemony at the Crossroads of American Government* (Philadelphia: Temple University Press, 1993).

to see "that the laws be faithfully executed" became, during FDR's presidency, virtually a responsibility to shape the laws before executing them.

Many of the New Deal programs were extensions of the traditional national government approach, which was described in Chapter 3 (see especially Table 3.1). But the New Deal went well beyond the traditional approach, adopting types of policies never before tried on a large scale by the national government; it began intervening in economic life in ways that had hitherto been reserved to the states. In other words, the national government discovered that it, too, had "police power" and could directly regulate individuals as well as provide roads and other services.

The new programs were such dramatic departures from the traditional policies of the national government that their constitutionality was in doubt. The Supreme Court in fact declared several of them unconstitutional, mainly on the grounds that in regulating the conduct of individuals or their employers, the national government was reaching beyond "*inter*state" and involving itself in "*intra*state"—essentially local—matters. Most of the New Deal remained in constitutional limbo until 1937, five years after Roosevelt was first elected and one year after his landslide 1936 reelection.

The turning point came with *National Labor Relations Board v. Jones and Laughlin Steel Corporation,* a case challenging the federal government's authority over the regulation of labor relations. The Supreme Court affirmed a federal role in the regulation of the national economy.[33] Since the end of the New Deal, the Supreme Court has never again seriously questioned the legitimacy of interventions of the national government in the economy or society.[34]

The most important constitutional effect of Congress's actions and the Supreme Court's approval of those actions during the New Deal was the enhancement of presidential power. Most major acts of Congress in this period involved significant exercises of control over the economy. But few programs specified the actual controls to be used. Instead, Congress authorized the president or, in some cases, a new agency to determine what the controls would be. Some of the new agencies were independent commissions responsible to Congress. But most of the new agencies and new programs of the New Deal were placed in the executive branch directly under presidential authority.

Technically this form of congressional act, as we noted earlier, is the delegation of power. In theory, the delegation of power works as follows: (1) Congress recognizes a problem, (2) Congress acknowledges that it has neither the time nor the expertise to deal with the problem, and (3) Congress therefore sets the basic policies

History Principle

By the end of the New Deal, the practice of significant management of the economy by the executive, as broadly defined by Congress, was firmly established.

History Principle

The New Deal's expanded role for the national government enhanced presidential power.

---

[33] *National Labor Relations Board v. Jones and Laughlin Steel Corporation,* 301 U.S. 1 (1937).

[34] Some will argue that there are exceptions to this statement. One was *National League of Cities v. Usery,* 426 U.S. 833 (1976), which declared unconstitutional Congress's effort to supply national minimum wage standards to state and local government employees. But the Court reversed itself on this nine years later, in *Garcia v. San Antonio Metropolitan Transit Authority,* 469 U.S. 528 (1985). Another was *Bowsher v. Synar,* 478 U.S. 714 (1986), which declared unconstitutional the part of the Gramm-Rudman law authorizing the comptroller general to make across-the-board budget cuts when total appropriations exceeded legally established ceilings. In 1999, executive authority was compromised somewhat by the Court's decision to question the Federal Communications Commission's authority to supervise telephone deregulation under the Telecommunications Act of 1996. But cases such as these are few and far between, and they touch on only part of a law, not the constitutionality of an entire program.

and then delegates to an agency the power to fill in the details. But in practice, Congress was delegating to the executive branch not merely the power to fill in the details but also real policy-making powers—that is, real legislative powers.

No modern government can avoid the delegation of significant legislative powers to the executive branch. But the fact remains that this delegation produced a fundamental shift in the American constitutional framework. During the 1930s, the growth of the national government through acts delegating legislative power tilted the national structure away from a Congress-centered government toward a president-centered government.[35] Make no mistake, Congress continues to be the constitutional source of policy. Legislative supremacy remains a constitutional fact of life, even at the beginning of the twenty-first century, because delegations are contingent. And not all delegations are the same. A Democratic Congress, for example, is unwilling to empower a Republican president and vice versa; unified governments are more likely than divided governments to engage in broad delegation.[36] In short, Congress can rescind these delegations of power, restrict them with subsequent amendments, and oversee the exercise of delegated power through congressional hearings, oversight agencies, budget controls, and other administrative tools. However, it is fair to say that presidential government has become an administrative fact of life as government by delegation has expanded greatly over the past century. The world of Woodrow Wilson's *Congressional Government* is forever changed. But Congress has many clubs behind its door with which to influence the manner in which the executive branch exercises its newly won power.

PRESIDENTIAL GOVERNMENT

The locus of policy decision making shifted to the executive branch because, as we just noted, Congress made delegations of authority to the president. Congress delegated authority to the executive for instrumental reasons, much as a principal delegates to an agent. An expanded agenda of political demands, necessitated first by economic crisis—the Great Depression—but also by an accumulation of the effects of nearly a century's worth of industrialization, urbanization, and greater integration into the world economy, confronted the national government, forcing Congress's hand. The legislature itself was limited in its ability to expand its own capacity to undertake these growing responsibilities, so delegation proved a natural

> **Rationality Principle**
>
> Congress delegates more power to the president as more demands are made on its agenda.

---

[35]The Supreme Court did in fact *dis*approve broad delegations of legislative power by declaring the National Industrial Recovery Act of 1933 unconstitutional on the grounds that Congress did not accompany the broad delegations with sufficient standards or guidelines for presidential discretion (*Panama Refining Co. v. Ryan*, 293 U.S. 388 [1935], and *Schechter Poultry Corporation v. United States*, 295 U.S. 495 [1935]). The Supreme Court has never reversed those two decisions, but neither has it really followed them. Thus broad delegations of legislative power from Congress to the executive branch can be presumed to be constitutional. See Sotirios A. Barber, *The Constitution and the Delegation of Congressional Power* (Chicago: University of Chicago Press, 1975).

[36]David Epstein and Sharyn O'Halloran, *Delegating Powers: A Transaction Cost Politics Approach to Policy Making under Separate Powers* (New York: Cambridge University Press, 1999).

administrative strategy. These acts of delegation gave a far greater role to the president, empowering this "agent" to initiate in his own right.

In the case of Franklin Roosevelt, it is especially appropriate to refer to his New Deal as launching an era of presidential government. Congress certainly retained many tools with which to threaten, cajole, encourage, and persuade its executive agent to do its bidding. But presidents in general, and Roosevelt in particular, are not *only* agents of the Congress and not *only* dependent on Congress for resources and authority. They are also agents of national constituencies for whom they are eager to demonstrate their capacity for leadership in executing constituency policy agendas.[37]

Likewise, congressional delegations of power are not the only resources available to a president. Presidents have at their disposal a variety of other formal and informal resources that have important implications for their ability to govern. Indeed, without these other resources, presidents would lack the ability—the tools of management and public mobilization—to make much use of the power and responsibility given to them by Congress. Let us first consider the president's formal or official resources and then turn to the more informal resources that affect a president's capacity to govern, in particular the president's base of popular support.

What Are the Formal Resources of Presidential Power?

The Cabinet   In the American system of government, the **cabinet** is the traditional but informal designation for the heads of all the major departments of the federal government (Figure 6.3). The cabinet has no constitutional status. In contrast to the United Kingdom and many other parliamentary countries, where the cabinet is the government, the American cabinet is not a collective body. It meets but makes no decisions as a group. Each appointment must be approved by the Senate, but cabinet members are not responsible to the Senate or to Congress at large. Cabinet appointments help build party and popular support, but the cabinet is not a party organ. The cabinet is made up of directors but is not a true board of directors.

Aware of this fact, the president tends to develop a burning impatience with and a mild distrust of cabinet members, to make the cabinet a rubber stamp for actions already decided on, and to demand results, or the appearance of results, more immediately and more frequently than most department heads can provide. Because cabinet appointees generally have not shared political careers with the president or with one another and because they may meet one another for the first time after their selection, the formation of an effective governing group out of this motley collection of appointments is unlikely. Although President Clinton's insistence on a cabinet diverse enough to resemble American society could be considered an act of political wisdom, it virtually guaranteed that few of his appointees had ever spent

[37] As the political scientist Terry Moe writes, "This is the rational basis for the institutional presidency. Throughout . . . [the twentieth] century, presidents have struggled to provide themselves with a structural capacity for leadership by building institutions of their own." See Terry M. Moe, "Presidents, Institutions, and Theory," in *Researching the Presidency: Vital Questions, New Approaches,* ed. George C. Edwards III, John H. Kessel, and Bert A. Rockman (Pittsburgh: University of Pittsburgh Press, 1993), p. 367.

FIGURE 6.3 The Institutional Presidency, 2007

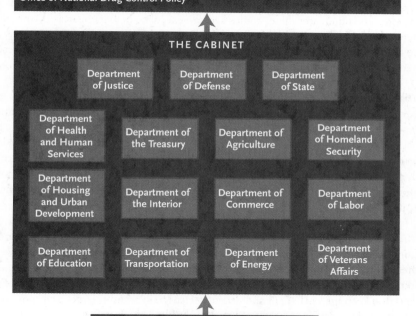

THE PRESIDENT

THE WHITE HOUSE STAFF

EXECUTIVE OFFICE OF THE PRESIDENT

White House Office
Office of Management and Budget
Council of Economic Advisers
National Security Council
President's Foreign Intelligence Advisory Board
Office of National Drug Control Policy

U.S. Trade Representative
Council on Environmental Quality
Office of Science and Technology Policy
Office of Administration

THE CABINET

Department of Justice

Department of Defense

Department of State

Department of Health and Human Services

Department of the Treasury

Department of Agriculture

Department of Homeland Security

Department of Housing and Urban Development

Department of the Interior

Department of Commerce

Department of Labor

Department of Education

Department of Transportation

Department of Energy

Department of Veterans Affairs

INDEPENDENT ESTABLISHMENTS AND GOVERNMENT CORPORATIONS

much time working together or even knew the policy positions or beliefs of the other appointees.[38]

Some presidents have relied more heavily on an "inner cabinet," the **National Security Council (NSC).** The NSC, established by law in 1947, is composed of the president, the vice president, the secretaries of state, defense, and the Treasury, the attorney general, the chair of the Joint Chiefs of Staff (as "statutory military adviser"), the director of national intelligence (as intelligence adviser), and other officials invited by the president. It has its own staff of foreign policy specialists run by the assistant to the president for national security affairs. For these highest appointments, presidents usually turn to people from outside Washington, often longtime associates. George W. Bush's inner cabinet was composed largely of former and proven senior staffers and cabinet members of former Republican administrations, most particularly Vice President Dick Cheney, Defense Secretary Robert Gates, Secretary of State Condoleezza Rice, national security adviser Stephen Hadley, and Attorney General Alberto Gonzales.

Presidents have obviously been uneven and unpredictable in their reliance on the NSC and other subcabinet bodies because executive management is inherently a personal matter. Despite all the personal variations, however, one generalization can be made: Presidents have increasingly preferred the White House staff to the cabinet as their means of managing the gigantic executive branch.

The White House Staff The **White House staff** is composed mainly of analysts and advisers.[39] Although many of the top White House staff members are given the title "special assistant" for a particular task or sector, the types of judgments they are expected to make and the kinds of advice they are supposed to give are a good deal broader and more generally political than those coming from the Executive Office of the President or the cabinet departments. The members of the White House staff also tend to be more closely associated with the president than other presidentially appointed officials.

From an informal group of fewer than a dozen people (popularly called the **Kitchen Cabinet**) and no more than four dozen at the height of FDR's prewar administration, the White House staff has grown substantially with each successive president.[40] Richard Nixon employed 550 people in 1972. President Carter, who found so many of the requirements of presidential power distasteful and publicly vowed to keep his staff small and decentralized, built an even larger and more centralized staff. President Clinton reduced the White House staff by 20 percent, but a large White House staff is still essential.

The White House staff is a crucial information source and management tool for the president. But it may also insulate the president from other sources of infor-

---

[38] *New York Times,* 23 December 1992, p. 1.

[39] A substantial portion of this section is taken from Lowi, *The Personal President,* pp. 141–50.

[40] All the figures since 1967, and probably since 1957, are understated because additional White House staff members have been on "detailed" service, borrowed from the military and various cabinet departments (some secretly assigned) and are not counted here because they were not on the White House payroll.

mation. Managing this trade-off between in-house expertise and access to independent outside opinion is a major challenge for the president. Sometimes it is botched, as when President George W. Bush depended too heavily on his staff for information about WMDs in Iraq, leading him to erroneous conclusions.[41]

The Executive Office of the President   The development of the White House staff can be appreciated only in its relation to the still-larger **Executive Office of the President (EOP)**. Created in 1939, the EOP is a major part of what is often called the institutional presidency—the permanent agencies that perform defined management tasks for the president. The most important and the largest EOP agency is the Office of Management and Budget (OMB). Its roles in preparing the national budget, designing the president's program, reporting on agency activities, and overseeing regulatory proposals make OMB personnel part of virtually every conceivable presidential responsibility. The status and power of the OMB have grown in importance with each successive president. The process of budgeting at one time was a bottom-up procedure, with expenditure and program requests passing from the lowest bureaus through the departments to "clearance" in OMB and hence to Congress, where each agency could be called in to reveal what its original request had been before it was revised by the OMB. Now the budgeting process is top-down: OMB sets the terms of discourse for agencies as well as for Congress. The director of OMB is now one of the most powerful officials in Washington.

The staff of the Council of Economic Advisers (CEA) constantly analyzes the economy and economic trends and attempts to give the president the ability to anticipate events rather than waiting and reacting to events. The Council on Environmental Quality was designed to do for environmental issues what the CEA does for economic issues. The members of the National Security Council meet regularly with the president to give advice on the large national-security picture. The staff of the NSC assimilates and analyzes data from all intelligence-gathering agencies (the CIA, and so on). Other EOP agencies perform more specialized tasks.

Somewhere between 1,500 and 2,000 highly specialized staffers work for EOP agencies.[42] The importance of each agency in the EOP varies according to the personal orientation of the president. For example, the NSC staff was of immense importance under President Nixon, especially because it served essentially as the personal staff of the presidential assistant Henry Kissinger before his elevation to the office of secretary of state. But it was of less importance to President George H. W. Bush, who looked outside the EOP altogether for military policy matters, turning much more to the Joint Chiefs of Staff and its chair at the time, General Colin Powell.

The Vice Presidency   The vice presidency is a constitutional anomaly, even though the office was created by the Constitution along with the presidency. The vice president exists for two purposes only: to succeed the president in case of death, resigna-

---

[41]See George Krause, "The Secular Decline in Presidential Domestic Policymaking: An Organizational Perspective," *Presidential Studies Quarterly* 34 (2004): 779–92. On the general issue, see James P. Pfiffner, ed., *The Managerial Presidency*, 2nd ed. (College Station: Texas A&M University Press, 1999).

[42]The actual number is difficult to estimate because, as with the White House staff, some EOP personnel, especially those in national-security work, are detailed to the office from outside agencies.

Executive Office of the President (EOP) The permanent agencies that perform defined management tasks for the president. Created in 1939, the EOP includes the Office of Management and Budget, the Council of Economic Advisers, the National Security Council, and other agencies.

tion, or incapacitation and to preside over the Senate, casting a tie-breaking vote when necessary.[43]

The main value of the vice presidency as a political resource for the president is electoral. Traditionally a presidential candidate's most important rule for the choice of a running mate is that he or she bring the support of at least one state (preferably a large one) not otherwise likely to support the ticket. It is very doubtful that John Kennedy would have won in 1960 without his vice-presidential candidate, Lyndon Johnson, and the contribution Johnson made to winning in Texas. Another rule holds that the vice-presidential nominee should provide some regional balance and, wherever possible, some balance among various ideological or ethnic subsections of the party. George W. Bush's choice of Dick Cheney in 2000 was completely devoid of direct electoral value, since Cheney comes from one of our least populous states (Wyoming, which casts only three electoral votes). But Cheney's stalwart right-wing record both in Congress and as President George H. W. Bush's secretary of defense helped to consolidate the support of the restive right wing of the Republican party. In 2008, Barack Obama named Senator Joseph Biden of Delaware as his running mate. Biden chaired the Senate Foreign Relations Committee and brought strong foreign policy experience to the ticket. Democrats hoped his working-class background would appeal to blue-collar voters in battleground states like Ohio and Pennsylvania. John McCain chose Alaska governor Sarah Palin as his running mate. Palin was very popular among the GOP's religious conservatives and helped to energize the party's "base," but her inexperience and apparent lack of familiarity with national issues led many voters to question her qualifications.

As the institutional presidency has grown in size and complexity, most presidents of the past twenty-five years have sought to use their vice president as a management resource after the election. George H. W. Bush, as President Reagan's vice president, was kept within the loop of decision making because Reagan delegated so much power. A copy of virtually every document made for Reagan was made for Bush, especially during the first term, when Bush's close friend James Baker was chief of staff. Former president Bush did not take such pains to keep Vice President Dan Quayle in the loop, but President Clinton relied greatly on his vice president, Al Gore, and Gore emerged as one of the most trusted and effective figures in the Clinton White House. Gore's most important task was to oversee the National Performance Review (NPR), an ambitious program to "reinvent" the way the federal government conducts its affairs. The presidency of George W. Bush has resulted in unprecedented power and responsibility for his vice president, Dick Cheney. Before becoming vice president, Cheney served for five years (1995–2000) as chief executive of Halliburton, the world's largest provider of oil and gas services, and developed the reputation, among supporters and critics, as a man who gets things done. Known as a hands-on vice president, he plays an active role in cabinet meetings and policy formation and directed the National Energy Policy Development Group, for which the Bush administration received some criticism when the Enron scandal unfolded in 2002. Cheney is widely viewed as one of the most—if not the most—influential vice presidents in American history.

---

[43]Article I, Section 3, provides that "the Vice President . . . shall be President of the Senate, but shall have no Vote, unless they be equally divided." This is the only vote the vice president is allowed.

The President and Policy   The president's powers and institutional resources, taken together, give the chief executive a substantial voice in the nation's policy-making processes. Strictly speaking, presidents cannot introduce legislation. Only members of Congress can formally propose new programs and policies. However, presidents often do send proposals to Congress. Congress, in turn, takes up these proposals by referring them to the relevant committee of jurisdiction. Sometimes these proposals are said to be dead on arrival, an indication that presidential preferences are at loggerheads with those in the House or Senate. This event is especially common during periods of divided government. In such circumstances, presidents and legislators engage in bargaining, although at the end of the day the status quo may prevail. Presidents are typically in a weak position in these circumstances, especially if they have grand plans to change the status quo.[44] During periods of unified government, the president has fellow copartisans in charge of each chamber; in these cases, the president may indeed seize the initiative, seeking to coordinate policy initiatives from the White House. The political scientist Charles Cameron suggests that the distinction between unified and divided government is quite consequential for presidential "style": It makes the chief executive either bargainer in chief or coordinator in chief.[45]

Congress has come to expect the president to propose the government's budget, and the nation has come to expect presidential initiatives to deal with major problems. Some of these initiatives have come in the form of huge packages of programs—Franklin Roosevelt's New Deal and Lyndon Johnson's Great Society. Sometimes presidents craft a single program they hope will have a significant effect on both the nation and their political fortunes. For example, George W. Bush made the war on terrorism the centerpiece of his administration. To fight this war, Bush brought about the creation of a new cabinet department, the Department of Homeland Security, and the enactment of such pieces of legislation as the Patriot Act to give the executive branch more power to deal with the terrorist threat. Going beyond terrorism, Bush also presided over the enactment of a huge expansion of the Medicare program to provide prescription drug benefits to senior citizens. All this from a president who was said to lack a popular ***mandate*** in the wake of the controversial 2000 election. Bush may have lacked a mandate, but the expressed and delegated powers of the office gave him the resources with which to prevail. Ironically his 2004 reelection victory was more substantial than his victory in 2000, but it failed to provide him much leverage on new policy initiatives. His efforts to reshape and reinvigorate the Social Security system and reform the estate tax have come to naught; the war in Iraq, the fight against terrorism, and the response to catastrophic hurricanes have squeezed other domestic initiatives off the active to-do list.

At one time, historians and journalists liked to debate the question of strong versus weak presidents. Today every president is strong. This strength is not so much a function of personal charisma or political savvy as it is a reflection of the increasing power of the institution of the presidency.

Collective-Action Principle

Whether government is divided or unified has a big influence on whether a president is a bargainer or a coordinator.

mandate A claim by a victorious candidate that the electorate has given him or her special authority to carry out promises made during the campaign.

○ ONLINE READING

---

[44]D. Roderick Kiewiet and Mathew D. McCubbins, *The Logic of Delegation: Congressional Parties and the Appropriations Process* (Chicago: University of Chicago Press, 1991).

[45]Cameron, "Bargaining and Presidential Power."

The Contemporary Bases of Presidential Power

In the nineteenth century, when Congress was America's dominant institution of government, its members sometimes treated the president with disdain. Today, however, no one would assert that the presidency is an unimportant institution. Presidents seek to dominate the policy-making process and claim the inherent power to lead the nation in time of war. The expansion of presidential power over the course of the past century has come about not by accident but as the result of an ongoing effort by successive presidents to enlarge the powers of the office. Some of these efforts have succeeded, and others have failed. As the framers of the Constitution predicted, presidential ambition has been a powerful and unrelenting force in American politics.

Generally presidents can expand their power by three means: party, popular mobilization, and administration. In the first instance, presidents may construct or strengthen national partisan institutions with which to exert influence in the legislative process and through which to implement their programs. Alternatively or in addition to the first tactic, presidents may use popular appeals to create a mass base of support that will allow them to subordinate their political foes. This tactic has sometimes been called the strategy of going public, or the "rhetorical" presidency.[46] In the third instance, presidents may seek to bolster their control of established executive agencies or create new administrative institutions and procedures that will reduce their dependence on Congress and give them a more independent governing and policy-making capability. Presidents' use of executive orders to achieve their policy goals in lieu of seeking to persuade Congress to enact legislation is, perhaps, the most obvious example.

Party as a Source of Power　All presidents have relied on the members and leaders of their own party to implement their legislative agendas. President George W. Bush, for example, has worked closely with congressional GOP leaders on such matters as energy policy and Medicare reform. But the president does not control his own party; party members have considerable autonomy. On immigration policy, for example, the Bush proposals in 2006 were supported in most respects by the Republican-controlled Senate. The Republican-controlled House, however, passed much more punitive policies. The two chambers, despite being controlled by the president's party, were unable to agree on a compromise and ended up settling on elements of the House bill that the president least desired. Nevertheless, he signed the measure in October 2006. The issue reemerged in 2007, but a comprehensive immigration reform proposal failed to pass in the Congress.

In America's system of separated powers, the president's party may be in the minority in Congress and unable to do much for the chief executive's programs (Figure 6.4). Consequently, although their party is valuable to chief executives, it has not been a fully reliable presidential tool. The more unified the president's party is in supporting his legislative requests, the more unified the opposition party is likely to be. Unless the majority of the president's party is very large, he must also appeal to the opposition to make up for the inevitable defectors within the ranks of his own party. Thus the president often poses as being above partisanship to win "bipartisan" support in Congress. But to the extent that he pursues a bipartisan strategy, he cannot throw himself fully

Collective-Action Principle

The more unified the president's party is in Congress, the more unified the opposition is likely to be.

---

[46]Kernell, *Going Public;* see also, Tulis, *The Rhetorical Presidency.*

FIGURE 6.4 The Presidential Batting Average: Presidential Success on Congressional Votes

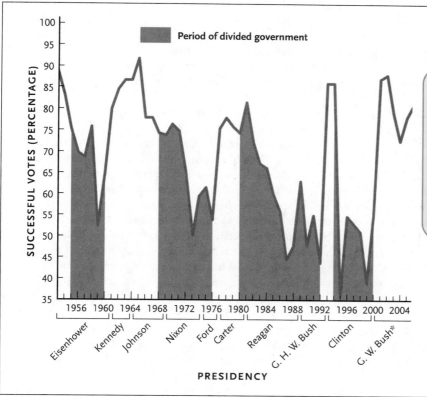

ANALYZING THE EVIDENCE

Presidential success ebbs and flows, especially with the partisan character of Congress. Compare success rates when the president and the legislature were of the same party (for example, Clinton's first two years) and when they were not (for example, Clinton's last six years).

SOURCE: *Congressional Quarterly Weekly Report,* 3 January 2004, p. 18.

NOTE: Percentages are based on votes on which presidents took a position.

*In 2001, the government was divided for only part of the year.

into building the party loyalty and the party discipline that would maximize the value of his own party's support in Congress. This is a dilemma for every president, particularly those faced with an opposition-controlled Congress.

The role of the filibuster in the Senate should not be underestimated in this context (see chapter 5). Even a president with a large majority in the House and a good working majority in the Senate may not have the 60 votes needed to shut down debate in the Senate. This is especially apparent in the case of presidential appointments, where individual senators can place a hold on the nomination, putting everyone on notice that the president's pursuit of a particular candidate will trigger a filibuster.[47] Filibuster power was especially prominent in 2005 as President Bush

---

[47] A powerful argument that invokes this logic is that of Keith Krehbiel in *Pivotal Politics: A Theory of U.S. Lawmaking* (Chicago: University of Chicago Press, 1998).

sought senate confirmation of federal judges and two Supreme Court justices. The Democrats, who were in the minority, were in a position to filibuster nominations they regarded as "extremist," forcing the president (and his majority partisans in the Senate) to negotiate. The Democrats lifted the filibuster threat in exchange for some moderation on the part of the president, and they have allowed up-or-down votes on some nominees. Because they cannot always rely on their party in Congress, contemporary presidents are more likely to use two other methods—popular mobilization and executive administration—to achieve their political goals.

Going Public   Popular mobilization as a technique of presidential power has its historical roots in the presidencies of Theodore Roosevelt and Woodrow Wilson and subsequently became a weapon in the political arsenals of most presidents after the mid-twentieth century. During the nineteenth century, it was considered rather inappropriate for presidents to engage in personal campaigning on their own behalf or in support of programs and policies. When Andrew Johnson broke this unwritten rule and made a series of speeches vehemently seeking public support for his Reconstruction program, even some of his most ardent supporters were shocked at what was seen as a lack of decorum and dignity. The president's opponents cited his "inflammatory" speeches in one of the articles of impeachment drafted by Congress pursuant to the first effort in American history to oust a sitting president.[48]

The president who used public appeals most effectively was Franklin Roosevelt. The political scientist Sidney Milkis observes that FDR was "firmly persuaded of the need to form a direct link between the executive office and the public."[49] FDR developed a number of tactics aimed at forging such a link. Like his predecessors, he often embarked on speaking trips around the nation to promote his programs. On one such tour, he told a crowd, "I regain strength just by meeting the American people."[50] In addition, FDR made limited but important use of the new electronic medium, the radio, to reach millions of Americans. In his famous "fireside chats," the president, or at least his voice, came into every living room in the country to discuss programs and policies and generally to assure Americans that Franklin Delano Roosevelt was aware of their difficulties and working diligently toward solutions. Another executive, Mayor Fiorello La Guardia of New York City, also "went public," using radio to read comic strips to Depression-era city children during a long newspaper strike. A brilliant political ploy, it deeply impressed voting-age citizens while entertaining the young ones.

Roosevelt was also an innovator in the realm of what now might be called press relations. When he entered the White House, FDR faced a mainly hostile press typically controlled by conservative members of the business establishment. As the president wrote, "All the fat-cat newspapers—85 percent of the whole—have been utterly opposed to everything the Administration is seeking."[51] Roosevelt hoped to be able to use

---

[48]Tulis, *The Rhetorical Presidency*, p. 91.

[49]Sidney M. Milkis, *The President and the Parties: The Transformation of the American Party System since the New Deal* (New York: Oxford University Press, 1993), p. 97.

[50]Quoted in James MacGregor Burns, *Roosevelt: The Lion and the Fox* (New York: Harcourt, Brace, 1956), p. 317.

[51]Ibid., p. 317.

the press to mold public opinion, but to do so he needed to circumvent the editors and publishers who were generally unsympathetic to his goals. To this end, the president worked to cultivate the reporters who covered the White House. Roosevelt made himself available for twice-weekly press conferences, during which he offered candid answers to reporters' questions and made certain to make important policy announcements that would provide the reporters with significant stories to file with their papers.[52] Roosevelt was the first president to designate a press secretary (Stephen Early), who was charged with organizing the press conferences and making certain that reporters observed the informal rules distinguishing presidential comments that were off the record from those that could be attributed directly to the president.

Every president since FDR has sought to craft a public relations strategy that emphasized his strengths and maximized his popular appeal. One Clinton innovation was to make the White House Communications Office an important institution within the EOP. In a practice continued by George W. Bush, the Communications Office became responsible not only for responding to reporters' queries but also for developing and implementing a coordinated communications strategy: promoting the president's policy goals, developing responses to unflattering news stories, and making certain that a favorable image of the president would, insofar as possible, dominate the news. George W. Bush's first communications director, Karen Hughes, sought to put the office "ahead of the news," constantly developing stories that would dominate the headlines, present the president in a favorable light, and deflect criticism. For example, after the administration responded to the September 11 terrorist attacks against the World Trade Center and the Pentagon with a massive military campaign in Afghanistan, the Communications Office developed several stories that made it difficult for administration critics to gain much traction. One such story concerned the brutal treatment of women by Afghanistan's fundamentalist Taliban regime, which was underlined in several speeches by First Lady Laura Bush and communicated to the press in hundreds of news releases. The wave of publicity the Communications Office was able to generate concerning the Taliban's harsh and demeaning posture toward women was one factor that made it extremely difficult for the Bush administration's liberal critics to utter even a word of protest regarding America's determined effort to oust the Taliban from power.[53]

In addition to using the media, recent presidents, particularly Bill Clinton, have reached out directly to the American public to gain its approval. President Clinton's enormously high public profile, as indicated by the number of public appearances he made (Figure 6.5), is a dramatic expression of the presidency as a ***permanent campaign*** for reelection. A study by the political scientist Charles O. Jones shows that President Clinton engaged in campaignlike activity throughout his presidency and was the most-traveled American president in history. In his first twenty months in office, he made 203 appearances outside Washington, compared with 178 by

permanent campaign Presidential politics in which all presidential actions are taken with reelection in mind.

○ ONLINE READING

---

[52]Kernell, *Going Public*, p. 79.

[53]Going public is a strategy well suited to a world of television with only a few major networks. A president is able to influence, if not control, the content of his coverage. With the proliferation of cable outlets, however, the president has less control. See Gerry Young and William Perkins, "Presidential Rhetoric, the Public Agenda, and the End of Presidential Television's Golden Age,'" *Journal of Politics* 67 (2005): 1190–1205.

FIGURE 6.5 Public Appearances by Presidents

ANALYZING
THE EVIDENCE

In the nineteenth century, presidents seldom made public speeches or other public appearances. By the end of the twentieth century, the number of times presidents went public had increased dramatically. What accounts for the growth in public appearances? What do presidents hope to accomplish through speeches and other public events? What risks do presidents take when they seek to develop and use popular support as a political tool?

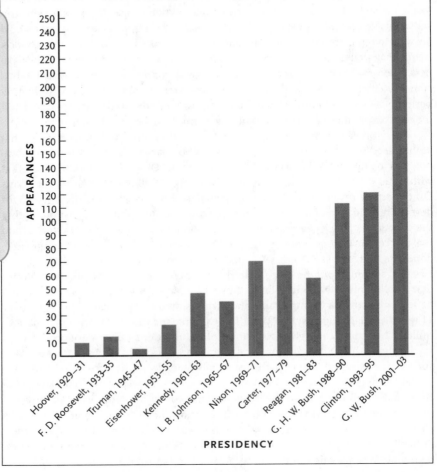

SOURCE: Samuel Kernell, *Going Public: New Strategies of Presidential Leadership*, 3rd ed. (Washington, D.C.: Congressional Quarterly Press, 1998), p. 118.

NOTE: Only the first two years of each term are included, because the last two years include many purely political appearances for the president's reelection campaign.

George H. W. Bush and 58 by Ronald Reagan.[54] During his first 100 days, President George W. Bush gave speeches and other public appearances in twenty-six states; the records of Clinton and former president Bush during their first 100 days were fifteen states each. During his second term, Bush's public appearances diminished, and by 2008 the president was giving few public speeches. During the 2008 campaign, Republican candidates seldom invited the unpopular president to appear with them.

[54]Charles O. Jones, *Passages to the Presidency: From Campaigning to Governing* (Washington, D.C.: Brookings Institution Press, 1998).

THE LIMITS OF GOING PUBLIC   Some presidents have been able to make effective use of popular appeals to overcome congressional opposition. Popular support, though, has not been a firm foundation for presidential power. To begin with, it is notoriously fickle. President Bush maintained an approval rating of over 70 percent for more than a year after the September 11 terrorist attacks. In 2003, however, his approval rating fell nearly twenty points as American casualties in Iraq mounted; by the end of 2005, it had fallen almost another twenty points, to the high 30s, where it remained through much of 2006. By the end of his presidency, Bush's approval rating had fallen to 24 percent. Such declines in popular approval during a president's term in office are nearly inevitable and follow a predictable pattern (Figure 6.6).[55] Presidents generate popular support by promising to undertake programs that will contribute directly to the well-being of large numbers of Americans. When presidential performance falls short of those promises and popular expectations, there is a sharp decline in public support and a collapse of presidential influence.[56]

Presidents have certainly not abandoned the tool of going public, but they no longer use it frequently as they once did—there has been, for example, a decline in presidential appearances on prime-time television over the past four administrations.[57] Instead, presidents have employed institutionalized public and media relations efforts more to create a generally favorable public image than to promote specific policies. Thus in 2002, President George W. Bush made several speeches to boost the proposed creation of the Homeland Security Department. At the same time, however, the White House Communications Office was engaged in a nonstop, seven-day-a-week effort to promote news and feature stories aimed at bolstering the president's more general public image. Stories emphasized the president's empathy for retirees hurt by the downturn of stock prices, the president's anger over corporate abuses, the president's concern for the environment, the president's determination to prevent terrorism, the president's support for Israel, and so forth. These are all examples of polishing one's image rather than going public on behalf of specific programs. Confronted with the limitations of a strategy of popular mobilization, presidents have shifted from an offensive strategy to a more defensive mode in this domain. The limitations of going public as a route to presidential power have also led contemporary presidents to make use of a third technique: expansion of their administrative capabilities.

The Administrative State

Contemporary presidents have increased the administrative capabilities of their office in three ways. First, they have enhanced the reach and power of the EOP. Second, they have sought to increase White House control over the federal bureaucracy. Third, they have expanded the role of executive orders and other instruments of direct presidential governance. Taken together, these components of what might be called the White House administrative strategy have given presidents a capacity to achieve their programmatic and policy goals even when they are unable to secure

---

[55] Lowi, *The Personal President.*

[56] Ibid., p. 11.

[57] Kernell, *Going Public,* p. 114.

FIGURE 6.6 Presidential Performance Ratings

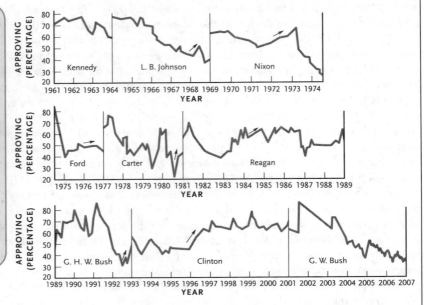

SOURCE: Courtesy of the Gallup Organization and Louis Harris and Associates.

NOTE: Arrows indicate preelection upswings.

congressional approval. Indeed, some recent presidents have been able to accomplish quite a bit without much congressional, partisan, or even public support.

The Executive Office of the President The Executive Office of the President has grown from 6 administrative assistants in 1939 to today's 39 assistants to the president, deputy assistants, and special assistants who work in the White House office, along with some 1,800 individuals staffing the nine divisions of the Executive Office.[58] The creation and growth of the White House staff give the president an enormously enhanced capacity to gather information, plan programs and strategies, communicate with constituencies, and exercise supervision of the executive branch. The staff multiplies the president's eyes, ears, and arms, serving as a critical instrument of presidential power.[59] In light of the degree to which Congress delegates to the executive branch, as described earlier in this chapter, the president has greatly enhanced his capacity as an agent of policy formulation and implementation.

---

[58] Harold W. Stanley and Richard G. Niemi, *Vital Statistics on American Politics, 2005–2006* (Washington, D.C.: Congressional Quarterly Press, 2005), pp. 250–51.

[59] Milkis, *The President and the Parties*, p. 128.

In particular, the OMB serves as a potential instrument of presidential control over federal spending and hence as a mechanism through which the White House has greatly expanded its power. The OMB has the capacity to analyze and approve not only budgetary requests but all legislative proposals but emanating from all federal agencies before they are submitted to Congress. This procedure, now a matter of routine, greatly enhanced the president's control over the entire executive branch. All executive orders also go through the OMB.[60] Thus in one White House agency the president has the means to exert major influence over the flow of money as well as the shape and content of national legislation.

Regulatory Review   A second tactic that presidents have used to increase their power and reach is the process of regulatory review, through which they have sought to control rule making by the agencies of the executive branch (see also Chapter 14). Whenever Congress enacts a statute, its actual implementation requires the promulgation of hundreds of rules by the agency charged with administering the law and giving effect to the will of Congress. Some congressional statutes are quite detailed and leave agencies with relatively little discretion. Typically, however, Congress enacts a relatively broad statement of legislative intent and delegates to the appropriate administrative agency the power to fill in many important details.[61] In other words, Congress typically says to an administrative agency, "Here is the problem. Deal with it."[62]

The discretion Congress delegates to administrative agencies has provided recent presidents with an important avenue for expanding their power. For example, President Clinton believed the president had full authority to order agencies of the executive branch to adopt such rules as the president thought appropriate. During the course of his presidency, Clinton issued 107 directives to administrators ordering them to propose specific rules and regulations. In some instances, the language of the rule to be proposed was drafted by the White House staff; in other cases, the president asserted a priority but left it to the agency to draft the precise language of the proposal. Presidential rule-making directives covered a wide variety of topics. For example, Clinton ordered the Food and Drug Administration (FDA) to develop rules designed to restrict the marketing of tobacco products to children. White House and FDA staffers then spent several months preparing nearly 1,000 pages of new regulations affecting tobacco manufacturers and vendors.[63] Republicans, of course, denounced Clinton's actions as a usurpation of power.[64] After he took office, however, President George W. Bush made no move to surrender the powers Clinton had claimed. Bush continued the Clinton-era practice of issuing presidential directives to agencies to spur them to issue new rules and regulations.

---

[60]Ibid., p. 160.

[61]The classic critique of this process is Lowi, *The End of Liberalism*.

[62]Kenneth Culp Davis, *Administrative Law Treatise* (St. Paul: West, 1958), p. 9.

[63]Elena Kagan, "Presidential Administration," *Harvard Law Review* 114 (2001): 2265.

[64]For example, Douglas W. Kmiec, "Expanding Power," in *The Rule of Law in the Wake of Clinton*, ed. Roger Pilon (Washington, D.C.: Cato Institute Press, 2000), pp. 47–68.

Governing by Decree: Executive Orders A third mechanism through which contemporary presidents have sought to enhance their power to govern unilaterally is the use of executive orders and other forms of presidential decrees, including executive agreements, national-security findings and directives, proclamations, reorganization plans, the signing of statements, and a host of others.[65] Executive orders have a long history in the United States and have been the vehicles for a number of important government policies, including the purchase of Louisiana, the annexation of Texas, the emancipation of the slaves, the internment of the Japanese, the desegregation of the military, the initiation of affirmative action, and the creation of important federal agencies, among them the EPA, the FDA, and the Peace Corps.[66]

While wars and national emergencies produce the highest volume of executive orders, such presidential actions also occur frequently in peacetime (Figure 6.7). In the realm of foreign policy, unilateral presidential actions in the form of executive agreements have virtually replaced treaties as the nation's chief foreign-policy instruments.[67] Presidential decrees, however, are often used for purely domestic purposes.

Presidents may not use executive orders to issue whatever commands they please. The use of such decrees is bound by law. If a president issues an executive order, proclamation, directive, or the like, in principle he does so pursuant to the powers granted to him by the Constitution or delegated to him by Congress, usually through a statute. When presidents issue such orders, they generally state the constitutional or statutory basis for their actions. For example, when President Truman ordered the desegregation of the armed services, he did so pursuant to his constitutional powers as commander in chief. In a similar vein, when President Johnson issued Executive Order No. 11246, he asserted that the order was designed to implement the 1964 Civil Rights Act, which prohibited employment discrimination. Where an executive order has no statutory or constitutional basis, the courts have held it to be void. The most important case illustrating this point is *Youngstown Sheet and Tube Company v. Sawyer*, the so-called steel seizure case of 1952.[68] Here the Supreme Court ruled that President Truman's seizure of the nation's steel mills during the Korean War had no statutory or constitutional basis and was thus invalid.

A number of court decisions, though, have established broad boundaries that leave considerable room for presidential action. By illustration, the courts have held that Congress might approve a presidential action after the fact or, in effect, ratify a presidential action through "acquiescence"—for example, by not objecting for long periods of time or by continuing to provide funding for programs established by executive orders. In addition, the courts have indicated that some areas, most notably the realm of military policy, are presidential in character, and they have allowed presidents wide latitude to make policy by executive decree. Thus within the very broad limits established by the courts, presidential orders can be and have been important policy tools.

---

[65] A complete inventory is provided in Harold C. Relyea, *Presidential Directives: Background and Review*, Congressional Research Service Report for Congress, 98–611 GOV, 9 November 2001.

[66] Terry M. Moe and William G. Howell, "The Presidential Power of Unilateral Action," *Journal of Law, Economics, and Organization* 15 (1999): 133–34.

[67] Ibid., p. 164.

[68] *Youngstown Sheet and Tube Company v. Sawyer*, 343 U.S. 579 (1952).

FIGURE 6.7 Significant Executive Orders, 1900–1995

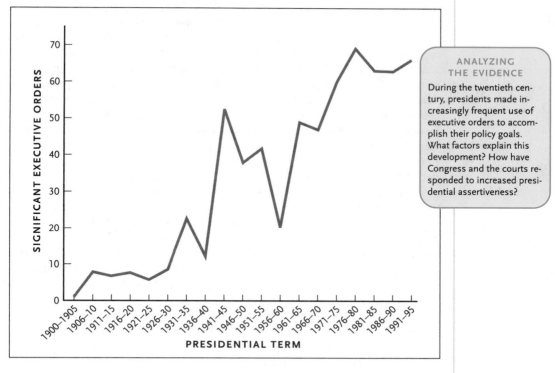

SOURCE: William G. Howell, "The President's Powers of Unilateral Action: The Strategic Advantages of Acting Alone" (Ph.D. diss., Stanford University, 1999).

ANALYZING THE EVIDENCE

During the twentieth century, presidents made increasingly frequent use of executive orders to accomplish their policy goals. What factors explain this development? How have Congress and the courts responded to increased presidential assertiveness?

President Clinton issued numerous orders designed to promote a coherent set of policy goals: protecting the environment, strengthening federal regulatory power, shifting the focus of America's foreign policy from unilateral to multilateral, expanding affirmative action programs, and helping organized labor in its struggles with employers.[69] As in his use of regulatory review, President Clinton was able to craft through executive orders a policy agenda that he could not accomplish through legislation. Faced with a hostile Congress, Clinton turned to unilateral instruments of executive power, including regulatory review, executive orders, and the like. Clinton certainly did not issue more executive orders than previous presidents. His innovation was to take an instrument that had been used sporadically and show that an activist president could develop and implement a significant policy agenda without legislation—a lesson that surely has not been lost on his successor.

Indeed, just as he continued the practice of using regulatory review as a policy instrument, President George W. Bush did not hesitate to use executive orders, issuing more than forty during his first year in office and continuing to employ this device (along with signing statements, described earlier) with great regularity

---

[69]Todd Gaziano, "The New 'Massive Resistance,'" *Policy Review*, May–June 1998, p. 283.

during his presidency. During his first months in office, Bush issued orders placing limits on the use of embryonic stem cells in federally funded research projects and prohibiting the use of federal funds to support international family-planning groups that provide abortion-counseling services. Subsequently Bush made very aggressive use of executive orders in response to the threat of terrorism, which the president declared to be his administration's most important policy agenda. In November 2001, for example, Bush issued a directive authorizing the creation of military tribunals to try noncitizens accused of involvement in acts of terrorism against the United States. The presidential directive also prohibits defendants from appealing their treatment to any federal or state court. In 2005 and 2006, it came to light that Bush had ordered the National Security Administration to conduct a massive program of domestic surveillance of telephone traffic involving suspected terrorists.

In addition, the president issued orders freezing the assets of groups and individuals associated with terrorism, providing expedited citizenship for foreign nationals serving in the U.S. military, and empowering the CIA to use all means possible to oust President Saddam Hussein of Iraq, whom Bush accused of plotting terrorist acts. In *Hamdan v. Rumsfeld,* the Supreme Court in June 2006 determined that the military tribunals established by Bush's executive order to try detainees at the U.S. naval base at Guantánamo Bay, Cuba, violated both the Uniform Code of Military Justice and the Geneva Conventions.[70]

While terrorism was certainly at the top of President Bush's agenda, he also issued a number of executive orders having to do with domestic policy. For example, the president was able to overcome congressional resistance to his efforts to increase domestic energy exploration and the rapid exploitation of domestic energy resources. Like Clinton, President Bush discovered that an executive order can often substitute for legislation. In May 2001, Bush signed an executive order that closely followed a recommendation from the American Petroleum Institute (API), an oil industry trade association, to free energy companies from a number of federal regulations.

The Advantages of the Administrative Strategy   Through the course of American history, party leadership and popular appeals have played important roles in presidential efforts to overcome political opposition. Both parties and appeals to the people continue to be instruments of presidential power. Reagan's tax cuts and Clinton's budget victories were achieved with strong partisan support. George W. Bush, lacking the oratorical skills of a Reagan or a Roosevelt, nevertheless made good use of sophisticated communications strategies to promote his agenda. Yet, as we saw, in the modern era, parties have waned in institutional strength while the effects of popular appeals have often proved evanescent. The limitations of the alternatives have increasingly impelled presidents to try to expand the administrative capabilities of the office and their own capacity for unilateral action as means of achieving their policy goals. And in recent decades, the expansion of the Executive Office, the development of regulatory review, and the use of executive orders, the signing of statements, and

[70] *Hamdan v. Rumsfeld,* 548 U.S. (2006).

the like have given presidents a substantial capacity to achieve significant policy results despite congressional opposition to their legislative agendas.

To be sure, the administrative strategy does not always succeed. In some instances over the years, as just noted, the federal courts have struck down unilateral actions by the president. And occasionally Congress acts to reverse presidential orders. For example, in 1999, Congress enacted legislation prohibiting the Department of Education from carrying out a presidential directive to administer national tests of reading and mathematics.[71] And before that, in 1996, in response to President Clinton's aggressive regulatory review program, the Republican-controlled Congress moved to strengthen its capacity to block the president's use of administrative directives by enacting the Congressional Review Act (CRA). This piece of legislation requires federal agencies to send all proposed regulations to Congress for review sixty days before they take effect. It also creates a fast-track procedure to allow the House and the Senate to enact a joint resolution of disapproval that would not only void the regulation but also prohibit the agency from subsequently issuing any substantially similar rule. The first test of the act came after Clinton left office. In the early weeks of the Bush administration, Congress passed a joint resolution repealing an ergonomics standard that had been supported by the Clinton administration and adopted by OSHA. President Bush, who opposed the standard, signed the resolution, and the ergonomics standard was voided. While this outcome may be seen as an effective effort by Congress to thwart a presidential directive, it seems clear that Congress was successful only because Clinton was out of office. Had his term not expired, Clinton would almost certainly have vetoed the resolution. Indeed, one reason Clinton was willing to sign the CRA into law in the first place was that the president retained the power to veto any action undertaken by Congress under the statute's authority.

In principle, perhaps, Congress could respond more vigorously than it has to unilateral policy making by the president. Certainly a Congress willing to impeach a president should have the mettle to overturn his administrative directives. But the president has significant advantages in such struggles with Congress. In battles over presidential directives and orders, Congress is on the defensive, reacting to presidential initiatives. The framers of the Constitution saw "energy," or the ability to take the initiative, as a key feature of executive power.[72] When the president takes action by issuing an order or an administrative directive, Congress must initiate the cumbersome and time-consuming lawmaking process, overcome internal divisions, and enact legislation that the president may ultimately veto. Moreover, as Terry Moe has argued, in such battles Congress faces a significant collective-action problem insofar as members are likely to be more sensitive to the substance of a president's actions and its effects on their constituents than to the more general implications of presidential power for the long-term vitality of their institution.[73]

---

[71]Kagan, "Presidential Administration," 2351.

[72]Alexander Hamilton, James Madison, and John Jay, *The Federalist Papers*, ed. Clinton L. Rossiter (New York: Signet, 1961) no. 70, pp. 423–30.

○ ONLINE READING

[73]Terry M. Moe, "The Presidency and the Bureaucracy: The Presidential Advantage," in *The Presidency and the Political System*, 7th ed., ed. Michael Nelson (Washington, D.C.: Congressional Quarterly Press, 2003), pp. 425–57.

Rationality Principle	Collective-Action Principle	Institution Principle	Policy Principle	History Principle
Under conditions of divided government, presidents may rationally want the protection of executive privilege from the partisan scrutiny of elements of Congress, and Congress may well suspect a president of hiding questionable activity behind a veil of executive privilege.	Vetoes are usually part of an intricate bargaining process involving the president and Congress.	By structuring the election of the president to be not by the people directly but by the electoral college, the framers sought to downplay presidential power.	Because of the president's veto power, Congress will alter the content of a bill to make it more to a president's liking.	The framers created a unitary executive; they wanted an energetic president but also one whose powers were limited.
	Presidential power should be analyzed in terms of the strategic interactions that a president has with other political actors.	The Constitution has established a presidency of expressed and delegated powers.	The outcome of congressional policy making depends greatly on the amount of leeway executive agencies have to interpret policies.	The presidency was strengthened somewhat in the 1830s with the introduction of a national convention system of nominating presidential candidates.
Bargaining between Congress and the president is strategic: The president tries to influence the legislators' beliefs about what they must do to keep the president from using the veto power.	The president can use public approval as a strategic resource.	There is tension in the separation of powers between the president and Congress over policy related to making war.		
	Whether government is divided or unified has a big influence on whether a president is a bargainer or a coordinator.	The president's constitutional role provides an opportunity for significant agenda setting by the executive for the Congress.		By the end of the New Deal, the practice of significant management of the economy by the executive, as broadly defined by Congress, was firmly established.
A president must weigh the advantages of vetoing legislation against the possible drop in his public approval.	The more unified the president's party is in Congress, the more unified the opposition is likely to be.	The veto power makes the president the most important single legislative leader.		
Congress delegates more power to the president as more demands are made on its agenda.		Congress delegates authority to the president but also maintains the means to influence how the executive branch exercises that power.		The New Deal's expanded role for the national government enhanced presidential power.

SUMMARY

The foundations for presidential government were laid in the Constitution by providing for a unitary executive. We reviewed these powers, focusing on expressed, delegated, and inherent variations. But we noted that the presidency was subordinated to congressional government during the nineteenth century and part of the twentieth, when the national government was relatively uninvolved in domestic functions and inactive or only sporadically involved in foreign affairs.

We traced the rise of modern presidential government after the much longer period of congressional dominance. There is no mystery in the shift to government centered on the presidency. Congress built the modern presidency not only by delegating to it the power to implement the vast new programs of the 1930s but also by delegating its own legislative power to make the policies themselves. The cabinet, the other top appointments, the White House staff, and the Executive Office of the President are some of the impressive formal resources of presidential power.

Finally, we focused on the president's formal and informal resources, in particular his political party and his access to the media and, through that, his access to the millions of Americans who make up the general public. But it was noted that these resources are not cost- or risk-free. The president's direct relationship with the public is his most potent modern resource but also the most problematic.

FOR FURTHER READING

Cameron, Charles M. *Veto Bargaining: Presidents and the Politics of Negative Power*. New York: Cambridge University Press, 2000.

ONLINE READING Canes-Wrone, Brandice. *Who Leads Whom? Presidents, Policy, and the Public*. Chicago: University of Chicago Press, 2006.

Deering, Christopher, and Forrest Maltzman. "The Politics of Executive Orders: Legislative Constraints on Presidential Power." *Political Research Quarterly* 52 (1999): 767–83.

Greenstein, Fred I. *The Presidential Difference: Leadership Style from FDR to Clinton*. Princeton, N.J.: Princeton University Press, 2001.

Kernell, Samuel. *Going Public: New Strategies of Presidential Leadership*. 3rd ed. Washington, D.C.: Congressional Quarterly Press, 1997.

Lowi, Theodore J. *The Personal President: Power Invested, Promise Unfulfilled*. Ithaca, N.Y.: Cornell University Press, 1985.

Milkis, Sidney M. *The President and the Parties: The Transformation of the American Party System since the New Deal*. New York: Oxford University Press, 1993.

———, and Michael Nelson. *The American Presidency: Origins and Development, 1776–2002*. 4th ed. Washington, D.C.: Congressional Quarterly Press.

Nelson, Michael, ed. *The Presidency and the Political System*. 8th ed. Washington, D.C.: Congressional Quarterly Press, 2005.

ONLINE READING Neustadt, Richard E. *Presidential Power and the Modern Presidents: The Politics of Leadership from Roosevelt to Reagan*. 1960. Rev. ed., New York: Free Press, 1990.

Pfiffner, James P. *The Modern Presidency*. 4th ed. Belmont, Calif.: Wadsworth, 2005.

Skowronek, Stephen. "Leadership by Definition: First Term Reflection on George W. Bush's Political Stance." *Perspectives on Politics* 3 (2005): 817–31.

———. *The Politics Presidents Make: Leadership from John Adams to Bill Clinton*. Cambridge, Mass.: Harvard University Press, 1997.

Tulis, Jeffrey. *The Rhetorical Presidency*. Princeton, N.J.: Princeton University Press, 1987.

What are the limits of executive power in a time of war? Some argue that the president, who is constitutionally delegated to act as the commander in chief, faces few constraints during times of war. Others believe that even in wartime, adherence to our constitutionally mandated separation of powers is vital. The principles of politics help us understand the debate over presidential power after September 11, as well as the larger institutional and historical context of executive authority.

The rationality principle suggests that all presidential administrations will attempt to extend their influence over public policy in competition with other branches of government.

The collective-action principle focuses us on the political makeup of all three branches of government. President Bush was in a strong position to extend his power during the first six years of his presidency, when he faced a Congress governed by his own party and, after the appointment of Justices John Roberts and Samuel Alito, a solidly conservative Supreme Court.

Finally, the history principle reminds us that the current state of presidential authority is in part a product of past events and experiences. Many in the Bush administration—such as Vice President Dick Cheney—believed that presidential authority had been significantly eroded since the Vietnam War and the resignation of Richard Nixon. A stronger presidency, according to this interpretation, is not just a response to September 11, but a return to the kind of robust and active executive seen in such presidents as Lincoln and FDR.

The New York Times, September 17, 2006

The Ruling on Tribunals: The Context; Court's Ruling Is Likely to Force Negotiations over Presidential Power

By David E. Sanger and Scott Shane

The Supreme Court's Guantánamo ruling on Thursday was the most significant setback yet for the Bush administration's contention that the Sept. 11 attacks and their aftermath have justified one of the broadest expansions of presidential power in American history.

President Bush and Vice President Dick Cheney spent much of their first term bypassing Congress in the service of what they labeled a "different kind of war." Now they will almost certainly plunge into negotiations they previously spurned, over the extent of the president's powers, this time in the midst of a midterm election in which Mr. Bush's wartime strategies and their consequences have emerged as a potent issue.

The ruling bolsters those in Congress who for months have been trying to force the White House into a retreat from its claims that Mr. Bush not only has the unilateral authority as commander in chief to determine how suspected terrorists are tried, but also to set the rules for domestic wiretapping, for interrogating prisoners and for pursuing a global fight against terror that many suspect could stretch for as long as the cold war did.

What the court's 5-to-3 decision declared, in essence, was that Mr. Bush and Mr. Cheney had overreached and must now either use the established rules of courts-martial or go back to Congress—this time with vastly diminished leverage—to win approval for the military commissions that Mr. Bush argues are the best way to keep the nation safe.

For Mr. Bush, this is not the first such setback. The court ruled two years ago that the giant prison at Guantánamo Bay, Cuba, was not beyond the reach of American courts and that prisoners there had some minimal rights.

Then, last year, came the overwhelming 90-to-9 vote in the Senate, over Mr. Cheney's strong objections, to ban "cruel, inhumane and degrading" treatment of prisoners. That forced Mr. Bush, grudgingly, to reach an accord with Senator John McCain, Republican of Arizona, on principles for interrogation, which are still being turned into rules.

As seen by Mr. Bush's critics, the court has finally reined in an executive who used the Sept. 11 attacks as a justification—or an excuse—to tilt the balance of power decidedly toward the White House.

"This is a great triumph for the rule of law and the separation of powers," said Bruce Ackerman, a professor of law and political science at Yale. "The

administration will have to go back to Congress and talk in a much more discriminating fashion about what we need to do."

Some allies of Mr. Bush reacted bitterly on Thursday, asserting that it was the court, rather than Mr. Bush, that had overreacted.

"Nothing about the administration's solution was radical or even particularly aggressive," said Bradford A. Berenson, who served from 2001 to 2003 as associate White House counsel. "What is truly radical is the Supreme Court's willingness to bend to world opinion and undermine some of the most important foundations of American national security law in the middle of a war."

At least rhetorically, the administration is giving no ground about the reach of the president's powers. Just 10 days ago, speaking here in Washington, Mr. Cheney cited the responses to Watergate and the Vietnam War as examples of where he thought Congress had "begun to encroach upon the power and responsibilities of the president," and said he had come to the White House with the view that "it was important to go back and try to restore that balance."

Since taking office, Mr. Bush and Mr. Cheney have largely tried to do so by fiat, sometimes with public declarations, sometimes with highly classified directives governing how suspects could be plucked from the battlefield or, in the case decided on Thursday, how they would be tried. The president's tone on Thursday, during a news conference with Prime Minister Junichiro Koizumi of Japan, suggested that he recognized he might now have to give ground.

Mr. Bush said he would be taking "the findings" of the Supreme Court "very seriously."

"One thing I'm not going to do, though, is I'm not going to jeopardize the safety of the American people," he said. But then he backtracked a bit, saying he would "work with Congress" to give legal foundation to the system he had already put in place.

To some degree, the court may have helped Mr. Bush out of a political predicament. He has repeatedly said he would like to close the detention center at Guantánamo, a recognition that the indefinite imprisonment of suspects without trial and the accusations that they have been mistreated were seriously undercutting American credibility abroad. But he set no schedule and said he was waiting for the court to rule.

"The court really rescued the administration by taking it out of this quagmire it's been in," said Michael Greenberger, who teaches the law of counterterrorism at the University of Maryland law school.

Now Congress, with the court's encouragement, may help the president find a way forward. For Senator Lindsey Graham, Republican of South Carolina, who said a legislative proposal on military commissions he sent to the White House 18 months ago "went nowhere," the ruling was a welcome restoration of the balance of power.

"The Supreme Court has set the rules of the road," Mr. Graham, a former military lawyer, said, "and the Congress and the president can drive to the destination together."

Supporters of the president emphasized that the question of how to balance suspects' rights against the need for intelligence on imminent attacks was always a daunting challenge, and that the ruling did not change that.

In fact, said Jack Goldsmith, who headed the Justice Department's Office of Legal Counsel in 2003 and 2004, the fact that no second attack has occurred on American soil is an achievement of the administration that is now complicating its political situation.

"The longer the president and the administration successfully prevent another attack," Mr. Goldsmith said, "the more people think the threat has abated and the more they demand that the administration adhere to traditional civil liberties protections."

In today's less panicky national mood, tough measures that few dared question as American forces first moved into Afghanistan, and then Iraq, are now the subject to nightly debate on cable television and of a small flotilla of court challenges.

But history suggests that this pendulum swing was inevitable. It took years, but history came to condemn the internment of Japanese-Americans during World War II, and to question Lincoln's suspension of habeas corpus during the Civil War.

Sooner or later, that same reversal was bound to happen to Mr. Bush and Mr. Cheney.

The question is how far it will swing back while they are still in office and while what Mr. Bush calls "the long war" continues around the globe.

Policy Principle

The Court, by establishing the appropriate rules and procedures, will help Congress and the president cooperate and reach a policy solution.

History Principle

The Bush administration was able to be very aggressive in asserting executive power immediately after September 11 precisely because there was no historical precedent for such an attack on American soil. Now, American politics may be returning to its historically normal path, with relatively equal institutions competing over policy.

The Executive Branch: Bureaucracy in a Democracy

ON MARCH 1, 2003, twenty-two federal agencies with responsibilities for combating international terrorism in the United States were combined in the Department of Homeland Security. By all accounts, this event marked the most dramatic reform of the federal bureaucracy since the establishment of the Department of Defense in 1947. However, that earlier transformation took forty years to be fully realized, a time frame that is unacceptable in the midst of a "hot" war on terrorism.

Soon after the catastrophic events of September 11, 2001, both Republicans and Democrats realized that the public was going to demand some ongoing response to the terrorist threat (beyond the immediate military response in Afghanistan).[1] But why did we end up with this particular solution—a new cabinet-level agency? A congressional investigation quickly revealed that serious security lapses and a lack of coordination among the various agencies with responsibility for domestic and foreign intelligence had occurred under the watch of both President Bill Clinton and President George W. Bush. Both political parties might be blamed if the government did not respond aggressively enough to the terrorist threat. Furthermore, the major alternative solution—the creation of a homeland-security "czar"—proved inadequate. Tom Ridge, ex-governor of Pennsylvania, did not have the power to hire and fire his subordinates. He did not have budgetary authority. He had little beyond his title. In this case, the lack of rules and procedures meant that Ridge had no power to shape bureaucratic outcomes. In the end, there seemed to be no alternative available to the president and members of Congress. The path to a cabinet-level agency was clear.

Institution Principle

Institutions are created by Congress to achieve policy goals.

---

[1] John W. Kingdon calls events that limit and focus our political options "windows of political opportunity." See his *Agendas, Alternatives, and Public Policies* (Boston: Little, Brown, 1984).

Eventually the Department of Homeland Security (DHS) was authorized by Congress. Did that mean the coordination problems faced by Ridge withered away? In fact, coordination becomes more difficult as the number of people and the diversity of goals or preferences grow. In the case of the DHS, the agencies brought under one umbrella are tremendously diverse (Table 7.1). Each of these agencies has gone down a particular path. Some of them (for example, the Customs Service and the Coast Guard) had developed a bureaucratic culture and an esprit de corps over more than two centuries, while others (such as the Transportation Security Administration) had grown aggressively in response to new threats. It is very difficult to set these agencies on a new course.

The birth pains of new government agencies are often traumatic, and agencies suffer midlife crises as well and even the decrepitude of old age.[2] Yet Americans depend on government bureaucracies to accomplish the most spectacular

---

[2]The Interstate Commerce Commission, the oldest regulatory agency (created in 1887), was put out of its misery in 1995.

Bureaucracy is necessary for implementing public policy. By implementing the laws and policies passed by elected officials, bureaucrats can be seen as agents of Congress and the presidency. As is the case in any principal-agent relationship, the agent (the bureaucracy) is delegated authority and has a certain amount of leeway for independent action. Despite the efforts of elected officials (the principals) to check departments and agencies (the agents), bureaucrats have their own goals and thus exercise their own influence on policy. The problem of controlling bureaucracy is a central concern for democracies. Although controlling the growth of bureaucracy is a major concern, the size of the federal bureaucracy has in fact kept pace with the economy and the needs of society. And because most Americans benefit in some way from programs implemented by government agencies, they are reluctant to cut back on the size and scope of these programs.

achievements as well as the most mundane. Even though bureaucracies provide essential services that all Americans rely on, they are often disparaged by politicians and the general public alike. Criticized as "big government," many federal bureaucracies come into public view only when they are charged with fraud, waste, and abuse.

Institution Principle

Bureaucracies are needed to achieve collective goals.

In emergencies, the national perspective on bureaucracy and, indeed, on big government shifts. After the September 11 terrorist attacks, all eyes turned to Washington. The federal government responded by strengthening and reorganizing the bureaucracy in order to undertake a new set of responsibilities designed to keep America safe. The war on terrorism has highlighted the extensive range of the tasks shouldered by the federal bureaucracy. Both routine and exceptional tasks require the organization, specialization, and expertise found in bureaucracies. Table 7.1 identifies the range of functions and activities brought under the jurisdiction of Homeland Security. Likewise, after a natural disaster like Hurricane Katrina in 2005, Americans look to government agencies to respond to the crisis.

In this chapter, we focus on the federal bureaucracy—the administrative structure that on a day-by-day basis is the American government. First, we define and describe bureaucracy as a social and political phenomenon. Second, we look in detail at American bureaucracy in action by examining the government's major administrative agencies, their role in the governmental process, and their political behavior. These details of administration are the very heart and soul of modern government.

WHY BUREAUCRACY?

Bureaucracies are commonplace because they touch so many aspects of daily life. Government bureaucracies implement the decisions made by the political process.

TABLE 7.1 The Shape of a Domestic Security Department, 2007

Department of Homeland Security	Agencies and Departments Now Part of the Main Divisions of the DHS	Previously Responsible Agency or Department
Border and Transportation Security Directorate	U.S. Customs Service	Treasury
	Immigration and Naturalization Service*	Justice
	Federal Protective Service†	
	Transportation Security Administration	Transportation
	Federal Law Enforcement Training Center	Treasury
	Animal and Plant Health Inspection Service*	Agriculture
	Office for Domestic Preparedness	Justice
Emergency Preparedness and Response Directorate	Federal Emergency Management Agency‡	
	Strategic National Stockpile and the National Disaster Medical System	Health and Human Services
	Nuclear Incident Response Team	Energy
	Domestic Emergency Support Teams	Justice
	National Domestic Preparedness Office	FBI
Science and Technology Directorate	CBRN (Chemical, Biological, Radiological and Nuclear) Countermeasures Programs	Energy
	Environmental Measurements Laboratory	Energy
	National BW (Biological Warfare) Defense Analysis Center	Defense
	Plum Island Animal Disease Center	Agriculture
Information Analysis and Infrastructure Protection Directorate§	Federal Computer Incident Response Center	General Services Administration
	National Communications System	Defense
	National Infrastructure Protection Center	FBI
	Energy Security and Assurance Program	Energy
Secret Service		Treasury
Coast Guard		Transportation

SOURCE: Department of Homeland Security, "History: Who Became Part of the Department?" (www.dhs.gov/xabout/history/editorial_0133.sht).

*Only partially under the aegis of DHS; some functions remain elsewhere.

†New.

‡Previously independent.

§Will analyze information provided by the CIA, the FBI, the Defense Intelligence Agency, the National Security Agency, and other agencies.

Bureaucracies are full of routine because routine ensures that services are delivered regularly and that each agency fulfills its mandate. For this reason, students often conclude that a consideration of bureaucracy is mechanical, routinized, and just plain boring. But that is a big mistake. Bureaucracy is not just about collecting garbage, training police, or mailing Social Security checks. Mainly, it is a reflection of political deals consummated by elected politicians, turf wars among government agents and private-sector suppliers and contractors, policy-delivery successes and failures in the eyes of the public, and to complete the circle, reactions to these by the very same elected officials who cut the deals in the first place. It is politics through and through.

Public bureaucracies are powerful because legislatures and chief executives—and, indeed, the people—delegate to them vast power to make sure a particular job is done, enabling the rest of us to be freer to pursue our private ends. The public sentiments that emerged after September 11 revealed this underlying appreciation of public bureaucracies. When faced with the challenge of making air travel safe again, the public strongly supported giving the federal government responsibility for airport security even though this meant increasing the size of the federal bureaucracy in order to make the security screeners federal workers. Former House majority whip Tom DeLay sought to forestall this growth in the federal government, declaring that "the last thing we can afford to do is erect a new bureaucracy that is unaccountable and unable to protect the American public."[3] But the antibureaucratic language that had been so effective before September 11 no longer resonated with a fearful public. Instead, there was a widespread belief that a public bureaucracy would provide more effective protection than the cost-conscious private companies that had been charged with airport security in the past. Bureaucrats across the federal government felt the new appreciation for their work. As one civil servant at the Pentagon put it, "The whole mood has changed. A couple of months ago we were part of the bloated bureaucracy. Now we're Washington's equivalent of the cops and firemen in New York."[4]

We can shed some systematic light on public attitudes toward government bureaucracy by examining one of the standard questions posed in election years by the American National Election Studies (ANES). As part of its survey of the American public, the ANES asks a range of questions, among which is "Do you think that people in the government waste a lot of money we pay in taxes, waste some of it, or don't waste very much of it?" While not perfect for eliciting from the public a nuanced assessment of bureaucratic performance, the question allows respondents to register a blunt evaluation. Results from the past several decades are given in Figure 7.1.

Public unhappiness with bureaucratic inefficiency grew during the 1960s and 1970s and became one of Ronald Reagan's campaign themes in the 1980 election.

---

[3]Janet Hook, "U.S. Strikes Back: Political Landscape; GOP Bypasses the Bipartisan Truce," *Los Angeles Times*, 14 October 2001, p. A8.

[4]R. W. Apple Jr., "White House Letter: Big Government Is Back in Style," *New York Times*, 23 November 2001, p. B2.

FIGURE 7.1 The Public Thinks There Is a Lot of Waste in Government

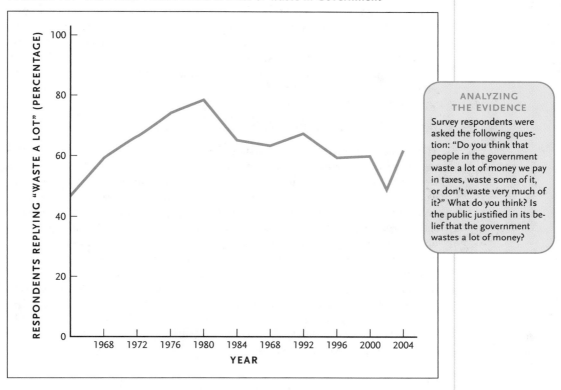

SOURCE: American National Election Studies, Cumulative Data File, 1948–2004, (www.electionstudies.org/index.htm).

During the administrations of Reagan, George H. W. Bush, and Bill Clinton, this unhappiness declined from nearly 80 percent of the survey respondents believing government "wastes a lot" in 1980 to just over 60 percent in 2004. This opinion has held steady in the low 60 percent range for twenty years, though there was a significant downward blip in 2002, just after September 11. But whatever honeymoon there might have been after the terrorist attacks, it appears that the public remains cynical about bureaucratic performance. The poor response of the Federal Emergency Management Agency (FEMA)—part of DHS—to the hurricane crises in the fall of 2005 and, especially, to charges of cronyism in personnel appointments surely contributed to further cynicism.

Despite this tendency to criticize bureaucracy, most Americans recognize that maintaining order in a large society is impossible without some sort of large governmental apparatus, staffed by professionals with some expertise in public administration. When we approve of what a government agency is doing, we give the phenomenon a positive name, administration; when we disapprove, we call the phenomenon bureaucracy.

Although the terms *administration* and *bureaucracy* are often used interchangeably, it is useful to distinguish between the two. *Administration* is the more general of the two terms; it refers to all the ways in which human beings might rationally coordinate their efforts to achieve a common goal. This applies to private as well as public organizations. ***Bureaucracy*** refers to the actual offices, tasks, and principles of organization that are employed in the most formal and sustained administration.

Bureaucratic Organization Enhances Efficiency

The core of bureaucracy is the division of labor. The key to bureaucratic effectiveness is the coordination of experts performing complex tasks. If each job is specialized to gain efficiencies, then each worker must depend on the output of other workers, and that dependence requires careful allocation of jobs and resources. Inevitably bureaucracies become hierarchical, often approximating a pyramid in form. At the base of the organization are workers with the fewest skills and specializations; one supervisor can deal with a relatively large number of these workers. At the next level of the organization, where there are more highly specialized workers, the supervision and coordination of work involves fewer workers per supervisor. Toward the top of the organization, a very small number of high-level executives engages in the "management" of the organization, meaning the organization and reorganization of all the tasks and functions, plus the allocation of the appropriate supplies and the distribution of the output of the organization to the market (if it is a private-sector organization) or to the public.

Bureaucracies Allow Governments to Operate

Bureaucracy, when used pejoratively, conjures up images of endless paperwork, red tape, and lazy, uncaring employees. But bureaucracy in fact represents a rather spectacular human achievement. By dividing up tasks, matching tasks to a labor force that develops appropriately specialized skills, routinizing procedure, and providing the incentive structure and oversight arrangements to get large numbers of people to operate in a coordinated, purposeful fashion, bureaucracies accomplish tasks and missions in a manner that would otherwise be unimaginable. The provision of an array of "government goods" as broad as the defense of people, property, and national borders or as narrow as a subsidy to a wheat farmer, a beef rancher, or a manufacturer of specialty steel requires organization, routines, standards, and at the end of the day, the authority that allows for someone to cut a check and put it in the mail. Bureaucracies are created to do these things. No large organization would be larger than the sum of its parts, and many would be smaller, without bureaucratizing its activities.

Bureaucracy also consolidates a range of complementary programs and insulates them from the predatory ambitions of out-of-sympathy political forces. Nothing in this world is permanent, but bureaucracies come close. By creating clienteles—in the legislature, the world of interest groups, and public opinion—a bureaucracy establishes a coalition of supporters, some of whom will fight to the end to keep it in place. It is a well-known rule of thumb that everyone in the political

Rationality Principle

Bureaucracies are the instruments through which policy objectives are secured.

bureaucracy The complex structure of offices, tasks, rules, and principles of organization that are employed by all large-scale institutions to coordinate the work of their personnel.

world cares deeply and intensely about a subset of policies and the agencies that produce them and opposes other policies and agencies, but not with nearly the same passion. Opponents, to succeed, must clear many hurdles, while proponents, to maintain the status quo, must marshal their forces only at a few veto points. In the final analysis, opponents typically meet obstacle after obstacle and eventually give up their uphill battles and concentrate on protecting and expanding what they care most deeply about. In a complex political system like that of the United States, it is much easier to do the latter. Politicians appreciate this fact of life. Consequently, both opponents and proponents of a particular set of governmental activities wage the fiercest battles at the time programs are enacted and a bureaucracy is created. Once created, these organizations assume a position of relative permanence.

So in response to the question of how bureaucracy makes government possible, there is an efficiency part to the answer and a credibility part. The creation of a bureau is a way to deliver government goods efficiently, and it is a device by which to tie one's hands, thereby providing a credible commitment to the long-term existence of a policy.

Bureaucrats Fulfill Important Roles

"Government by offices and desks" conveys to most people a picture of hundreds of office workers shuffling millions of pieces of paper. There is a lot of truth in that image, but we have to look more closely at what papers are being shuffled and why. More than fifty years ago, an astute observer defined bureaucracy as "continuous routine business."[5] Almost any organization succeeds by reducing its work to routines, with each routine being given to a different specialist. But specialization separates people from one another; one worker's output becomes another worker's input. The timing of the relationships is essential, requiring the workers to stay in communication with each other. In fact, bureaucracy was the first information network. Voluminous routine came as bureaucracies grew and specialized. It's no small irony that as bureaucracies have grown, the term *bureaucrat* has come to connote sluggishness and inefficiency.

Bureaucrats Implement Laws   Bureaucrats, whether in public or in private organizations, communicate with one another to coordinate all the specializations within their organization. This coordination is necessary to carry out the primary task of bureaucracy, which is ***implementation***—that is, implementing the objectives of the organization as laid down by its board of directors (if a private company) or by law (if a public agency). In government, the "bosses" are ultimately the legislature and the elected chief executive. As we saw in Chapter 1, in a principal-agent relationship it is the principal who stipulates what he wants done, relying on the agent's concern for her reputation, appropriate incentives, and other control mechanisms to secure compliance with his wishes. Thus it may be argued that legislative principals establish bureaucratic agents—in departments, bureaus,

 Collective-Action Principle
Coordination among bureaucrats is necessary to carry out the primary task of bureaucracy: implementation.

implementation
The efforts of departments and agencies to translate laws into specific bureaucratic routines.

---

[5]Arnold Brecht and Comstock Glaser, *The Art and Technique of Administration in German Ministries* (Cambridge, Mass.: Harvard University Press, 1940), p. 6.

Institution Principle

Legislative principals establish bureaucratic agents to implement policies.

Institution Principle

Congress also delegates authority to bureaucrats to make law through the procedures of rule making and administrative adjudication.

rule making A quasi-legislative administrative process that produces regulations by government agencies.

administrative adjudication The application rules and precedents to specific cases to settle disputes with regulated parties.

agencies, institutes, and commissions of the federal government—to implement the policies promulgated by Congress and the president.

Bureaucrats Make and Enforce Rules When the bosses—Congress, in particular, when it is making the law—are clear in their instructions to bureaucrats, implementation is a fairly straightforward process. Bureaucrats translate the law into specific routines for each employee of an agency. But what happens to routine administrative implementation when there are several bosses who disagree as to what the instructions ought to be? The agent of multiple principals who disagree among themselves often finds himself or herself in a bind. The agent must chart a delicate course, seeking to do the best he or she can and trying not to offend any of the bosses too much. This requires yet another job for the bureaucrats: interpretation. Interpretation is a form of implementation in that the bureaucrats have to carry out what they believe to be the intentions of their superiors. But when bureaucrats have to interpret a law before implementing it, they are in effect engaging in lawmaking.[6] Congress often deliberately delegates to an administrative agency the responsibility of lawmaking. Members of Congress often conclude that some area of industry needs regulating or some area of the environment needs protection, but they are unwilling or unable to specify just how that should be done. In such situations, Congress delegates to the appropriate agency a broad authority within which the bureaucrats have to make law, through the procedures of ***rule making*** and ***administrative adjudication***.

Rule making is exactly the same as legislation; in fact, it is often referred to as quasi-legislation. The rules issued by government agencies provide more detailed and specific indications of what a policy will actually mean. For example, the Forest Service is charged with making policies that govern the use of national forests. Just before President Clinton left office, the agency issued rules that banned new road building and development in the forests. This was a goal long sought by environmentalists and conservationists. In 2005, the Forest Service relaxed the rules, allowing states to make proposals for building new roads within the national forests. Just as the timber industry opposed the Clinton rule banning road building, environmentalists have challenged the new ruling and have sued the Forest Service in federal court for violating clean-water and endangered-species legislation.

New rules proposed by an agency take effect only after a period of public comment. Reaction from the people or businesses that are subject to the rules may cause an agency to modify the rules they first issue. The rule-making process is thus a highly political one. Once rules are approved, they are published in the *Federal Register* and have the force of law.

Bureaucrats Settle Disputes Administrative adjudication is very similar to what the judiciary ordinarily does: apply rules and precedents to specific cases to settle

---

[6]When bureaucrats engage in interpretation, the result is what political scientists call bureaucratic drift. Bureaucratic drift occurs because, as we've suggested, the "bosses" (in Congress) and the agents (within the bureaucracy) don't always share the same purposes. Bureaucrats also have their own agendas to fulfill. There exists a vast body of political science literature on the relationship between Congress and the bureaucracy. For a review, see Kenneth A. Shepsle and Mark S. Bonchek, *Analyzing Politics: Rationality, Behavior, and Institutions* (New York: Norton, 1997), pp. 355–68.

disputes. In administrative adjudication, the agency charges the person or business suspected of violating the law. The ruling in an adjudication dispute applies only to the specific case being considered. Many regulatory agencies use administrative adjudication to make decisions about specific products or practices. For example, product recalls are often the result of adjudication. To take another example, the National Labor Relations Board (NLRB) has used case-by-case administrative adjudication in a great many instances. One large class of cases involves union certification. Groups of workers seek the right to vote on the creation of a union or the right to affiliate with an existing union as their bargaining agent and are opposed by their employers, who assert that relevant provisions of labor law do not apply. The NLRB, takes testimony case by case, considers evidence, and makes determinations for one side or the other, acting essentially like a court.

In sum, bureaucrats in government do essentially the same things that bureaucrats in large private organizations do, and neither type deserves the disrespect embodied in the term *bureaucrat*. But because of the authoritative, coercive nature of government, far more constraints are imposed on public bureaucrats than on private bureaucrats, even when their jobs are the same. Public bureaucrats are required to maintain a far more thorough paper trail. They are also subject to a great deal more access by the public—newspaper reporters, for example, have access to public bureaucrats. And public access has been vastly facilitated in the past thirty years; the adoption of the Freedom of Information Act (FOIA) in 1966 gave ordinary citizens the right of access to agency files and agency data so that they might determine whether those files (and data) contain derogatory information about them and learn what the agency is doing in general.

Finally, citizens are given opportunities to participate in the decision-making processes of public agencies. This kind of access is limited by time, money, and expertise, but it does exist, and it occupies a great deal of the time of mid-level and senior public bureaucrats. Such public exposure and access serve a purpose, but they also cut down significantly on the efficiency of public bureaucrats. Thus much of the lower levels of efficiency in public agencies can be attributed to the political, judicial, legal, and publicity restraints put on public bureaucrats.

Politics

We have provided two main answers to the question "Why bureaucracy?": (1) Bureaucracies enhance efficiency, and (2) they are the instruments of policy implementation. We would be remiss if we didn't include a third important answer: Legislatures find it valuable to delegate.

In principle, the legislature could make all bureaucratic decisions itself, writing very detailed legislation each year, dotting every *i* and crossing every *t*. In some jurisdictions—tax policy, for example—this is in fact done. Tax policy is promulgated in significant detail by the House Ways and Means Committee, the Senate Finance Committee, and the Joint Committee on Taxation. The Internal Revenue Service, the administrative agency charged with implementation, engages in relatively less discretionary activity than many other regulatory and administrative agencies. But this is the exception.

The norm is for statutory authority to be delegated to the bureaucracy, sometimes with specificity but often in relatively vague terms. The bureaucracy is expected to fill in the gaps. This, however, is not a blank check to exercise unconstrained discretion. The bureaucracy is expected to be guided by legislative intent, and it will be held to account by the legislature's oversight of bureaucratic performance. The latter is monitored by the staffs of relevant legislative committees, which also serve as repositories for complaints from affected parties.[7] Poor performance or the exercise of discretion inconsistent with the preferences of the important legislators invites sanctions ranging from the browbeating of senior bureaucrats to the trimming of budgets and the clipping of authority.

The delegation relationship will be revisited later in this chapter. For now, simply note that over and above the more conventional reasons for bureaucracy, politicians find it convenient to delegate many of the nuts-and-bolts decisions to bureaucratic agents. We will take up the reasons shortly.

HOW IS THE EXECUTIVE BRANCH ORGANIZED?

Cabinet departments, agencies, and bureaus are the operating parts of the bureaucratic whole. These parts can be separated into four general types: (1) cabinet departments, (2) independent agencies, (3) government corporations, and (4) independent regulatory commissions.

Although Figure 7.2 is an organizational chart of the Department of Agriculture, any other department could have been used as an illustration. At the top is the head of the department, called the secretary of the department. Below the department head and his or her deputy are several top administrators, such as the general counsel and the chief financial officer, whose responsibilities cut across the various departmental functions and provide the secretary with the ability to manage the entire organization. Of equal status are the undersecretaries and assistant secretaries, each of whom has management responsibilities for a group of operating agencies, which are arranged vertically below each of the undersecretaries.

The next tier, generally called the bureau level, is the highest level of responsibility for specialized programs. The names of these "bureau-level agencies" are often very well known to the public: the Forest Service and the Food Safety and Inspection Service are two examples. Sometimes they are officially called bureaus, as in the FBI, which is a bureau in the Department of Justice. Nevertheless, *bureau* is also the generic term for this level of administrative agency. Within the bureaus, there are divisions, offices, services, and units—sometimes designating agencies of the same status, sometimes designating agencies of lesser status.

Not all government agencies are part of cabinet departments. A second type of agency, the independent agency, is set up by Congress outside the departmental structure altogether, even though the president appoints and directs the heads of

[7] See Mathew D. McCubbins and Thomas Schwartz, "Congressional Oversight Overlooked: Police Patrols versus Fire Alarms," *American Journal of Political Science* 28 (1984): 165–79.

FIGURE 7.2 Organizational Chart of the Department of Agriculture

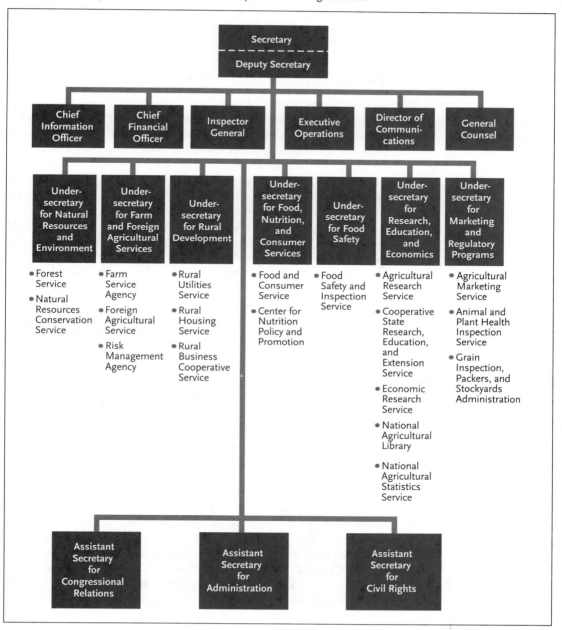

SOURCE: U.S. Department of Agriculture (www.usda.gov/img/content/org_chart_enlarged.jpg).

this type of agency. Independent agencies usually have broad powers to provide public services that are either too expensive or too important to be left to private initiatives. Some examples of independent agencies are the National Aeronautics and Space Administration (NASA), the Central Intelligence Agency (CIA), and the Environmental Protection Agency (EPA). Government corporations are a third type of government agency but are more like private businesses performing and charging for a market service, such as delivering the mail (the United States Postal Service) or transporting railroad passengers (Amtrak).

Yet a fourth type of agency is the independent regulatory commission, given broad discretion to make rules. The first regulatory agencies established by Congress, beginning with the Interstate Commerce Commission in 1887, were set up as independent regulatory commissions because Congress recognized that regulatory agencies are mini-legislatures, whose rules are the same as legislation but require the kind of expertise and full-time attention that is beyond the capacity of Congress. Until the 1960s, most of the regulatory agencies that were set up by Congress, such as the Federal Trade Commission (1914) and the Federal Communications Commission (1934), were independent regulatory commissions. But beginning in the late 1960s and early 1970s, all new regulatory programs, with two or three exceptions (such as the Federal Election Commission), were placed within existing departments and made directly responsible to the president. Since the 1970s, no new major regulatory programs have been established, independent or otherwise.

There are too many agencies in the executive branch to identify, much less to describe, so a simple classification of agencies will be helpful. Instead of dividing the bureaucracy into four general types, as we did above, an alternative classification organizes each agency by its mission, as defined by its jurisdiction: clientele agencies, agencies for maintenance of the Union, regulatory agencies, and redistributive agencies. We shall examine each of these types of agencies, focusing on both their formal structure and their place in the political process.

Clientele Agencies Serve Particular Interests

The entire Department of Agriculture is an example of a *clientele agency.* So are the Departments of the Interior, Labor, and Commerce. Although all administrative agencies have clienteles, certain agencies are singled out and called clientele agencies because they are directed by law to foster and promote the interests of their clientele. For example, the Department of Commerce and Labor was founded in 1903 as a single department "to foster, promote, and develop the foreign and domestic commerce, the mining, the manufacturing, the shipping, and fishing industries, and the transportation facilities of the United States."[8] It remained a single department until 1913, when the law created the separate departments of Commerce and Labor, with each statute providing for the same obligation: to support and foster their respective clientele.[9] The

---

clientele agencies
Departments or bureaus of government whose mission is to promote, serve, or represent a particular interest.

---

[8] *U.S. Statutes at Large* 32 (1903): 825; 15 U.S. Code 1501.

[9] For a detailed account of the creation of the Department of Commerce and Labor and its split into separate departments, see Theodore J. Lowi, *The End of Liberalism: The Second Republic of the United States,* 2nd ed. (New York: Norton, 1979), pp. 78–84.

Department of Agriculture serves the many farming interests that, taken together, are the largest economic sector of the United States (agriculture accounts for one fifth of the total U.S. domestic output).

Most clientele agencies locate a relatively large proportion of their total personnel in field offices dealing directly with their clientele. The Extension Service of the Department of Agriculture is among the most familiar, with its numerous local "extension agents" who consult with farmers on farm productivity. These same agencies also seek to foster the interests of their clientele by providing "functional representation"—that is, they try to learn what their clients' interests and needs are and then operate almost as a lobby in Washington on their behalf. In addition to the Departments of Agriculture, the Interior, Labor, and Commerce, other clientele agencies include five of the newest cabinet departments: Housing and Urban Development (HUD), created in 1965; Transportation (DOT), created in 1966; Energy (DOE), created in 1977; Education (ED), created in 1979; and Health and Human Services (HHS), created in 1979.[10]

Policy Principle

The policies of clientele agencies promote the interests of their clientele.

Agencies for the Maintenance of the Union Keep the Government Going

Agencies for the maintenance of the Union could be called public-order agencies were it not for the fact that the Constitution entrusts to the state governments so many of the vital functions of public order, such as the police. But some agencies vital to maintaining national bonds do exist in the national government, and they can be grouped for convenience into three categories: (1) agencies for managing the sources of government revenue, (2) agencies for controlling conduct defined as a threat to internal national security, and (3) agencies for defending American security from external threats. The departments of greatest power in these three areas are Treasury, Justice, Defense, State, and Homeland Security.

Revenue Agencies   The Internal Revenue Service (IRS) is the most important revenue agency. The IRS is also one of the federal government's largest bureaucracies. Over 100,000 employees are spread throughout four regions, sixty-three districts, ten service centers, and hundreds of local offices. In 2007, more than 139 million returns were filed. The IRS collected more than $2.7 trillion in taxes from individuals and corporations.

Agencies for Internal Security   As long as the country is not in a state of insurrection, most of the task of maintaining the Union takes the form of legal work, and the main responsibility for that lies with the Department of Justice. It is indeed a luxury, and rare in the world, when national unity can be maintained by routines of civil law rather than imposed by military force. The largest and most important agency in the Justice Department is the Criminal Division, which is responsible for enforcing all the federal criminal laws except a few specifically assigned to other divisions. Criminal

---

[10]Until 1979, the Department of Education and the Department of Health and Human Services were joined in a single department, Health, Education, and Welfare (HEW), which was established by Congress in 1953.

litigation is actually done by the U.S. attorneys. There is a presidentially appointed U.S. attorney assigned to each federal judicial district, and he or she supervises the work of assistant U.S. attorneys. The work or jurisdiction of the Antitrust and Civil Rights Divisions is described by their official names. Although it looms so very large in American folklore, the FBI is simply another bureau of the Department of Justice. The FBI handles no litigation but instead serves as the information-gathering agency for all the other divisions.

In 2002, Congress created the Department of Homeland Security to coordinate the nation's defense against the threat of terrorism. The new department is responsible for a number of tasks, including protecting commercial airlines from would-be hijackers.

Agencies for External National Security Two departments occupy center stage here, State and Defense. There are a few key agencies outside State and Defense that also have external national-security functions. They are treated in this chapter only as bureaucratic phenomena and as examples of the political problems relevant to administration.

Although diplomacy is generally considered the primary task of the State Department, diplomatic missions make up only one of its organizational dimensions. The State Department is also composed of geographic, or regional, bureaus concerned with all problems within the defined regions of the world; "functional" bureaus, which handle such things as economic and business affairs, intelligence, and research; and international organizations and bureaus of internal affairs, which handle such areas as security, finance and management, and legal issues.

Despite the importance of the State Department in foreign affairs, fewer than 20 percent of all U.S. government employees working abroad are directly under its authority. By far the largest number of career government professionals working abroad are under the authority of the Defense Department.

The creation of the Department of Defense by legislation enacted between 1947 and 1949 was an effort to unify the two historic military departments, the War Department and the Navy Department, and integrate into them a new department, the Air Force Department. Real unification did not occur, however. Instead, the Defense Department added more pluralism to national security.

America's primary political problem with its military has not been the historic one of how to keep the military out of the politics of governing, a problem that has plagued so many countries in Europe and Latin America. The American military problem is instead one of the lower politics of the pork barrel. President Clinton's long list of proposed military-base closings, a major part of his budget-cutting drive for 1993, caused a firestorm of opposition even in his own party, with some of the opposition coming from members of Congress who otherwise prominently favored significant reductions in the Pentagon budget. Emphasis on jobs rather than strategy and policy means pork-barrel use of the military for political purposes. This is a classic way for a bureaucracy to defend itself politically in a democracy. It is the distributive tendency, in which the bureaucracy ensures political support among elected officials by making sure to distribute things—military bases, contracts, facilities, and jobs—to the states and districts that elected the legislators. As is commonly known, it is hard to bite the hand that feeds you! Thus the best way to

Policy Principle

The military pork barrel is an example of the distributive tendency in Congress.

understand the military in American politics is to study it within the bureaucratic framework that is used to explain the domestic agencies.

Regulatory Agencies Guide Individual Conduct

As we saw in Chapter 3, our national government did not even begin to get involved in the regulation of economic and social affairs until the late nineteenth century. Until then, regulation was strictly a state and local affair. The federal *regulatory agencies* are, as a result, relatively new, most dating from the 1930s. But they have come to be extensive and important. In this section, we look at these regulatory agencies as an administrative phenomenon, with its attendant politics.

The United States has no "department of regulation," but it has many regulatory agencies. Some of these are bureaus within departments, such as the Food and Drug Administration (FDA) in the Department of Health and Human Services, and the Occupational Safety and Health Administration (OSHA) in the Department of Labor. Other regulatory agencies are independent regulatory commissions—for example, the Federal Trade Commission (FTC). But whether departmental or independent, an agency or commission is regulatory if Congress delegates to it relatively broad powers over a sector of the economy or a type of commercial activity and authorizes it to make rules governing the conduct of people and businesses within that jurisdiction. Rules made by regulatory agencies have the force and effect of legislation; indeed, the rules they make are referred to as *administrative legislation.* And when these agencies make decisions or orders settling disputes between parties or between the government and a party, they are acting like courts.

Because regulatory agencies exercise a tremendous amount of influence over the economy and because their rules are a form of legislation, Congress was at first loath to turn them over to the executive branch as ordinary agencies under the control of the president. Consequently, most of the important regulatory programs were delegated to independent commissions with direct responsibility to Congress rather than to the White House. This is the basis of the 1930s reference to them as the "headless fourth branch."[11] With the rise of presidential government, most recent presidents have supported more regulatory programs but have successfully opposed the expansion of regulatory independence. The 1960s and 1970s witnessed the adoption of an unprecedented number of new regulatory programs but only four new independent commissions.

Agencies of Redistribution Implement Fiscal or Monetary and Welfare Policies

Welfare agencies and fiscal or monetary agencies are responsible for the transfer of hundreds of billions of dollars annually between the public and the private spheres, and through such transfers these agencies influence how people and corporations spend and invest trillions of dollars annually. We call them agencies of redistribution

regulatory agencies Departments, bureaus, or independent agencies whose primary mission is to eliminate or restrict certain behaviors defined as negative in themselves or negative in their consequences.

administrative legislation Rules made by regulatory agencies and commissions.

---

[11]*Final Report of the President's Committee on Administrative Management* (Washington, D.C.: Government Printing Office, 1937). The term *headless fourth branch* was invented by a member of the committee staff, the Cornell University government professor Robert Cushman.

because they influence the amount of money in the economy and because they directly influence who has money, who has credit, and whether people will want to invest or save their money rather than spend it.

Fiscal and Monetary Agencies   The best generic term for governmental activity affecting or relating to money is *fiscal* policy. However, we choose to make a further distinction, reserving *fiscal* for taxing and spending policies and using *monetary* for policies having to do with banks, credit, and currency.

Administration of fiscal policy is primarily performed in the Treasury Department. Today, in addition to administering and policing income tax and other tax collections, the Treasury is responsible for managing the enormous federal debt. The Treasury Department also prints the currency that we use, but currency represents only a tiny proportion of the entire money economy. Most of the trillions of dollars used in the transactions that make up the private and public sectors of the American economy exist on printed accounts and computers, not in currency.

Another important fiscal agency (although for technical reasons it is called an agency of monetary policy) is the ***Federal Reserve System,*** headed by the Federal Reserve Board. The Federal Reserve System (the Fed) has authority over the credit rates and lending activities of the nation's most important banks. Established by Congress in 1913, the Fed is responsible for adjusting the supply of money to both the needs of banks in the different regions and the commerce and industry in each. It also ensures that banks do not overextend themselves by adopting lending policies that are too liberal. The basis for this responsibility is the fear that if there is a sudden economic scare, a run on a few banks might be contagious and cause another terrible crash like the one in 1929. The Federal Reserve Board sits at the top of a pyramid of twelve district Federal Reserve Banks, which are "bankers' banks," serving the monetary needs of the hundreds of member banks in the national bank system. In 2008, the Federal Reserve and the Treasury worked to resolve the nation's financial crisis, which had been touched off by a sharp decline in housing prices, a collapse in the value of hundreds of billions of dollars in mortgage-backed securities, and steep declines in the stock market. To avert a total financial meltdown, the Federal Reserve and the Treasury worked together to shore up the banking system and bolster stock prices, investing hundreds of billions of taxpayer dollars in financial institutions to ensure their stability.

Welfare Agencies   No single government agency is responsible for all the programs making up the "welfare state." The largest agency in the field is the Social Security Administration (SSA), which manages the social insurance aspects of Social Security and Supplemental Security Income (SSI). As the baby-boom generation ages, a growing bloc of voters (and their children) have become concerned about the solvency of this system. Many argue that without some adjustments in benefit schedules or taxes, the present population will begin drawing down the enormous amount of funds in the Social Security Trust Fund in two decades and exhaust it in forty years.

Agencies in the Department of Health and Human Services administer Temporary Assistance to Needy Families (TANF) and Medicaid, and the Department of Agriculture is responsible for the Food Stamp Program. With the exception of Social

Federal Reserve System (the Fed) Consisting of twelve Federal Reserve districts, the Fed facilitates exchanges of cash, checks, and credit; it regulates member banks; and it uses monetary policies to fight inflation and deflation.

Security, these are *means-tested* programs, requiring applicants to demonstrate that their total annual cash earnings fall below an officially defined poverty line. These public-assistance programs create a large administrative burden.

In August 1996, virtually all of the means-tested public-assistance programs were legally abolished as national programs and "devolved" to the states (see also Chapter 3). However, for the five years between fiscal 1996 and fiscal 2001, there was still a great deal of national administrative responsibility because federal funding of these programs continued through large, discretionary block grants to each state. Other aspects of state welfare activity were policed by federal agencies, and all of that required about the same size administrative capacity in welfare as existed before. Those who expected some kind of revolution after adoption of the Personal Responsibility and Work Opportunity Reconciliation Act of 1996 were in for a disappointment.

THE PROBLEM OF BUREAUCRATIC CONTROL

Two centuries, millions of employees, and trillions of dollars after the founding, we must return to James Madison's observation that "you must first enable the government to control the governed; and in the next place oblige it to control itself."[12] Today the problem is the same, but the form has changed. Our problem today is bureaucracy and our inability to keep it accountable to elected political authorities.

Bureaucrats Have Their Own Motivational Considerations

The economist William Niskanen proposed that we consider a bureau or department of government as analogous to a division of a private firm and conceive of the bureaucrat just as we would the manager who runs that division.[13] In particular, Niskanen stipulated for the purposes of modeling bureaucratic behavior that a bureau chief or department head be thought of as a maximizer of his or her budget (just as the private-sector counterpart is a maximizer of his or her division's profits).

There are quite a number of motivational bases on which bureaucratic budget maximizing might be justified. A cynical (though some would say realistic) basis for budget maximizing is that the bureaucrat's own compensation is often tied to the size of his or her budget. Not only might bureaus with large budgets have higher-salaried executives with more elaborate fringe benefits but there also may be enhanced opportunities for career advancement, travel, a poshly appointed office, possibly even a chauffeur-driven limousine.

A second, related motivation for large budgets is nonmaterial personal gratification. An individual understandably enjoys the prestige and respect that comes from running a major enterprise. You can't take these things to the bank or put them on your family's dinner table, but your sense of esteem and your stature are

Rationality Principle

One view of bureaucratic behavior is that bureaucrats are motivated to maximize their budgets.

---

[12]Alexander Hamilton, James Madison, and John Jay, *The Federalist Papers*, ed. Clinton L. Rassiter (New York: New American Library, 1961), no. 51.

[13]William A. Niskanen Jr., *Bureaucracy and Representative Government* (Chicago: Aldine, 1971).

surely buoyed by the conspicuous fact that your bureau or division has a large budget. That you are also boss of a large number of subordinates, made possible by a large bureau budget, is another aspect of this sort of ego gratification.

But personal salary, "on-the-job consumption," and power tripping are not the only forces driving a bureaucrat toward gaining as large a budget as possible. Some bureaucrats, perhaps most, actually *care* about their mission.[14] They initially choose to go into public safety, or the military, or health care, or social work, or education—as police officers, soldiers, hospital managers, social workers, and teachers, respectively—because they believe in the importance of helping people in their community. As they rise through the ranks of a public bureaucracy and assume management responsibilities, they take this mission orientation with them. Thus as chief of detectives in a big-city police department, as head of procurement in the air force, as director of nursing services in a public hospital, as supervisor of the social work division in a county welfare department, or as assistant superintendent of a town school system, individuals try to secure as large a budget as they can to succeed in achieving the mission to which they have devoted their professional lives.

Whether for cynical, self-serving motives or for the noblest of public purposes, it is entirely plausible that individual bureaucrats seek to persuade others (typically legislators or taxpayers) to provide them with as many resources as possible. Indeed, it is sometimes difficult to distinguish the saint from the sinner because each sincerely argues that he or she needs more to do more. This is one nice feature of Niskanen's assumption of budget maximizing: It doesn't really matter *why* a bureaucrat is interested in a big budget; what matters is simply that he or she wants more resources rather than fewer.

Critics of the budget-maximizing theory call into question its assumption about the passivity of the legislature. The legislature, the only customer of the bureau's product, in essence tells the bureau how much it is willing to pay for various production levels. The critics suggest that this is akin to a customer walking onto a used-car lot and telling the salesman precisely how much he or she is willing to spend for each vehicle.[15]

In a representative democracy, it may be difficult for the legislature to keep silent about its own willingness to pay. The bureau, at any rate, can do some research to judge the preferences of various legislators based on who their constituents are. But legislators can do research, too. Indeed, we suggested in Chapter 5 that the collection, evaluation, and dissemination of information—in this case information about the production costs of bureaucratic supply—are precisely the things in which specialized legislative committees engage. Committees hold hearings, request documentation on production, assign investigatory staff to various research tasks, and query bureau personnel on the veracity of their data and their use of the lowest-cost technologies (making it more difficult for the bureau to disguise on-the-job consumption). After the fact, the committees engage in oversight, making sure that what the legislature was told at the time when authorization and appropriations

ONLINE READING

[14]John Brehm and Scott Gates, *Working, Shirking, and Sabotage: Bureaucratic Response to a Democratic Public* (Ann Arbor: University of Michigan Press, 1997).

[15]This and other related points are drawn from Gary J. Miller and Terry M. Moe, "Bureaucrats, Legislators, and the Size of Government," *American Political Science Review 77*, no. 2 (June 1983): 297–323.

were voted actually holds in practice. In short, the legislature can be much more proactive than the Niskanen budget-maximizing theory gives it credit for. And in the real world, the legislature is more proactive, as we shall see later in this chapter.

Before leaving motivational considerations, it should be remarked that budget maximizing is not the only objective that bureaucrats pursue. It needs to be emphasized and reemphasized that career civil servants and high-level political appointees are *politicians*. They spend their professional lives pursuing political goals, bargaining, forming alliances and coalitions, solving cooperation and collective-action problems, making policy decisions, operating within and interfacing with political institutions—in short, doing what other politicians do. They do not have elections to win, but even elections affect their conditions of employment by determining the composition of the legislature and the partisan and ideological complexion of the chief executive. Bureaucrats are politicians beholden to other politicians for authority and resources. They are servants of many masters.

As politicians subject to the oversight and authority of others, bureaucrats must make contingency plans. They must be strategic and forward thinking. Whichever party wins control of the House or the Senate, whichever candidate wins the presidency, whoever becomes chair of the legislative committee with authorization or appropriation responsibility over their agency, life will go on and bureau chiefs will have to adjust to the prevailing political winds. To protect and expand authority and resources, bureaucratic politicians seek, in the form of autonomy and discretion, insurance against political change. They don't always succeed in acquiring this freedom, but they do try to insulate themselves from changes in the broader political world.[16] So bureaucratic motivations include budget-maximizing behavior, to be sure, but bureaucrats also seek the autonomy to weather changes in the political atmosphere and the discretion and flexibility to achieve their goals.

Control of the Bureaucracy Is a Principal-Agent Problem

Two broad categories of control mechanisms enable a principal to guard against opportunistic or incompetent agent behavior. They may be illustrated by a homeowner (the principal) who seeks out a contractor (the agent) to remodel a kitchen. The first category is employed before the fact and depends on the reputation an agent possesses. One guards against selecting an incompetent or corrupt agent by relying on various methods for authenticating the promises made by the agent. These include advice from people you trust (your neighbors who just had their kitchen remodeled), certification by various official boards (an association of kitchen contractors), letters of recommendation and other testimonials, credentials (specialized training programs), and interviews. Before-the-fact protection relies on the assumption that an agent's reputation is a valuable asset that he or she does not want to depreciate.

The second class of control mechanisms operates after the fact. Payment may be made contingent on completion of various tasks by specific dates, so that it may

---

[16]For an expanded view of bureaucratic autonomy and insulation with historical application to the U.S. Department of Agriculture and the Post Office Department, see Daniel P. Carpenter, *The Forging of Bureaucratic Autonomy: Reputations, Networks, and Policy Innovation in Executive Agencies, 1862–1928* (Princeton, N.J.: Princeton University Press, 2001).

be withheld for nonperformance. Alternatively, financial incentives (for example, bonuses) for early or on-time completion may be part of the arrangement. The agent may be required to post a bond that would be forfeited for lack of performance. An inspection process, after the work is completed, may lead to financial penalties, bonuses, or possibly even legal action. Of course, the principal can always seek legal relief for breach of contract, either in the form of an injunction stipulating that the agent comply or in the form of an order demanding that the agent pay damages.

How does the principal-agent problem apply to the president's and Congress's control of the bureaucracy?

Suppose the legislation that created the EPA required that after ten years new legislation be passed renewing its existence and mandate. The issue facing the House, the Senate, and the president in their consideration of renewal involves how much authority to give this agency and how much money to permit it to spend. Suppose the House is conservative on environmental issues and prefers limited authority and a limited budget. The Senate wants the agency to have wide-ranging authority but is prepared to give it only slightly more resources than the House is (because of its concern with the budget deficit). The president is happy to split the difference between House and Senate on the matter of authority but feels beholden to environmental types and is thus prepared to shower the EPA with resources. Bureaucrats in the EPA want more authority than even the Senate is prepared to grant and more resources than even the president is willing to grant. Eventually relevant majorities in the House and the Senate (including the support of relevant committees) and the president agree on a policy reflecting a compromise among their various points of view.

The bureaucrats are not particularly pleased with this compromise because it gives them considerably less authority and funding than they had hoped for. If they flout the wishes of their principals and implement a policy exactly to their liking, they risk the unified wrath of the House, the Senate, and the president. Undoubtedly the politicians would react with new legislation (and they would also presumably find other political appointees and career bureaucrats at the EPA to replace the current bureaucratic leadership). If, however, the EPA implements some policy located between its own preferences and the preferences of its principals, it might be able to get away with it.

Thus we have a principal-agent relationship in which a political principal—a collective principal consisting of the president and coalitions in the House and Senate—formulates policy and creates an implementation agent to execute its details. The agent, however, has policy preferences of its own and, unless subjected to further controls, will inevitably implement a policy that drifts toward its ideal.

A variety of controls might conceivably restrict this **bureaucratic drift**. Indeed, legislative scholars often point to congressional hearings in which bureaucrats may be publicly humiliated, annual appropriations decisions that may be used to punish out-of-control bureaus, and watchdog agents, like the Government Accountability Office, that may be used to monitor and scrutinize the bureau's performance. But these all come after the fact and may be only partially credible threats to the agency.

Before-the-Fact Controls The most powerful before-the-fact political weapon is the appointment process. The adroit control of the political stance of a given bureau by the president and Congress, through their joint powers of nomination and confirmation

Rationality Principle

Bureaucratic drift occurs because the policy preferences of bureaucratic agents differ from those of members of Congress or the president.

bureaucratic drift
The oft-observed phenomenon of bureaucratic implementation that produces policy more to the liking of the bureaucracy than to the original intention of the legislation that created it, but without triggering a political reaction from elected officials.

(especially if they can arrange for appointees who closely share the political consensus on policy) is a self-enforcing mechanism for ensuring reliable agent performance.

A second powerful before-the-fact weapon is procedural controls. The general rules and regulations that direct the manner in which federal agencies conduct their affairs are contained in the Administrative Procedure Act. This act is almost always the boilerplate of legislation creating and renewing federal agencies. It is not uncommon, however, for an agency's procedures to be tailored to suit particular circumstances.

Coalitional Drift as a Collective-Action Problem   Not only do politicians want the legislative deals that they strike to be faithfully implemented, but they also want those deals to endure. This is especially problematic in American political life, with its shifting alignments and absence of permanent political cleavages. Today's coalition transforms itself overnight. Opponents today are partners tomorrow, and vice versa. A victory today, even one implemented in a favorable manner by the bureaucracy, may be undone tomorrow. What is to be done?

To some extent, legislative structure is disinclined to undo legislation. If such a coalition votes for handsome subsidies to grain farmers, say, it is very hard to reverse this policy without the gatekeeping and agenda-setting resources of members on the House and Senate Agriculture Committees, yet their members undoubtedly participated in the initial deal and are unlikely to turn against it. But even these structural units are unstable; old politicians depart and new ones are enlisted.

In short, legislatively formulated and bureaucratically implemented output is subject to **coalitional drift**.[17] To prevent shifting coalitional patterns among politicians from endangering carefully fashioned policies, one thing the legislature might do is insulate the bureaucracy and its implementation activities from legislative interventions. If an enacting coalition makes it difficult for its *own* members to intervene in implementation, then it also makes it difficult for enemies of the policy to disrupt the flow of bureaucratic output. This political insulation can be provided by giving bureaucratic agencies long lives, their political heads long terms of office and wide-ranging administrative authority, and other political appointees overlapping terms of office and secure sources of revenue. This insulation comes at a price, however. The civil servants and political appointees of bureaus insulated from political overseers are thereby empowered to pursue independent courses of action. Protection from coalitional drift comes at the price of an increased potential for bureaucratic drift. It is one of the great trade-offs in the field of intergovernmental relations.

The President as Chief Executive Can Direct Agencies

In 1937, President Franklin Roosevelt's Committee on Administrative Management gave official sanction to an idea that had been growing increasingly urgent: "The president needs help." The national government had grown rapidly during the preceding

---

[17]This idea, offered as a supplement to the analysis of bureaucratic drift, is found in Murray J. Horn and Kenneth A. Shepsle, "Administrative Process and Organizational Form as Legislative Responses to Agency Costs," *Virginia Law Review* 75 (1989): 499–509. It is further elaborated in Kenneth A. Shepsle, "Bureaucratic Drift, Coalitional Drift, and Time Consistency," *Journal of Law, Economics, and Organization* 8 (1992): 111–18.

Institution Principle

The appointment process and procedural controls allow the president and Congress some before-the-fact control over bureaucratic agents.

Collective-Action Principle

Coalitional drift increases the difficulty of the long-term implementation of policy.

Policy Principle

Bureaucratic drift and coalitional drift are contrary tendencies. Fixing them often involves a trade-off.

coalitional drift The prospect that enacted policy will change because the composition of the enacting coalition is temporary and provisional.

twenty-five years, but the structures and procedures necessary to manage the burgeoning executive branch had not yet been established. The response to the call for help for the president initially took the form of three management policies: (1) All communications and decisions that related to executive policy decisions must pass through the White House; (2) to cope with such a flow, the White House must have an adequate staff of specialists in research, analysis, legislative and legal writing, and public affairs; and (3) the White House must have additional staff to follow through on presidential decisions—to ensure that those decisions are made, communicated to Congress, and carried out by the appropriate agency.

Establishing a management capacity for the presidency began in earnest with FDR, but it did not stop there. The story of the modern presidency can be told largely as a series of responses to the plea for managerial help. Indeed, each expansion of the national government into new policies and programs in the twentieth century was accompanied by a parallel expansion of the president's management authority. This pattern began even before FDR's presidency, with the policy innovations of President Woodrow Wilson between 1913 and 1920. Congress responded to Wilson's policies with the 1921 Budget and Accounting Act, which conferred on the White House agenda-setting power over budgeting. The president, in his annual budget message, transmits comprehensive budgetary recommendations to Congress. Because Congress retains ultimate legislative authority, a president's proposals are sometimes said to be dead on arrival on Capitol Hill. Nevertheless, the power to frame deliberations is potent and constitutes an important management tool. Each successive president has continued this pattern of setting the congressional agenda, creating what we now know as the managerial presidency.

For example, although President Clinton was often criticized for the way he managed his administration (Clinton's easygoing approach led critics to liken his management style to college bull sessions, complete with pizza and all-nighters), he also inaugurated one of the most systematic efforts to change the way government does business in his National Performance Review. Heavily influenced by the theories of management consultants who prize decentralization, customer responsiveness, and employee initiative, Clinton sought to infuse these new practices into government.[18]

George W. Bush was the first president with a graduate degree in business. His management strategy followed a standard business-school dictum: Select skilled subordinates and delegate responsibility to them. Bush followed this model closely in his appointment of highly experienced officials to cabinet positions. Especially noteworthy was his selection of Dick Cheney as vice president. Cheney was an old Washington hand with experience in Congress and previous administrations. (He was the first President Bush's secretary of defense and President Gerald Ford's chief of staff.) The second President Bush relied heavily on his vice president's insider abilities. Indeed, at the outset of his term, Bush often appeared overshadowed by these appointees (by the vice president in particular). Many observers had the impression that Bush did not lead his own administration. The president's performance during the war in Afghanistan and the war on terrorism temporarily dispelled many doubts about his executive capabilities. These doubts were to reemerge as the results in Iraq came

---

[18] See John Micklethwait, "Managing to Look Attractive," *New Statesman*, 8 November 1996, p. 24.

FIGURE 7.3 Congress, the President, and the Executive Branch

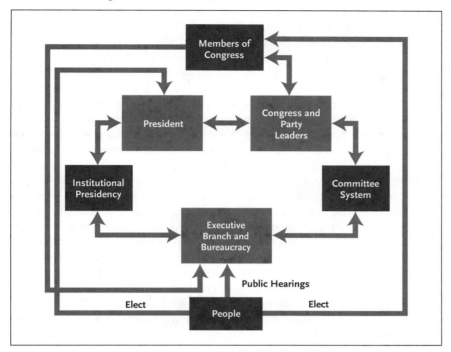

slowly and unevenly and the administration's handling of relief to New Orleans and the Gulf Coast after Hurricane Katrina was seen as incompetent.

The story of the modern presidency can be told largely as a series of responses to the rise of big government. Each expansion of the national government in the twentieth century was accompanied by a parallel expansion of presidential management authority. The executive bureaucracy and the institutional presidency are right in the middle of the separation-of-powers administrative state (Figure 7.3).

 History
Principle

Each expansion of the national government is accompanied by a parallel expansion of presidential management authority.

Congress Can Promote Responsible Bureaucracy through Oversight and Incentives

Congress is constitutionally essential to responsible bureaucracy because the key to governmental responsibility is legislation. When a law is passed and its intent is clear, then the president knows what to "faithfully execute," and the responsible agency understands what is expected of it. In our modern age, legislatures rarely make laws directly for citizens; most laws are really instructions to bureaucrats and their agencies. But when Congress enacts vague legislation, agencies must rely on their own interpretations. The president and the federal courts step in to tell them what the legislation intended. And so do intensely interested organized groups. But when everybody—from the president to the courts to interest groups—gets involved in the interpretation of legislative intent, to whom is the agency responsible?

The answer lies in the process of *oversight.* The more legislative power Congress has delegated to the executive, the more it has sought to get back into the game through committee and subcommittee oversight of the agencies. The standing committee system in Congress is well suited for oversight, inasmuch as most of the congressional committees and subcommittees are organized with jurisdictions roughly parallel to one or more executive departments or agencies. Appropriations committees as well as authorization committees have oversight powers, as do their respective subcommittees. In addition to these, there is a committee on government operations in both the House and the Senate, each with oversight powers not limited by departmental jurisdiction.

The best indication of Congress's oversight efforts is the use of public hearings, before which bureaucrats and other witnesses are summoned to discuss and defend agency budgets and decisions. The data drawn from systematic studies of congressional committee and subcommittee hearings and meetings show dramatically that Congress has tried through oversight to keep pace with the expansion of the executive branch. Between 1950 and 1980, the annual number of committee and subcommittee meetings in the House of Representatives rose steadily. Yet beginning in 1980 in the House and 1978 in the Senate, the number of committee and subcommittee hearings and meetings slowly began to decline. New questions about the ability of Congress to exercise oversight arose when the Republicans took over Congress in 1995. Reductions in committee staffing and an emphasis on using investigative oversight to uncover scandal meant that much less time was spent on programmatic oversight. Moreover, congressional Republicans complained that they could not get sufficient information about programs from the White House to conduct effective oversight. Congressional records show that in 1991–92, when Democrats controlled the House, they issued reports on fifty-five federal programs, whereas in 1997–98 the Republican Congress issued only fourteen.[19] On matters of major national importance, multiple committees may initiate oversight hearings simultaneously. No less than a dozen congressional committees (along with the Justice Department and the Securities and Exchange Commission) launched investigations into the collapse of the giant energy company Enron.

Although congressional oversight is potent because of Congress's power to make—and therefore change—the law, often the most effective and the most influential control over bureaucratic accountability is the power of the purse—the ability of the House and Senate committees and subcommittees on appropriations to look at agency performance through the microscope of the annual appropriations process. This process makes bureaucrats attentive to Congress, especially members of the relevant authorizing committee and appropriations subcommittee, because they know that Congress has a chance each year to reduce their authority or funding.[20] A more recent evaluation of the budget and appropriations process by the National Performance Review expressed one serious concern about oversight through appropriation: Pressure to cut appropriations "has put a premium on preserving particular programs, projects, and activities from Executive Branch as well as congressional ac-

oversight The effort by Congress, through hearings, investigations, and other techniques, to exercise control over the activities of executive agencies.

---

[19]Richard E. Cohen, "Crackup of the Committees," *National Journal,* 31 July 1999, p. 2214.

[20]See Aaron Wildavsky, *The New Politics of the Budgetary Process,* 2nd ed. (New York: HarperCollins, 1992), pp. 15–16.

tion."[21] This may be another explanation for why there may be some downsizing but almost no terminations of federal agencies.

Oversight can also be carried out by individual members of Congress. Such inquiries addressed to bureaucrats are considered standard congressional "casework" and can turn up significant questions of public responsibility even when the motive is only to meet the demand of an individual constituent. Oversight also very often takes place through communications between congressional staff and agency staff. Congressional staff has been enlarged tremendously since the Legislative Reorganization Act of 1946, and the legislative staff, especially the staff of the committees, is just as professionalized and specialized as the staff of an executive agency. In addition, Congress has created for itself three quite large agencies whose obligations are to engage in constant research on problems taking place in the executive branch: the Government Accountability Office, the Congressional Research Service, and the Congressional Budget Office. Each is designed to give Congress information independent of the information it can get through hearings and other communications directly with the executive branch.[22]

Congressional Oversight: Abdication or Strategic Delegation? Congress often grants the executive-branch bureaucracies discretion in determining certain features of a policy during the implementation phase. Although the complexities of governing a modern industrialized democracy make the granting of discretion necessary, some argue that Congress not only gives unelected bureaucrats too much discretion but also delegates too much policy-making authority to them. Congress, they say, has transferred so much power that it has created a "runaway bureaucracy" in which unelected officials accountable neither to the electorate nor to Congress make important policy decisions.[23] By enacting vague statutes that give bureaucrats broad discretion, so the argument goes, members of Congress effectively abdicated their constitutionally designated roles and effectively removed themselves from the policy-making process. Ultimately this extreme delegation has left the legislative branch weak and ineffectual and has dire consequences for the health of our democracy.

Others claim that even though Congress may possess the tools to engage in effective oversight, it fails to use them simply because we do not see Congress actively engaging in much oversight activity.[24] However, Mathew McCubbins and Thomas

---

[21]National Performance Review, *From Red Tape to Results: Creating a Government That Works Better and Costs Less* (Washington, D.C.: Government Printing Office, 1993), p. 42.

[22]Until 1983, there was still another official tool of legislative oversight, the legislative veto. Each executive agency was obliged to submit to Congress proposed decisions or rules. These were to lie before both houses for thirty to sixty days; then, if Congress took no explicit action by a one-house or two-house resolution to veto a proposed measure, it became law. The legislative veto was declared unconstitutional by the Supreme Court in 1983 on the grounds that it violated the separation of powers because the resolutions Congress passed to exercise its veto were not subject to a presidential veto, as required by the Constitution. See *Immigration and Naturalization Service v. Chadha*, 462 U.S. 919 (1983). On the congressional staff more generally, see Robert H. Salisbury and Kenneth A. Shepsle, "Congressman as Enterprise," *Legislative Studies Quarterly* 6 (1981): 559–76.

[23]Lowi, *The End of Liberalism*; and Lawrence C. Dodd and Richard L. Schott, *Congress and the Administrative State* (New York: Wiley, 1979).

[24]Morris S. Ogul, *Congress Oversees the Bureaucracy: Studies in Legislative Supervision* (Pittsburgh: University of Pittsburgh Press, 1976); and Peter Woll, *American Bureaucracy*, 2nd ed. (New York: Norton, 1977).

Schwartz argue that these critics have focused on the wrong type of oversight and have missed a type of oversight that benefits members of Congress in their bids for reelection.[25] McCubbins and Schwartz distinguish between two types of oversight: police patrol and fire alarm. Under the police-patrol variety, Congress systematically initiates investigation into the activity of agencies. Under the fire-alarm variety, members of Congress do not initiate investigations but wait for adversely affected citizens or interest groups to bring bureaucratic perversions of legislative intent to the attention of the relevant congressional committee. To make sure that individuals and groups bring these violations to members' attention—to set off the fire alarm, so to speak—Congress passes laws that help individuals and groups make claims against the bureaucracy, granting them legal standing before administrative agencies and federal courts.

McCubbins and Schwartz argue that fire-alarm oversight is more efficient than the police-patrol variety, given costs and the electoral incentives of members of Congress. Why should members spend their scarce resources (mainly time) to initiate investigations without having any evidence that they will reap electoral rewards? Police-patrol oversight can waste taxpayers' dollars too, because many investigations will not turn up any evidence of violations of legislative intent. It is much more cost-effective for members to conserve their resources and then claim credit for fixing the problem (and saving the day) after the fire alarms have been sounded. (Also see Analyzing the Evidence, p. 312)

On the other hand, bureaucratic drift might be contained if Congress spent more of its time clarifying its legislative intent and less of its time on oversight activity. If its original intent in the law were clearer, Congress could then afford to defer to presidential management to maintain bureaucratic responsibility. Bureaucrats are more responsive to clear legislative guidance than to anything else. But when Congress and the president are at odds (or coalitions within Congress are at odds), bureaucrats have an opportunity to evade responsibility by playing one branch off against the other.

Collective-Action Principle

When Congress and the president are at odds (or coalitions within Congress are at odds), bureaucrats have an opportunity to evade responsibility.

HOW CAN BUREAUCRACY BE REDUCED?

Americans like to complain about bureaucracy. Americans don't like big government because big government means big bureaucracy, and bureaucracy means the federal service—about 2.7 million civilian and 1.5 million military employees.[26] Promises to cut the bureaucracy are popular campaign appeals; "cutting out the fat," with big reductions in the number of federal employees, is held out as a sure-fire way of cutting the deficit.

Despite fears of bureaucratic growth getting out of hand, however, the federal service has hardly grown at all during the past thirty years; it reached its peak post-

ONLINE READING ○ [25]McCubbins and Schwartz, "Congressional Oversight Overlooked."

[26]This is just under 99 percent of all national government employees. About 1.4 percent work for the legislative branch and the federal judiciary. See Office of Management and Budget, *Budget of the U.S. Government, Fiscal Year 2004, Historical Tables* (Washington, D.C.: Government Printing Office, 2003), table 17.5, p. 306.

FIGURE 7.4 Employees in the Federal Service: Total Number as a Percentage of the Workforce

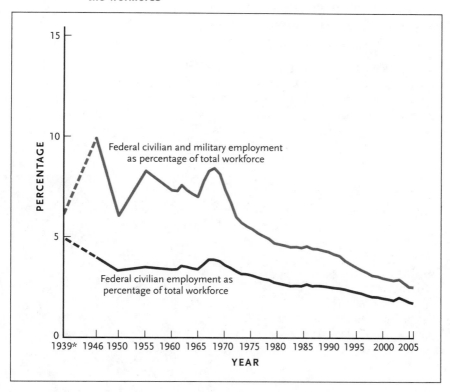

SOURCE: Tax Foundation, *Facts and Figures on Government Finance* (Baltimore: Johns Hopkins University Press, 1990), pp. 22, 44; Office of Management and Budget, *Budget of the U.S. Government, Fiscal Year 2002, Historical Tables* (Washington, D.C.: Government Printing Office, 2001), p. 304; and U.S. Bureau of Labor Statistics, "Employment Status of the Civilian Population by Sex and Age," *Labor Force Statistics from the Current Population Survey* (stats.bls.gov/webapps/legacy/cpsatab1.htm), table A1.

NOTE: Workforce includes unemployed persons.

*Lines between 1939 and 1946 are broken because they connect the last prewar year with the first postwar year, disregarding the temporary ballooning of federal employees, especially in the military, during the war years.

war level in 1968 with 2.9 million civilian employees plus an additional 3.6 million military personnel (a figure swollen by the war in Vietnam). The number of civilian federal executive-branch employees has since remained close to that figure. The growth of the federal service is even less imposing when placed in the context of the total workforce and compared to the size of state and local public employment, which was 18.7 million in 2004.[27] Figure 7.4 indicates that since 1950 the ratio of

---

[27]Ibid.

Oversight of the Executive Branch

Although we often think of the Congress as a lawmaking body, it also carries out another important task—checking the executive branch through the oversight process. If Congress thinks the bureaucracy is no longer serving the public's interest as defined by the legislative branch, it can use its oversight powers to put the agency back on track. In recent years, it has been suggested that Congress may be neglecting its oversight responsibilities. Let us consider how oversight has varied over time, and why measuring the effectiveness of oversight may be difficult.

GOVERNMENT EFFICIENCY AND BUREAUCRATIC OVERSIGHT HEARINGS[1]

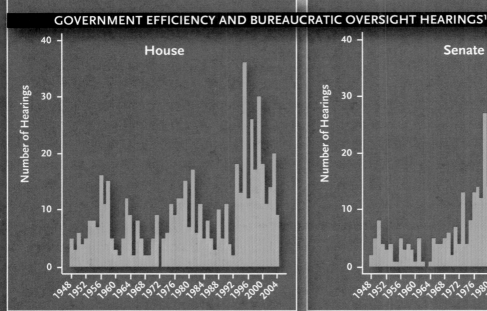

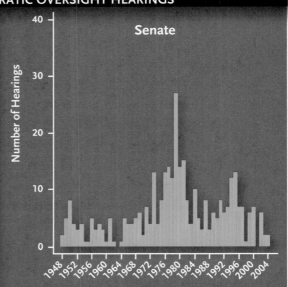

▲

Congressional hearings are an important tool used to oversee the bureaucracy. The House holds more hearings than the Senate: On average during this period, the House held 9.6 hearings per year while the Senate held only 6.1. We also see two periods where the number of hearings increased dramatically. Both chambers began to hold more hearings in the mid- to late 1970s in the wake of the Watergate scandal and the Vietnam War, and hearings in the House increased significantly after a new Republican majority was elected in 1994.

▲

According to congressional scholars Norman Ornstein and Thomas Mann, in recent years oversight of the bureaucracy across a range of policies has virtually collapsed.[2] Since the 1990s, the Senate has lagged well behind the House in holding oversight hearings. In fact, there were no Senate oversight hearings in 2001 and only two each in 2003 and 2004.

[1]Source: Policy Agendas Project, Center for American Politics and Public Policy, University of Washington.
[2]Norman J. Ornstein and Thomas Mann. 2006. "When Congress Checks Out." *Foreign Affairs* 85(6): 67–82.

Measuring the effectiveness of oversight may be difficult because it depends on the type of oversight Congress is using. Mathew McCubbins and Thomas Schwartz define two types of oversight: Police Patrols and Fire Alarms.

Under the police-patrol method, Congress systematically initiates investigations into the activity of agencies. The goal is to catch and punish enough violators so that the rest of the bureaucracy will be discouraged from straying too far from legislative intent. However, Congress cannot monitor all agencies at once. Police-patrol oversight is especially difficult because of the vast number of employees spread out over many government departments and agencies. The table below lists the number of employees in each of the fifteen executive Cabinet departments and the six largest independent agencies.

EXECUTIVE BRANCH EMPLOYEES

Executive Departments		Independent Agencies	
Defense	616,000	Social Security Administration	65,000
Veterans Affairs	234,000	National Aeronautics and Space Administration	20,000
Homeland Security	149,000	Environmental Protection Agency	18,000
Justice	103,000		
Agriculture	102,000	Tennessee Valley Authority	13,000
Treasury	95,000	General Services Administration	13,000
Interior	71,000		
Health and Human Services	61,000	Federal Deposit Insurance Corporation	5,000
Transportation	57,000		
Commerce	36,000		
Labor	16,000		
Energy	15,000		
State	13,000		
Housing and Urban Development	10,000		
Education	4,000		

Source: Bureau of Labor Statistics, U.S. Department of Labor, *Career Guide to Industries, 2006–07 Edition*, Federal Government, Excluding the Postal Service, www.bls.gov/oco/cg/cgs041.htm (accessed June 11, 2007).

The fire-alarm method relies on the public. Members of Congress do not initiate investigations but wait for adversely affected citizens or interest groups to bring bureaucratic perversions of legislative intent to the attention of the relevant congressional committee. McCubbins and Schwartz argue that this method is more effective because, "Instead of sniffing for fires, Congress places fire-alarm boxes on street corners, builds neighborhood fire houses and sometimes dispatches its own hook-and-ladder in response to an alarm."[3] Since concerned citizens are out looking for bureaucratic fires, members of Congress will have more time to engage in other activities, such as securing reelection.

[3]Mathew McCubbins and Thomas Schwartz. 1984. "Congressional Oversight Overlooked: Police Patrols and Fire Alarms." *American Journal of Political Science* 28(1): 165–179.

FIGURE 7.5 Annual Federal Outlays

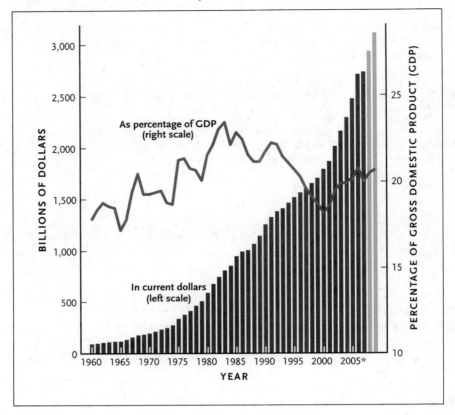

SOURCE: Office of Management and Budget, *Budget of the U.S. Government, Fiscal Year 2008, Historical Tables* (Washington, D.C.: Government Printing Office, 2008).

*Data for 2008–9 are estimated.

federal service employment to the total workforce has been fairly steady, declining only slightly in the past twenty-five years. Another useful comparison is to be found in Figure 7.5: Although the dollar increase in federal spending shown by the bars looks impressive, the red line indicates that even here the national government has simply kept pace with the growth of the economy.

In sum, the national government is indeed very large, but the federal service has not been growing any faster than the economy or the society. The same is roughly true of the growth pattern of state and local public personnel. Our bureaucracy keeps pace with our society, despite our seeming dislike for it, because we cannot operate the control towers, the prisons, the Social Security system, and other essential elements of the state without it. And we certainly could not conduct a war in Iraq without a gigantic military bureaucracy.

History Principle

The size of the federal bureaucracy has kept pace with the growth of the economy and the needs of society.

Nevertheless, some Americans continue to argue that bureaucracy is too big and that it should be reduced. In the 1990s, Americans seemed particularly enthusiastic about reducing (or to use the popular contemporary word, *downsizing*) the federal bureaucracy.

Termination

The only *certain* way to reduce the size of the bureaucracy is to eliminate programs. Variations in the levels of federal personnel and expenditures demonstrate the futility of trying to make permanent cuts in existing agencies. Furthermore, most agencies have a supportive constituency that will fight to reinstate any cuts that are made. Termination is the only way to ensure an agency's reduction, and it is a rare occurrence.

The Republican-led 104th Congress (1995–96) was committed to the termination of programs. Newt Gingrich, the Speaker of the House, took Congress by storm with his promises of a virtual revolution in government. But when the dust had settled at the end of the first session of the first Gingrich-led Congress, no significant progress had been made toward downsizing through the termination of agencies and programs.[28] The only two agencies eliminated were the Office of Technology Assessment, which provided research for Congress, and the Advisory Council on Intergovernmental Relations, which studied the relationship between the federal government and the state. Significantly, neither of these agencies had a strong constituency to defend it.[29]

The overall lack of success in terminating bureaucracy is a reflection of Americans' love-hate relationship with the national government. As antagonistic as Americans may be toward bureaucracy in general, they grow attached to the services rendered and protections offered by particular bureaucratic agencies—that is, they fiercely defend their favorite agencies while perceiving no inconsistency between that defense and their antagonistic attitude toward the bureaucracy in general. A good case in point was the agonizing problem of closing military bases in the wake of the end of the cold war, when the United States no longer needed so many bases. Because every base is in some congressional member's district, it proved impossible for Congress to decide to close any of them. Consequently, between 1988 and 1990, Congress established the Defense Base Closure and Realignment Commission to decide on base closings. Even though the matter is now out of Congress's hands altogether, the process has been slow and agonizing.

Elected leaders have come to rely on a more incremental approach to downsizing the bureaucracy. They have done much by budgetary means, reducing the budgets of all agencies across the board by small percentages and cutting some poorly supported agencies by larger amounts. Yet these changes are still incremental, leaving the existence of agencies unaddressed.

History Principle

Americans have grown attached to the programs implemented by government agencies and are thus reluctant to cut back on their size and scope.

----

[28] A thorough review of the first session of the 104th Congress can be found in "Republican's Hopes for 1996 Lie in Unfinished Business," *Congressional Quarterly Weekly Report*, 6 January 1996, pp. 6–18.

[29] The Interstate Commerce Commission, created in 1887, was also terminated in 1995, by which time many of its functions had been dispersed to other agencies. In that year, its remaining functions were transferred to the newly created Surface Transportation Board.

An additional approach has been taken to thwart the highly unpopular regulatory agencies, which are so small (relatively) that cutting their budgets contributes virtually nothing to reducing the deficit. This approach is called **deregulation**, simply defined as a reduction in the number of rules promulgated by regulatory agencies. But deregulation by rule reduction is still incremental and has certainly not satisfied the hunger of the American public in general and Washington representatives in particular for a genuine reduction in the size of the bureaucracy.

Devolution

The next best approach to genuine reduction in the size of the bureaucracy is **devolution**—downsizing the federal bureaucracy by delegating the implementation of programs to state and local governments. Indirect evidence for this is seen in Figure 7.6, which shows the increase in state and local government employment against a backdrop of flat or declining federal employment. This evidence suggests a growing share of governmental actions taking place on the state and local levels.

Devolution often alters the pattern of who benefits most from government programs. In the early 1990s, a major devolution in transportation policy sought to open up decisions about transportation to a new set of interests. Since the 1920s, transportation policy had been dominated by road-building interests in the federal and state governments. Many advocates for cities and many environmentalists believed that the emphasis on road building hurt cities and harmed the environment. The 1992 reform, initiated by environmentalists, put more power into the hands of metropolitan planning organizations and lifted many federal restrictions on how the money should be spent. Reformers hoped that these changes would open up the decision-making process so that those advocating alternatives to road building, such as mass transit, bike paths, and walkways, would have more influence over how federal transportation dollars were spent. Although the pace of change has been slow, devolution has indeed brought new voices to decisions about transportation spending, and alternatives to highways have received increasing attention.

Often the central aim of devolution is to provide more efficient and more flexible government services. Yet by its very nature, devolution entails variation across the states. In some states, government services may improve as a consequence of devolution. In other states, services may deteriorate as the states use devolution as an opportunity to cut spending and reduce services. This has been the pattern in the implementation of the welfare reform passed in 1996, the most significant devolution of federal social programs in many decades. Some states, such as Wisconsin, have used the flexibility of the reform to design innovative programs that respond to clients' needs; other states, such as Idaho, have virtually dismantled their welfare programs. Because the legislation placed a five-year lifetime limit on receiving welfare, the states will take on an even greater role in the future as existing clients lose their eligibility for federal benefits. Welfare reform has been praised by many for reducing welfare rolls and responding to the public desire that welfare be a temporary program. At the same time, it has placed more low-income women and their children at risk of being left with no form of assistance at all.

deregulation The policy of reducing or eliminating regulatory restraints on the conduct of individuals or private institutions.

devolution The policy of removing a program from one level of government by deregulating it or passing it down to a lower level, such as from the national government to the state and local governments.

FIGURE 7.6 Government Employment

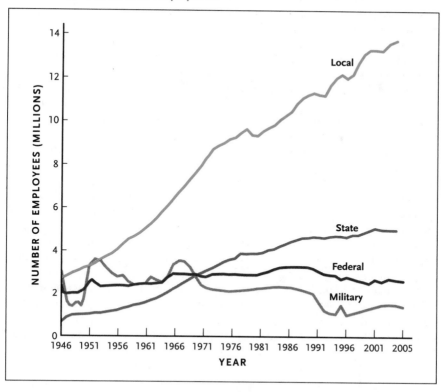

SOURCE: U.S. Bureau of the Census, *Statistical Abstract of the United States 2006* (Washington, D.C.: Government Printing Office, 2006), pp. 297, 330.

NOTE: Federal government employment figures include civilians only. Military employment figures include only active-duty personnel.

This variation is the dilemma that devolution poses. To a point, variation can be considered one of the virtues of federalism. But in a democracy there are dangers inherent in large variations in the provision of services and benefits.

Privatization

Privatization, another downsizing option, seems like a synonym for termination, but that is true only at the extreme. Most of what is called privatization is not termination at all but the provision of government goods and services by private contractors under direct government supervision. Except for top-secret strategic materials, virtually all of the production of military hardware, from boats to bullets, is done on a privatized basis by private contractors. Billions of dollars of research services are bought under contract by governments; these private contractors are universities as well as ordinary industrial corporations and private think tanks. ***Privatization*** simply means that a public purpose is provided under contract by a private company. But such programs are

privatization The act of moving all or part of a program from the public sector to the private sector.

still very much government programs; they are paid for by government and supervised by government. Privatization downsizes the government only in that the workers providing the service are no longer counted as part of the government bureaucracy.

The central aim of privatization is to reduce the cost of government. When private contractors can perform a task as well as a government but for less money, taxpayers win. Government workers are generally unionized and, therefore, receive good pay and generous benefits. Private-sector workers are less likely to be unionized, and private firms often provide lower pay and fewer benefits. For this reason, public-sector unions have been one of the strongest voices arguing against privatization. Other critics of privatization observe that private firms may not be more efficient or less costly than government. This is especially likely when there is little competition among private firms and public bureaucracies are not granted a fair chance to bid in the contracting competition. When private firms have a monopoly on service provision, they may be more expensive than government.

There are important questions about how private contractors can be held accountable. As one analyst of Pentagon spending put it, "The Pentagon is supposed to be representing the taxpayer and the public interest—its national security. So it's really important to have transparency, to be able to see these competitions and hold people accountable."[30] As security has become the nation's paramount concern, new worries about privatization have surfaced. Some Pentagon officials fear that too many tasks vital to national security may have already been contracted out and that national security might best be served by limiting privatization.

The new demands of domestic security have altered the thrust of bureaucratic reform. The emphasis on reducing the size of government that was so prominent during the previous two decades is gone. Instead, there is an acceptance of the idea that the federal government will grow as needed to ensure the safety of American citizens. The administration's security effort, focusing the entire federal bureaucracy on a single central mission, will require unprecedented levels of coordination among federal agencies. Despite the strong agreement on the goal of fighting terrorism, the effort to streamline the bureaucracy by focusing on a single purpose is likely to face considerable obstacles along the way. Reform of public bureaucracies is always complex because strong constituencies may attempt to block changes that they believe will harm them. Initiatives that aim to improve coordination among agencies can easily provoke political disputes if the proposed changes threaten to alter the access of groups to the bureaucracy. And groups that oppose bureaucratic changes can appeal to Congress to intervene on their behalf. As the respected reform advocate Donald Kettl said of the effort to reinvent government, "Virtually no reform that really matters can be achieved without at least implicit congressional support."[31] In wartime, many obstacles to bureaucratic reform are lifted. But the war on terrorism is an unusual war that will be fought over an extended period of time. Whether the unique features of this war improve or limit the prospects for bureaucratic reform remains to be seen.

---

[30]Ellen Nakashima, "Defense Balks at Contract Goals: Essential Services Should Not Be Privatized, Pentagon Tells OMB," *Washington Post*, 30 January 2002, p. A21.

[31]Quoted in Stephen Bar, "Midterm Exam for 'Reinvention': Study Cites 'Impressive Results' but Calls for Strategy to Win Congressional Support," *Washington Post*, 19 August 1994, p. A25.

Rationality Principle	Collective-Action Principle	Institution Principle	Policy Principle	History Principle
Bureaucracies are the instruments through which policy objectives are secured.	Coordination among bureaucrats is necessary to carry out the primary task of bureaucracy: implementation.	Institutions are created by Congress to achieve policy goals.	The policies of clientele agencies promote the interests of their clientele.	Each expansion of the national government is accompanied by a parallel expansion of presidential management authority.
One view of bureaucratic behavior is that bureaucrats are motivated to maximize their budgets.	Coalitional drift increases the difficulty of the long-term implementation of policy.	Bureaucracies are needed to achieve collective goals.	The military pork barrel is an example of the distributive tendency in Congress.	The size of the federal bureaucracy has kept pace with the growth of the economy and the needs of society.
Bureaucratic drift occurs because the policy preferences of bureaucratic agents differ from those of members of Congress or the president.	When Congress and the president are at odds (or coalitions within Congress are at odds), bureaucrats have an opportunity to evade responsibility.	Legislative principals establish bureaucratic agents to implement policies.	Bureaucratic drift and coalitional drift are contrary tendencies. Fixing them often involves a trade-off.	Americans have grown attached to the programs implemented by government agencies and thus are reluctant to cut back on their size and scope.
		Congress also delegates authority to bureaucrats to make law through the procedures of rule making and administrative adjudication.		
		The appointment process and procedural controls allow the president and Congress some before-the-fact control over bureaucratic agents.		
		In conferring budgetary agenda power on the president, the Budget and Accounting Act accelerated the development of the managerial presidency.		

SUMMARY

Most American citizens possess less information and more misinformation about bureaucracy than about any other feature of government. We therefore began this chapter with an elementary definition of bureaucracy, identifying its key characteristics and demonstrating the extent to which bureaucracy is not only a phenomenon but also an American phenomenon. In the second section of the chapter, we showed how all essential government services and controls are carried out by bureaucracies—or, to be more objective, by administrative agencies. Following a very general description of the types of bureaucratic agencies in the executive branch, we divided up the agencies of the executive branch into four categories according to mission: clientele agencies, agencies for maintaining the Union, regulatory agencies, and redistributive agencies. These categories illustrate the varieties of administrative experience in American government. Although the bureaucratic phenomenon is universal, not all the bureaucracies are the same in the way they are organized, in the degree of their responsiveness, or in the way they participate in the political process. "Bureaucracy in a Democracy" is the subtitle and the theme of this chapter not because we have succeeded in democratizing bureaucracies but because it is the never-ending challenge of politics in a democracy.

FOR FURTHER READING

Aberbach, Joel, and Bert A. Rockman. *In the Web of Politics: Three Decades of the U.S. Federal Executive*. Washington, D.C.: Brookings Institution, 2000.

Arnold, Peri E. *Making the Managerial Presidency: Comprehensive Reorganization Planning, 1905–1980*. Princeton, N.J.: Princeton University Press, 1986.

ONLINE READING ○ Brehm, John, and Scott Gates. *Working, Shirking, and Sabotage: Bureaucratic Response to a Democratic Public*. Ann Arbor: University of Michigan Press, 1997.

Downs, Anthony. *Inside Bureaucracy*. Boston: Little, Brown, 1966.

Esman, Milton J. *Government Works: Why Americans Need the Feds*. Ithaca, N.Y.: Cornell University Press, 2000.

Goodsell, Charles. *The Case for Bureaucracy*. 4th ed. Washington, D.C.: Congressional Quarterly Press, 2003.

Heclo, Hugh. *On Thinking Institutionally*. Boulder, Colo.: Paradigm, 2007.

Kerwin, Cornelius M. *Rulemaking*. 3rd ed. Washington, D.C.: Congressional Quarterly Press, 2003.

Kettl, Donald F., and James Fesler. *The Politics of the Administrative Process*. 3rd ed. Washington, D.C.: Brookings Institution, 2005.

Light, Paul C. *The True Size of Government*. Washington, D.C.: Brookings Institution, 1999.

Meier, Kenneth J., and John Bohte. *Politics and the Bureaucracy*. 5th ed. Belmont, Calif.: Wadsworth, 2006.

Seidman, Harold. *Politics, Position, and Power: The Dynamics of Federal Organization*. 5th ed. New York: Oxford University Press, 1998.

ONLINE READING ○ Wilson, James Q. *Bureaucracy: What Government Agencies Do and Why They Do It*. New York: Basic Books, 1989.

The public has been cynical about bureaucratic performance in recent decades. In response, presidents from Jimmy Carter onward have attempted to reduce the size of the federal bureaucracy. Total federal and military employment as a percentage of the total workforce has, in fact, been declining since 1970. Yet total federal expenditures have increased and the government has taken on new responsibilities, especially after September 11. The principles of politics help us understand how a federal government, under increased public scrutiny, can reduce the number of government employees while simultaneously increasing its power and spending.

Both Congress and the executive branch are acting according to the rationality principle: the electorate does not want to give up existing programs, but the public also is critical of excessive federal authority and spending. Thus, the branches have sought policy solutions that will satisfy both of these goals. As we discussed in this chapter, these policies have taken two forms: devolution and privatization.

The story below describes privatization. The federal government ostensibly reduces its workforce by contracting out to private firms. This policy solution reflects the belief among the public that private firms are more efficient than "bureaucrats." The problem, however, is one that is endemic to collective-action problems. The executive branch, Congress, and the public all seem inclined toward privatization, but the "public good" is often lost in the process of forging policy outcomes.

The New York Times, February 4, 2007

In Washington, Contractors Take On Biggest Role Ever

By Scott Shane and Ron Nixon

In June, short of people to process cases of incompetence and fraud by federal contractors, officials at the General Services Administration responded with what has become the government's reflexive answer to almost every problem.

They hired another contractor.

It did not matter that the company they chose, CACI International, had itself recently avoided a suspension from federal contracting; or that the work, delving into investigative files on other contractors, appeared to pose a conflict of interest; or that each person supplied by the company would cost taxpayers $104 an hour. Six CACI workers soon joined hundreds of other private-sector workers at the G.S.A., the government's management agency.

Without a public debate or formal policy decision, contractors have become a virtual fourth branch of government. On the rise for decades, spending on federal contracts has soared during the Bush administration, to about $400 billion last year from $207 billion in 2000, fueled by the war in Iraq, domestic security and Hurricane Katrina, but also by a philosophy that encourages outsourcing almost everything government does.

Contractors still build ships and satellites, but they also collect income taxes and work up agency budgets, fly pilotless spy aircraft and take the minutes at policy meetings on the war. They sit next to federal employees at nearly every agency; far more people work under contracts than are directly employed by the government. Even the government's online database for tracking contracts, the Federal Procurement Data System, has been outsourced (and is famously difficult to use).

The contracting explosion raises questions about propriety, cost and accountability that have long troubled watchdog groups and are coming under scrutiny from the Democratic majority in Congress. While flagrant cases of fraud and waste make headlines, concerns go beyond outright wrongdoing.

* * *

The contracting surge has raised bipartisan alarms. A just-completed study by experts appointed by the White House and Congress, the Acquisition Advisory Panel, found that the trend "poses a threat to the government's long-term ability to perform its mission" and could "undermine the integrity of the government's decision making."

The House Committee on Oversight and Government Reform, whose new Democratic chairman, Representative Henry A. Waxman of California, added the word "oversight" to signal his intentions, begins a series of investigative hearings on Tuesday focusing on contracts in Iraq and at the Department of Homeland Security.

"Billions of dollars are being squandered, and the taxpayer is being taken to the cleaners," said Mr. Waxman, who got an "F" rating last year from the Contract Services Association, an industry coalition. The chairman he succeeded, Representative Thomas M. Davis III, Republican of Virginia, earned an "A."

David M. Walker, who as comptroller general of the United States leads the Government Accountability Office, has urged Congress to take a hard look at the proper limits of contracting. * * *

"There's something civil servants have that the private sector doesn't," Mr. Walker said in an interview. "And that is the duty of loyalty to the greater good—the duty of loyalty to the collective best interest of all rather than the interest of a few. Companies have duties of loyalty to their shareholders, not to the country."

Even the most outspoken critics acknowledge that the government cannot operate without contractors, which provide the surge capacity to handle crises without expanding the permanent bureaucracy. Contractors provide specialized skills the government does not have. And it is no secret that some government executives favor contractors because they find the federal bureaucracy slow, inflexible or incompetent.

Stan Soloway, president of the Professional Services Council, which represents government contractors, acknowledged occasional chicanery by contractors and too little competition in some areas. But Mr. Soloway asserted that critics had exaggerated the contracting problems.

"I don't happen to think the system is fundamentally broken," he said. "It's remarkable how well it works, given the dollar volume."

* * * Wariness of government contracting dates at least to 1941, when Harry S. Truman, then a senator, de-

clared, "I have never yet found a contractor who, if not watched, would not leave the government holding the bag."

But the recent contracting boom had its origins in the "reinventing government" effort of the Clinton administration, which slashed the federal work force to the lowest level since 1960 and streamlined outsourcing. Limits on what is "inherently governmental" and therefore off-limits to contractors have grown fuzzy. * * *

* * *

If the government is exporting some traditional functions to contractors, it is also inviting contractors into agencies to perform delicate tasks. The State Department, for instance, pays more than $2 million a year to BearingPoint, the consulting giant, to provide support for Iraq policy making, running software, preparing meeting agendas and keeping minutes.

State Department officials insist that the company's workers, who hold security clearances, merely relieve diplomats of administrative tasks and never influence policy. But the presence of contractors inside closed discussions on war strategy is a notable example of what officials call the "blended work force."

That blending is taking place in virtually every agency. When Polly Endreny, 29, sought work last year with the National Oceanographic and Atmospheric Administration, she was surprised to discover that most openings were with contractors.

"The younger generation is coming in on contracts," said Ms. Endreny, who likes the arrangement. * * *

She said her pay was "a little higher" than that of comparable federal workers, and she gets dental coverage they do not. Such disparities can cause trou-

ble. A recent study of one NOAA program where two-thirds of the work force were contractors found that differences in salary and benefits could " substantially undermine staff relations and morale."

The shift away from open competition affects more than morale. One example among many: with troops short in Iraq, Congress in 2003 waived a ban on the use of private security guards to protect military bases in the United States. The results for the first $733 million were dismal, investigators at the Government Accountability Office found.

The Army spent 25 percent more than it had to because it used sole-source contracts at 46 of 57 sites, the investigators concluded. And screening of guards was so lax that at one base, 61 guards were hired despite criminal records, auditors reported. Yet the Army gave the contractors more than $18 million in incentive payments intended to reward good performance. * * *

* * *

History Principle

The rules regarding "inherently governmental" functions are changing, as government has to adapt to new technologies and new public policies.

Collective-Action Principle

A "blended" workforce means that the private contractors and the governmental agencies have a shared interest in making sure that the system continues. After all, some of the same people who are running the private firms were previously working for the government agencies.

8

The Federal Courts: Structure and Strategies

GEORGE W. BUSH won the 2000 presidential election. The final battle in the race was not decided in the electoral arena, however, and did not involve the participation of ordinary Americans. Instead, the battle was fought in the courts, in the Florida state legislature, and in the executive institutions of the Florida state government by small groups of attorneys and political activists. During the course of the dispute, some forty lawsuits were filed in the Florida circuit and supreme courts, the U.S. District Court, the U.S. Court of Appeals, and the U.S. Supreme Court.[1] The two campaigns together amassed nearly $10 million in legal fees during the month of litigation. In most of the courtroom battles, the Bush campaign prevailed. Despite two setbacks before the all-Democratic Florida Supreme Court, Bush's attorneys won most of the circuit court cases and the ultimate clash before the U.S. Supreme Court in a narrow 5–4 vote.

During the arguments before the Supreme Court, it became clear that the conservative majority was determined to prevent a Gore victory. Conservative justices were sharply critical of the arguments presented by Vice President Al Gore's lawyers and openly sympathetic to the arguments made by Bush's lawyers. The conservative justice Antonin Scalia went so far as to intervene when the Bush attorney Theodore Olson responded to a question from Justices David Souter and Ruth Bader Ginsburg. Scalia evidently sought to ensure that Olson did not concede too much to the Gore argument. "It's part of your submission, I think," Scalia said, "that there is no wrong when a machine does not count those ballots that it's not supposed to count?" Scalia was seeking to remind Olson that when voter error rendered ballots unreadable by a tabulating machine, it was not appropriate for a court to order them

---

[1]"In the Courts," *San Diego Union-Tribune*, 7 December 2000, p. A14.

counted by hand. "The voters are instructed to detach the chads entirely," Scalia said, "and if the machine does not count those chads where those instructions are not followed, there isn't any wrong." Olson was happy to accept Scalia's reminder.[2]

The liberal justice John Paul Stevens said the majority opinion smacked of partisan politics. The opinion, he said, "can only lend credence to the most cynical appraisal of the work of judges throughout the land." He concluded, "Although we may never know with complete certainty the identity of the winner of this year's presidential election, the identity of the loser is perfectly clear. It is the nation's confidence in the judge as an impartial guardian of the rule of law."[3] Justice Stevens's eloquent dissent did not change the outcome. Throughout the nation, Democrats saw the majority opinion of the Supreme Court as a blatantly partisan decision.

---

[2]Linda Greenhouse, "U.S. Supreme Court Justices Grill Bush, Gore Lawyers in Effort to Close the Book on Presidential Race," *New Orleans Times-Picayune*, 12 December 2000, p. 1.

[3]Dissenting opinion of Justice John Paul Stevens in *Bush v. Gore* 531 U.S. 98 (2000).

Although they are free from electoral considerations and constrained by precedents in ways that elected policy makers are not, federal judges and Supreme Court justices are politicians with political goals and preferences. In this sense, we can conceive of courts as political institutions. By treating courts as political institutions, we can understand them as settlers of disputes, coordinators, and interpreters of rules. In deciding cases, judges and justices must seek to reconcile their policy goals and judicial philosophies on the one hand with existing precedents on the other.

Rationality Principle

Judges have political goals and policy preferences and act to achieve them.

Policy Principle

Courts are not legislative bodies, but many important policy issues are, nevertheless, decided by the judiciary.

Nevertheless, the contest was over. The next day Al Gore made a speech conceding the election, and on December 18, 2000, 271 presidential electors—the constitutionally prescribed majority—cast their votes for George W. Bush.

What does the court battle over Florida's twenty-five electoral votes reveal about the power of courts and judges in the American political system? First of all, it shows that judges are similar to other politicians in that they have political goals and policy preferences and they act accordingly so that those goals and preferences are realized. While thinking of judges as legislators in robes is antithetical to the view that judges rule according to a well-thought-out judicial philosophy based on constitutional law, there is evidence that strategic thinking on the part of judges is also a factor in their decision-making process. Second, this battle illustrates the political power that the courts now exercise. Over the past fifty years, the prominence of the courts has been heightened by the sharp increase in the number of major policy issues that have been fought and decided in the judicial realm. But since judges are not elected and accountable to the people, what does this shift in power mean for American democracy?

In this chapter, we examine the judicial process first, including the types of cases that the federal courts consider and the types of laws with which they deal. Second, we assess the organization and structure of the federal court system and explain how judges are appointed to the courts. Third, we analyze courts as political institutions and consider their roles in the political system. Fourth, we consider judicial review and how it makes the Supreme Court a lawmaking body. Fifth, we examine the flow of cases through the courts and various influences on the Supreme Court's decisions. Finally, we analyze the process of judicial decision making and the power of the federal courts in the American political process, looking in particular at the growth of judicial power in the United States.

THE JUDICIAL PROCESS

Originally a court was the place where a sovereign ruled—where a king and his entourage governed, and judging—settling disputes between citizens—was part of

TABLE 8.1 Types of Laws and Disputes

Type of Law	Type of Case or Dispute	Form of Citation
Criminal law	Cases arising out of actions that violate laws protecting the health, safety, and morals of the community. The government is always the plaintiff.	*U.S. (or state) v. Jones* *Jones v. U.S. (or state)* if Jones lost and is appealing
Civil law	Law involving disputes between citizens or between a government and a citizen where no crime is alleged. Two general types are contract law and tort law. *Contract cases* are disputes that arise over voluntary actions. *Tort cases* are disputes that arise out of obligations inherent in social life. Negligence and slander are examples of torts.	*Smith v. Jones* *New York v. Jones* *U.S. v. Jones* *Jones v. New York*
Public law	All cases in which the powers of government or the rights of citizens are involved. The government is the defendant. *Constitutional law* involves judicial review of the basis of a government's action in relation to specific clauses of the Constitution as interpreted in Supreme Court cases. *Administrative law* involves disputes over the statutory authority, jurisdiction, or procedures of administrative agencies.	*Jones v. U.S. (or state)* *In re Jones* *Smith v. Jones* if a license or statute is at issue in their private dispute

governing. Over time, however, the function of settling disputes was slowly separated from the king and the king's court and made into a separate institution of government. Courts have taken over from kings the power to settle controversies by hearing the facts on both sides and deciding which side possesses the greater merit. But because judges are not kings, they must have a basis for their authority. That basis in the United States is the Constitution and the law. Courts decide cases by applying the relevant law or principle to the facts.

Court cases in the United States proceed under two broad categories of law: criminal and civil. One form of civil law, public law, is so important that we consider it as a separate category (Table 8.1).

Cases of ***criminal law*** are those in which the government charges an individual with violating a statute that has been enacted to protect the public health, safety, morals, or welfare. In criminal cases, the government is always the ***plaintiff*** (the party that brings charges) and alleges that a criminal violation has been committed by a named ***defendant.*** Most criminal cases arise in state and municipal courts and

criminal law The branch of law that deals with disputes or actions involving criminal penalties (as opposed to civil law). It regulates the conduct of individuals, defines crimes, and provides punishment for criminal acts.

plaintiff The individual or organization that brings a complaint in court.

defendant The individual or organization charged with a complaint in court.

involve matters ranging from traffic offenses to robbery and murder. While the great bulk of criminal law is still a state matter, a large and growing body of federal criminal law deals with such matters as tax evasion, mail fraud, and the sale of narcotics. Defendants found guilty of criminal violations may be fined or sent to prison.

Cases of *civil law* involve disputes between individuals or between individuals and the government where no criminal violation is charged. Unlike criminal cases, the losers in civil cases cannot be fined or sent to prison, although they may be required to pay monetary damages for their actions. In a civil case, the one who brings a complaint is the plaintiff and the one against whom the complaint is brought is the defendant. The two most common types of civil cases involve contracts and torts. In a typical contract case, an individual or corporation charges that it has suffered because of another's violation of a specific agreement between the two. For example, the Smith Manufacturing Corporation may charge that Jones Distributors failed to honor an agreement to deliver raw materials at a specified time, causing Smith to lose business. Smith asks the court to order Jones to compensate it for the damage allegedly suffered. In a typical tort case, one individual charges that he or she has been injured by another's negligence or malfeasance. Medical malpractice suits are one example of tort cases.

In deciding cases, courts apply statutes (laws) and legal *precedents* (prior decisions). State and federal statutes often govern the conditions under which contracts are and are not legally binding. Jones Distributors might argue that it was not obliged to fulfill its contract with the Smith Corporation because actions by Smith—the failure to make promised payments—constituted fraud under state law. Attorneys for a physician being sued for malpractice, on the other hand, may search for prior instances in which courts ruled that actions similar to those of their client did not constitute negligence. Such precedents are applied under the doctrine of **stare decisis,** a Latin phrase meaning "let the decision stand."

A case becomes a matter of a third category, *public law,* when a plaintiff or defendant in a civil or criminal case seeks to show that his or her case involves the powers of government or the rights of citizens as defined under the Constitution or by statute. One major form of public law is constitutional law, under which a court will examine the government's actions to see if they conform to the Constitution as it has been interpreted by the judiciary. Thus what began as an ordinary criminal case may enter the realm of public law if a defendant claims that his or her constitutional rights were violated by the police. Another important arena of public law is administrative law, which involves disputes over the jurisdiction, procedures, or authority of administrative agencies. Under this type of law, civil litigation between an individual and the government may become a matter of public law if the individual asserts that the government is violating a statute or abusing its power under the Constitution. For example, landowners have asserted that federal and state restrictions on land use constitute violations of the Fifth Amendment's restrictions on the government's ability to confiscate private property. Recently the Supreme Court has been very sympathetic to such claims, which effectively transform an ordinary civil dispute into a major issue of public law.

Most of the Supreme Court cases we will examine in this chapter involve judgments concerning the constitutional or statutory basis of the actions of government agencies. As we shall see, it is in this arena of public law that Court decisions can have significant consequences for American politics and society.

civil law A system of jurisprudence, including private law and governmental actions, for settling disputes that do not involve criminal penalties.

precedents Prior cases whose principles are used by judges as the bases for their decisions in present cases.

stare decisis Literally, "let the decision stand." The doctrine whereby a previous decision by a court applies as a precedent in similar cases until that decision is overruled.

public law Cases involving the action of public agencies or officials.

THE ORGANIZATION
OF THE COURT SYSTEM

Types of Courts

In the United States, systems of courts have been established both by the federal government and by the governments of the individual states. Both systems have several levels, as shown in Figure 8.1. Nearly 99 percent of all court cases in the United States are heard in state courts. The overwhelming majority of criminal cases, for example, involve violations of state laws prohibiting such actions as murder, robbery, fraud, theft, and assault. If such a case is brought to trial, it will be heard in a state *trial court* in front of a judge and sometimes a jury, who will determine whether the defendant violated state law. If the defendant is convicted, he or she may appeal the conviction to a higher court, such as a state *court of appeals,* and from there to a state's *supreme court.* Similarly, in civil cases, most litigation is brought in the courts established by the state in which the activity in question took place. For example, a patient bringing suit against a physician for malpractice would file the suit in the appropriate court in the state where the alleged malpractice occurred. The judge hearing the case would apply state law and state precedent to the matter at hand. (It should be noted that in both criminal and civil matters, most cases are settled before trial through negotiated agreements between the parties. In criminal cases, these agreements are called plea bargains. Such bargains may affect the severity of the charge and/or the severity of the sentence.)

In addition, the U.S. military operates its own court system under the Uniform Code of Military Justice, which governs the behavior of men and women in the armed services. On rare occasions, the government has constituted special military tribunals to hear cases deemed inappropriate for the civil courts. Such tribunals tried Nazi saboteurs apprehended in the United States during World War II. More recently, President George W. Bush ordered the creation of military tribunals to try individuals suspected of acts of terrorism against the United States.

Federal Jurisdiction

Cases are heard in the federal courts if they involve federal laws, treaties with other nations, or the U.S. Constitution; these areas are the official jurisdiction of the federal courts. In addition, any case in which the U.S. government is a party is heard in the federal courts. If, for example, an individual is charged with violating a federal criminal statute, such as evading the payment of income taxes, charges would be brought before a federal judge by a federal prosecutor. Civil cases involving the citizens of more than one state and in which more than $70,000 is at stake may be heard in either the federal or the state courts, usually depending on the preference of the plaintiff.

But even if a matter belongs in federal court, how do we know which federal court should exercise jurisdiction over the case? The answer to this seemingly simple question is somewhat complex. The jurisdiction of each federal court is derived from the U.S. Constitution and federal statutes. Article III of the Constitution gives the Supreme Court appellate jurisdiction in all federal cases and original jurisdiction in

trial court The first court to hear a criminal or civil case.

court of appeals A court that hears the appeals of trial-court decisions.

supreme court The highest court in a particular state or in the United States. This court primarily serves an appellate function.

FIGURE 8.1 The U.S. Court System

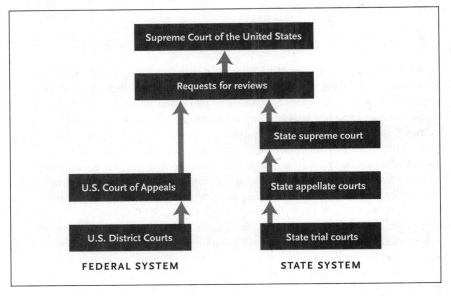

Supreme Court of the United States

Requests for reviews

State supreme court

U.S. Court of Appeals   State appellate courts

U.S. District Courts   State trial courts

FEDERAL SYSTEM   **STATE SYSTEM**

cases involving foreign ambassadors and issues in which a state is a party. Article III assigns original jurisdiction in all other federal cases to the lower courts that Congress was authorized to establish. Over the years, as Congress enacted statutes creating the federal judicial system, it specified the jurisdiction of each type of court it established. For the most part, Congress has assigned jurisdictions on the basis of geography. The nation is currently, by statute, divided into ninety-four judicial districts, including one court for each of three U.S. territories: Guam, the U.S. Virgin Islands, and the Northern Marianas. Each of the ninety-four U.S. district courts exercises jurisdiction over federal cases arising within its territorial domain. The judicial districts are, in turn, organized into eleven regional circuits and the District of Columbia circuit (Figure 8.2). Each circuit court exercises appellate jurisdiction over cases heard by the district courts within its region.

Geography is not the only basis for federal court jurisdiction. Congress has also established several specialized courts that have nationwide original jurisdiction in certain types of cases. These include the U.S. Court of International Trade, created to deal with trade and customs issues, and the U.S. Court of Federal Claims, which handles damage suits against the United States. Congress has, in addition, established a court with nationwide appellate jurisdiction. This is the U.S. Court of Appeals for the Federal Circuit, which hears appeals involving patent law and those arising from the decisions of the trade and claims courts. Other federal courts assigned specialized jurisdictions by Congress include the U.S. Court of Appeals for Veterans Claims, which exercises exclusive jurisdiction over cases involving veter-

FIGURE 8.2 Geographic Boundaries of U.S. Courts of Appeals and U.S. District Courts

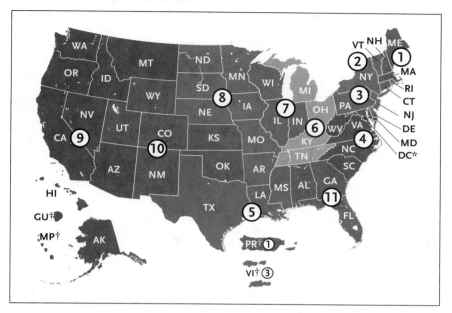

SOURCE: Administrative Office of the U.S. Courts (www.uscourts.gov/images/Circuit Map.pdf).

* The District of Columbia has its own circuit, called the D.C. Circuit.

† U.S. Postal Service abbreviations for Guam (GU), Northern Mariana Island (MP), Puerto Rico (PR), and the U.S. Virgin Islands (VI).

ans' claims, and the U.S. Court of Appeals for the Armed Forces, which deals with questions of law arising from trials by court-martial.

With the exception of the claims court and the Court of Appeals for the Federal Circuit, these specialized courts were created not in accordance with Article III of the Constitution but by Congress on the basis of the powers the legislature exercises under Article I. Article III was designed to protect judges from political pressure by granting them life tenure and prohibiting reduction of their salaries while they serve. The judges of Article I courts, by contrast, are appointed by the president for fixed terms of fifteen years and are not protected by the Constitution from salary reduction. As a result, these so-called legislative courts are generally viewed as less independent than the courts established under Article III of the Constitution. The three territorial courts were also established under Article I, and their judges are appointed for ten-year terms.

The appellate jurisdiction of the federal courts also extends to cases originating in the state courts. In both civil and criminal cases, a decision of the highest state court can be appealed to the U.S. Supreme Court by raising a federal issue. Appellants might assert, for example, that they were denied the right to counsel or otherwise deprived of the *due process* guaranteed by the federal Constitution, or they might assert that important issues of federal law were at stake in the case. The U.S. Supreme Court is not obligated to accept such appeals and will accept them only if it believes that the matter has considerable national significance. (We shall return to this topic later in this chapter.) In addition, in criminal cases defendants who have been convicted in a state court may request a *writ of* **habeas corpus** from a federal district court. Sometimes known as the Great Writ, *habeas corpus* is a court order to the authorities to release a prisoner deemed to be held in violation of his or her legal rights. In 1867, its distrust of southern courts led Congress to authorize federal district judges to issue such writs to prisoners they believed had been deprived of their constitutional rights in state court. Generally speaking, state defendants seeking a federal writ of *habeas corpus* must show that they have exhausted all available state remedies and raise issues not previously raised in their state appeals. Federal courts of appeals and, ultimately, the U.S. Supreme Court have appellate jurisdiction over federal district court *habeas* decisions.

Over the past three decades, the caseload of the federal courts has nearly quadrupled, to nearly 350,000 cases a year. This has come about because Congress has greatly expanded the number of federal crimes, particularly in the realm of drug possession and sale. Behavior that was once exclusively a state criminal question has, to some extent, come within the reach of federal law. In 1999, Chief Justice William Rehnquist criticized Congress for federalizing too many offenses and intruding unnecessarily into areas that should be handled by the states.[4] About 80 percent of federal cases end in the district courts, and the remainder are appealed to the circuit courts. In the past five years, moreover, between 8,500 and 9,500 circuit court decisions per year were appealed to the Supreme Court. Most of the cases filed with the Supreme Court are dismissed without a ruling on their merits. The Court has broad latitude to decide what cases it will hear and generally listens only to those it deems to raise the most important issues. Thus in the last five years, between 84 and 91 cases per year were given full-dress Supreme Court review (the nine justices actually sitting *en banc*—in full court—and hearing lawyers argue the case).[5]

Although the federal courts hear only a small fraction of all the civil and criminal cases decided each year in the United States, their decisions are extremely important. It is in the federal courts that the Constitution and federal laws that govern all Americans are interpreted and their meaning and significance established. Moreover, it is in the federal courts that the powers and limitations of the increasingly powerful national government are tested. Finally, through their power to review the decisions of the state courts, it is ultimately the federal courts that dominate the American judicial system.

Federal Trial Courts

The federal district courts are trial courts of general jurisdiction, and their cases are, in form, indistinguishable from cases in the state trial courts.

due process The guarantee that no citizen may be subjected to arbitrary action by national or state government.

writ of *habeas corpus* A court order demanding that an individual in custody be brought into court and shown the cause for detention. *Habeas corpus* is guaranteed by the Constitution and can be suspended only in cases of rebellion or invasion.

---

[4] Roberto Suro, "Rehnquist: Too Many Offenses Are Becoming Federal Crimes," *Washington Post*, 1 January 1999, p. A2.

[5] Administrative Office of the U.S. Courts (www.uscourts.gov), 2006.

There are eighty-nine district courts in the fifty states, one each in the District of Columbia and Puerto Rico, and one in each of the three U.S. territories. There are 663 district judgeships. District judges are assigned to district courts according to the workload; the busiest of these courts may have as many as 28 judges. Only one judge is assigned to each case, except where statutes provide for three-judge courts to deal with special issues. The routines and procedures of the federal district courts are essentially the same as those of the lower state courts except that federal procedural requirements tend to be stricter. States, for example, do not have to provide a grand jury, a twelve-member trial jury, or a unanimous jury verdict. Federal courts must provide all these things. As we saw above, in addition to the district courts, cases are handled by several specialized courts, including the U.S. Tax Court, the Court of Federal Claims, and the Court of International Trade.

Federal Appellate Courts

Roughly 20 percent of all lower-court cases, along with appeals of some federal agency decisions, are subsequently reviewed by a federal appeals court. As noted, the country is divided into twelve judicial circuits, each with a U.S. Court of Appeals. Every state and the District of Columbia are assigned to the circuit in the continental United States that is closest to it. A thirteenth appellate court, the U.S. Court of Appeals for the Federal Circuit, is defined by subject matter (patent law and decisions of trade and claims courts) rather than geographic jurisdiction.

Except for cases selected for review by the Supreme Court, decisions made by the appeals courts are final. Because of this finality, certain safeguards have been built into the system. The most important is the provision of more than one judge for every appeals case. Each court of appeals has from three to twenty-eight permanent judgeships, depending on the workload of the circuit. Although normally three judges hear appealed cases, in some instances a larger number of judges sit together *en banc*.

Another safeguard is provided by the assignment of a Supreme Court justice as the circuit justice for each of the twelve circuits. The circuit justice deals with requests for special action by the Supreme Court. The most frequent and best-known action of circuit justices is that of reviewing requests for stays of execution when the full Court is unable to do so—mainly during the summer, when the Court is in recess.

The Supreme Court

The Supreme Court is America's highest court. Article III of the Constitution vests "the judicial Power of the United States" in the Supreme Court, and this court is supreme in fact as well as form. The Supreme Court is made up of a chief justice and eight associate justices. The **chief justice** presides over the Court's public sessions and conferences. In the Court's actual deliberations and decisions, however, the chief justice has no more authority than his colleagues. Each justice casts one vote. The chief justice, though, is always the first to speak and the last to vote when the justices deliberate. In addition, if the chief justice has voted with the majority, he decides which of the justices will write the formal opinion for the Court. To some extent, the influence of the chief justice is a function of his leadership ability. Some

chief justice The justice on the Supreme Court who presides over the Court's public sessions.

chief justices, such as Earl Warren, have been able to lead the court in a new direction. In other instances, a forceful associate justice, such as Felix Frankfurter, is the dominant figure on the Court.

The Constitution does not specify the number of justices that should sit on the Supreme Court; Congress has the authority to change the Court's size. In the early nineteenth century, there were six Supreme Court justices; later there were seven. Congress set the number of justices at nine in 1869, and the Court has remained that size ever since. In 1937, President Franklin D. Roosevelt, infuriated by several Supreme Court decisions that struck down New Deal programs, asked Congress to enlarge the Court so that he could add sympathetic justices to the bench. Although Congress balked at Roosevelt's "Court-packing" plan, the Court gave in to FDR's pressure and began to take a more favorable view of his policy initiatives. The president, in turn, dropped his efforts to enlarge the Court. The Court's surrender to FDR came to be known as "the switch in time that saved nine."[6]

How Judges Are Appointed

Federal judges are appointed by the president and are generally selected from the more prominent or politically active members of the legal profession. Many federal judges previously served as state court judges or state or local prosecutors. Before the president formally nominates a candidate for a district judgeship, however, the senators from the nominee's state must indicate that they support him or her. This is an informal but seldom violated practice called *senatorial courtesy.* If one or both senators from a prospective nominee's home state belong to the president's political party, the president will almost invariably consult them and secure their blessing for the nomination. Because the president's party in the Senate will rarely support a nominee opposed by a home-state senator from their ranks, this arrangement gives these senators virtual veto power over appointments to the federal bench in their own states. Senators often see such a nomination as a way to reward important allies and contributors in their states. If the state has no senator from the president's party, the governor or members of the state's House delegation may make suggestions. In general, presidents endeavor to appoint judges who possess legal experience and good character and whose partisan and ideological views are similar to theirs. During the presidencies of Richard Nixon, Ronald Reagan, and George H. W. Bush, most federal judicial appointees were conservative Republicans. Indeed, Bush established an advisory committee to screen judicial nominees to make certain their legal and political philosophies were sufficiently conservative. Bill Clinton's appointees to the federal bench, on the other hand, tended to be liberal Democrats. Following the example of Jimmy Carter, Clinton also made a major effort to appoint women and African Americans to the federal courts. Nearly half his nominees were drawn from these groups.

Once the president has formally nominated an individual, the nominee must be considered by the Senate Judiciary Committee and confirmed by a majority vote

Collective-Action Principle

Appointments to the federal bench involve informal bargaining (senatorial courtesy) as well as formal bargaining (Senate confirmation).

senatorial courtesy The practice whereby the president, before formally nominating a person for a federal judgeship, finds out whether the senators from the candidate's state support the nomination.

---

[6]For an alternative view, see David R. Mayhew, "Supermajority Rule in the Senate," *PS: Political Science and Politics* 36 (2003): 31–36

in the full Senate. In recent years, the Senate Judiciary Committee has sought to signal the president when it has qualms about a judicial nomination. After the Republicans won control of the Senate in 1994, for example, the Judiciary Committee chair, Orrin Hatch of Utah, let President Clinton know that he considered two of the president's nominees to be too liberal. The president withdrew the nominations.

Federal appeals court nominations follow much the same pattern. Because appeals court judges preside over jurisdictions that include several states, however, senators do not have as strong a role in proposing potential candidates. Instead, potential candidates are generally suggested to the president by the Justice Department or by important members of the administration. The senators from the nominee's state are still consulted before the president formally acts.

During President George W. Bush's first two years in office, Democrats controlled the Senate and used their majority on the Judiciary Committee to block eight of the president's first eleven federal court nominations. After the GOP won a narrow Senate majority in the 2002 national elections, Democrats used a filibuster to block action on several other federal appeals court nominees. Both Democrats and Republicans saw struggles over lower-court slots as practice and preparation for all-out partisan warfare over the next Supreme Court vacancy. President Bush occasionally followed a successful strategy when nominees were victimized by partisan fighting. Instead of withdrawing a nominee blocked by Democrats in the Senate, he waited until the Senate was in recess and then appointed the nominee provisionally, the appointment lasting until the end of the Congress. The appointment then terminated unless the president resubmitted the nomination.

If political factors play an important role in the selection of district and appellate court judges, they are decisive when it comes to Supreme Court appointments. Because the high court has so much influence over American law and politics, virtually all presidents have made an effort to select justices who share their own political philosophy. Presidents Ronald Reagan and George H. W. Bush, for example, appointed five justices whom they believed to have conservative perspectives: Sandra Day O'Connor, Antonin Scalia, Anthony Kennedy, David Souter, and Clarence Thomas. Reagan also elevated William Rehnquist to the position of chief justice. Reagan and George H. W. Bush sought appointees who believed in reducing government intervention in the economy and supported the moral positions taken by the Republican party in recent years, particularly opposition to abortion. However, not all the Reagan and Bush appointees fulfilled their sponsors' expectations. David Souter, for example, appointed by President George H. W. Bush, has been attacked by conservatives as a turncoat for his decisions on school prayer and abortion rights. Nevertheless, through their appointments, Reagan and George H. W. Bush were able to create a far more conservative Supreme Court. For his part, President Clinton endeavored to appoint liberal justices. He named Ruth Bader Ginsburg and Stephen Breyer to the Court, hoping to counteract the influence of the Reagan and Bush appointees.

In 2005, President George W. Bush was given an opportunity to put his own stamp on the Supreme Court after Justice O'Connor announced her decision to retire and Chief Justice Rehnquist died (Table 8.2). Bush quickly nominated federal appeals court judge John Roberts, initially to replace O'Connor and then as Chief Justice after Rehnquist's death. Roberts, a moderate conservative with a brilliant

TABLE 8.2 Supreme Court Justices, 2007

Name	Year of Birth	Prior Experience	President Who Made the Appointment	Year of Appointment
John G. Roberts Jr.,* Chief Justice	1955	Federal judge	G. W. Bush	2005
John Paul Stevens	1920	Federal judge	Ford	1975
Antonin Scalia	1936	Federal judge	Reagan	1986
Anthony M. Kennedy	1936	Federal judge	Reagan	1988
David Hackett Souter	1939	Federal judge	G. H. W. Bush	1990
Clarence Thomas	1948	Federal judge	G. H. W. Bush	1991
Ruth Bader Ginsburg	1933	Federal judge	Clinton	1993
Stephen G. Breyer	1938	Federal judge	Clinton	1994
Samuel A. Alito Jr.	1950	Federal judge	G. W. Bush	2006

*Appointed chief justice by George W. Bush in 2005.

legal record, provoked some Democratic opposition but was confirmed without much difficulty. Bush's next nominee, though, sparked an intense battle within the president's party. To the surprise of most observers, the president named a long-time associate, White House counsel Harriet Miers, to replace O'Connor. Many Republicans viewed Miers as merely a Bush crony who lacked judicial qualifications and was insufficiently supportive of conservative causes. Opposition to Miers within the GOP was so intense that Democrats remained gleefully silent as the president was forced to allow her to withdraw her name from consideration. In the wake of the Miers debacle, President Bush turned to a more conventional nominee, federal appeals court judge Samuel Alito, who pleased conservative Republicans. Democrats and liberal political forces attempted to block the nomination but ultimately failed, and Alito was confirmed in February 2006. Senator John Kerry (D-Mass.) led a brief filibuster that was easily overcome, with many of his Democratic colleagues voting to end it.

Typically in recent years, after the president has named a nominee, interest groups opposed to the nomination have mobilized opposition in the media, the public, and the Senate. When former president Bush proposed the conservative judge Clarence Thomas in 1991, for example, liberal groups launched a campaign to discredit the nominee. After extensive research into his background, opponents of the nomination were able to produce evidence suggesting that Thomas had sexually harassed a former subordinate, Anita Hill, a charge Thomas steadfastly denied. After contentious Senate Judiciary Committee hearing, highlighted by testimony by Thomas and Hill, Thomas narrowly won confirmation.

Likewise, conservative interest groups carefully scrutinized Bill Clinton's more liberal nominees, hoping to find information about them that would sabotage their appointments. During his two opportunities to name Supreme Court justices, Clinton was compelled to drop several potential appointees because of information unearthed by political opponents.

These struggles over judicial appointments indicate the growing intensity of partisanship in the United States today. They also indicate how much importance competing political forces attach to Supreme Court appointments. Because the contending forces see the outcome as critical, they are willing to engage in a fierce struggle when Supreme Court appointments are at stake.

The matter of judicial appointments became an important issue in the 2000 and 2004 elections. Democrats charged that if he were elected president, George W. Bush would appoint conservative judges who might, among other things, reverse the *Roe v. Wade* decision[7] and curb abortion rights. Bush would say only that he would seek judges who would uphold the Constitution without reading their own political biases into the document. In 2008, both Democrats and Republicans pointed to the composition of the federal judiciary as an important campaign issue. Both Obama and McCain promised to appoint only the best-qualified judges and to use no political "litmus test" in choosing their appointees, but it seemed clear that "best-qualified" meant different things to Democrats and Republicans.

HOW DO COURTS WORK AS POLITICAL INSTITUTIONS?

Judges are central players in important political institutions, and this role makes them politicians. To understand what animates judicial behavior, we need to place the judge or justice in context by considering the role of the courts in the political system more generally. In doing so, we emphasize the role of the courts as dispute resolvers, coordinators, and interpreters of rules.

Dispute Resolution

So much productive activity occurs in a modern society because its members do not have to devote substantial resources to protecting themselves and their property or monitoring compliance with agreements.[8] For any potential violation of person or property or defection from an agreement, all parties know in advance that an aggrieved party may take an alleged violator to court. The court, in turn, serves as a venue in which the facts of a case are established, punishment is meted out to violators, and compensation awarded to victims. An employee, for example, may sue his

---

[7] *Roe v. Wade,* 410 U.S. 113 (1973).

[8] If extraordinary resources had to be devoted to those activities, their rising cost would cause the frequency of productive activities to decline. Indeed, because the costs of negotiating, monitoring, and enforcing agreements (what political economists call transaction costs) can be very high, they are a serious impediment to social interaction and productive activities of all sorts. Economizing on them—by providing the services of courts and judges, for example—is one of the modern state's great contributions to social welfare.

or her employer for allegedly violating the terms of a privately negotiated employment contract. Or a consumer may sue a producer for violating the terms of a product warranty. The court, then, is an institution that engages in fact-finding and judgment. It provides the service of dispute resolution. In criminal cases, the "aggrieved party" is not only the victim of the crime but also the entire society whose laws have been violated.

Coordination

Dispute resolution occurs after the fact—that is, after a dispute has occurred. We may also think of courts and judges as before-the-fact coordination mechanisms inasmuch as the anticipation of legal consequences allows private parties to form rational expectations and thereby coordinate their actions in advance of possible disputes. A prospective embezzler, estimating the odds of getting caught, prosecuted, and subsequently punished, may think twice about cheating his partner. Conversely, the legal system can work as an incentive: Two acquaintances, for example, may confidently entertain the possibility of going into business together, knowing that the sword of justice hangs over their collaboration.

In this sense, the court system is as important for what it doesn't do as for what it does. The system of courts and law coordinates private behavior by providing incentives and disincentives for specific actions. To the extent that these work, there are fewer disputes to resolve and thus less after-the-fact dispute resolution for courts and judges to engage in.

Collective-Action Principle

The legal system coordinates private behavior by providing incentives and disincentives for specific actions.

Rule Interpretation

Dispute resolution and coordination affect private behavior and the daily lives of ordinary citizens tremendously. Judges, however, are not entirely free agents. In matching the facts of a specific case to judicial principles and statutory guidelines, judges must engage in interpretive activity: They must determine what particular statutes or judicial principles mean, which of them fit the facts of a particular case, and then, having determined this, ascertain the disposition of the case at hand. Does the statute of 1927 regulating the electronic transmission of radio waves apply to television, cellular phones, ship-to-shore radios, fax machines, and e-mail? Does the law governing the transportation of dangerous substances, passed in 1937, apply to nuclear fuels, infected animals, and artificially created biological hazards? Often the enacting legislative body has not been entirely clear about the scope of the legislation it passed.

Interpreting the rules is probably the single most important activity in which higher courts engage. This is because the court system is hierarchical in the sense that judgments by higher courts constrain the discretion of judges in lower courts. If the Supreme Court rules that nuclear fuels are covered by the 1937 law on transporting dangerous substances, then lower courts must render subsequent judgments in a manner consistent with this ruling.

As we shall see in the following section, courts and judges engage not only in statutory interpretation but in constitutional interpretation as well. Here they interpret the provisions of the U.S. Constitution, determining their scope and content. In determining, for example, whether the act of Congress regulating the transportation of dangerous substances from one state to another is constitutional, the justices of the Supreme Court might appeal to the commerce clause of the Constitution (allowing the federal government to regulate interstate commerce) to justify the constitutionality of the act. On the other hand, a Supreme Court majority might also rule that a shipment of spent fuel rods from a nuclear reactor in Kansas City to a nuclear-waste facility outside St. Louis is *not* covered by this law because the shipment took place entirely within the boundaries of a single state and thus did not constitute interstate commerce.

In short, judges and justices are continually engaged in elaborating, embellishing, even rewriting the rules by which private and public life are organized. However, judicial interpretation—elaboration, embellishment, and "redrafting"—of statutes is naturally subject to review. Statutory interpretation, even if it is conducted by the highest court in the land, is exposed to legislative review. If Congress is unhappy with a specific statutory interpretation, then it may amend the legislation so as to overcome the Court's objection or even reverse its ruling. In January 2005, for example, the Supreme Court struck down the mandatory-sentencing rules enacted by Congress in 1984.[9] The rules severely limited judicial discretion in the realm of sentencing and had long been resented by the bench. Members of Congress vowed to reinstate the guidelines through new legislation. Senator Jeff Sessions (R-Ala.) said, "The challenge will be to . . . re-create the guidelines in a way that will meet the court's test."[10] Of course, if the court makes a *constitutional* ruling, Congress cannot then abrogate that ruling through new legislation. Congress would need to commence the process of constitutional amendment to overturn a constitutional interpretation with which it disagreed.

THE POWER OF JUDICIAL REVIEW

The phrase *judicial review* refers to the power of the judiciary to examine and, if necessary, invalidate actions undertaken by the legislative and executive branches. The phrase is sometimes also used to describe the scrutiny that appellate courts give to the actions of trial courts, but strictly speaking, that is an improper usage. A higher court's examination of a lower court's decisions might be called appellate review, but it is not judicial review (Figure 8.3).

Judicial Review of Acts of Congress

Because the Constitution does not give the Supreme Court the power of judicial review of congressional enactments, the Court's exercise of it may be seen as something of a usurpation. Among the proposals debated at the Constitutional

judicial review The power of the courts to declare actions of the legislative and executive branches invalid or unconstitutional. The Supreme Court asserted this power in *Marbury v. Madison* (1803).

---

[9] *United States v. Booker*, 543 U.S. 220 (2005).

[10] Quoted in Carl Hulse and Adam Liptak, "New Fight over Controlling Punishments Is Widely Seen," *New York Times*, 13 January 2005, p. A27.

FIGURE 8.3 Judicial Review

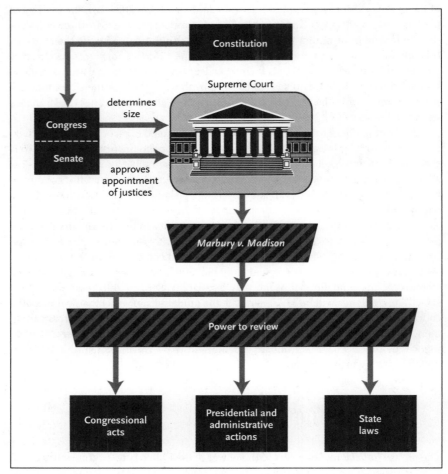

Convention was one to create a council composed of the president and the judiciary that would share the veto power over legislation. Another proposal was to route all legislation through both the Court and the president; overruling a veto by either one would have required a two-thirds vote of the House and the Senate. Those and other proposals were rejected by the delegates, and no further effort was made to give the Supreme Court review power over the other branches. This does not prove that the framers of the Constitution opposed judicial review, but it does indicate that "if they intended to provide for it in the Constitution, they did so in a most obscure fashion."[11]

---

[11]C. Herman Pritchett, *The American Constitution* (New York: McGraw-Hill, 1959), p. 138.

Disputes over the intentions of the framers were settled in 1803 in the case of *Marbury v. Madison.*[12] In that case, William Marbury sued Secretary of State James Madison for Madison's failure to complete Marbury's appointment to a lower judgeship that had been initiated by the outgoing administration of President John Adams. Quite apart from the details of the case, Chief Justice John Marshall, speaking on behalf of the court, used the case to declare a portion of a law unconstitutional. In effect, he stated that while the substance of Marbury's request was not unreasonable, the Court's jurisdiction in the matter was based on a section of the Judiciary Act of 1789, which the Court declared unconstitutional.

Although Congress and the president have often been at odds with the Court, its legal power to review acts of Congress has not been seriously questioned since 1803. One reason is that judicial power has been accepted as natural, if not intended. Another reason is that during the early years of the Republic, the Supreme Court was careful to use its power sparingly, striking down only two pieces of legislation during the first seventy-five years of its history. One of these decisions was the 1857 *Dred Scott* ruling, which invalidated the Missouri Compromise and helped precipitate the Civil War. In *Dred Scott v. Sandford,* Chief Justice Roger Taney wrote in the Court's majority opinion that the fact that a slave, Dred Scott, had been transported to a free state (Illinois) and a free territory (Wisconsin) before returning to the slave state of Missouri did not alter the fact that he was property.[13] This ruling had the effect of invalidating a portion of the Missouri Compromise of 1820, thus permitting slavery in all the country's territories. In recent years, with the power of judicial review securely accepted, the Court has been more willing to use it. Between 1986 and 2007, the Supreme Court struck down more than thirty-six acts of Congress.

Judicial Review of State Actions

The power of the Supreme Court to review state legislation or other state action and to determine its constitutionality is neither granted by the Constitution nor inherent in the federal system. But the logic of the **supremacy clause** of Article VI of the Constitution—which declares the Constitution and laws made under its authority to be the supreme law of the land—is very strong. Furthermore, in the Judiciary Act of 1789, Congress conferred on the Supreme Court the power to reverse state constitutions and laws whenever they are clearly in conflict with the U.S. Constitution, federal laws, or treaties.[14] This power gives the Supreme Court jurisdiction over all of the millions of cases handled by American courts each year.

The civil rights area abounds with examples of state laws that were overturned because the statutes violated the guarantees of due process and equal protection contained in the Fourteenth Amendment to the Constitution. For example, in the 1954 case of *Brown v. Board of Education,* the Court overturned statutes in Kansas, South Carolina, Virginia, and Delaware that either required or permitted segregated public schools, on the basis that such statutes denied black schoolchildren equal

History Principle

Since *Marbury v. Madison* (1803), the power of judicial review has not been in question.

supremacy clause
A clause of Article VI of the Constitution that states that all laws passed by the national government and all treaties are the supreme laws of the land and superior to all laws adopted by any state or any subdivision.

---

[12] *Marbury v. Madison,* 1 Cranch 137 (1803).

[13] *Dred Scott v. Sandford,* 60 U.S. 393 (1857).

[14] This review power was affirmed by the Supreme Court in *Martin v. Hunter's Lessee,* 14 U.S. 304 (1816).

ONLINE READING

ONLINE READING

protection of the law.[15] In 1967 in *Loving v. Virginia*, the Court invalidated a Virginia statute prohibiting interracial marriages.[16] State statutes in other areas are equally subject to challenge. In *Griswold v. Connecticut*, the Court invalidated a Connecticut statute prohibiting the general distribution of contraceptives to married couples, on the basis that the statute violated the couples' right to marital privacy.[17]

Judicial Review of Federal Agency Actions

Although Congress makes the law, as we saw in Chapters 5 and 7, Congress can hardly administer the thousands of programs it has enacted and must delegate power to the president and to a huge bureaucracy to achieve its purpose. For example, if Congress wishes to improve air quality, it cannot possibly anticipate all the conditions and circumstances that may arise over the years with respect to its general goal. Inevitably Congress must delegate to the executive substantial discretionary power to make judgments about the best ways to bring about improved air quality in the face of changing circumstances. Thus, over the years, almost any congressional program will result in thousands and thousands of pages of administrative regulations developed by executive agencies nominally seeking to implement the will of Congress.

The issue of delegation of power has led to a number of court decisions over the past two centuries, generally involving the question of the scope of the delegation. Courts have also been called on to decide whether the rules and regulations adopted by federal agencies are consistent with Congress's express or implied intent.

As presidential power expanded during the New Deal era, one measure of increased congressional subordination to the executive was the enactment of laws that contained few if any principles limiting executive discretion. Congress enacted legislation, often at the president's behest, that gave the executive virtually unfettered authority to address a particular concern. For example, the Emergency Price Control Act of 1942 authorized the executive to set "fair and equitable" prices without offering any indication of what those terms might mean. Although the Court initially challenged these delegations of power to the president during the New Deal, a confrontation with President Franklin Roosevelt caused the Court to retreat from its position. Perhaps as a result, no congressional delegation of power to the president has been struck down as impermissibly broad since then. In the last two decades in particular, the Supreme Court has found that as long as federal agencies developed rules and regulations "based upon a permissible construction" or "reasonable interpretation" of Congress's statute, the judiciary would accept the views of the executive branch.[18] Generally the courts give considerable deference to administrative agencies as long as those agencies have engaged in a formal rule-making process and can show that they have carried out the conditions prescribed by the various statutes governing agency rule making. These statutes include the 1946 Administrative Procedure Act, which re-

---

[15] *Brown v. Board of Education*, 347 U.S. 483 (1954).

[16] *Loving v. Virginia*, 388 U.S. 1 (1967).

[17] *Griswold v. Connecticut*, 381 U.S. 479 (1965).

[18] *Cookman Realty Group, Inc. v. West Virginia Division of Environmental Protection*, no. 30116 (W.Va. S. Ct. App. 2002).

quires agencies to notify parties affected by proposed rules and to allow them ample time to comment on such rules before they go into effect.

Judicial Review and Presidential Power

The federal courts are also called on to review the actions of the president. As we saw in Chapter 6, presidents have increasingly made use of unilateral executive powers rather than relying on congressional legislation to achieve their objectives. On many occasions, presidential orders and actions have been challenged in the federal courts by members of Congress and by individuals and groups opposing the president's policies. In recent years, assertions of presidential power in such realms as foreign policy, war and emergency powers, legislative power, and administrative authority have, more often than not, been upheld by the federal bench. Indeed, the federal judiciary has sometimes taken extraordinary presidential claims that were made for limited and temporary purposes and rationalized them—that is, the Court has converted them into routine and permanent instruments of presidential government. Take, for example, Richard Nixon's sweeping claims of executive privilege. In *United States v. Nixon,* the Court, to be sure, rejected the president's refusal to turn over tape recordings to congressional investigators. For the first time, though, the justices recognized the validity of the principle of executive privilege and discussed the situations in which such claims might be appropriate.[19] This judicial recognition of executive privilege encouraged Presidents Bill Clinton and George W. Bush to base broad claims on that principle during their terms in office.[20] Executive privilege has even been invoked to protect the deliberations of the vice president from congressional scrutiny, in the case of Dick Cheney's consultations with representatives of the energy industry.

This pattern of judicial deference to presidential authority is also manifest in the Supreme Court's recent decisions regarding President Bush's war on terrorism. In June 2004, the Supreme Court ruled on three cases involving the president's antiterrorism initiatives and claims of executive power and in two of them appeared to place some limits on presidential authority. Indeed, the justices had clearly been influenced by revelations that U.S. troops had abused prisoners in Iraq, and the justices sought in these cases to make a statement against the absolute denial of procedural rights to individuals in the custody of U.S. military authorities. But while the Court's decisions were widely hailed as reining in the executive branch, they fell far short of stopping presidential power in its tracks.

The most important of these cases was *Hamdi v. Rumsfeld.*[21] Yaser Esam Hamdi, apparently a Taliban soldier, was captured by American forces in Afghanistan in late 2001 and brought to the United States. Hamdi was classified as an enemy combatant and denied civil rights, including the right to counsel, despite

---

[19] *United States v. Nixon,* 418 U.S. 683 (1974).

[20] On Clinton, see Jonathan Turley, "Paradise Lost: The Clinton Administration and the Erosion of Executive Privilege," *Maryland Law Review* 60 (2001): 295. On Bush, see Jeffrey P. Carlin, "*Walker v. Cheney:* Politics, Posturing, and Executive Privilege," *Southern California Law Review* 76 (November 2002): 235.

[21] *Hamdi v. Rumsfeld,* 542 U.S. 507 (2004).

the fact that he was born in Louisiana and held U.S. citizenship. A federal district court ordered that he be given unmonitored access to counsel. This ruling was reversed by the U.S. Court of Appeals for the Fourth Circuit, however. In its opinion, the court held that in the national-security realm, the president wields "plenary and exclusive power." In essence, said the court, the president had virtually unfettered discretion in dealing with emergencies, and it was inappropriate for the judiciary to saddle presidential decisions with what the court called the "panoply of encumbrances associated with civil litigation."

In June 2004, the Supreme Court ruled that Hamdi was entitled to a lawyer and "a fair opportunity to rebut the government's factual assertions." However, the Supreme Court affirmed that the president possessed the authority to declare a U.S. citizen an enemy combatant and order that such an individual be held in federal detention. Several of the justices intimated that once designated an enemy combatant, a U.S. citizen might be tried before a military tribunal, with the normal presumption of innocence suspended. In 2006, in *Hamdan v. Rumsfeld,* the Court ruled that the military commissions established to try enemy combatants and other detainees violated both the Uniform Code of Military Justice and the Geneva Conventions.[22]

Thus the Supreme Court did assert that presidential actions were subject to judicial scrutiny and placed some constraints on the president's power. But at the same time, the Court affirmed the president's single most important claim: the unilateral power to declare individuals, including U.S. citizens, "enemy combatants" who could be detained by federal authorities under adverse legal circumstances.

Judicial Review and Lawmaking

Policy Principle

By interpreting existing statutes as well as the Constitution, judges make law.

Much of the work of the courts involves the application of statutes to a particular case at hand. Over the centuries, however, judges have developed a body of rules and principles of interpretation that are not grounded in specific statutes. This body of judge-made law is called common law.

The appellate courts are in another realm. Their rulings can be considered laws, but they are laws governing only the behavior of the judiciary. They influence citizens' conduct only because, in the words of Justice Oliver Wendell Holmes Jr. (who served on the Supreme Court from 1902 to 1932), lawyers make "prophecies of what the courts will do in fact."[23]

Institution Principle

Because the court system is hierarchical, decisions by higher courts constrain the discretion of lower-court judges.

The written opinion of an appellate court is about halfway between common law and statutory law. It is judge-made and draws heavily on the precedents of previous cases. In that it tries to articulate the rule of law controlling the case in question and future cases like it, it is like a statute. But a statute addresses itself to the future conduct of citizens, whereas a written opinion addresses itself mainly to the willingness or ability of courts in the future to take cases and render favorable opinions.

An example may help clarify the distinction. In *Gideon v. Wainwright,* the Supreme Court ordered a new trial for Clarence Earl Gideon, an indigent defendant, because he had been denied the right to legal counsel. This ruling said to all trial

---

[22] *Hamdan v. Rumsfeld,* 548 U.S. (2006).

[23] Oliver Wendell Holmes Jr., "The Path of the Law," *Harvard Law Review* 10 (1897): 457.

judges and prosecutors that henceforth they would be wasting their time if they cut corners in the trials of indigent defendants.[24] The Court was thereby predicting what it would and would not do in future cases of this sort. It also invited thousands of prisoners to appeal their convictions.

Many areas of civil law have been constructed in the same way—by judicial messages to other judges, some of which are codified eventually in legislative enactments. It has become "the law," for example, that employers are liable for injuries in the workplace without regard to negligence. But the law in this instance is simply a series of messages to lawyers that they should advise their corporate clients not to appeal injury decisions.

In the realm of criminal law, almost all the dramatic changes in the treatment of criminals and persons accused of crimes have been made by the appellate courts, especially the Supreme Court. The Supreme Court brought about a veritable revolution in the criminal process with three cases over less than five years. The first, *Gideon v. Wainwright*, in 1963, was just discussed. The second, *Escobedo v. Illinois*, in 1964, gave suspects the right to remain silent and the right to have counsel present during questioning.[25] But the decision left confusion that allowed differing decisions to be made by lower courts. In the third case, *Miranda v. Arizona*, in 1966, the Supreme Court cleared up the confusion by setting forth what is known as the Miranda rule: Arrested people have the right to remain silent, the right to be informed that anything they say can be held against them, and the right to counsel before and during police interrogation.[26]

One of the most significant changes brought about by the Supreme Court was the revolution in legislative representation unleashed by the 1962 case of *Baker v. Carr*.[27] In this landmark case, the Supreme Court held that it could no longer avoid reviewing complaints about the apportionment of seats in state legislatures. Following that decision, the federal courts went on to force reapportionment of all state, county, and local legislatures in the country.

As these various cases illustrate, the appellate courts are intimately involved in creating and interpreting laws. Many experts on court history and constitutional law criticize the federal appellate courts for being too willing to introduce radical change, even when the experts agree with the general direction of the changes. Often they are troubled by the willingness of the courts (especially the Supreme Court) to jump into such cases prematurely—before the constitutional issues have been fully clarified by decisions of district and appeals courts in many related cases in various parts of the country.[28] But from the perspective of the appellate judiciary, and especially the Supreme Court, the situation is one of choosing between the lesser of two evils: They must take the cases as they come and then weigh the risks of opening new options against the risks of embracing the status quo.

---

[24] *Gideon v. Wainwright*, 372 U.S. 335 (1963).

[25] *Escobedo v. Illinois*, 378 U.S. 478 (1964).

[26] *Miranda v. Arizona*, 384 U.S. 436 (1966).

[27] *Baker v. Carr*, 369 U.S. 186 (1962).

[28] See Philip B. Kurland, *Politics, the Constitution, and the Warren Court* (Chicago: University of Chicago Press, 1970).

THE SUPREME COURT IN ACTION

How Cases Reach the Supreme Court

Given the millions of disputes that arise every year, the job of the Supreme Court would be impossible if it were not able to control the flow of cases and its own caseload. The Supreme Court has original jurisdiction in a limited variety of cases defined by the Constitution. Original jurisdiction includes (1) cases between the United States and one of the fifty states, (2) cases between two or more states, (3) cases involving foreign ambassadors or other ministers, and (4) cases brought by one state against citizens of another state or against a foreign country. The most important of these cases are disputes between states over land, water, or old debts. Generally the Supreme Court deals with these cases by appointing a "special master," usually a retired judge, to hear the case and present a report. The Supreme Court then allows the states involved in the dispute to present arguments for or against the master's opinion.[29]

Rules of Access   Over the years, the courts have developed specific rules that govern which cases within their jurisdiction they will and will not hear. Thus the Court is an institution very much in control of its own agenda, which, according to the institution principle, gives it a great deal of independence to follow the preferences of its members. To have access to the courts, cases must meet certain criteria that are initially applied by the trial court but may be reconsidered by appellate courts. These rules of access can be broken down into three major categories: case or controversy, standing, and mootness.

Both Article III of the Constitution and Supreme Court decisions define judicial power as extending only to "cases and controversies." This means that the case before a court must be an actual controversy, not a hypothetical one, with two truly adversarial parties. The courts have interpreted this language to mean that they do not have the power to render advisory opinions to legislatures or agencies about the constitutionality of proposed laws or regulations. Furthermore, even after a law is enacted, the courts will generally refuse to consider its constitutionality until it is actually applied.

Parties to a case must also have *standing*—that is, they must show that they have a substantial stake in the outcome of the case. The traditional requirement for standing has been that one must show injury to oneself; that injury can be personal, economic, or even aesthetic, for example. In order for a group or class of people to have standing (as in class action suits), each member must show specific injury. This means that a general interest in the environment, for instance, does not provide a group with a sufficient basis for standing.

The third criterion in determining whether the Supreme Court will hear a case is *mootness.* In theory, this requirement disqualifies cases that are brought too

Institution Principle

The courts have developed specific rules of access that govern which cases within their jurisdiction they will hear.

standing The right of an individual or an organization to initiate a court case.

mootness A criterion used by courts to avoid hearing cases that no longer require resolution.

---

[29]Walter F. Murphy, "The Supreme Court of the United States," in *Encyclopedia of the American Judicial System: Studies of the Principal Institutions and Processes of Law,* ed. Robert J. Janosik (New York: Scribner, 1987).

late—after the relevant facts have changed or the problem has been resolved by other means. The criterion of mootness, however, is subject to the discretion of the courts, which have begun to relax the rules pertaining to this criterion, particularly in cases in which a situation that has been resolved is likely to come up again. In the abortion case of *Roe v. Wade*, for example, the Supreme Court rejected the lower court's argument that because the pregnancy had already come to term, the case was moot. The Court agreed to hear the case because no pregnancy was likely to outlast the lengthy appeals process.

Putting aside the formal criteria, the Supreme Court is most likely to accept cases that involve conflicting decisions by the federal circuit courts, cases that present important questions of civil rights or civil liberties, and cases in which the federal government is the appellant.[30] Ultimately, however, the question of which cases are accepted can come down to the preferences and priorities of the justices. If a number of justices believe that the Court should intervene in a particular area of policy or politics, they are likely to look for a case or cases that will serve as vehicles for judicial intervention. For many years, for example, the Court was not interested in considering challenges to affirmative action or other programs designed to provide particular benefits to minorities. In recent years, however, several of the Court's more conservative justices have been eager to push back the limits of affirmative action and racial preference and have therefore accepted a number of cases that would allow them to do so. In 1995, the Court's decisions in *Adarand Constructors v. Pena*, *Missouri v. Jenkins*, and *Miller v. Johnson* placed new restrictions on federal affirmative action programs, school desegregation efforts, and attempts to increase minority representation in Congress through the creation of "minority districts" (see Chapter 10).[31] Similarly, because some justices have felt that the Court had gone too far in restricting public support for religious ideas, the Court accepted the case of *Rosenberger v. University of Virginia*. This case was brought by a Christian student group against the University of Virginia, which had refused to provide student activities funds to support the group's magazine, *Wide Awake*. Other student publications received subsidies from the activities fund, but university policy prohibited grants to religious groups. Lower courts supported the university, finding that support for the magazine would violate the Constitution's prohibition of government support for religion. The Supreme Court, however, ruled in favor of the students' assertion that the university's policies amounted to support for some ideas but not others. The Court said this violated the students' First Amendment right of freedom of expression.[32]

Most cases reach the Supreme Court through a **writ of** certiorari (Figure 8.4). *Certiorari* is an order to a lower court to deliver the records of a particular case to be reviewed for legal errors. The term is sometimes shortened to *cert,* and cases deemed to merit *certiorari* are referred to as *certworthy*. An individual who loses in a

 Rationality Principle

The Supreme Court accepts cases based on the preferences and priorities of the justices.

---

[30]Gregory A. Caldeira and John R. Wright, "Organized Interests and Agenda Setting in the U.S. Supreme Court," *American Political Science Review* 82, no. 4 (December 1988): 1109–27.

[31]*Adarand Constructors v. Pena*, 115 U.S. 200 (1995); *Missouri v. Jenkins*, 515 U.S. 70 (1995); *Miller v. Johnson*, 515 U.S. 900 (1995).

[32]*Rosenberger v. University of Virginia*, 515 U.S. 819 (1995).

writ of *certiorari* A formal request by an appellant to have the Supreme Court review a decision of a lower court. *Certiorari* is from a Latin word meaning "to make more certain."

FIGURE 8.4 Reaching the Supreme Court through *Certiorari*

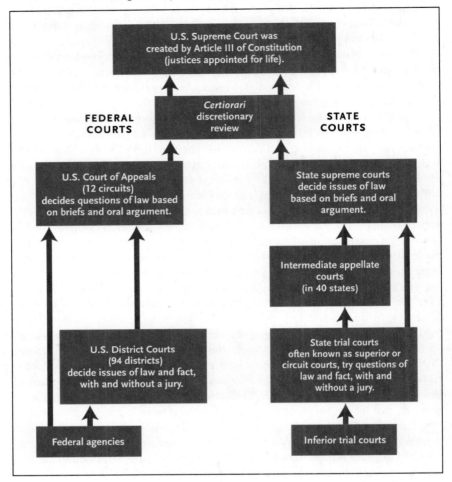

lower federal court or a state court and wants the Supreme Court to review the decision has ninety days to file a petition for a writ of *certiorari* with the clerk of the U.S. Supreme Court. There are two types of petitions: paid petitions and petitions *in forma pauperis* (in the form of a pauper). The former requires the payment of filing fees, submission of a certain number of copies, and compliance with a variety of other rules. For *in forma pauperis* petitions, which are usually filed by prison inmates, the Court waives the fees and most other requirements.

Since 1972, most of the justices have participated in a "*certiorari* pool" in which their law clerks work together to evaluate the petitions. Each petition is reviewed by one clerk, who writes a memo summarizing the facts and issues and making a recommendation for all the justices participating in the pool. Clerks for the other justices add their comments to the memo. After the justices have reviewed the memos, any one of them may place any case on the discuss list, which is circulated by the chief justice. If a case is not placed on the discuss list, it is automatically denied *certiorari*. Cases placed on the discuss list are considered and voted on during the justices' closed-door conference.

For *certiorari* to be granted, four justices must be convinced that the case satisfies Rule 10 of the Rules of the U.S. Supreme Court. Rule 10 states that *certiorari* is not a matter of right but is to be granted only when there are special and compelling reasons. These include conflicting decisions by two or more circuit courts, conflicts between circuit courts and state courts of last resort, conflicting decisions by two or more state courts of last resort, decisions by circuit courts on matters of federal law that should be settled by the Supreme Court, and a circuit court decision on an important question that conflicts with a Supreme Court decision. It should be clear from this list that the Court will usually take action under only the most compelling circumstances—when there are conflicts among the lower courts about what the law should be, when an important legal question has been raised in the lower courts and not definitively answered, and when a lower court deviates from the principles and precedents established by the high court. The support of four justices is needed for *certiorari*, and few cases are able to satisfy this requirement. In recent sessions, although thousands of petitions have been filed (Figure 8.5), the Court has granted *certiorari* to hardly more than eighty petitioners each year—about 1 percent of those seeking a Supreme Court review.

A handful of cases reach the Supreme Court through avenues other than *certiorari*. One of these is the writ of certification. This writ can be used when a U.S. Court of Appeals asks the Supreme Court for instructions on a point of law that has never been decided. A second alternative avenue is the writ of appeal, which is used to appeal the decision of a three-judge district court.

Controlling the Flow of Cases

In addition to the judges themselves, two other actors play an important role in shaping the flow of cases through the federal courts: the solicitor general and the federal law clerks.

The Solicitor General If any single person has greater influence than the individual justices over the work of the Supreme Court, it is the solicitor general of the United States. The solicitor general is third in status in the Justice Department (below the attorney general and the deputy attorney general), but he or she is the top government lawyer in virtually all cases before the appellate courts in which the government is a party. Although others can regulate the flow of cases, the solicitor general has the greatest control, with no review of his or her actions by any higher authority in the executive branch. More than half the Supreme Court's total workload consists of cases under the direct charge of the solicitor general.

The solicitor general exercises especially strong influence by screening cases long before they approach the Supreme Court; indeed, the justices rely on the solicitor general to "screen out undeserving litigation and furnish them with an agenda to

Collective-Action Principle

Four of the nine Supreme Court justices need to agree to review a case.

FIGURE 8.5 Cases Filed in the U.S. Supreme Court

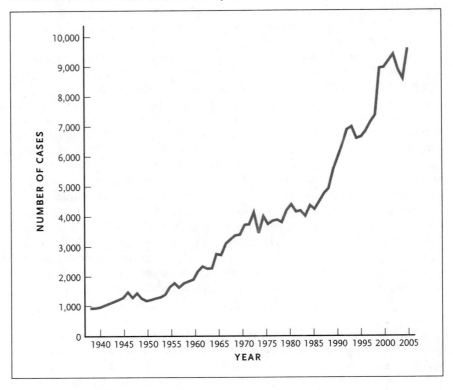

SOURCE: Years 1938–69: successive volumes of U.S. Bureau of the Census, *Statistical Abstract of the United States* (Washington, D.C.: Government Printing Office); 1970–83: Office of the Clerk of the Supreme Court; 1984–99: reprinted with permission from *The United States Law Week* (Washington, D.C.: Bureau of National Affairs), vol. 56, 3102; vol. 59, 3064; vol. 61, 3098; vol. 63, 3134; vol. 65, 3100; vol. 67, 3167; vol. 69, 3134 (copyright © Bureau of National Affairs Inc.); 2000–2002: successive volumes of U.S. Bureau of the Census, *Statistical Abstract of the United States.*

NOTE: Graph indicates the number of cases filed in the term beginning in the year indicated.

hear government cases that deserve serious consideration."[33] Typically more requests for appeals are rejected than are accepted by the solicitor general. Agency heads may lobby the president or otherwise try to circumvent the solicitor general, and a few of the independent agencies have a statutory right to make direct appeals, but without the solicitor general's support these are seldom reviewed by the Court.

The solicitor general, by writing an **amicus curiae** ("friend of the court") brief, can enter a case even when the federal government is not a direct litigant. A "friend

amicus curiae
"Friend of the court," an individual or group who is not party to a lawsuit but seeks to assist the court in reaching a decision by presenting an additional brief.

---

[33]Robert Scigliano, *The Supreme Court and the Presidency* (New York: Free Press, 1971), p. 162. For an interesting critique of the solicitor general's role during the Reagan administration, see Lincoln Caplan, "Annals of the Law," *New Yorker,* 17 August 1987, pp. 30–62.

of the court" is not a direct party to a case but has a vital interest in its outcome. Thus when the government has such an interest, the solicitor general can file as *amicus curiae,* or the Court can invite such a brief because it wants an opinion in writing. Other interested parties may file briefs as well.

In addition to exercising substantial control over the flow of cases, the solicitor general can shape the arguments used before the Court. Indeed, the Court tends to give special attention to the way the solicitor general characterizes the issues. The solicitor general is the person appearing most frequently before the Court and, theoretically at least, the most disinterested. The credibility of the solicitor general is not hurt when several times each year he or she comes to the Court to withdraw a case with the admission that the government has made an error.[34]

Law Clerks Every federal judge employs law clerks to research legal issues and assist with the preparation of opinions. Each Supreme Court justice is assigned four clerks. The clerks are almost always honors graduates of the nation's most prestigious law schools. A clerkship with a Supreme Court justice is a great honor and generally indicates that the fortunate individual is likely to reach the very top of the legal profession. One of the most important roles performed by the clerks is screening the thousands of petitions for writs of *certiorari* that come before the Court.[35] It is also likely that some justices rely heavily on their clerks for advice in writing opinions and deciding whether an individual case ought to be heard by the Court. It is often rumored that certain opinions were actually written by a clerk rather than a justice.[36] Although such rumors are difficult to substantiate, it is clear that at the end of long judicial careers, justices such as William O. Douglas and Thurgood Marshall had become so infirm that they were compelled to rely on the judgments of their law clerks.

The Supreme Court's Procedures

The Preparation The Supreme Court's decision to accept a case is the beginning of what can be a lengthy and complex process (Figure 8.6). First, the attorneys on both sides must prepare *briefs*—written documents in which the attorneys explain why the Court should rule in favor of their client. The document filed by the individual bringing the case is called the petitioner's brief. It summarizes the facts of the case and presents the legal basis on which the Supreme Court is being asked to overturn the lower court's decision. The document filed by the side that prevailed in the lower

---

[34]On the strategic and informational role played by the solicitor general, see Kevin McGuire, "Explaining Executive Success in the U.S. Supreme Court," *Political Research Quarterly* 51 (1998): 505–26. Also see Michael Bailey, Brian Kamoie, and Forrest Maltzman, "Signals from the Tenth Justice: The Political Role of the Solicitor General in Supreme Court Decision Making." *American Journal of Political Science* 49 (2005): 72–85.

[35]H. W. Perry Jr., *Deciding to Decide: Agenda Setting in the United States Supreme Court* (Cambridge, Mass.: Harvard University Press, 1991).

[36]Edward Lazarus, *Closed Chambers: The First Eyewitness Account of the Struggles inside the Supreme Court* (New York: Times Books, 1998).

briefs Written documents in which attorneys explain—using case precedents—why the Court should rule in favor of their client.

ONLINE READING

FIGURE 8.6 The Supreme Court's Decision-Making Process

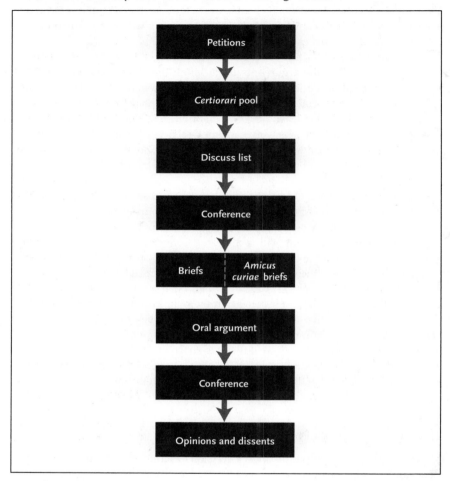

court is called the respondent's brief. It explains why the Supreme Court should affirm the lower court's verdict. The petitioners then file a brief answering and attempting to refute the points made in the respondent's brief. This document is called the petitioner's reply brief. Briefs are filled with references to precedents specifically chosen to show that other courts have frequently ruled in the same way that the Supreme Court is being asked to rule.

As the attorneys prepare their briefs, they often ask sympathetic interest groups for their help by means of *amicus curiae* briefs. In a case involving separation of church and state, for example, liberal groups such as the American Civil Liberties Union (ACLU) and People for the American Way are likely to be asked to file *amicus* briefs in support of strict separation, whereas conservative religious groups, the

Family Research Council or Focus on the Family, for example, are likely to file *amicus* briefs advocating increased public support for religious ideas. Often dozens of briefs will be filed on each side of a major case.

Oral Argument The next stage of a case is **oral argument,** in which attorneys for both sides appear before the Court to present their positions and answer the justices' questions. Each attorney has only a half hour to present his or her case, and this time includes interruptions for questions. Certain members of the Court, such as Justice Antonin Scalia, are known to interrupt attorneys dozens of times. Others, such as Justice Clarence Thomas, seldom ask questions. Oral argument can be very important to the outcome of a case. It allows justices to better understand the heart of a case and raise questions that might not have been addressed in the opposing sides' briefs. It is not uncommon for justices to go beyond the strictly legal issues and ask opposing counsel to discuss the implications of the case for the Court and the nation at large.[37]

The Conference After oral argument, the Court discusses the case in its Wednesday or Friday conference. The chief justice presides over the conference and speaks first; the other justices follow in order of seniority. The Court's conferences are secret, and no outsiders are permitted to attend. The justices discuss the case and eventually reach a decision on the basis of a majority vote. As the case is discussed, justices may try to influence or change one another's opinions. At times, this may result in compromise decisions.

Opinion Writing After a decision has been reached, one of the members of the majority is assigned to write the **opinion.** This assignment is made by the chief justice or the most senior justice in the majority if the chief justice is on the losing side. The assignment of the opinion can make a significant difference to the interpretation of a decision, as its wording and emphasis can have important implications for future litigation. Thus in assigning an opinion, the justices must give serious thought to the impression the case will make on lawyers and the public, as well as to the probability that one justice's opinion will be more widely accepted than another's.[38]

One of the more dramatic instances of this tactical consideration occurred in 1944, when Chief Justice Harlan Fiske Stone chose Justice Felix Frankfurter to write the opinion in the "white primary" case *Smith v. Allwright,* which overturned the southern practice of prohibiting black participation in primaries. The day after Stone made the assignment, Justice Robert Jackson wrote a letter to Stone arguing that Frankfurter, a foreign-born Jew from New England, would not win over the South with his opinion, regardless of his brilliance. Stone accepted the advice and

Institution Principle

The Supreme Court's procedures allow various individuals and groups to influence the decision-making process.

oral argument The stage in Supreme Court proceedings in which attorneys for both sides appear before the Court to present their positions and answer questions posed by the justices.

opinion The written explanation of the Supreme Court's decision in a particular case.

---

[37]On the consequences of oral argument for decision making, see Timothy R. Johnson, Paul J. Wahlbeck, and James F. Spriggs II, "The Influence of Oral Arguments on the U.S. Supreme Court," *American Political Science Review* 100, no. 1 (February 2006): 99–113.

[38]For this and other strategic aspects of the Court's process, see Forrest Maltzman, James F. Spriggs II, and Paul J. Wahlbeck, *Crafting Law on the Supreme Court: The Collegial Game* (New York: Cambridge University Press, 2001).

substituted Justice Stanley F. Reed, an American-born Protestant from Kentucky and a southern Democrat in good standing.[39]

Once the majority opinion is drafted, it is circulated to the other justices. Some members of the majority may agree with both the outcome and the rationale but wish to emphasize or highlight a particular point and so draft a concurring opinion, called a *regular concurrence.* In other instances, one or more justices may agree with the majority but disagree with the rationale presented in the majority opinion. Then the justices may draft a *special concurrence,* explaining their disagreements with the majority. The pattern of opinions that emerge on a case ultimately depends on bargaining among the justices, as suggested by the collective-action principle.

†††† Collective-
Action
Principle

Bargaining among
justices figures
prominently at the
opinion-drafting
stage.

Dissent Justices who disagree with the majority decision of the Court may choose to publicize the character of their disagreement in the form of a *dissenting opinion.* The dissenting opinion is generally assigned by the senior justice among the dissenters. Dissents can be used to express irritation with an outcome or to signal to defeated political forces in the nation that their position is supported by at least some members of the Court. Ironically, the most dependable way an individual justice can exercise a direct and clear influence on the Court is to write a dissent. Because there is no need to please a majority, dissenting opinions can be more eloquent and less guarded than majority opinions. The current Supreme Court often produces 5–4 decisions, with dissenters writing long and detailed opinions that, they hope, will help them convince a swing justice to join their side on the next round of cases dealing with a similar topic. Thus, for example, Justice David Souter wrote a thirty-four-page dissent in a 2002 case upholding the use of government-funded school vouchers to pay for parochial-school tuition. Souter called the decision "a dramatic departure from basic Establishment Clause principle" and went on to say that he hoped it would be reconsidered by a future court.[40]

Dissent plays a special role in the work and impact of the Court because it amounts to an appeal to lawyers all over the country to keep bringing cases of the sort at issue. Therefore, an effective dissent influences the flow of cases through the Court as well as the arguments that will be used by lawyers in later cases.

JUDICIAL DECISION MAKING

The judiciary is conservative in its procedures, but its effect on society can be radical. That effect depends on a variety of influences, two of which stand out above the rest. The first is the individual members of the Supreme Court, their attitudes and goals, and their relationships with one another. The second is the other branches of government, particularly Congress.

regular concurrence
A concurring opinion
that agrees with the
outcome and the majority's rationale but
highlights a particular
legal point.

special concurrence
A concurring opinion
that agrees with the
outcome but disagrees with the rationale presented by
the majority opinion.

dissenting opinion
A decision written by
a justice who voted
with the minority
opinion in a particular
case, in which the justice fully explains the
reasoning behind his
or her opinion.

---

[39] *Smith v. Allwright,* 321 U.S. 649 (1944).

[40] Warren Richey, "Dissenting Opinions as a Window on Future Rulings," *Christian Science Monitor,* 1 July 2002, p. 1.

The Supreme Court Justices

The Supreme Court explains its decisions in terms of law and precedent. But although law and precedent do have an effect on the Court's deliberations and eventual decisions, it is the Supreme Court that decides what laws mean and what importance precedents will have. Throughout its history, the Court has shaped and reshaped the law. If any individual judges in the country influence the federal judiciary, the Supreme Court justices are the ones who do.

From the 1950s to the 1980s, the Supreme Court took an activist role in such areas as civil rights, civil liberties, abortion, voting rights, and police procedures. For example, the Supreme Court was more responsible than any other governmental institution for breaking down America's system of racial segregation. The Supreme Court virtually prohibited states from interfering with the right of a woman to seek an abortion and sharply curtailed state restrictions on voting rights. And it was the Supreme Court that placed restrictions on the behavior of local police and prosecutors in criminal cases.

But since the early 1980s, resignations, deaths, and new appointments have led to many shifts in the mix of philosophies and ideologies represented on the Court. In a series of decisions between 1989 and 2001, the conservative justices appointed by Ronald Reagan and George H. W. Bush were able to swing the Court to a more conservative position on civil rights, affirmative action, abortion rights, property rights, criminal procedure, voting rights, desegregation, and the power of the national government.

The importance of ideology was very clear during the Court's 2000–2001 term. In important decisions, the Court's most conservative justices—Scalia, Thomas, and Rehnquist, usually joined by Kennedy—generally voted as a bloc.[41] Indeed, Scalia and Thomas voted together in 99 percent of all cases. At the same time, the Court's most liberal justices—Breyer, Ginsburg, Souter, and Stevens—also generally formed a bloc, with Ginsburg and Breyer and Ginsburg and Souter voting together 94 percent of the time.[42] Justice O'Connor, a moderate conservative, was the swing vote in many important cases.[43] This ideological division led to a number of important 5–4 decisions. In the Florida election law case, *Bush v. Gore*, Justice O'Connor joined with the conservative bloc to give Bush a 5–4 victory. Indeed, more than 33 percent of all the cases heard by the Court in its 2000–2001 term were decided by a 5–4 vote. In the Court's 2003–4 term, eight of the fourteen most important cases were also decided by a 5–4 margin.

However, precisely because the Court has been so evenly split in recent years, the conservative bloc has not always prevailed. On some issues Justice O'Connor or Justice Kennedy sided with the liberal camp, producing a 5–4 and, sometimes, a 6–3 victory for the liberals. In the 2003 case of *Missouri v. Seibert*, for example, Justice

---

[41]Linda Greenhouse, "In Year of Florida Vote, Supreme Court Also Did Much Other Work," *New York Times*, 2 July 2001, p. A12.

[42]Charles Lane, "Laying Down the Law," *Washington Post*, 1 July 2001, p. A6.

[43]For an insightful discussion about identifying the swing justice on the Court, see Andrew D. Martin, Kevin M. Quinn, and Lee Epstein, "The Median Justice on the U.S. Supreme Court," *North Carolina Law Review* 83 (2005): 1275–1322.

Consensus on the U.S. Supreme Court

For much of the nineteenth century and through the early part of the twentieth century, the Supreme Court publicly operated under what many considered to be a "norm of consensus." Justices believed that unanimity in decision making would serve to strengthen the authority of the Court and its rulings, even if disagreements persisted in private.[1] Over time, however, this behavioral norm appears to have declined among the justices serving on the Court.

▶ The proportion of unanimous decisions handed down by the Court declined sharply between 1930 and 1950, dropping from 90 percent of the cases heard to less than 20 percent. While a number of changes occurred within the judiciary during this period, no definitive explanation exists to account for this trend. Since the 1950s, there has been a modest increase in the proportion of unanimous decisions, but not to anywhere near the level that was common prior to the 1930s.

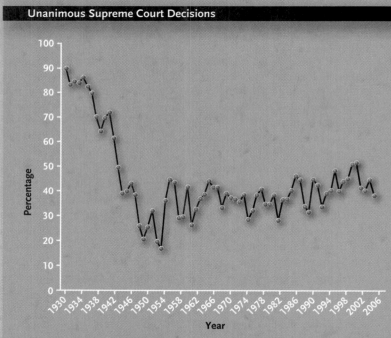

Unanimous Supreme Court Decisions

Source: Lee Epstein, Jeffrey A. Segal, Harold J. Spaeth, and Thomas G. Walker. 2003. *The Supreme Court Compendium: Data Decisions, and Developments.* 3rd edition. (Washington, DC: CQ Press, 2003).

[1]On these points, see Lee Epstein, Jeffrey A. Segal, and Harold J. Spaeth. 2001. "The Norm of Consensus on the U.S. Supreme Court." *American Journal of Political Science* 45 (April): 362–377.

As Alexander Hamilton observed in *Federalist* 78, the federal judiciary was designed to be the weakest of the three branches of government. Given that the Supreme Court is reliant upon the other branches of government to enforce its decisions, it is much easier to defend a unanimous Court decision than one that reveals a sharp divide among the justices.

▶

Federalist 78

The judiciary…has no influence over either the sword or the purse; no direction either of the strength or of the wealth of the society; and can take no active resolution whatever. It may truly be said to have neither FORCE nor WILL, but merely judgment; and must ultimately depend upon the aid of the executive arm even for the efficacy of its judgments.[2]

◀

What are the implications of the precipitous decline in unanimous decisions after 1930? Unanimously decided cases are less likely to be interpreted differently by lower court judges who consider these decisions to be established precedents, whereas decisions supported by a bare majority of justices may not be followed as strictly. Indeed, the proportion of Supreme Court cases decided by a one-vote margin has been steadily increasing since 1930.

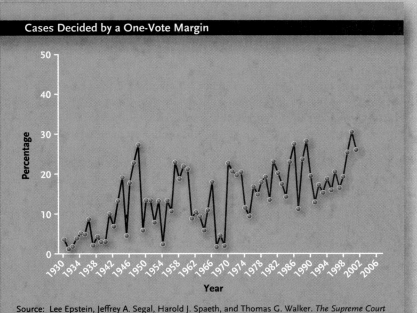

Cases Decided by a One-Vote Margin

Percentage / Year

Source: Lee Epstein, Jeffrey A. Segal, Harold J. Spaeth, and Thomas G. Walker. *The Supreme Court Compendium: Data Decisions, and Developments*. 3rd edition. (Washington, DC: CQ Press, 2003).

[2]Alexander Hamilton, *Federalist* No. 78, in *The Federalist Papers*, edited by Clinton Rossiter. (New York, Penguin: 1961).

Kennedy joined a 5–4 majority to strengthen Miranda rights.[44] Similarly, in *McConnell v. Federal Election Commission*, Justice O'Connor joined the liberal bloc to uphold the validity of the Bipartisan Campaign Reform Act.[45] On abortion, women's rights, and affirmative action, Justice O'Connor often joined the liberal bloc. With the departure of O'Connor and her replacment by Alito in 2006, many anticipated a series of new 5–4 decisions favoring the conservatives under new chief justice John Roberts.[46] In 2007, for example, the Court upheld the Partial Birth Abortion Act—a law favored by conservatives—by a 5–4 majority. However, the Court's policy influence comes not from the "horse race" results often trumpeted by the media, but from the written opinions providing the constitutional or statutory rationale for policy in the future. These opinions establish the guidelines that govern how federal courts must decide similar cases in the future. The departure of Justice O'Connor shifted the center of the Court (the part that proves pivotal in formulating opinions) to Justice Kennedy, who by many measures does not significantly differ from O'Connor in his jurisprudence. The Court's policies will probably drift rightward, but only from O'Connor's position to Kennedy's, not nearly as dramatic a difference as that between O'Connor and Alito.[47]

Activism and Restraint   One element of judicial philosophy is the issue of activism versus restraint. Over the years, some justices have believed that courts should interpret the Constitution according to the stated intentions of its framers and defer to the views of Congress when interpreting federal statutes. Justice Felix Frankfurter, for example, advocated judicial deference to legislative bodies and avoidance of the "political thicket," in which the Court would entangle itself by deciding questions that were essentially political rather than legal in character. Advocates of *judicial restraint* are sometimes called strict constructionists because they look strictly to the words of the Constitution in interpreting its meaning.

The alternative to restraint is *judicial activism.* Activist judges such as Chief Justice Earl Warren believe that the Court should go beyond the words of the Constitution or a statute to consider the broader societal implications of its decisions. Activist judges sometimes strike out in new directions, promulgating new interpretations or inventing new legal and constitutional concepts when they believe them to be socially desirable. For example, Justice Harry Blackmun's opinion in *Roe v. Wade* was based on a constitutional right to privacy that is not found in the words of the Constitution but was, rather, based on the Court's prior decision in *Griswold v. Connecticut*. Blackmun and the other members of the majority in the *Roe* case argued that the right to privacy is implied by other constitutional provisions. In this instance of judicial activism, the Court knew the result it wanted to achieve and was not afraid to make the law conform to the desired outcome.

judicial restraint The judicial philosophy whereby its adherents refuse to go beyond the text of the Constitution in interpreting its meaning.

judicial activism The judicial philosophy that posits that the Court should see beyond the text of the Constitution or a statute to consider broader societal implications for its decisions.

[44]*Missouri v. Seibert*, 542 U.S. 600 (2004).

[45]*McConnell v. Federal Election Commission*, 540 U.S. 93 (2003).

[46]Adam Liptak, "Entrances and Exits: The New 5-to-4 Supreme Court," *New York Times*, 22 April 2007.

[47]For a development of this argument, see David W. Rohde and Kenneth A. Shepsle, "Advising and Consenting in the 60-Vote Senate," *Journal of Politics* vol. 69, no. 3 (August 2007): forthcoming.

Political Ideology   The second component of judicial philosophy is political ideology. The liberal or conservative attitudes of justices play an important role in their decisions.[48] The philosophy of activism versus restraint is sometimes a smokescreen for political ideology. In the past, liberal judges have been activists, willing to use the law to achieve social and political change, whereas conservatives have been associated with judicial restraint. Conservative politicians often castigate "liberal activist" judges and call for the appointment of conservative jurists who will refrain from reinterpreting the law. It is interesting, however, that in recent years some conservative justices who have long called for restraint have become activists in seeking to undo some of the work of liberal jurists over the past three decades. To be sure, some liberal jurists are activists and some conservatives have been advocates of restraint, but the relationship is by no means one to one. Indeed, the Rehnquist Court, dominated by conservatives, was among the most activist Courts in American history, striking out in new directions in areas such as federalism and election law.

In our discussion of congressional politics in Chapter 5, we described legislators as policy oriented. In conceiving of judges as legislators in robes, we are effectively claiming that judges, like other politicians, have policy preferences that they seek to implement.

Other Institutions of Government

Congress   At both the national and the state level in the United States, courts and judges are players in the policy game because of the separation of powers. Essentially this means that the legislative branch formulates policy (defined constitutionally and institutionally by a legislative process), the executive branch implements policy (according to well-defined administrative procedures and subject to initial approval by the president or the legislative override of his veto), and the courts, when asked, rule on the faithfulness of the legislated and executed policy, either to the substance of the statute or to the Constitution itself. The courts, that is, may strike down an administrative action either because it exceeds the authority granted in the relevant statute (statutory rationale) or because the statute itself exceeds the authority granted the legislature by the Constitution (constitutional rationale).

If the Court declares the administrative agent's act as outside the permissible bounds prescribed by the legislation, we suppose the Court's majority opinion can declare whatever policy it wishes. If the legislature is unhappy with this judicial action, then it may either recraft the legislation (if the rationale for striking it down was statutory)[49] or initiate a constitutional amendment that would enable the stricken policy to pass constitutional muster (if the rationale for originally striking it down was constitutional).

---

[48]C. Herman Pritchett, *The Roosevelt Court: A Study in Judicial Politics and Values* (New York: Macmillan, 1948); Jeffrey A. Segal and Harold J. Spaeth, *The Supreme Court and the Attitudinal Model* (New York: Cambridge University Press, 1993); and by the same authors, *The Supreme Court and Attitudinal Model Revisited* (New York: Cambridge University Press, 2002).

[49]William N. Eskridge Jr., "Overriding Supreme Court Statutory Interpretation Decisions," *Yale Law Journal* 101 (1991): 331–55.

In reaching their decisions, Supreme Court justices must anticipate Congress's response. As a result, judges will not always vote according to their true preferences because doing so may provoke Congress to enact legislation that moves the policy further from what the judges prefer. By voting for a lesser preference, the justices can get something they prefer to the status quo without provoking congressional action to overturn their decision. The most famous example of this phenomenon is the "switch in time that saved nine," when two justices voted in favor of New Deal legislation, the constitutionality of which they doubted, to diminish congressional support for President Roosevelt's plan to "pack" the Court by increasing the number of justices. In short, the interactions between the Court and Congress are part of a complex strategic game.[50]

The President   The president's most direct influence on the Court is the power to nominate justices. Presidents typically nominate judges who they believe are close to their policy preferences and close enough to the preferences of a majority of senators, who must confirm the nomination.

Yet the efforts by presidents to reshape the federal judiciary are not always successful. Often in American history, judges have surprised and disappointed the presidents who named them to the bench. Justice Souter, for example, has been far less conservative than President George H. W. Bush and the Republicans who supported Souter's appointment in 1990 thought he would be. Likewise, Justices O'Connor and Kennedy disappointed conservatives by opposing limitations on abortion.

Nevertheless, with a combined total of twelve years in office, Reagan and Bush were able to exercise a good deal of influence on the composition of the federal district and appellate courts. By the end of Bush's term, he and Reagan together had appointed nearly half of all the federal judges. Thus, whatever impact Reagan and Bush ultimately had on the Supreme Court, their federal appointments have certainly had a continuing influence on the temperament and behavior of the district and circuit courts.

President Clinton promised to appoint more liberal jurists to the district and appellate courts and to increase the number of women and minorities serving on the federal bench. During his first two years in office, Clinton held to this promise (Figure 8.7). More than 50 percent of his 128 judicial nominees were women or members of minority groups.[51] A large number of judicial vacancies remained unfilled, however, when the Republicans took control of Congress at the end of 1994. Soon after the election, Senator Orrin Hatch of Utah, the new chair of the Senate Judiciary Committee, indicated his intention to oppose any nominee he deemed too liberal. Hatch's attitude prompted the Clinton White House to withdraw some nominations and to search for district and appellate nominees who would be more acceptable to the Republicans.[52]

---

[50] A fully strategic analysis of the maneuvering among legislative, executive, and judicial branches in the separation-of-powers arrangement choreographed by the U.S. Constitution may be found in William N. Eskridge Jr. and John Ferejohn, "The Article I, Section 7, Game," *Georgetown Law Review* 80 (1992): 523–65. The entire issue of this journal is devoted to the theme of strategic behavior in American institutional politics.

[51] *Chicago Daily Law Bulletin*, 5 October 1994.

[52] R. W. Apple Jr., "A Divided Government Remains, and with It the Prospect of Further Combat," *New York Times*, 7 November 1996, p. B6.

FIGURE 8.7 Diversity of Federal District Court Appointees

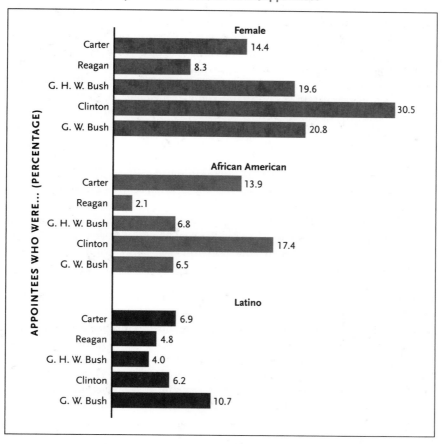

Female
- Carter: 14.4
- Reagan: 8.3
- G. H. W. Bush: 19.6
- Clinton: 30.5
- G. W. Bush: 20.8

African American
- Carter: 13.9
- Reagan: 2.1
- G. H. W. Bush: 6.8
- Clinton: 17.4
- G. W. Bush: 6.5

Latino
- Carter: 6.9
- Reagan: 4.8
- G. H. W. Bush: 4.0
- Clinton: 6.2
- G. W. Bush: 10.7

Y-axis: APPOINTEES WHO WERE... (PERCENTAGE)

SOURCE: Harold W. Stanley and Richard G. Niemi, *Vital Statistics on American Politics, 2001–2002* (Washington, D.C.: Congressional Quarterly Press, 2001), pp. 277–79, plus updates by the authors.

During President George W. Bush's first term in office, Senate Democrats fought a pitched battle with the White House to block judicial nominees they deemed too conservative. Ten of Bush's nominees to the circuit courts were blocked by Democratic filibusters, though Bush infuriated Democrats by giving two of them, Charles Pickering Sr. and William Pryor, temporary recess appointments. Democrats had hoped to block Bush's nominees until the 2004 elections and then see a Democratic president chosen. After Bush's reelection, however, the battle resumed, and Republicans threatened to change the Senate rules to prevent a continuation of the Democrats' filibuster. As noted earlier, this threat, known as the nuclear option, was ultimately shelved by the Republicans.

The Implementation of Supreme Court Decisions

The president and the rest of the executive branch, along with Congress, the states, the lower courts, and a variety of private organizations and individuals also play key roles in the implementation of Supreme Court decisions. Once the high court has made a decision, a variety of other government agencies must put it into effect. The lower courts must understand and apply to new cases the principles asserted by the Supreme Court. The executive branch must enforce the Court's decision. State legislators and governors must implement the decision in their own jurisdictions. And often individuals and organizations must take action in the courts and in the political arena to demand that the Supreme Court's verdicts be fully implemented. At each of these stages, opposition on the part of the revelant actors may delay full national implementation of a Supreme Court decision, sometimes for years.

For example, if lower-court judges strongly disagree with a Supreme Court decision, they may use a variety of tactics to avoid fully implementing it. Lower-court judges may, for example, avoid applying the case by disposing of similar cases on technical or procedural grounds. In a similar vein, they may apply the case as narrowly as possible or declare that some portion of the Court's opinion was merely "dicta"—useful as guidance but not binding.

As to executive agencies, most Supreme Court decisions must be implemented by federal, state, and local agencies. If these agencies are unsympathetic to the Court's decision, they may obstruct, delay, or even refuse to accept them. In the nineteenth century, President Andrew Jackson famously refused to obey a Supreme Court decision, declaring, "John Marshall has made his decision. Now let him enforce it." While few executives or executive agencies have been as overtly defiant as Jackson, many have quietly ignored or sought to circumvent the Court. For example, many local school boards have searched for years for ways to circumvent the high court's various rulings prohibiting religious observance in the public schools.

Strategic Behavior in the Supreme Court

In describing the role and effect of the Supreme Court, we have occasionally referred to the strategic opportunities the Court provides. It is useful to gather some of them in one place to stitch together a more consistent strategic interpretation. Let's divide this strategic behavior into three stages. Stage 1 begins with a period of "normal" politics—in (local or national) legislatures, (local or national) executive and regulatory agencies, political processes like elections, and the stuff of everyday life involving interactions among public and private entities (citizens, corporations, nonprofits, voluntary associations, governments). Conflict arises, and interested parties must decide what to do: live with the results, pursue normal political channels using legislatures and agencies to resolve the conflict, or move the conflict into the courts. Stage 2 involves a court responding to its environment, with judges both reacting to demands from the outside and fashioning their own behavioral strategies within the legal process. Stage 3 involves what happens once a court renders a decision and how the actors in stages 1 and 2 anticipate the decision and adjust their behavior to its expectations. Although our discussion could be developed for all courts, we will focus on the U.S. Supreme Court. Indeed, we will narrow things even further by devoting the bulk of our remarks to the internal strategic environment of the Supreme Court at stage 2, when it both reacts to developments that have preceded its being drawn into a conflict (stage 1) and anticipates what will happen if it responds in a particular manner (stage 3).

Stage 1   Assume that a conflict has arisen and appeals have been made through normal channels. Administrative and regulatory agencies, for example, often have well-defined procedures for appealing a ruling within the agency, with the opportunity of a subsequent appeal to a court always being available. Dissatisfied with the outcome, one of the parties moves the dispute to the courts, and at some point in the process the option of appeal to the U.S. Supreme Court is available. The aggrieved party has a decision to make. It is a calculated, strategic decision in three respects.

First, an appeal will consume resources that might otherwise be redeployed and used for different purposes. A prospective appellant must weigh an appeal against this "opportunity cost." The Sierra Club, for example, might use resources to appeal a lower-court decision on environmental protection to the Supreme Court or, alternatively, devote some of those same resources to lobby Congress on other issues.

Second, a high-court appeal sometimes competes with alternative political moves. An interest group like the Sierra Club that lost its lower-court appeals might find it more sensible to lobby Congress for a change in the National Environmental Protection Act to ameliorate the condition addressed in the legal proceedings.

Third, all options are uncertain propositions whose resolution stretches out over time. Regarding uncertainty, a prospective appellant must recognize that the probability of successfully getting to the Court is slim, and even if it succeeds in obtaining *certiorari*, it may not win on the merits of its case. Regarding the time dimension, even if the appellant wins, the process may take years, making the delayed victory bittersweet.

Ultimately these strategic calculations revolve around what an appellant can expect in pursuing an appeal—that is, what might happen in stages 2 and 3. Let us turn to them.[53]

Stage 2   As we have already reported, thousands of cases are appealed to the Supreme Court. The decision to appeal from a lower federal or state court is consummated in a petition for a writ of *certiorari*. The nine justices of the Supreme Court (or, more accurately, their clerks) must sort through these petitions and, according to the **rule of four,** build their docket each session: A case is added to the docket if four justices vote to include it. The Court, in short, has the power to create its own agenda. Appellants for each session are competing with about 10,000 others to claim one of fewer than 100 slots.

---

[53]There are subtleties to the strategies of appellants. They may seek an appeal to the Supreme Court, for example, as a bluff to induce the winner in the lower court to accommodate in advance some of their preferences—in effect, to settle out of court. Why might the lower-court winners be induced to accommodate the losers? There are at least two reasons: first, to avoid the exorbitant costs of fighting an appeal to the Supreme Court and, second, to avoid the prospect that their victory in the lower court may be reversed.

rule of four The rule that *certiorari* will be granted only if four justices vote in favor of the petition.

In building their docket for the current session of the Court, how do justices think about the available options? They support some cases undoubtedly out of a strong belief that an area is ripe for constitutional clarification. They support others out of an interest in the development of legal principles in a particular area of the law—criminal rights, privacy, First Amendment, abortion, affirmative action, federal-state relations, and so on—or in the belief that contradictory decisions in lower courts need to be sorted out. They may oppose certain appeals because they believe a particular case will not provide a sufficiently clear-cut basis for clarifying a legal issue. That is, even though a case might attract the interest of a justice on substantive grounds or might be perceived by a justice as containing procedural errors that could lead to a reversal, he or she might not support *certiorari* because of a strategic calculation that it is not a particularly good vehicle or that it would be prudent to wait until a better vehicle comes up through the appeals process in a subsequent session.[54]

Once a case is included on the docket and oral arguments have been delivered by the attorneys for the litigants and *amicus curiae* briefs filed by other interested parties, the case becomes the subject of two decisions.[55] The first takes place after it is discussed by the justices in one of the regularly scheduled conferences during the Court's term. When discussion has concluded and all attempts at persuasion have come to an end, there is a vote on the merits—a vote in favor of the appeal or against it. In principle, this vote affects only the parties to the case, either affirming or reversing the lower-court decision.

It is the second decision that has a wider bearing. Having decided one way or the other, the justices must determine whether there is agreement on the reasons for their decision. The most senior justice on the winning side—the chief justice if he is in this group—assigns a colleague to write the majority opinion or keeps it for himself to write. This is a highly strategic decision because the Court's impact over and above its effect on the contesting parties depends on the reasons it gives for the decision at hand. The reasons of a Court majority set legal precedent for similar cases in the future, thus influencing litigation in lower courts. If the majority cannot agree among themselves on why they decided as they did, there is no binding effect on other comparable cases. Drafting an opinion that can attract the signatures of at least five justices is therefore of pivotal significance. A justice on the winning side who stakes out an extreme position relative to the others is unlikely to be able to draft such an opinion, so moderate members of the Court usually do the heavy lifting of opinion drafting for especially controversial cases. Of course, in some cases a majority may agree on the merits of a case but are unable to come to a consensus on the reasons. In such cases, there will be no majority opinion, though each justice is free to write his or her own opinion (possibly co-signed by others), either supporting or dissenting from the decision on the merits, giving his or her particular reasons.

---

[54] An excellent discussion of this facet of Supreme Court decision making is found in Perry, *Deciding to Decide*.

[55] On the strategic decisions of *amicus* groups, see Thomas Hansford, "Information Provision, Organizational Constraints, and the Decision to Submit an Amicus Brief in a U.S. Supreme Court Case," *Political Research Quarterly* 57 (2004): 219–30.

These opinions have no binding effect on future lower-court cases but may still serve a strategic signaling role, conveying to the lower courts and the legal community where a justice stands on the issues involved in the case at hand.[56]

Stage 3   The Supreme Court is not an island unto itself. It is the top rung of one branch in a separation-of-powers system. Its decisions are not automatically implemented; it must depend on executive agencies for implementation and on lower courts for enforcement of its dicta. In fact, it ultimately depends on the willingness of others, especially ordinary citizens, to conform to its rulings. In some instances, the Court may worry about resistance. Throughout the 1940s and 1950s, for example, there were concerns that issues relating to integration would meet with popular disapproval and defiance in the South. Indeed, in the famous *Brown* decision desegregating public schools in 1954, Chief Justice Earl Warren worried about precisely this. When he wrote the majority opinion for the Court, he strategically softened some of its language in order to attract the signatures of all nine justices. The 9–0 decision and opinion served as a signal to a potentially defiant South that the Court was united and that it would take a very long time (the time to replace at least five justices) before there would be any prospect of reversal—that is, resistance would not pay off in the near or medium term.

In addition to compliance, enforcement, and resistance, the Court must also worry about reversal. On a decision taken by the Court on a statutory issue—for example, on whether an existing law covers a particular situation—majorities in both houses of Congress and the president may pass a new statute reversing the Court's interpretation. If, for example, the Court rules that the Radio Act of 1927 does not cover transmissions by cellular phones and Congress and the president think otherwise, then Congress may pass legislation, and the president may sign it into law, amending the Radio Act of 1927 to allow for its provisions to govern the regulation of cell phones. The Court may well say "what the law is" (to quote Justice Oliver Wendell Holmes), but Congress and the president are free to change the law.[57]

For decisions taken by the Court on constitutional (as opposed to statutory) grounds, no mere revision of existing law is sufficient to reverse the Court; an amendment to the Constitution is required. President George W. Bush, for example, has given his blessing to efforts to amend the Constitution to reverse the *Roe v. Wade* decision permitting a woman to choose an abortion in the first two trimesters of her pregnancy.

At the end of the day, the Supreme Court is the final legal authority on whether governmental and interpersonal practices satisfy statutory or Constitutional scrutiny. But as Yogi Berra put it, "It ain't over till it's over." The other branches of government must be taken into account as justices vote on cases and write legal opinions; the justices are not free agents. Hence strategic calculation cannot ever be far from their thinking.

---

[56]For an insightful discussion of the strategic elements influencing how the senior justice in the winning coalitions assigns opinion writing, see David W. Rohde, "Policy Goals, Strategic Choice, and Majority Opinion Assignments in the U.S. Supreme Court," *Midwest Journal of Political Science* 16 (1972): 652–82.

[57]On the strategic interaction among Court, Congress, and the President, see Eskridge and Ferejohn, "The Article I, Section 7, Game."

JUDICIAL POWER AND POLITICS

One of the most important institutional changes to occur in the United States during the past half century has been the striking transformation of the role and power of the federal courts and the Supreme Court in particular. Understanding how this transformation came about is the key to understanding the contemporary role of the courts in America.

Traditional Limitations on the Federal Courts

For much of American history, the power of the federal courts was subject to five limitations.[58] First, courts were constrained by judicial rules of standing that limited access to the bench. Claimants who simply disagreed with governmental action or inaction could not obtain access. Access to the courts was limited to individuals who could show that they were particularly affected by the government's behavior in some area. This limitation on access to the courts diminished the judiciary's capacity to forge links with important political and social forces. Second, courts were traditionally limited in the character of the relief they could provide. In general, courts acted to offer relief or assistance only to individuals and not to broad social classes, again inhibiting the formation of alliances between the courts and important social forces. Third, courts lacked enforcement powers of their own and were compelled to rely on executive or state agencies to ensure compliance with their edicts. If the executive or state agencies were unwilling to assist the courts, judicial enactments could go unheeded.

Fourth, federal judges are, of course, appointed by the president (with the consent of the Senate). As a result, the president and Congress can shape the composition of the federal courts and ultimately, perhaps, the character of judicial decisions. Finally, Congress has the power to change both the size and the jurisdiction of the Supreme Court and other federal courts. For example, Franklin Roosevelt's "court packing" plan encouraged the justices to drop their opposition to New Deal programs. In many areas, federal courts obtain their jurisdiction not from the Constitution but from congressional statutes. On a number of occasions, Congress has threatened to take matters out of the Court's hands when it was unhappy with the Court's policies.[59]

As a result of these five limitations on judicial power, through much of their history the chief function of the federal courts was to provide judicial support for executive agencies and to legitimate acts of Congress by declaring them consistent with constitutional principles. Only on rare occasions did the federal courts dare to challenge Congress or the executive.[60]

---

[58] For limits on judicial power, see Alexander M. Bickel, *The Least Dangerous Branch: The Supreme Court at the Bar of Politics* (Indianapolis: Bobbs-Merrill, 1962).

[59] See Walter F. Murphy, *Congress and the Court: A Case Study in the American Political Process* (Chicago: University of Chicago Press, 1962).

[60] Robert A. Dahl, "The Supreme Court and National Policy Making," *Journal of Public Law* 6 (1958): 279.

Two Judicial Revolutions

Since World War II, however, the role of the federal judiciary has been strengthened and expanded. There have actually been two judicial revolutions in the United States since the war. The first and most visible of these was the substantive revolution in judicial policy. As we saw in Chapter 4, in policy areas—including school desegregation, legislative apportionment, and criminal procedure, as well as obscenity, abortion, and voting rights—the Supreme Court was at the forefront of a series of sweeping changes in the role of the U.S. government and, ultimately, the character of American society.[61]

At the same time that the courts were introducing important policy innovations, they were bringing about a second, less visible revolution. During the 1960s and 1970s, the Supreme Court and other federal courts began a series of institutional changes in judicial procedures that had major consequences by fundamentally expanding the power of the courts in the United States. First, the federal courts liberalized the concept of standing to permit almost any group seeking to challenge the actions of an administrative agency to bring its case before the federal bench. In 1971, for example, the Supreme Court ruled that public interest groups could use the National Environmental Policy Act to challenge the actions of federal agencies by claiming that the agencies' activities might have adverse environmental consequences.[62] Congress helped make it even easier for groups dissatisfied with government policies to bring their cases to the courts by adopting Title 42, Section 1988, of the U.S. Code, which permits the practice of "fee shifting." Section 1988 allows citizens who successfully bring a suit against a public official for violating their constitutional rights to collect their attorneys' fees and costs from the government. Thus Section 1988 encourages individuals and groups to bring their problems to the courts rather than to Congress or the executive branch. These changes have given the courts a far greater role in the administrative process than ever before.

In a second institutional change, the federal courts broadened the scope of relief to permit themselves to act on behalf of broad categories or classes of persons in "class action" cases, rather than just on behalf of individuals.[63] A ***class action suit*** is a procedural device that permits a large number of persons with common interests to join together under a representative party to bring or defend a lawsuit. In 1999, for example, a consortium of several dozen law firms filed a class action suit against firearms manufacturers on behalf of victims of gun violence. Claims could ultimately amount to billions of dollars. Some of the same law firms had been involved earlier in the decade in a massive class action suit against cigarette manufacturers on behalf of the victims of tobacco-related illnesses. This suit eventually led to a settlement in which the tobacco companies agreed to pay out several billion dollars. The beneficiaries of the settlement included the treasuries of all fifty states, which received compensation for costs allegedly borne by the states in treating illnesses

Institution Principle

During the 1960s and 1970s, the courts liberalized the concept of standing.

Rationality Principle

Reducing the expected costs of litigation, through fee switching and class actions, increased the frequency of court challenges.

class action suit A lawsuit in which a large number of persons with common interests join together under a representative party to bring or defend a lawsuit, as when hundreds of workers join together to sue a company.

---

[61] Martin Shapiro, "The Supreme Court: From Warren to Burger," in *The New American Political System*, ed. Anthony King (Washington, D.C.: American Enterprise Institute, 1978).

[62] *Citizens to Preserve Overton Park v. Volpe*, 401 U.S. 402 (1971).

[63] See "Developments in the Law—Class Actions," *Harvard Law Review* 89 (1976): 1318.

caused by tobacco use. Of course, the attorneys who brought the case also received an enormous settlement, splitting more than $1 billion. Continuing litigation against tobacco firms remains to be resolved.

In the third major judicial change, the federal courts began to employ so-called structural remedies, in effect retaining jurisdiction of cases until a court's mandate had been implemented to its satisfaction.[64] The best-known of these instances was the effort by federal judge W. Arthur Garrity to operate the Boston school system from his bench to ensure its desegregation. Between 1974 and 1985, Judge Garrity issued fourteen decisions relating to different aspects of the Boston school desegregation plan that had been developed under his authority and put into effect under his supervision.[65]

Through these three judicial mechanisms, the federal courts paved the way for an unprecedented expansion of national judicial power. In essence, liberalization of the rules of standing and expansion of the scope of judicial relief drew the federal courts into link with important social interests and classes while the introduction of structural remedies enhanced the courts' ability to serve these constituencies. Thus during the 1960s and 1970s the power of the federal courts expanded in the same way the power of the executive expanded during the 1930s: through links with constituencies—such as groups advocating civil rights, consumers' rights, gay rights, women's rights, and environmental issues—that staunchly defended the Supreme Court in its battles with Congress, the executive, or other interest groups.

During the 1980s and early 1990s, the Reagan and Bush administrations sought to end the relationship between the Court and liberal political forces. The conservative judges appointed by these Republican presidents modified the Court's position in areas such as abortion, affirmative action, and judicial procedure, though not as completely as some conservatives had hoped. In June 2003, for example, the Court handed down a series of decisions that pleased many liberals and outraged conservative advocacy groups. Within a period of one week, the Supreme Court affirmed the validity of affirmative action, reaffirmed abortion rights, strengthened gay rights, offered new protection to individuals facing the death penalty, and issued a ruling in favor of a congressional apportionment plan that dispersed minority voters across several districts—a practice that appeared to favor the Democrats.[66] It is interesting, however, that the current Court has not been eager to surrender the expanded powers carved out by earlier Courts. In a number of decisions during the 1980s and 1990s, the Court was willing to make use of its expanded powers on behalf of interests it favored.[67] In the 1992 case of *Lujan v. Defenders of Wildlife*, the Court seemed to retreat to a conception of standing more restrictive than that affirmed by liberal activist jurists.[68]

---

[64] See Donald L. Horowitz, *The Courts and Social Policy* (Washington, D.C.: Brookings Institution, 1977).

[65] *Morgan v. McDonough*, 540 F. 2nd 527 (1 Cir., 1976); *cert. denied* 429 U.S. 1042 (1977).

[66] David Van Drehle, "Court That Liberals Savage Proves to Be Less of a Target," *Washington Post*, 29 June 2003, p. A18.

[67] Mark Silverstein and Benjamin Ginsberg, "The Supreme Court and the New Politics of Judicial Power," *Political Science Quarterly* 102 (Fall 1987): 371–88.

[68] *Lujan v. Defenders of Wildlife*, 504 U.S. 555 (1992).

Rather than representing an example of judicial restraint, however, the *Lujan* case was a direct judicial challenge to congressional power. The case involved an effort by an environmental group, the Defenders of Wildlife, to make use of the 1973 Endangered Species Act to block the expenditure of federal funds being used by the governments of Egypt and Sri Lanka for public works projects. Environmentalists charged that the projects threatened the habitats of several endangered species of birds and that the expenditure of federal funds to support the projects therefore violated the 1973 act. The Interior Department claimed that the act affected only domestic projects.[69]

The Endangered Species Act, like a number of other pieces of liberal environmental and consumer legislation enacted by Congress, encourages citizen suits— suits by activist groups not directly harmed by the action in question—to challenge government policies that they deem to be inconsistent with the act. Justice Scalia, however, writing for the Court's majority in the *Lujan* decision, reasserted a more traditional conception of standing, requiring those bringing suit against a government policy to show that the policy is likely to cause *them* direct and imminent injury.

Had Scalia stopped at this point, the case might have been seen as an example of judicial restraint. Scalia went on, however, to question the validity of any statutory provision for citizen suits. Such legislative provisions, according to Justice Scalia, violate Article III of the Constitution, which limits the federal courts to consideration of actual "Cases" and "Controversies." This interpretation strips Congress of its capacity to promote the enforcement of regulatory statutes by encouraging activist groups not directly affected or injured to be on the lookout for violations that could provide the basis for lawsuits. This enforcement mechanism—which conservatives liken to bounty hunting—was an extremely important congressional instrument and played a prominent part in the enforcement of such pieces of legislation as the 1990 Americans with Disabilities Act. Thus the *Lujan* case offers an example of judicial activism rather than judicial restraint; even the most conservative justices are reluctant to surrender the powers now wielded by the Court.[70]

SUMMARY

Millions of cases come to trial every year in the United States. The great majority— nearly 99 percent—are tried in state and local courts. The types of law are civil, criminal, and public. There are three types of courts that hear cases: trial, appellate, and (state) supreme courts.

[69]Linda Greenhouse, "Court Limits Legal Standing in Suits," *New York Times*, 13 June 1992, p. 12.

[70]On the role of the Supreme Court in forcing conformity with existing law, a discussion of the Court's enforcement of civil rights in unions as another example is found in Paul Frymer, "Acting When Elected Officials Won't: Federal Courts and Civil Rights Enforcement in U.S. Labor Unions, 1935–85," *American Political Science Review* 97, no. 3 (August 2003): 483–99.

Rationality Principle	Collective-Action Principle	Institution Principle	Policy Principle	History Principle
Judges have political goals and policy preferences and act to achieve them.	Appointments to the federal bench involve informal bargaining (senatorial courtesy) as well as formal bargaining (Senate confirmation).	Because the court system is hierarchical, decisions by higher courts constrain the discretion of lower-court judges.	Courts are not legislative bodies, but many important policy issues are nevertheless decided by the judiciary.	Since *Marbury v. Madison* (1803), the power of judicial review has not been in question.
The Supreme Court accepts cases based on the preferences and priorities of the justices.	The legal system coordinates private behavior by providing incentives and disincentives for specific actions.	The courts have developed specific rules of access that govern which cases within their jurisdiction they will hear.	By interpreting existing statutes as well as the Constitution, judges make law.	In the last fifty years, the power of the judiciary has been strengthened and expanded.
Reducing the expected costs of litigation, through fee switching and class actions, increased the frequency of court challenges.	Four of the nine Supreme Court justices need to agree to review a case.	The Supreme Court's procedures allow various individuals and groups to influence the decision-making process.		
	Bargaining among justices figures prominently at the opinion-drafting stage.	During the 1960s and 1970s, the courts liberalized the concept of standing.		
	In reaching their decisions, Supreme Court judges must anticipate Congress's response.			

There are two kinds of federal cases: (1) civil cases involving disputes between individuals or disputes between the government and an individual in which no criminal violation is charged and (2) cases involving federal criminal statutes or state criminal cases that have been made issues of public law. Judicial power extends only to cases and controversies. Litigants must have standing to sue, and courts neither hand down opinions on hypothetical issues nor take the initiative. Sometimes appellate courts even return cases to the lower courts for further trial.

The organization of the federal judiciary provides for original jurisdiction in the federal district courts, specialized courts, and federal regulatory agencies.

Each district court is in one of the twelve appellate districts, called circuits, presided over by a court of appeals. Appellate courts admit no new evidence; their rulings are based solely on the records of the court proceedings or agency hearings that led to the original decision. Appeals court rulings are final unless the Supreme Court chooses to review them.

The Supreme Court has some original jurisdiction, but its major job is to review lower-court decisions involving substantial issues of public law. There is no explicit constitutional authority for the Supreme Court to review acts of Congress. Nonetheless, the 1803 case of *Marbury v. Madison* established the Court's right to review congressional acts. The supremacy clause of Article VI and the Judiciary Act of 1789 give the Court the power to review state constitutions and laws.

Cases reach the Court mainly through the writ of *certiorari*. The Supreme Court controls its caseload by issuing few writs and handing down clear opinions that enable lower courts to resolve future cases without further review.

Both appellate and Supreme Court decisions, including the decision not to review a case, make law. The effect of such law usually favors the status quo. Yet many revolutionary changes in the law have come about through appellate court and Supreme Court rulings—in the criminal process, apportionment, and civil rights.

The judiciary as a whole is subject to two major influences: (1) the individual members of the Supreme Court, who have lifetime tenure, and (2) the other branches of government, particularly Congress.

The influence of an individual member of the Supreme Court is limited when the Court is polarized, and close votes in a polarized Court impair the value of the decision rendered. Writing the majority opinion for a case is an opportunity for a justice to influence the judiciary. But the need to frame an opinion in such a way as to develop majority support on the Court may limit such opportunities. Dissenting opinions can have more effect than the majority opinion; they stimulate a flow of cases around the issue at hand.

The solicitor general is the most important single influence outside the Court itself because he or she controls the flow of cases brought by the Justice Department and shapes the argument in those cases. But the flow of cases is a force in itself, which the Department of Justice cannot entirely control.

Social problems give rise to similar cases that ultimately must be adjudicated and appealed. Some interest groups try to develop such case patterns as a means of gaining power through the courts.

In recent years, the importance of the federal judiciary—the Supreme Court in particular—has increased substantially as the courts have developed new tools of judicial power and forged alliances with important forces in American society.

FOR FURTHER READING

Abraham, Henry J. *The Judicial Process: An Introductory Analysis of the Courts of the United States, England, and France.* 7th ed. New York: Oxford University Press, 1998.

ONLINE READING ○ Baum, Lawrence. *The Puzzle of Judicial Behavior.* Ann Arbor: University of Michigan Press, 1997.

ONLINE READING ○ Bickel, Alexander M. *The Least Dangerous Branch: The Supreme Court at the Bar of Politics.* Indianapolis: Bobbs-Merrill, 1962.

Epstein, Lee, and Jack Knight. *The Choices Justices Make.* Washington, D.C.: Congressional Quarterly Press, 1998.

ONLINE READING ○ Kahn, Ronald. *The Supreme Court and Constitutional Theory, 1953–1993.* Lawrence: University Press of Kansas, 1994.

O'Brien, David M. *Storm Center: The Supreme Court in American Politics.* 7th ed. New York: Norton, 2005.

ONLINE READING ○ Perry, H. W., Jr. *Deciding to Decide: Agenda Setting in the United States Supreme Court.* Cambridge, Mass.: Harvard University Press, 1991.

Segal, Jeffrey A., and Harold J. Spaeth. *The Supreme Court and the Attitudinal Model Revisited.* New York: Cambridge University Press, 2002.

Silverstein, Mark. *Judicious Choices: The New Politics of Supreme Court Confirmations.* New York: Norton, 1994.

Tribe, Laurence H. *Constitutional Choices.* Cambridge, Mass.: Harvard University Press, 1985.

There is no "natural" level of activity for the Supreme Court. The number and types of cases that come before the Court in a given year are determined partly by other actors and other political institutions. Of course, the justices ultimately decide which cases to hear, but it is only by placing the Court within the larger political, institutional, and historical context that we can analyze the nature of its caseload.

The institution principle directs us to the rules and procedures by which cases come before the Court. The Court determines which cases it is willing to hear—but it cannot force issues onto its docket. They must emerge out of the appeals process from lower courts or from challenges to new laws passed by Congress. As this story shows, if the federal government is winning cases in the lower courts, it has no reason to appeal. And if Congress has been passing fewer laws, this circumstance will also reduce the Court's docket.

At the same time, the rationality principle focuses on the preferences of the actors on the Court—the justices and their staff. According to this article, the justices may prefer a smaller docket. That is because in a divided Court many decisions are reached with a bare 5–4 majority, making it less likely that an individual justice will accept a case: The risk of a loss—and establishing a new constitutional precedent that he or she does not agree with—is too great.

The New York Times, December 17, 2006

Case of the Dwindling Docket Mystifies the Supreme Court

BY LINDA GREENHOUSE

On the Supreme Court's color-coded master calendar, which was distributed months before the term began on the first Monday in October, Dec. 6 is marked in red to signify a day when the justices are scheduled to be on the bench, hearing arguments.

The courtroom, however, was empty on Wednesday, and for a simple reason: The court was out of cases. The question is, where have all the cases gone?

Last year, during his Senate confirmation hearing, Chief Justice John G. Roberts Jr. said he thought the court had room on its docket and that it "could contribute more to the clarity and unifor- mity of the law by taking more cases."

But that has not happened. The court has taken about 40 percent fewer cases so far this term than last. It now faces noticeable gaps in its calendar for late winter and early spring. . . .

The number of cases the court decided with signed opinions last term, 69, was the lowest since 1953 and fewer than half the number the court was deciding as recently as the mid-1980s. And aside from the school integration and global warming cases the court heard last week, along with the terrorism-related cases it has decided in the last few years, relatively few of the cases it is deciding speak to the core of the country's concerns.

The reasons for the decline all grow out of forces building for decades. The federal government has been losing fewer cases in the lower courts and so has less reason to appeal. As Congress enacts fewer laws, the justices have fewer statutes to interpret. And justices who think they might end up on the losing side of an important case might vote not to take it.

In a divided court, in a divided country, the court's reduced role is perhaps not surprising, nor is it necessarily a bad thing. "In the post–Bush v. Gore era, the court may be concerned about taking the wrong case and making an unpopular decision," said Frederick Schauer, a professor at the John F. Kennedy School of Government at Harvard. * * *

Professor Schauer argued in a recent and much-discussed Harvard Law Review article that the court's work "had only minimal direct engagement with the central issues of the nation's public and policy agenda." * * * He said, "I think they like being under the radar."

In private conversations, the justices themselves insist that nothing so profound is going on, but rather seem mystified at what they perceive as a paucity of cases that meet the court's standard criteria. The most important of those criteria is whether a case raises a question that has produced conflicting decisions among the lower federal courts.

But there are still plenty of lower-court conflicts that go unresolved, said Thomas C. Goldstein, a Supreme Court practitioner and close student of court statistics who wrote last week on the popular Scotusblog that the justices were "on the cusp of the greatest shortfall in filling the court's docket in recent memory, and likely in its modern history."

"I don't think we're at the end of history and have fixed all the problems," Mr. Goldstein said in an interview.

One theory is that the court is so closely divided that neither the liberals nor the conservatives want to risk granting a case in which, at the end of the day, they might not prevail. To grant a case takes four votes, which can be a heartbreaking distance from the five votes it takes to win. Scholars of the court call this risk-averse behavior "defensive denial."

While such behavior may account for a portion of the shortfall, it can hardly provide a global explanation, because only a relative handful of the 8,000 appeals that reach the court each term are ideologically charged.

Other, more neutral explanations provide likely pieces of the puzzle.

One is the decreasing number of appeals filed on behalf of the federal government by the solicitor general's office. Over the decades, the Supreme Court has granted cases filed by the solicitor general's office at a high rate. In the mid-1980s, the office was filing more than 50 petitions per term. But as the lower federal courts have become more conservative and the government has lost fewer cases, the number has plummeted, opening a substantial hole in the court's docket.

As recently as the court's 2000 term, the solicitor general filed 24 petitions, of which 17 were granted. Last term, it filed 10, of which the court granted 4. This term, the solicitor general has filed 13 petitions; the court has granted 5, denied 3 and is still considering the rest.

Another explanation lies across the street from the Supreme Court, in Congress.

Over the years, about half the court's docket has been made up not of constitutional cases, but of cases requiring

Collective-Action Principle

The justices range from liberal to conservative, but none of them wants to be on the losing side of a case. "Defensive denial" thus encourages collective agreement to limit the number of cases on the docket.

Rationality Principle

The justices on the Court may feel that the Court is under particular scrutiny after its role in the 2000 presidential election. As a result, they find it in their political self-interest to be less aggressive for some period of time.

the justices to interpret federal statutes. Statutes from the 1970s, including major environmental laws, antidiscrimination laws and Erisa, the employee-benefits law, have been staples of the court's docket for decades. But as Congress's willingness to pass new laws has waned, the flow of statutory cases has begun to dry up.

Another possible explanation is the method by which the justices screen the thousands of petitions. Eight of the justices, all except Justice John Paul Stevens, pool their law clerks and have only one clerk make the initial recommendation for each case.

The recommendation is not binding, of course. But there is a built-in "institutional conservatism" in which law clerks are afraid to look overly credulous and so are reluctant to recommend a grant. * * *

The sharpest drop in opinions came after William H. Rehnquist became chief justice in 1986. He had made clear his belief that the court under Chief Justice Warren E. Burger was taking too many cases, and Congress assisted in 1988 by eliminating from the court's jurisdiction a category of "mandatory" appeals to which the justices collectively had long objected.

In the early 1990s, after the number of decisions dropped to 107 from 145 in the space of five terms, Chief Justice Rehnquist responded to reporters' questions by commenting wryly that the Supreme Court would be the first institution of American government to fulfill Karl Marx's prophecy of the withering away of the state.

He was kidding, of course. The late chief justice believed in a muscular role for the court, and went on to show that he could accomplish more with less.

The question now, on a docket dominated by cases that only a law professor could love, is how much less. * * *

Institution Principle

The Court's docket is determined in large part by other institutions of government —most importantly Congress. A more divided Congress has found it difficult to pass large-scale regulatory and social legislation. This results in fewer cases coming before the Court.

History Principle

We may view the current Court's docket as small only when compared in historical context with the Warren and Burger Courts (a period when major changes, such as those in civil rights, were decided by the Courts). It is possible, however, that we have entered a new historical path for the Court, where it will have a smaller docket.

Part Three | Politics

Public Opinion

IN MARCH 2003, American and British military forces invaded Iraq with the express intent of disarming Iraq's military and driving Iraqi president Saddam Hussein from power. The invasion followed months of diplomatic wrangling and an ultimately unsuccessful effort by President George W. Bush and British prime minister Tony Blair to win UN support for military action against Iraq. In the months before the war, many Americans were dubious about the need to attack Iraq. For example, according to a CBS News poll taken during the first week of March 2003, only 50 percent of those responding thought removing Saddam from power was worth the potential costs of war, and 43 percent thought it was not worth it. The same poll reported that only 55 percent of Americans approved of the way President Bush was handling the situation with Iraq. Once the American and British invasion of Iraq began, however, popular support for U.S. military action rose by twenty-four points, to 77 percent.

Many commentators attributed support for the war to a rally-round-the-flag effect that is commonly seen when a president leads Americans into battle. Pundits predicted that support for the war and the president would drop if fighting turned out to be prolonged or inconclusive. And the pundits were right. A week after the 2006 midterm elections, a CNN poll reported that only 33 percent of those surveyed approved of U.S. policy in Iraq, and 63 percent were opposed to it. In a CBS poll at about the same time, only 34 percent approved of President Bush's job performance, and 61 percent disapproved of it (Figure 9.1).

It also quickly became apparent that support for the president and his war policy varied considerably according to demographic and political factors. Men were more supportive than women of the president's policies, indicating a continuation of the gender gap that has been a persistent feature of American public opinion. Race was also a factor, with African Americans much more critical than whites of President Bush and his goals. In addition, partisanship was important. Republicans were nearly unanimous in their approval of President Bush's policies, while Democrats were more closely divided on the wisdom of going to war. Partisan politics, it seems, did not stop at the water's edge.

Even as popular support for his policies eroded, President Bush remained steadfast. The president won reelection in 2004 despite doubts about his handling of the Iraq situation, and he was determined to bring about the creation of a pro-American regime in that nation. The president attempted to halt the downward trend of popular approval for his policies by hinting that American forces might be reduced after the 2005 Iraqi elections and by continuously restating the need to promote democracy in the Middle East. At the same time, though, President Bush made it clear that his policies would not respond to shifts in popular opinion. The president reminded Americans that he planned to do his duty as he saw it, regardless of the vicissitudes of public sentiment. Even after a stinging rebuke in the 2006 midterm congressional elections, President Bush has remained steadfast in "staying the course" in Iraq, though support for that policy even among politicians has wavered.

Underlying political beliefs formed through political socialization often cohere into a political ideology. As a result, ideology can work for some citizens as an information shortcut by allowing them to form an opinion on an issue or a candidate while economizing on the cost of becoming informed of the details. Some analysts consider it rational for citizens to be only partially informed about politics and to form political opinions either by drawing on their ideological leanings or by following the cues of others, such as government officials, leaders of interest groups, and members of the media. This creates a dilemma: Those who have more knowledge of politics will tend to have more influence on political outcomes. This dilemma in turn contributes to a gulf between public opinion and public policy. This gulf is explained in part by how institutions shape outcomes. An institutional framework based on representative government limits the extent to which public opinion affects policy outcomes.

These events underline many issues raised in this chapter. Do Americans know enough to form meaningful opinions about important policy issues? What factors account for differences in opinion? To what extent can the government manipulate popular sentiment? To what extent do—or should—the government's policies respond to public opinion?

Public opinion is the term used to denote the values and attitudes that people have about issues, events, and personalities. Although the terms are sometimes used interchangeably, it is useful to distinguish between values or beliefs on the one hand and attitudes or opinions on the other. ***Values (or beliefs)*** are made up of a person's basic orientation to politics. Values represent deep-rooted goals, aspirations, and ideals that shape an individual's perceptions of political issues and events. Liberty, equality, and democracy are basic political values that most Americans hold. Another useful term for understanding public opinion is *ideology*. ***Political ideology*** refers to a complex and interrelated set of beliefs and values that, as a whole, form a general philosophy about government. As we shall see, liberalism and conservatism are important ideologies in America today. For example, the idea that governmental solutions to problems are inherently inferior to private-sector solutions is a belief held by many Americans. This general belief, in turn, may lead individuals to have negative views of specific government programs even before they know much about them. An ***attitude (or opinion)*** is a specific view about a particular issue, personality, or event. An individual may have an attitude toward American policy in Iraq or an opinion about George W. Bush. The attitude or opinion may have emerged from a broad belief about military intervention or Republicans, but an attitude itself is very specific. Some attitudes may be short-lived.

One reason why public policy and public opinion may not always coincide is, of course, that ours is a representative government, not a direct democracy. The framers of the Constitution thought that our nation would be best served by a sys-

public opinion Citizens' attitudes about political issues, leaders, institutions, and events.

values (or beliefs) The basic principles that shape a person's opinions about political issues and events.

political ideology A cohesive set of beliefs that form a general philosophy about the role of government.

attitude (or opinion) A specific preference on a specific issue.

FIGURE 9.1 President Bush's Falling Approval Rating

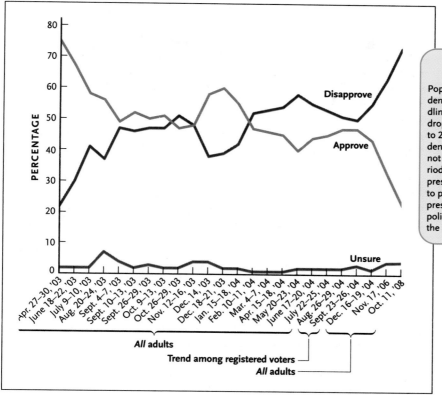

SOURCE: ABC News/*Washington Post* poll, 16–19 December 2004 (www.pollingreport.com), CNN poll 17 November 2006, *Washington Post* poll, 11 October 2008.

NOTE: *N* = 1,004 adults nationwide. Margin of error is ±3.

ANALYZING THE EVIDENCE

Popular approval of President George W. Bush's handling of the situation in Iraq dropped sharply from 2003 to 2004, although the president's policies in Iraq did not change during this period. Does this mean the president was indifferent to public opinion? Should presidents change their policies in response to the polls?

tem of government that allowed the elected representatives of the people an opportunity to reflect and consider their decisions rather than by a government that bowed immediately to shifts in popular sentiment. A century after the founding, however, the populist movement averred that government was too far removed from the people and introduced the initiative and the referendum, procedures that allow for direct popular legislation. A number of states allow policy issues to be placed on the ballot, where they are resolved by a popular vote. Some modern-day populists believe that initiative and referendum processes should be adopted at the national level as well. Whether this would lead to greater responsiveness, however, is an open question, to which we shall return.

In this chapter, we examine the role of public opinion in American politics. First, we examine the political values and beliefs that help Americans form their perceptions of the political process. After reviewing basic American political values, we analyze how values and beliefs are formed and how certain processes and institutions influence their formation. We conclude this first section by considering the

Institution Principle

One reason why policy may not be consistent with opinion is that the United States is a representative government, not a direct democracy.

ways in which values and beliefs can cumulate to create political ideologies. Second, we see how general values and beliefs help shape more specific attitudes and opinions. In this discussion we consider the role of political knowledge and the influence of political leaders, private groups, and the media. We see why there appear to be so many differences of opinion among Americans. Third, we assess the science of gathering and measuring public opinion. Finally, we assess the effect of public opinion on the government and its policies. We ask: Is the U.S. government responsive to public opinion? Should it be?

WHAT ARE THE ORIGINS OF PUBLIC OPINION?

Opinions are products of an individual's personality, social characteristics, and interests. They mirror who a person is, what she wants, and the manner in which she is embedded in her family, community, and the broader economy and society. But opinions are also shaped by institutional, political, and governmental forces that make it more likely that citizens will hold some beliefs and less likely that they will hold others.

Common Fundamental Values

Today most Americans share a common set of political beliefs. First, they generally believe in *equality of opportunity*—they assume that all individuals should be allowed to seek personal and material success. Moreover, Americans generally believe that such success should be linked to personal effort and ability rather than family connections or other forms of special privilege. Second, Americans strongly believe in individual freedom. They typically support the notion that government interference with individuals' lives and property should be kept to the minimum consistent with the general welfare (although in recent years Americans have grown accustomed to greater levels of government intervention than would have been deemed appropriate by the founders of liberal theory). Third, most Americans believe in democracy. They presume that everyone should have the opportunity to take part in the nation's governmental and policy-making processes and have some say in determining how they are governed (Figure 9.2).[1]

Of course, support for abstract principles does not always carry over to affirmation of these same principles in concrete situations. For example, Americans who believe in individual freedom in the abstract may still support policies that limit freedom, especially if such policies are said to be necessary to combat crime or thwart terrorism. Nevertheless, widespread acceptance of a principle establishes a general benchmark or standard that can be difficult to dispute. During the 1960s, for instance, one reason the civil rights movement focused on voting rights was that the principle of access to the ballot box was so firmly established in the United

equality of opportunity A universally shared American ideal, according to which all have the freedom to use whatever talents and wealth they possess to reach their full potential.

[1]For a discussion of the political beliefs of Americans, see Everett Carll Ladd, *The American Ideology* (Storrs, Conn.: Roper Center, 1994).

FIGURE 9.2 Americans' Support for Fundamental Values

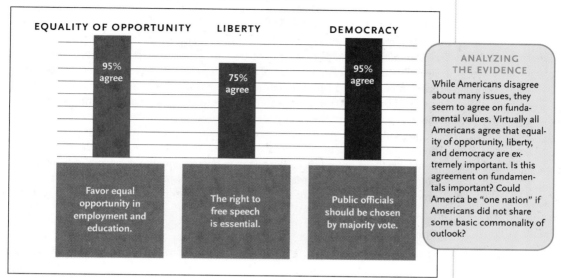

EQUALITY OF OPPORTUNITY   LIBERTY   DEMOCRACY

95% agree

75% agree

95% agree

Favor equal opportunity in employment and education.

The right to free speech is essential.

Public officials should be chosen by majority vote.

ANALYZING THE EVIDENCE

While Americans disagree about many issues, they seem to agree on fundamental values. Virtually all Americans agree that equality of opportunity, liberty, and democracy are extremely important. Is this agreement on fundamentals important? Could America be "one nation" if Americans did not share some basic commonality of outlook?

SOURCES: Gallup Poll, 2001; Roper Poll, 2002; and Robert S. Erikson, Norman R. Luttbeg, and Kent L. Tedin, *American Public Opinion: Its Origins, Content, and Impact,* 4th ed. (New York: Macmillan, 1991), p. 108.

States that opponents of voting rights for African Americans found it virtually impossible to form an intellectual basis from which to defend their position.

Agreement on fundamental political values, though certainly not absolute, is probably more widespread in the United States than anywhere else in the Western world. During the course of Western political history, competing economic, social, and political groups have put forward a variety of radically divergent views, opinions, and political philosophies. And although America was never socially or economically homogeneous, two forces that were extremely powerful and important sources of ideas and beliefs elsewhere in the world were relatively weak or absent in the United States. First, the United States never had the feudal aristocracy that had dominated so much of European history. Second, for reasons including America's prosperity and the early availability of political rights, no socialist movements comparable to those that developed in nineteenth-century Europe were ever able to establish themselves in the United States. As a result, during the course of American history there existed neither an aristocracy to assert the virtues of inequality, special privilege, and a rigid class structure nor a powerful communist or socialist party to seriously challenge the desirability of limited government and individualism.[2]

 History Principle

The absence of either a feudal or a socialist tradition in the United States allowed for the emergence of a consensus on liberal democracy.

---

[2]See Louis Hartz, *The Liberal Tradition in America: An Interpretation of American Political Thought since the Revolution* (New York: Harcourt, Brace, 1955).

Obviously the principles that Americans espouse have not always been put into practice. For two centuries, Americans were able to believe in the principles of equality of opportunity and individual liberty while denying them in practice to generations of African Americans. Yet as we observed earlier, the strength of those principles ultimately helped Americans overcome practices that deviated from them. Proponents of slavery and, later, of segregation were defeated in the arena of public opinion because their practices differed so sharply from the fundamental principles accepted by most Americans. Ironically, in contemporary politics Americans' fundamental commitment to equality of opportunity has led to divisions over racial policy. In particular, both proponents and opponents of affirmative action programs cite their belief in equality of opportunity as the justification for their position. Proponents see these programs as necessary to ensure equality of opportunity, while opponents believe that affirmative action constitutes preferential treatment for some groups—a clear violation of the principle of equality of opportunity.[3]

Political Socialization

Individuals' attitudes about political issues and personalities tend to be shaped by their underlying political beliefs and values. For example, an individual who has basically negative feelings about government intervention in America's economy and society would probably be predisposed to oppose the development of new healthcare and social programs. Similarly, someone who distrusts the military would likely be suspicious of any call for the use of American troops. The processes through which such underlying political beliefs and values are formed, considered collectively, are called *political socialization.*

The process of political socialization is important. Probably no nation and certainly no democracy could survive if its citizens did not share some fundamental beliefs. If Americans had few common values or perspectives, it would be very difficult for them to reach agreement on particular issues. In contemporary America, some elements of the socialization process tend to produce differences in outlook, whereas others promote similarities. Four of the most important *agents of socialization* that foster differences in political perspectives are the family, membership in social groups, education, and prevailing political conditions. Although these factors cannot fully explain the development of any one individual's political outlook, let us consider the ways in which they tend to influence most people.

The Family Most people acquire their initial orientation to politics from their family. Although relatively few parents spend much time teaching their children about politics, political conversations occur in many households, and children tend to absorb the political views of their parents and other caregivers, perhaps without realizing it. Studies have suggested, for example, that party preferences are initially acquired at home. Children raised in households in which the primary caregivers are Democrats tend to become Democrats themselves, whereas children raised in homes where their care-

political socialization The induction of individuals into the political culture; the process of learning the underlying beliefs and values on which the political system is based.

agents of socialization The social institutions, including families and schools, that help shape individuals' basic political beliefs and values.

---

[3]Paul M. Sniderman and Edward G. Carmines, *Reaching beyond Race* (Cambridge, Mass.: Harvard University Press, 1997).

givers are Republicans tend to favor the GOP.[4] Similarly, children reared in politically liberal households are more likely than not to develop a liberal outlook, whereas children raised in politically conservative settings are prone to see the world through conservative lenses. Obviously, not all children absorb their parents' political views. For instance, two of the four children of Ronald Reagan, a conservative Republican president, rejected their parents' conservative values. The late president's son Ron supported the Democrat John Kerry in the 2004 presidential race. Moreover, even those children whose views are initially shaped by parental values may change their mind as they mature and experience political life for themselves. Nevertheless, the family is an important initial source of political orientation for everyone.

Social Groups Another important source of divergent political orientations and values is the social groups to which individuals belong. Social groups include those to which individuals belong involuntarily—gender and racial groups, for example—as well as those to which people belong voluntarily—such as political parties, labor unions, religious organizations, and educational and occupational groups. Some social groups have both voluntary and involuntary attributes. For example, individuals are born with a particular social-class background, but as a result of their own efforts they may move up—or down—the class structure.

Membership in social groups can affect political values in a variety of ways. Membership in a particular group can give individuals important experiences and perspectives that shape their views of political and social life. The experiences of blacks and whites, for example, can differ significantly. Blacks are a minority and have been victims of persecution and discrimination throughout American history. Blacks and whites also have different educational and occupational opportunities, often live in separate communities, and may attend separate schools. Such differences tend to produce distinctive political outlooks. For example, in 1995 blacks and whites had very different reactions to the murder trial of the former football star O. J. Simpson, who was accused of killing his ex-wife and one of her friends. Approximately 70 percent of the white Americans surveyed believed that Simpson was guilty, based on the evidence presented by the police and prosecutors. But an identical 70 percent of the black Americans surveyed immediately after the trial believed that the police had fabricated evidence and had sought to convict Simpson of a crime he had not committed, their beliefs presumably based on their experiences with and perceptions of the criminal justice system.[5] In a similar vein, the Reverend Al Sharpton's 2003–4 campaign for the Democratic presidential nomination was not taken seriously by most white voters and received little attention from the mainstream news media. Black voters, on the other hand, were quite attuned to Sharpton's candidacy, which received considerable coverage in the African American news media. Indeed, Sharpton received considerable financial backing from black media executives.[6]

---

[4]See Angus Campbell, Philip E. Converse, Warren E. Miller, and Donald E. Stokes, *The American Voter* (New York: Wiley, 1960), p. 147. We shall discuss psychological attachments to political parties, called party identification, in Chapter 11.

[5]Richard Morin, "Poll Reflects Division over Simpson Case," *Washington Post*, 8 October 1995, p. A31.

[6]Paul Farhi, "Black Media Barons Back Sharpton Bid," *Washington Post*, 9 November 2003, p. A4.

FIGURE 9.3 Disagreement among Blacks and Whites

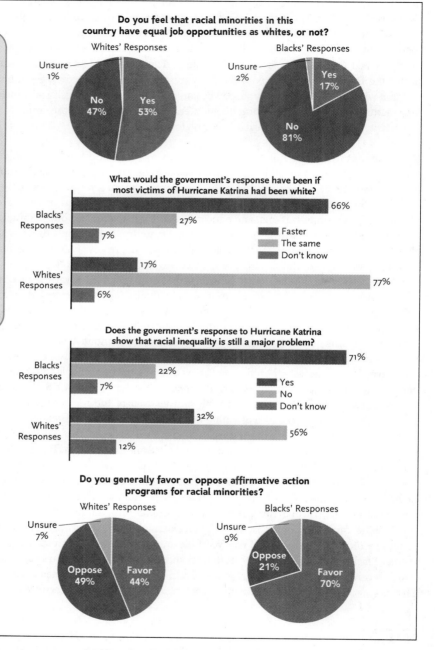

SOURCE: Gallup polls, 8–25 June 2006 and 12–15 June 2003 (www.pollingreport.com); Pew Research Center for the People and the Press, "The Black and White of Public Opinion," 31 October 2005 (people-press.org/commentary).

TABLE 9.1 Partisan Division in the Latino Community

Background	Democratic (%)	Republican (%)
Cuban	17	52
Mexican	47	18
Puerto Rican	50	17

SOURCE: Pew Hispanic Center/Kaiser Family Foundation, "The 2004 National Survey of Latinos: Politics and Civic Participation," July 2004 (www.kff.org/kaiserpolls).

ANALYZING THE EVIDENCE

Members of America's Latino community share a linguistic and cultural heritage, but they are not politically homogeneous. For example, most Mexican Americans and Puerto Rican Americans are staunchly Democratic, whereas most Cuban Americans are loyal Republicans. What factors might account for these differences?

According to other recent surveys, blacks and whites in the United States differ on a number of issues. For example, in surveys conducted by the Pew Research Center, clear majorities of whites supported the ideas that government should do more to guarantee food and shelter (62 percent in a 2003 survey) and generally help the needy (55 percent in a 2005 survey). Much larger majorities of blacks expressed support for the guarantee of food and shelter (80 percent) and the provision of help for the needy (72 percent).[7] Other issues show a similar pattern of disagreement, reflecting the differences in experience, background, and interests between blacks and whites in America (Figure 9.3).

Of course, disagreements between blacks and whites are not the only important racial or ethnic differences to be found in contemporary America. Latinos are another major American subgroup with distinctive opinions on some public issues. For example, 54 percent of Latinos surveyed in 2004 by the Pew Hispanic Center viewed education as the most important issue facing America. In the general population, however, only 5 percent of those surveyed attached such importance to education. Often immigrants or the children of immigrants, Hispanics view education as the ticket to a better life in America and attach great value to educational opportunity. As a population currently moving to the United States, Latinos also have a distinctive view of immigration. A 2004 Pew Hispanic Center survey found that more than 60 percent of Latinos believe that immigration is good for America. Among non-Latinos, though, more than 60 percent believe that immigration poses a major threat to the country. The Latino community is itself divided into subgroups based on national origin. Latinos of Mexican, Puerto Rican, Cuban, and Central American descent have distinctive opinions and even partisan loyalties (Table 9.1) Cuban Americans, for example, tend to be Republican and conservative, whereas Puerto Rican Americans are more likely to be liberal and Democratic. These differences, in turn, are related to each group's level of education, economic status, and history.

---

[7]Pew Research Center for the People and the Press, "The Black and White of Public Opinion," 31 October 2005 (people-press.org/commentary).

TABLE 9.2 Should Same-Sex Marriage Be Legalized?

Religious Group	In Favor (%)	Opposed (%)
White evangelical Protestant	14	78
White nonevangelical Protestant	42	47
White non-Hispanic Catholic	33	58
Black Protestant	19	74
Secular	63	27

SOURCE: Pew Research Center for the People and the Press, "Pragmatic Americans Liberal and Conservative on Social Issues: Most Want Middle Ground on Abortion," 3 August 2006 (people-press.org/reports).

Cubans tend to be wealthier and better educated than other Latinos and have traditionally viewed the Republican party as a foe of the Communist regime that forced them (or their parents or grandparents) to flee Cuba. Puerto Ricans, by contrast, tend to be poorer and to depend more on the social services championed by the Democratic party.

Religion has become another important source of variation in opinion. In recent years, contending political forces have placed a number of religious and moral issues on the national political agenda. The Republican party, in particular, has emphasized its support for traditional "family values" and its opposition to abortion, same-sex marriage, and other practices opposed by conservative religious leaders. It is not surprising that public opinion on these issues differs along religious lines, with evangelical Protestants being most supportive of traditional values and respondents identifying themselves as "secular" manifesting the least support for them. Take the issue of same-sex marriage, for example (Table 9.2).

Men and women have important differences of opinion as well. Reflecting differences in social roles, political experience, and occupational patterns, women tend to be less militaristic than men on issues of war and peace, more likely than men to favor measures to protect the environment, and more supportive than men of government social and health-care programs (Table 9.3). Perhaps because of these differences on issues, women are more likely than men to vote for Democratic candidates, while men have become increasingly supportive of the GOP.[8] This tendency for men's and women's opinions to differ is called the **gender gap.** Perhaps surprisingly, the gender gap has virtually vanished on the abortion issue. An August 2006 Pew Research Center poll indicated that men and women are nearly identical—52 percent versus 51 percent—on the issue of allowing abortion

gender gap A distinctive pattern of voting behavior reflecting the differences in views between women and men.

---

[8]For data, see Center for American Women and Politics, Eagleton Institute of Politics, Rutgers, State University of New Jersey, "Sex Differences in Voter Turnout," 2005 (www.cawp.rutgers.edu/Facts5.html).

TABLE 9.3 Disagreements among Men and Women on Issues of War and Peace

Government Action	Approve of Action (%)	
	Men	Women
Continued troop commitment in Iraq (2005)	57	48
Brokering a cease-fire in Yugoslavia instead of using NATO air strikes (1999)	44	51
Ending the ban on homosexuals in the military (1993)	34	51
Engaging in a military operation against a Somali warlord (1993)	72	60
Going to war against Iraq (1991)	72	53

SOURCE: Gallup polls, 1991, 1993, and 1999; *Washington Post*, 2005.

in general or on a limited basis, and 46 percent of both men and women believe abortion should always or almost always be illegal.[9]

As we shall see in Chapter 11, political party membership can be another factor affecting political orientation. Partisans tend to rely on party leaders and spokespersons for cues on the appropriate position to take on major political issues. In recent years, congressional redistricting and partisan realignment in the South have reduced the number of conservative Democrats and all but eliminated liberal Republicans from Congress and positions of prominence in the party. As a result, the leadership of the Republican party has become increasingly conservative and that of the Democratic party has become more and more liberal. These changes in the positions of party leaders have been reflected in the views of party adherents and sympathizers in the general public. According to recent studies, differences between Democratic and Republican partisans on a variety of political and policy questions are greater today than they were during any other period for which data are available. On issues of national security, for example, Republicans have become very "hawkish," whereas Democrats have become quite "dovish." In 2008, 81 percent of the Republicans surveyed opposed a timetable for withdrawing from Iraq, while 75 percent of Democrats favored such a timetable.[10]

Membership in a social group can affect individuals' political orientations in another way: through the efforts of groups themselves to influence their members. Labor unions, for example, often seek to "educate" their members through meetings,

---

[9]Pew Research Center for the People and the Press, "Pragmatic Americans Liberal and Conservative on Social Issues: Most Want Middle Ground on Abortion," 3 August 2006 (people-press.org/reports).

[10]ABC/*Washington Post* poll, July 2008.

rallies, and literature. These activities are designed to shape union members' understanding of politics and make them more amenable to supporting the political positions favored by union leaders. Similarly, organization can sharpen the effect of membership in an involuntary group. Women's groups, black groups, religious groups, and the like usually endeavor to structure their members' political views through intensive educational programs. The importance of such group efforts can be seen in the impact of group membership on political opinion. Women who belong to women's organizations, for example, are more likely than women without such group affiliation to differ from men in their political views.[11] Other analysts have found that African Americans who belong to black organizations are more likely than blacks who lack such affiliations to differ from whites in their political orientation.[12]

In many cases, no particular efforts are required by groups to affect their members' beliefs and opinions. Often individuals will consciously or unconsciously adapt their views to those of the groups with which they identify. For example, an African American who is dubious about affirmative action is likely to come under considerable peer pressure and internal pressure to modify his or her views. In this and other cases, dissenters are likely to gradually shift their own views to conform to those of the group. The political psychologist Elisabeth Noelle-Neumann has called this process the "spiral of silence."[13]

Another way in which membership in social groups can affect political beliefs is through what might be called objective political interests. On many economic issues, for example, the interests of the rich and the poor differ significantly. Inevitably, these differences of interest will produce differences of political outlook. James Madison and other framers of the Constitution thought that the inherent gulf between the rich and the poor would always be the most important source of conflict in political life. Certainly today struggles over tax policy, welfare policy, health-care policy, and so forth are fueled by differences of interest between wealthier and poorer Americans. In a similar vein, objective differences of interest between "senior citizens" and younger Americans can lead to very different views on such diverse issues as health-care policy, Social Security, and criminal justice.

It is worth pointing out again that, like the other agencies of socialization, group membership can never fully explain a given individual's political views. Group membership is conducive to particular outlooks, but it is not determinative. It is also worth pointing out, in line with the rationality principle, that objective interests, while not always determinative, exert a strong influence on opinions and behavior—hence the small number of black Republicans and socialist businesspeople.

Differences in Education A third important source of differences in political perspectives is a person's education. In some respects, of course, schooling is a great

---

[11]Pamela Johnston Conover, "The Role of Social Groups in Political Thinking," *British Journal of Political Science* 18 (1988): 51–78.

[12]See Michael C. Dawson, *Behind the Mule: Race and Class in African-American Politics* (Princeton, N.J.: Princeton University Press, 1994).

[13]Elisabeth Noelle-Neumann, *The Spiral of Silence: Public Opinion, Our Social Skin* (Chicago: University of Chicago Press, 1984).

TABLE 9.4 Education and Public Opinion

Issue	Level of Education			
	Grade School	High School	Some College	College Graduate
Women and men should have equal roles.	38	75	83	80
Abortion should never be allowed.	21	10	7	4
The government should adopt national health insurance.	35	47	42	39
The United States should not concern itself with other nations' problems.	45	26	20	8
Government should see to fair treatment in jobs for African Americans.	49	28	30	45
Government should provide fewer services to reduce government spending.	8	17	19	27

SOURCE: American National Election Studies, 2004 data, Center for Political Studies, University of Michigan (electionstudies.org).

NOTE: The figures show the percentage of respondents in each category agreeing with the statement.

> **ANALYZING THE EVIDENCE**
>
> What factors might explain the relationship between education and opinion? Some commentators believe that many college courses have a liberal political orientation. Do you agree? How have your college courses affected your opinions on social and political issues?

equalizer. Governments use public education to try to teach all children a common set of civic values. It is mainly in school that Americans acquire their basic belief in liberty, equality, and democracy. In history classes, students are taught that the founders fought for the principle of liberty. Through participation in class elections and student government, students are taught the virtues of democracy. In the course of studying such topics as the Constitution, the Civil War, and the civil rights movement, students are taught the importance of equality. These lessons are repeated at every grade level in a variety of contexts. No wonder they are such an important element in Americans' beliefs.

At the same time, however, differences in educational attainment are strongly associated with differences in political outlook. In particular, those who attend college are often exposed to philosophies and modes of thought that will forever distinguish them from their friends and neighbors who do not pursue college diplomas. Table 9.4 outlines some general differences of opinion that are found between college graduates and other Americans. One of the major differences is in levels of political participation. College graduates vote, write letters to the editor, join campaigns, take part in protests, and generally make their voices heard.

Political Conditions   A fourth set of factors shaping political orientation and values has to do with the conditions under which individuals and groups are recruited into and involved in political life—that is, the circumstances in which an individual comes of age politically. Although political beliefs are influenced by family background and group membership, the precise content and character of these views is, to a large extent, determined by political circumstances. For example, many Americans who came of political age during the Great Depression and World War II developed an intense loyalty to President Franklin Roosevelt and became permanently attached to his Democratic party. In a similar vein, the Vietnam War and the social upheavals of the 1960s produced lasting divisions among Americans of the baby-boom generation. Indeed, arguments over Vietnam persisted into the 2004 presidential election, some thirty years after American troops left Southeast Asia. Perhaps the September 11 terrorist attacks and ongoing threats to America's security will have a lasting impact on the political orientation of contemporary Americans.

In a similar vein, the views held by members of a particular group can shift drastically over time as political circumstances change. For example, white southerners were staunch members of the Democratic party from the Civil War through the 1960s. As members of this political group, they became key supporters of liberal New Deal and post–New Deal social programs that greatly expanded the size and power of the national government. Since the 1960s, however, southern whites have shifted in large numbers to the Republican party. Now they provide a major base of support for efforts to scale back social programs and sharply reduce the size and power of the national government. The South's move from the Democratic to the Republican camp took place because of white southern opposition to the Democratic party's racial policies and because of determined Republican efforts to win white southern support. It was not a change in the character of white southerners but a change in the political circumstances in which they found themselves that induced this major shift in political allegiances and outlook in the South.

The moral of this story is that a group's views cannot be inferred simply from the character of the group. College students are not inherently radical or inherently conservative. Jews are not inherently liberal. Southerners are not inherently conservative. Men are not inherently militaristic. Any group's political outlooks and orientations are shaped by the political circumstances in which the group finds itself, and those outlooks can change as circumstances change. Quite probably, the generation of American students now coming of political age will have a very different view of the use of American military power than their parents, members of a generation who reached political consciousness during the 1960s, when opposition to the Vietnam War and military conscription were important political phenomena.

Political Ideology

As we have seen, people's beliefs about government can vary widely. But for some individuals the set of underlying orientations, ideas, and beliefs through which they understand and interpret politics fits together in a political ideology.

In America today, people often describe themselves as liberals or conservatives. Liberalism and conservatism are political ideologies that include beliefs about the role of the government, ideas about public policies, and notions about which groups

History Principle

Changing political circumstances and events can be the impetus for major shifts in opinion. For example, with the changing landscape of race relations and race-related policies beginning in the 1960s, southern whites have become a major source of support for the Republican party.

Rationality Principle

Ideologies serve as informational shortcuts, allowing individuals to arrive at a view on an issue or a candidate while economizing on the cost of becoming informed of the details.

in society should properly exercise power. Historically, these terms were defined somewhat differently. As recently as the nineteenth century, a liberal was an individual who favored freedom from state control, while a conservative was someone who supported the use of governmental power and favored continuation of the influence of church and aristocracy in national life.

Today the term *liberal* has come to imply support for political and social reform; extensive government intervention in the economy; the expansion of federal social services; more vigorous efforts on behalf of the poor, minorities, and women; and greater concern for consumers and the environment. In social and cultural areas, liberals generally support abortion rights and oppose state involvement with religious institutions and religious expression. In international affairs, liberal positions are usually seen as including support for arms control, opposition to the development and testing of nuclear weapons, support for aid to poor nations, opposition to the use of American troops to influence the domestic affairs of developing nations, and support for international organizations such as the United Nations. Of course, liberalism is not monolithic. For example, among individuals who view themselves as liberal, many support American military intervention when it is tied to a humanitarian purpose, as in the case of America's military action in Kosovo in 1998–99. Most liberals initially supported President George W. Bush's war on terrorism even when some of the president's actions seemed to curtail civil liberties.

By contrast, the term *conservative* today is used to describe those who generally support the social and economic status quo and are suspicious of efforts to introduce new political formulas and economic arrangements. Conservatives believe strongly that a large and powerful government poses a threat to citizens' freedom. Thus in the domestic arena conservatives generally oppose the expansion of governmental activity, asserting that solutions to social and economic problems can be developed in the private sector. Conservatives in particular oppose efforts to impose government regulation on business, pointing out that such regulation is frequently economically inefficient and costly and can ultimately lower the entire nation's standard of living. As for social and cultural positions, many conservatives oppose abortion and support school prayer. In international affairs, conservatism has come to mean support for the maintenance of American military power. Like liberalism, conservatism is far from a monolithic ideology. Some conservatives support many government social programs. George W. Bush, a Republican, called himself a compassionate conservative to indicate that he favored programs that assist the poor and the needy. Other conservatives oppose efforts to outlaw abortion, arguing that government intrusion in this area is as misguided as government intervention in the economy. Such a position is sometimes called libertarian. The real political world is far too complex to be seen in terms of a simple struggle between liberals and conservatives.

Liberal and conservative differences manifest themselves in a variety of contexts. For example, the liberal approach to increasing airline safety in October 2001 was to create a workforce of federal employees who would screen and inspect passengers' luggage. The conservative approach was to call for better training of existing employees and better supervision of private-sector screeners. To some extent, contemporary liberalism and conservatism can be seen as blends of the fundamental American political values of liberty and equality. For liberals, equality is often the

liberal A liberal today generally supports political and social reform; extensive government intervention in the economy; the expansion of federal social services; more vigorous efforts on behalf of the poor, minorities, and women; and greater concern for consumers and the environment.

conservative Today this term refers to those who generally support the social and economic status quo and are suspicious of efforts to introduce new political formulas and economic arrangements. Many conservatives also believe that a large and powerful government poses a threat to citizens' freedoms.

How Polarized Is Public Opinion?

In the past several years, Americans have heard a lot about how divided they are. The American public is portrayed as increasingly "polarized"—with two camps, red and blue, that are far apart on key political questions. In particular, some have argued that America is experiencing a "culture war" over hot-button social issues, such as abortion and gay marriage. But how accurate is this characterization?

▶

In this map, red states are those won by President Bush in 2004, and blue states are those won by John Kerry. Here, the United States looks very polarized. The South and much of the Midwest appear Republican. The West Coast and the Northeast appear Democratic. But this map is misleading.

◀

What happens if we break down the map by counties instead of states? Even within red and blue states, there are areas where the majority votes differently. There are pockets of "blue" even in the Deep South and lots of "red" on the West Coast.

▶

Even more importantly, every state and county includes both Democrats and Republicans, making its true partisan color a shade of purple. If we color each county not based on whether Bush or Kerry won, but based on the percent of the vote that each of them received, the country hardly looks divided. Instead, much of the country is neither red nor blue.

The portrayal of a "culture war" between Democrats and Republicans is also misleading. While Americans have different opinions on issues such as abortion and gay marriage, these differences have increased only a little, if at all. For example, consider abortion. For over twenty-five years, the American National Election Study has asked the following question:

▶

Which one of these opinions best agrees with your view?

1. By law, abortion should never be permitted.

2. The law should permit abortion only in cases of rape, incest, or when the woman's life is in danger.

3. The law should permit abortion for reasons other than rape, incest, or danger to the woman's life, but only after the need for the abortion has been clearly established.

4. By law, a woman should always be able to obtain an abortion as a matter of personal choice.

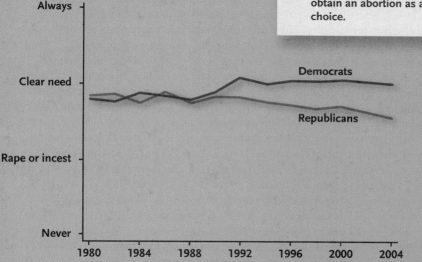

◀

The average opinions of Democrats and Republicans have diverged somewhat over time, but both groups are still quite close to the middle. Democrats do not unanimously support abortion under all circumstances, and Republicans do not unanimously oppose abortion under any circumstance. The term "culture war" seems an exaggeration.

Americans have not become more polarized on many issues, but there are two big exceptions: attitudes about President George W. Bush and attitudes toward the Iraq War. In the immediate aftermath of the September 11 terrorist attacks, both Republicans and Democrats tended to approve of President Bush. Over time, however, the gap between Republicans and Democrats increased dramatically. The gap with regard to the Iraq War also increased.

	October 2001	October 2003	June 2007
Approve of Bush			
Democrats	88%	53%	10%
Independents	92%	68%	32%
Republicans	99%	92%	74%
Believe Iraq War was worth fighting			
Democrats	–	50%	14%
Independents	–	70%	35%
Republicans	–	91%	70%

most important of the core values. Liberals are willing to tolerate government intervention in such areas as college admissions and business decisions to help remedy
high levels of race, class, or gender inequality. For conservatives, on the other hand,
liberty is the core value. Conservatives oppose most efforts by the government, however well intentioned, to intrude into private life or the marketplace. This simple formula for distinguishing liberalism and conservatism is of course not always
accurate because political ideologies seldom lend themselves to neat or logical char-
acterizations. Conservatives, for example, are sometimes more tolerant of, and liberals more resistant to, government intervention in social policy realms involving the
family, marriage, homosexuality, and abortion.

Often political observers search for logical connections among the various positions identified with liberalism or conservatism, and they are disappointed or puzzled
when they are unable to find a set of coherent philosophical principles that define and
unite the several elements of either set of beliefs. On the liberal side, for example,
what is the logical connection between opposition to U.S. government intervention in
the affairs of foreign nations and calls for greater intervention in America's economy
and society? On the conservative side, what is the logical relationship between opposition to government regulation of business and support for a ban on abortion?

Frequently, the relationships among the various elements of liberalism or the several aspects of conservatism are *political* rather than *logical*. One underlying basis of liberal views is that all or most of them represent criticisms of or attacks on the foreign
and domestic policies and cultural values of the business and commercial strata that
have been prominent in the United States for the past century. In some measure, the
tenets of contemporary conservatism represent this elite's defense of its positions
against its enemies, who include organized labor, minority groups, and some intellectuals and professionals. Thus liberals attack business and commercial elites by advocating more government regulation, including consumer protection and environmental
regulation; opposition to weapons programs; and support for expensive social programs. Conservatives counterattack by asserting that government regulation of the
economy is ruinous and that military weapons are needed in a changing world.

Of course, it is important to note that many people who call themselves liberals
or conservatives accept only part of the liberal or conservative ideology. Although it
appears that Americans have adopted a more conservative outlook on some issues,
their views in other areas have remained largely unchanged or have even become
more liberal in recent years. Thus many individuals who are liberal on social issues
are conservative on economic issues. There is certainly nothing illogical about these
mixed positions. They simply indicate the relatively open and fluid character of
American political debate.

PUBLIC OPINION AND POLITICAL KNOWLEDGE

As they read newspapers, listen to the radio, watch television, and chat with their
friends and associates, citizens are constantly confronted by new political events, issues, and personalities. Often they will be asked what they think about a particular
issue or whether they plan to support a particular candidate. Indeed, in our democ-

racy we expect every citizen to have views about the major problems of the day as well as opinions about who should be entrusted with the nation's leadership.

Some Americans know quite a bit about politics, and many have general views and hold opinions on several issues. Few Americans, though, devote sufficient time, energy, or attention to politics to really understand or evaluate the myriad issues with which they are bombarded on a regular basis. In fact, many studies have shown that the average American knows very little about politics. In one major study, for example, only 25 percent of respondents could name their two senators, only 29 percent could name their U.S. representative, and fewer than half knew that the Constitution's first ten amendments are called the Bill of Rights.[14] Evidence that half of America's citizens—particularly those who have not attended college—are so unaware of the nation's history and politics is troubling.

Yet ignorance is probably a predictable and inevitable fact of political life. Some analysts have argued that political attentiveness is costly; it means spending time at the very least, and often money as well, to collect, organize, and digest political information.[15] Balanced against this cost to an individual is the very low probability that he or she will, on the basis of this costly information, take an action that would not otherwise have been taken *and* that such a departure in behavior would make a beneficial difference to him or her *and* that such a difference, if it existed, would exceed the cost of acquiring the information in the first place. Because individuals anticipate that informed actions taken by them will rarely make much difference while the costs of informing oneself are often not trivial, especially for those with little education to begin with, it is rational to remain ignorant. In other words, the rationality principle suggests that many people should more profitably devote their personal resources—particularly their time—to more narrowly personal matters. This idea is in turn suggested by the collective-action principle, in which the bearing of burdens—such as the cost of becoming informed—is not likely to have much impact in a mass political setting. A more moderate version of "rational" ignorance recognizes that some kinds of information are inexpensive to acquire, such as sound bites from the evening news, or can be pleasant, such as reading the front page of the newspaper while drinking a cup of coffee. In such cases, an individual may become partially informed, but usually not in detail.

Precisely because becoming truly knowledgeable about politics requires a substantial investment of time and energy, many Americans seek to acquire political information and to make political decisions on the cheap, using shortcuts that seem to relieve them of having to engage in information gathering and evaluation. One "inexpensive" way to become informed is to take cues from trusted others—the local minister, the television commentator or newspaper editorialist, an interest-group leader, friends, and relatives.[16] Sometimes the cue giver is distrusted, in which case

 Rationality Principle

Some argue that the relatively high cost of gathering political information makes staying uninformed rational and therefore not surprising.

---

[14]Michael X. Delli Carpini and Scott Keeter, *What Americans Know about Politics and Why It Matters* (New Haven, Conn.: Yale University Press, 1996), pp. 307–28.   ○ ONLINE READING

[15]Anthony Downs, *An Economic Theory of Democracy* (New York: Harper & Row, 1957).

[16]For a discussion of the role of information in democratic politics, see Arthur Lupia and Mathew D. McCubbins, *The Democratic Dilemma: Can Citizens Learn What They Need to Know?* (New York: Cambridge University Press, 1998).

the cue leads the receiver in the opposite direction. For example, if a liberal is told that Republican leaders are backing a major overhaul of the Social Security system, he or she will probably not read thousands of pages of economic projections before exhibiting suspicion of the president's efforts. Along the same lines, a common shortcut for political evaluation and decision making is to assess new issues and events through the lenses of one's general beliefs and orientation. Thus if a conservative learns of a plan to expand federal social programs, he or she might express opposition to the endeavor without carefully pondering the specifics of the proposal.

Neither of these shortcuts is entirely reliable, however. Taking cues from others may lead individuals to accept positions that they would not support if they had more information. And general ideological orientations are usually poor guides to decision making in concrete instances. For one thing, especially when applied to discrete issues, most individuals' beliefs turn out to be filled with contradictions. For example, what position should a liberal take on immigration? Should a liberal favor keeping America's borders open to poor people from all over the world, or should he or she be concerned that America's open borders create a pool of surplus labor that permits giant corporations to drive down the wages of poor American workers? Many other issues defy easy ideological characterization. What should liberals think about the financial rescue plan enacted by Congress in 2008? How should conservatives view America's military actions in Iraq? Each of these policies combines a mix of issues and is too complex to lend itself to simple ideological interpretation.

While understandable and perhaps inevitable, widespread inattentiveness to politics weakens American democracy in two ways. First, those who lack political information or resort to inadequate shortcuts to acquire and assess information cannot effectively defend their political interests and can easily become victims or losers in political struggles. Second, the presence of large numbers of politically inattentive or ignorant individuals means that the political process can be more easily manipulated by the various institutions and forces that seek to shape public opinion.

As to the first of these problems, in our democracy millions of ordinary citizens take part in political life, at least to the extent of voting in national elections. Those with little knowledge of the election's issues or candidates or procedures can find themselves acting against their own preferences and interests. One example is U.S. tax policy. Over the past several decades, the United States has substantially reduced the rate of taxation for its wealthiest citizens.[17] Tax cuts signed into law by President Bush in 2001 and mostly maintained throughout the decade provided a tax break mainly for the top 1 percent of the nation's wage earners, and further tax cuts proposed by the president offered additional benefits to this privileged stratum. It is surprising, however, that polling data showed that millions of middle-class and lower-middle-class Americans who did not stand to benefit from the president's tax cuts seemed to favor them nonetheless. The explanation appears to be a lack of political knowledge. Millions of individuals who were unlikely to derive much advantage from President Bush's tax policy thought they would. The politi-

> **Policy Principle**
>
> Government policies disproportionately reflect the goals and interests of citizens with higher levels of income and education because these individuals tend to have more knowledge of politics and are more willing to act on it.

---

[17]One of the most detailed analyses of the distribution of the tax burden in advanced industrial democracies in the past half century is Thomas Piketty and Emmanuel Saez, "How Progressive Is the U.S. Federal Tax System? Historical and International Perspectives," working paper 12404, National Bureau of Economic Research, 2006 (www.nber.org/papers/w12404).

cal scientist Larry Bartels has called this phenomenon "misplaced self-interest."[18] Upper-bracket taxpayers, who are usually served by an army of financial advisers, are unlikely to suffer from this problem. Knowledge may not always translate into political power, but lack of knowledge is almost certain to translate into political weakness. And according to the policy principle, the lack of knowledge and concomitant political weakness mean policy disappointment.

SHAPING OPINION: POLITICAL LEADERS, PRIVATE GROUPS, AND THE MEDIA

The fact that many Americans are inattentive to politics and lack even basic political information renders public opinion and the political process more easily susceptible to manipulation. Although direct efforts to influence opinion don't always succeed, three forces play especially important roles in shaping opinion. These are the government, private groups, and the news media.

Collective-Action Principle

Widely held political ideas may be the product of orchestrated campaigns by government, organized groups, or the media.

Government and the Shaping of Public Opinion

All governments attempt, to a greater or lesser extent, to influence, manipulate, or manage their citizens' beliefs. But the extent to which public opinion is affected by government public relations efforts is probably limited. The government—despite its size and power—is only one source of information in the United States. Very often government claims are disputed by the media, interest groups, and at times opposing forces within the government itself. Often, too, government efforts to manipulate public opinion backfire when the public is made aware of the government's tactics. Thus in 1971 the government's efforts to build popular support for the Vietnam War were hurt when CBS News aired its documentary *The Selling of the Pentagon*, which purported to reveal the extent and character of government efforts to sway popular sentiment. In this documentary, CBS demonstrated the techniques, including planted news stories and faked film footage, that the government had used to misrepresent its activities in Vietnam. These revelations, of course, undermined popular trust in all government claims.

A hallmark of the administration of President Bill Clinton was the steady use of election-campaign-type techniques to bolster popular enthusiasm for White House initiatives. The president established a political "war room" similar to the one that operated in his campaign headquarters. In the presidential version, representatives from all cabinet departments met daily to discuss and coordinate the president's public relations efforts. Many of the same consultants and pollsters who directed the successful Clinton campaign were also employed in the selling of the president's programs.[19]

---

[18]Larry M. Bartels, "Homer Gets a Tax Cut: Inequality and Public Policy in the American Mind," *Perspectives on Politics* 3 (2005): 15–31.

[19]Gerald F. Seib and Michael K. Frisby, "Selling Sacrifice," *Wall Street Journal*, 5 February 1993, p. 1.

After he assumed office in 2001, George W. Bush asserted that political leaders should base their programs on their own conception of the public interest, not on the polls. This did not mean that Bush ignored public opinion, however. He relied on the pollster Jan van Lohuizen to conduct a low-key operation, sufficiently removed from the limelight to allow the president to renounce polling while he continued to make use of survey data.[20] At the same time, the Bush White House developed an extensive public relations program, led initially by the former presidential aide Karen Hughes, to bolster popular support for the president's policies. Hughes, working with the conservative TV personality Mary Matalin, coordinated White House efforts to maintain popular support for the administration's war against terrorism. These efforts included presidential speeches, media appearances by administration officials, numerous press conferences, and thousands of press releases presenting the administration's views.[21] The White House also made a substantial effort to sway opinion in foreign countries, even sending officials to present the administration's views on television networks serving the Arab world.

Another example of a Bush administration effort to shape public opinion is a series of commercials it produced at taxpayer expense in 2004 to promote the new Medicare prescription drug program. The commercials, prominently featuring the president, were designed to look like news stories and were aired in English and Spanish by hundreds of local television stations. Called a video news release, this type of commercial is designed to give viewers the impression that they are watching a real news story. The presumption is that viewers are more likely to believe what they think is news coverage than material they know to be advertising. Democrats, of course, accused the administration of conducting a partisan propaganda campaign with public funds, but Republicans pointed out that the Clinton administration had engaged in similar practices.

In January 2005, it was revealed that the administration had paid the conservative African American radio pundit Armstrong Williams to comment favorably on its educational policies. Williams received $240,000 in taxpayer dollars for touting the administration's programs but never indicated that he was being paid for his support. Presumably, listeners were never aware that they were hearing what amounted to government propaganda disguised as editorial commentary. Rational politicians push the envelope in manipulating the information environment to show themselves off in the most favorable light. Sometimes they get caught.

Private Groups and the Shaping of Public Opinion

We have already seen how the government tries to shape public opinion. But the ideas that become prominent in political life are also developed and spread by important economic and political groups searching for issues that will advance their causes. Rational political entrepreneurs pursue strategies that—an application of the collective-action principle—give the groups they lead a decided advantage in

---

[20] Joshua Green, "The Other War Room," *Washington Monthly*, April 2002.

[21] Peter Marks, "Adept in Politics and Advertising, Four Women Shape a Campaign," *New York Times*, 11 November 2001, p. B6.

the political arena in comparison with latent, unorganized groups. In some instances, in the hope of bringing others over to their side, private groups espouse values they truly believe in. Take, for example, the campaign against so-called partial birth abortion, which resulted in the Partial Birth Abortion Ban Act of 2003. Proponents of the act believed that prohibiting particular sorts of abortions would be a first step toward eliminating all abortions, something they view as a moral imperative.[22] In other cases, however, groups will promote principles designed mainly to further hidden agendas of political and economic interests. One famous example is the campaign against cheap imported handguns—the so-called Saturday-night specials—that was covertly financed by the domestic manufacturers of more expensive firearms. The campaign's organizers claimed that cheap handguns pose a grave risk to the public and should be outlawed. The real goal, though, was not safeguarding the public but protecting the economic well-being of the domestic gun industry. A more recent example is the campaign against the alleged "sweatshop" practices of some American companies manufacturing their products in third world countries. This campaign is mainly financed by U.S. labor unions seeking to protect their members' jobs by discouraging American firms from manufacturing their products abroad.[23]

Typically, ideas are marketed most effectively by groups with access to financial resources, public or private institutional support, and sufficient skill or education to select, develop, and draft ideas that will attract interest and support. Thus the development and promotion of conservative themes and ideas in recent years have been greatly facilitated by the millions of dollars that conservative corporations and business organizations such as the U.S. Chamber of Commerce and the Public Affairs Council spend each year on public information and what is now called in corporate circles "issues management." In addition, conservative business leaders have contributed millions of dollars to such conservative institutions as the Heritage Foundation, the Hoover Institution, and the American Enterprise Institute.[24] Many of the ideas that helped those on the right influence political debate were first developed and articulated by scholars associated with institutions such as these.

Although they do not usually have access to financial assets that match those available to their conservative opponents, liberal intellectuals and professionals have ample organizational skills, access to the media, and practice in creating, communicating, and using ideas. During the past three decades, the chief vehicle through which liberal intellectuals and professionals have advanced their ideas has been the "public interest group," an institution that relies heavily on voluntary contributions of time, effort, and interest on the part of its members. Through groups like Common Cause, the National Organization for Women, the Sierra Club, Friends of the Earth, and Physicians for Social Responsibility, intellectuals and professionals have been able to use their organizational skills and educational resources to develop and

Collective-Action Principle

One of the jobs of leaders of well-organized interest groups is seeking out issues around which they can mobilize group members. Organized interests are at a decided advantage in this respect, compared with latent, unorganized interests.

---

[22]Cynthia Gorney, "Gambling with Abortion," *Harper's Magazine*, November 2004, pp. 33–46.

[23]David P. Baron and Daniel Diermeier, "Strategic Activism and Nonmarket Strategy," *Journal of Economics and Management Strategy* (2006).

[24]See David Vogel, "The Power of Business in America: A Reappraisal," *British Journal of Political Science* 13 (1983): 19–44.

promote ideas.[25] Often research conducted at universities and liberal "think tanks" such as the Brookings Institution provides the ideas on which liberal politicians rely. For example, the welfare reform plan introduced by the Clinton administration in 1994 originated with the work of the Harvard professor David Ellwood. Ellwood's academic research led him to the conclusion that the nation's welfare system would be improved if services to the poor were expanded in scope but limited in duration. His idea was adopted by the 1992 Clinton presidential campaign, which was searching for a position on welfare that would appeal to both liberal and conservative Democrats. The Ellwood plan seemed perfect: It promised liberals an immediate expansion of welfare benefits, yet it held out to conservatives the idea that welfare recipients would receive benefits for only a limited time. The Clinton welfare reform plan even borrowed phrases from Ellwood's book *Poor Support*.[26]

The journalist and author Joe Queenan has correctly observed that although political ideas can erupt spontaneously, they almost never do. Instead, he says,

> issues are usually manufactured by tenured professors and obscure employees of think tanks. . . . It is inconceivable that the American people, all by themselves, could independently arrive at the conclusion that the depletion of the ozone layer poses a dire threat to our national well-being, or that an immediate, across-the-board cut in the capital-gains tax is the only thing that stands between us and the economic abyss. The American people do not have that kind of sophistication. *They have to have help* [emphasis added].[27]

The Media and the Shaping of Public Opinion

The communications media are among the most powerful forces operating in the marketplace of ideas. The mass media are not simply neutral messengers for ideas developed by others. Instead, the media have an enormous effect on popular attitudes and opinions. Over time, the ways in which the mass media report political events help shape the underlying attitudes and beliefs from which opinions emerge.[28] For example, for the past thirty years, the national news media have relentlessly investigated personal and official wrongdoing on the part of politicians and public officials. This continual media presentation of corruption in government and venality in politics has undoubtedly fostered the general attitude of cynicism and distrust that exists in the general public.

At the same time, the ways in which media coverage interprets or frames specific events can have a major impact on popular responses to and opinions about these events.[29] Because media framing can be important, the Bush administration sought to persuade broadcasters to follow its lead in its coverage of terrorism and

---

[25] See David Vogel, "The Public Interest Movement and the American Reform Tradition," *Political Science Quarterly* 96 (Winter 1980): 607–27.

[26] Jason DeParle, "The Clinton Welfare Bill Begins Trek in Congress," *New York Times*, 15 July 1994, p. 1.

[27] Joe Queenan, "Birth of a Notion," *Washington Post*, 20 September 1992, p. C1.

[28] John R. Zaller, *The Nature and Origins of Mass Opinion* (New York: Cambridge University Press, 1992).

[29] See Shanto Iyengar, *Is Anyone Responsible? How Television Frames Political Issues* (Chicago: University of Chicago Press, 1991); and Iyengar, *Do the Media Govern?* (Thousand Oaks, Calif.: Sage, 1997).

America's response to it in the months after the September 11 attacks. Broadcasters, who found themselves targets of anthrax-contaminated letters apparently mailed by terrorists, needed little persuasion. For the most part, the media praised the president for his leadership and presented the administration's military campaign in Afghanistan and domestic antiterrorism efforts in a positive light. Even newspapers like the *New York Times,* which had strongly opposed Bush in the 2000 election and questioned his fitness for the presidency, asserted that he had grown into the job. In the aftermath of the 2003 invasion of Iraq, however, media coverage of the Bush administration became more critical. Formerly supportive media accused the president of failing both to anticipate the chaos and violence of postwar Iraq and to develop a strategy that would allow America to extricate itself from its involvement in that country. The president, for his part, accused the media of failing to present an accurate picture of his administration's success in Iraq.

During the 2008 campaign, the media were often accused of bias. Hillary Clinton claimed that the media supported her rival, Barack Obama, throughout the campaign. And in the general election most of the mainstream media presented a respectful but unflattering view of John McCain while almost always dismissing attacks against Democratic candidate Barack Obama as partisan sniping. McCain's running mate, Sarah Palin, was savaged by the media, which published and broadcast every rumor that could be found about her on the Internet. At one point, the *New York Times* had to retract an account based upon gossip from *US* magazine that Palin was a supporter of right-wing columnist Pat Buchanan and had been a member of an Alaska separatist group.

The efforts of the government, private groups, and the media would almost certainly affect public opinion even if Americans were knowledgeable about politics and possessed the analytic abilities of philosophers. But widespread political ignorance makes the task of those who wish to manipulate opinion all the easier. Perhaps even a more attentive public might have believed the government's false claims that Iraq possessed weapons of mass destruction, but an uninformed public was easily persuaded. Indeed, tens of millions of Americans continued to believe Iraq had WMDs even after the claim had been definitively disproved.[30] Perhaps a better informed public would have understood that most Americans would not benefit from recently enacted tax changes, but a naive public was easily misled. More generally, while a more astute public might see through efforts by interest groups and the media to camouflage selfish interests behind campaigns purporting to serve higher goals, a credulous public is more easily deceived. All in all, Americans' lack of political interest and awareness makes public opinion an easy target for manipulation. However, as the 2006 elections proved (see Chapter 10), a competitive political environment permits attempts at manipulation to be countered and successful manipulations reversed.

---

[30]Mark Danner, "How Bush Really Won," *New York Review of Books,* 13 January 2005, p. 51.

MEASURING PUBLIC OPINION

As recently as fifty years ago, American political leaders gauged public opinion by people's applause and the size of crowds at meetings. This direct exposure to the people's views did not necessarily produce accurate knowledge of public opinion. It did, however, give political leaders confidence in their public support—and therefore confidence in their ability to govern by consent.

Abraham Lincoln and Stephen Douglas debated each other seven times in the summer and autumn of 1858, two years before they became presidential nominees. Their debates took place before audiences in parched cornfields and courthouse squares. A century later most presidential debates, although seen by millions, take place before a few reporters and technicians in television studios that might as well be on the moon. The public's response cannot be experienced directly. This distance between leaders and followers is one of the agonizing problems of modern democracy. The media provide information to millions of people, but they are not yet as efficient at providing leaders with information. Is government by consent possible where the scale of communication is so large and impersonal? To compensate for the decline in their ability to experience public opinion for themselves, leaders have turned to science, in particular the science of opinion polling.

It is no secret that politicians and public officials make extensive use of *public opinion polls* to help decide whether to run for office, what policies to support, how to vote on important legislation, and what types of appeals to make in their campaigns. President Lyndon Johnson was famous for carrying the latest Gallup and Roper poll results in his pocket, and it is widely believed that he began to withdraw from politics because the polls reported losses in public support. All recent presidents and other major political figures have worked closely with polls and pollsters.

Constructing Public Opinion from Surveys

The population in which pollsters are interested is usually quite large. To conduct their polls, they first choose a *sample* of the total population. The selection of this sample is important. Above all, it must be representative: The views of those in the sample must accurately and proportionately reflect the views of the whole. To a large extent, the validity of the poll's results depends on the sampling procedure used.

Sampling Techniques and Selection Bias The most common techniques for choosing such a sample are probability sampling and random digit dialing. In the case of *probability sampling*, the pollster begins with a list of the population to be surveyed. This list is called the sampling frame. After each member of the population has been assigned a number, a table of random numbers or a computerized random selection process is used to pick those members of the population to be surveyed.

It is important to emphasize, first, that a sample selected in this manner produces a subset of the population that is representative of the population—it is a microcosm, so to speak. It is also important to point out that whatever is learned about this representative sample can also be attributed to the larger population with a high level of assurance. (We shall discuss potential errors in generalizing to the full population shortly.) This technique is appropriate when the entire population can be identified. For example, all students registered at Texas colleges and universities can be identified from college records, and a sample of them can easily be drawn. When the pollster is interested in a national sample of Americans, however, this technique is not feasible, as no complete list of Americans exists.[31] National samples are usually drawn using a technique called *random digit dialing*—in which a computerized random-number generator produces a list of as many ten-digit numbers as the pollster deems necessary. Given that more than 95 percent of American households have telephones, this technique usually results in a random national sample. With the growth in cell-phone use, however, and the enactment of "do-not-call" legislation to discourage telemarketers, random digit dialing has become less reliable. (We shall elaborate on this shortly.)

The importance of sampling was brought home early in the history of political polling. A 1936 *Literary Digest* poll predicted that the Republican presidential candidate, Alf Landon, would defeat the Democrat, Franklin D. Roosevelt, in that year's election. The election of course ended in a Roosevelt landslide. The main problem with the survey was what is called *selection bias* in drawing the sample. The pollsters had relied on telephone directories and automobile registration rosters to produce a sampling frame. During the Great Depression, however, only wealthy Americans owned telephones and automobiles. Thus the millions of working-class Americans who constituted Roosevelt's principle base of support were excluded from the sample. A more recent instance of polling error caused by selection bias occurred during the 1998 Minnesota gubernatorial election. A poll conducted by the *Minneapolis Star Tribune* just six weeks before the election showed the former professional wrestler Jesse Ventura running a distant third to the Democratic candidate, Hubert Humphrey III, who seemed to have the support of 49 percent of the electorate, and the Republican, Norm Coleman, whose support stood at 29 percent. Only 10 percent of those polled said they were planning to vote for Ventura. On election day, Ventura outpolled both Humphrey and Coleman. Analysis of exit-poll data showed why the preelection polls had been so wrong. In an effort to be accurate, preelection pollsters' predictions often take account of the likelihood that respondents will actually vote. They do this by polling only people who have voted in the past or correcting for past frequency of voting. The *Star Tribune* poll was conducted only among individuals who had voted in the previous election. Ventura, however, brought to the polls not only individuals who had not voted in the last election but also many people who had never voted before in their lives. Approximately 12 percent of Minnesota's voters in 1998 said they came to the polls only because Ventura was on the ballot. This surge in turnout was facilitated by the fact that Minnesota permits same-day voter registration. Thus the pollsters were wrong because Ventura changed the composition of the electorate.[32]

---

[31] Herbert Asher, *Polling and the Public* (Washington, D.C.: Congressional Quarterly Press, 2001), p. 64.

[32] Carl Cannon, "A Pox on Both Our Parties," in *The Enduring Debate: Classic and Contemporary Readings in American Politics*, 2nd ed., ed. David T. Canon, Anne Khademian, and Kenneth R. Mayor (New York: Norton, 2000), p. 389.

random digit dialing A poll in which respondents are selected at random from a list of ten-digit telephone numbers, with every effort made to avoid bias in the construction of the sample.

selection bias A polling error in which the sample is not representative of the population being studied, so that some opinions are over- or underrepresented.

In recent years, the issue of selection bias has been further complicated by the fact that growing numbers of individuals refuse to answer pollsters' questions or use answering machines and caller ID to screen unwanted calls. If pollsters could be certain that those who responded to their surveys simply reflected the views of those who refused to respond, there would be no problem. Some studies suggest, however, that the views of respondents and nonrespondents can differ, especially along social-class lines. Middle- and upper-middle-class individuals are more likely to be willing to respond to surveys than their working-class counterparts.[33] Thus far, "nonresponse bias" has not undermined a major national survey, but the possibility of a future *Literary Digest* fiasco should not be ignored.

Sample Size The degree of reliability in polling is also a function of sample size. For polls of citizens of the United States, the typical size of a sample ranges from 450 to 1,500 respondents. This number reflects a trade-off between cost and degree of precision desired. A larger and hence more costly sample size is associated with greater precision in making generalizations to the full population than is a smaller sample size.

The chance that the sample used does not accurately represent the population from which it is drawn is called the **sampling error**, or *margin of error*. The sampling error measures the range of possibilities for a particular characteristic of a population based on the estimate of that characteristic in the sample drawn. The margin of error acknowledges that any given sample may not be perfectly representative of the full population. A typical survey of 1,500 respondents, for example, will have a sampling error of approximately 3 percent. When a preelection poll indicates that 51 percent of voters surveyed favor the Republican candidate and 49 percent support the Democratic candidate, the outcome is in fact too close to call because it is within the margin of error of the survey. A figure of 51 percent means that between 54 and 48 percent of voters in the population favor the Republicans, while a figure of 49 percent indicates that between 52 and 46 percent of all voters support the Democrats. Thus in this example, any outcome ranging from a 54–46 Republican victory to a 48–52 Republican loss is consistent with the survey evidence. The precision of the poll in this case does not permit a clear prediction of a winner.

Table 9.5 shows how accurate two of the major national polling organizations have been in predicting the outcome of presidential elections. In both the 2000 and the 2004 presidential elections, for example, in light of a 3 percent margin of error, both the Harris and the Gallup organizations predicted a "dead heat." Pollsters have been mostly correct in their predictions.[34]

Survey Design Even with reliable sample procedures, surveys may fail to reflect the true distribution of opinion within a target population. One frequent source of

---

[33]John Goyder, Keith Warriner, and Susan Miller, "Evaluating Socio-economic Status Bias in Survey Nonresponse," *Journal of Official Statistics* 18, no. 1 (2002): 1–11.

[34]For a recent paper on the difficulties with polls, especially in trying to assess the preferences of specific subgroups in the population, see David Leal, Matt Barreto, Jongho Lee, and Rodolfo O. de la Garza, "The Latino Vote in the 2004 Election," *PS: Political Science and Politics* 38 (January 2005): 41–49.

sampling error A polling error that arises on account of the small size of the sample.

TABLE 9.5 Two Pollsters and Their Records

Year	Presidential Candidates	Harris	Gallup	Actual Outcome
2008	Obama	50	51	53
	McCain	44	43	46
2004	Bush, G. W.	49	49	51
	Kerry	48	49	48
	Nader	1	1	0
2000	Bush, G. W.	47	48	48
	Gore	47	46	49
	Nader	5	4	3
1996	Clinton	51	52	49
	Dole	39	41	41
	Perot	9	7	8
1992	Clinton	44	44	43
	Bush, G. H. W.	38	37	38
	Perot	17	14	19
1988	Bush, G. H. W.	51	53	54
	Dukakis	47	42	46
1984	Reagan	56	59	59
	Mondale	44	41	41
1980	Reagan	48	47	51
	Carter	43	44	41
	Anderson		8	
1976	Carter	48	48	51
	Ford	45	49	48
1972	Nixon	59	62	61
	McGovern	35	38	38
1968	Nixon	40	43	43
	Humphrey	43	42	43
	Wallace	13	15	14
1964	Johnson	62	64	61
	Goldwater	33	36	39
1960	Kennedy	49	51	50
	Nixon	41	49	49
1956	Eisenhower	NA*	60	58
	Stevenson		41	42
1952	Eisenhower	47	51	55
	Stevenson	42	49	44
1948	Truman	NA*	44.5	49.6
	Dewey		49.5	45.1

SOURCE: Data from the Harris survey and the Gallup poll, Chicago Tribune–New York News Syndicate, various press releases, 1964–2008. Courtesy of Louis Harris & Associates and the Gallup Organization.

NOTE: Figures are percentages. All except those for 1948 are rounded.
*Not asked

FIGURE 9.4 It Depends on How You Ask

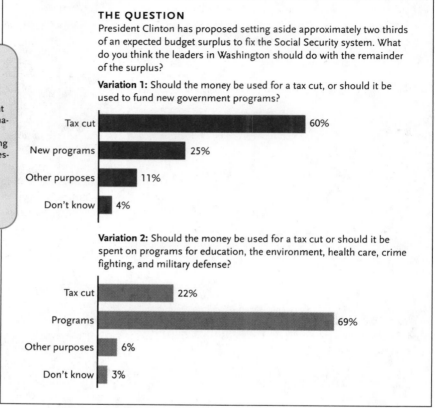

THE QUESTION

President Clinton has proposed setting aside approximately two thirds of an expected budget surplus to fix the Social Security system. What do you think the leaders in Washington should do with the remainder of the surplus?

Variation 1: Should the money be used for a tax cut, or should it be used to fund new government programs?

Tax cut	60%
New programs	25%
Other purposes	11%
Don't know	4%

Variation 2: Should the money be used for a tax cut or should it be spent on programs for education, the environment, health care, crime fighting, and military defense?

Tax cut	22%
Programs	69%
Other purposes	6%
Don't know	3%

SOURCE: Pew Research Center for the People and the Press, reported in the *New York Times*, 30 January 2000.

ANALYZING THE EVIDENCE

The public's desire for tax cuts can be hard to measure. Pollsters asking what should be done with the nation's budget surplus got different results, depending on the specifics of the question. What differences in the two versions of the question do you think account for the different answers?

measurement error is the wording of survey questions. The precise words used in a question can have an enormous effect on the answers a survey elicits. The validity of survey results can also be adversely affected by poorly formatted questions, a faulty ordering of questions, inappropriate vocabulary, ambiguous questions, or questions with built-in biases. Often seemingly minor differences in the wording of a question can convey vastly different meanings to respondents and thus produce quite different response patterns (Figure 9.4). For example, for many years the University of Chicago's National Opinion Research Center has asked respondents whether they think the federal government is spending too much, too little, or about the right amount of money on "assistance for the poor." Answering the question posed this way, about two thirds of all respondents seem to believe that the government is spending too little. However, the same survey also asks whether the government spends too much, too little, or about the right amount for "welfare." When the word

measurement error
The failure to identify the true distribution of opinion within a population because of errors such as ambiguous or poorly worded questions.

welfare is substituted for *assistance for the poor,* about half of all respondents indicate that too much money is being spent.[35]

Push Polling   In recent years, another form of bias has been introduced into surveys by the use of a technique called *push polling.* This technique involves asking a respondent a loaded question about a political candidate, with the question designed to elicit the response sought by the pollster and, simultaneously, to shape the respondent's perception of the candidate in question. For example, during the 1996 New Hampshire presidential primary, push pollsters employed by the campaign of one of Lamar Alexander's rivals called thousands of voters to ask, "If you knew that Lamar Alexander had raised taxes six times in Tennessee, would you be less inclined or more inclined to support him?"[36] More than 100 consulting firms across the nation now specialize in push polling, which is not a conventional use of legitimate survey methods and has been condemned by the American Association for Public Opinion Researchers.[37] Calling push polling the "political equivalent of a drive-by shooting," Representative Joe Barton (R-Tex.) launched a congressional investigation into the practice.[38] Push polls may be one reason why Americans are becoming increasingly skeptical of the practice of polling and increasingly unwilling to answers pollsters' questions.[39]

Illusion of Salience   In the early days of a political campaign, when voters are asked which candidates they do or do not support, the answer they give often has little significance because the choice is not yet important to them. Their preferences may change many times before the election. This is part of the explanation for the phenomenon of the postconvention "bounce" in the popularity of presidential candidates, which is observed after Democratic and Republican national nominating conventions. Respondents' preferences reflected the amount of attention a candidate had received during the conventions rather than strongly held views.

The issues that are truly uppermost in the minds of voters at the time of an election, called *salient interests,* are often difficult to forecast very far in advance. These are interests that are of more than ordinary concern to respondents in a survey or to voters in the electorate. Politicians, social scientists, journalists, or pollsters who assume that something is important to the public when in fact it is not are creating an *illusion of salience.* This illusion can be created and fostered by polls despite careful controls in sampling, interviewing, and data analysis. In fact, the

> **push polling** A polling technique in which the questions are designed to shape the respondent's opinion.
>
> **salient interests** Attitudes and views that are especially important to the individual holding them.
>
> **illusion of salience** The impression conveyed by polls that something is important to the public when it actually is not.

---

[35]Michael R. Kagay and Janet Elder, "Numbers Are No Problem for Pollsters, Words Are," *New York Times,* 9 August 1992, p. E6.

[36]Donn Tibbetts, "Draft Bill Requires Notice of Push Polling," *Manchester Union Leader,* 3 October 1996, p. A6.

[37]See www.aapor.org.pdfs/2003/2003pushpollstatement.pdf.

[38]Amy Keller, "Subcommittee Launches Investigation of Push Polls," *Roll Call,* 3 October 1996, p. 1.

[39]For a discussion of the growing difficulty of persuading people to respond to surveys, see John Brehm, *Phantom Respondents* (Ann Arbor: University of Michigan Press, 1993).

illusion is strengthened by the credibility that science gives survey results. The problem of salience has become especially acute as a result of the proliferation of media polls. The television networks and major national newspapers all make heavy use of opinion polls. Polls are also commissioned by local television stations and local and regional newspapers.

On the positive side, polls allow journalists to make independent assessments of political realities, assessments not influenced by the partisan claims of politicians. At the same time, however, media polls can allow journalists to make news when none exists. Polling diminishes journalists' dependence on news makers. A poll commissioned by a news agency can provide the basis for a good story even when candidates, politicians, and other news makers are not engaging in especially newsworthy activities. Thus on days when little or nothing is taking place in a political campaign, poll results, especially apparent changes in candidates' popularity margins, can provide exciting news. Several times during the 2008 presidential campaign, for example, small changes in the relative standing of the Democratic and Republican candidates produced banner headlines around the country. Stories about what the candidates actually did or said often took second place to reporting the "horse race."

Because rapid and dramatic shifts in candidates' margins tend to take place when voters' preferences are least fully formed, it is interesting that horse-race news is most likely to make the headlines when it is least significant. In other words, media interest in poll results is inversely related to the salience of voters' opinions and the significance of the polls' findings. However, by influencing perceptions, especially those of major contributors, media polls can influence political realities.

Bandwagon Effect One of the most noted polling problems is the **bandwagon effect,** which occurs when polling results influence people to support the candidate marked as the probable victor. Some scholars argue that the bandwagon effect can be offset by an "underdog effect," in favor of the candidate who is trailing in the polls.[40] However, a candidate who demonstrates a lead in the polls usually finds it considerably easier to raise campaign funds than does a candidate whose poll standing is poor. With these additional funds, poll leaders can often afford to pay for television time and other campaign activities that will cement their advantage.

HOW DOES PUBLIC OPINION INFLUENCE GOVERNMENT POLICY?

One of the fundamental notions on which the U.S. government was founded is that "the public" should not be trusted when it comes to governing. The framers designed institutions that, although democratic, somewhat insulated governmental

bandwagon effect
A shift in electoral support to the candidate whom public opinion polls report as the front-runner.

---

[40]See Michael Traugott, "The Impact of Media Polls on the Public," in *Media Polls in American Politics,* ed. Thomas E. Mann and Gary Orren (Washington, D.C.: Brookings Institution, 1992), pp. 125–49.

decision making from popular pressure. For example, the indirect election of senators and presidents was supposed to prevent the government from being too dependent on the vagaries of public opinion.

Research from the 1950s and 1960s indicates that the framers' concerns were well founded. Individual-level survey analysis reveals that the respondents lacked fundamental political knowledge and had ill-formed opinions about government and public policy.[41] Their answers seemed nothing more than "doorstep opinions"— opinions given off the top of the head. When an individual was asked the same questions at different times, he or she often gave different answers. The dramatic and unpredictable changes seemed to imply that the public was indeed unreliable as a guide for political decisions.

The political scientists Benjamin Page and Robert Shapiro take issue with the notion that the public should not be trusted when it comes to policy making.[42] They contend that public opinion at the aggregate level is coherent and stable and that it moves in a predictable fashion in response to changing political, economic, and social circumstances.

How is this possible, given what previous studies have found? Page and Shapiro hypothesize that the individual-level responses are plagued by various types of errors that make people's opinions seem incoherent and unstable.When a large number of individual-level responses to survey questions are added up to produce an aggregate public opinion, the errors, or "noise," in the individual responses, if more or less random, will cancel one another out, revealing a collective opinion that is stable, coherent, and meaningful. From their results, Page and Shapiro concluded that the general public can indeed be trusted when it comes to governing.

In democratic nations, leaders should pay heed to public opinion, and most evidence suggests that they do. There are many instances in which public policy and public opinion do not coincide, but in general the government's actions are consistent with citizens' preferences. One study, for example, found that between 1935 and 1979, in about two thirds of all cases significant changes in public opinion were followed within one year by changes in government policy consistent with the shift in the popular mood.[43] Other studies have come to similar conclusions about public opinion and government policy at the state level.[44] Do these results imply that elected leaders merely pander to public opinion? The answer is no.

A recent study on the role that public opinion played during the failed attempt to enact health-care reform in the early days of the Clinton presidency found that public opinion polls had very little influence on individual members of Congress,

---

[41]Campbell et al., *The American Voter;* Philip E. Converse, "The Nature of Belief Systems in Mass Publics," in *Ideology and Discontent,* ed. David E. Apter (New York: Free Press, 1964).

[42]Benjamin I. Page and Robert Y. Shapiro, *The Rational Public: Fifty Years of Trends in Americans' Policy Preferences* (Chicago: University of Chicago Press, 1992).

[43]Benjamin I. Page and Robert Y. Shapiro, "Effects of Public Opinion on Policy," *American Political Science Review* 77, no. 1 (March 1983): 175–90.

[44]Robert S. Erikson, Gerald C. Wright, and John P. McIver, *Statehouse Democracy: Public Opinion and Policy in the American States* (New York: Cambridge University Press, 1993).

who used these polls first to justify positions they had already adopted and then to shape public thinking on the issue. In other words, opinion and policy were related because policy makers shaped opinion to support paths they already planned to take. This pattern is consistent with the opinion-manipulation efforts we examined earlier in this chapter. However, the study also found that congressional party leaders based their health-care legislation strategies on their concerns about the effects of public opinion on the electoral fortunes of individual members of Congress. Leaders' concerns about public opinion thus help explain why the congressional policy-making process follows public opinion even though individual members of Congress do not.[45] The salience of health care has remained high for more than a decade since the failure of Clinton's effort. During the 2008 presidential campaign, both Barack Obama and John McCain presented complex and ambitious health-care reform proposals in response to the public's continuing concern with the issue.

There are always areas of disagreement between opinion and policy. For example, the majority of Americans favored stricter government control of handguns for years before Congress adopted the modest restrictions on firearms purchases embodied in the 1994 Brady gun-control bill and the amendment of the 1968 Omnibus Crime Control and Safe Streets Act. Similarly, most Americans, blacks as well as whites, oppose school busing to achieve racial balance, yet such busing continues to be used in many parts of the nation. Most Americans are also far less concerned with the rights of the accused than the federal courts seem to be. And most Americans oppose U.S. military intervention in other nations' affairs, yet such intervention continues to take place and often wins public approval after the fact.

Several factors can contribute to a lack of consistency between opinion and government policy. First, the nominal majority on a particular issue may not be as intensely committed to its preference as the adherents of the minority viewpoint. An intensely committed minority may often be more willing to commit its time, energy, efforts, and resources to the affirmation of its opinions than an apathetic majority, even if it is large. In the case of firearms, for example, although the proponents of gun control are in the majority by a wide margin, most do not regard the issue as one of critical importance to themselves and are not willing to commit much effort to advancing their cause. The opponents of gun control, by contrast, are intensely committed, well organized, and well financed and as a result are usually able to carry the day. In accordance with the institution principle, the collective-action principle, and the policy principle, intense commitment, organization, and financial resources are potent assets in the legislature, the executive bureaucracy, and the courts.

A second important reason why public policy and public opinion may not coincide has to do with the character and structure of the American system of government. The framers of the Constitution, as we saw in Chapter 2, sought to create a system of government that was based on popular consent but did not invariably and automatically translate shifting popular sentiments into public policies. As a result,

---

[45] Lawrence R. Jacobs, Eric D. Lawrence, Robert Y. Shapiro, and Steven S. Smith, "Congressional Leadership of Public Opinion," *Political Science Quarterly* 113 (Spring 1998): 21–41.

the American governmental process includes arrangements such as an appointed judiciary that can produce policy decisions that may run contrary to prevailing popular sentiment—at least for a time.

Perhaps the inconsistencies between opinion and policy could be resolved if we made broader use of a mechanism currently employed by a number of states: the ballot initiative. This procedure allows propositions to be placed on the ballot and voted into law by the electorate, bypassing most of the normal machinery of representative government. In recent years, several important propositions sponsored by business and conservative groups have been enacted.[46] For example, California's Proposition 209, approved by the state's voters in 1996, prohibited state and local government agencies in California from using race or gender preferences in hiring, contracting, or university admissions decisions. Responding to conservatives' success, liberal groups launched a number of ballot initiatives in 2000. In Washington State, for example, voters were asked to consider propositions sponsored by teachers unions that would have required annual cost-of-living raises for teachers and more than $1.8 billion in additional state spending over the next six years.[47]

Initiatives such as these seem to provide the public with an opportunity to express its will. During the 2008 election, propositions on social issues—gay marriage, stem-cell research, immigration—were on the ballot in many states, bypassing stalled efforts of the normal political process. The major problem, however, is that government by initiative offers little opportunity for reflection and compromise. Voters are presented with a proposition, usually sponsored by a special interest group, and are asked to take it or leave it. Perhaps the true will of the people, not to mention their best interest, lies somewhere between the positions taken by the various interest groups. Perhaps California voters might have preferred some compromise position on same-sex marriage rather than the *yes* or *no* vote required by Proposition 8. In a representative assembly, as opposed to a referendum campaign, a compromise position might have been achieved that would have been more satisfactory to all the residents of the state. This capacity for compromise is one reason the framers of the U.S. Constitution strongly favored representative government rather than direct democracy.[48]

When all is said and done, however, there can be little doubt that in general the actions of the American government do not remain out of line with popular sentiment for very long. A major reason for this is, of course, the electoral process, to which we shall next turn. Lest we become too complacent, however, we should not forget that the close relationship between government and opinion in America may also be in part a result of the government's success in molding opinion.

Institution Principle

Policy and opinion are not always consistent because policy is the product of institutional processes and public opinion is but one of many influences on these processes.

---

[46]David Broder, *Democracy Derailed: Initiative Campaigns and the Power of Money* (New York: Harcourt, 2000).

[47]Robert Tomsho, "Liberals Take a Cue from Conservatives: This Election, the Left Tries to Make Policy with Ballot Initiatives," *Wall Street Journal*, 6 November 2000, p. A12.

[48]For the classic treatment of take-it-or-leave-it referendums and initiatives, see Thomas Romer and Howard Rosenthal, "Political Resource Allocation, Controlled Agendas, and the Status Quo," *Public Choice* 33 (1978): 27–44.

Rationality Principle	Collective-Action Principle	Institution Principle	Policy Principle	History Principle
Objective political interests fuel individuals' political beliefs. Ideologies serve as informational shortcuts, allowing individuals to arrive at a view on an issue or a candidate while economizing on the cost of becoming informed of the details. Some argue that the relatively high cost of gathering political information makes staying uninformed rational and therefore not surprising.	Widely held political ideas may be the product of orchestrated campaigns by government, organized groups, or the media. One of the jobs of leaders of well-organized interest groups is seeking out issues around which they can mobilize group members. Organized interests are at a decided advantage in this respect, compared with latent, unorganized interests.	One reason why policy may not be consistent with opinion is that the United States is a representative government, not a direct democracy. Policy and opinion are not always consistent because policy is the product of institutional processes and public opinion is but one of many influences on these processes.	Government policies disproportionately reflect the goals and interests of citizens with higher levels of income and education because these individuals tend to have more knowledge of politics and are more willing to act on it.	The absence of either a feudal or a socialist tradition in the United States allowed for the emergence of a consensus on liberal democracy. Changing political circumstances and events can be the impetus for major shifts in opinion. For example, with the changing landscape of race relations and race-related policies beginning in the 1960s, southern whites have become a major source of support for the Republican party.

SUMMARY

All governments claim to obey public opinion, and in democracies politicians and political leaders actually try to do so.

The American government does not directly regulate opinions and beliefs in the sense that dictatorial regimes often do. Opinion is regulated by an institution that the government constructed and maintains: the marketplace of ideas. In this marketplace, opinions and ideas compete for support. In general, opinions supported by upper-class groups have a better chance of succeeding than those advanced mainly by the lower classes.

Americans share a number of values and viewpoints but often classify themselves as liberal or conservative in their basic orientation. The meaning of these terms has changed greatly over the past century. Once liberalism meant opposition to big government, yet today liberals favor an expanded role for the government. And once conservatism meant support for state power and aristocratic rule, but today conservatives oppose government regulation, at least of business affairs.

Although the United States relies mainly on market mechanisms to regulate opinion, even our government intervenes to some extent, seeking to influence both particular opinions and, more important, the general climate of political opinion. Political leaders' increased distance from the public makes it difficult for them to gauge public opinion. Until recently, public opinion on some issues could be gauged better by studying mass behavior than by studying polls. Population characteristics are also useful in estimating public opinion on some subjects.

The modern scientific approach to determining public opinion is random sample polling. One advantage of this method is that elections can be very accurately predicted; using a model of behavior, pollsters are often able to predict better than the voters themselves how voters will mark their ballots. A second advantage is that polls provide information on the bases and conditions of voting decisions. They make it possible to assess trends in attitudes and the influence of ideology on attitudes.

There are also problems with polling, however. The illusion of salience can encourage politicians to confront too many trivial issues. Even with scientific polling, politicians cannot be certain that they understand public opinion. Their recognition of this limitation may function as a valuable restraint, however.

FOR FURTHER READING

Althaus, Scott. *Collective Preferences and Democratic Politics.* New York: Cambridge University Press, 2003.

Erikson, Robert S., and Kent L. Tedin. *American Public Opinion: Its Origins, Content, and Impact.* 6th ed. New York: Longman, 2001.

Gallup, George, and Saul Forbes Rae. *The Pulse of Democracy: The Public-Opinion Poll and How It Works.* New York: Simon & Schuster, 1940.

Ginsberg, Benjamin. *The Captive Public: How Mass Opinion Promotes State Power.* New York: Basic Books, 1986.

Herbst, Susan. *Numbered Voices: How Opinion Polling Has Shaped American Politics.* Chicago: University of Chicago Press, 1993.

Key, V. O. *Public Opinion and American Democracy.* New York: Knopf, 1961.

ONLINE READING ○ Lee, Taeku. *Mobilizing Public Opinion.* Chicago: University of Chicago Press, 2002.

Lippmann, Walter. *Public Opinion.* New York: Harcourt, Brace, 1922.

Mueller, John. *Policy and Opinion in the Gulf War.* Chicago: University of Chicago Press, 1994.

Neuman, W. Russell. *The Paradox of Mass Politics: Knowledge and Opinion in the American Electorate.* Cambridge, Mass.: Harvard University Press, 1986.

Page, Benjamin I., and Robert Y. Shapiro. *The Rational Public: Fifty Years of Trends in Americans' Policy Preferences.* Chicago: University of Chicago Press, 1992.

Roll, Charles W., and Albert H. Cantril. *Polls: Their Use and Misuse in Politics.* New York: Basic Books, 1972.

ONLINE READING ○ Stimson, James A. *Public Opinion in America: Moods, Cycles, and Swings.* 2nd ed. Boulder, Colo.: Westview Press, 1998.

Sussman, Barry. *What Americans Really Think: And Why Our Politicians Pay No Attention.* New York: Pantheon Books, 1988.

Zaller, John R. *The Nature and Origins of Mass Opinion.* New York: Cambridge University Press, 1992.

Since the first public opinion research was conducted in the 1950s, scholars have observed that the public is not well informed about nor very interested in foreign policy. The principles of politics help us understand why this is perhaps not surprising. For most Americans, it is not rational to spend much time thinking about foreign policy. The countries involved are far away, the issues are complicated, and the outcomes seldom affect Americans' daily lives the way that, say, a popular federal program or a spike in the unemployment rate might.

Furthermore, foreign policy institutions are not designed to give the public a strong voice. Intelligence agencies are necessarily secretive, and the president makes most foreign policy decisions, generally without debate in Congress. Even the congressional committees that deal with foreign policy issues hold many of their hearings behind closed doors.

However there are periods when public opinion matters in foreign affairs. One such instance is in the midst of a "rally," such as occurred after the September 11 terrorist attacks. In these cases, collective action on the part of politicians is easy, since the public tends to throw its support behind the current president and other political leaders. Other situations, such as the war in Iraq, are more complicated. Public opinion on the war is deeply divided along partisan lines, which makes it politically rational for politicians to reflect those divisions.

The New York Times, July 30, 2006

Partisan Divide on Iraq Exceeds Split on Vietnam

By Robin Toner and Jim Rutenberg

No military conflict in modern times has divided Americans on partisan lines more than the war in Iraq, scholars and pollsters say—not even Vietnam. And those divisions are likely to intensify in what is expected to be a contentious fall election campaign.

The latest New York Times/CBS News poll shows what one expert describes as a continuing "chasm" between the way Republicans and Democrats see the war. Three-fourths of the Republicans, for example, said the United States did the right thing in taking military action against Iraq, while just 24 percent of the Democrats did. Independents split down the middle.

"The present divisions are quite without precedent," said Ole R. Holsti, a professor of political science at Duke University and the author of "Public Opinion and American Foreign Policy."

The Vietnam War caused a wrenching debate that echoes to this day and shaped both parties, but at the time, public opinion did not divide so starkly on party lines. * * * The partisan divide on Iraq has fluctuated but endured across two intensely fought campaigns in which war and peace—and the overarching campaign against terrorism—have figured heavily. Each party has its internal differences, especially on future strategy for Iraq. But the overall divide is a defining feature of the fall campaign.

 History Principle

Many people still view American foreign policy through the lens of Vietnam, even though the conflict ended more than three decades ago. Political leaders struggle with the political legacy of Vietnam and the lessons it provides for Iraq.

The White House's top political advisers are advancing a strategy built around national security, arguing that Iraq is a central front in the battle against global terrorism and that opposition to the war is tantamount to "cutting and running" in a broader struggle to keep America safe.

After three years of conflict, Democrats argue that the Bush administration's policies in Iraq should not be equated with a stronger, safer America. Senator Harry Reid, the Democratic leader, said recently, "Nearly everywhere you look—from the Middle East to Asia—America's enemies have been emboldened by the administration's mismanagement of Iraq."

The voters, at times, are even more impassioned. Representative Henry J. Hyde, Republican of Illinois and chairman of the International Relations Committee, said that voters, pro or con, were treating the war the way they treated the mention of Richard M. Nixon in the 1974 post-Watergate midterm campaign. "Nobody is tepid on this issue," said Mr. Hyde, who is planning to retire.

Many experts and members of both parties say they worry about the long-term consequences of such bitter partisan polarization and its effect on the longstanding tradition—although one often honored in the breach—that foreign policy is built on bipartisan trust and consensus.

"The old idea that politics stops at the water's edge is no longer with us, and I think we've lost something as a result," said John C. Danforth, a former senator and an ambassador to the United Nations under President Bush. Senator Richard J. Durbin, Democrat of Illinois, said, "There used to be some unwritten rules when it came to foreign policy."

These divisions do not run across foreign policy. The latest poll shows no comparable partisan gap, for example, in attitudes toward the fighting between Israel and Hezbollah in Lebanon. On Capitol Hill, even as lawmakers position themselves furiously over Iraq, they produce big bipartisan majorities on issues like * * * nuclear deals with India or * * * resolutions expressing support for Israel.

But compared with past conflicts— from Vietnam to the war in the Persian Gulf to Afghanistan—the war in Iraq evoked strong partisan passions from the start.

* * *

* * * The difference in the way Democrats and Republicans viewed the Vietnam War—specifically, whether sending American troops was a mistake—never exceeded 18 percentage points between 1966 and 1973. In the most recent Times/CBS poll on Iraq, the partisan gap * * * was 50 percentage points.

* * *

The overall shift in public opinion on the war largely depends on how independents fall—and lately, they have been agreeing more with the Democrats. * * *

Christopher F. Gelpi, a political scientist at Duke, said the only partisan divide that came close to the division over Iraq occurred during President Ronald Reagan's military action in Grenada, but it was much smaller.

Experts cited several reasons for the extent of this partisan divide: Mr. Bush is a polarizing president in an intensely partisan age, they say. Gary C. Jacobson, a political scientist at the University of California, San Diego, said, "The divisions on the war exacerbate the divisions on Bush, and the divisions on Bush exacerbate the divisions on the war."

Democrats are generally more skeptical about the use of force, especially

Policy Principle

Democratic leaders and candidates found it in their electoral interests to attack Republicans on the war even though, in the long run, this may undermine the nation's ability to speak with one voice on foreign policy.

without broad international support, and the course of the war has seemed to justify their doubts.

Republicans have been fiercely loyal to Mr. Bush for his handling of the fight against terrorism and see Democratic critiques as counterproductive to that effort.

Partisan passions have also been heightened, some analysts said, by the use of national security issues in the past campaigns.

* * *

Democrats say the Republicans repeatedly broke the old rules, treating national security as a wedge issue to make Democrats look weak and unacceptable, especially in 2004. "George Bush decided to make foreign policy partisan in a way that Ronald Reagan or the first George Bush never did," said Senator Charles E. Schumer of New York, chairman of the Democratic Senatorial Campaign Committee.

Representative Rahm Emanuel of Illinois, the chairman of the Democratic Congressional Campaign Committee, said, "The divisions over Iraq and national security are the house that Karl Rove and George Bush built."

But Ken Mehlman, chairman of the Republican National Committee, said the war and national security were entirely appropriate issues for election campaigns.

"I don't think we're politicizing the war," Mr. Mehlman said. "I think the fact that there are legitimate and important differences, and it is the job of a campaign to clarify between individual candidates on what is the central question our nation faces, which is: How do you win this global war on terror?"

Mr. Mehlman said presidents from both parties had used war as a campaign rallying point throughout history. But, he said, national security has been especially important to the Republican Party since the Reagan days, as Democrats in the post-Vietnam era have become increasingly antiwar.

* * *

Three months before the midterm elections, the exchanges are already rough. * * * In independent interviews, two senior Republican strategists said that the war on terror—with Iraq as its central front—had been the single most effective motivator for base voters in internal party polls this year. Even so, some strategists said the continued violence in Iraq was a drag on many of their candidates, especially in moderate districts.

* * *

Analysts in both parties say the intensity of Democratic feeling against the war will be a powerful motivator in this fall's elections. The sentiment is perhaps most apparent in the Connecticut primary challenge to Senator Jospeh I. Lieberman, a strong supporter of the war.

A variety of experts in both parties said they worried about the aftermath of intense partisanship.

"This era in general feels excessively partisan, and national security has been put right into the mix of intense partisan debate," said Thomas E. Donilon, a lawyer and a former assistant secretary of state in the Clinton administration. "And it's a mistake in terms of the president developing support for his position on these tough issues."

Richard N. Haass, president of the Council on Foreign Relations, who until June 2003 served as director of policy planning for the State Department, said all nuance got lost in a campaign debate.

You end up with very stark choices: quote, stay the course, versus, quote, cut and run," Mr. Haass said. "And in reality, a lot of policy needs to be made between them."

* * *

Collective-Action Principle

Political candidates often speak to the public as if there are only two extreme options. This way, if one group wins office, as the Democrats did in 2006, they can unite effectively behind a common goal to change policy.

10 Elections

OVER THE PAST TWO CENTURIES, elections have come to play a significant role in the political processes of most nations. Democratic electoral systems, such as those that have evolved in the United States and western Europe, allow opposing forces to compete against and even replace current officeholders. In democracies, elections can also serve as institutions of legitimation and as safety valves for social discontent.[1] But beyond these functions, democratic elections facilitate popular influence, promote leadership accountability, and offer groups in society a measure of protection from the abuse of governmental power. Citizens exercise influence through elections by determining who should control the government. The chance to decide who will govern is an indirect opportunity for ordinary citizens to make choices about the policies, programs, and directions of governmental action. In the United States, for example, recent Democratic and Republican candidates have differed significantly on issues of taxing, social spending, and government regulation. As American voters have chosen between the two parties' candidates, they have also made choices about these issues.

Nominally, of course, a democratic election is the collective selection of leaders and representatives. In terms now familiar to the reader, elections are occasions in which multiple principals—the citizens—choose political agents to act on their behalf. There are two kinds of problems that face even the most rational of citizen principals in these circumstances. Electoral rules and arrangements

---

[1]See Daron Acemoglu and James A. Robinson, "Why Did the West Extend the Franchise? Democracy, Inequality, and Growth in Historical Perspective," *Quarterly Journal of Economics* 115 (2000): 1167–1200.

may be characterized and ultimately assessed as mechanisms for coming to grips with these.

The first problem facing citizens participating in a democratic election, known as the adverse selection problem, is a consequence of hidden information. When selecting one alternative over another, we are often incompletely informed about just what we are choosing. Many aspects or features of our choices are hidden from view and become apparent only long after the choice has been made. Thus in choosing Candidate A over Candidate B, exactly what are we getting? To some degree, candidates for office are pigs in a poke. We may know some things about them and some other things about their opponents, but even in a world of investigative reporters, paparazzi, and blogs, we can't always know what we've selected. It may turn out badly, but then again, it may not. The candidates themselves in large measure affect what we know about them, and it is often in their interest to hide or shroud in ambiguity items about themselves that, though possibly highly relevant to citizens' choices, might harm their electoral prospects. The solution to this

Elections can be perceived as institutional opportunities for multiple principals—the citizenry—to select agents—their elected officials—to act on their behalf, even though citizens usually have imperfect information about candidates and don't know how their agents will act once in office. Like any institutional arrangement, the electoral process is subject to rules and regulations that affect outcomes. In addition to the composition of the electorate, the "rules of the game"—what it takes to win and the size and composition of electoral districts—as well as the means of limiting popular involvement in elections—such as the electoral college—all play important roles in translating popular sentiment and votes into electoral outcomes. Voters decide based on multiple criteria, including partisan loyalty, issues, and candidates' characteristics. When issues dominate a campaign, candidates tend to converge toward the median voter. Voter turnout in the United States is low because candidates and parties often fail to mobilize voters and institutional barriers to participation—such as registration requirements—are too high for many Americans. But on the whole, elections remain important because they socialize and institutionalize political participation within the system.

---

adverse selection problem is openness and transparency: a wide-open and free-wheeling electoral process, a competitive political opposition, and an activist press. During the course of campaigns, information comes to light—from investigative reporting, opposition research, or sometimes even leaks from a candidate's own organization—that damages a candidate's competitive position.[2] Thus Governor Sarah Palin's vice-presidential nomination in 2008 was undermined by allegations that Palin had abused her authority as governor to bring about the dismissal of an Alaska state trooper who had been divorced from Palin's sister. Throughout the campaign, Palin's background, which was largely unfamiliar to voters, was vigorously investigated by the press.

---

[2] A classic example of adverse selection is the presidential selection of Supreme Court justices. Often a president finds that these men and women turn out much differently than expected. It is unlikely, for example, that President Dwight Eisenhower would have chosen Earl Warren, a former governor of California and the 1948 Republican vice-presidential candidate, to be chief justice of the Supreme Court had he known of Warren's liberal leanings. Nor would he have appointed Justice William Brennan, who turned out to be among the most liberal justices on the Court in the twentieth century. In Eisenhower's final press conference, he was asked by a reporter if he had made any mistakes while president. He said, "Two, and they're both sitting on the Supreme Court." President Richard Nixon, to give another example, appointed Harry Blackmun, the justice who later crafted the famous pro-choice opinion *Roe v. Wade* (410 U.S. 113 [1973]). Finally, there was the near-fateful decision of President George H. W. Bush in his elevation of David Souter, a federal judge, to the Supreme Court. Souter, in December 2000, joined the minority (only one vote short of a majority) that would have ordered the popular vote in the Florida presidential election recounted, an action that might well have denied President George W. Bush the presidency.

adverse selection problem The problem of incomplete information—of choosing alternatives without fully knowing the details of available options.

The second problem facing voters is known as ***moral hazard***. If adverse selection is a problem caused by hidden information, then moral hazard is a problem produced by hidden action. That is, it is the problem of agents who, once selected, cannot easily be monitored. Political leaders do many things that are public, such as making speeches, attaching their names as sponsors of legislation, and voting on legislative motions. But behind this public visibility are many private acts that are imperfectly observed at best. These veiled encounters used to take place in the proverbial smoke-filled rooms of Washington, but today they take place in the private dining rooms of Capitol Hill, where deals are struck between legislators and special interests, or in the wink-and-nod conversations between presidents and large donors (who may get to spend a night in the Lincoln Bedroom of the White House or hitch a ride on *Air Force One*).[3] Political agents can use their political power and the bully pulpits that public office provides to advance these special interests without a more general public awareness. Moral hazard makes the public vulnerable to abuses of the power delegated to elected agents. The solution to moral hazard is found in the way elections are conducted. If agents have strong incentives to renew their contracts—to be reelected or advance to a higher office—they will take care not to abuse their delegated power, or at least not to take risks that, if discovered, could damage their political reputation. Giving incumbents the incentive of possible reelection—indeed, tolerating small advantages that incumbency gives in electoral contests—will encourage them to moderate the inclination to strike private deals. The incentives that elections provide for agents are enhanced by other factors mitigating moral hazard, especially transparency and publicity. Various solution— moving the places where real decisions get made to more visible venues, opening these venues to public scrutiny, and empowering publicizers (the press, the political opposition)—both dampen the motive and diminish the opportunities for hidden actions that are contrary to more public purposes. For example, congressional procedures have become more transparent: Committee hearings and bill-drafting sessions are open, legislative votes in committee and on the floor are recorded, and records of campaign contributions are publicly available, providing increased visibility of an incumbent's record in office to his or her electoral constituency. A contemporary example of hidden action is earmarking, an activity taken by legislators on behalf of special interests. A legislator engages in earmarking by burying in a complex several-hundred-pages-long appropriations bill an item giving a monetary benefit to a special interest (who, in turn, may have contributed generously to the legislator's campaign). Having recaptured the House in the 2006 elections, the Democrats promised to reform this practice. In particular, they promised to deal directly with the moral hazard problem by requiring that every earmark identify the legislator sponsoring it.

Elections, then, promote political accountability because the threat of defeat at the polls exerts pressure on those in power to conduct themselves in a responsible

 Rationality Principle

Elections allow multiple principals— citizens—to choose political agents to act on their behalf. But citizens usually have imperfect information about candidates and don't know how they will act once in office.

moral hazard Not knowing all aspects of the actions taken by an agent (nominally on behalf of the principal but potentially at the principal's expense).

---

[3]Clinton's secretary of commerce, the late Ron Brown, a former head of the Democratic National Committee, used the frequent occasions of foreign travel required of his cabinet post to bring along many a Democratic fat cat. Republican officeholders, of course, are no less vigilant in rewarding their fat-cat contributors.

manner and to take account of popular interests and wishes when they make their decisions. As James Madison observed in the *Federalist Papers*, elected leaders are

> compelled to anticipate the moment when their power is to cease, when their exercise of it is to be reviewed, and when they must descend to the level from which they were raised, there forever to remain unless a faithful discharge of their trust shall have established their title to a renewal of it.[4]

In this chapter, we shall look first at the formal structure and setting of American elections. Second, we shall see how—and what—voters decide when they take part in elections. Third, we shall focus on recent national elections, including the 2008 election. Fourth, we shall discuss the role of money in the election process, particularly in recent elections. Finally, we shall assess the place of elections in the American political process, raising the important question, "Do elections matter?"[5]

HOW DOES GOVERNMENT REGULATE THE ELECTORAL PROCESS?

In earlier chapters, we suggested that the relationship between citizens and elected politicians is an instance of a principal-agent relationship (see Chapter 1). There are two basic approaches to this relationship: the consent approach and the agency approach. The consent approach emphasizes the historical reality that the right of the citizen to participate in his or her own governance, mainly through the act of voting or other forms of consent, arises from an existing governmental order aimed at making it easier for the governors to govern by legitimating their rule. By giving their consent, citizens provide this legitimation. The agency approach treats the typical citizen as someone who would much rather devote scarce time and effort to his or her own private affairs than spend that time and effort on governance. As the rationality principle implies, he or she therefore chooses to delegate governance to agents—politicians—who are controlled through elections. In this approach, the control of agents is emphasized.

Whether they are seen as a means to control delegates (the agency approach) or legitimate governance by politicians (the consent approach), elections allow citizens to participate in political life on a routine and peaceful basis. Indeed, American voters have the opportunity to select and, if they so desire, depose some of their most important leaders. In this way, Americans have a chance to intervene in and influence the government's programs and policies. Yet it is important to recall that elections are not spontaneous affairs. Instead, they are formal governmental institutions. Although elections allow citizens a chance to participate in politics, they also

Collective-Action Principle

Elections are a mechanism for channeling and limiting political participation to actions within the system.

---

[4]Alexander Hamilton, James Madison, and John Jay, *The Federalist Papers*, ed. Clinton L. Rossiter (New York: New American Library, 1961), no. 57, p. 352.

[5]For the most up-to-date research on analyzing elections, see Rebecca B. Morton, *Analyzing Elections* (New York: Norton, 2006).

allow the government a chance to exert a good deal of control over when, where, how, and which of its citizens will participate. Electoral processes are governed by a variety of rules and procedures that provide those in power with a significant opportunity to regulate the character—and perhaps also the consequences—of mass political participation.

Thus elections provide governments with an excellent opportunity to regulate and control popular involvement. Three general forms of regulation have played especially important roles in the electoral history of the Western democracies. First, governments often attempt to regulate the composition of the electorate to diminish the electoral weight of groups they deem undesirable. Second, governments frequently seek to manipulate the translation of voters' choices into electoral outcomes. Third, virtually all governments attempt to insulate policy-making processes from electoral intervention through regulation of the relationship between electoral decisions and the composition or organization of the government.

Institution Principle

The electoral process is governed by a variety of rules and procedures that provide those in power with an opportunity to regulate the character and consequences of political participation.

Electoral Composition

Perhaps the oldest and most obvious device used to regulate voting and its consequences is manipulation of the electorate's composition. In the earliest elections in western Europe, for example, the suffrage was generally limited to property owners and others who could be trusted to vote in a manner acceptable to those in power. To cite just one illustration, property qualifications in France before 1848 limited the electorate to 240,000 of some 7 million men over the age of twenty-one.[6] Of course, no women were permitted to vote. During the same era, other nations manipulated the electorate's composition by assigning unequal electoral weights to different classes of voters. The 1831 Belgian constitution, for example, assigned individuals anywhere from one to three votes, depending on their property holdings, education, and social position.[7] But even in the context of America's ostensibly universal and equal suffrage in the twentieth century, the composition of the electorate was still subject to manipulation. Some states manipulated the vote by the discriminatory use of poll taxes and literacy tests or by such practices as placing polls and scheduling voting hours such as to depress participation by one or another group.[8] Today many states disenfranchise felons and ex-felons, dramatically reducing the participation of some groups in the population.[9] The most important example of

[6]Stein Rokkan, *Citizens, Elections, Parties: Approaches to the Comparative Study of the Processes of Development* (New York: McKay, 1970), p. 149. Also see Acemoglu and Robinson, "Why Did the West Extend the Franchise?"

[7]John A. Hawgood, *Modern Constitutions since 1787* (New York: Van Nostrand, 1939), p. 148.

[8]In the aftermath of the 2004 presidential election, in which Ohio proved a pivotal state in George W. Bush's victory, it has been alleged that Republicans engaged in this sort of manipulation. In the county in which Kent State University (a Democratic stronghold) is located, very few voting machines were made available, producing long lines and waiting times of up to nine hours. Republican-leaning suburban locations, on the other hand, were adequately provisioned with machines. Similar stories about Democratic manipulations also circulated after the election.

[9]According to some unofficial estimates, for example, Alabama has disenfranchised more than one quarter of young African American men.

FIGURE 10.1 Voter Turnout around the World, 1945–2006

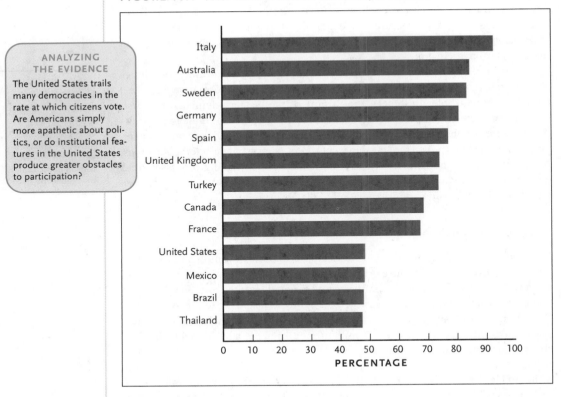

SOURCE: International Institute of Democracy and Electoral Assistance

NOTE: Average between 1945 and 2006.

the regulation of the American electorate's composition is our unique registration requirements.

Levels of voter participation in twentieth-century American elections were quite low compared with those of the other Western democracies (Figure 10.1).[10] Indeed, voter participation in presidential elections in the United States had barely averaged 50 percent (Figure 10.2). Turnout in the 2000 presidential election was 51 percent of voting-age Americans; in 2008, it was approximately 63 percent. During the nineteenth century, by contrast, voter turnout in the United States was extremely high, considerably larger than it is today.[11]

---

[10]See Walter Dean Burnham, "The Changing Shape of the American Political Universe," American Political Science Review 59, no. 1 (March 1965): 7–28. It should be noted that other democracies, like India and Switzerland, have even lower turnout rates, as do some of the new democracies in eastern Europe.

[11]See statistics of the U.S. Bureau of the Census and the Federal Election Commission. For voting statistics for 1960 to 2004, see "National Voter Turnout in Federal Elections: 1960–2004," at www.infoplease.com/ipa/A0781453.html.

FIGURE 10.2 Voter Turnout in Presidential Elections

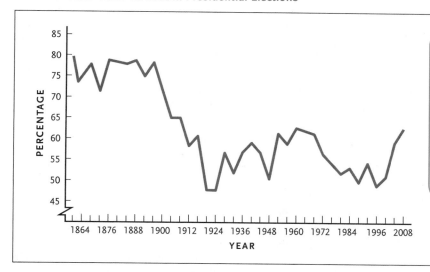

ANALYZING THE EVIDENCE

Voter turnout for American presidential elections was significantly higher in the nineteenth century than in the twentieth. What institutional change caused the sharp decline in turnout between 1890 and 1910? Why did this change have such a dramatic effect? Did it have any positive outcomes?

SOURCES: For 1860–1928, U.S. Bureau of the Census, *Historical Statistics of the United States, Colonial Times to 1970* (www.census.gov/prod/www/abs/statab.html); pt. 2, p. 1071; for 1932–92, U.S. Bureau of the Census, *Statistical Abstract of the United States*, 1993 (Washington, D.C.: Government Printing Office, 1993), p. 284; for 1996–2008, Federal Election Commission data.

NOTE: Data reflect the population of eligible voters; the percentage of the voting-age population that voted would be smaller.

Before delving too deeply into the quantitative data, a few qualifying remarks are in order: A turnout rate is a ratio comparing the number of people who voted to some baseline population. The numerator of this ratio is relatively uncontroversial—it is the number of individuals who present themselves at a polling station or submit an absentee ballot. (There may be some ambiguity because some people do not vote for every office on the ballot, so the actual voting rate for president, for example, is usually higher than that for county recorder or town sheriff. But this is a relatively minor ambiguity. Walter Burnham calls this the "fall-off rate."[12])

The real problem with quantitative presentations lies in defining the baseline population—the denominator of the turnout ratio. Some use the voting-age population, which is those eighteen years or older residing in the United States. (Of course, this voting age was set by the Twenty-sixth Amendment, ratified in 1971.) But this figure may be misleading in at least two ways. It incorrectly *includes* noncitizens and ineligible felons as well as eligible citizens who have failed to register. Furthermore, it incorrectly *excludes* overseas eligible voters. Other analysts use the population of eligible voters, certainly the more relevant denominator of the turnout ratio. But there are problems here as well. Cross-national comparisons may be misleading because eligibility requirements differ among countries.

---

[12]Burnham, "The Changing Shape of the American Political Universe."

Over-time comparisons may also be misleading because eligibility criteria within the same country change over time. In the United States, for example, the Nineteenth Amendment, ratified in 1920, extended the vote to women and the Twenty-sixth Amendment lowered the voting age to eighteen; both amendments changed the denominator of the turnout ratio.

Finally, we should point out that some turnout rates, such as those calculated for a series of elections in a country, are often reported as an average over several years (as in Figure 10.1). Such averages often pool different kinds of elections. In the United States, such measures include elections during presidential years as well as those in off-years (just congressional elections). Because off-year turnout is low, this practice pulls down the U.S. average compared with that of countries in which only national elections are counted.[13] Even with various refinements by leading experts, the denominator of the turnout rate may still be "too large" for the United States, thereby making America look less participatory than other democracies. In particular, most estimates do not sufficiently take into account the number of felons, and especially ex-felons, stricken from the voting rolls.[14]

As Figure 10.2 indicates, the critical years during which voter turnout declined across the United States were those between 1890 and 1910. These years coincide with the adoption of laws across much of the nation requiring eligible citizens to appear personally at a registrar's office to register to vote some time before the actual date of an election. Personal registration was one of several "Progressive" reforms of political practices initiated at the beginning of the twentieth century. The ostensible purpose of registration was to discourage fraud and corruption. But to many Progressive reformers, *corruption* was a code word, referring to the type of politics practiced in the large cities, where political parties had organized immigrant and ethnic populations. Reformers not only objected to the corruption that surely was a facet of party politics in this period but also opposed the growing political power of urban populations and their leaders.

Personal registration imposed a new burden on potential voters and altered the format of American elections. Under the registration systems adopted after 1890, it became the duty of individual voters to secure their own eligibility. This duty could prove to be a significant burden for potential voters, for a number of reasons. First, during a personal appearance before the registrar, individuals seeking to vote were (and are) required to furnish proof of identity, residence, and citizenship. While the inconvenience of registration varied from state to state, usually voters could register only during business hours on weekdays. Many potential voters could not afford to lose a day's pay in order to register. Second, voters were usually required to register well before the next election, in some states up to several months earlier. Third, because most personal registration laws required a periodic purge of the election rolls, ostensibly to keep them up-to-date, voters often had to re-register to maintain their eligibility. Thus, although personal registration requirements helped diminish the

History Principle

Between 1890 and 1910, voter turnout declined in the United States as a result of new registration requirements. Since that time, turnout has remained low in comparison with the nineteenth century.

---

[13] For an excellent discussion of these and related issues, consult Michael P. M. McDonald and Samuel Popkin, "The Myth of the Vanishing Voter," *American Political Science Review* 95, no. 4 (December 2001): 963–74.

[14] Jeff Manza, Christopher Uggen, *Locked Out: Felon Disenfranchisement and American Democracy* (New York: Cambridge University Press, 2006).

widespread electoral corruption that accompanied a completely open voting process, they also made it much more difficult for citizens to participate in the electoral process. Rational citizens with busy lives might well be expected to forgo political participation as its complications and costs increase.

Registration requirements in particular depress the participation of those with little education and low income because registration requires a greater degree of political involvement and interest than does the act of voting itself. To vote, a person need only be concerned with the particular election campaign at hand. Yet requiring individuals to register before a coming election forces them to make a decision to participate on the basis of an abstract interest in the electoral process rather than a simple concern with a specific campaign. Such an abstract interest in electoral politics is largely a product of education. Those with relatively little education may become interested in political events once the stimuli of a particular campaign become salient, but by that time it may be too late to register. As a result, personal registration requirements not only diminish the size of the electorate but also tend to create an electorate that is, in the aggregate, less representative of the voting-age population. The electorate is better educated, has a higher income and social status, and includes fewer African Americans and other minorities than the citizenry as a whole (Figure 10.3).

Over the years, voter registration restrictions have been modified somewhat to make registration easier. In 1993, for example, Congress approved and President Bill Clinton signed the "motor voter" bill to ease voter registration by allowing individuals to register when they applied for driver's licenses, as well as in public-assistance and military-recruitment offices.[15] In many jurisdictions, casting a vote automatically registers the voter for the next election. In Europe, there is typically no registration burden on the individual voter; voter registration is handled automatically by the government. This is one reason why voter turnout rates in Europe are higher than those in the United States.

Another factor explaining low rates of voter turnout in the United States is the relative weakness of the American party system. During the nineteenth century, American political party machines employed hundreds of thousands of workers to organize and mobilize voters and bring them to the polls. The result was an extremely high rate of turnout, typically more than 90 percent of eligible voters.[16] But political party machines began to decline in strength in the early twentieth century and by now have largely disappeared. Without party workers to encourage them to go to the polls and even take them there if necessary, many eligible voters will not participate. In the absence of strong parties, participation rates drop the most among poorer and less-educated citizens. Because of the absence of strong political parties, the American electorate is smaller and skewed more toward the middle class than toward the population of all those potentially eligible to vote.[17]

Rationality Principle

As registration costs rise, the number of citizens participating may be expected to decrease.

---

[15] Helen Dewar, "'Motor Voter' Agreement Is Reached," *Washington Post,* 28 April 1993, p. A6.

[16] Erik W. Austin and Jerome M. Clubb, *Political Facts of the United States since 1789* (New York: Columbia University Press, 1986), pp. 378–79.

[17] In the 2004 election, both parties devoted considerable resources to targeting potential new voters, helping them register, and mobilizing them on Election Day. Elevated turnout in the election reflects this effort.

FIGURE 10.3 Differences in Voter Registration Rates by Social Group, 2004

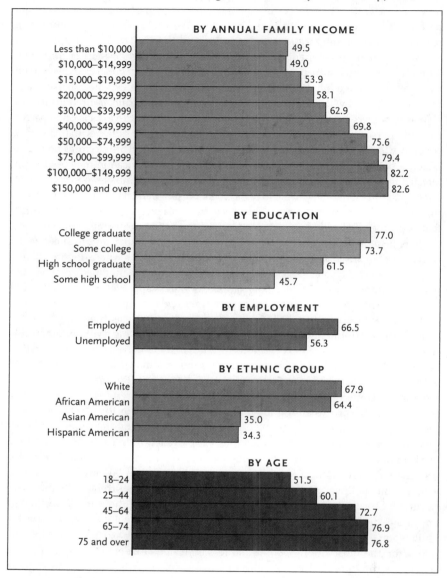

SOURCE: U.S. Bureau of the Census, Population Division, Education and Social Stratification Branch, "Voting and Registration in the Election of November 2004," April 2005, (www.census.gov/population/www/socdemo/voting/cps2004).

Translating Voters' Choices into Electoral Outcomes

With the exception of America's personal registration requirements, contemporary governments generally do not try to limit the composition of their electorate. Instead, they prefer to allow everyone to vote and then manipulate the outcome of the election. This is possible because there is more than one way to decide the relationship between individual votes and electoral outcome.[18] There are any number of possible rules that can be used to determine how individual votes will be translated. And as suggested by the institution principle, these rules and arrangements will be highly consequential for the results. Two types of regulations are especially important: the rules that set the criteria for victory and the rules that define electoral districts.

The Criteria for Winning   In some nations, to win a seat in the parliament or other representative body, a candidate must receive a majority (50 percent plus 1) of all the votes cast in the relevant district. This type of electoral system, called a ***majority system,*** was used in the primary elections of most southern states until recent years. Generally, majority systems have a provision for a second, or "runoff," contest between the two top candidates if the initial contest draws so many contestants that none receives an absolute majority of the votes cast.

In other nations, candidates for office need not receive an absolute majority of the votes cast to win an election. Instead, victory is awarded to the candidate who receives the greatest number of votes in a given election regardless of the actual percentage of votes this represents. Thus a candidate who received 40 percent of the votes cast may win the contest so long as no rival receives more votes. This type of electoral process is called a ***plurality system,*** and it is the system used in almost all general elections in the United States. There are different types of plurality systems. The one currently used in the United States in congressional and presidential elections is characterized by single-member districts, where each district elects a single representative, and what is known as a first-past-the-post system, where only the candidate who receives the most votes is elected. In Taiwan, by contrast, members are elected in multi-member districts, typically with three or five seats per district; the top three (or top five) vote getters are elected.[19]

In some electoral systems, multiple representatives are selected from each district, constituency, or region according to a third electoral system, called ***proportional representation.*** Under proportional rules, competing political parties are awarded legislative seats roughly in proportion to the percentage of the popular vote they receive. For example, a party that won 30 percent of the votes would receive roughly 30 percent of the seats in the parliament or other representative body. In the

majority system A type of electoral system in which, to win a seat in a representative body, a candidate must receive a majority (50 percent plus 1) of all the votes cast in the relevant district.

plurality system A type of electoral system in which victory goes to the individual who gets the most votes in an election, but not necessarily a majority of the votes cast.

proportional representation A multiple-member-district system that allows each political party representation in proportion to its percentage of the vote.

---

[18]This general proposition is developed extensively in William H. Riker, *Liberalism against Populism: A Confrontation between the Theory of Democracy and the Theory of Social Choice* (San Francisco: Freeman, 1982).

[19]For an accessible analysis of the different types of plurality systems and a model for analyzing electoral systems, see Kenneth A. Shepsle and Mark S. Bonchek, *Analyzing Politics: Rationality, Behavior, and Institutions* (New York: Norton, 1997), pp. 178–87.

United States, proportional representation is used by many states in presidential primary elections. In these primaries, candidates for the Democratic and Republican nominations are awarded convention delegates in rough proportion to the percentage of the popular vote that they received in the primary. Early in the twentieth century, proportional-representation systems were employed in many American cities, including New York, to elect city councils. Today these systems have nearly disappeared. Cambridge, Massachusetts, is one of the last cities to use such a system in city-council elections. Elections to the New York City school board are also still conducted using a proportional-representation system.

Institution Principle

The rules that set the criteria for winning an election have an effect on the outcome.

Generally, systems of proportional representation work to the electoral advantage of smaller political parties, while majority and plurality systems tend to help larger and more powerful forces. This is because in legislative elections, proportional representation reduces, whereas majority and plurality rules increase, the number of votes that political parties must receive to win legislative seats. For instance, in European parliamentary elections, a Green party that wins 10 percent of the national vote will also receive approximately 10 percent of the parliamentary seats. In American congressional elections, by contrast, a Green party winning only 10 percent of the popular vote would probably receive no congressional seats at all.[20] Obviously, choices among types of electoral systems can have important political consequences. Competing forces often seek to establish an electoral system that each believes will serve its political interests while undermining the fortunes of its opponents. In 1937, for example, New York City Council seats were awarded on the basis of proportional representation. This system led to the selection of several Communist party council members. During the 1940s, to prevent the election of Communists, the city adopted a plurality system. Under the new rule, the tiny Communist party was unable to muster enough votes to secure a council seat. In a similar vein, the introduction of proportional representation for the selection of delegates to the Democratic party's 1972 national convention was designed in part to maximize the voting strength of minority groups and, not entirely coincidentally, to improve the electoral chances of the candidates they were most likely to favor.[21]

---

[20]For an argument that plurality systems are governance oriented whereas proportional systems are representation oriented, see Shepsle and Bonchek, *Analyzing Politics*, pp. 188–91. This argument derives from the famous Duverger's law, an argument that plurality systems encourage two-party competition (with one party or the other securing a majority of seats in the legislature), whereas proportional systems encourage multiparty competition (with many parties holding seats in the legislature, with the very frequent outcome that no party commands a majority on its own and thus parties must build coalitions in order to govern). Thus plurality systems "manufacture" government (majority legislative parties) but squeeze out a lot of political diversity. Proportional systems encourage diversity but require that majority coalitions be "built" after the election. The law was first described systematically by the French political scientist Maurice Duverger in his *Political Parties, Their Organization and Activity in the Modern State*, trans. Barbara North and Robert North (New York: Wiley, 1954).

[21]See Nelson W. Polsby and Aaron Wildavsky, *Presidential Elections: Strategies of American Electoral Politics*, 5th ed. (New York: Scribner's, 1980).

Electoral Districts   Despite the occasional use of proportional representation and majority voting systems, most electoral contests in the United States are decided on the basis of plurality rules. Rather than seeking to manipulate the criteria for victory, American politicians have usually sought to influence the electoral outcome by manipulating the organization of electoral districts. Congressional-district boundaries in the United States are redrawn by governors and state legislatures every ten years, after the decennial census determines the number of House seats to which each state is entitled (Figure 10.4). The manipulation of electoral districts to increase the likelihood of one or another outcome is called ***gerrymandering***, in honor of the nineteenth-century Massachusetts governor Elbridge Gerry, who was alleged to have designed a district in the shape of a salamander to promote his party's interests.

The principle of gerrymandering is a simple one. Different distributions of voters among districts produce different electoral outcomes; those in a position to control the arrangements of districts are also in a position to manipulate the results. The Analyzing the Evidence unit on page 436 shows how this works, using a hypothetical state to explain some basic strategies the party in power might use to influence elections through manipulation of district lines, as well as a real-world example of how this affects electoral outcomes.

Until recent years, gerrymandering to dilute the voting strength of racial minorities was employed by many state legislatures. One of the more common strategies involved redrawing congressional boundary lines in such a way as to divide and disperse a black population that would otherwise have constituted a majority within the original district. This form of racial gerrymandering, sometimes called cracking (the opposite of the Highway 85 strategy just described), was used in Mississippi during the 1960s and 1970s to prevent the election of a black congressman. Historically, the black population in Mississippi was clustered in the western half of the state, along the Mississippi Delta. From 1882 until 1966, the Delta constituted one congressional district. Although blacks constituted a clear majority within the district (66 percent in 1960), the continuing election of white congressmen was ensured simply because blacks were denied the right to register and vote. With Congress's passage of the Voting Rights Act of 1965, however, the Mississippi state legislature moved swiftly to minimize the potential voting power of blacks by redrawing congressional district lines in such a way as to fragment the black population in the Delta into four of the state's five congressional districts. Mississippi's gerrymandering scheme was preserved in the state's redistricting plans in 1972 and 1981 and helped prevent the election of any black representative until 1986, when Mike Espy became the first African American since Reconstruction to represent Mississippi in Congress.

In recent years, federal law has encouraged what is sometimes called benign gerrymandering, designed to increase minority representation in Congress. The 1982 amendments to the Voting Rights Act of 1965 encouraged the creation of legislative districts with predominantly African American or Hispanic American populations by requiring states, when possible, to draw district lines that take account of concentrations of African American and Hispanic American voters. These amendments were initially supported by Democrats, who assumed that minority-controlled districts would guarantee the election of Democratic members of Congress. However, Republicans have championed these efforts, reasoning that if minority voters were concentrated in their own districts, Republican prospects in other districts would be

gerrymandering
The apportionment of voters in districts in such a way as to give unfair advantage to one political party.

FIGURE 10.4 Congressional Redistricting

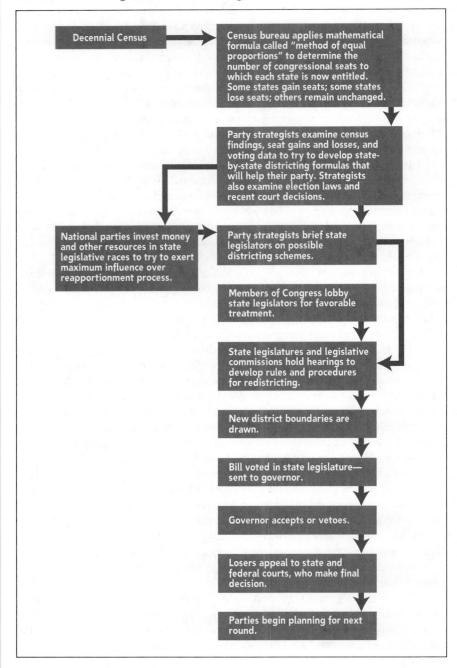

Decennial Census

Census bureau applies mathematical formula called "method of equal proportions" to determine the number of congressional seats to which each state is now entitled. Some states gain seats; some states lose seats; others remain unchanged.

Party strategists examine census findings, seat gains and losses, and voting data to try to develop state-by-state districting formulas that will help their party. Strategists also examine election laws and recent court decisions.

National parties invest money and other resources in state legislative races to try to exert maximum influence over reapportionment process.

Party strategists brief state legislators on possible districting schemes.

Members of Congress lobby state legislators for favorable treatment.

State legislatures and legislative commissions hold hearings to develop rules and procedures for redistricting.

New district boundaries are drawn.

Bill voted in state legislature—sent to governor.

Governor accepts or vetoes.

Losers appeal to state and federal courts, who make final decision.

Parties begin planning for next round.

enhanced.[22] Moreover, Republicans hoped some Democratic incumbents might be forced from office to make way for minority representatives. In some cases, the Republicans' theory has proved correct. As a result of the creation of a number of new minority districts in 1991, several long-term white Democrats lost their congressional seats. The 1993 Supreme Court decision in *Shaw v. Reno,* however, opened the way for challenges by white voters to the drawing of these districts. In the 5–4 majority opinion, Justice Sandra Day O'Connor wrote that if district boundaries were so "bizarre" as to be inexplicable on any grounds other than an effort to ensure the election of minority group members to office, white voters would have reason to assert that they had been the victims of unconstitutional racial gerrymandering.[23] In its 1995 decision in *Miller v. Johnson,* the Court questioned the entire concept of benign racial gerrymandering by asserting that the use of race as a "predominant factor" in the drawing of district lines was presumptively unconstitutional. However, the Court held open the possibility that race could be *one* of the factors taken into account in legislative redistricting.[24] Similarly, in *Bush v. Vera* the Court ruled that three Texas congressional districts with black or Hispanic majorities were unconstitutional because state officials put too much emphasis on race in drawing boundaries. "Voters," said the Court, "are more than mere racial statistics."[25] In *Shaw v. Hunt,* the Court struck down a North Carolina black-majority voting district for similar reasons.[26] In the 1997 case of *Abrams v. Johnson,* the Court upheld a new Georgia congressional- district map that eliminated two of the state's three black-majority districts.[27] In *Georgia v. Ashcroft* in 2003, the Court rejected a Georgia state senate districting plan because it diluted minority votes, making it harder for minorities to elect candidates they preferred.[28]

Traditionally, district boundaries have been redrawn only once a decade, following the national census. In recent years, however, the Republican party has adopted an extremely aggressive redistricting strategy, in some instances not waiting for a new census before launching a redistricting effort that could serve its political interests. In Texas, for example, after the GOP took control of both houses of the state legislature in the 2002 elections, Republican lawmakers sought to enact a redistricting plan that promised to shift as many as five congressional seats to the Republican column. This Republican effort was masterminded by Tom DeLay, a Texan who was then majority leader in the U.S. House of Representatives. DeLay saw an opportunity to increase the

---

[22] Roberto Suro, "In Redistricting, New Rules and New Prizes," *New York Times,* 6 May 1990, sec. 4, p. 5. A more recent examination is found in Gary W. Cox and Jonathan Katz, *Elbridge Gerry's Salamander: The Electoral Consequences of the Reapportionment Revolution* (New York: Cambridge University Press, 2002).

[23] *Shaw v. Reno,* 509 U.S. 630 (1993); Linda Greenhouse, "Court Questions Districts Drawn to Aid Minorities," *New York Times,* 29 June 1993, p. 1. See also Joan Biskupic, "Court's Conservatism Unlikely to Be Shifted by a New Justice," *Washington Post,* 30 June 1993, p. 1.

[24] *Miller v. Johnson,* 515 U.S. 900 (1995).

[25] *Bush v. Vera,* 517 U.S. 952 (1996).

[26] *Shaw v. Hunt,* 517 U.S. 899 (1996).

[27] *Abrams v. Johnson,* 521 U.S. 74 (1997).

[28] *Georgia v. Ashcroft,* 539 U.S. 461 (2003). A recent assessment of the political and legal environment in which redistricting takes place may be found in David Epstein, Rodolfo O. de la Garza, Sharyn O'Halloran, and Richard Pildes, eds., *The Future of the Voting Rights Act* (New York: Russell Sage Foundation, 2006).

The Electoral Impact of Congressional Redistricting

The method by which electoral districts are drawn may directly impact who gets elected from those districts. Recent decades have witnessed more states utilizing independent commissions or panels to redraw congressional districts in an attempt to limit partisanship in the districting process, but the majority of states still rely on state legislatures to reapportion House seats. At the same time, technological innovations such as Geographic Information Systems (GIS) software allow mapmakers to be extremely precise in terms of how individual voters are allocated among districts. As a result, congressional redistricting has become a focal point for party strategy.

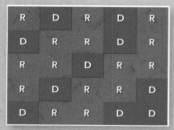

 Consider a hypothetical state where Republicans represent 60% of voters and Democrats represent the remaining 40% of voters. As a result of population changes during the preceding decade, this state now has five congressional districts. Assuming members of the state legislature want to create congressional districts with approximately the same number of people, there are several ways to draw district boundaries.

 For instance, a state legislature controlled by a Republican majority could draw congressional districts so that Republican voters clearly dominate three of the five districts and Democratic voters dominate the remaining two. In this scenario, the Republicans could expect their candiates to win three of the five House districts.

SCENARIO 1

SCENARIO 2

Another possibility might arise if the Republican state legislature decides to make the districts slightly more competitive, but also attempts to gain control of all five House districts in the upcoming election.

Suppose that the Democrats are in control of the state legislature. With the same distribution of voters in the state, they could draw the districts to favor Democrats as much as possible (with Democratic voters dominating three of the districts).

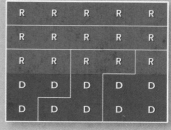

SCENARIO 3

IOWA DISTRICTS, 2000

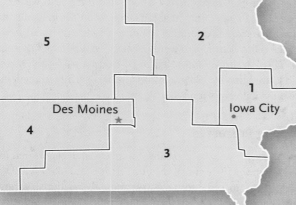

◀ By contrast, a non-partisan independent commission or panel may draw more-competitive districts, with a more even distribution of Republican and Democratic voters. A real-world example from Iowa (which employs an independent commission) shows district boundaries before and after the 2002 redistricting cycle.

IOWA DISTRICTS, 2002

▶ Note how the district boundaries changed in an effort to promote greater levels of competition throughout the state. This is reflected by the incumbent vote share inthe subsequent election. The more-competitive districts created after 2002 meant that incumbents could be challenged more easily, and as a result, Iowa incumbents received a smaller share of votes in the 2004 elections.

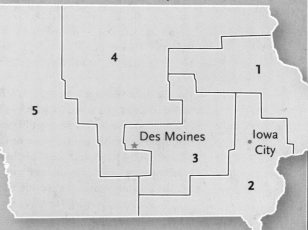

THE OUTCOME

Incumbent vote share, 2000 House races in Iowa	62.4%
Incumbent vote share, 2004 House races in Iowa	56%

30   40   50   60   70

Republican majority in the House and reduce Democratic prospects of regaining control of Congress. In an effort to block DeLay's plan, a group of fifty-one Democratic legislators refused to attend state legislative sessions, leaving the Texas legislature without a quorum and unable to conduct its business. The legislature's Republican leadership ordered the state police to apprehend the missing Democrats and return them to the state capitol. The Democrats responded by escaping to Oklahoma, beyond the jurisdiction of the Texas police. Eventually, the Democrats capitulated, and the GOP was able to enact its redistricting plan. In the 2004 election, the first under the new plan, the Republicans defeated four Democratic incumbents and won three of the five seats in which no incumbent was running. This Republican gain was equal to the total Republican gain in the House nationally. The redistricting plan was challenged in court by the League of United Latin American Citizens on the grounds that it violated the voting rights of Hispanic Americans. The case reached the Supreme Court in 2006, and parts of the redistricting plan were rejected.[29] A similar GOP redistricting effort in Colorado failed when it was ruled unconstitutional by the state's supreme court. The court declared that the Colorado constitution permitted the legislature to redistrict the state only once every ten years.

Insulating Decision-Making Processes

Virtually all governments attempt at least partially to insulate decision-making processes from electoral intervention. The most obvious forms of insulation are the confinement of popular elections to only some governmental positions, various modes of indirect election, and lengthy tenure in office. In the United States, the framers of the Constitution intended that only members of the House of Representatives would be subject to direct popular selection. The president and members of the Senate were to be indirectly elected for rather long terms to allow them, as the *Federalist Papers* put it, to avoid "an unqualified complaisance to every sudden breeze of passion, or to every transient impulse which the people may receive."[30]

The Electoral College   In the early history of popular voting, nations often made use of indirect elections. In such elections, voters would choose the members of an intermediate body. These members would in turn select public officials. The assumption underlying such processes was that ordinary citizens were not qualified to choose their leaders and could not be trusted to do so directly. The last vestige of this procedure in America is the ***electoral college,*** the group of electors who formally select the president and vice president of the United States.

When Americans go to the polls on Election Day, they are technically not voting directly for presidential candidates. Instead, voters within each state are choosing among slates of electors who have been nominated by political parties some months earlier. The electors who are chosen in the presidential race are pledged to support their own party's presidential candidate. In each state (except Maine and Nebraska), the slate that wins casts all the state's electoral votes for its

electoral college
The presidential electors from each state who meet in their respective state capitals after the popular election to cast ballots for president and vice president.

---

[29]*League of Latin American Citizens v. Perry,* 548 U.S. (2006).

[30]Hamilton, Madison, and Jay, *The Federalist Papers,* no. 71, p. 432.

party's candidate.[31] Each state is entitled to a number of electoral votes equal to the number of the state's senators and representatives combined, for a total of 538 electoral votes for the fifty states and the District of Columbia. Occasionally, an elector breaks his or her pledge and votes for the other party's candidate. In 1976, for example, when the Republicans carried the state of Washington, one Republican elector from that state refused to vote for Gerald Ford, the Republican presidential nominee. More recently, a Democratic elector from Washington, D.C., refused to vote for Al Gore in 2000 because he believed Gore to be insufficiently supportive of D.C. statehood. Many states have now enacted statutes formally binding electors to their pledges, but some constitutional authorities doubt whether such statutes are enforceable.

In each state, the electors whose slate has won proceed to the state's capital on the Monday after the second Wednesday in December and formally cast their ballots. These are sent to Washington and tallied by Congress in January, and the name of the winner is formally announced. In the event that no candidate receives a majority of all electoral votes, the names of the top three candidates are to be submitted to the House, where each state may cast one vote. Whether a state's vote would be decided by a majority, a plurality, or some other fraction of the state's delegates would be determined under rules established by the House.

In 1800 and 1824, the electoral college failed to produce a majority for any candidate. In the election of 1800, Thomas Jefferson, the Democratic-Republican party's presidential candidate, and Aaron Burr, that party's vice-presidential candidate, received an equal number of votes in the electoral college, throwing the election into the House of Representatives. (The Constitution at that time made no distinction between presidential and vice-presidential candidates, specifying only that the individual receiving a majority of electoral votes would be named president.) Some members of the Federalist party in Congress suggested that they should seize the opportunity to damage the Republican cause by supporting Burr and denying Jefferson the presidency. The Federalist leader Alexander Hamilton put a stop to this mischievous notion, however, and made certain that his party supported Jefferson. Hamilton's actions enraged Burr and helped lead to the infamous duel between the two men, in which Hamilton was killed. The Twelfth Amendment, ratified in 1804, was designed to prevent a repetition of such a situation by providing for separate electoral college votes for president and vice president.

In the 1824 election, four candidates—John Quincy Adams, Andrew Jackson, Henry Clay, and William Crawford—divided the electoral vote; not one of them received a majority. The House of Representatives eventually chose Adams over the others, even though Jackson won more electoral and popular votes. This choice was the result of the famous "corrupt bargain" in which Clay threw his support to Adams, the eventual winner, and was subsequently named secretary of state. After

---

[31] State legislatures determine the system by which electors are selected, and almost all states use this "winner-take-all" system. Maine and Nebraska, however, provide that one electoral vote goes to the winner in each congressional district and two electoral votes go to the winner statewide. In 2004, a proposition on the Colorado ballot to divide electoral votes as in Maine and Nebraska was defeated 2–1.

1824, the two major political parties had begun to dominate presidential politics to such an extent that by December of each election year, only two candidates remained for the electors to choose between, thus ensuring that one would receive a majority. This situation freed the parties and the candidates from having to plan campaigns that culminated in Congress, and Congress quickly ceased to dominate the presidential selection process.

On all but three occasions since 1824, the electoral vote has simply ratified the nationwide popular vote. Because electoral votes are won on a state-by-state basis, it is mathematically possible for a candidate who receives a nationwide popular plurality to fail to carry states whose electoral votes would add up to a majority. Thus in 1876, Rutherford Hayes was the winner in the electoral college despite receiving fewer popular votes than his rival, Samuel Tilden. In 1888, Grover Cleveland received more popular votes than Benjamin Harrison but received fewer electoral votes. And in 2000, Al Gore outpolled his opponent, George W. Bush, but lost the electoral college by a mere four electoral votes. In 2004, President Bush won both the popular vote and an electoral majority in his successful reelection bid. In doing so, Bush became the first candidate since Ronald Reagan in 1984 to win a clear majority of the popular vote. In 2008, Barack Obama won both a large majority of electoral votes and a significant 53 percent majority of the popular vote.

In the modern era, the electoral college has a profound effect on the nature of campaigning. Imagine an election with no electoral college, in which the winner of the popular vote is elected. Campaigns in this scenario would focus on votes wherever they may be found. Resources—for television ads, candidates' visits, or securing local endorsements—would be invested wherever the vote yield was expected to be fruitful. In a world *with* an electoral college, on the other hand, votes in a state matter only if they can move that state into the candidate's column. There was no point in 2008, for example, for either Obama or McCain to devote scarce campaign resources to Massachusetts (a sure Obama state) or Texas (a sure McCain state); instead, they focused on places that were contestable: Ohio, Florida, and Pennsylvania. A contest with no electoral college would entail a wide-open national campaign with votes sought out everywhere. A contest with an electoral college, in contrast, concentrates campaign activity in contestable states.

Frequency of Elections   Less obvious are the insulating effects of electoral arrangements that permit the direct and even frequent popular election of public officials but tend to fragment the impact of elections on the government's composition. In the United States, for example, the constitutional provision for staggered terms of service in the Senate was designed to diminish the effect of shifts in electoral sentiment on the Senate as an institution. Because only one third of its members are selected every two years, the composition of the institution is partially protected from changes in electoral preferences. This arrangement prevents what the *Federalist Papers* called "mutability in the public councils arising from a rapid succession of new members."[32]

---

[32]Hamilton, Madison, and Jay, *The Federalist Papers*, no. 62.

Size of Electoral Districts   The division of the nation into relatively small geographically based constituencies for the purpose of selecting members of the House of Representatives was in part designed to have a similar effect. Representatives were to be chosen frequently. And although not prescribed by the Constitution, the fact that each was to be selected by a discrete constituency was thought by James Madison and others to diminish the government's vulnerability to mass popular movements.

In a sense, the House of Representatives was compartmentalized for several reasons. First, by dividing the national electorate into small districts, the importance of local issues would increase. Second, the salience of local issues would mean that a representative's electoral fortunes would be more closely tied to factors peculiar to his or her own district than to national responses to issues. Third, given a geographic principle of representation, national groups would be somewhat fragmented, while the formation of local forces that might or might not share common underlying attitudes would be encouraged. No matter how well represented individual constituencies might be, the influence of voters on national policy questions would be fragmented. In Madison's terms, the influence of "faction" would thus become "less likely to pervade the whole body than some particular portion of it."[33]

The Ballot   Another example of an American electoral arrangement that tends to fragment the impact of mass elections on the government's composition is the Australian ballot (named for its country of origin). Before the introduction of this official ballot in the 1890s, voters cast ballots according to political parties. Each party printed its own ballots, listed only its own candidates for each office, and employed party workers to distribute its ballots at the polls. This ballot format had two important consequences. First, the party ballot precluded secrecy in voting. Because each party's ballot was distinctive in size and color, it was not difficult for party workers to determine how individuals intended to vote. This, of course, facilitated the intimidation and bribery of voters. Second, the format of the ballot prevented split-ticket voting. Because only one party's candidates appeared on any ballot, it was difficult for a voter to cast anything other than a straight party vote.

The official *Australian ballot* represented a significant change in electoral procedure. The new ballot was prepared and administered by the state rather than the parties. Each ballot was identical and included the names of all candidates for office. This reform, of course, increased the secrecy of voting and reduced the possibility of voter intimidation and bribery. Because all ballots were identical in appearance, even the voter who had been threatened or bribed might still vote as he or she wished, without the knowledge of party workers. But perhaps even more important, the Australian-ballot reform made it possible for voters to make their choices on the basis of the individual merits of a party's candidates rather than on the collective merits. Because all candidates for the same office now appeared on the same ballot, voters were no longer forced to choose a straight party ticket. It was indeed the introduction of the Australian ballot that gave rise to the phenomenon of split-ticket voting in American elections.[34]

Australian ballot An electoral format that presents the names of all the candidates for any given office on the same ballot. Introduced at the end of the eighteenth century, the Australian ballot replaced the partisan ballot and facilitated split-ticket voting.

---

[33]Ibid., no. 10.

[34]Jerold G. Rusk, "The Effect of the Australian Ballot Reform on Split Ticket Voting: 1876–1908," *American Political Science Review* 64, no. 4 (December 1970): 1220–38.

Ticket splitting is especially prevalent in states that use the "office-block" ballot format, which does not group candidates by their partisan affiliations. By contrast, the "party-column" format places all the candidates affiliated with a given party in the same row or column. The former facilitates ticket splitting, whereas the latter encourages straight-ticket voting.

It is this second consequence of the Australian-ballot reform that tends to fragment the impact of American elections on the government's composition. Before the reform of the ballot, it was not uncommon for an entire incumbent administration to be swept from office and replaced by an entirely new set of officials. In the absence of a real possibility of split-ticket voting, any desire on the part of the electorate for change could be expressed only as a vote against all candidates of the party in power. Because of this, there always existed the possibility, particularly at the state and local levels, that an insurgent slate committed to policy change could be swept into power. The party ballot thus increased the potential effect of elections on the government's composition. Although this potential may not always have been realized, the party ballot at least increased the chance that electoral decisions could lead to policy changes. By contrast, because it permitted choice on the basis of candidates' individual appeals, the Australian ballot lessened the likelihood that the electorate would sweep an entirely new administration into power. Ticket splitting led to increasingly divided partisan control of government.

The ballots used in the United States are a mix of forms developed as long ago as the 1890s, when the states took over the printing of ballots from the political parties. They were modified during the 1940s and 1950s, when voting machines and punch-card ballots were introduced, and they were further updated in some jurisdictions during the 1990s, when more modern and more accurate computerized voting methods were introduced. The choice of ballot format is a county decision, and within any state various counties may use different formats, depending on local resources and preferences. For example, the Palm Beach County butterfly ballot, which in 2000 seemed to confuse many voters, was selected by Democratic election officials who thought its larger print would help elderly, predominantly Democratic voters read the names of the candidates. Often, as turned out to be the case in Florida, neighboring counties use completely different ballot systems. For example, the city of Baltimore introduced voting machines many years ago and continues to use them. Baltimore County, Maryland, uses more modern ballots, which are optically scanned by computers. Neighboring Montgomery County employs a cumbersome punch-card system that requires voters to punch different cards on both sides, a bewildering process that usually results in large numbers of spoiled ballots. In some states, including Florida, different precincts within the same county may use different voting methods, causing still more confusion.

As became only too evident during the struggle over Florida's votes in 2000, America's overall balloting process is awkward, confusing, riddled with likely sources of error and bias and in cases of close races, incapable of producing a result that will stand up to scrutiny. Results can take several days to process, and every recount appears to produce a slightly different result. Often, too, the process of counting and recounting is directed by state and county officials with political axes to grind. The Votomatic punch-card machines used in a number of Florida counties are notoriously unreliable, but they are popular with many county governments because they are inexpensive. About 37 per-

Institution Principle

The electoral college and the Australian ballot are two instances of changes in electoral rules that can affect the outcomes of elections.

cent of the precincts in America's 3,140 counties used Votomatic or similar machines in the 2000 election.[35] However, voters often find it difficult to insert the punch cards properly, frequently punch the wrong hole, or do not sufficiently perforate one or more chads to allow the punch cards to be read by the counting machine. Votomatic and other punch-card voting devices generally yield a much higher rate of spoiled votes than other voting methods. A study of the last four presidential elections of the twentieth century determined that approximately 2 percent of all ballots were spoiled or unmarked. The incidence of spoiled ballots was highest in those counties using punch-card voting machines.[36] Indeed, a 1988 Florida Senate race was won by the Republican, Connie Mack, in part because of thousands of spoiled Votomatic ballots. To make matters worse, precinct-level election officials—often elderly volunteers—may not understand the rules themselves, and they are therefore unable to help voters with questions. These difficulties would not have been subject to public scrutiny as long as they affected only local races. In 2000, however, America's antiquated electoral machinery collapsed under the weight of a presidential election, revealing its flaws for all to see. Despite these problems, electoral officials are often reluctant to change voting methods because changes can affect the outcome of the next election in ways that might counter the officials' preferences.

Direct Democracy: The Referendum and the Recall

In addition to voting for candidates, twenty-four states also provide for referendum voting. The ***referendum*** process allows citizens to vote directly on proposed laws or other governmental actions. In recent years, voters in several states have voted to set limits on tax rates, block state and local spending proposals, and prohibit social services for illegal immigrants. Although it involves voting, a referendum is not an election. The election is an institution of representative government. Through an election, voters choose officials to act for them. The referendum, by contrast, is an institution of direct democracy; it allows voters to govern directly without intervention by government officials. The validity of referendum results, however, are subject to judicial action. If a court finds that a referendum outcome violates the state or national constitution, it can overturn the result. This happened in the case of a 1995 California referendum curtailing social services to illegal aliens.[37] It should be emphasized that the issues that emerge as referendum subjects are of the "hot-button" variety. It is not clear that these often emotional issues, which require deliberation and reflection, are the ones best dealt with by direct democracy. In other words, referendum issues are often adversely selected.

Twenty-four states also permit various forms of the initiative. Whereas the referendum described above allows citizens to affirm or reject a policy produced by legislative action, the ***initiative*** provides citizens with a way forward in the face of legislative inaction. This is done by placing a policy proposal (legislation or a state

referendum The practice of referring a measure proposed or passed by a legislature to the vote of the electorate for approval or rejection.

initiative A process by which citizens may petition to place a policy proposal on the ballot for public vote.

---

[35] Chad Terhune and Joni James, "Presidential Race Brings Attention to Business of Voting Machines," *Wall Street Journal*, 16 November 2000, p. A16.

[36] See Caltech/MIT Voting Technology Project (www.vote.caltech.edu).

[37] *League of United Latin American Citizens v. Wilson*, 908 F. Supp. 755 (C.D. Calif., 1995).

constitutional amendment) on the ballot to be approved or disapproved by the electorate. To have a place on the ballot, a petition must be accompanied by a minimum number of voters' signatures—a requirement that varies from state to state—that have been certified by the state's secretary of state.

The initiative is also vulnerable to adverse selection. Ballot propositions involve policies that the state legislature cannot (or does not want to) resolve. Like referendum issues, these are often highly emotional and, consequently, not always well suited to resolution in the electoral arena. One of the "virtues" of the initiative is that it may force action. That is, leaders in the legislature may induce recalcitrant legislators to move on controversial issues by using as a threat the possibility that a worse outcome will result from inaction.[38]

Legal provisions for *recall* elections exist in eighteen states. The recall is an electoral device that was introduced by early-twentieth-century Populists to allow voters to remove governors and other state officials from office before the expiration of their term. Federal officials such as the president and members of Congress are not subject to recall. Generally speaking, a recall effort begins with a petition campaign. For example, in California—the site of a tumultuous recall battle in 2003—if 12 percent of those who voted in the last general election sign petitions demanding a special recall election, one must be scheduled by the state board of elections. Such petition campaigns are relatively common, but most fail to garner enough signatures to bring the matter to a statewide vote. In California in 2003, however, a conservative Republican member of Congress, Darrell Issa, led a successful effort to recall Governor Gray Davis, a Democrat. Voters were unhappy about the state's economy and dissatisfied with Davis's performance: They blamed him for the state's $38 billion budget deficit. Issa and his followers were able to secure enough signatures to force a vote, and in October 2003 Davis became the second governor in American history to be recalled by his state's electorate (the first was North Dakota governor Lynn Frazier, who was recalled in 1921). Under California law, voters in a special recall election are also asked to choose a replacement for the official whom they dismiss. Californians in 2003 elected the movie star Arnold Schwarzenegger to be their governor. Although critics charged that the Davis recall had been a "political circus," the campaign had the effect of greatly increasing voter interest and involvement in the political process. More than 400,000 new voters registered in California in 2003, many drawn into the political arena by the opportunity to participate in the recall campaign.

The referendum, initiative, and recall all entail shifts in agenda-setting power. The referendum gives an impassioned electoral majority the opportunity to reverse legislation that displeases them, thus affecting the initial strategic calculations of institutional agenda setters (who want to get as much of what they want *without* its being subsequently reversed). The initiative has a similar effect on institutional agenda setters, but here it inclines them toward action rather than inaction. Combining the two, an institutional agenda setter is caught on the two horns of an institutional dilemma: Do I act, risking a reversal via referendum, or do I maintain the status quo, risking an overturn via initiative? The recall complements both of these, keeping institutional

recall The removal of a public official by popular vote.

---

[38]This point is developed in Morton Bennedsen and Sven Feldmann, "Lobbying Legislatures," *Journal of Political Economy* 110 (2002): 919–46.

agenda setters on their toes to avoid being ousted. As the institution principle implies, these arrangements do not just provide citizens with governance tools. They also affect the strategic calculations of institutional politicians—legislators and governors.

HOW DO VOTERS DECIDE?

Thus far, we have focused on the election as an institution. But the election is also a process in which millions of individuals make decisions and choices. Three types of factors influence voters' decisions at the polls: partisan loyalty, issues, and candidates' characteristics.

Partisan Loyalty

Many studies have shown that most Americans identify more or less strongly with one of the two major political parties. Partisan loyalty was strong during the 1940s and 1950s, declined for the next five decades, and has recently ticked up, reaching the levels it enjoyed in the 1950s. Most voters today feel a certain sense of identification or kinship with the Democratic or Republican party. This sense of identification is often handed down from parents to children and is reinforced by social and cultural ties. Partisan identification predisposes voters in favor of their party's candidates and against those of the opposing party. Partisanship is most likely to assert itself in the less-visible races, where issues and candidates are not very well known. Races for state legislatures, for example, are often decided by voters' party ties. However, even at the level of the presidential contest, in which issues and candidates' personalities become very important, many Americans supported John McCain or Barack Obama in 2008 largely because of partisan loyalty (Figure 10.5). Once formed, partisan loyalties are resistant to change. But sufficiently strong events and experiences may have the effect of eroding or even reversing them. White men in the South, for example, have been transformed over the last fifty years from strong partisans of the Democratic party to independents and even supporters of the Republican party. Voters tend to keep their party affiliations unless some crisis causes them to reexamine the bases of their loyalties and conclude that they have not given their support to the appropriate party. During these relatively infrequent periods, millions of voters can change their party ties. For example, at the beginning of the New Deal era, between 1932 and 1936, millions of former Republicans transferred their allegiance to Franklin Roosevelt and the Democratic party.

Partisan loyalty should be understood as more than a psychological attachment (although it certainly is that as well). It is also an informational shortcut—a way for voters to economize on information collection and processing. In many circumstances, it may be "enough" simply to know what party label a particular candidate wears. Any extra information—issue positions or personal attributes—may not influence the voter's choice once the partisan content has been taken on board. For example, once a particular voter learns that a candidate is a Democrat, he or she knows that the candidate is likely to be the preferred alternative; for another voter, however, that simple fact may be enough to cause him or her to vote

FIGURE 10.5 The Effect of Party Identification on the Vote for President, 2008

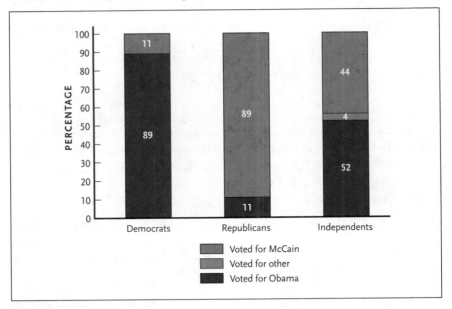

for the other guy! In the second half of the twentieth century, party labels began losing their capacity to signal likely characteristics of candidates, with the result that more and more voters found their partisan attachments weakening or disappearing altogether. The rise in the proportion of the electorate now identifying only weakly with a party or declaring themselves independents is testimony to this fact.[39]

In the next chapter, Figure 11.2 shows the relative decline in Democratic partisanship, the flatness of Republican identification, and the steep rise in those professing to be independents. Accompanying the long-term trend in party attachments, however, are ebbs and flows. As voters sorted themselves out between the parties, with more southerners becoming Republicans and moderates and liberals moving toward the Democrats, there was an uptick in partisan attachment in the 1990s. Parties, it would seem, by clarifying themselves ideologically, have become useful informational shortcuts again.[40]

---

[39]For a detailed assessment of the political use of information-economizing devices like party labels, see Arthur Lupia and Mathew D. McCubbins, *The Democratic Dilemma: Can Citizens Learn What They Need to Know?* (New York: Cambridge University Press, 1998). For the classic argument that party loyalty is a *variable*, not a constant, and that the voter updates party loyalty on the basis of his or her experience with the parties and their candidates, see Morris P. Fiorina, *Retrospective Voting in American National Elections* (New Haven, Conn.: Yale University Press, 1981).

ONLINE READING ○ [40]See Larry M. Bartels, "Partisanship and Voting Behavior, 1952–1956," *American Journal of Political Science* 44 (2000): 35–50; and Marc Hetherington, "Resurgent Mass Partisanship: The Role of Elite Polarization," *American Political Science Review* 95, no. 3 (September 2001): 619–31.

Issues

Issues and policy preferences are a second factor influencing voters' choices at the polls. Voters may cast their ballot for the candidate whose position on economic issues they believe to be closest to their own. Similarly, they may select the candidate who has what they believe to be the best record on foreign policy. Issues are more important in some races than others. If candidates actually "take issue" with one another—that is, if they articulate and publicize very different positions on important public questions—then voters are more likely to be able to identify and act on whatever policy preferences they may have.[41]

The ability of voters to make choices on the basis of issue or policy preferences is diminished, however, if competing candidates do not differ substantially or do not focus their campaigns on policy matters. Very often candidates deliberately take the safe course and emphasize topics that will not be offensive to any voters. Thus candidates often trumpet their opposition to corruption, crime, and inflation. Presumably, few voters favor these things. While it may be perfectly reasonable for candidates to take the safe course and remain as inoffensive as possible, this strategy makes it extremely difficult for voters to make their issue or policy preferences the bases for their choices at the polls.

Similarly, a paucity of useful and discriminating information during a campaign can induce the "wrong" decision by "knowledge-challenged" voters. Some analysts claimed that in 2000 Al Gore snatched defeat from the jaws of victory in just this way. In his efforts to distance himself from his scandal-plagued predecessor, he failed to remind voters of Clinton's great successes—eight years of peace and prosperity. Consequently, voters who may have been prepared to overlook Gore's party label because of the Clinton administration's achievements—moderate Republicans, for example—were not given much opportunity to do so.[42] An example from the 2004 presidential campaign also illustrates this. During that campaign, John Kerry provided abundant information about his views on the war in Iraq, but they straddled so many sides of the issue that they confused rather than informed voters. At one point, Kerry began emphasizing in campaign speeches that he had voted against a war appropriation in Senate deliberations but had voted for it a few minutes later. Analysts believe his straddling was an attempt to establish his credentials with antiwar voters while not alienating those who supported the war. This mixed strategy earned Kerry the label of "flip flopper" in Republican campaign advertising.

Voters' choice of issues usually involves a mix of their judgments about the past behavior of competing parties and candidates and their hopes and fears about

---

[41]Issue preferences and partisan loyalty are often suggested as separate factors influencing the voter's decision. Along with Morris Fiorina, however, let us reiterate that partisan identification is not merely a psychological attachment (like Boston's love affair with the Red Sox). There is a heavy dose of issue content to party identification. If a party consistently moves away from issue positions important to voters, then partisan attachment weakens. Voters are subsequently less likely to use the partisan label as an informational shortcut.

[42]This argument is spelled out in Morris P. Fiorina, Samuel Abrams, and Jeremy Pope, "The 2000 U.S. Presidential Election: Can Retrospective Voting Be Saved?" *British Journal of Political Science* 33 (2003): 163–87.

candidates' future behavior. Political scientists call choices that focus on future behavior *prospective voting* and those based on past performance *retrospective voting.* To some extent, whether prospective or retrospective evaluation is more important in a particular election depends on the strategies of the competing candidates. Candidates always endeavor to define the issues of an election in terms that will serve their interests. Incumbents running during a period of prosperity will seek to take credit for the economy's happy state and define the election as revolving around their record of success. This strategy encourages voters to make retrospective judgments. By contrast, an insurgent running during a period of economic uncertainty will tell voters it is time for a change and ask them to make prospective judgments. Thus Bill Clinton focused on change in 1992 and on prosperity in 1996 and through well-crafted media campaigns was able to define voters' agenda of choices.

In 2004, President Bush emphasized his efforts to protect the nation from terrorists and his strong commitment to religious and moral values. On the other hand, the Democratic candidate, John Kerry, attacked Bush's decision to invade Iraq, questioned the president's leadership in the war on terrorism, and charged that the president's economic policies had failed to produce prosperity. When asked by exit pollsters which issue mattered most in deciding how they voted for president, 22 percent of all voters cited moral values as their chief concern. More than 80 percent of these voters supported President Bush. The economy was cited as the most important issue by 20 percent of those who voted, and 80 percent of those Americans voted for Senator Kerry. Terrorism ranked third in terms of the percentage of voters who indicated it was the most important issue for them. President Bush received more than 80 percent of the votes of those Americans concerned mainly with terrorism. The 2006 midterm elections were portrayed by Democrats as a referendum on President Bush's conduct of the war in Iraq. There was a considerable swing of votes to the Democrats, even in districts that had supported Bush over Kerry in 2004, with the result that the Democrats picked up twenty-five seats in the House and six in the Senate.[43]

When voters engage in issue voting, competition between two candidates has the effect of pushing the candidates' issue positions toward the middle of the distribution of voters' preferences. This is known as the median-voter theorem, made famous by Duncan Black and Anthony Downs.[44] To see the logic of this claim, imagine a series of possible stances on a policy issue as points along a line, stretching from 0 to 100 (Figure 10.6). A voter is represented by an "ideal" policy and preferences, which decline as policy moves away from this ideal. Thus voters in group 1 prefer policy X_1 most, and their preference declines as the policy moves to the left or right of X_1. Voters whose ideal policy lies between, say, 0 and 25 are said to be liberal on this policy (groups 1 and 2), those whose ideal lies between 75

 **Rationality Principle**

Issue voting motivates candidates to converge toward the preferences of the median voter.

prospective voting
Voting based on the imagined future performance of a candidate.

retrospective voting
Voting based on the past performance of a candidate.

---

[43]William F. Connelly Jr., "Wall vs. Wave?" *The Forum* 4, no. 3 (2006; www.bepress.com/forum/vol4/1553/art3).

[44]See Duncan Black, *The Theory of Committees and Elections,* 2nd ed. (Boston: Kluwer, 1998); and Anthony Downs, *An Economic Theory of Democracy* (New York: Harper & Row, 1957). A general, accessible treatment of this subject is found in Shepsle and Bonchek, *Analyzing Politics,* chap. 5.

FIGURE 10.6 The Median-Voter Theorem

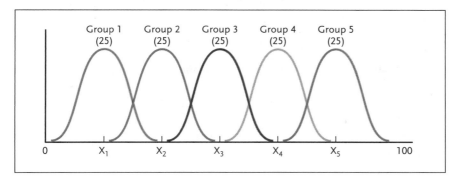

and 100 are conservative (groups 4 and 5), and those whose favorite policy is be-tween 25 and 75 are moderate (group 3). An issue voter cares only about issue po-sitions, not partisan loyalty or candidates' characteristics, and would, therefore, vote for the candidate whose announced policy is closest to his or her own most preferred policy.

Consider now an electorate of 125 voters evenly distributed among the five groups shown in Figure 10.6.[45] The middle group contains the median voter be-cause half or more of this electorate has an ideal policy at or to the left of X_3 (groups 1, 2, and 3) and half or more has an ideal policy at or to the right of X_3 (groups 3, 4, and 5). Group 3 is in the driver's seat, as the following reasoning suggests. If a can-didate announces X_3 as his policy—the most preferred alternative of the median voter—and if his opponent picks any point to the right, then the median voter and all those with ideal policies to the left of the median voter's (groups 1–3) will support the first candidate. They constitute a majority, by definition of the median, so this candidate will win. Suppose instead that the opponent chose as her policy some point to the left of the median ideal policy. Then the median voter and all those with ideal policies to the right of the median voter's (groups 3–5) will support the first candidate—and he wins, again. In short, the median-voter theorem says that the candidate whose policy position is closest to the ideal policy of the median voter will defeat the other candidate in a majority contest. We can conclude from this brief analysis that issue voting encourages candidate convergence (in which both candi-dates move to cozy up to the position of the median voter). Even when voters are not exclusively issue voters, two-candidate competition still encourages a tendency to-ward convergence, although it may not fully run its course.[46]

Policy Principle

The median-voter the-orem predicts policy moderation on the part of candidates.

---

[45] For the sake of this illustration, we've put 25 voters in each group. One argument is the same with any distribution of voters among the groups.

[46] This convergence will also be a moderating force as candidates move toward what they believe will ap-peal to voters in the middle. But if the middle of the voter distribution of preferences tilts toward the right or the left, it may not be very moderate. If X_3, for example, were barely to the left of X_4, then the median voter would be fairly right wing rather than in the middle of the issue dimension.

The Economy As we identify the strategies and tactics employed by opposing political candidates and parties, we should keep in mind that the best-laid plans of politicians often go awry. Election outcomes are affected by a variety of forces that candidates for office cannot fully control. Among the most important of these is the condition of the economy. If voters are satisfied with their economic prospects, they tend to support the party in power, while voters' unease about the economy tends to favor the opposition. Thus George H. W. Bush lost in 1992 during an economic downturn even though his victory in the Persian Gulf War had briefly given him a 90 percent favorable rating in the polls. And Bill Clinton won in 1996 during an economic boom even though voters had serious concerns about his moral fiber. Over the past quarter century, the Consumer Confidence Index, calculated by the Conference Board, a business research group, has been a fairly accurate predictor of presidential outcomes. The index is based on surveys asking voters how optimistic they are about the future of the economy. It would appear that a generally rosy view, indicated by a score greater than 100, augurs well for the party in power. An index score of less than 100, suggesting that voters are pessimistic about the economy's trend, suggests that incumbents should worry about their job prospects (Figure 10.7).

Candidate Characteristics

Candidates' personal attributes always influence voters' decisions. The more important characteristics that affect voters' choices are race, ethnicity, religion, gender, geography, and social background. In general, voters prefer candidates who are closer to themselves in terms of these categories. Voters presume that such candidates are likely to have views and perspectives close to their own. Moreover, they may be proud to see someone of their ethnic, religious, or geographic background in a position of leadership. This is why, for many years, politicians sought to "balance the ticket," making certain that their party's ticket included members of as many important groups as possible.

Just as a candidate's personal characteristics may attract some voters, so they may repel others. Many voters are prejudiced against candidates of certain ethnic, racial, or religious groups. And for many years, voters were reluctant to support the political candidacy of women, although this tendency appears to be changing.

Voters also pay attention to candidates' personality characteristics, such as their "decisiveness," "honesty," and "vigor." In recent years, integrity has become a key election issue. In the 2000 presidential race, Al Gore chose Joe Lieberman as his running mate in part because Lieberman had been sharply critical of Bill Clinton's moral lapses. The senator's presence on the Democratic ticket thus helped defuse the GOP's efforts to link Gore to Clinton's questionable character. In the 2004 presidential race, President Bush and the Republicans accused Senator Kerry of being inconsistent, a "flip flopper" who continuously changed his position when it was expedient to do so. Bush, on the other hand, emphasized his own constancy. "I say what I mean and I do what I say" was the president's frequent refrain. The president also pointed to his strong religious commitment as evidence of his exemplary character. For their part, Democrats emphasized Senator Kerry's intelligence, empathy for ordinary Americans, and record of wartime heroism, which, they said, stood in sharp contrast to Bush's own somewhat blemished mil-

FIGURE 10.7 Consumer Confidence and Presidential Elections

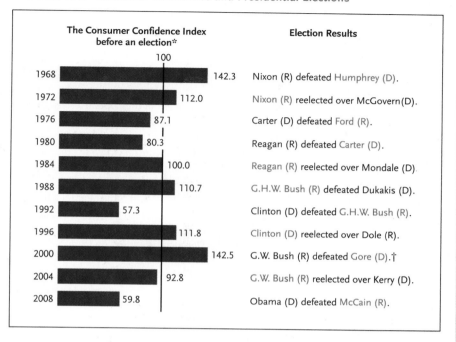

The Consumer Confidence Index before an election*	Election Results
1968 — 142.3	Nixon (R) defeated Humphrey (D).
1972 — 112.0	Nixon (R) reelected over McGovern (D).
1976 — 87.1	Carter (D) defeated Ford (R).
1980 — 80.3	Reagan (R) defeated Carter (D).
1984 — 100.0	Reagan (R) reelected over Mondale (D).
1988 — 110.7	G.H.W. Bush (R) defeated Dukakis (D).
1992 — 57.3	Clinton (D) defeated G.H.W. Bush (R).
1996 — 111.8	Clinton (D) reelected over Dole (R).
2000 — 142.5	G.W. Bush (R) defeated Gore (D).†
2004 — 92.8	G.W. Bush (R) reelected over Kerry (D).
2008 — 59.8	Obama (D) defeated McCain (R).

SOURCE: *Bloomberg Markets.*

NOTE: The candidate representing the incumbent party appears in red.

*Survey was bimonthly before 1977, so figures for 1968, 1972, and 1976 are for October; from 1980 on, they are for September.

†Gore won the popular vote, but Bush was elected by the Electoral College.

itary record. In the end, the GOP's characterization of Kerry as a "flip flopper" and Bush as an individual with deep moral and religious commitments seemed to resonate with voters. Among those who said that it was important for the president to take a clear stand on issues, 80 percent voted for President Bush; among those for whom strong religious faith was important, 90 percent voted for Bush; and among those who cited honesty as the candidate quality that mattered most, more than 70 percent gave their votes to Bush. On the other hand, among Americans who thought a president should be empathic and care about people like them, 75 percent supported Kerry; and among those who thought intelligence was the most important personal characteristic of a president, 91 percent voted for Kerry and only 9 percent for Bush.[47]

---

[47]Individual qualities and chararacteristics are known in the political science literature as valence issues. See Stephen Ansolabehere and James Snyder, "Valence Politics and Equilibrium in Spatial Election Models," *Public Choice* 103 (2000): 327–36; and Timothy Groseclose, "A Model of Candidate Location When One Candidate Has a Valence Advantage," *American Journal of Political Science* 45 (2001): 862–86.

THE 2008 ELECTION

The 2008 presidential election was in some ways predictable—voters wanted a change from a very unpopular Republican administration and, perhaps predictably, elected a Democrat—but in many ways the 2008 race was a groundbreaking departure from politics as usual. In 2008, for the first time in the nation's history, Americans elected an African American to the White House as Illinois senator Barack Obama led the Democratic party to a solid electoral victory, securing 53 percent of the popular vote versus 46 percent for Republican candidate Senator John McCain. Obama won a 365-to-173 majority in the Electoral College (see Figure 10.8), far more than the 270 electoral votes needed to claim the presidency. The 2008 presidential election was also notable because of the prominence of women candidates. Hillary Clinton's strong campaign for the Democratic nomination shattered the notion that a woman couldn't compete seriously for the nation's highest office, and John McCain's selection of Sarah Palin as his running mate seemed based at least partly on the advantages of having a woman on the ticket. The 2008 campaigns also brought about a significant shift in the electoral map, as states like Virginia that hadn't supported a Democratic candidate in decades went from "red" to "blue."

The Democrats increased their strength in both houses of Congress, adding at least six seats in the Senate, giving them a larger majority, with four more seats still up for grabs pending recounts in the days after the election. Democrats had hoped to reach the magical sixty-seat total that would prevent GOP filibusters from blocking votes on Democratic bills. Democrats also gained at least twenty-two seats in the House of Representatives (eight were still undecided at the end of the night) to win a 254-to-173 majority in the lower chamber, with more seats possible. Further embarrassing the Republicans, incumbent GOP senators in New Hampshire (John Sununu) and North Carolina (Elizabeth Dole) were ousted by Democratic challengers. Because of enormous interest in the campaign, the increasing use of absentee and pre-Election Day voting, and well-financed voter registration drives conducted mainly by the Democrats, more than 120 million Americans cast ballots in 2008, a number comparable to the level of turnout reached in 2004.

The Path to 2008: Modern Electoral Politics and Race

At one level, the 2008 results are not so surprising. Outgoing Republican president George W. Bush had become one of the most unpopular chief executives in American history, the nation seemed mired in never-ending and inconclusive wars in Iraq and Afghanistan, and, to make matters even worse, the nation's fall 2008 financial crisis appeared to presage a deep economic recession. Was there any reason the GOP could even hope to survive the triple whammy of recession, war, and an extraordinarily unpopular Republican president? One reason Republicans might have hoped for survival in 2008 was the matter of race. Democrat Barack Obama is the son of a black African father and white Kansan mother and was the first nonwhite major party presidential candidate in American history. Given America's tangled racial politics and sometimes violent racial antagonisms, many observers questioned whether white Americans were prepared to elect a black man to the highest office in the land. As late as September 2008, polls showed that more than one-third

FIGURE 10.8 Distribution of Electoral Votes in the 2008 Presidential Election

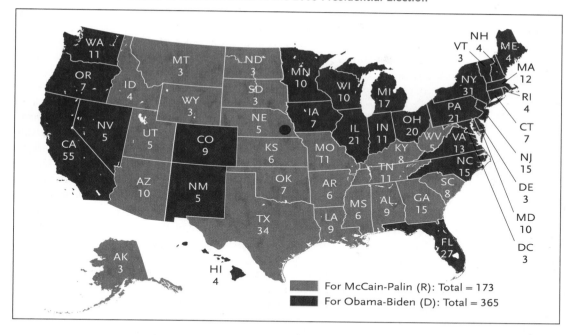

For McCain-Palin (R): Total = 173
For Obama-Biden (D): Total = 365

of white Democratic and Independent voters harbored misgivings about the idea of a black president. That tens of millions of whites did vote for the Democratic candidate is a reflection both of Obama's unique attributes and of underlying changes in American race relations over the past several decades.

Race in Twentieth-Century Elections   To understand the significance of the 2008 election, a bit of political history is in order. The roots of Obama's victory go back nearly half a century to the civil rights movement of the 1960s. In the New Deal era, the majority of northern blacks joined the Democratic party, which they saw as the party of economic opportunity. Yet in the 1950s and early 1960s, when civil rights protests against the southern system of racial segregation and political exclusion initially broke out in the South, national Democratic leaders were reluctant to commit their support to the black cause. The white South had been a solid Democratic bastion since the end of Reconstruction and was a linchpin of Democratic power in the Congress and the White House. Indeed, during this era, many black Americans believed that the Republican party, which had no ties to the South, was more likely to take up their cause than the Democrats. In 1960, nearly as many northern black voters cast ballots for Richard Nixon as for John F. Kennedy.

Though Kennedy is often remembered as having been a staunch supporter of civil rights, his administration was cautious and anxious not to offend white southerners. After Kennedy's assassination, Democratic liberals secured the support of President Lyndon Johnson. Though a southerner, and knowing that his support for black civil rights would alienate the white South, Johnson felt a personal moral commitment to the civil rights cause and was also anxious to win the favor of the upper-middle-class intellectuals and professionals who had been devoted to Kennedy. Prodded by Johnson and against the backdrop of increasingly violent southern resistance to peaceful civil rights protests, Congress enacted the 1965 Voting Rights Act, under whose auspices federal voting officials presided over the registration of millions of African American voters in the former Confederacy.

Democratic support for black voting rights and affirmative action infuriated millions of white southerners and, at the same time, angered many blue-collar northern Democrats over what they saw as preferential treatment for blacks when they, themselves, were engaged in day-to-day economic struggles. With the Democratic party divided by racial conflicts and struggles over the Vietnam War, and with Johnson choosing not to run for reelection, the 1968 election was won by Republican Richard Nixon, who launched what he called his "southern strategy," to bring disaffected southern whites into the Republican camp. Nixon attacked racial preferences and declared that the civil rights movement had gone too far in its demands. In response to Nixon's appeals, millions of southern whites began to shift their political allegiance to the Republican party.

Ronald Reagan built upon but significantly modified Nixon's efforts. After taking office in 1980, Reagan eschewed the sorts of racial appeals that had been made by Nixon eight years earlier. Instead, Reagan used patriotic and religious symbols that would resonate not only among white southerners but also among blue-collar white northerners. Reagan and his advisers turned to "family values" issues, especially abortion, to appeal to Catholic and Protestant religious conservatives in the North and South.

As for the Democrats during this period, the nation's racial politics and racial polarization posed significant political dilemmas, especially at the presidential level. Championing the cause of civil rights had helped Democratic liberals greatly expand their power within the Democratic party but had undermined the party's fortunes in national presidential elections. Racial divisions were one reason that the Democrats lost seven of ten presidential elections between 1968 and 2004, electing only two presidents in a forty-year period. Efforts by Democratic presidential candidates to rebuild their party's support among southern whites and blue-collar northerners were hampered by the harsh racial arithmetic of American politics. In the wake of the Voting Rights Act, the Democratic party depended upon African Americans for more than 20 percent of its votes in national presidential elections. Yet, at the same time, and for a somewhat larger percentage of Democratic and Independent voters, the Democrats relied upon whites who, for one or another reason, were unfriendly to blacks.

The 2000 and 2004 Elections   In 2000 and 2004, George W. Bush generally followed the electoral game plan developed by Ronald Reagan. In 2000, Bush's own ineptitude and general voter satisfaction with the economics, if not the public morality, of the Clinton years, almost cost the Republicans the presidency. In fact, Bush lost the popular vote, but thanks to the vagaries of the Electoral College system and the intervention of the Supreme Court, Bush became America's forty-third president.

As president, Bush reacted forcefully to the September 11, 2001, terrorist attacks against the United States and temporarily saw his standing in the polls rise to a stratospheric 90 percent level. Over the next two years, however, sluggish economic growth and the Bush administration's miscues in Iraq seemed to offer the Democrats an opportunity to reclaim the White House. Bush, however, made enormous efforts to register and mobilize the Republican base. Though Bush's dismal performance in the 2004 presidential debates briefly seemed to threaten his reelection, the Republican base rallied to his side and handed him a solid electoral victory.

Virtually unnoticed during the 2000 and 2004 elections, and during Bush's years in office, was a decline in the racial polarization of American politics. Some Americans, to be sure, continued to harbor animosities toward one another, but race seemed to be less salient in the political arena. To some extent, the credit for this development should go to Ronald Reagan. Reagan had made a deliberate decision to drop the racially charged Republican rhetoric of the Nixon years in favor of a focus on patriotism and religious values. This shift in rhetoric was not total and absolute, but it meant that the number of overtly racial appeals and even racial code words found in political debate gradually diminished and that issues of race were gradually deemphasized on the national political battlefield. It was significant that George W. Bush, a conservative president, appointed African Americans, such as former secretaries of state Colin Powell and Condoleezza Rice, and other nonwhite candidates to high government positions. Democrats accused Bush and the Republicans of racial tokenism, but these tokens were important.

In an atmosphere in which racially charged rhetoric was on the decline, other social processes could begin to have an effect. After the civil rights revolution of the 1960s, and the erosion of America's many systems of segregation, both legal and customary, blacks and whites were more likely to live in the same neighborhoods, attend the same schools, work in the same factories and offices, serve in the military together, and frequent the same stores, restaurants, and entertainment venues. For many Americans, the end of segregation opened the way for a gradual lessening of racial antagonisms over the course of several decades. The nation's demographics also changed during this period. A huge influx of immigrants from Latin America as well as Asia and the Middle East meant that America was no longer a land of black and white. It now included many shades of brown as well, complicating the nation's racial divisions. In this new America, explicitly racist appeals from politicians would seem out-of-step and illegitimate.

The 2008 Campaigns

In this political landscape of shifting race relations and frustration with a Republican administration, Democrats saw that 2008 offered a major opportunity to reclaim the White House. Democratic strategists were determined not to repeat the errors of 2000 and 2004. In the 2006 congressional elections, the Democrats picked up momentum, winning majorities in both houses of Congress for the first time since 1994. By 2006, the electorate was already blaming the GOP for a sluggish economy and seemingly endless war. As voters became increasingly dissatisfied with the policies promoted by President Bush and supported by his Republican allies in Congress, it appeared that the stage was set for a Democratic victory in 2008.

The 2008 Primaries   The 2008 Democratic and Republican primaries and caucuses to select the parties' candidates for the presidency began January 3 with the Iowa

Democratic caucuses. The actual campaigns, of course, began early in 2007, as ambitious politicians assessed their chances and started the long process of raising the tens of millions of dollars required to launch a presidential candidacy. On the Republican side, the front-runner was John McCain. The Arizona senator had campaigned for the Republican nomination in 2000 only to be defeated by Bush in a primary contest remembered for the victor's smear tactics. McCain, the son and grandson of U.S. Navy admirals, was a Vietnam War hero. McCain had a distinguished career in the Senate and was the chief sponsor of several major pieces of legislation, including the McCain-Feingold campaign reform law. Despite his national prominence, McCain was generally not well liked in Republican circles. Traditional business-oriented Republicans might have preferred Mitt Romney, a successful businessperson and former governor of Massachusetts, but the GOP's evangelical Protestant cadres did not like the idea of Romney, a Mormon, as their party's candidate. Social conservatives supported former Arkansas governor and evangelical minister Mike Huckabee, an articulate politician whose sense of humor made him a successful guest on *Saturday Night Live*. Establishment Republicans, however, thought Huckabee was too closely associated with the party's religious element and would have no chance in a national campaign. Other Republicans, Ron Paul, Rudy Giuliani, and Fred Thompson, excited little interest. After losing the Iowa caucuses to Huckabee and struggling to raise money, McCain regained his political and financial footing and was able to drive his opponents from the race. McCain had effectively secured the Republican nomination by the beginning of March.

Clinton versus Obama On the Democratic side, the early front-runner for the presidential nomination was New York senator and former first lady Hillary Rodham Clinton. Senator Clinton was famous, her husband was extraordinarily popular among Democrats, and her contacts and position as a New York senator meant that she would be able to count on tens of millions of dollars in campaign contributions. Most pundits predicted an easy Clinton victory. Other Democratic contenders included former North Carolina senator and 2004 vice-presidential candidate John Edwards, former New Mexico governor Bill Richardson, Congressman Dennis Kucinich, former Alaska senator Mike Gravel, and senators Joe Biden, Chris Dodd, and Barack Obama. Biden, Dodd, and Richardson, along with Gravel and Kucinich, generated relatively little interest and quickly dropped out. Edwards was popular among his fellow trial lawyers, who contributed enough money to his campaign to keep him in through the end of January, though with little chance of success. The surprise of the Democratic primary contest was, of course, Illinois senator Barack Obama.

Obama was a first-term senator, having arrived in Washington in 2004. He had won a measure of national celebrity by delivering a rousing keynote address at the 2004 Democratic national convention. Many Democrats' first opportunity to see Obama as a serious contender came in the Democratic debates. The Illinois senator was not necessarily more articulate, more knowledgeable, or more passionate about important issues than Clinton, Edwards, and the others, but observers were impressed that at debate after debate the virtually unknown senator stood toe to toe with his more seasoned and famous opponents and held his own. Obama's impressive performance electrified liberal Democrats, excited young voters, intrigued the media, and ignited the enthusiasm of black Democrats, even if most were initially dubious that Obama could succeed. This enthusiastic response to Obama's debate appearances swelled the ranks of Obama supporters, inspired donors to write checks, and gave Obama the means to compete against Clinton.

Throughout the primaries, Clinton and Obama battled furiously in state after state. Obama was particularly popular with younger voters and with liberals who resented what they saw as Clinton's early equivocation on the Iraq war. Black politicians—many of whom had considered Bill Clinton an important ally during his presidency—initially supported Hillary Clinton, assuming she would win. But as their constituents rallied to Obama and it became clear that Obama's candidacy actually had a chance, the Illinois senator was able to garner overwhelming black support. Some pundits said it was ironic that the first woman to mount a serious presidential bid and the first black person to mount such a bid were pitted against one another. For the news media, however, in this battle of the firsts, Obama's candidacy was the more important first.

By late spring, it became clear that Obama would be the Democratic presidential nominee. The result was close. Under Democratic rules, 2,118 delegates were needed to win the nomination. In the various primaries and caucuses, Obama had won 1,763 delegates to Clinton's 1,640. This effectively left the decision to the party's 796 "superdelegates," party officials and notables chosen to attend the convention. At the outset, most superdelegates had backed Clinton. As the race wore on, however, sentiment shifted toward Obama. Some saw Obama as the better candidate, while others worried that black Democrats—20 percent of the party's electoral strength—would stay home on Election Day if Obama was denied the nomination. With 438 superdelegates supporting Obama, he could count on 2,201 votes. Clinton briefly weighed taking her candidacy to the floor of the convention to be decided there, but ultimately, on June 3, withdrew and announced that she and her husband would staunchly support Obama in the general election.

The General Election   At the August 2008 Democratic national convention, speaker after speaker extolled Obama's virtues, and even Bill Clinton gave a speech in which he strongly supported Obama. Obama chose Delaware senator Joseph Biden as his vice-presidential running mate. Biden, chair of the Senate Foreign Relations Committee, was selected at least partly in response to questions about Obama's scant foreign policy experience. In addition, Biden had working-class roots in Pennsylvania. Democrats hoped that Biden would appeal to the so-called Joe Six-pack voters, blue-collar workers whom the Democrats needed in such battleground states as Ohio and Pennsylvania.

The Republican convention, which opened a few days after the Democratic convention ended, began without much fanfare. Although John McCain had won the primary battle and was respected for his military service, he was not an especially beloved figure among rank-and-file Republicans. Nevertheless, McCain energized Republicans when he chose little-known Alaska governor Sarah Palin as his vice-presidential running mate and "introduced" her to the GOP base at the convention. Palin, a religious conservative who opposed abortion, excited many Republicans who had been cool toward McCain. Unfortunately for the GOP, Palin's star faded rapidly as the inexperienced governor proved unequal to the demands of a national campaign. In television interviews, including one with Katie Couric on CBS, Palin seemed to know little about current political issues and problems and could do no more than repeat Republican talking points that she seemed to have committed to memory. Despite her reasonable performance in the nationally televised vice-presidential debate, Palin was declared "clearly out of her league," even by staunchly Republican commentators, who wondered aloud if Palin could seriously be entrusted with the presidency if anything happened to McCain.

Despite the brief surge of enthusiasm generated by the selection of Palin, the McCain ticket struggled throughout the campaign. From the beginning, the deck seemed stacked against the Republicans. Despite his assertions of independence, the fact remained that McCain was a Republican and, hence, was tied to the Bush administration. Obama and the Democrats, moreover, held an enormous fund-raising advantage over McCain and the Republicans. Knowing that he would have difficulty raising money from traditional GOP donors, McCain had decided to accept public funding for the general election. This would give his campaign some $84 million to spend on organizing, advertising, and voter registration. McCain hoped Republican party fund-raising would add considerably to this figure. Obama, on the other hand, became the first major party candidate since the law was enacted to forgo general election public funding. As a consequence, Obama was able to step up his Internet and conventional fund-raising, which eventually produced in the neighborhood of $700 million, an astonishing total that more than doubled the previous record, which had been set by the Republicans in 2004. His campaign's extraordinary fund-raising prowess gave Obama and the Democrats some $200 million more to spend than was available to McCain and the Republicans.

Lack of money was not McCain's only problem. In September 2008, the nation experienced a serious financial crisis that began with a decline in home sales and a wave of mortgage foreclosures and continued with billions of dollars of losses in mortgage-based securities. Since all these events took place while the Republicans controlled the White House, the Democrats were quick to blame the Bush administration's economic policies for the crisis.

The Debates   Obama helped his cause enormously in the three televised presidential debates held in September and October. He responded with evident knowledge and intelligence to questions on domestic and foreign policy. So, for that matter, did McCain. But McCain, the Washington veteran, was expected to have answers to policy questions. Obama was the newcomer who had been chided for his inexperience. Like Kennedy, Reagan, and Clinton before him, Obama bore the burden of reassuring voters that he measured up to the job of being president. In the debates, Obama spoke clearly and incisively on education, economic policy, health policy, and the wars in Iraq and Afghanistan. Even more important was Obama's manner. By contrast with the often twitchy McCain, Obama was smooth, calm, and reassuring. Many commentators observed that Obama appeared "presidential" and that this helped more and more Americans feel comfortable with his candidacy. Following the debates, Obama's approval ratings rose steadily and the McCain campaign faltered.

Obama's Victory Throughout October, Obama consistently led by single-digit margins in the national polls. Given the faltering economy, an unpopular president, and the Democrats' enormous financial advantage, the GOP should have been heading for a train wreck of epic proportions, and yet, until Obama's lead increased in late October, McCain trailed by only three to five points in the polls. Some analysts of opinion data thought the problem was race. A white Democratic candidate, according to some mathematical models of public opinion, would have enjoyed a much stronger lead in the polls, perhaps an additional six or seven points. Some analysts worried whether Obama's lead was even as strong as it looked. These analysts pointed to the so-called Bradley effect, a phantom lead produced when white voters, reluctant to display overt signs of racism, lie to pollsters about their intentions. This is allegedly what happened in 1982, when Los Angeles mayor Tom Bradley lost the California gubernatorial race after leading his white opponent in the polls.

In the end, racial antipathy did not determine the outcome of the 2008 presidential election. Though many forces were at work, Obama's victory was made possible by the softening of racial antagonisms in the United States over the past half-century and the delegitimization of overtly racist rhetoric in the public forum. But the election of a black president does not mean the end of racism in America. Obama is an exceptional individual—a graduate of the Harvard Law School with a white mother, an African rather than an African American father, and raised by white grandparents. Some Democratic canvassers emphasized these facts to white voters, describing their candidate as a man from a multiracial background whose father was an African intellectual, not an American from the inner city.

Does Obama's victory represent the end of racism and the birth of a new America? Or is Obama an exception? Only time will help us to fully understand the significance of the 2008 election.

CAMPAIGN FINANCE

Modern national political campaigns are fueled by enormous amounts of money. In 2008, incumbent candidates in competitive House races typically spent close to $2 million to hold on to their seats. The average winner in Senate races spent more than $4 million. In recent years, some Senate contests have cost $25 million or more. In the 2008 presidential race, the two parties and their candidates spent more than $1.5 billion. Hundreds of millions more were spent by individuals and groups who ran independent ads seeking to influence the outcome of the presidential contest.

Sources of Campaign Funds

In 2008, according to the Center for Responsive Politics, roughly $3 billion was spent by candidates for federal offices. About 10 percent of this total came from political action committees (PACs), mainly in support of congressional races, and the remainder from individual donors. Several million individuals donated money to political campaigns in 2008, some in contributions of as little as $5 or $10. One of the sources of Barack Obama's fund-raising advantage in the 2008 campaign was his ability to generate more than two million small and medium-size contributions. Another $500 million in 2008 was raised and spent by individuals and advocacy groups—the so-called 527s and 501c(4) groups operating outside the structure of the Democratic and Republican campaigns.

Individual Donors Politicians spend a great deal of time asking people for money. Money is solicited via direct mail, over the phone, and in numerous face-to-face meetings. Under federal law, individuals may donate as much as $2,300 per candidate per election, $5,000 per PAC per calendar year (to a maximum of $65,000), $28,500 per national party committee per calendar year, and $10,000 to state and local party committees per calendar year (to a maximum of $42,700). Federal rules also impose an overall limit on individual contributors of $108,200 per election cycle. Individuals may also contribute freely to 527 committees and to 501c(4) groups. 527 donations are a matter of public record, but 501c(4)s are not required to disclose their donor lists. Individuals may also attempt to enhance their influence by raising and "bundling" their contributions with those of friends and associates. Many Washington lobbyists curry favor with politicians through vigorous bundling efforts.

Political Action and 527 Committees *Political action committees (PACs)* are organizations established by corporations, labor unions, or interest groups to channel the contributions of their members into political campaigns. Under the terms of the 1971 Federal Election Campaign Act, which governs campaign finance in the United States, PACs are permitted to make larger contributions to any given candidate than individuals are allowed to make. Individuals may donate a maximum of $2,000 to any single candidate, but a PAC may donate as much as $5,000 to each candidate. Moreover, allied or related PACs often coordinate their campaign contributions, greatly increasing the amount of money a candidate receives from an interest group. As a result, PACs have become central to campaign finance in the United States. Many critics assert that PACs corrupt the political process by allowing corporations and other interests to influence politicians with large contributions. It is by no means clear, however, that PACs corrupt the political process any more than large, individual contributions do.

More than 4,500 PACs are registered with the Federal Election Commission (FEC), which oversees campaign finance practices in the United States. Nearly two thirds of all PACs represent corporations, trade associations, and other business and professional groups. Alliances of bankers, lawyers, doctors, and merchants all sponsor PACs. One example is the National Beer Wholesalers Association Political Action Committee, which for many years was known as Six PAC. Labor unions also sponsor PACs, as do ideological, public interest, and nonprofit groups. For example, the National Rifle Association sponsors a PAC, as does the Sierra Club. Many congressional and party leaders have also established PACs, known as leadership PACs, to provide funding for their political allies.

In recent years, PACs and individuals have contributed hundreds of millions of dollars—so-called hard money—to political campaigns. But although they have been important fund-raising tools, they have been overshadowed by the so-called

political action committees (PACs) Private groups that raise and distribute funds for use in election campaigns.

soft money contributed to the political parties and then recycled into campaigns. Soft money is money that is not contributed directly to a candidate and is thus not subject to the limitations of the Federal Election Campaign Act. As a result, well-heeled individuals and interests often preferred to make large, anonymous soft-money contributions to parties rather than—or in addition to—relatively small and publicly recorded contributions directly to PACs and candidates. By 2000, as much as $3 in soft money was spent for every $1 of hard money given directly and thus subject to FEC regulation. The 2002 Bipartisan Campaign Reform Act outlawed many, albeit not all, forms of soft money, thus increasing the importance of political action committees in the funding process.

Another important source of soft money has been **527 committees.** Expenditures by these committees are "soft" because they are not given to or coordinated with any specific candidate's campaign. Technically, then, this money does not finance candidates' campaigns. Indeed, 527 committee advertisements cannot directly endorse a candidate. But by using soft-money expenditures to register voters with serious Democratic propensities, as the 527 committee financed by the billionaire George Soros did in 2004, or to attack John Kerry's Vietnam service record, as the Swift Boat Veterans for Truth did, the 527 committees' efforts had clear and significant candidate- and party-specific effects.

The Candidates　On the basis of the Supreme Court's 1976 decision in *Buckley v. Valeo*, the right of individual candidates to spend their *own* money on their campaigns for office is a constitutionally protected matter of free speech and is not subject to limitation.[48] Thus extremely wealthy candidates often contribute millions of dollars to their own campaigns. Jon Corzine, for example, spent approximately $60 million of his own funds in a successful New Jersey Senate bid in 2000, launching a political career that has included his election as governor of New Jersey in 2005.

Independent Spending　As noted above, some forms of spending are also free from regulation: private groups, political parties, and wealthy individuals, engaging in what is called ***issue advocacy,*** may spend as much as they wish in order to help elect one candidate or defeat another, as long as their expenditures are not coordinated with any candidate's campaign. Many business and ideological groups engage in such activities. Some estimates suggest that groups and individuals spent as much as $509 million on issue advocacy—generally through television advertising—during the 2000 elections.[49] In 2004 and 2008, they also spent hundreds of millions of dollars.

Some groups are careful not to mention particular candidates in their issue ads, to avoid any suggestion that they might merely be fronts for a candidate's campaign committee. Most issue ads, however, are attacks on the opposing

527 committees Tax-exempt organizations that engage in political activities, often through unlimited "soft-money" contributions. The committees are not restricted by current law on campaign finance, thus exploiting a loophole in the Internal Revenue Service code.

issue advocacy Independent spending by individuals or interest groups that supports a campaign issue but is not directly tied to a particular candidate.

○　ONLINE READING

---

[48] *Buckley v. Valeo,* 424 U.S. 1 (1976).

[49] Kathleen Hall Jamieson, "Issue Advertising in the 1999–2000 Election Cycle," Annenberg Public Policy Center, University of Pennsylvania, 1 February 2001. (www.annenbergpublicpolicycenter.org/issuead502_01_2001_1999-2000issueadvocacy.pdf). Subsequent election cycles produced even greater spending.

candidate's record or character. In 2000 and 2004, liberal groups ran ads bashing Bush's record on capital punishment, tax reform, and Social Security. Conservative groups attacked the Democratic candidates' views on gun ownership, abortion, and environmental regulation. In the 2008 national elections, the top 527s were mainly, albeit not exclusively, supportive of the Democrats.

Public Funding   The Federal Election Campaign Act also provides for public funding of presidential campaigns. As they seek a major party presidential nomination, candidates become eligible for public funds by raising at least $5,000 in individual contributions of $250 or less in each of twenty states. Candidates who reach this threshold may apply for federal funds to match, on a dollar-for-dollar basis, all individual contributions of $250 or less that they receive. The funds are drawn from the Presidential Election Campaign Fund. Taxpayers can contribute $1 to this fund, at no additional cost to themselves, by checking a box on the first page of their federal income-tax returns. Major party presidential candidates receive a lump sum (currently nearly $90 million) during the summer before the general election. They must meet all their campaign expenses from this money—that is, they may not accept other contributions. Under current law, no candidate is required to accept public funding for either the nominating races or the presidential election. Candidates who do not accept public funding are not affected by any expenditure limits. Thus in 1992, Ross Perot financed his own presidential bid and was not bound by the $55 million limit to which the Democratic and Republican candidates were held that year. Perot did accept public funding in 1996. In 2008, John McCain accepted public funding for the general election campaign, receiving $84 million, but Barack Obama declined, choosing to rely on his own fund-raising prowess. Obama was ultimately able to outspend McCain by a wide margin. As a result, many observers believe that the 2008 race will be the last time that a major-party candidate forgos fund-raising in favor of public funding.

Third-party candidates are eligible for public funding only if they received at least 5 percent of the vote in the previous presidential race. This stipulation effectively blocks preelection funding for third-party or independent candidates, although a third party that wins more than 5 percent of the vote can receive public funding after the election. In 1980, John Anderson convinced banks to lend him money for an independent candidacy on the strength of poll data showing that he would receive more than 5 percent of the vote and would thus obtain public funds with which to repay the loans.

Campaign Finance Reform

The United States is one of the few advanced industrial nations that permit individual candidates to accept large private contributions from individual or corporate donors. Most other countries either mandate public funding of campaigns or, as in the case of Great Britain, require that large private donations be made to political parties rather than to individual candidates. The logic of such a requirement is that a contribution that might seem very large to an individual candidate would weigh much less heavily if made to a national party. Thus the chance of a donor's buying influence would be reduced.

After the 1996 and 2000 national elections, efforts were made to enact reform measures, but these failed. In 2002, however, a scandal involving contributions made by Enron, the giant Texas energy company that was subsequently embroiled in a much bigger scandal and collapsed in bankruptcy, gave reformers the ammunition they needed to bring about a set of changes in election law in the form of the Bipartisan Campaign Reform Act (BCRA). One of the changes brought about by BCRA was a ban on campaign spending by the national party organizations, which had previously used hundreds of millions of dollars in soft-money contributions from corporations, unions, and individuals to influence electoral contests. The long-term effects of this reform remain to be seen. Perhaps banning soft money will reduce the influence of wealthy donors, but at the same time, eliminating soft money is likely to weaken the national parties—now among the few sources of coherence in America's fragmented political process. In the short term at least, the Democratic party seems to be suffering from the soft-money ban more than the Republican party is. The Democratic party had come to depend on a relatively small number of well-heeled contributors who wrote large checks to the national party. The Republicans, on the other hand, have developed a broader base of smaller contributors who are accustomed to sending money directly to individual candidates. These hard-money contributions are not affected by the new law.[50] In the 2004 election, 527 committees, though not able to spend directly on particular campaigns, took up some of this slack, with Democrats outspending Republicans via this route.

DO ELECTIONS MATTER?

What is the place of elections in the American political process? Unfortunately, recent political trends, such as the increasing importance of money, raise serious questions about the continuing ability of ordinary Americans to influence their government through electoral politics.

Why Is Voter Turnout So Low?

Despite the sound and the fury of contemporary American politics, one very important fact stands out: Participation in the American political process is abysmally low. For every registered voter who voted in the 2000 elections, for example, one stayed home. There was a slight increase in voter turnout in 2004, however.

Competition and Voter Turnout Throughout much of American history, the major parties have been the principal agents responsible for giving citizens the motivation and incentive to vote. One of the most interesting pieces of testimony to

---

[50]Adam Nagourney, "McCain Feingold School Finds Many Bewildered," *New York Times*, 19 February 2003, p. A23.

TABLE 10.1 Federal Campaign Finance Regulation

The Rules for Campaign Contributions

Who	may contribute . . .	to . . .	if . . .
Individuals	up to $2,300	a candidate	they are contributing to a single candidate in a single election.
Individuals	up to $28,500	a national party committee.	
Individuals	up to $5,000	a PAC.	
PACs	up to $5,000	a candidate	they contribute to the campaigns of at least five candidates.
Individuals and PACs	unlimited funds	a 527 committee	the funds are used for issue advocacy and the 527 committee's efforts are not coordinated with any political campaign.
Individuals and PACs	up to $10,000	a state party committee	the money is used for voter registration and get-out-the-vote efforts.

The Rules for Campaign Advertising

Who	may not finance . . .	if . . .
Unions, corporations, and nonprofit organizations	broadcast issue ads mentioning federal candidates	they occur within sixty days of a general election or thirty days of a primary.

the lengths to which parties have been willing to go to induce citizens to vote is a list of Chicago precinct captains' activities in the 1920s and 1930s. Among other matters, these party workers helped constituents obtain food, coal, and money for rent; gave them advice in dealing with juvenile and domestic problems; helped them obtain government and private jobs; adjusted taxes; helped with permits, zoning, and building-code problems; served as liaisons with social, relief, and medical agencies; provided legal assistance and help in dealing with government agen-

The Rules for Presidential Primaries and Elections

Candidates . . .	may receive . . .	if . . .
In primaries	federal matching funds, dollar for dollar, up to $5 million	they raise at least $5,000 in each of twenty states in contributions of $250 or less.
In general elections	full federal funding (but may spend no more than their federal funding)	they belong to a major party (minor-party candidates may receive partial funding).
In any election	money from independent groups (PACs and 527 committees)	the groups' efforts are not tied directly to the official campaign.

Important Definitions for Campaign Finance Regulation

- **Political action committee (PAC):** Private group that raises and distributes funds for use in election campaigns.

- **527 committee:** Tax-exempt organization that engages in political activities, often through unlimited "soft-money" contributions. The committee is not restricted by current law on campaign finance, thus exploiting a loophole in the Internal Revenue Service code.

- **501(c)4:** Not for profit group that may engage in unlimited political spending so long as amount spent does not exceed 50 percent of its budget. Unlike the 527s, 501(c)4s are not required to disclose contributor and recipient information.

- **Hard money:** Contributions by individuals and PACs to a particular political campaign. These contributions are subject to federal regulation.

- **Federal matching funds:** Federal funds that match, dollar for dollar, all individual contributions of $250 or less received by a candidate. To qualify, the candidate must raise at least $5,000 in individual contributions of $250 or less in each of twenty states.

- **Federal Election Commission:** The commission that oversees campaign finance practices in the United States.

cies; handed out Christmas baskets; and attended weddings and funerals.[51] Obviously, all these services were provided in the hope of winning voters' support at election time. And the efforts, in turn, became even more compelling as the competition between parties heated up. Hence party competition has long been

---

[51]Harold F. Gosnell, *Machine Politics, Chicago Model,* rev. ed. (Chicago: University of Chicago Press, 1968), chap. 4.

recognized as a key factor in stimulating voting. As the political scientists Stanley Kelley, Richard Ayres, and William Bowen note, competition not only gives citizens an incentive to vote but also gives politicians an incentive to get them to vote.[52]

The parties' competitive efforts to attract citizens to the polls are not their only influence on voting. Individual voters, as we have seen, tend to form psychological ties to parties. Although the strength of partisan ties in the United States has declined over the last fifty years (despite a recent upsurge), a majority of Americans continue to identify with either the Republican or the Democratic party. Party loyalty gives citizens a stake in election outcomes that encourages them to take part with considerably greater regularity than those who lack partisan ties.[53] Even when both legal facilitation and competitiveness are weak, party loyalists vote with great regularity.

In recent decades, as we shall see in Chapter 11, the importance of parties as a political force in the United States has diminished considerably. The decline of parties is undoubtedly one of the factors responsible for the relatively low rates of voter turnout that characterize American national elections. To an extent, federal and state governments and even, more recently, PACs, 527 committees, and individual candidates' organizations have directly assumed some of the burden of voter mobilization that was once assigned to the parties.

The 1993 motor voter bill was a step, though a hesitant one, in the direction of expanded voter participation. This act requires all states to allow voters to register by mail when they renew their driver's license (twenty-eight states had already instituted similar mail-in procedures). Motor voter did result in some increases in voter registration. Thus far, however, few of the newly registered individuals have gone to the polls to cast their ballots. After 1996, the percentage of newly registered voters who appeared at the polls actually dropped.[54] More interesting and more promising is the fact that many states have liberalized absentee balloting, thus reducing the cost of voting. Same-day registration—currently used in several states, including Minnesota—could boost turnout by several percentage points. Instituting weekend voting or, alternatively, making Election Day a federal holiday would make it easier for Americans to go to the polls.

Diminished turnout in the United States may be due in part to the way we structure elections. The median-voter theorem suggests that, with only one winner in a winner-takes-all system, candidates head for the center of the distribution of voters' ideal policies and toward one another, much as Bill Clinton succeeded in doing in 1992 and 1996 and George W. Bush did in 2000. This sometimes produces disillusionment, even disgust, in voters who find, in the immortal words of the late third-party candidate George Wallace, "there ain't a

---

[52]Stanley Kelley Jr., Richard E. Ayres, and William G. Bowen, "Registration and Voting: Putting First Things First," *American Political Science Review* 61, no. 2 (June 1967): 359–70; and William H. Riker and Peter C. Indeshook, "A Theory of the Calculus of Voting," *American Political Science Review* 62, no. 1 (March 1968): 25–42.

[53]See Angus Campbell, Philip E. Converse, Warren E. Miller, and Donald E. Stokes, *The American Voter* (New York: Wiley, 1960).

[54]Peter Baker, "Motor Voter Apparently Didn't Drive Up Turnout," *Washington Post*, 6 November 1996, p. B7.

dime's worth of difference" between the candidates. Many citizens conclude that there is not much point to going to the polls. Turnout, according to this view, is a consequence not only of candidates' failing to mobilize voters but also of their failure, on account of the inexorable pull of the median voter, to differentiate themselves and thus inspire voters.

Is It Rational to Vote? Compared with other democracies, voter turnout in national elections in the United States is extremely low (see Figure 10.1). It is usually around 50 percent for presidential elections and between 30 and 40 percent for midterm elections. In other Western democracies, turnout regularly exceeds 80 percent. In defense of American citizens, it should be pointed out that occasions for voting as a form of civic activity occur more frequently in the United States than in other democracies. More offices are filled by election in the United States than elsewhere—indeed, more offices per capita are filled by election, which is somewhat startling given how large a democracy the United States is; many of these posts are filled by appointment in other democracies. Especially unusual in this respect are elected judges in many jurisdictions and elected local "bureaucrats" (like the local sheriff and the proverbial town dogcatcher). In addition, there are primaries as well as general elections, and in many states there are initiatives and referendums to vote on, too. It is a wonder that American citizens don't suffer from some form of democratic fatigue! Though many scholars have tried to answer the question, "Why is turnout so low?" others have argued that the real question should be "Why is turnout so high?" That is, why does anyone turn out to vote at all?

Certainly the collective-action principle suggests as much: If the electorate is large and there is little likelihood that any individual participant will make a difference, then many citizens will not be inclined to vote if the costs of participation are not negligible. So if we think of voter turnout in terms of cost-benefit analysis, it isn't obvious why people vote.[55] There are many costs to voting. People must take time from their busy schedules, possibly incurring a loss of wages, to show up at the polls. In many states, voters have to overcome numerous hurdles just to register. If an individual wants to cast an informed vote, he or she must also spend time learning about the candidates and their positions.

Voters must bear these costs no matter what the outcome of the election, yet it is extremely unlikely that an individual's vote will affect the outcome, unless the vote makes or breaks a tie. Just making a close election one vote closer by voting for the loser or making the winner one vote more secure by voting for her doesn't matter much. As the saying goes, closeness counts only in horseshoes and dancing. It is almost certain that if an individual did not incur the costs of voting and stayed home instead, the election results would be the same. The probability of a single vote

Rationality Principle

Because the chance of affecting an election is low, it is not plainly irrational to stay home and not participate.

---

[55]W. Riker and Ordeshook, "A Theory of the Calculus of Voting." Riker and Ordeshook argue that someone caring about the *benefits* from securing the victory of his or her favorite candidate over the opponent, after all the *costs* of voting have been taken into account, will also want to weigh the likelihood that his or her vote is decisive. Because the probability of any voter tipping the balance is bound to be low—indeed, infinitesimal in a moderately large electorate—the benefits will have to be extraordinarily large relative to the costs to motivate participation. Hence Riker and Ordeshook wonder why turnout is "so high" and look to reasons other than the simple (some say "simplistic") cost-benefit analysis for the explanation.

being decisive in a presidential election is about 1 in 10 million.[56] Given the tiny probability that an individual's vote will determine whether the candidate he or she prefers is elected, it seems as if those who turn out to vote are behaving irrationally.[57]

One possible solution to this puzzle is that people are motivated by more than just their preferences for electing a particular candidate—they are, in fact, satisfying the desire to fulfill their duty as citizens, and this benefit exceeds the costs of voting.[58] Yet this hypothesis still does not provide an adequate answer to the question of the rationality of voting—it speaks only to the fact that people value the *act of voting* itself. That is, people have a "taste" for voting. But one cannot say, based on the rationality principle, where tastes come from,[59] and therefore one cannot say much about voter turnout.

John Aldrich offers another possible solution: He looks at the question from the politician's point of view.[60] Candidates calculate how much to invest in campaigns based on their probability of winning. In the unlikely event that an incumbent appears beatable, the challengers often invest heavily in their own campaigns because they believe the investment has a good chance of paying off. In response to these strong challenges, incumbents not only work harder to raise campaign funds but also spend more of what they raise.[61] Parties seeking to maximize the number of positions they control in the government may also shift resources to help out the candidates in these close races.

More vigorous campaigns will generally lead to increased turnout. The increase is not necessarily due to citizens' reacting to the closeness of the race (that is, the perception that their vote may affect the outcome) but to the greater effort and resources that candidates put into close races, which in turn reduce the costs of voting. Candidates share some of the costs of voting by helping citizens register and by getting them to the polls on Election Day. Heated advertising campaigns reduce the voters' costs of becoming informed (because candidates flood the public with information about themselves). This decrease in costs to individual voters in what strategic politicians perceive to be a close race at least partially explains why rational individuals would turn out to vote. Thus the major registration and mobilization efforts by politicians and 527 committees in 2004 and 2008 produced an increase in turnout. By the same token, lower effort in non-presidential-election years is associated with much lower turnout.

Rationality Principle

Given the tiny probability that an individual's vote will determine the winner of an election, candidates need to reduce the cost of voting for citizens in order to mobilize them.

---

[56] Andrew Gelman, Gary King, and John Boscardin, "Estimating the Probability of Events That Have Never Occurred: When Is Your Vote Decisive?" *Journal of the American Statistical Association* 93, no. 441 (March 1998): 1–9.

[57] A *strategic* cost-benefit analysis plays out the following reasonable argument: If everyone determines that his or her vote doesn't matter and no one votes, then *my* vote will determine the outcome! This kind of strategic conjecturing has been analyzed in Thomas Palfrey and Howard Rosenthal, "Voter Participation and Strategic Uncertainty," *American Political Science Review* 79, no. 1 (March 1985): 62–79. They conclude that once all the back-and-forth conjecturing is done, the question of why anyone participates remains.

[58] This was Riker and Ordeshook's line of argument. They claim, in effect, that there is an *experiential* as well as an *instrumental* rationale for voting. In more economic terms, this is the view that voting is a form of consumption as much as it is a type of investment. For a brief and user-friendly development of this logic, see Shepsle and Bonchek, *Analyzing Politics*, pp. 251–59.

[59] Brian Barry, *Sociologists, Economists, and Democracy* (London: Collier-Macmillan, 1970).

[60] John H. Aldrich, "Rational Choice and Turnout," *American Journal of Political Science* 37 no. 1 (February 1993): 246–78.

[61] Jacobson and Kernell, *Strategy and Choice in Congressional Elections*, 2nd ed.

Why Do Elections Matter as Political Institutions?

Voting choices and electoral outcomes can be extremely important in the United States. Yet observing the relationships among voters' choices, leadership selection, and policy decisions is only part of the significance of democratic elections. Important as they are, voters' choices and electoral results may still be less consequential for government and politics than the simple fact of voting itself. The fact of mass electoral participation can be more significant than what or how citizens decide once they participate. Thus electoral participation has important consequences in that it socializes and institutionalizes political action.

First, democratic elections socialize political activity. Voting is not a natural or spontaneous phenomenon. It is an institutionalized form of mass political involvement. That individuals vote rather than engage in some other form of political behavior is a result of national policies that create the opportunity to vote and discourage other political activities relative to voting. Elections transform what might otherwise consist of sporadic, citizen-initiated acts into a routine public function. This transformation expands and democratizes mass political involvement. At the same time, however, elections help preserve the government's stability by containing and diverting potentially more disruptive or dangerous forms of mass political activity. By establishing formal avenues for mass participation and accustoming citizens to their use, government reduces the threat that volatile, unorganized political involvement can pose to the established order.[62]

Second, elections bolster the government's power and authority. Elections help increase popular support for political leaders and for the regime itself. The formal opportunity to participate in elections serves to convince citizens that the government is responsive to their needs and wishes. Moreover, elections help persuade citizens to obey. Electoral participation increases popular acceptance of taxes and military service, on which the government depends. Elections—particularly democratic elections—substitute consent for coercion as the foundation of governmental power.

Finally, elections institutionalize mass influence in politics. Democratic elections permit citizens to select and depose public officials routinely, and elections can serve to promote popular influence over officials' conduct. This influence over the conduct of officials operates even if actual voter participation is not high. Thus despite the problems of inducing participation as described by the collective-action principle, the mere possibility of participation constrains the actions of elected politicians.

 Institution Principle

Elections matter because they socialize and institutionalize political action.

SUMMARY

Allowing citizens to vote represents a calculated risk on the part of power holders. On the one hand, popular participation can generate consent and support for the government. On the other hand, the right to vote may give ordinary citizens more influence in the governmental process than political elites would like.

---

[62] Acemoglu and Robinson, "Why Did the West Extend the Franchise?"

Rationality Principle	Collective-Action Principle	Institution Principle	Policy Principle	History Principle
Elections allow multiple principals—citizens—to choose political agents to act on their behalf. But citizens usually have imperfect information about candidates and don't know how they will act once in office.	Elections are a mechanism for channeling and limiting political participation to actions within the system.	The electoral process is governed by a variety of rules and procedures that provide those in power with an opportunity to regulate the character and consequences of political participation.	The median-voter theorem predicts policy moderation on the part of candidates.	Between 1890 and 1910, voter turnout declined in the United States as a result of new registration requirements. Since that time, turnout has remained low in comparison with the nineteenth century.
As registration costs rise, the number of citizens participating may be expected to decrease.		The rules that set the criteria for winning an election have an effect on the outcome.		
Issue voting motivates candidates to converge toward the preferences of the median voter.		The electoral college and the Australian ballot are two instances of changes in electoral rules that can affect the outcome of elections.		
At least until recent years, political parties have been the primary agents for giving citizens the motivation and incentive to vote.		Instituting new election laws, such as same-day voter registration, could increase turnout.		
Because the chance of affecting an election is low, it is not plainly irrational to stay home and not participate.		Elections matter because they socialize and institutionalize political action.		
Given the tiny probability that an individual's vote will determine the winner of an election, candidates need to reduce the cost of voting for citizens in order to mobilize them.				

Voting is only one of many possible types of political participation. The significance of voting is that it is an institutional and formal mode of political activity. Voting is organized and subsidized by the government. This makes it both more limited and more democratic than other forms of participation.

All governments regulate voting to influence its effects. The most important forms of regulation include the bases of the electorate's composition, the way in which voters' choices are translated into electoral outcomes, and the insulation of policy-making processes from electoral intervention.

Voters' choices themselves are based on partisanship, issues, and candidates' personalities. Which of these criteria will be most important varies over time and depends on the factors that opposing candidates choose to emphasize in their campaigns.

Campaign funds in the United States are provided by small, direct-mail contributions, large gifts, PACs, 527 committees, political parties, candidates' personal resources, and public funding. Campaign finance is regulated by the Federal Election Campaign Act of 1971. Since the passage of that act, there have been continuing efforts to dampen the influence of money on elections.

Regardless of what voters decide, elections are important institutions because they socialize political activity, increase government authority, and institutionalize popular influence in political life.

FOR FURTHER READING

Bartels, Larry M. "What's the Matter with *What's the Matter with Kansas?" Quarterly Journal of Political Science* 1 (2006): 201–26.   ○ ONLINE READING

Brady, David W. *Critical Elections and Congressional Policy Making*. Palo Alto, Calif.: Stanford University Press, 1988.

Carmines, Edward G., and James A. Stimson. *Issue Evolution: Race and the Transformation of American Politics*. Princeton, N.J.: Princeton University Press, 1989.

Conway, M. Margaret. *Political Participation in the United States*. 3rd ed. Washington, D.C.: Congressional Quarterly Press, 2000.

Fowler, Linda L. *Candidates, Congress, and the American Democracy*. Ann Arbor: University of Michigan Press, 1994.

Ginsberg, Benjamin, and Martin Shefter. *Politics by Other Means: Politicians, Prosecutors, and the Press from Watergate to Whitewater*. 3rd ed. New York: Norton, 2002.

Green, Donald, and Alan Gerber. *Get Out the Vote: How to Increase Voter Turnout*. Washington, D.C.: Brookings Institution, 2004.   ○ ONLINE READING

Lau, Richard, and David Redlawsk, *How Voters Decide*. New York: Cambridge University Press, 2006.

Morton, Rebecca B. *Analyzing Elections*. New York: Norton, 2006.

Piven, Frances Fox, and Richard A. Cloward. *Why Americans Don't Vote*. New York: Pantheon, 1988.

Reichley, A. James, ed. *Elections American Style*. Washington, D.C.: Brookings Institution, 1987.

Tate, Katherine. *From Protest to Politics: The New Black Voters in American Elections*. Cambridge, Mass.: Harvard University Press, 1994.

Witt, Linda, Karen M. Paget, and Glenna Matthews. *Running as a Woman: Gender and Power in American Politics*. New York: Free Press, 1994.

Conventional wisdom holds that voters reward incumbents when the economy is strong and penalize them when the economy is lagging. The principles of politics help us understand why voters behave this way. Most voters prefer a strong economy, so the rational choice is to reelect an incumbent from the party that has overseen one. Political parties, interest groups, and candidate organizations will often focus on the economy as a way to motivate collective action (voting) on the part of citizens. Not surprisingly, then, the political outcome in the face of a strong economy is often a victory for incumbents from the governing party.

So what happened in 2006, when the economy was robust, but voters paid little attention? First, even though the median voter position on the economy benefited Republicans, voter discontent over the war in Iraq overwhelmed positive views of the economy. Thus, following the rationality principle, most Democratic candidates focused on the median voter on this issue, to the exclusion of all others—and many Republicans followed suit.

Second, the principles of politics are not simply about policy positions, they are also about policy beliefs. It is irrational to reward a party for their policies if you do not believe that they can continue those policies in the future. As the story below shows, while Republicans should have been rewarded for strong economic growth, voters remained pessimistic about the future. It may not seem reasonable for voters to feel pessimistic about the economy based on the war, but if they do feel this way, it is not irrational for them to vote accordingly. And so they did, throwing out the Republican majority in both the House and the Senate in 2006.

The New York Times, October 24, 2006

This Time, It's Not the Economy

By Eduardo Porter

In many ways, the economy has not looked so good in a long time.

The price of gas at the pump has tumbled since midsummer. Unemployment has fallen to its lowest level in more than five years. On Wall Street, the Dow Jones industrial average has finally returned to its glory days of the late 1990's, setting records almost daily.

President Bush, in hopes of winning credit for his party's stewardship of the economy, is spending two days this week campaigning on the theme that the economy is purring. "No question that a strong economy is going to help our candidates," Mr. Bush said in a CNBC interview yesterday, "primarily because they have got something to run on, they can say our economy's good because I voted for tax relief."

But Republican candidates do not seem to be getting any traction from the glowing economic statistics with midterm elections just two weeks away.

The economy is virtually nowhere to be found among the campaign ads of embattled Republican incumbents fighting to hold onto their House or Senate seats. Nor is it showing up as a strong weapon in the arsenal of Republican governors defending their jobs from Democrats.

"I don't know of another election cycle in which the economy was so good, yet the election prospects for the incumbent party looked so bad," said Frank Luntz, a Republican strategist. "If something goes wrong, Republicans are to blame. If something goes right, Republicans don't get credit."

The only place that the economy has emerged as a major campaign theme has been in the aging industrial heartland around the Great Lakes, where the bleak economic prospects are being deployed against incumbents, Republicans and Democrats alike. But where the economic winds seem to be blowing their way, voters appear unwilling to hear that Republican policies made it so.

Disenchantment over the war in Iraq has morphed into disillusionment over the direction of the country, breeding distrust in the administration's policies, surveys suggest. Moreover, concerned by weak wage growth, costly health care and eroding benefits, many middle-class voters do not see the economy improving for them.

"Voters overwhelmingly don't approve of the president on the economy," said Amy Walter, a senior editor at the Cook Political Report, a nonpartisan firm that handicaps political races. "It comes down to the issue of credibility. And so many voters feel so pessimistic about the direction of the country."

Richard Curtin, who runs the University of Michigan's consumer surveys, has found that even as consumer confidence has improved since gasoline prices took a tumble in August, the White House has gotten no credit for the gain.

"The one indicator that didn't improve," Mr. Curtin said, "was confidence in the government's economic policies."

For many voters, the overall issue has faded in importance as the economy has managed to grow steadily in recent years. In late 2003, The New York Times/CBS News poll found, 4 in 10 voters said either the economy or jobs was the most pressing problem facing the nation. This month, only 13 percent shared that concern.

But Republicans' inability to harness an improving economy in their political favor appears mostly to be a function of the weight of other big national issues stacked against them. Prime among them are voters' growing concerns about the costs of the war in Iraq, fed by a stream of American casualties displayed every night on television.

The seeming morass in Iraq has hurt Republicans in more ways than one, analysts say, contributing to the notion that the country is heading in the wrong direction and fueling distrust in the administration of President Bush that has leaked out to other fronts—including his management of the economy.

* * *

It has been some time since the public last trusted Republicans more than Democrats on economic issues.

Of voters polled in the latest New York Times/CBS News national survey this month, 60 percent rated the economy as either good or very good, up from 56 percent in September.

But voters favor Democrats over Republicans as stewards of the economy by 51 to 36 percent. The 15-point margin, which remained the same as in September, is the widest since the survey first included the question in 1984.

Republicans have a tough act to follow. President Bush pointed out yesterday that employers have added 6.6 million jobs since August 2003, finally gaining ground after a long decline in employment over most of his first term. But the figure falls well short of the nine million jobs created during the same period of the Clinton administration.

Still, the National Republican Congressional Committee believes that the improving economy provides a good issue for many Republicans to run on, and has spent money on TV commercials praising the administration's economic track record in several Midwest districts and upstate New York.

A few candidates have taken this tack, but most have done so sparingly. Some Republican challengers are using the economy as a campaign issue in places where it is doing poorly.

Perhaps the biggest challenge Republicans face to take credit for an improving economy is that for many voters, their economic prospects do not feel as great as overall statistics might imply. Rather than celebrate the stock market's gains and the overall growth of the economy, many voters are worried about the wages of ordinary workers, which have just started to improve after several years of falling short or barely keeping up with inflation.

The tens of millions of people lacking health insurance and the steady shrinkage in traditional pensions have also added to the sense of personal insecurity.

Consider Florida's 22nd Congressional District, stretching along the Atlantic coast in Broward and Palm Beach Counties, north of Miami. Employment in the district has grown at three times the national average over the last three years, according to an analysis by Moody's Economy.com. Unemployment there is well under the national level.

But the Republican incumbent, E. Clay Shaw Jr., running neck and neck with Ron Klein, a Democrat, has steered away from celebrating the area's sunny economic prospects. Instead, he has pointed to his record on the environment, talked about how he disagreed with President Bush's attempt to privatize Social Security, and accused Mr. Klein of being in the pocket of sugar companies.

And concerns over how fair the prosperous economy has been to most Americans appear to be hurting Republican prospects even among those who see themselves as doing relatively well.

Republican leaders might still try to use an improving economy for a final campaign push. Mr. Luntz, the Republican strategist, said economic issues should help the party in Florida, Georgia and the Carolinas.

Mr. Collegio of the National Republican Campaign Committee said the campaign group planned a flurry of advertisements warning that, as they see it, Democrats will hurt the economy by raising taxes.

Still, even that tried-and-true Republican theme may not work so well this year.

"In these races you just pray for a Republican claiming that tax cuts are the reason for the good economy," said Stanley Greenberg, a Democratic pollster. "Candidates don't do it because the public doesn't believe it. And a candidate who claimed it would seem out of touch."

History
Principle

The Republicans have a reputation historically as careful stewards of the economy. However, a burgeoning deficit during unified Republican control may erode the GOP's traditional advantage in this area.

Political Parties

11

WE OFTEN REFER TO THE UNITED STATES as a nation with a two-party system. By this we mean that in the United States the Democratic and Republican parties compete for office and power. Most Americans believe that party competition contributes to the health of the democratic process. Certainly, we are more than just a bit suspicious of those nations that claim to be ruled by their people but do not tolerate the existence of opposing parties.

The idea of party competition was not always accepted in the United States. In the early years of the Republic, parties were seen as a threat to the social order. In his 1797 Farewell Address, President George Washington admonished his countrymen to shun partisan politics:

> Let me . . . warn you in the most solemn manner against the baneful effects of the spirit of party, generally. This spirit . . . exists under different shapes in all governments, more or less stifled, controlled, or repressed; but in those of the popular form it is seen in its greatest rankness and is truly their worst enemy.

Often those in power viewed the formation of political parties by their opponents as acts of treason that merited severe punishment. Thus in 1798 the Federalist party, which controlled the national government, in effect sought to outlaw its Democratic-Republican opponents through the infamous Alien and Sedition Acts, which among other things made it a crime to publish or say anything that might tend to defame or bring into disrepute either the president or Congress. Under this law, twenty-five individuals—including several Republican newspaper editors—were arrested and convicted.[1]

---

[1]See Richard Hofstadter, *The Idea of a Party System: The Rise of Legitimate Opposition in the United States, 1780–1840* (Berkeley: University of California Press, 1969).

These efforts to outlaw political parties obviously failed. By the mid-nineteenth century, American politics was dominated by powerful party organizations that inspired enormous voter loyalty, controlled electoral politics, and through elections exercised immense influence over government and policy in the United States. In recent years, these party organizations have had competition from the candidates themselves. Electoral politics has become a candidate-centered affair in which individual candidates for office build their own campaign organizations while voters make choices based on both their reactions to the candidates and their loyalty to the parties. Party organization, as we saw in Chapter 5, continues to be an important factor in Congress. In general, the party system in American politics, in its role in organizing both elections and government, has fluctuated in importance.[2]

In this chapter, we examine the realities underlying the changing conceptions of political parties.

---

[2] For an excellent discussion of the fluctuating role of political parties in the United States and the influence of government on that role, see John J. Coleman, *Party Decline in America: Policy, Politics, and the Fiscal State* (Princeton, N.J.: Princeton University Press, 1996).

Political parties act as solutions to collective-action problems in terms of electoral choice and collective choice in the policy-making process and to problems related to the ambitions of politicians. In elections, parties facilitate collective action by helping candidates attract campaign funds, assemble campaign workers, and mobilize voters. Parties also facilitate a voter's choice by providing cues or brand names to simplify the complex choices voters are given. In terms of policy making, parties work as permanent coalitions of individuals with shared goals and interests and thus facilitate cooperation in Congress. Finally, parties help regulate ambition by resolving competition among party members. Parties represent evolving coalitions of different groups in society, and over time the nature of those coalitions and thus the nature of party politics have changed. That is, the collective-action problems that parties seek to overcome are historically determined.

As long as political parties have existed, they have been criticized for introducing selfish, "partisan" concerns into public debate and national policy. Yet political parties are extremely important to the proper functioning of a democracy. As we shall see, parties expand popular political participation, promote more effective choice in elections, and smooth the flow of public business in the Congress. Our problem in America today is not that political life is too partisan but that our parties are not strong enough to function effectively. This is one reason why America has such low levels of popular political involvement. Nevertheless, parties continue to play an important if uneven role in the American political process. For one thing, tens of millions of Americans identify strongly with one or the other major party.[3] Many Republican partisans would not dream of voting for a Democrat, and many Democratic partisans viewed the 2004 reelection of George W. Bush as a national tragedy. The 2006 midterm elections, however, in which the Democrats captured both houses of Congress, revealed a preference of many voters to strip the Republicans of unified control of the government. Many Democratic identifiers rallied to the support of their party's legislative candidates while some Republican voters deserted theirs. In 2008, partisanship strongly reasserted itself with nearly 90 percent of Democrats and Republicans supporting their own parties' candidates.

In recent years, a growing ideological gulf between the two parties has translated into rancorous debate on many policy issues in Congress and in the state legislatures. And yet contemporary American political parties lack the discipline and organizational coherence of their nineteenth-century forebears. Once, parties dominated the electoral process, but today's party leaders control neither candidates' nominations nor campaigns for political office. For the most part, modern-day candidates are self-selected and manage and finance their own campaigns. At one time,

ONLINE READING

[3]For an analysis of partisanship in the second half of the twentieth century, see Larry M. Bartels, "Partisanship and Voting Behavior, 1952–1996," *American Journal of Political Science* 44 (2000): 35–50.

powerful party barons ruled Capitol Hill, dispensing rewards and punishments and imposing discipline on the legislative process. Today congressional party leaders depend on the cooperation of their legislative troops. Reforms enacted in 2002, such as the elimination of soft money, will likely further erode party strength in America.

What should become clear in this chapter is that the role of parties in the electoral arena and the halls of government is constantly changing, flowing in some eras but ebbing in others, stronger in some arenas but weaker in others. In our examination of political parties in America, we look first at party formation and organization and at the place of parties in the American political process. Second, we discuss the role of parties in election campaigns and the policy process. Third, we consider why America has a two-party system, we trace the history of the major parties, and we look at some of the third parties that have come and gone over the past two centuries. Finally, we address the significance and changing role of parties in American politics today and answer the question, "Is the party over?"

WHY DO POLITICAL PARTIES FORM?

Political parties, like interest groups, are organizations seeking influence over government. Ordinarily, they can be distinguished from interest groups on the basis of their orientation. A party seeks to control the entire government by electing its members to office, thereby controlling the government's personnel. Interest groups, through campaign contributions and other forms of electoral assistance, are also concerned with electing politicians—in particular, those who are inclined in their policy direction. But interest groups ordinarily do not sponsor candidates directly, and between elections they usually accept government and its personnel as givens and try to influence government policies through them. They are *benefit seekers,* whereas parties are composed mainly of *office seekers.*[4]

Political parties organize because of three problems with which politicians and other political activists must cope. The first is the problem of collective action. This is chiefly an outgrowth of elections in which a candidate for office must attract campaign funds, assemble a group of activists and workers, mobilize prospective voters, and persuade them to vote for him or her. Collective action is also a problem *inside* government, where kindred spirits in a legislature must arrange for, and then engage in, cooperation. The second problem for which parties are sometimes the solution is that of collective choice of policy.[5] The give-and-take within a legislature and

---

[4]This distinction is from John H. Aldrich, *Why Parties? The Origin and Transformation of Party Politics in America* (Chicago: University of Chicago Press, 1995).

[5]A slight variation on this theme is emphasized by Gary W. Cox and Mathew D. McCubbins in *Legislative Leviathan: Party Government in the House* (Berkeley: University of California Press, 1993). They suggest that parties in the legislature are electoral machines whose purpose is to preserve and enhance party reputation, thereby giving meaning to the party labels when elections are contested. By keeping order within their ranks, parties make certain that individual actions by members do not discredit the party label. This is an especially challenging task for party leaders when there is diversity within each party, as has often been the case in American political history.

ONLINE READING

between the legislature and the executive can make or break policy success and subsequent electoral success. The third problem follows from the fact that fellow politicians, like members of any organization, seek success simultaneously for the organization and for themselves. This problem of ambition can undermine the collective aspirations of fellow partisans unless astutely managed. We briefly examine each of these problems below.

To Facilitate Collective Action in the Electoral Process

Collective-Action Principle

Parties facilitate collective action in the electoral process by helping candidates attract campaign funds, assembling campaign workers, and mobilizing voters.

Political parties as they are known today developed along with the expansion of suffrage and can be understood only in the context of elections. The two are so intertwined that American parties actually take their structure from the electoral process. The shape of party organization in the United States has followed a simple rule: For every district where an election is held, there should be some kind of party unit. These units provide the brand name, the resources—both human and financial—the "buzz," and the link to the larger national organization, which all help the party's candidates arouse interest in their candidacy, stimulate commitment, and ultimately overcome the free riding that diminishes turnout in general elections.

Party organization is also generally an essential ingredient for effective electoral competition by groups lacking substantial economic or institutional resources. Party building has typically been the strategy pursued by groups that must organize the collective energies of large numbers of individuals to counter their opponents' superior material means or institutional standing. Historically, disciplined and coherent party organizations were generally developed first by groups representing the political aspirations of the working classes. Parties, the French political scientist Maurice Duverger notes, "are always more developed on the Left than on the Right because they are always more necessary on the Left than on the Right."[6] Compared with political parties in Europe, parties in the United States have always seemed weak. They have no criteria for party membership—no cards for their members to carry, no dues to pay, no obligatory participation in any activity, no notion of exclusiveness. Throughout much of the twentieth century, they were relatively weak, unable to control nominations, campaigns, or the legislative process. In the 1990s and in the first decade of the twenty-first century, we have observed an uptick in strength, both in Congress and in the electoral process.

To Resolve Collective Choice in the Policy-Making Process

Policy Principle

Parties help resolve collective choice in the policy-making process by acting as permanent coalitions of individuals with similar policy goals.

Political parties are also essential elements in the process of making policy. Within the government, parties are coalitions of individuals with shared or overlapping interests who, as a rule, will support one another's programs and initiatives. Even though there may be areas of disagreement within each party, a common party label in and of itself gives party members a reason to cooperate. Because they are permanent coalitions, parties greatly facilitate the policy-making process. If alliances had

---

[6]See Maurice Duverger, *Political Parties: Their Organization and Activity in the Modern State*, trans. Barbara North and Robert North (New York: Wiley, 1954), p. 426.

to be formed from scratch for each legislative proposal, the business of government would slow to a crawl or halt altogether. Parties create a basis for coalition and thus sharply reduce the time, energy, and effort needed to advance a legislative proposal. For example, in January 1998, when President Bill Clinton considered a series of new policy initiatives, he met first with the House and Senate leaders of the Democratic party. Although some congressional Democrats disagreed with the president's approach to a number of issues, all felt they had a stake in cooperating with Clinton in order to burnish the party's image in preparation for the next round of national elections. Without the support of a party, the president would be compelled to undertake the daunting and probably impossible task of forming a completely new coalition for every policy proposal—a virtually impossible task.

To Deal with the Problem of Ambition

Parties are important vehicles that enable individual politicians to achieve their ambitions. The very "brand names" they provide are often a significant electoral asset. Moreover, once their candidates are elected, parties provide these politicians, who share principles, causes, and constituencies, with a basis for coordination, common cause, cooperation, and joint enterprise. But individual ambition, sometimes in the background but often in the foreground, constantly threatens to undermine any bases for cooperation. Political parties, by regulating career advancement, providing for the orderly resolution of ambitious competition, and attending to the post-career care of elected and appointed party officials, do much to rescue coordination and cooperation and permit fellow partisans to pursue common causes where feasible. Simple devices like primaries, for example, provide a context in which clashing electoral ambitions may be resolved. Representative partisan bodies, like the Democratic Committee on Committees in the House (with comparable bodies for the Republicans and for both parties in the Senate), resolve competing claims for power positions. In short, politics consists not of foot soldiers walking in lockstep but, rather, of ambitious and autonomous individuals seeking power. The unchecked and unregulated burnishing of individual careers is a formula for chaos and destructive competition in which the dividends of cooperation are rarely reaped. Political parties constitute organizations of relatively kindred spirits who try to capture some of those dividends by providing a structure in which ambition is not suppressed altogether but is not so destructive either.

 Rationality Principle

By regulating career advancement and resolving competition, parties help deal with the threat to cooperation posed by ambitious individuals.

WHAT FUNCTIONS DO PARTIES PERFORM?

Parties are mainly involved in nominations and elections—providing the candidates for office, getting out the vote, and facilitating mass electoral choice. That is, they help solve the problems of collective action and ambition to which we alluded earlier. They also influence the institutions of government—providing leadership as well as organization of the various congressional committees and activities on the floor in each chamber. That is, they help solve the problem of collective choice concerning institutional arrangements and policy formulation that we also noted earlier.

Recruiting Candidates

One of the most important but least noticed party activities is the recruitment of candidates for local, state, and national office. Each election year, candidates must be found for thousands of state and local offices as well as for congressional seats. Where an incumbent is not running for reelection, party leaders attempt to identify strong candidates and interest them in entering the campaign. One reason for the great success of the Democrats in the 2006 midterm elections was the heightened role played by their campaign committees in the House and Senate and, especially, the active recruitment of new candidates by Rahm Emanuel (D-Ill.) and Charles Schumer (D-N.Y.), chairs respectively of the Democratic Congressional Campaign Committee and the Democratic Senatorial Campaign Committee.[7] In 2008, the Democrats not only worked to recruit strong candidates but also made sure to provide them with solid financial support, taking advantage of the Democratic party's massive financial advantage in that year.

An ideal candidate will have an unblemished record and the capacity to raise enough money to mount a serious campaign. Party leaders are usually not willing to provide financial backing to candidates who are unable to raise substantial funds on their own. For a House seat, this can mean several hundred thousand dollars; for a Senate seat, a serious candidate must be able to raise several million dollars. Often party leaders have difficulty finding attractive candidates and persuading them to run. In recent years, party leaders in several states have reported that many potential congressional candidates declined the opportunity to run for office, saying they were reluctant to leave their homes and families for the hectic life of a member of Congress. Candidate recruitment has become particularly difficult in an era when political campaigns often involve mudslinging and candidates must assume that their personal lives will be intensely scrutinized in the press.[8]

Nominating Candidates

Article I, Section 4, of the Constitution makes only a few provisions for elections. It delegates to the states the power to set the "Times, Places and Manner of holding Elections," even those for U.S. senators and representatives. It does, however, reserve to Congress the power to make such laws if it chooses to do so. The Constitution has been amended from time to time to expand the right to participate in elections. Congress has also occasionally passed laws about elections, congressional districting, and campaign practices. But the Constitution and the laws are almost completely silent on nominations, setting only citizenship and age requirements for candidates. The president must be at least thirty-five years of age, a natural-born citizen, and a resident of the United States for fourteen years. A senator must be at least thirty, a U.S. citizen for at least nine years, and a resident of the state he or she represents. A member of the House must be at least twenty-five, a U.S. citizen for seven years, and a resident of the state he or she represents.

---

[7]See Adam Nagourney, "Eyeing '08: Democrats Nurse Freshmen at Risk," *New York Times*, 22 December 2006.

[8]For an excellent analysis of the parties' role in recruitment, see Paul S. Herrnson, *Congressional Elections: Campaigning at Home and in Washington* (Washington, D.C.: Congressional Quarterly Press, 1995).

FIGURE 11.1 Types of Nominating Processes

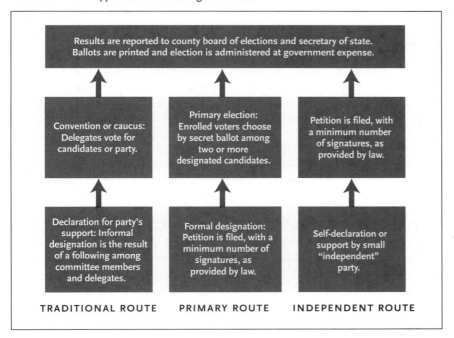

Nomination is the process by which a party selects a single candidate to run for each elective office. Nomination is the parties' most serious and difficult business. The nominating process can precede the election by many months (Figure 11.1), as it does when the many candidates for the presidency are eliminated from consideration through a grueling series of debates and state primaries until there is only one survivor in each party—the party's nominee.

Nomination by Convention A nominating convention is a formal caucus bound by a number of rules that govern participation and nominating procedures. Conventions are meetings of delegates elected by party members from the relevant county (a county convention) or state (a state convention). Delegates to each party's national convention (which nominates the party's presidential candidate) are chosen by party members on a state-by-state basis; there is no single national delegate selection process.

Nomination by Primary Election In primary elections, party members select the party's nominees directly rather than selecting convention delegates who then select the nominees. Primaries are far from perfect replacements for conventions because it is rare that more than 25 percent of the enrolled voters participate. Nevertheless, they are replacing conventions as the dominant method of nomination.[9] At the present

nomination The process by which political parties select their candidates for election to public office.

---

[9]For a discussion of some of the effects of primary elections, see Peter F. Galderisi and Benjamin Ginsberg, "Primary Elections and the Evanescence of Third Party Activity in the United States," in *Do Elections Matter?* ed. Benjamin Ginsberg and Alan Stone (Armonk, N.Y.: Sharpe, 1986), pp. 115–30.

time, only a small number of states, including Connecticut, Delaware, and Utah, provide for state conventions to nominate candidates for statewide offices, and even those states also use primaries whenever a substantial minority of delegates has voted for one of the defeated aspirants.

Generally speaking, candidates chosen in primary elections tend to be more aggressive and more ambitious individuals, whereas those selected by party conventions are more likely to have mastered the arts of compromise and collegiality. The shift from party conventions to primary elections for the nomination of presidential candidates is one reason contemporary presidents tend to be more ambitious and, indeed, more driven than their nineteenth-century predecessors. Party conventions tend to choose candidates who can get along, whereas primary elections tend to favor politicians with the energy and enterprise to mount a public campaign.[10] Thus there is a "selection" effect that results from the particular institutional arrangement a state employs. Institutions matter in this case because they encourage or discourage particular types of candidates, as the institution principle suggests.

Primary elections fall mainly into two categories—closed and open. In a **closed primary**, participation is limited to individuals who have previously declared their affiliation by registering with the party. In an **open primary**, individuals declare their party affiliation on the day of the primary election. To do so, they simply go to the polling place and ask for the ballot of a particular party. The open primary allows each voter to consider candidates and issues before deciding whether to participate and in which party's contest to participate. Open primaries, therefore, are less conducive to strong political parties. But in either case, primaries are more open than conventions or caucuses to new issues and new types of candidates.

Getting Out the Vote

The election period begins immediately after the nominations. Historically, this has been a time of glory for the political parties, whose popular base of support is fully displayed. All the paraphernalia of party committees and all the committee members are activated in the form of local party workforces.

The first step in the electoral process involves voter registration. This aspect of the process takes place all year round. There was a time when party workers were responsible for virtually all of this kind of electoral activity, but they have been supplemented (and in many states virtually displaced) by civic groups such as the League of Women Voters, unions, and chambers of commerce.

Those who have registered have to decide on Election Day whether to go to the polling place, stand in line, and vote for the various candidates and referendums on the ballot. Political parties, candidates, and campaigning can make a big difference in persuading eligible voters to vote. Because it is costly for voters to participate in elections and because many of the benefits that winning parties bestow are public goods (that is, parties cannot exclude any individual from enjoying them), people will often free ride by enjoying the benefits without incurring the costs of electing

Institution Principle

Primary elections tend to favor aggressive and ambitious politicians, whereas conventions tend to favor those who have mastered the arts of compromise and collegiality.

closed primary A primary election in which voters can participate in the nomination of only those candidates of the party in which they have been enrolled for a period of time before primary day.

open primary A primary election in which voters can choose on the day of the primary which party to enroll in to select candidates for the general election.

---

[10]Matthew Crenson and Benjamin Ginsberg, *Presidential Power: Unchecked and Unbalanced* (New York: Norton, 2007).

the party that provided the benefits. This is the free-rider problem (see Chapter 1), and parties are important because they help overcome it by mobilizing the voters to support the candidates.

In recent years, not-for-profit groups like America Votes have made an effort to register and mobilize voters. To comply with election law, these groups are nominally independent of the political parties. In reality, though, such not-for-profits are shadow appendages of the two parties, with liberal groups working to mobilize Democratic voters and conservative groups laboring to mobilize Republicans. In 2008, the Democrats, with the support of liberal groups like ACORN, registered several million new voters—many members of minority groups and young people—who helped Democratic candidates sweep to power.

On any general election ballot, there are likely to be only two or three candidacies for which the nature of the office and the characteristics and positions of the candidates are well-known to voters. But what about the choices for judges, the state comptroller, the state attorney general, and many other elective positions? Without partisan cues, voters are likely to find it extremely difficult to make informed choices about these candidates. And what about referendums? This method of making policy choices is being used more and more as a means of direct democracy. A referendum may ask, "Should there be a new bond issue for financing the local schools?" "Should there be a constitutional amendment to increase the number of county judges?" The typical referendum question is one on which few voters have a clear and knowledgeable position. Parties and campaigns help most by giving information when voters must choose among obscure candidates and vote on unclear referendums.

Facilitating Mass Electoral Choice

Parties facilitate mass electoral choice. It is often argued that we should vote for the "best person" regardless of his or her party affiliation. But as the late Harvard political scientist V. O. Key pointed out, in the absence of party labels, voters would be constantly confronted by a bewildering array of "new faces, new choices" and might have considerable difficulty making informed decisions. Without a doubt, their own party identifications and candidates' party affiliations help voters make reasonable choices.

Parties lower the information costs of participating by providing a kind of "brand-name" recognizability—that is, voters know with a substantial degree of accuracy what positions a candidate will take just by identifying the candidate's party affiliation. In addition, parties give elections a kind of sporting-event atmosphere, with voters treating parties like teams that they can support and cheer on to victory. This enhances the entertainment value of participating in elections. Parties also direct the flow of government benefits, such as patronage jobs, to those who put the party in power. These and other activities encourage individuals to identify with and support one of the two parties.[11]

Although political parties continue to be significant in the United States, the role of party organizations in electoral politics has clearly declined over the past three decades. This decline, and the partial replacement of the party by new forms of

Collective-Action Principle

Parties can help mobilize voters who are potential free riders.

Rationality Principle

Parties can lower the cost of voting by facilitating a voter's choice.

---

[11]On the concept of party as brand name, see Cox and McCubbins, *Legislative Leviathan*.

electoral technology (discussed later in this chapter), is one of the most important developments in twentieth- and twenty-first-century American politics.

Influencing National Government

The ultimate test of the party system is its relationship to and influence on the institutions of government and the policy-making process. Thus it is important to examine the party system in relation to Congress and the president.

Parties and Policy   One of the most familiar observations about American politics is that the two major parties try to be all things to all people and are therefore indistinguishable from each other. Data and experience give some support to this observation. Parties in the United States are not programmatic or ideological, as they have sometimes been in Britain or other parts of Europe. But this does not mean that there are no differences between them. During the era of Ronald Reagan, important differences emerged between the positions of Democratic and Republican party leaders on a number of key issues, and these differences are still apparent. For example, the national leadership of the Republican party supports high levels of military spending, cuts in social programs, tax relief for middle- and upper-income voters, tax incentives to businesses, and the "social agenda" backed by members of conservative religious denominations. The national Democratic leadership, on the other hand, supports expanded social welfare spending, cuts in military spending, increased regulation of business, and a variety of consumer and environmental programs. Even with these notable differences, it is still appropriate to describe American parties as nonprogrammatic and nonideological because as "big tents," each party covers a wide range of policy orientations among its politicians.

Yet the two parties' basic positions reflect differences in philosophy and, therefore, in the core constituencies to which the parties seek to appeal. The Democratic party at the national level seeks to unite organized labor, the poor, members of racial minorities, and liberal upper-middle-class professionals. The Republicans, by contrast, appeal to business, upper-middle- and upper-class groups in the private sector, and social conservatives. Often party leaders will seek to develop issues that they hope will add new groups to their party's constituent base. During the 1980s, for example, under the leadership of President Reagan, the Republicans devised a series of "social issues," including support for school prayer, opposition to abortion, and opposition to affirmative action, designed to cultivate the support of white southerners. This effort was extremely successful in increasing Republican strength in the once solidly Democratic South. In the 1990s, under the leadership of President Clinton, who called himself a "new Democrat," the Democratic party sought to develop social programs designed to solidify the party's base among working-class and poor voters and somewhat conservative economic programs aimed at attracting the votes of middle- and upper-middle-class voters.

As these examples suggest, parties do not always support policies because they are favored by their constituents. Instead, party leaders can play the role of policy entrepreneurs, seeking ideas and programs that will expand their party's base of support while eroding that of the opposition. In recent years, for example, leaders of both major political parties have sought to develop ideas and programs they hoped would appeal to America's most rapidly growing electoral bloc: Latino voters. Thus

Policy Principle

Policies typically reflect the goals of the party in power.

President George W. Bush recommended a number of proposals designed to help Latinos secure U.S. residence and employment. Democrats, for their part, have proposed education and social service programs designed to appeal to the needs of Latino immigrants. While in 2004 each party claimed to be satisfied with its long-term strategy for building Latino support, the 2006 election campaign produced much more one-sided results. A hard-line view on immigration, especially from Latin America, put Republicans at a competitive disadvantage, and several prominent Republican incumbents in the Southwest lost their seats. By 2008, several years of Democratic efforts produced even more significant results as Barack Obama won the support of a large majority of Latino voters.

It is one of the essential characteristics of party politics in America that a party's programs and policies often lead, rather than follow, public opinion. Like their counterparts in the business world, party leaders seek to identify and develop "products" (programs and policies) that will appeal to the public. The public, of course, has the ultimate voice. With its votes, it decides whether or not to "buy" the new policy offerings.

Through members elected to office, both parties have made efforts to translate their general goals into concrete policies. Republicans, for example, implemented tax cuts, increased defense spending, cut social spending, and enacted restrictions on abortion during the 1980s and 1990s. Democrats were able to defend consumer and environmental programs against GOP attacks and sought to expand domestic social programs in the late 1990s. During his two terms in office, President George W. Bush sought substantial cuts in federal taxes, "privatization" of the Social Security system, and a larger role for Republican-allied faith-based organizations in the administration of federal social programs. In the context of the nation's campaign against terrorism, Bush sought to shift America's defense posture from an emphasis on deterrence to a doctrine of preemptive strikes against perceived threats.

The Parties and Congress   Congress, in particular, depends more on the party system than is generally recognized. First, the speakership of the House is essentially a party office. All the members of the House take part in the election of the Speaker, but the actual selection is made by the ***majority party.*** When the majority party caucus presents a nominee to the entire House, its choice is then invariably ratified in a straight party-line vote.

The committee system of both houses of Congress is also a product of the two-party system. Although the rules organizing committees and the rules defining the jurisdiction of each committee are adopted like ordinary legislation by the whole membership, all other features of the committees are shaped by the parties. For example, each party is assigned a quota of members for each committee, depending on the percentage of total seats held by the party. On the rare occasions when an independent or third-party candidate is elected, the leaders of the two parties must agree against whose quota this member's committee assignments will count. Presumably, the member will not be able to serve on any committee until the question of quota is settled.[12]

Collective-Action Principle

Cooperation in Congress is facilitated by the party system.

majority party The party that holds the majority of legislative seats in either the House or the Senate.

---

[12]Scott A. Frisch and Sean Q. Kelly, *Committee Assignment Politics in the U.S. House of Representatives* (Norman: University of Oklahoma Press, 2006).

As we saw in Chapter 5, the assignment of individual members to committees is a party decision. Each party has a "committee on committees" to make such decisions. Whether to grant permission to transfer to another committee is also a party decision. Moreover, who will advance up the committee ladder toward the chair is a party decision. Since the late nineteenth century, most advancements have been automatic, based on the length of continuous service on the committee. This seniority system has existed only because of the support of the two parties, and each party can depart from it by a simple vote. During the 1970s, both parties reinstituted the practice of reviewing each chairmanship, voting anew every two years on whether each chair would be continued. In 2001, Republicans lived up to their 1995 pledge to limit House committee chairs to three terms. Existing chairs were forced to step down but were generally replaced by the next most senior Republican member of each committee. (Even after they were reduced to minority status after the 2006 elections, Republicans stuck to this policy. Republican chairs in the 109th Congress who had served three terms were not permitted to serve as ranking minority member in the 110th Congress.)

President and Party   As we saw earlier, the party that wins the White House is always led, in title anyway, by the president. The president normally depends on fellow party members in Congress to support legislative initiatives. At the same time, members of the president's party in Congress hope that the president's programs and personal prestige will help them raise campaign funds and secure reelection. During his two terms in office, President Clinton had a mixed record as party leader. In the realm of trade policy, Clinton sometimes found more support among Republicans than among Democrats. In addition, although Clinton proved to be an extremely successful fund-raiser, congressional Democrats often complained that he failed to share his largesse with them. At the same time, however, a number of Clinton's policy initiatives seemed calculated to strengthen the Democratic party as a whole. Clinton's early health-care initiative would have linked millions of voters to the Democrats for years to come, much as Franklin Roosevelt's Social Security program had done in a previous era. But by the middle of Clinton's second term, the president's acknowledgement of his sexual affair with a White House intern threatened his position as party leader. Initially, Democratic candidates nationwide feared that the scandal would undermine their chances for election, and many moved to distance themselves from the president. The Democrats' surprisingly good showing in the 1998 elections, however, strengthened Clinton's position and gave him another chance to shape the Democratic agenda.

Between the 1998 and 2000 elections, however, the president's initiatives on Social Security and nuclear disarmament failed to make much headway in a Republican-controlled Congress. The GOP was not prepared to give Clinton anything for which Democrats could claim credit in the 2000 elections. Lacking strong congressional leadership, however, the GOP did agree to many of Clinton's budgetary proposals in 1999 and dropped its own plan for large-scale cuts in federal taxes.

When he assumed office in 2001, President George W. Bush called for a new era of bipartisan cooperation, and the new president did receive the support of some Democratic conservatives. Generally, however, Bush depended on near-unanimous backing from his own party in Congress to implement his plans for cutting taxes as well as other elements of his program. After the terrorist attacks of September 11, both parties united behind Bush's military response. By the end of the president's first term, however, the parties were sharply divided on the administration's policies in Iraq, economic policy, Social Security reform, abortion, other social issues, and the need for enhanced governmental law-enforcement powers to combat terrorism. Ultimately, Bush relied mainly on Republican support to achieve his goals.

PARTIES AND THE ELECTORATE

Political parties are more than just organizations and leaders; they are made up of millions of rank-and-file members. Individual voters tend to develop *party identification* with one of the political parties. Although it is a psychological tie, party identification also has a rational component.[13] Voters generally form attachments to parties that reflect their views and interests. Once those attachments are formed, however, they are likely to persist and even be handed down to children unless some very strong factors convince individuals that their party is no longer an appropriate object of their affections. In some sense, party identification is similar to brand loyalty in the marketplace: Consumers choose a brand of automobile for its appearance or mechanical characteristics and stick with it out of loyalty, habit, and unwillingness to reexamine their choices constantly, but they may eventually switch if the old brand no longer serves their interests.

Although the strength of partisan ties in the United States seems to have declined in the 1960s and 1970s, most Americans continue to identify with either the Republican party or the Democratic party (Figure 11.2). The Analyzing the Evidence unit in this chapter takes a closer look at how political scientists study trends in partisanship. Party identification gives citizens a stake in election outcomes that goes beyond the race at hand. This is why strong party identifiers are more likely than other Americans to go to the polls and, of course, are more likely than others to support the party with which they identify. *Party activists* are drawn from the ranks of the strong identifiers. Activists are those who not only vote but also contribute their time, energy, and effort to party affairs. Activists ring doorbells, stuff envelopes, attend meetings, and contribute money to the party cause. No party could succeed without the thousands of volunteers who undertake the mundane tasks needed to keep the organization going. It is worth noting that attachment to a party does not guarantee voting for that party's candidates, though it does reflect a tendency. Strong identifiers do almost always, and weak identifiers do most of the time.

Group Affiliations

The Democratic and Republican parties are America's only national parties. They are the only political organizations that draw support from most regions of the

party identification
An individual voter's psychological ties to one party or another.

party activists Partisans who contribute time, energy, and effort to support their party and its candidates.

[13] For what is perhaps still the best discussion of the bases of party identification, see Arthur S. Goldberg, "Social Determinism and Rationality as Bases of Party Identification," *American Political Science Review* 63, no. 1 (March 1969): 5–25. For a more recent article weighing in on economic versus social determinants of party attachments, see Larry M. Bartels, "What's the Matter with *What's the Matter with Kansas?*" *Quarterly Journal of Political Science* 1 (2006): 201–26.

FIGURE 11.2 Americans' Party Identification

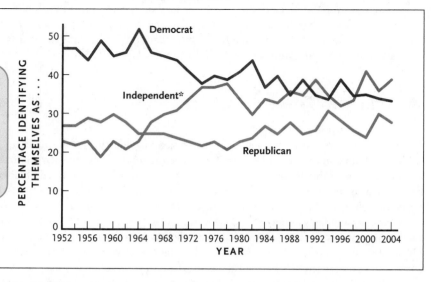

SOURCE: Harold W. Stanley and Richard G. Niemi, *Vital Statistics on American Politics, 2001–2002* (Washington, D.C.: Congressional Quarterly Press, 2001), p. 115; *American National Election Studies, the ANES Guide to Public Opinion and Electoral Behavior* (www.election-studies.org).

*Includes independents who report "leaning" toward one of the parties.

country and from Americans of every racial, economic, religious, and ethnic group. The two parties do not draw equal support from members of every social stratum, however. When we refer to the Democratic or Republican coalition, we mean the groups that generally support one or the other party. In the United States today, a variety of group characteristics are associated with party identification. These include race and ethnicity, gender, religion, class, ideology, and region.

Race and Ethnicity   Since the 1930s and Franklin Roosevelt's New Deal, African Americans have been overwhelmingly Democratic in their party identification. More than 90 percent of African Americans describe themselves as Democrats and support Democratic candidates in national, state, and local elections. Approximately 25 percent of the Democratic party's support in presidential races comes from African American voters.

Latino voters do not form a monolithic bloc, by contrast. Cuban Americans are generally Republican in their party affiliation, whereas Mexican Americans favor the Democrats by a small margin. Other Latino voters, including those from Puerto Rico, are overwhelmingly Democratic.[14] Asian Americans tend to be divided as well, but along class lines. The Asian American community's influential business and

---

[14]As noted earlier, Latinos shifted toward the Democrats in the 2006 election, but this trend need not represent a permanent change in party attachment.

professional stratum identifies with the Republicans, but less-affluent Asian Americans tend to support the Democrats.

Gender   Women are somewhat more likely to support Democrats, and men are somewhat more likely to support Republicans, in surveys of party affiliation. This difference is known as the ***gender gap.*** In 1996, the gender gap was pronounced: Women voted for Clinton 54 percent of the time, and only 43 percent of voting men did so. In the 2000 election, the gender gap closed, but only slightly, but in 2008 women supported Obama by a 56 to 43 percent margin over McCain, while men divided nearly evenly, with 50 percent backing Obama and 48 percent voting for McCain.

Religion   Jews are among the Democratic party's most loyal constituent groups and have been since the New Deal. Nearly 90 percent of all Jewish Americans describe themselves as Democrats, although the percentage is declining among younger Jews. Catholics were once a strongly pro-Democratic group as well but have been shifting toward the Republican party since the 1970s, when the GOP began to focus on abortion and other social issues deemed important to Catholics. Protestants are more likely to identify with the Republicans than with the Democrats. Protestant fundamentalists, in particular, have been drawn to the GOP's conservative stands on social issues, such as school prayer and abortion. After his victory in the 2000 election, George W. Bush announced that his administration would seek to award federal grants and contracts to religious groups to reward religious conservatives for their loyalty to the GOP and to ensure that they would have a continuing stake in Republican success. In 2008, Protestants supported McCain by a 54 to 45 percent margin, while members of other religious groups backed Obama—Catholics by a margin of 54 to 46 percent, and Jews by a more lopsided 78 to 21 percent margin.

Class   Upper-income Americans are considerably more likely to affiliate with the Republicans, whereas lower-income Americans are far more likely to identify with the Democrats. This divide reflects the differences between the two parties on economic issues. In general, the Republicans support cutting taxes and social spending—positions that reflect the interests of the wealthy. The Democrats, however, favor increased social spending, even if this requires increasing taxes—a position consistent with the interests of less-affluent Americans. One important exception to this principle is that relatively affluent individuals who work in the public sector or such related institutions as foundations and universities also tend to affiliate with the Democrats. Such individuals are likely to appreciate the Democratic party's support for an expanded role of government and high levels of public spending. White voters with less than a college education (a measure of class) have become less strongly affiliated with the Democrats over time, but this trend is restricted almost entirely to the South. (Outside the South, voters with less than a college education have declined in their support of Democratic presidential candidates by only one percentage point in the last fifty years.) This "southern" effect reflects the general sorting out of partisan attachments as voting rights have been extended to African Americans in the South.[15]

gender gap A distinctive pattern of voting behavior reflecting the differences in views between women and men.

---

[15] Bartels, "What's the Matter with *What's the Matter with Kansas?*"

Ideology Ideology and party identification are very closely linked. Most individuals who describe themselves as conservatives identify with the Republican party, whereas most who call themselves liberals support the Democrats. This division has increased in recent years as the two parties have taken very different positions on social and economic issues. Before the 1970s, when party differences were more blurred, it was not uncommon to find Democratic conservatives and Republican liberals. Both of these species are rare today. The Voting Rights Act of 1965 was a watershed event in American politics. Over the next two decades, African American voting in the South grew dramatically, and Republicans began offering southern whites alternatives to the Democratic party. One consequence is that each party became clearer ideologically, leaving little room for conservative Democrats and moderate Republicans.

Region Between the Civil War and the 1960s, the "Solid South" was a Democratic bastion. Today the South is becoming solidly Republican, as is much of the West and Southwest. The area of greatest Democratic party strength is the Northeast. The Midwest is a battleground, more or less evenly divided between the two parties.

The explanations for these regional variations are complex. Southern Republicanism has come about because conservative white southerners identify the Democratic party with the civil rights movement and liberal positions on abortion, school prayer, and other social issues. Republican strength in the South and the West is related to the weakness of organized labor in these regions, as well as to the dependence of the two regions on military programs supported by the Republicans. Democratic strength in the Northeast is a function of the continuing influence of organized labor in the large cities of this region, as well as the region's large population of minority and elderly voters, who benefit from Democratic social programs. In the 2006 elections, one of the biggest shifts toward the Democrats occurred in the Rocky Mountain West, where Democrats unexpectedly won a number of congressional races and governorships. This trend reflects in part the shift in the population to this region, including in particular people who value the environment and demand public services.

Age Age is another factor associated with partisanship. At the present time, individuals younger than fifty are fairly evenly divided between Democrats and Republicans, whereas those older than fifty are much more likely to be Democrats. There is nothing about a particular numerical age that leads to a particular party loyalty. Instead, individuals from the same age cohort are likely to have experienced a similar set of events during the period when they formed their party loyalties. Thus Americans between the ages of fifty and sixty-four came of political age during the cold war, the Vietnam War and the civil rights movement, and those older than sixty-five are the product of the Great Depression and World War II. Apparently among voters whose initial perceptions of politics were shaped during these periods, more responded favorably to the role played by the Democrats than to the actions of the Republicans. It is interesting that among the youngest group of Americans, a group that came of age during an era of political scandals that tainted both parties, the majority describe themselves as independents.

Figure 11.3 indicates the relationship between party identification and a number of social criteria. Race, religion, and income seem to have the greatest influence

FIGURE 11.3 Party Identification by Social Groups

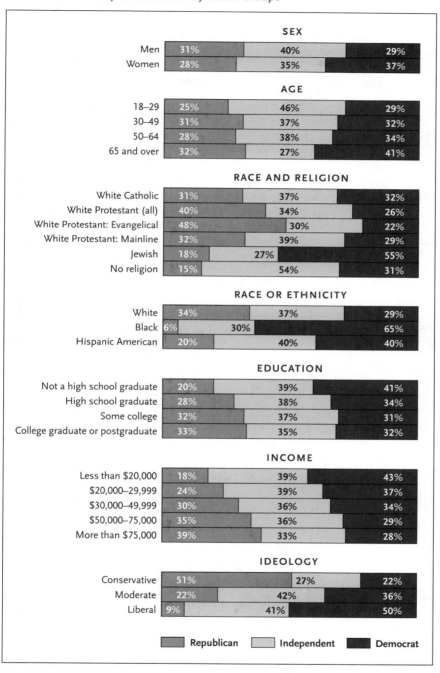

SOURCE: Pew Research Center for the People and the Press, "Democrats Gain Edge in Party Identification," 26 July 2004 (people-press.org/commentary/pdf/95.pdf).

Is Partisanship in Decline?

Since 1948, researchers at the University of Michigan have collected survey data during election years as part of the American National Election Studies (ANES). The purpose of these surveys is to offer systematic explanations of election outcomes through individual-level surveys of ordinary citizens who participate in these elections. Because these data have been collected over an extended period, they have contributed to a much better understanding of changes in voting behavior over time.

Among the survey questions is a measure of how strongly voters and non-voters identify with a particular political party. Rather than using just three broad categories (Democrat, Republican, independent), the ANES uses a seven-point scale to assess partisanship. By separating out "strong" and "weak" partisan identifiers from independent "leaners" and "pure" independents, we gain a more nuanced understanding of trends in partisanship.

Democrat			Independent		Republican	
Strongly Democrat	Weakly Democrat	Independent Leans Democrat	Pure Independent	Independent Leans Republican	Weakly Republican	Strongly Republican

Interestingly, in the ANES data we observe a sizeab[le] decline in the number of strong partisan identifiers beginning in the 1960s and continuing into the 197[0s] and 1980s. This trend has been documented elsewhere by scholars, who suggest that large segments of the American public have steadily bee[n] drifting away from the major parties since the 1950[s]

[1]Martin P. Wattenberg. *The Decline of American Political Parties: 1952–1994*. (Cambridge, Mass.: Harvard University Press, 1996).

But is partisanship really in decline? By 1996, the proportion of citizens strongly identifying with the two major parties was almost as high as it was during the 1950s. When we factor in the proportion of weak identifiers and independent leaners over this entire period, we observe that the aggregate number of Americans identifying with the parties has remained fairly constant since the 1950s, even if the intensity of citizen preferences for the parties has clearly changed over time.

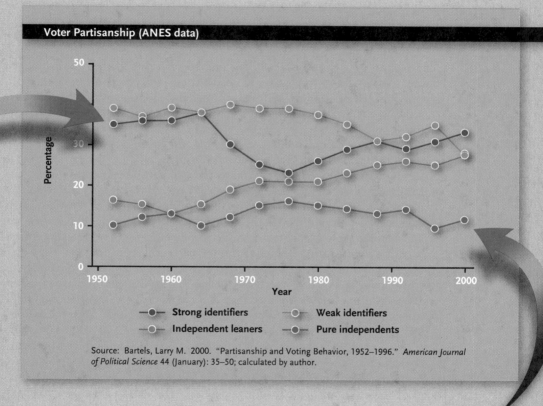

Voter Partisanship (ANES data)

Source: Bartels, Larry M. 2000. "Partisanship and Voting Behavior, 1952–1996." *American Journal of Political Science* 44 (January): 35–50; calculated by author.

There has not been a marked increase in the number of "pure" independents over this period, suggesting that parties may be as relevant today as they were 50 years ago. The lesson here is how one thinks about the seven-point scale of partisanship affects the types of conclusions one draws about American political behavior.

on Americans' party affiliations. None of these social characteristics is inevitably linked to partisan identification, however. There are black Republicans, southern white Democrats, Jewish Republicans, and even an occasional conservative Democrat. The general party identifications just discussed are broad tendencies that both reflect and reinforce the issue and policy positions the two parties take in the national and local political arenas.

PARTY SYSTEMS

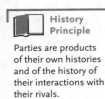

History Principle

Parties are products of their own histories and of the history of their interactions with their rivals.

Our understanding of political parties would be incomplete if we considered only their composition and roles. America's political parties compete with each other for offices, policies, and power and as malleable institutions have adapted to the demands of the time and age. In short, the history of each party is inextricably linked to that of its major rival. Historians often call the constellation of parties that are important at any given moment a nation's party system. The most obvious feature of a party system is the number of major parties competing for power. Usually the United States has had a two-party system, meaning that only two parties have a serious chance to win national elections. Of course, we have not always had the same two parties, and as we shall see, minor parties often put forward candidates.

The term *party system,* however, refers to more than just the number of parties competing for power. It also connotes the organization of the parties, the balance of power between and within party coalitions, the parties' social and institutional bases, and the issues and policies around which party competition is organized. Seen from this broader perspective, the character of a nation's party system can change even though the number of parties may remain the same and even when the same two parties seem to be competing for power. Today's American party system is very different from the party system of fifty years ago even though the Democrats and the Republicans continue to be the major competing forces (Figure 11.4). The character of a nation's party system can have profound consequences for the relative influence of social forces, the importance of political institutions, and even the types of issues and policies that reach the nation's political agenda. For example, the contemporary American political parties mainly compete for the support of different groups of middle-class Americans. One reason for this is that less affluent Americans participate less often in the political process than do wealthier Americans (see Figure 10.3). As a result, issues that concern the middle and upper-middle classes—such as the environment, health care, retirement benefits, and taxation—are very much on the political agenda, while issues that concern working-class and poorer Americans, such as welfare and housing, receive short shrift from both parties.[16] Of course, throughout America's history the creation of new issues did not just happen. Rather they

---

[16]See Matthew Crenson and Benjamin Ginsberg, *Downsizing Democracy: How America Sidelined Its Citizens and Privatized Its Public* (Baltimore: Johns Hopkins University Press, 2002).

FIGURE 11.4 How the Party System Evolved

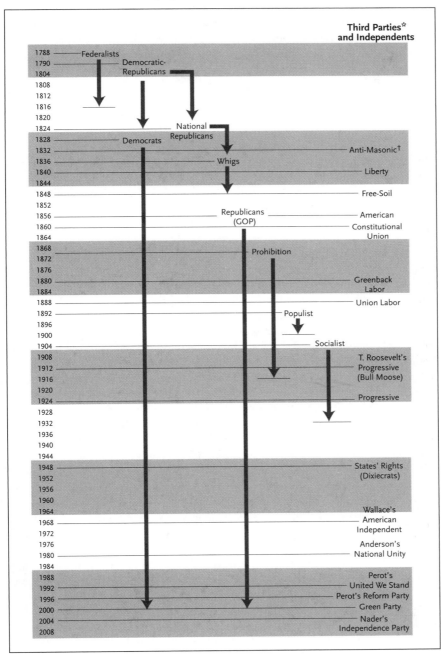

*In some cases, there was even a fourth party. Most of the parties listed here existed for only one term.

†The Anti-Masonics not only had the distinction of being the first third party but also were the first party to hold a national nominating convention and the first to announce a party platform.

Rationality Principle

Political entrepreneurs introduce issues in order to mobilize voters and steer them to their cause.

were the fruit of political entrepreneurs looking for opportunities to undermine the prevailing political orthodoxy and its political beneficiaries.[17]

Over the course of American history, changes in political forces and alignments have produced six party systems, each with distinctive political institutions, issues, and patterns of political power and participation. Of course, some political phenomena have persisted across party systems. Conflicts over the distribution of wealth, for example, are an enduring feature of American political life. But even such phenomena manifest themselves in different ways during different political eras.

The First Party System: Federalists and Democratic-Republicans

Although George Washington and, in fact, many other leaders of the time deplored partisan politics, the two-party system emerged early in the history of the new Republic. Competition in Congress between northeastern mercantile and southern agrarian factions led Alexander Hamilton and the northeasterners to form a cohesive voting bloc within Congress. The southerners, led by Thomas Jefferson and James Madison, responded by attempting to organize a popular following to change the balance of power within Congress. When the northeasterners replied to this southern strategy, the result was the birth of America's first national parties—the Democratic-Republicans, whose primary base was in the South, and the Federalists, whose strength was greatest in the New England states. The Federalists spoke mainly for New England mercantile groups and supported protective tariffs to encourage manufacturers, the assumption of the states' Revolutionary War debts, the creation of a national bank, and resumption of commercial ties with England. The Democratic-Republicans opposed these policies, favoring instead free trade, the promotion of agrarian over commercial interests, and friendship with France.

Collective-Action Principle

The first American political parties were formed mainly to overcome collective-action problems in Congress.

The rationale behind the formation of both parties was primarily that they would be a means by which to institutionalize existing voting blocs in Congress around a cohesive policy agenda. Although the Federalists and the Democratic-Republicans competed in elections, their ties to the electorate were loose. In 1800, the American electorate was small, and deference was an important political factor, with voters generally expected to follow the lead of local political and religious leaders and community notables. Nominations were informal, without rules or regulations. Local party leaders would simply gather the party elites, and they would agree on the person, usually one of them, who would be the candidate. The meetings where candidates were nominated were generally called caucuses. In this era, before the introduction of the secret ballot, many voters were reluctant to publicly defy the views of influential members of their community. In this context, the Democratic-Republicans and the Federalists organized political clubs and developed newspapers and newsletters

---

[17] Such entrepreneurial efforts are not always successful; history mainly tends to remember the successful ones. For an intriguing development of this notion, see William H. Riker, *Liberalism against Populism: A Confrontation between the Theory of Democracy and the Theory of Social Choice* (San Francisco: Freeman, 1982), esp. chaps. 8 and 9. See also Andrew J. Polsky, "When Business Speaks: Political Entrepreneurship, Discourse, and Mobilization in American Partisan Regimes," *Journal of Theoretical Politics* 12 (2002): 451–72; and Kenneth A. Shepsle, "Losers in Politics (and How They Sometimes Become Winners): William Riker's Heresthetic," *Perspectives on Politics* 1 (2003): 307–15.

designed to mobilize elite opinion and relied on local elites to bring along their followers. In the election of 1800, Jefferson defeated the incumbent Federalist president, John Adams, and led his party to power. Over the ensuing years, the Federalists gradually weakened. The party disappeared altogether after the pro-British sympathies of some Federalist leaders during the War of 1812 led to charges that the party was guilty of treason.

The Second Party System: Democrats and Whigs

From the collapse of the Federalists until the 1830s, America had only one political party, the Democratic-Republicans. This period of one-party politics is sometimes known as the Era of Good Feelings, to indicate the absence of party competition. Throughout this period, however, there was intense factional conflict within the Democratic-Republican party, particularly between the supporters and opponents of General Andrew Jackson, America's great military hero of the War of 1812. Jackson was one of five significant candidates for president in 1824 and won the most popular and electoral votes but a majority of neither, throwing the election into the House of Representatives. Jackson's opponents united to deny him the presidency, but Jackson won election in 1828 and again in 1832.

Jackson was greatly admired by millions of ordinary Americans living on the nation's farms and in its villages, and the Jacksonians made the most of the general's appeal to the common people by embarking on a program of suffrage expansion that would give Jackson's impecunious but numerous supporters the right to vote. To bring growing numbers of voters to the polls, the Jacksonians built political clubs and held mass rallies and parades, laying the groundwork for a new and more popular politics. Jackson's vice president and eventual successor, Martin Van Buren, was the organizational genius behind the Jacksonian movement, establishing a central party committee, state party organizations, and party newspapers. In response to widespread complaints about cliques of party leaders dominating the nominations at party caucuses and leaving no place for other party members who wanted to participate, the Jacksonians also established the state and national party conventions as the forums for nominating presidential candidates. The conventions gave control of the presidential nominating process to the new state party organizations that the Jacksonians had created and expected to control. As the political scientist John Aldrich has argued, unlike any political leader before him, Van Buren appreciated the possibilities for mass mobilization and the necessity of a well-oiled national organization to overcome free riding and other collective-action problems.[18] With a keen sense of what it took to organize a party for electoral competition, Van Buren produced institutional solutions to collective-action problems, leaving as a historical legacy the blueprint for the modern mass-based political party.

The Jacksonians, whose party came to be known as the Democratic party, were not without opponents, however, especially in the New England states, and during the 1830s groups opposing Jackson for reasons of personality and politics united to form a new political force—the Whig party—thus giving rise to the

---

[18]See Aldrich, *Why Parties?* chap. 4.

second American party system. During the 1830s and 1840s, the Democrats and the Whigs built party organizations throughout the nation, and both sought to enlarge their bases of support by expanding the suffrage through the elimination of property restrictions and other barriers to voting—at least voting by white men. This would not be the last time that party competition paved the way for expansion of the electorate. Support for the new Whig party was stronger in the Northeast than in the South and the West and stronger among mercantile groups than among small farmers. Hence to some measure the Whigs were the successors of the Federalists. Many, though not all, Whigs favored a national bank, a protective tariff, and federally sponsored internal improvements. The Jacksonians opposed all three policies. Yet conflict between the two parties revolved around personalities as much as policies. The Whigs were a diverse group, united more by opposition to the Democrats than by agreement on programs. In 1840, the Whigs won their first presidential election under the leadership of General William Henry Harrison, a military hero known as Old Tippecanoe. The 1840 election marked the first time in American history that two parties competed for the presidency in every state in the Union. The Whig campaign carefully avoided issues—because different party factions disagreed on most matters—and emphasized the personal qualities and heroism of the candidate. The Whigs also invested heavily in campaign rallies and entertainment to win the hearts, if not exactly the minds, of the voters. The 1840 campaign came to be called the hard-cider campaign to denote the then-common practice of using food and, especially, drink to elicit electoral favor.

In the late 1840s and early 1850s, conflicts over slavery produced sharp divisions within both the Whig and the Democratic parties, despite the efforts of party leaders like Henry Clay and Stephen Douglas to develop sectional compromises that would bridge the increasing gulf between the North and the South. By 1856, the Whig party had all but disintegrated under the strain. The 1854 Kansas-Nebraska Act overturned the Missouri Compromise of 1820 and the Compromise of 1850, which together had hindered the expansion of slavery in the American territories. The Kansas-Nebraska Act gave each territory the right to decide whether to permit slavery. Opposition to this policy led to the formation of a number of antislavery parties, with the Republicans emerging as the strongest of the new forces.[19] They drew their membership from existing political groups—former Whigs, Know-Nothings of the American Party, Free-Soilers, and antislavery Democrats. In 1856, the party's first presidential candidate, John C. Frémont, won one third of the popular vote and carried eleven states.

The early Republican platforms appealed to commercial as well as antislavery interests. The Republicans favored homesteading, internal improvements, the construction of a transcontinental railroad, and protective tariffs, as well as the containment of slavery. In 1858, the Republican party won control of the House of Representatives; in 1860, the Republican presidential candidate, Abraham Lincoln, was victorious. Lincoln's victory strengthened southern calls for secession from the Union and led, soon thereafter, to all-out civil war.

---

[19]See William E. Gienapp, *The Origins of the Republican Party, 1852–1856* (New York: Oxford University Press, 1994).

The Third Party System: Republicans and Democrats, 1860–96

During the course of the war, President Lincoln depended heavily on Republican governors and state legislatures to raise troops, provide funding, and maintain popular support for a long and bloody military conflict. The secession of the South had stripped the Democratic party of many of its leaders and supporters, but the Democrats nevertheless remained politically competitive throughout the war and nearly won the 1864 presidential election due to war weariness on the part of the northern public. With the defeat of the Confederacy in 1865, some congressional Republicans sought to convert the South into a Republican bastion through Reconstruction, a program that enfranchised newly freed slaves while disenfranchising many white voters and disqualifying many white politicians from seeking office. Reconstruction collapsed in the 1870s as a result of divisions within the Republican party in Congress and violent resistance to the program by southern whites. With the end of Reconstruction, the former Confederate states regained full membership in the Union and full control of their internal affairs. Throughout the South, African Americans were deprived of political rights, including the right to vote, despite post–Civil War constitutional guarantees to the contrary. The post–Civil War South was solidly Democratic in its political affiliation, and with a firm southern base, the national Democratic party was able to confront the Republicans on a more or less equal basis. From the end of the Civil War to the 1890s, the Republican party remained the party of the North, with strong business and middle-class support, while the Democratic party was the party of the South, with support from working-class and immigrant groups in the North. Republican candidates campaigned by waving the "bloody shirt" of the Civil War and urging their supporters to "vote the way you shot." Democrats emphasized the issue of the tariff, which they claimed was ruinous to agricultural interests.

Party Machines as a Strategic Innovation   It was during the third party system that party entrepreneurs were most successful at turning party organizations into well-oiled machines. In the nineteenth and early twentieth centuries, many cities and counties, and even a few states on occasion, had such well organized parties that they were called ***party machines*** and their leaders were called bosses. Party machines depended heavily on the patronage of the spoils system, the party's power to control government jobs. Patronage worked as a selective benefit for anyone the party wished to attract to its side. With thousands of jobs to dispense to the party faithful, party bosses were able to recruit armies of political workers, who in turn mobilized millions of voters. During the height of the party machines, party and government were virtually interchangeable. Just as the creation of mass parties by Van Buren and other political entrepreneurs of the second party system solved a collective-action problem, the well-oiled machines used the selective incentives of patronage and nomination to maintain their organizations and diminish free riding. Many organizational aspects of party politics, in short, involve the ingenuity of rational politicians and leaders grappling with problems of coordination and collective action, as the rationality principle and the collective-action principle suggest.

Many critics condemned party machines as antidemocratic and corrupt. They argued that machines served the interests of powerful businesses and did not help

party machines In the late nineteenth and early twentieth centuries, the local party organizations that controlled local politics through patronage and the nominations process.

the working people who voted for them. But one of the most notorious machine leaders in American political history, George Washington Plunkitt of New York City's Tammany Hall, considered machine politics and the spoils system to be "patriotic." Plunkitt grasped a simple, central fact about purposeful behavior and overcoming the collective-action problem. To create and retain political influence and power, "you must study human nature and act accordin'." He argued with some acumen that the country was built by political parties, that the parties needed such patronage to operate and thrive, and that if patronage was withdrawn, the parties would "go to pieces." As we shall see next, Plunkitt was somewhat prescient in making this observation.

Institutional Reforms of the Progressives   As the nineteenth century gave way to the twentieth, the excessive powers and abuses of party machines and their bosses led to one of the great reform movements in American history, the so-called Progressive Era. Many Progressive reformers were undoubtedly motivated by a sincere desire to rid politics of corruption and improve the quality and efficiency of government in the United States. But simultaneously, from the perspective of middle- and upper-class Progressives and the financial, commercial, and industrial elites with whom they were often associated, the weakening or elimination of party organization would also mean that power could more readily be acquired and retained by the "best men"—that is, those with wealth, position, and education.

The list of anti-party reforms of the Progressive Era is a familiar one. As we saw in Chapter 10, the introduction of voter registration laws required eligible voters to register in person well before an election. The Australian-ballot reform took away the parties' privilege of printing and distributing ballots and thus introduced the possibility of split-ticket voting (see also Chapter 10). The introduction of nonpartisan local elections eroded grassroots party organization. The extension of "merit systems" for administrative appointments stripped party organizations of their vitally important access to patronage and thus reduced party leaders' capacity to control the nomination of candidates.

These reforms obviously did not destroy political parties as entities, but taken together they did substantially weaken party organizations in the United States. After the beginning of the twentieth century, the strength of American political parties gradually diminished, and voter turnout declined precipitously. Between the two world wars, organization remained the major tool available to contending electoral forces, but in most areas of the country the "reformed" state and local parties that survived the Progressive Era gradually lost their organizational vitality and coherence and became less effective campaign tools. While most areas of the nation continued to boast Democratic and Republican party groupings, reform did mean the elimination of the permanent mass organizations that had been the parties' principal campaign weapons.

The Fourth Party System, 1896–1932

During the 1890s, profound and rapid social and economic changes led to the emergence of a variety of protest parties, including the Populist party, which won the support of hundreds of thousands of voters in the South and the West. The Populists appealed mainly to small farmers but also attracted western mining interests and urban workers. In the 1892 presidential election, the Populist party carried four states and elected governors in eight states. In 1896, the Democrats in effect adopted the Populist party platform and nominated William Jennings Bryan, a Democratic senator with pronounced Populist sympathies, for the presidency. The Republicans nominated the conservative senator William McKinley. In the ensuing campaign, northern and midwestern business made an all-out effort to defeat what it saw as a radical threat from the Populist-Democratic alliance. When the dust settled, the Republicans had won a resounding victory. In the nation's metropolitan regions, especially in the Northeast and upper Midwest, workers became convinced that the Populist-Democratic alliance threatened the industries that provided their jobs, while immigrants were frightened by the nativist rhetoric employed by some Populist orators and writers. The GOP had carried the northern and midwestern states and confined the Democrats to their bastions in the South and the Far West. For the next thirty-six years, the Republicans were the nation's majority party, carrying seven of nine presidential elections and controlling both houses of Congress in fifteen of eighteen contests. The Republican party of this era was very much the party of American business, advocating low taxes, high tariffs, and a minimum of government regulation. The Democrats were far too weak to offer much opposition. Southern Democrats, moreover, were more concerned with maintaining the region's autonomy on issues of race to challenge the Republicans on other fronts.

The Fifth Party System: The New Deal Coalition, 1932–68

Soon after the Republican candidate Herbert Hoover won the 1928 presidential election, the nation's economy collapsed. The Great Depression, which produced unprecedented economic hardship, stemmed from a variety of causes, but from the perspective of millions of Americans the Republican party had not done enough to promote economic recovery. In 1932, Americans elected Franklin D. Roosevelt and a solidly Democratic Congress. FDR developed a program for economic recovery that he dubbed the New Deal, under the auspices of which the size and reach of America's national government was substantially increased. The federal government took responsibility for economic management and social welfare to an extent that was unprecedented in American history. FDR designed many of his programs specifically to expand the political base of the Democratic party. He rebuilt the party around a nucleus of unionized workers, upper-middle-class intellectuals and professionals, southern farmers, Jews, Catholics, and northern African Americans (few blacks in the South could vote) that made the Democrats the nation's majority party for thirty-six years. Republicans groped for a response to the New Deal but often wound up supporting popular New Deal programs like Social Security in what was sometimes derided as "me-too" Republicanism.

The New Deal coalition was severely strained during the 1960s by conflicts over President Lyndon Johnson's Great Society initiative, civil rights, and the Vietnam War. A number of Johnson's Great Society programs, designed to fight poverty and racial discrimination, involved the empowerment of local groups that were often at odds with established city and county governments. These programs touched off battles between local Democratic political machines and the national administration that split the Democratic coalition. For its part, the struggle over civil rights initially divided northern Democrats, who supported the civil rights cause, and white southern Democrats, who defended the system of racial segregation. Subsequently, as the civil rights movement launched a northern campaign aimed at securing access to jobs and education and an end to racial discrimination in such realms as housing, northern Democrats also experienced a split, often along class lines, with blue-collar workers tending to vote Republican. The struggle over the Vietnam War further divided the Democrats, with upper-income liberal Democrats strongly opposing the Johnson administration's decision to send U.S. forces to fight in Southeast Asia. These schisms within the Democratic party provided an opportunity for the GOP to return to power, which it did in 1968 under the leadership of Richard Nixon.

The Sixth Party System?

In the 1960s, conservative Republicans argued that me-tooism was a recipe for continual failure and sought to reposition the GOP as a genuine alternative to the Democrats. In 1964, for example, the Republican presidential candidate, Barry Goldwater, author of a book titled *The Conscience of a Conservative,* argued in favor of substantially reduced levels of taxation and spending, less government regulation of the economy, and the elimination of many federal social programs. Although Goldwater was defeated by Lyndon Johnson, the ideas he espoused continue to be major themes of the Republican party. The Goldwater message, however, was not enough to lead Republicans to victory. It took Richard Nixon's "southern strategy" to give the GOP the votes it needed to end Democratic dominance of the political process. Nixon appealed strongly to disaffected white southerners and, with the help of the independent candidate and former Alabama governor George Wallace, sparked the shift of voters that eventually gave the once-hated "party of Lincoln" a strong position in all the states of the former Confederacy. In the 1980s, under the leadership of Ronald Reagan, Republicans added another important group to their coalition: religious conservatives who were offended by Democratic support of abortion rights as well as alleged Democratic disdain for traditional cultural and religious values.

While Republicans built a political base with economic and social conservatives and white southerners, the Democratic party maintained its support among unionized workers and upper-middle-class intellectuals and professionals. Democrats also appealed strongly to racial minorities. The 1965 Voting Rights Act had greatly increased the participation of black voters in the South and helped the Democratic party retain some congressional and Senate seats in the South. And while the GOP appealed to social conservatives, the Democrats appealed strongly to Americans concerned about abortion rights, gay rights, feminism, environmentalism, and other progressive social causes. The result so far has been a small but growing edge for the GOP. Three of the four presidents elected between 1980 and 2004 have been Republicans, and during the Clinton era Republicans took control of the House of Representatives for the first time in decades. The 2000 presidential election ended in a virtual tie, with the Democratic presidential candidate, Al Gore, outpolling George W. Bush by 500,000 votes out of more than 100 million cast. But Republicans nevertheless captured the White House and both houses of Congress. It was the first time since 1888 that the winner of the popular vote failed to win the presidency. In 2004,

Bush defeated the Democratic challenger, John Kerry, by more than 3 million votes, and Republicans increased their majorities in the House and Senate. In 2006, however, the Democrats took control of both the House and the Senate, and in 2008 they won the presidency while adding to their congressional strength. Perhaps these solid Democratic wins mark the beginning of a new party system in the United States, with the Democrats now in the majority and the GOP returned to minority status.

The shift of much of the South from the Democratic to the Republican camp, along with the other developments mentioned above, meant that each political party became ideologically more homogeneous after the 1980s. Today there are few liberal Republicans or conservative Democrats. One consequence of this development is that party loyalty in Congress, which had been weak between the 1950s and the 1970s, became a more potent force. Battles over such matters as the Clinton impeachment, for example, resulted in nearly straight party-line voting in the House and Senate. On other matters, including budgetary priorities, judicial appointments, and foreign policy, party-line voting has become far more common than it was in prior years (see Chapter 5).[20]

To some extent, ideology has replaced organization as the glue holding together each party's coalition. But in the long run, ideology is often an unreliable basis for party unity. Within the Republican coalition, social conservatives are often at odds with economic conservatives, whereas among Democrats proponents of regulatory reform and economic internationalism are frequently at odds with traditional liberals, who favor big government and protecting American workers from foreign competition. The party workers of yesteryear supported the leadership almost no matter what. Today's more ideologically motivated party activists feel free to withhold support if they disagree with the leadership's goals and plans. Because of internal divisions in the Republican party, for example, GOP congressional leaders have adopted a strategy of avoiding votes on the many issues that might split the party.[21] The price of unity based on ideology can be the inability to act.

The ideological gap between the two parties has been exacerbated by two other factors: each party's dependence on ideologically motivated activists and the changes in the presidential nominating system that were introduced during the 1970s. Democratic political candidates depend heavily on the support of liberal activists—such as feminists, environmentalists, and civil libertarians—to organize and finance their campaigns, while Republican political candidates depend equally on the support of conservative activists, including religious fundamentalists. In the nineteenth century, political activists were motivated more by party loyalty and political patronage than by programmatic concerns. Today's issue-oriented activists, by contrast, demand that politicians demonstrate strong commitments to moral principles and political causes in exchange for their support. The demands of party activists have tended to push

---

[20]The classic statement of the connection between cohesive legislative parties and ideological homogeneity within party ranks is found in David W. Rohde, *Parties and Leaders in the Post-reform House* (Chicago: University of Chicago Press, 1991). An elaboration of this argument is presented in Gary W. Cox and Mathew D. McCubbins, *Setting the Agenda: Responsible Party Government in the U.S. House of Representatives* (New York: Cambridge University Press, 2005).

[21]Isaiah J. Poole, "Votes Echo Electoral Themes," *Congressional Quarterly Weekly Report*, 11 December 2004, pp. 2906–8.

ONLINE READING

Democrats further to the political left and Republicans further to the political right. Often efforts by politicians to reach compromises on key issues are attacked by party activists as "sellouts," leading to stalemates on such matters as the budget and judicial appointments.

The second factor exacerbating the parties' ideological split, the changes in the presidential nominating system, took place in response to the Democratic party's defeat in 1968. Liberal forces, guided by the so-called McGovern-Fraser Commission on party reform, succeeded in changing the rules governing Democratic presidential nominations to reduce the power of party officials and party professionals while increasing the role of issue-oriented activists. Among other changes, the new rules required national convention delegates to be chosen in primaries and caucuses rather than by each state party's central committee, as had previously been the practice in many states. Subsequently, Republican activists were able to bring about similar changes in the GOP's rules, so that today in both parties presidential nominating processes are strongly influenced by precisely the sorts of grassroots activists who are often inclined to oppose centrist or pragmatic politicians in favor of those appearing to manifest ideological purity. As a result, elections have tended to pit liberal Democrats against conservative Republicans. Observers of post–World War II American political parties often dubbed them Tweedledum and Tweedledee, but the two parties today differ sharply on a number of social, economic, and foreign-policy issues. Compare, for example, Democratic and Republican legislative priorities at the opening of the 110th Congress, in January 2007. Republicans emphasized support of Iraq war policy, immigration reform, and new laws to strengthen marriage and discourage abortion. The Democrats emphasized expanding social programs, protecting the jobs of unionized workers, bringing an end to operations in Iraq, and strengthening abortion rights. The 2008 Democratic and Republican platforms reflected the same partisan differences, setting the stage for a contentious legislative session.

American Third Parties

Although the United States is said to possess a two-party system, we have always had more than two parties. Typically, ***third parties*** in the United States have represented social and economic protests that, for one or another reason, were not given voice by the two major parties.[22] Such parties have had a good deal of influence on ideas and elections in the United States. The Populists, a party centered in the rural areas of the West and the Midwest during the late nineteenth century, and the Progressives, spokesmen for the urban middle classes in the late nineteenth and early twentieth centuries, are among the most important examples. More recently, Ross Perot, who ran in 1992 and 1996 as an independent, impressed some voters with his folksy style in the presidential debates and garnered

---

[22]For a discussion of third parties in the United States, see Daniel A. Mazmanian, *Third Parties in Presidential Elections* (Washington, D.C.: Brookings Institution, 1974).

third parties Parties that organize to compete against the two major American political parties.

TABLE 11.1 Parties and Candidates, 2008

Candidate	Party	Vote Total	Percentage of Vote
Barack Obama	Democratic	64,629,649	53
John McCain	Republican	56,887,996	46
Ralph Nader	Independent	667,045	0.5
Robert L. Barr, Jr.	Libertarian	493,987	0.4
Charles O. Baldwin	Independent	177,690	0.1
Alan Keyes	Independent	35,299	0

SOURCE: elections.foxnews.com/tracker.html (accessed 11/6/08).

almost 19 percent of the votes cast in the 1992 presidential election. Earlier, George Wallace received almost 10 percent of the vote in 1968, and John Anderson received about 5 percent in 1980.

Table 11.1 lists the top candidates in the 2008 presidential election, including third-party and independent candidates. In addition to the candidates listed in Table 11.1, the Green Party, the Socialist Party, the Prohibition Party, and several other parties nominated candidates for the presidency in 2008. In order to have even any realistic chance of winning, a candidate needs to appear on the ballot in at least enough states to reach a total of 270 electoral votes. However, most of the third-party and independent candidates in 2008 did not appear on the ballot in enough states to have any hope of winning. The third-party and independent candidates gained no electoral votes for president, and most of them disappeared immediately after the presidential election. Third-party candidacies also arise at the state and local levels. In New York, the Liberal and Conservative parties have been on the ballot for decades. In 1998, Minnesota elected a third-party governor, the former professional wrestler Jesse Ventura. In 2002, the Green Party candidate for governor in Massachusetts, Jill Stein, may have affected the race between Mitt Romney and his Democratic rival by drawing votes away from the Democrats in a close race. And in 2006, the entertainer Kinky Friedman mounted a somewhat credible campaign running as an independent candidate for the governorship of Texas.

Although the Republican party, founded as a third party in the 1850s, was only the third American political party ever to make itself permanent (by replacing the Whigs and becoming the Democrats' major competitor), other third parties have enjoyed an influence far beyond their electoral size. That is because large parts of their programs were adopted by one or both of the major parties, which sought to appeal to the voters mobilized by the new party and so expand their own electoral strength. The Democratic party, for example, became a great deal more liberal when it adopted most of the Progressive program early in the twentieth century. Many Socialists felt that President Roosevelt's New Deal had adopted most of their party's program, including old-age pensions, unemployment compensation, an agricultural marketing program, and laws guaranteeing workers the right to organize into unions.

This kind of influence explains the short lives of third parties. Their causes are usually eliminated by the ability of the major parties to absorb their programs and draw their supporters into the mainstream. There are, of course, additional reasons for the short duration of most third parties. One is the typical limitation of their electoral support to one or two regions. Populist support, for example, was primarily midwestern. The 1948 Progressive party, with Henry Wallace as its candidate, drew nearly half its votes from the state of New York. The American Independent party polled nearly 10 million popular votes and 45 electoral votes for George Wallace in 1968—the most electoral votes ever polled by a third-party candidate. But all of Wallace's electoral votes and the majority of his popular vote came from the states of the Deep South.

Americans usually assume that only the candidates nominated by one of the two major parties have any chance of winning an election. Thus a vote cast for a third-party or an independent candidate is often seen as a wasted vote. Voters who would prefer a third-party candidate may feel compelled to vote for the major party candidate whom they regard as the lesser of two evils to avoid wasting their vote in a futile gesture. Third-party candidates must struggle—usually without success—to overcome the perception that they cannot win. Thus in 2004, many liberals who admired Ralph Nader nevertheless urged him not to mount an independent bid for the presidency for fear he would siphon liberal votes from the Democrats, as he had in 2000. Some former Naderites participated in efforts to keep Nader off the ballot in a number of states. Ultimately Nader did mount a presidential campaign but received 2.5 million fewer votes in 2004 than in 2000. Most of his former adherents, knowing he could not win, voted for John Kerry. In 2008, Nader was on the ballot again, but received just over half a million votes. The other leading third-party and independent candidates in 2008 seemed more likely to siphon votes from the Republicans. For example, Bob Barr, the Libertarian candidate, ran on a platform of smaller government, lower taxes, and more individual freedom. Independent candidates Charles Baldwin and Alan Keyes were social conservatives. However, none won more than half a million votes, so their direct impact on the outcome was negligible.

As many scholars have pointed out, third-party prospects are also hampered by America's **single-member-district** plurality election system. In many other nations, several individuals can be elected to represent each legislative district. This is called a system of **multiple-member districts.** With this type of system, the candidates of weaker parties have a better chance of winning at least some seats. For their part, voters are less concerned about wasting ballots and usually more willing to support minor-party candidates.

Reinforcing the effects of the single-member district (as noted in Chapter 10), plurality voting rules generally have the effect of setting what could be called a high threshold for victory. To win a plurality race, candidates usually must secure many more votes than they would need under most European systems of proportional representation. For example, to win an American plurality election in a single-member district with only two candidates, a politician must win more than 50 percent of the votes cast. To win a seat in a European multi-member district under proportional-

single-member district An electorate that is allowed to elect only one representative from each district—the typical method of representation in the United States.

multiple-member district An electorate that selects several candidates at large from an entire district, with each voter given the number of votes equivalent to the number of seats to be filled.

representation rules, a candidate may need to win only 15 or 20 percent of the votes cast. This high threshold in American elections discourages minor parties and encourages the various political factions that might otherwise form minor parties to minimize their differences and remain within the major-party coalitions.[23]

It would nevertheless be incorrect to assert (as some scholars have maintained) that America's single-member plurality election system guarantees that only two parties will compete for power in all regions of the country. All that can be said is that American election law depresses the number of parties likely to survive over long periods of time in the United States. There is nothing magical about two. Indeed, the single-member plurality election system can also discourage second parties. After all, if one party consistently receives a large plurality of the vote, people may eventually come to see their vote even for the second party as a wasted effort. This happened to the Republican party in the Deep South before World War II.

Of the two most successful third-party efforts of the last half century, by George Wallace in 1968 and Ross Perot in 1992, it is useful to compare the candidates' relative fates. In the last Gallup public opinion poll before the 1968 election, Hubert Humphrey, the Democrat, and Richard Nixon, the Republican, were in a near dead heat, with 43 percent and 42 percent of the vote respectively. George Wallace was the preferred choice of about 14 percent of the electorate, with some voters still undecided. In the actual balloting, Nixon barely won the popular vote, and Wallace's share shrank to less than 10 percent: Wallace lost more than one third of his support. Fast forward to 1992, when the final Gallup poll showed the Democrat, Bill Clinton, leading the Republican, George H. W. Bush, by about five percentage points (43–38). Perot was the first preference of about 19 percent. In the final balloting, Perot got approximately that share—there was virtually no loss of support. In each case, the third-party candidate had little chance of winning. But in the Humphrey-Nixon contest, the margin was razor thin, and many Wallace supporters, not wanting to waste their vote, opted for the lesser of evils. In the Clinton-Bush race, Clinton was comfortably in the lead at the end, so Perot supporters felt less pressure to desert their favorite in order to make a difference in the contest between the two leaders. In each case, voters reflected the rationality principle in their deliberations. (Indeed, there is evidence in the 2000 race between Al Gore, the Democrat, and George W. Bush, the Republican, that the third-party candidate Ralph Nader did better in those states where either Bush or Gore was nearly certain of winning, whereas his support dwindled in more closely contested states.)

 Institution Principle

Third-party prospects for electoral success are hampered by America's single-member-district plurality election system.

THE ROLE OF PARTIES TODAY

As a result of Progressive reform, American party organizations entered the twentieth century with rickety substructures. As the use of civil service, primary elections, and the other Progressive innovations spread during the period between the two world wars, the strength of party organizations continued to be eroded. By the end of World War II, political scientists were already bemoaning the absence of party discipline and "party responsibility" in the United States.

---

[23]See Duverger, *Political Parties.*

High-Tech Politics and the Rise of Candidate-Centered and Capital-Intensive Politics

This erosion of the parties' organizational strength set the stage for the introduction of new political techniques. These new methods represented radical departures from the campaign practices perfected during the nineteenth century. In place of manpower and organization, contending forces began to employ intricate electronic communications techniques to attract electoral support. This new political technology includes six basic elements: polling, the broadcast media, phone banks, direct mail, professional public relations, and the Internet.

Polling   Surveys of voter opinion provide the information that candidates and their staffs use to craft campaign strategies. Candidates employ polls to select issues, assess their own strengths and weaknesses (as well as those of the opposition), check voter response to the campaign, and determine the degree to which various constituent groups are susceptible to campaign appeals. Virtually all contemporary campaigns for national and statewide office, as well as many local campaigns, make extensive use of opinion surveys. As we saw in Chapter 9, President Clinton made extensive use of polling data during and after the 1996 presidential election to shape his rhetoric and guide his policy initiatives.

The Broadcast Media   Extensive use of the electronic media, television in particular, has become the hallmark of the modern political campaign. One commonly used broadcast technique is the 30- or 60-second television spot advertisement—such as George H. W. Bush's "Willie Horton" ad in 1988 or Lyndon Johnson's famous "daisy girl" ad in 1964—which permits the candidate's message to be delivered to a target audience before uninterested or hostile viewers can psychologically or physically tune it out. In the 2008 campaign, a McCain ad depicted a stormy sea and asked whether Obama had enough experience to pilot the nation through rough weather. At the same time, a variety of Obama ads featured ordinary Americans worrying that McCain's health policy proposals would leave them and their families without coverage for major illnesses.

Television spot ads and other media techniques are designed to establish candidate name recognition, create a favorable image of the candidate and a negative image of the opponent, link the candidate to desirable groups in the community, and communicate the candidate's stands on selected issues. Spot ads can have an important electoral impact. Generally, media campaigns attempt to follow the guidelines indicated by a candidate's polls, emphasizing issues and personal characteristics that appear important in the poll data. The broadcast media are now so central to modern campaigns that most candidates' activities are tied to their media strategies. Candidate activities are designed expressly to stimulate television news coverage. For instance, members of Congress running for reelection or for president often sponsor committee or subcommittee hearings to generate publicity.

Phone Banks   Through the broadcast media, candidates communicate with voters en masse and impersonally. Phone banks, on the other hand, allow campaign workers to make personal contact with hundreds of thousands of voters. Personal contacts of this sort are thought to be extremely effective. Again, poll data serve to identify the groups that will be targeted for phone calls. Computers select phone numbers from areas in which members of these groups are concentrated. Staffs of paid or volunteer callers, using computer-assisted dialing systems and prepared scripts, then place calls to deliver the candidate's message. The targeted groups are generally those identified by polls as either uncommitted or weakly committed, as well as strong supporters of the candidate who are contacted simply to encourage them to vote. In recent elections the use of previously recorded phone messages has grown. Tactically, this entails trading off the personal touch for a capacity to reach much larger target populations.

Direct Mail   Direct mail serves both as a vehicle for communicating with voters and as a mechanism for raising funds. The first step in a direct-mail campaign is the purchase or rental of a computerized mailing list of voters deemed to have some particular perspective or social characteristic. Often sets of magazine subscription lists or lists of donors to various causes are employed. For example, a candidate interested in reaching conservative voters might rent subscription lists from the *National Review;* a candidate interested in appealing to liberals might rent subscription lists from *The New York Review of Books* or from *The New Republic.* Considerable fine-tuning is possible. After obtaining the appropriate mailing lists, candidates usually send pamphlets, letters, and brochures describing themselves and their views to voters believed to be sympathetic. Different types of mail appeals are made to different electoral subgroups. Often the letters sent to voters are personalized. The recipient is addressed by name in the text and the letter appears to have been signed by the candidate. Of course, these "personal" letters are written and even signed by a computer.

In addition to its use as a political advertising medium, direct mail has become an important source of campaign funds. Computerized mailing lists permit campaign strategists to pinpoint individuals whose interests, background, and activities suggest that they may be potential donors to the campaign. Letters of solicitation are sent to these potential donors. Some of the money raised is then used to purchase additional mailing lists. Direct-mail solicitation can be enormously effective.

Professional Public Relations   Modern campaigns and the complex technology on which they rely are typically directed by professional public relations consultants. Virtually all serious contenders for national and statewide office retain the services of professional campaign consultants.[24] Increasingly, candidates for local office, too, have come to rely on professional campaign managers. Consultants offer candidates the expertise necessary to conduct accurate opinion polls, produce television commercials, organize direct-mail campaigns, and make use of sophisticated computer analyses.

The Internet   Most candidates for office set up a Web site as an inexpensive means of establishing a public presence. The 1998 election saw increased use of the Internet by political candidates. Virtually all statewide candidates, as well as many candidates for Congress and local offices, developed Web sites providing contact information, press releases, speeches, photos, and information on how to volunteer, contact the candidate, or donate money to the campaign. During his campaign, Florida governor

[24]Larry Sabato, *The Rise of Political Consultants: New Ways of Winning Elections* (New York: Basic Books, 1981). Also see various issues of the journal *Campaigns and Elections,* which is aimed in part at the growing number of professional political consultants.

Jeb Bush sold "Jebwear," articles of clothing emblazoned with his name, through his Web site.

During the 2004 presidential primaries, as noted above, Democratic hopeful Howard Dean made extensive use of the Internet as a communication and fund-raising tool. Thousands of bloggers maintained discussion forums that promoted Dean's candidacy and solicited funds. By the end of 2003, Dean had amassed a war chest of more than $15 million. The full potential of the Internet as a campaign tool began to be realized in 2008. Directed by several Trippi protégés, the Obama campaign harnessed the power of social networking to build an Internet community of several million people who mobilized support for the ticket and generated several hundred million dollars in campaign funds, mostly in small contributions, for Obama and the Democrats. Campaigns will never be the same.

Labor-Intensive to Capital-Intensive Politics

The displacement of organizational methods by the new political technology is, in essence, a shift from labor-intensive to capital-intensive competitive electoral practices. Campaign tasks were once performed by masses of party workers with some cash. These tasks now require fewer personnel but a great deal more money, for the new political campaign depends on polls, computers, and other electronic paraphernalia. This shift has given the advantage to groups with the ability to raise a great deal of money, a phenomenon that has served the political interests of the GOP and those of wealthy donors within the Democratic party. Such is the harsh logic of fund-raising.

Contemporary Party Organizations

In the United States, party organizations exist at virtually every level of government (Figure 11.5). These organizations are usually committees made up of a number of active party members. State law and party rules prescribe how such committees are constituted. Usually, committee members are elected at a local party meeting—called a *political caucus*—or as part of the regular primary election. The best-known examples of these committees are at the national level: the Democratic National Committee and the Republican National Committee.

The National Convention   At the national level, the party's most important institution is the national convention. The convention is attended by delegates from each of the states; as a group, they nominate the party's presidential and vice-presidential candidates, draft the party's campaign platform for the presidential race, and approve changes in the rules and regulations governing party procedures. Before World War II, presidential nominations occupied most of the time, energy, and effort expended at the national convention. The nomination process required days of negotiation and compromise among state party leaders and often required many ballots before a nominee was selected. In recent years, however, presidential candidates have essentially nominated themselves by winning enough delegate support in primary elections to win the official nomination on the first ballot. The convention itself has played little or no role in selecting the candidates.

The convention's other two tasks, establishing the party's rules and establishing its platform, remain important. Party rules can determine the relative influence of competing factions within the party and can increase or decrease the party's chances

political caucus A normally closed meeting of a political or legislative group to select candidates, plan strategy, or make decisions regarding legislative matters.

Figure 11.5 How American Parties Are Organized

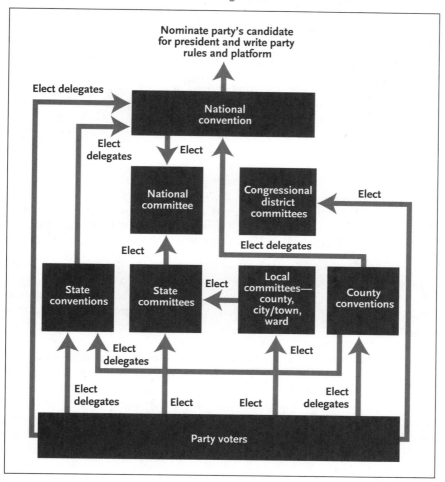

for electoral success. In 1972, for example, the Democratic National Convention adopted a new set of rules favored by the party's liberal wing, according to which state delegations to the Democratic convention are required to include women and members of minority groups in rough proportion to those groups' representation among the party's membership in their state. The convention also approves the party platform. Platforms are often dismissed as platitude-laden documents that are seldom read by voters. Furthermore, the parties' presidential candidates make little use of the platforms in their campaigns; usually they prefer to develop and promote their own themes. Nonetheless, the platform should be understood as a "treaty" in which the various party factions attending the convention state their terms for supporting the ticket.

The National Committee Between conventions, each national political party is technically headed by its national committee. For the Democrats and Republicans, these are called the Democratic National Committee (DNC) and the Republican Na-

 Institution Principle

Party rules can determine the relative influence of competing factions within the party and can increase or decrease the party's chances for electoral success.

tional Committee (RNC) respectively. These national committees raise campaign funds, head off factional disputes within the party, and endeavor to enhance the party's media image. Since 1972, the size of staff and the amount of money raised have increased substantially for both national committees. The actual work of each committee is overseen by its chairperson. Other committee members are generally major party contributors or fund-raisers and serve in a largely ceremonial capacity.

For the party that controls the White House, the national committee chair is appointed by the president. Typically, this means that that party's national committee becomes little more than an adjunct to the White House staff. For a first-term president, the committee devotes the bulk of its energy to the reelection campaign. The national committee chair of the party that is not in control of the White House is selected by the committee itself and usually takes a broader view of the party's needs, raising money and performing other activities on behalf of the party's members in Congress and in the state legislatures. In 2008, the DNC was headed by Howard Dean, who crafted a fifty-state strategy for the 2008 elections, believing that with a strong financial advantage and a weak GOP presidential ticket, Democrats could win House and Senate seats in states where Republicans had been dominant for years.

Congressional Campaign Committees   Each party forms House and Senate campaign committees to raise funds for the House and Senate election campaigns. Their efforts may or may not be coordinated with the activities of the national committees. For the party that controls the White House, the national committee and the congressional campaign committees are often rivals because both groups are seeking donations from the same people but for different candidates: the national committee seeks funds for the presidential race while the congressional campaign committees approach the same contributors for support for the congressional contests. In recent years, the Republican party has attempted to coordinate the fund-raising activities of all its committees. Republicans have sought to give the GOP's national institutions the capacity to invest funds in those close congressional, state, and local races where they can do the most good. The Democrats have been slower to coordinate their various committee activities, and this may have placed them at a disadvantage in recent congressional and local races. The efforts of the parties to centralize and coordinate fund-raising activities have helped bring about greater party unity in Congress. As members have come to rely on the leadership for campaign funds, they have become more likely to vote with the leadership on major issues. All in all, campaign committees have begun to resemble large-scale campaign consulting firms, hiring full-time political operatives and evolving into professional organizations. In 2008, the Democratic Senatorial Campaign Committee (DSSC) was headed by Senator Charles Schumer of New York. The Democratic Congressional Campaign Committee (DCCC) was chaired by Representative Chris Van Hollen of Maryland. Because the Democrats had been able to raise far more money than their Republican rivals, the DSSC and DCCC were able to strengthen Democratic incumbents and help Democratic challengers mount strong bids, even in normally Republican bastions. These efforts contributed to impressive Democratic gains in both houses of Congress.

State and Local Party Organizations   Each of the two major parties has a central committee in each state. The parties traditionally also have county committees and, in some instances, state senate district committees, judicial district committees, and

Collective-Action Principle

The efforts of the parties to centralize and coordinate fund-raising activities have helped bring about greater party unity in Congress.

in larger cities, citywide party committees and local assembly district "ward" committees as well. Congressional districts may also have party committees. Some cities also have precinct committees.[25]

State and local party organizations are very active in recruiting candidates, conducting voter registration drives, and providing financial assistance to candidates. In many respects, federal election law has given state and local party organizations new life, permitting them to spend unlimited amounts of money on "party-building" activities such as voter registration and get-out-the-vote drives. As a result, the national party organizations, which have enormous fund-raising abilities but are limited by law in the amount of money they can spend on candidates, transfer millions of dollars each year to the state and local organizations. The state and local parties, in turn, spend these funds, sometimes called soft money, to promote the candidacies of national, state, and local candidates. In this process, as local organizations have become linked financially to the national parties, American political parties have become somewhat more integrated and nationalized than ever before. At the same time, the state and local party organizations have come to control large financial resources and play important roles in elections despite the collapse of the old patronage machines.

The Contemporary Party as Service Provider to Candidates

Party leaders have adapted parties to the modern age. Parties as organizations are more professional, better financed, and better organized than ever before.[26] Political scientists argue that parties have evolved into "service organizations," which, although they no longer hold a monopoly over campaigns, still provide services to candidates, without which it would be extremely difficult for them to win and hold office.

Many politicians, however, are able to raise funds, attract volunteers, and win office without much help from the local party organizations. Once in office, these politicians often refuse to submit to party discipline; instead, they steer an independent course. They are often supported by voters who see independence as a virtue and party discipline as "boss rule." Analysts refer to this pattern as a candidate-centered politics, to distinguish it from a political process in which parties are the dominant forces. The problem with a candidate-centered politics is that it tends to be associated with low turnout, high levels of special-interest influence, and a lack of effective decision making. In short, many of the problems that have plagued American politics in recent years can be traced directly to the independence of American voters and politicians and the candidate-centered nature of American national politics.

Politicians, especially legislative politicians, have a collective-action problem. Because they possess considerable independence, they are able to chart an independent political course—hence candidate-centered politics. But so, too, can their fellow partisans. The result is that the party label, on which all rely, is undermined and comes to stand for nothing. (It is thus no accident that more and more voters call themselves independents as parties have become big tents from which a cacophony of signals is

---

[25] Well-organized political parties—especially the famous old machines of New York, Chicago, and Boston—provide for "precinct captains" and a fairly tight group of party members around them. Precinct captains were usually members of long standing in neighborhood party clubhouses.

[26] See Aldrich, *Why Parties?* chap. 8.

emitted.) Legislative leaders, in an effort to protect the party label, provide entrepreneurial direction to their co-partisans. They seek to reduce the exercise of "too much" independence because every such instance entails negative external effects on the party's reputation. Legislative leadership, in short, enables partisans to rein in one another's independence (which each is so sorely tempted to exercise). While each politician is thus constrained (somewhat) in the fine-tuning of his or her political behavior to meet the needs of individual constituencies, he or she nevertheless benefits from maintaining an unblemished party label. As party delegations in Congress have become more homogeneous in recent years, party leaders have been in a better position to exercise this type of control, ultimately to the benefit of co-partisans. This scenario is but another aspect of the "service-organization" conception of the modern political party.[27]

Collective-Action Principle

Candidate-centered politics has produced a collective-action problem for co-partisans. Legislative leadership enables them to cooperate to reduce the effects of individual independence on one another.

Parties and Democracy

Political parties make democratic government possible. We often do not appreciate that democratic government is a contradiction in terms. Government implies policies, programs, and decisive action. Democracy, on the other hand, implies an opportunity for all citizens to participate fully in the governmental process. The contradiction is that full participation by everyone is often inconsistent with getting anything done. At what point should participation stop and governance begin? How can we make certain that popular participation will result in a government capable of making decisions and developing needed policies? Strong political parties are a partial antidote to the inherent contradiction between participation and government. Strong parties can both encourage popular involvement and convert participation into effective government.

SUMMARY

Political parties seek to control government by controlling its personnel. Elections are one means to this end. Thus parties take shape from the electoral process. The formal principle of party organization is this: For every district in which an election is held—from the entire nation to the local district, county, or precinct—there should be some kind of party unit.

Nominating and electing are the basic functions of parties. Originally, nominations were made in party caucuses, and individuals who ran as independents had a difficult time getting on the ballot. In the 1830s, dissatisfaction with the cliquish caucuses led to nominating conventions. Although these gave the presidency a popular base, they, too, proved unsatisfactory. Primaries now have more or less replaced the conventions. There are both closed and open primaries. The former are more supportive of strong political parties than the latter. Contested primaries sap party strength and financial resources, but they nonetheless serve to resolve important social conflicts and recognize new interest groups. In campaigning, the mass communications

ONLINE READING ○   [27]This argument is developed in great detail in Rohde, *Parties and Leaders in the Post-reform House,* and in the two books by Cox and McCubbins, *Legislative Leviathan* and *Setting the Agenda.*

Rationality Principle	Collective-Action Principle	Institution Principle	Policy Principle	History Principle
By regulating career advancement and resolving competition, parties help deal with the threat to cooperation posed by ambitious individuals. Parties can lower the cost of voting by facilitating a voter's choice. Political entrepreneurs introduce issues in order to mobilize voters and steer them to their cause.	Parties facilitate collective action in the electoral process by helping candidates attract campaign funds, assembling campaign workers, and mobilizing voters. Parties can help mobilize voters who are potential free riders. Cooperation in Congress is facilitated by the party system. The first American political parties were formed mainly to overcome collective-action problems in Congress. The efforts of the parties to centralize and coordinate fund-raising activities have helped bring about greater party unity in Congress. Candidate-centered politics has produced a collective-action problem for co-partisans. Legislative leadership enables them to cooperate to reduce the effects of individual independence on one another.	Primary elections tend to favor aggressive and ambitious politicians, whereas conventions tend to favor those who have mastered the arts of compromise and collegiality. Third-party prospects for electoral success are hampered by America's single-member-district plurality election system. Party rules can determine the relative influence of competing factions within the party and can increase or decrease the party's chances for electoral success.	Parties help resolve collective choice in the policy-making process by acting as permanent coalitions of individuals with similar policy goals. Policies typically reflect the goals of the party in power.	Parties are products of their own histories and of the history of their interactions with their rivals. The erosion of the strength of party organizations set the stage for the introduction of new political campaign techniques and the rise of candidate-centered campaigns.

media and mass mailings are important. Thus campaign funds are crucial to success.

Congress is organized around the two-party system. The House speakership is a party office. Parties determine the makeup of congressional committees, including their chairs, which are no longer based entirely on seniority.

The two-party system dominates U.S. politics. While the two parties agree on some major issues, the Democrats generally favor higher levels of social spending funded by higher levels of taxation than the GOP is willing to support. Republicans favor lower levels of domestic activity on the part of the federal government but also support federal action on a number of social and moral issues such as abortion. Even though party affiliation means less to Americans than it once did, partisanship remains important.

Third parties are short-lived for several reasons: They have limited electoral support, the tradition of the two-party system is strong, and a major party often adopts their platforms. Single-member districts with two competing parties also discourage third parties.

In recent years, the role of parties in political campaigns has been partially supplanted by the use of new political technologies. These include polling, the broadcast media, phone banks, direct-mail fund-raising and advertising, professional public relations, and the Internet. These techniques are enormously expensive and have led to a shift from labor-intensive to capital-intensive politics.

FOR FURTHER READING

ONLINE READING Aldrich, John H. *Why Parties? The Origin and Transformation of Party Politics in America.* Chicago: University of Chicago Press, 1995.

Beck, Paul Allen, and Marjorie Randon Hershey. *Party Politics in America.* 10th ed. New York: Longman, 2003.

Chambers, William N., and Walter Dean Burnham, eds. *The American Party Systems: Stages of Political Development.* 2nd ed. New York: Oxford University Press, 1975.

Coleman, John J. *Party Decline in America: Policy, Politics, and the Fiscal State.* Princeton, N.J.: Princeton University Press, 1996.

Cox, Gary W., and Mathew D. McCubbins. *Legislative Leviathan: Party Government in the House.* Berkeley: University of California Press, 1993.

ONLINE READING ————. *Setting the Agenda: Responsible Party Government in the U.S. House of Representatives.* New York: Cambridge University Press, 2005.

Hofstadter, Richard. *The Idea of a Party System: The Rise of Legitimate Opposition in the United States, 1780–1840.* Berkeley: University of California Press, 1969.

Kayden, Xandra, and Eddie Mahe Jr. *The Party Goes On: The Persistence of the Two-Party System in the United States.* New York: Basic Books, 1985.

Milkis, Sidney M. *The President and the Parties: The Transformation of the American Party System since the New Deal.* New York: Oxford University Press, 1993.

Rohde, David W. *Parties and Leaders in the Post-reform House.* Chicago: University of Chicago Press, 1991.

Shafer, Byron, ed. *Beyond Realignment? Interpreting American Electoral Eras.* Madison: University of Wisconsin Press, 1991.

ONLINE READING Sundquist, James L. *Dynamics of the Party System: Alignment and Realignment of Political Parties in the United States.* Washington, D.C.: Brookings Institution, 1983.

ONLINE READING Wattenberg, Martin P. *The Decline of American Political Parties, 1952–1996.* Cambridge, Mass.: Harvard University Press, 1998.

According to the median voter theorem, political candidates should converge on the median, leading to policy moderation and centrist political campaigns. But what happens when we put an institution—political parties—into the mix? Some argue that, contrary to the median voter theorem, parties encourage policy divergence among candidates, and as a consequence, polarize our political system. How can this be? How do rational, self-interested candidates who want to win office end up polarizing voters because of the party label?

Almost every candidate in the American political system runs under a party label, so the rationality principle tells us that parties must be valuable for something. Parties facilitate collective action in the electoral system by helping candidates organize their campaigns. In Chapter 10, we saw that parties help voters choose among competing candidates, and many institutions, such as the Congress, are organized by party organizations. So association with a party is a valuable label for most political candidates—it helps them win office, and once there, helps them keep their seat.

Party leaders have their own interests, however, and some people argue that the parties encourage candidates to diverge from the center because the parties want to maintain a clear "brand label." This makes it easier for parties to recruit activists and attract donors (facilitating collective action) and to resolve collective choices in the policy-making process by presenting distinctive policy preferences.

So what about non-partisan elections? Do we see centrist behavior in these systems? The answer, not surprising once you know the principles of politics, is no. Interest groups and "non-partisan" voter organizations appear that look and function much as the political party does, only without the traditional party label.

The New York Times, October 28, 2006

Moderate Republicans Feeling Like Endangered Species

By Carl Hulse

Facing the loss of fellow moderates in the Nov. 7 elections, Republican centrists in the House and Senate are faulting Congressional and party leaders for pursuing a strategy dominated by conservative themes.

Leading moderates say Republicans concentrated on social wedge issues like same-sex marriage while pressing national security almost to the exclusion of popular wage and health policies that could have helped endangered Republicans in the Northeast and the Midwest

"There wasn't an impetus to help develop a political and legislative plan that incorporated the broad umbrella of philosophy in our party," said Senator Olympia J. Snowe, Republican of Maine, whom experts expect to be easily re-elected. "I think they always operated under the wrong assumption

History Principle

Based on their experience in elections since 2000, the Republican party leadership believed that a loyal party base would be large enough to lead to victory in 2006.

that you just appeal to the base and no more than that."

Ms. Snowe and other moderates, while holding out hope that most of their counterparts would hang on, were dismayed by the prospect of depleted ranks, saying it could lead to a more polarized Congress.

Two Senate Republicans often found in the small moderate bloc, Lincoln Chafee of Rhode Island and Mike DeWine of Ohio, are in serious jeopardy. Two leading House moderates are retiring, another lost a primary, and at least six others are in difficult re-election fights in Connecticut, New Hampshire, New York, Ohio, Pennsylvania and elsewhere.

The centrists said heavy losses outside strongholds in the South and parts of the West and Midwest could imperil the party's future. They say Republicans cannot sustain a long-term majority unless the party thrives throughout the country.

"There are some people who, because they are so pure and so sure of themselves, they are willing to run the risk of having the Republican Party no longer be national but be more regional," said Representative Sherwood L. Boehlert of New York, a respected moderate who is retiring. "They think they can maintain their majority as a regional party."

Conservatives say the overall party message was developed to draw the most loyal voters to the polls by emphasizing bedrock principles. The leader of one group that backed conservative candidates in Republican primaries, angering the moderate wing, said some moderates were in trouble simply because they strayed too far, alienating Republicans without attracting Democrats

"We have people who are certainly well left of the center of the Republican conference on all issues, including economic and growth issues," said the leader, Pat Toomey, a former congressman from Pennsylvania who heads the Club for Growth. "I'm not hoping they lose. But if they do, I think we will be able to recapture those seats with pro-growth candidates who distance themselves from Democrats."

Even conservatives acknowledge that the push did not make it easy for candidates in close races in New England and Ohio.

"It is a real quandary," Senator John Cornyn, Republican of Texas, said. "It is true that in order to motivate folks there has been an appeal made to turn out our conservatives, which by definition doesn't help those who are not as in tune with the base."

In past election cycles, Republican moderates, like their right-leaning Democratic colleagues in the South, have survived by emphasizing differences with their own party on pivotal issues. Independent voters at home have indicated a willingness to back their lawmakers and draw a distinction between them and the party.

But this year, given the Iraq war, dissatisfaction with President Bush and a series of Republican scandals, some voters no longer seem willing to separate the two.

"It appears we have finally pushed them far enough to vote for the Democratic Party," said Sarah Chamberlain Resnick, executive director of the Republican Mainstreet Partnership. "As a loyal Republican, I think that is scary."

Democrats have also made a concerted effort against vulnerable Republican moderates, which Senator

Collective-Action Principle

Republican Party strategists have to choose between staking out a conservative position that will mobilize a core group of voters, or taking a more moderate position that will appeal to a broader segment of voters—but may be so weak and indistinct that they end up attracting fewer voters overall.

Rationality Principle

Voting decisions are instrumental, but historically, congressional elections have often turned more on local and state politics than on national politics. In 2006, the war in Iraq nationalized the election, so moderate Republicans were unable to run away from Iraq or President Bush.

Susan Collins, another Republican of Maine, said was not much of a reward for those willing to try to work with the opposition party.

"There is no one who has voted more often with the Democrats than Linc Chafee," Ms. Collins said. "Yet that didn't stop them from going after him with everything they had. That is a good lesson."

Ms. Collins and Ms. Snowe noted that although voters indicate a strong desire for bipartisanship, some lawmakers most likely to be punished are the very ones who have reached across the aisle.

Representative Rahm Emanuel of Illinois, chairman of the Democratic Congressional Campaign Committee, made no apologies for focusing on Republican moderates and said Republicans should blame the party leaders for its approach.

"They left these guys to fend for themselves in districts that have been trending Democratic," Mr. Emanuel said. "What we did was recruit and fully fund our candidates."

Republicans leaning toward the middle on social, environmental and spending matters have been raising the alarm for months, saying the party was missing opportunities to bolster moderate candidates with measures on raising the minimum wage, expanding stem cell research and ethics reform.

But the minimum-wage increase died when it was tied to a move to repeal the estate tax, President Bush vetoed the stem cell measure, and the drive for ethics reform collapsed.

"I don't think the agenda has been particularly helpful," said Representative Michael N. Castle, Republican of Delaware, who said some Republicans had been dismissive of the centrists until the leadership was desperate for votes on major bills.

"I will be the first to say there are those in the Republican Party who feel moderates are essential only in terms of numbers," Mr. Castle said.

While Republican moderates struggle to maintain their numbers, some top Democratic challengers are from the more moderate wing of that party, raising the prospect that some gains will come from the right.

That possibility also gives Republican moderates hope that even if they number fewer, they could potentially band with Democrats in the center to influence measures.

"I think," Ms. Collins said, "the moderates in both parties could be empowered."

Policy Principle

GOP leaders believed that they needed a distinct conservative message in the election, and President Bush opposed many of these moderate measures on principle. The result was a strongly conservative policy message that hurt moderate Republicans.

12   Groups and Interests

FOR MORE THAN TWO DECADES, lobbyists for senior citizens, led by AARP (formerly called the American Association of Retired Persons), sought to add a prescription drug benefit to the Medicare program, on which most seniors depend for their health care. Many members of Congress opposed such a benefit because it would cost hundreds of billions of dollars. The pharmaceutical industry also feared that a Medicare prescription plan would open the way for government regulation of drug prices as well as other aspects of the industry. Through its political arm, the Pharmaceutical Research and Manufacturers of America (PhRMA), the pharmaceutical industry is one of the most powerful lobbies in Washington. Drug-company executives and corporate political action committees have contributed nearly $100 million to political campaigns since 2000, and a number of drug-industry lobbyists and executives were major donors to and fund-raisers for George W. Bush's presidential campaigns. The drug industry's political clout was, for years, an enormous impediment to the enactment of a Medicare prescription drug plan.

By the early 2000s, however, the industry had begun to face a number of economic and political problems. First, the high prices charged for prescription drugs were producing enormous pressure in Congress to reduce the patent protection enjoyed by drug-company products in order to allow cheaper generic drugs to enter the marketplace more rapidly. Second, many consumers had discovered that they could purchase drugs in Canada and Europe for as much as 75 percent less than what they paid in the United States. These foreign purchases, while illegal, are difficult to monitor and are costing the drug companies millions of dollars in profits. Finally, growing numbers of senior citizens were not able to afford their prescription drugs at all and so were simply not buying medicine—another source of lost profit for the industry.

In the face of these problems, PhRMA changed its lobbying strategy. Rather than continue to resist a Medicare drug plan, the industry moved to craft a plan of its own.

In 2002, the pharmaceutical industry formed an alliance with several other health-industry groups, including nursing home and hospital interests, to develop a new Medicare bill. AARP had a number of misgivings about the bill but lent its support, calculating that once a law was enacted, the "senior lobby" could secure favorable amendments over the ensuing years. The resulting legislation, enacted by Congress in November 2003, after the drug industry spent nearly $40 million lobbying on its behalf, appeared to be perfectly tailored to suit the industry's needs. Under the plan, Medicare subsidizes drug purchases for all seniors who agree to pay a modest monthly fee. The plan prohibits the government from attempting to force the companies to lower drug prices, leaves in place the ban on imported drugs, and does not address the issue of generic drugs. Since it began operation in 2006, the Medicare prescription plan has helped boost industry profits at a cost of tens of billions of dollars a year to the federal treasury. PhRMA's nursing home and hospital allies also won favorable treatment under the plan.[1] Seniors at long last got their drug

---

[1]Thomas B. Edsall, "2 Bills Would Benefit Top Bush Fundraisers," *Washington Post*, 22 November 2003, p. 1.

Inasmuch as an interest group is an organization in which a group of individuals work to achieve common policy-related goals, the difficulties associated with collective action are particularly acute. To overcome the obstacles to collective action, groups must provide individuals with incentives to join. Group politics is also organized in part by the goal-oriented activities of political entrepreneurs. Despite the obstacles to collective action, the number and types of interest groups in American politics proliferated throughout the twentieth century. Moreover, recognizing the importance of institutions in influencing political outcomes, groups strategically seek out institutional venues they believe will be most hospitable to their goals and interests.

plan, but in a form that cost the nation an enormous amount of money in funds that are being transferred from the pockets of hard-pressed middle-class taxpayers to the coffers of an already fabulously wealthy industry.

After the 2006 elections gave the Democrats control of both houses of Congress, Democratic leaders promised to take a new look at the prescription drug plan. In particular, they talked about undoing the provisions of the law that ban imported drugs and prohibit the government from attempting to lower drug prices. Some Democrats said the drug industry should be forced to give up some of its patent protection to allow more generics to enter the marketplace. The pharmaceutical industry responded quickly by hiring dozens of new Democratic lobbyists, who can be expected to have influence with the new leadership in Congress. These lobbyists included former staffers in the administration of President Bill Clinton—Joel Johnson, Steve Ricchetti, and Charles Brain—as well as George Crawford, a former chief of staff to the new House Speaker, Nancy Pelosi.[2] The pharmaceutical industry was not about to let a mere election interfere with its new source of income.

The story of the pharmaceutical industry illustrates several of our key principles of politics. First, pharmaceutical manufacturers and other interests engaged in political action for very definite purposes. The industry in particular was very much aware of its economic interests and based its support for or opposition to particular pieces of legislation on its calculation of the economic gain it was likely to reap. Second, to achieve their political purposes, firms and interests banded together and engaged in a collective effort to influence members of Congress, the president, and other key policy makers. Members of this coalition negotiated with one another to identify a policy approach on which they could all agree and then sought to bring about the enactment of legislation that reflected this approach. Third, control of a key policy-making institution matters a great deal. The pharmaceutical industry had devoted a great deal of effort to building ties to the Republican leadership of Con-

---

[2]Jeffrey H. Birnbaum, "In the Loop on K Street," *Washington Post*, 16 January 2007, p. A17.

gress. When Democrats ousted the GOP in 2006, the industry moved quickly to cultivate a relationship with the new leaders of America's premier lawmaking institution. Finally, history matters. In the United States, government control of the manufacture, distribution, and pricing of a product is historically viewed with considerable suspicion. This historical bias against government interference in the marketplace gave the manufacturers an advantage in arguing against government efforts to lower the prices of the drugs it was purchasing for Medicare recipients.

In this chapter, we examine some of the antecedents and consequences of interest-group politics in the United States. We analyze the group basis of politics, the problems that result from collective action, and some solutions to these problems. We seek to understand the character of the interests promoted by interest groups. We assess the growth of interest-group activity in recent American political history, including the emergence of "public interest" groups. We review and evaluate the strategies that competing groups use in their struggle for influence. Finally, we assess the question, Are interest groups too influential in the political process?

WHAT ARE THE CHARACTERISTICS OF INTEREST GROUPS?

An *interest group* is an organized group of individuals or organizations that makes policy-related appeals to government. Individuals form groups and engage in collective action to increase the chance that their views will be heard and their interests treated favorably by the government. Interest groups are organized to influence governmental decisions; they are sometimes referred to as lobbies.

Interest groups are sometimes confused with political action committees. The difference is that PACs focus on winning elections, and interest groups focus on influencing elected officials. Another distinction we should make is that interest groups differ from political parties: Interest groups tend to concern themselves with the *policies* of government; parties tend to concern themselves with the *personnel* of government.

Interest Groups Not Only Enhance Democracy . . .

There are an enormous number of interest groups in the United States, and millions of Americans are members of one or more groups, at least to the extent of paying dues or attending an occasional meeting. By representing the interests of such large numbers of people and encouraging political participation, organized groups can and do enhance American democracy. Organized groups educate their members about issues that affect them. Groups lobby members of Congress and the executive branch, engage in litigation, and generally represent their members' interests in the political arena. Groups mobilize their members for elections and grassroots lobbying efforts, thus encouraging participation. Interest groups also monitor government programs to make certain that they do not adversely affect their members. In all these ways, organized interests can be said to promote democratic politics.

interest group An organized group of individuals or organizations that makes policy-related appeals to government.

But Also Represent the Evils of Faction

The framers of the American Constitution feared the power that could be wielded by organized interests. James Madison wrote:

> The public good is disregarded in the conflict of rival [factions], . . . citizens . . . who are united and actuated by some common impulse of passion, or of interest, adverse to the rights of other citizens, or to the permanent and aggregate interests of the community.[3]

Yet the founding fathers believed that interest groups thrived because of freedom—the freedom, enjoyed by all Americans, to organize and express their views. To the framers, this problem presented a dilemma. If the government were given the power to regulate or in any way forbid efforts by organized interests to interfere in the political process, it would in effect have the power to suppress freedom. The solution to this dilemma was presented by Madison:

> Take in a greater variety of parties and interest [and] you make it less probable that a majority of the whole will have a common motive to invade the rights of other citizens. . . . [Hence the advantage] enjoyed by a large over a small republic.[4]

According to the Madisonian theory, a good constitution encourages multitudes of interests so that no single interest can ever tyrannize the others. The basic assumption is that competition among interests will produce balance and compromise, with all the interests regulating one another.[5] Today this Madisonian principle of regulation is called *pluralism*. According to pluralist theory, all interests are and should be free to compete for influence in the United States. Moreover, according to pluralist doctrine, the outcome of this competition is compromise and moderation, because no group is likely to be able to achieve any of its goals without accommodating itself to some of the views of its many competitors.[6]

There are tens of thousands of organized groups in the United States, but the huge number of interest groups competing for influence does not mean that all interests are fully and equally represented in the American political process. As we shall see, the political deck is heavily stacked in favor of those interests able to organize and wield substantial economic, social, and institutional resources on behalf of their cause. This means that within the universe of interest-group politics, it is political power—not some abstract conception of the public good—that is likely to prevail. Moreover, this means that interest-group politics, taken as a whole, is a political format that works more to the advantage of some types of interests than others. In general, a politics in which interest groups predominate is a politics with a distinctly upper-class bias.

pluralism The theory that all interests are and should be free to compete for influence in the government. The outcome of this competition is compromise and moderation.

ONLINE READING ○

---

[3]Alexander Hamilton, James Madison, and John Jay, *The Federalist Papers*, ed. Clinton L. Rossiter (New York: New American Library, 1961), no. 10, p. 78.

[4]Ibid., p. 83.

[5]Ibid.

[6]The best statement of the pluralist view is in David B. Truman, *The Governmental Process: Political Interests and Public Opinion* (New York: Knopf, 1951), chap. 2.

Organized Interests Are Predominantly Economic

When most people think about interest groups, they immediately think of groups with a direct and private economic interest in governmental actions, and, indeed, economic interest is one of the main purposes for which individuals and groups engage in political action. Interest groups are generally supported by groups of producers or manufacturers in a particular economic sector. Examples of this type of group include the National Petrochemical Refiners Association, the American Farm Bureau Federation, and the National Federation of Independent Business, which represents small-business owners. At the same time that broadly representative groups like these are active in Washington, specific companies—like Disney, Shell, IBM, and General Motors—may be active on certain issues that are of particular concern to them.

Labor organizations are equally active lobbyists. The AFL-CIO, the United Mine Workers, and the International Brotherhood of Teamsters are all groups that lobby on behalf of organized labor. In recent years, lobbies have arisen to further the interests of public employees, the most significant among these being the American Federation of State, County, and Municipal Employees.

Professional lobbies like the American Bar Association and the American Medical Association have been particularly successful in furthering their interests in state and federal legislatures. Financial institutions, represented by organizations like the American Bankers Association and America's Community Bankers, although often less visible than other lobbies, also play an important role in shaping legislative policy.

Recent years have witnessed the growth of a powerful "public interest" lobby purporting to represent interests whose concerns are not addressed by traditional lobbies. These groups have been most visible in the consumer protection and environmental policy areas, although public interest groups cover a broad range of issues. The Natural Resources Defense Council, the Union of Concerned Scientists, and Common Cause are all examples of public interest groups.

The perceived need for representation on Capitol Hill has generated a public-sector lobby in the past several years, including the National League of Cities and the "research" lobby. The latter group comprises universities and think tanks, such as Harvard University, the Brookings Institution, and the American Enterprise Institute, that have an interest in obtaining government funds for research and support. Indeed, universities have expanded their lobbying efforts even as they have reduced faculty positions and course offerings and increased tuition.[7]

All Groups Require Money and Leadership, and Most Need Members

Although there are many interest groups, most share certain key organizational components. First, most groups must attract and keep members. Usually, groups appeal to members not only by promoting political goals or policies that they favor

---

[7]Betsy Wagner and David Bowermaster, "B.S. Economics," *Washington Monthly*, November 1992, pp. 19–21.

but also by providing them with direct economic or social benefits. Thus, for example, AARP, which promotes the interests of senior citizens, at the same time offers members a variety of insurance benefits and commercial discounts. Similarly, many groups whose goals are chiefly economic or political also seek to attract members through social interaction and good fellowship. Thus the local chapters of many national groups provide their members with a congenial social environment while collecting dues that finance the national office's political efforts.

Second, every group must build a financial structure capable of sustaining an organization and funding the group's activities. Most interest groups rely on yearly membership dues and voluntary contributions from sympathizers. Many also sell members some ancillary services, such as insurance and vacation tours. Third, every group must have a leadership and decision-making structure. For some groups, this structure is very simple. For others, it can involve hundreds of local chapters that are melded into a national apparatus. Finally, most groups include an agency that actually carries out the group's tasks. This may be a research organization, a public relations office, or a lobbying office in Washington or a state capital.

Group Membership Has an Upper-Class Bias

Membership in interest groups is not randomly distributed in the population. People with higher incomes, higher levels of education, and management or professional occupations are much more likely to become members of groups than are those who occupy the lower rungs on the socioeconomic ladder.[8] Well-educated upper-income business and professional people are more likely to have the time and the money, and to have acquired through the educational process the concerns and skills, needed to play a role in a group or association. Moreover, for business and professional people, group membership may provide personal contacts and access to information that can help advance their careers. At the same time, corporate entities—businesses and the like—usually have ample resources to form or participate in groups that seek to advance their causes.

The result is that interest-group politics in the United States tends to have a very pronounced upper-class bias. Certainly, there are many interest groups and political associations that have a working-class or lower-class membership—labor organizations or welfare-rights organizations, for example—but the great majority of interest groups and their members are drawn from the middle and upper-middle classes. In general, the "interests" served by interest groups are the interests of society's haves. Even when interest groups take opposing positions on issues and policies, the conflicting positions they espouse usually reflect divisions among upper-income strata rather than conflicts between upper and lower classes.

In general, to obtain adequate political representation, forces from the bottom rungs of the socioeconomic ladder must be organized on the massive scale associated with political parties. Parties can organize and mobilize the collective energies of large numbers of people who, as individuals, may have very limited resources. Inter-

---

[8]Kay Lehman Schlozman and John T. Tierney, *Organized Interests and American Democracy* (New York: Harper & Row, 1986), p. 60.

est groups, on the other hand, generally organize smaller numbers of the better-to-do. Thus the relative importance of political parties and interest groups in American politics has far-ranging implications for the distribution of political power in the United States. As we saw in Chapter 11, political parties have declined in influence in recent years. Interest groups, on the other hand, as we shall see shortly, have become much more numerous, more active, and more influential in American politics.

Groups Form in Response to Changes in the Political Environment

If interest groups and our concerns about them were a new phenomenon, we would not have begun this chapter with James Madison. As long as there is government, as long as government makes policies that add value or impose costs, and as long as there is liberty to organize, interest groups will abound. And if government expands, so will interest groups. There was, for example, a spurt of growth in the national government during the 1880s and 1890s, arising largely from the first government efforts at economic intervention to fight large monopolies and regulate some aspects of interstate commerce. In the latter decade, a parallel spurt of growth occurred in national interest groups, including the imposing National Association of Manufacturers and numerous other trade associations. Many groups organized around specific agricultural commodities as well. This period also marked the beginning of the expansion of trade unions as interest groups. Later, in the 1930s, interest groups with headquarters and representation in Washington began to grow significantly, concurrent with that decade's expansion of the national government.

Over the past forty years, there has been an enormous increase both in the number of interest groups seeking to play a role in the American political process and in the extent of their opportunity to influence that process. The total number of interest groups in the United States today is not known. There are certainly tens of thousands of groups at the national, state, and local levels. One indication of the proliferation of such groups' activity is the growth over time in the number of PACs attempting to influence U.S. elections. Nearly six times as many PACs operated in 2008 as in the 1970s (Figure 12.1). A *New York Times* report, for example, noted that during the 1970s, expanded federal regulation of the automobile, oil, gas, education, and health-care industries impelled each of these interests to increase substantially its efforts to influence the government's behavior. These efforts, in turn, had the effect of spurring the organization of other groups to augment or counter the activities of the first.[9] Similarly, federal social programs have occasionally sparked political organization and action on the part of clientele groups seeking to influence the distribution of benefits and, in turn, the organization of groups opposed to the programs or their cost. For example, federal programs and court decisions in such areas as abortion and school prayer were the stimuli for political action and organization by fundamentalist religious groups. These groups include the Christian Coalition of America, the Family Research Council, the Traditional Values Coalition, Focus on the Family, and Christian Voice. Struggles over such issues as abortion and gay marriage have

History Principle

The explosion of interest-group activity has its origins in the expansion of the role of government, especially since the 1960s.

---

[9]John Herbers, "Special Interests Gaining Power as Voter Disillusionment Grows," *New York Times*, 14 November 1978.

FIGURE 12.1 PAC Count, 1974–2008

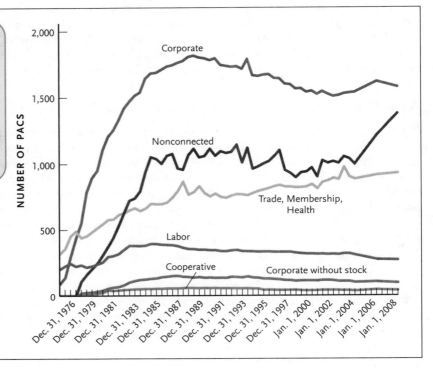

SOURCE: Federal Election Commission, "FEC Records Slight Increase in the Number of PACs," 17 January 2008 (www.fec.gov/press/press2008/20080117paccount.html).

helped these groups expand their membership roles and build a network of state and local chapters. As we have noted, religious conservatives played key roles in George W. Bush's presidential victories in both 2000 and 2004. In response, Bush launched his so-called faith-based initiative. Under the terms of this program, federal grants and contracts were given to religious organizations to provide social services to children, seniors, and others. By using so-called faith-based groups as federal contractors, Bush sought to reward religious conservatives for their loyalty to the GOP and ensure that these groups had a continuing stake in Republican success.

Another factor accounting for the explosion of interest-group activity in recent years was the emergence of a new set of forces in American politics that can collectively be called the new politics movement, a movement made up of upper-middle-class professionals and intellectuals for whom the civil rights and antiwar movements were formative experiences, just as the Great Depression and World War II had been for their parents. The crusade against racial discrimination and the Vietnam War led these young men and women to see themselves as a political force in opposition to the public policies and politicians associated with the nation's postwar regime. In more recent years, the forces of new politics have focused their attention on such issues as environmental protection, women's rights, and nuclear disarmament.

Members of the new politics movement constructed or strengthened public interest groups such as Common Cause, the Sierra Club, the Environmental Defense Fund, Physicians for Social Responsibility, the National Organization for Women, and the various organizations formed by the consumer activist Ralph Nader. Through these groups, new politics forces were able to influence the media, Congress, and even the judiciary and enjoyed a remarkable degree of success during the late 1960s and early 1970s in securing the enactment of policies they favored. New politics activists also played a major role in securing the enactment of environmental, consumer, and occupational health and safety legislation.

Among the factors contributing to the rise and success of new politics forces was technology. In the 1970s and 1980s, computerized direct-mail campaigns allowed public interest groups to reach hundreds of thousands of potential sympathizers and contributors. Today the Internet and e-mail serve the same function. Electronic communication allows relatively small groups to efficiently identify and mobilize their adherents throughout the nation. Individuals with perspectives that might be in the minority everywhere can become conscious of one another and mobilize for national political action through the magic of electronic politics. For example, only a handful of Americans scattered across the nation might be intensely concerned with the protection of whales and other aquatic mammals. These individuals form an active and vocal community on the Internet, however. They communicate with one another, reach out to potential sympathizers, and bombard politicians with e-mail. In this way, the Internet can facilitate group formation and political action, overcoming the limitations of geography and numbers.

HOW AND WHY DO INTEREST GROUPS FORM?

Pluralist theory argues that because individuals in the United States are free to join or form groups that reflect their common interests, interest groups should easily form whenever a change in the political environment warrants their formation. If this argument is correct, groups should form roughly in proportion to people's interests. We should find a greater number of organizations around interests shared by a greater number of people. The evidence for this pluralist hypothesis is weak, however. Kay Schlozman and John Tierney examined interest groups that represent people's occupations and economic roles.[10] Using census data and lists of interest groups, they compared how many people in the United States have particular economic roles and how many organizations represent those roles in Washington. For example, they found that (in the mid-1980s) 4 percent of the population was looking for work, but only a handful of organizations represented the unemployed in Washington.[11]

There is a considerable disparity in Washington representation across categories of individuals in the population, as Table 12.1 suggests. Schlozman and

---

[10]Schlozman and Tierney, *Organized Interests and American Democracy*.

[11]Of course, the *number* of organizations is at best only a rough measure of the extent to which various categories of citizens are represented in the interest-group world of Washington.

TABLE 12.1 Who Is Represented by Organized Interests?

ANALYZING THE EVIDENCE

What types of interests are most likely to be represented by interest groups? If interest-group politics is biased in favor of the wealthy and the powerful, should we curb group politics? What was James Madison's answer? Do you agree with Madison?

Economic Role of the Individual	U.S. Adults (%)	Orgs. (%)	Type of Org. in Washington	Ratio of Orgs. to Adults
Managerial/administrative	7	71.0	Business association	10.10
Professional/technical	9	17.0	Professional association	1.90
Student/teacher	4	4.0	Educational organization	1.00
Farmworker	2	1.5	Agricultural workers' organization	0.75
Unable to work	2	0.6	Organization for the handicapped	0.30
Other nonfarm workers	41	4.0	Union	0.10
Homemaker	19	1.8	Women's organization	0.09
Retired	12	0.8	Senior citizens' organization	0.07
Looking for work	4	0.1	Unemployment organization	0.03

Tierney note, for example, that there are at least a dozen groups representing senior citizens, but none for the middle-aged. Ducks Unlimited is an organization dedicated to the preservation of ducks and their habitats; turkeys, on the other hand, have no one working on their behalf. The pluralists' inability to explain why groups form around some interests and not others led some scholars to investigate the dynamics of collective action. Mancur Olson's work, mentioned in Chapter 1 and discussed later in this chapter, is the most well-known challenge to the pluralists. It is in Olson's insights that we find the basis for interest-group formation.

Interest Groups Facilitate Cooperation

Groups of individuals pursuing some common interest or shared objective—maintenance of a hunting and fishing habitat, creation of a network for sharing computer software, lobbying for favorable legislation, playing a Beethoven symphony, and so on—consist of individuals who bear some cost or make some contribution on behalf of the joint goal. Each member of the Possum Hollow Rod and Gun Club may, for example, pay annual dues and devote one weekend a year to cleaning up the rivers and forests of the club-owned game preserve.

We can think of this in an analytic fashion, somewhat removed from any of these examples, as an instance of two-person cooperation writ large. Accordingly, each one of a very large number of individuals has, in the simplest situation, two options in his or her behavioral repertoire: "contribute" or "don't contribute" to achieving the jointly shared objective. If the number of contributors to the group enterprise is sufficiently large, a group goal is achieved. However, there is a twist. If the group goal is achieved, then every member of the group enjoys its benefits, whether he or she contributed to its achievement or not.

FIGURE 12.2 The Prisoner's Dilemma

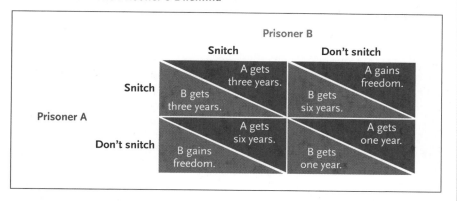

The Prisoner's Dilemma   Researchers often rely on the metaphor of the prisoner's dilemma when theorizing about social situations of collective action. According to this metaphor, two prisoners (A and B) who are accused of jointly committing a crime are kept in separate interview rooms. The arresting officers do not have enough evidence to persuade a judge to give the prisoners the maximum sentence, so the officers hope that one of the prisoners will provide the additional evidence they require. The prisoners know that the officers have scant evidence against them and that they will probably receive a less severe sentence or escape punishment altogether if they remain silent. Each prisoner is offered the same plea bargain: "Testify against the other prisoner in exchange for freedom, provided that your accomplice does not also testify against you. Remain silent, and you will possibly get the maximum sentence if your accomplice testifies against you."

If you assume that prisoners A and B are self-interested, rational actors (who, given the choice between the two alternatives, will choose the one that offers the best deal) and that they prefer less jail time to more, then they will face an unpleasant choice. Notice that in Figure 12.2, prisoner A is better off choosing to snitch no matter what prisoner B does. If B chooses to snitch, then A's choice to snitch gets A a three-year jail term, but a don't-snitch choice by A results in six years for A—clearly worse. On the other hand, if B chooses not to snitch, then A gets no jail time if he snitches instead of one year if he also chooses not to snitch. In short, A is always better off snitching. But this situation is symmetrical, so it follows that B is better off snitching, too. If both prisoners snitch, the prosecutor is able to convict both of them, and each serves three years. If they had both been *irrational* and kept silent, they would have gotten only one year each! In terms of game theory (from which the prisoner's dilemma is drawn), each player has a dominant strategy—snitching is best no matter what the other player does—and this leads paradoxically to an outcome in which each player is *worse* off.

The prisoner's dilemma provides the insight that rational individual behavior does not always lead to rational collective results. The logic of this situation is very compelling—if A appreciates the dilemma and realizes that B appreciates the dilemma, then A will still be drawn to the choice of snitching. The reasons for this are the temptation to get off scot-free (if he testifies and his accomplice doesn't) and

Collective-Action Principle

The prisoner's dilemma, a type of collective-action problem, explains why cooperation in groups can be difficult to achieve.

the *fear* of being suckered. The dilemma is brilliant because it applies to a wide range of circumstances.

Consider the swamp-clearing example described in Chapter 1, in which each person benefits from a drained swamp even if he or she does not provide the required effort. As long as enough other people do so, any individual can ride free on the efforts of the others. This is a multi-person prisoner's dilemma because not providing effort, like snitching, is a dominant strategy, yet if everyone avails himself or herself of it, it leads to an unwanted outcome: a mosquito-infested swamp. The prospect of free riding, as we shall see next, is the bane of collective action.

Rationality Principle

In a group setting, rational individuals have an incentive to free ride.

The Logic of Collective Action   Mancur Olson, writing in 1965, essentially took on the political science establishment by noting that the pluralist assumption of the time—that common interests among individuals are automatically transformed into group organization and collective action—was problematic. Individuals are tempted to free ride on the efforts of others, have difficulty coordinating multiple objectives, and may even have differences of opinion about which common interest to pursue (conflicts of interest).

Olson was at his most persuasive when talking about large groups and mass collective action, like many of the antiwar demonstrations and civil rights rallies of the 1960s. In these circumstances, the world of politics is a bit like the swamp-clearing example, where each individual has a rational strategy of not contributing. The logic of collective action makes it difficult to induce participation in and contribution to collective goals.

Olson claimed that this difficulty is severest in large groups, for three reasons. First, large groups tend to be anonymous. Each household in a city is a taxpaying unit and may share the wish to see property taxes lowered. It is difficult, however, to forge a group identity or induce households to contribute effort or activity for the cause of lower taxes on such a basis. Second, in the anonymity of the large-group context, it is especially plausible to claim that no one individual's contribution makes much difference. Should the head of a household kill the better part of a morning writing a letter to his city council member in support of lower property taxes? Will it make much difference? If hardly anyone else writes, then the council member is unlikely to pay much heed to this one letter; on the other hand, if the council member is inundated with letters, would one more have a significant additional effect? Finally, there is the problem of enforcement. In a large group, are other group members going to punish a slacker? By definition, they cannot prevent the slacker from receiving the benefits of collective action, should those benefits materialize. (Every property owner's taxes will be lowered if anyone's is.) But more to the point, in a large, anonymous group it is often hard to know who has and who has not contributed, and because there is only the most limited sort of group identity, it is hard for contributors to identify, much less take action against, slackers. As a consequence, many large groups that share common interests fail to mobilize at all—they remain *latent*.

This same problem plagues small groups, too, as the swamp-clearing problem in Chapter 1 reveals. But Olson argued that small groups manage to overcome the problem of collective action more frequently and to a greater extent than their larger counterparts. Small groups are more personal, and their members are therefore more vulnerable to interpersonal persuasion. In small groups, individual contributions may make a more noticeable difference, so that individuals feel that their contributions are more essential. Contributors in small groups, moreover, often know who they are and who the slackers are. Thus punishment, ranging from subtle judgmental pressure to social ostracism, is easier to effect.

In contrast to large groups that often remain latent, Olson called these small groups *privileged,* because of their advantage in overcoming the free-riding, coordination, and conflict-of-interest problems of collective action. It is for these perhaps counterintuitive reasons that small groups often prevail over, or enjoy greater privileges relative to, larger groups. These reasons, therefore, help explain why we so often see producers win out over consumers, owners of capital win out over owners of labor, and a party's elite win out over its mass members.

Selective Benefits: A Solution to the Collective-Action Problem

Despite the free-rider problem, interest groups offer numerous incentives to join. Most important, as Olson shrewdly noted in a profound theoretical insight, they make various "selective benefits" available only to group members (see Chapter 1). These benefits can be informational, material, solidary, or purposive. Table 12.2 gives some examples of the range of benefits in each of these categories.

Informational benefits are the most widespread and important category of selective benefits offered to group members. Information is provided through conferences, training programs, and newsletters and other periodicals sent automatically to those who have paid membership dues.

Material benefits include anything that can be measured monetarily, such as special services, goods, and even money. A broad range of material benefits can be offered by groups to attract members. These benefits often include discount purchasing, shared advertising, and perhaps most valuable of all, health and retirement insurance.

Another option identified in Table 12.2 is that of *solidary benefits.* The most notable of this class of benefits are the friendship and "networking" opportunities that membership provides. Another benefit that has become extremely important to many of the newer nonprofit and citizens' groups is what has come to be called consciousness-raising. One example of this can be seen in the claims of many women's organizations that active participation conveys to each member of the organization an enhanced sense of her own value and a stronger ability to advance individual as well as collective civil rights. A similar solidary or psychological benefit has been the mainstay of the appeal of group membership to discouraged and disillusioned African Americans since their emergence as a constitutionally free and equal segment of the population.

A fourth type of benefit involves the appeal of the purpose of an interest group. The benefits of religious interest groups provide us with the best examples of such *purposive benefits.* The Christian Right is a powerful movement made up of a number of interest groups that offer virtually no material benefits to their members. The growth and the success of these groups depend on the religious identification and affirmation of their members. Many such religiously based interest groups have arisen, especially at state and local levels, throughout American history. For example, both

Collective-Action Principle

Selective benefits are one solution to the collective-action problem.

informational benefits Special newsletters, periodicals, training programs, conferences, and other information provided to members of groups to entice others to join.

material benefits Special goods, services, or money provided to members of groups to entice others to join.

solidary benefits Selective benefits of group membership that emphasize friendship, networking, and consciousness-raising.

purposive benefits Selective benefits of group membership that emphasize the purpose and accomplishments of the group.

TABLE 12.2 Selective Benefits of Interest-Group Membership

Category	Benefits
Informational benefits	Conferences
	Professional contacts
	Training programs
	Publications
	Coordination among organizations
	Research
	Legal help
	Professional codes
	Collective bargaining
Material benefits	Travel packages
	Insurance
	Discounts on consumer goods
Solidary benefits	Friendship
	Networking opportunities
Purposive benefits	Advocacy
	Representation before government
	Participation in public affairs

SOURCE: Adapted from Jack L. Walker Jr., *Mobilizing Interest Groups in America: Patrons, Professions, and Social Movements* (Ann Arbor: University of Michigan Press, 1991), p. 86.

the abolition and the prohibition movements were driven by religious interest groups whose main attractions were nonmaterial benefits.

Ideology itself, or the sharing of a commonly developed ideology, is another important nonmaterial benefit. Many of the most successful interest groups of the past twenty years have been citizens' groups or public interest groups whose members are brought together largely around shared ideological goals, including government reform, election and campaign reform, civil rights, economic equality, "family values," or even opposition to government itself.

Political Entrepreneurs Organize and Maintain Groups

In a review of Olson's book, Richard Wagner noticed that Olson's arguments about groups and politics in general, and his theory of selective incentives in particular, had very little to say about the internal workings of groups.[12] In Wagner's experience, however, groups often came into being and then were maintained in good working order, not only because of selective incentives but also because of the ex-

---

[12]Richard Wagner, "Pressure Groups and Political Entrepreneurs," *Papers on Non-market Decision Making* 1 (1966): 161–70.

traordinary efforts of specific individuals—leaders, in ordinary language, or "political entrepreneurs" in Wagner's more colorful expression.

Wagner was motivated to raise the issue of group leaders because, in his view, Olson's theory was too pessimistic. Mass organizations in the real world—labor unions, consumer associations, senior citizens' groups, environmental organizations—all exist, some persisting and prospering over long periods. Contrary to Olson's suggestions, they seem to somehow get jump-started in the real world. Wagner suggests that a special kind of theory of selective incentives is called for. Specifically, he argues that certain selective benefits may accrue to those who organize and maintain otherwise latent groups.

Senator Robert Wagner (no relation) in the 1930s and Congressman Claude Pepper in the 1970s each had private reasons—electoral incentives—to try to organize laborers and the elderly, respectively. Wagner, a Democrat from New York, had a large constituency of working men and women who would reward him by reelecting him—a private, conditional payment—if he bore the cost of organizing workers (or at least bore the cost of facilitating their organization). And this he did. The law that bears his name, the Wagner Act of 1935, made it much easier for unions to organize in the industrial North.[13] Likewise, Claude Pepper, a Democratic congressman with a large number of elderly constituents in his South Miami district, saw it as serving his own electoral interests to provide the initial investment of effort to organize the elderly as a political force.

In general, a political entrepreneur is someone who sees a prospective dividend from cooperation. This is another way of saying that there is a latent group that, if it were to become manifest, would enjoy the fruits of collective action. For a price, whether in votes (as in the cases of Wagner and Pepper), a percentage of the dividend, nonmaterial glory, or other perks, the entrepreneur bears the costs of organizing, expends effort to monitor individuals for slacker behavior, and sometimes even imposes punishment on slackers (such as expelling them from the group and denying them any of its selective benefits).

 Rationality Principle

Organizing collective action can provide private benefits to a political entrepreneur.

To illustrate this phenomenon, there is a story about a British tourist who visited China in the late nineteenth century. She was appalled to see teams of men pulling barges along the Chang (Yangtze) River, overseen by whip-wielding masters. She remarked to her guide that such an uncivilized state of affairs would never be tolerated in modern societies like those in the West. The guide, anxious to please but concerned that his employer had come to a wildly erroneous conclusion, hastily responded, "Madam, I think you misunderstand. The man carrying the whip is *employed* by those pulling the barge. He noticed that it is generally difficult, if you are pulling your weight along a tow path, to detect whether any of your team members are pulling theirs or, instead, whether they are free riding on your labors. He convinced the workers that his entrepreneurial services were required and that they should hire him. For an agreed-on compensation, he monitors each team member's effort level, whipping those who shirk in their responsibilities. Notice, madam, that

---

[13]The Wagner Act made it possible for unions to organize by legalizing the so-called closed shop. If a worker took a job in a closed shop or plant, he or she was *required* to join the union there. "Do not contribute" was no longer an option, so that workers in closed shops could not free ride on the efforts made by others to improve wages and working conditions.

he rarely ever uses the whip. His mere presence is sufficient to get the group to accomplish the task."

Thus political entrepreneurs, such as the whip-wielding driver, may be thought of as complements to Olsonian selective incentives in that both provide ways of motivating groups to accomplish collective objectives. Indeed, if selective incentives *resolve* the paradox of collective action, then political entrepreneurs *dissolve* the paradox. Both are helpful, and sometimes both are needed to initiate and maintain collective action. Groups that manage, perhaps on their own, to get themselves organized with a low level of activity often take the next step of *creating* leaders and leadership institutions to increase the activity level and the resulting cooperation dividends. Richard Wagner, in other words, took Olson's theory of selective incentives and suggested an alternative explanation, one that made room for institutional solutions to the problem of collective action.

HOW DO INTEREST GROUPS INFLUENCE POLICY?

Interest groups work to improve the probability that they and their policy interests will be heard and treated favorably by all branches and levels of the government. The quest for political influence or power takes many forms. Insider strategies include gaining access to key decision makers and using the courts. Outsider strategies include going public and using electoral politics. These strategies do not exhaust all the possibilities, but they paint a broad picture of ways in which groups use their resources in the fierce competition for power.

Many groups employ a mix of insider and outsider strategies. For example, environmental groups like the Sierra Club lobby members of Congress and key congressional staff members, participate in bureaucratic rule making by offering comments and suggestions to agencies on new environmental rules, and bring lawsuits under various environmental acts, like the Endangered Species Act, which authorizes groups and citizens to come to court if they believe the act is being violated. At the same time, the Sierra Club attempts to influence public opinion through media campaigns and to influence electoral politics by supporting candidates who they believe share their environmental views and by opposing candidates who they view as foes of environmentalism.

In some cases, lobbyists' efforts to influence lawmakers raise serious ethical and legal questions. In March 2006, for example, the powerful Washington lobbyist Jack Abramoff was sentenced to nearly six years in federal prison for fraud, tax evasion, and conspiracy to bribe public officials. For many years, Abramoff had helped his clients gain favorable treatment from important members of Congress, including the former House majority leader Tom DeLay, in exchange for campaign contributions and cash payments. DeLay, along with another Abramoff crony, Robert Ney of Ohio, resigned from Congress after Abramoff made a plea deal and began providing information to federal prosecutors. Abramoff is the latest in a long line of unethical lobbyists, sometimes called influence peddlers, to wind up in prison. Often, though, the line between outright bribery and efforts by lobbyists to raise money for politicians in the hopes of future favors is very thin. Many Washington lobbyists double as fund-raisers for political campaigns. Though such activities do not constitute bribes, members of Congress are certainly likely to listen to the views of lobbyists on whom they rely heavily for campaign cash.

Direct Lobbying

Lobbying is an attempt by a group to influence the policy process through persuasion of government officials. Most Americans tend to believe that interest groups exert their influence through direct contact with members of Congress, but lobbying encompasses a broad range of activities that groups engage in with all sorts of government officials and the public as a whole.

The 1946 Federal Regulation of Lobbying Act defined a lobbyist as "any person who shall engage himself for pay or any consideration for the purpose of attempting to influence the passage or defeat of any legislation of the Congress of the United States." The 1995 Lobbying Disclosure Act requires all organizations employing lobbyists to register with Congress and disclose whom they represent, whom they lobby, what they are lobbying for, and how much they are paid. More than 7,000 organizations, collectively employing many thousands of lobbyists, are currently registered.

Lobbying involves a great deal of activity on the part of someone speaking for an interest. Lobbyists badger and buttonhole legislators, administrators, and committee staff members with facts about pertinent issues and facts or claims about public support of them.[14] Lobbyists can serve a useful purpose in the legislative and administrative process by providing this kind of information. In 1978, during debate on a bill to expand the requirement for lobbying disclosures, Democratic senators Edward Kennedy of Massachusetts and Dick Clark of Iowa joined with Republican senator Robert Stafford of Vermont to issue the following statement: "Government without lobbying could not function. The flow of information to Congress and to every federal agency is a vital part of our democratic system."[15]

Lobbying Members of Congress Interest groups also have substantial influence in setting the legislative agenda and in helping craft the language of legislation (Figure 12.3). Today sophisticated lobbyists win influence by providing information about policies to busy members of Congress. As one lobbyist noted, "You can't get access without knowledge. . . . I can go in to see John Dingell [chairman of the House Committee on Energy and Commerce], but if I have nothing to offer or nothing to say, he's not going to want to see me."[16] In recent years, interest groups have also begun to build broader coalitions and comprehensive campaigns around particular policy issues.[17] These coalitions do not rise from the grassroots but instead are put together

---

[14]For discussions of lobbying, see Jeffrey M. Berry, *Lobbying for the People: The Political Behavior of Public Interest Groups* (Princeton, N.J.: Princeton University Press, 1977); and John R. Wright, *Interest Groups and Congress: Lobbying, Contributions, and Influence* (Boston: Allyn & Bacon, 1996).

[15]"The Swarming Lobbyists," *Time*, 7 August 1978, p. 15.

[16]Daniel Franklin, "Tommy Boggs and the Death of Health Care Reform," *Washington Monthly*, April 1995, p. 36.

[17]Marie Hojnacki, "Interest Groups' Decisions to Join Alliances or Work Alone," *American Journal of Political Science* 41 (1997): 61–87; Kevin W. Hula, *Lobbying Together: Interest Group Coalitions in Legislative Politics* (Washington, D.C.: Georgetown University Press, 1999).

lobbying An attempt by a group to influence the policy process through persuasion of government officials.

FIGURE 12.3 How Interest Groups Influence Congress

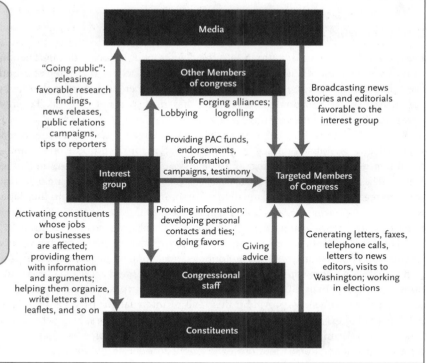

by Washington lobbyists who launch comprehensive campaigns that combine simulated grassroots activity with information and campaign funding for members of Congress.

Some interest groups are able to place their lobbyists directly on congressional staffs. In 2007, several experienced lobbyists and Washington insiders were "borrowed" by the new Democratic leadership to help organize the business of the new Congress. For example, Dennis Fitzgibbons, a lobbyist for DaimlerChrysler, was hired as chief of staff of the House Energy and Commerce Committee. In his capacity as an auto lobbyist, Fitzgibbons attempted to block efforts to force automakers to make vehicles more fuel efficient or to manufacture vehicles that would use alternative fuels. In his new job, Fitzgibbons plays a powerful role on the panel that will make the legislative decisions about these issues. At the same time, the House Democratic whip, James Clyburn of South Carolina, appointed Matt Gelman a senior adviser. Gelman will be on leave from Microsoft Corporation, where he serves as director of federal government affairs, a position to which he plans to return.[18] Both Fitzgibbons and Gelman said that they would not allow their roles as lobbyists to affect their new positions. These individuals, however, could be seen as "stealth lobby-

---

[18]Birnbaum, "In the Loop on K Street."

ists," unlikely to forget the needs of the corporations for which they recently worked and to which they were likely to return.

Not every interest group can embed a stealth lobbyist in Congress. Many, however, do the next best thing: They hire the spouses and relatives of members of Congress or important staffers to lobby for them. One extensive study of the congressional appropriations process conducted in 2006 found thirty instances in which lobbyists related to members and senior staffers of the House and Senate appropriations committees sought money in the appropriation bills their family members helped to write. In twenty-two cases, relatives were able to get specific language inserted in bills that guaranteed money for their clients.[19] Important members of Congress married to lobbyists include Representative John Dingell (D-Mich.), Senator Joe Lieberman (D-Conn.), and Representative Roy Blunt (R-Mo.).

Some interest groups have strong ties to the Democrats and others to the Republicans. Most interest groups, however, endeavor to maintain good relations with both political parties and are prepared to work with the party in power to achieve their legislative goals. When Republicans controlled Congress, trade associations and corporate interests hired Republican lobbyists and built close ties to the GOP leadership. In 2007, as Democrats returned to power, the same interest groups hired Democratic lobbyists and worked to build close ties to the new Democratic leadership. And when it came to campaign contributions, corporate interests cheerfully backed both sides, making sure to befriend the winners, whoever they might be.[20]

What happens to interests that do not engage in extensive lobbying? They often find themselves "Microsofted." In 1998, the software giant was facing antitrust action from the Justice Department and had few friends in Congress. One member of the House, Representative Billy Tauzin (R-La.), told Microsoft chairman Bill Gates that without an extensive investment in lobbying, the corporation would continue to be "demonized." Gates responded by quadrupling Microsoft's lobbying expenditures and hiring a group of lobbyists with strong ties to Congress. The result was congressional pressure on the Justice Department, resulting in a settlement of the Microsoft suit on terms favorable to the company. Similarly, in 1999, members of Congress advised Wal-Mart that its efforts to win approval to operate savings and loans in its stores were doomed to failure if the retailer did not greatly increase its lobbying efforts. "They don't give money. They don't have congressional representation—so nobody here cares about them," said one influential member. Like Microsoft, Wal-Mart learned its lesson, hired more lobbyists, and got what it wanted.[21]

Providing access is only one of the many services lobbyists perform. Lobbyists often testify on behalf of their clients at congressional committee and agency hearings; lobbyists sometimes help their clients identify potential allies with whom to construct coalitions; lobbyists provide research and information to government officials; lobbyists often draft proposed legislation or regulations to be introduced by

---

[19]Matt Kelley and Peter Eisler, "Relatives Have Inside Track in Lobbying for Tax Dollars," *USA Today,* 17 October 2006, p. 1.

[20]"Cash Flow: Congress Changes Hands—or Does It?" *Washington Post,* 7 January 2007, p. B2.

[21]Common Cause, "The Microsoft Playbook: A Report from Common Cause," 25 September 2000 (www.commoncause.org).

friendly lawmakers; lobbyists talk to reporters, place ads in newspapers, and organize letter-writing, e-mail, and telegram campaigns. Lobbyists also play an important role in fund-raising, helping to direct clients' contributions to members of Congress and presidential candidates.

Lobbying the President   All these efforts and more are needed when the target of a lobbying campaign is the president of the United States. So many individuals and groups clamor for the president's time and attention that only the most skilled and well-connected members of the lobbying community can hope to influence presidential decisions. One Washington lobbyist who filled this bill was Tom Kuhn, president of the Edison Electric Institute, a lobbying organization representing the electric power industry. Kuhn was a friend and former college classmate of President George W. Bush. In 2000, Kuhn was among the leading "Pioneers"—individuals who raised at least $100,000 for the Bush election campaign. Later the electric power companies represented by Kuhn gave nearly $20 million to congressional candidates in the 2001–2 election cycle. Kuhn's close relationship with the president and his efforts on behalf of the president's election gave the lobbyist enormous leverage with the White House. During the 2000 transition, candidates for a presidential nomination to head the Environmental Protection Agency felt compelled to pay "courtesy calls" to Kuhn. Subsequently, Kuhn led a successful effort to delay and weaken proposed EPA controls on electric power plant emissions of mercury, a toxic substance linked to neurological damage, especially in children.[22] This victory for the electric power lobby promised to save the industry hundreds of millions of dollars a year and illustrates the influence that can be brought to bear by a powerful lobbyist.

Lobbying the Executive Branch   Even when an interest group is very successful at getting its bill passed by Congress and signed by the president, the prospect of full and faithful implementation of that law is not guaranteed. Often a group and its allies do not pack up and go home as soon as the president turns their lobbied-for law over to the appropriate agency. On average, 40 percent of interest-group representatives regularly contact both legislative and executive branch organizations, whereas 13 percent contact only the legislative branch and 16 percent contact only the executive branch.[23]

   In some respects, interest-group access to the executive branch is promoted by federal law. The Administrative Procedure Act, first enacted in 1946 and frequently amended, requires most federal agencies to provide notice and an opportunity for comment before implementing proposed rules and regulations. So-called notice-and-comment rule making is designed to allow interests an opportunity to make their views known and participate in the implementation of federal legislation that affects them. In 1990, Congress enacted the Negotiated Rulemaking Act to encourage administrative agencies to engage in direct and open negotiations with affected

Policy Principle

Public policy can reveal the impact of lobbying.

---

[22]"Edison Electric Institute Lobbying to Weaken Toxic Mercury Standards," *Tri-State News* (Pike County, Pa., Orange County, N.Y., Sussex County, N.J.), 28 February 2003 (http://tristatenews.com).

[23]John P. Heinz, Edward O. Laumann, Robert L. Nelson, and Robert H. Salisbury, *The Hollow Core: Private Interests in National Policy Making* (Cambridge, Mass.: Harvard University Press, 1993).

interests when developing new regulations. These two pieces of legislation, which have been strongly enforced by the federal courts, have played an important role in opening the bureaucratic process to interest-group influence. Today few federal agencies would consider attempting to implement a new rule without consulting affected interests, who are sometimes known in Washington as "stakeholders."[24]

Cultivating Access Exerting influence on Congress or government agencies by providing their members with information about issues, support, and even threats of retaliation requires easy and constant access to decision makers. One interesting example of why groups need to cultivate and maintain access is provided by the dairy farmers. Through the 1960s, dairy farmers were part of the powerful coalition of agricultural interests that had full access to Congress and the Department of Agriculture. During the 1960s, a series of disputes over commodities prices broke out between the dairy farmers and the producers of corn, grain, and other agricultural commodities. Dairy farmers, whose cows consume grain, prefer low commodities prices, whereas grain producers obviously prefer high prices. The commodities producers won the battle, and Congress raised commodities prices, in part at the expense of the dairy farmers. In the 1970s, the dairy farmers left the agriculture coalition, set up their own lobby and political action groups, and became heavily involved in public relations campaigns and both congressional and presidential elections. Thus the dairy farmers lost their traditional access and had to pursue an "outsider" strategy. Indeed, the political fortunes of the dairy operations were badly hurt when they were accused of making illegal contributions to President Richard Nixon's reelection campaign in 1972.

Collective-Action Principle

Lobbying and cultivating access require coordination across the legislative and executive branches.

Cultivating access usually requires considerable time and effort, and a successful long-term strategy for gaining access may entail the sacrifice of short-run influence. For example, many of the most important organized interests in agriculture devote far more time and resources to cultivating the staff and trustees of state agriculture schools and county agents back home than to buttonholing members of Congress or bureaucrats in Washington.

Regulations on Lobbying As a result of the constant access to important decision makers that lobbyists seek out and require, stricter guidelines regulating the actions of lobbyists have been adopted in the last decade. For example, as of 1993, businesses may no longer deduct from their taxes the cost of lobbying. Trade associations must report to members the proportion of their dues that goes to lobbying, and that proportion may not be reported as a business expense. The most important attempt to limit the influence of lobbyists was the 1995 Lobbying Disclosure Act, which significantly broadened the definition of people and organizations that must register as lobbyists. According to the filings under this act, there were almost 11,500 lobbyists working the halls of Congress in 2006.

In 1996, Congress passed legislation limiting gifts from a single source to $50 and no more than $100 annually. It also banned the practice of honoraria, which

---

[24] For an excellent discussion of the political origins of the Administrative Procedure Act, see Martin Shapiro, "APA: Past, Present, Future," *Virginia Law Review* 72 (1986): 447–92.

had been used by special interests to supplement congressional salaries. But Congress did not limit the travel of representatives, senators, their spouses, or congressional staff members. Interest groups can pay for congressional travel as long as a trip is related to legislative business and is disclosed on congressional reports within thirty days. On these trips, meals and entertainment expenses are not limited to $50 per event and $100 annually. The rules of Congress allow its members to travel on corporate jets as long as they pay an amount equal to first-class airfare.

In 2007, congressional Democrats secured the enactment of a package of ethics rules designed to fulfill their 2006 campaign promise to bring an end to lobbying abuses. The new rules prohibited lobbyists from paying for most meals, trips, parties, and gifts for members of Congress. Lobbyists were also required to disclose the amounts and sources of small campaign contributions they collected from clients and "bundled" into large contributions. And interest groups were required to disclose the funds they used to rally voters to support or oppose legislative proposals. As soon as these new rules were enacted, lobbyists and politicians hurried to find ways to cirumvent them, and it remains to be seen whether these reforms will have any major impact.

Using the Courts

Institution Principle

Groups can turn to the courts if they are not successful in the legislative and executive branches.

Interest groups sometimes turn to the courts to augment other avenues of access. They can use the courts to affect public policy in at least three ways: (1) by bringing suit directly on behalf of the group itself, (2) by financing suits brought by individuals, and (3) by filing a companion brief as *amicus curiae* (literally, "friend of the court") to an existing court case.

Among the most significant modern illustrations of the use of the courts as a strategy for political influence are those that accompanied the "sexual revolution" of the 1960s and the emergence of the movement for women's rights. Beginning in the mid-1960s, a series of cases was brought into the federal courts in an effort to force the definition of a right to privacy in sexual matters. The effort began with a challenge to state restrictions on obtaining contraceptives for nonmedical purposes, a challenge that was effectively made in *Griswold v. Connecticut,* in which the Supreme Court held that states could neither prohibit the dissemination of information about, nor prohibit the actual use of, contraceptives by married couples. That case was soon followed by *Eisenstadt v. Baird,* in which the Court held that the states could not prohibit the use of contraceptives by single persons any more than it could prohibit their use by married couples. One year later, in the 1973 case of *Roe v. Wade,* the Court held that states could not impose an absolute ban on voluntary abortions. Each of these cases, as well as others, were part of the Court's enunciation of a constitutional doctrine of privacy.[25]

The 1973 abortion case sparked a controversy that brought conservatives to the fore on a national level. Conservative groups then made extensive use of the courts to whittle away the scope of the privacy doctrine. They obtained rulings, for exam-

---

[25]*Griswold v. Connecticut,* 381 U.S. 479 (1965); *Eisenstadt v. Baird,* 405 U.S. 438 (1972); *Roe v. Wade,* 410 U.S. 113 (1973).

ple, that prohibit the use of federal funds to pay for voluntary abortions. And in 1989, right-to-life groups were able to use a strategy of litigation that significantly undermined the *Roe v. Wade* decision—namely, in the case of *Webster v. Reproductive Health Services,* which restored the right of states to place restrictions on abortion.[26]

Another extremely significant set of contemporary illustrations of the use of the courts as a strategy for political influence are those found in the history of the National Association for the Advancement of Colored People. The most important of these court cases was *Brown v. Board of Education,* in which the Supreme Court held that legal segregation of the schools was unconstitutional.[27]

Business groups are also frequent users of the courts, because of the number of government programs that apply to them. Litigation involving large businesses is most mountainous in such areas as taxation, antitrust issues, interstate transportation, patents, and product quality and standardization. Often a business is brought to litigation against its will by virtue of initiatives taken against it by other businesses or by government agencies. But many individual businesses bring suit themselves to influence government policy. Major corporations and their trade associations pay tremendous amounts of money each year in fees to the most prestigious Washington law firms. Some of this money is expended in gaining access. A great proportion of it, however, is used to keep the best and most experienced lawyers prepared to represent the corporations in court or before administrative agencies when necessary.

The forces of the new politics movement made significant use of the courts during the 1970s and 1980s, and judicial decisions were instrumental in advancing their goals. Facilitated by changes in the rules governing access to the courts (the rules of standing are discussed in Chapter 8), the new politics agenda was clearly visible in court decisions handed down in several key policy areas. In environmental policy, new politics groups were able to force federal agencies to pay attention to environmental issues even when the agencies were not directly involved in activities related to environmental quality.

Mobilizing Public Opinion

Going public is a strategy that attempts to mobilize the widest and most favorable climate of opinion. Many groups consider it imperative to maintain this climate at all times, even when they have no issue to fight about. An increased use of this kind of strategy is usually associated with modern advertising. As early as the 1930s, political analysts were distinguishing between the "old lobby" of direct group representation before Congress and the "new lobby" of public relations professionals' addressing the public at large in order to reach Congress.[28]

One of the best-known ways of going public is to use institutional advertising. A casual scan of important mass-circulation magazines and newspapers will

going public The act of launching a media campaign to build popular support.

---

[26] *Webster v. Reproductive Health Services,* 492 U.S. 490 (1989).

[27] *Brown v. Board of Education,* 347 U.S. 483 (1954).

[28] Pendleton Herring, *Group Representation before Congress* (1928; repr., New York: Russell & Russell, 1967). See also Kenneth W. Kollman, *Outside Lobbying: Public Opinion and Interest Group Strategies* (Princeton, N.J.: Princeton University Press, 1998).

○ ONLINE READING

provide numerous examples of expensive and well-designed ads by the major oil, automobile, and steel companies, other large corporations, and trade associations. The ads show how much these organizations are doing for the country, for the protection of the environment, or for the defense of the American way of life. Their purpose is to create and maintain a strongly positive association between the organization and the community at large in the hope that the community's favorable feelings can be drawn on as needed for specific political campaigns later on.

During any month in 2007, for example, members of the radio or television audience might have been exposed to an advertisement sponsored by a consortium of defense contractors touting the virtues of antiballistic missile systems. Presumably few members of the audience were interested in purchasing such a weapons system, but positive feelings among constituents might encourage members of Congress to support its acquisition. During the same month, viewers and listeners might have been treated to ads touting the virtues of pork, poultry, and dairy products, all sponsored by consortia of producers. The purpose of such ads is to give Americans a positive feeling toward the products—a feeling that can be harnessed by the industry in the event of health scares or other problems that might arise in the future.

Many groups resort to protest because they lack the resources, contacts, or experience to use other political strategies. The sponsorship of boycotts, sit-ins, mass rallies, and marches by Martin Luther King's Southern Christian Leadership Conference and related organizations in the 1950s and 1960s is one of the most significant and successful cases of going public—in this case by calling attention to abuses—to create a more favorable climate of opinion. The success of these events inspired similar efforts on the part of women. Organizations such as the National Organization for Women used public strategies in their drive for legislation and in their efforts to gain ratification of the equal rights amendment. In 1993, gay rights groups organized a mass rally in their effort to eliminate restrictions on military service and other forms of discrimination against individuals based on their sexual preference.

Another form of going public is the grassroots lobbying campaign. In such a campaign, a lobby group mobilizes ordinary citizens throughout the country to write their representatives in support of the group's position. A grassroots campaign can cost anywhere from $40,000 to sway the votes of one or two crucial members of a committee or subcommittee to millions of dollars to mount a national effort aimed at the Congress as a whole. During the past several years, grassroots lobbying campaigns have played an important role in battles over presidential appointments. In 2005, President George W. Bush was presented with an opportunity to fill two Supreme Court vacancies, one occasioned by the death of Chief Justice William Rehnquist and the other by the retirement of Justice Sandra Day O'Connor. Immediately, liberal and conservative advocacy groups mobilized for battle. In particular, pro-choice and pro-life groups saw the two Supreme Court appointments as a decisive point in the long-standing national struggle over abortion. Pro-choice groups feared that Bush would appoint justices hostile to abortion rights, while pro-life groups feared that he would not. As each side urged its members to pressure Congress, hundreds of thousands of calls, letters, telegrams, and e-mails flooded Capitol Hill. These campaigns had a major impact on the appointment process, forcing

Collective-Action Principle

One means groups use to overcome collective-action problems is to mobilize public opinion in their support.

President Bush to withdraw the name of one nominee, Harriet Miers and very nearly derailing a second nominee, Samuel Alito.

Grassroots lobbying campaigns have been so effective in recent years that a number of Washington consulting firms specialize in them. Firms such as Bonner and Associates, for example, will generate grassroots telephone campaigns on behalf of or in opposition to important legislative proposals.

Grassroots lobbying has become more prevalent in Washington over the last couple of decades because the adoption of congressional rules limiting gifts to members has made traditional lobbying more difficult. This circumstance makes all the more compelling the question of whether grassroots campaigning has reached an intolerable extreme. One case in particular illustrates the extremes of "Astroturf" lobbying (a play on the brand name of an artificial grass used on many sports fields). In 1992, ten giant companies in the financial services, manufacturing, and high-tech industries began a grassroots campaign and spent millions of dollars to influence a decision in Congress to limit the ability of investors to sue for fraud. Retaining an expensive consulting firm, these corporations paid for the use of specialized computer software to persuade Congress that there was "an outpouring of popular support for the proposal." Thousands of letters from individuals flooded Capitol Hill. Many of the letters were written and sent by people who sincerely believed that investor lawsuits are often frivolous and should be curtailed. But much of the mail was phony, generated by the Washington-based campaign consultants; the letters came from people who had no strong feelings, or even no opinion at all, about the issue. More and more people, including leading members of Congress, are becoming skeptical of such methods, charging that these are not genuine *grass-roots* campaigns but instead represent *Astroturf* lobbying. Such "Astroturf" campaigns have increased in frequency in recent years as members of Congress grow more and more skeptical of Washington lobbyists and far more concerned about demonstrations of support for a particular issue by their constituents. But after the firms spent millions of dollars and generated thousands of letters to members of Congress in their attempt to influence legislation affecting investors' ability to sue for fraud, they came to the somber conclusion that "it's more effective to have 100 letters from your district where constituents took the time to write and understand the issue," because "Congress is sophisticated enough to know the difference."[29]

The Center for Responsive Politics, a "watchdog" group, estimates that the total cost of lobbying activities at the federal level in 2005 was $2.28 billion. This figure includes grassroots groups that spent a few thousand dollars and organizations like the U.S. Chamber of Commerce, which spent $243 million. The federal figure does not include lobbying at the state and local levels, but the amount spent to influence state legislatures and city and county councils is staggering. In 2005, according to the Center for Public Integrity, lobbyists spent $240 million to influence California lawmakers, $175 million in Texas, $150 million in New York, $130 million in Pennsylvania, more than $50 million apiece in Massachusetts and Minnesota, and slightly less than $50 million apiece in Washington, Maryland, Wisconsin, and

---

[29]Jane Fritsch, "The Grass Roots, Just a Free Phone Call Away," *New York Times*, 23 June 1995, pp. A1 and A22.

Michigan. All told, $1.16 billion was spent in forty-two states that require lobbyists to report their expenditures.

Using Electoral Politics

In addition to attempting to influence members of Congress and other government officials, interest groups seek to use the electoral process to elect the right legislators in the first place and ensure that those who are elected will owe them a debt of gratitude for their support. To put matters into perspective, groups invest far more resources in lobbying than in electoral politics. Nevertheless, financial support and campaign activism can be important tools for organized interests.

Political Action Committees   By far, the most common electoral strategy employed by interest groups is that of giving financial support to the parties or to particular candidates. But such support can easily cross the threshold into outright bribery. Therefore, Congress has occasionally made an effort to regulate this strategy. For example, the Federal Election Campaign Act of 1971 (amended in 1974) limits campaign contributions and requires that each candidate or campaign committee provide the full name and address, occupation, and principal business of each person who contributes more than $100. These provisions have been effective up to a point, considering the rather large number of embarrassments, indictments, resignations, and criminal convictions in the aftermath of the Watergate scandal.

The Watergate scandal itself was triggered when Republican "dirty tricksters" were caught breaking into the office of the Democratic National Committee in the Watergate apartment complex in Washington. An investigation quickly revealed numerous violations of campaign finance laws, involving millions of dollars that was passed from corporate executives to President Nixon's reelection committee. Many of these revelations were made by the famous Ervin Committee, whose official name and jurisdiction was the Senate Select Committee on Presidential Campaign Activities.

Reaction to Watergate produced further legislation on campaign finance in 1974 and 1976, but the effect has been to restrict individual rather than interest-group campaign activity. Individuals may now contribute no more than $2,000 to any candidate for federal office in any primary or general election. A political action committee, however, can contribute $5,000, provided it contributes to at least five different federal candidates each year. Beyond this, the laws permit corporations, unions, and other interest groups to form *political action committees (PACs)* and pay the costs of soliciting funds from private citizens for the PACs.

Electoral spending by interest groups has been increasing steadily despite the flurry of reform following Watergate. Table 12.3 presents a dramatic picture of the growth of PACs as the source of campaign contributions. The dollar amounts for each year indicate the growth in electoral spending. The number of PACs has also increased significantly—from 608 in 1974 to nearly 4,000 in 2004 (Figure 12.1). Although the reform legislation of the 1970s attempted to reduce the influence of special interests over elections, the effect has been almost the exact opposite. Opportunities for legally influencing campaigns are now widespread.

Given the enormous cost of television commercials, polls, computers, and other elements of the new political technology (see Chapter 11), most politicians are

political action committees (PACs) Private groups that raise and distribute funds for use in election campaigns.

TABLE 12.3 Presidential Campaign Receipts for PAC Contributions (in millions of dollars)

	1996	2000	2004
Primary Campaigns			
Winner of Republican primary	44.9	95.5	269.6
Winner of Democratic primary	42.5	48.1	234.6
All others	160.9	208.0	169.7
General Election Campaigns			
Major party grants	123.6	135.2	149.2
Republican candidate's legal and accounting expenditures	3.5	9.0	12.2
Democratic candidate's legal and accounting expenditures	4.2	11.5	8.9
Reform grant		12.6	
Conventions			
Major party grants	24.7	27.0	29.8
Host city of Republican convention	24.2	70.8	85.7
Host city of Democratic convention	20.4	29.3	56.8
Reform grant		2.5	
Total	449.0	649.5	1,016.5
Independent expenditures for candidates	0.6	12.7	85.7
Independent expenditures against candidates	0.8	2.0	106.7
Communication costs for	2.4	10.9	11.9
Communication costs against	0.3	0.6	0.4
Electioneering communications			40.8

SOURCE: Federal Election Commission.

eager to receive PAC contributions and are at least willing to give a friendly hearing to the needs and interests of contributors. It is probably not the case that most politicians simply sell their votes to the interests that fund their campaigns. But there is considerable evidence to support the contention that interest groups' campaign contributions do influence the overall pattern of political behavior in Congress and the state legislatures.

Indeed, PACs and campaign contributions provide organized interests with such a useful tool for gaining access to the political process that calls to abolish PACs have been quite frequent among political reformers. Concern about PACs grew through the 1980s and 1990s, creating a constant drumbeat for reform of federal election laws. Proposals were introduced in Congress on many occasions, perhaps the most celebrated being the McCain-Feingold bill. When it was originally proposed in 1996, that bill was aimed at reducing or eliminating PACs. But in a stunning about-face, when campaign finance reform was adopted in 2002 as the Bipartisan Campaign Reform Act (BCRA), it did not restrict PACs in any significant way. Rather, it eliminated unrestricted soft-money donations to the national political parties (see Chapter 10). One consequence of this reform was the creation of a host of 527 committees, named after the section of the tax code that defines them, which are often directed by former party officials but are nominally unaffiliated with the parties. These organizations are free to raise and spend as much money as they can. In addition to 527 committees, issue advocacy groups (501C3 and 501C4) are also permitted to engage in political spending under BCRA. For a fuller discussion of spending rules, see Chapter 10.

Campaign Activism Financial support is not the only way in which organized groups seek influence through electoral politics. Sometimes activism can be even more important than campaign contributions.

In 2008, a number of advocacy groups supporting the Democratic party made a concerted effort to register and mobilize millions of new voters, who they hoped would support Democratic candidates. Organized labor, of course, targeted union households. Civil rights groups worked to register African Americans. And a number of new groups, including MoveOn.org, labored to reach young people via the Internet. Their presumption was that young voters would disproportionately favor the Democrats.

Republicans, for their part, worked with church groups and such advocates of conservative causes as the National Rifle Association and the National Federation of Independent Business to register and mobilize voters likely to support the GOP. Ultimately, the Democrats were more successful than their Republican counterparts. Young people and African Americans came to the polls in larger-than-usual numbers to help hand the Democratic party and Barack Obama a solid victory.

The Initiative Another political tactic sometimes used by interest groups is sponsorship of ballot initiatives at the state level. The *initiative,* a device adopted by a number of states around 1900, allows proposed laws to be placed on the general election ballot and submitted directly to the state's voters. This procedure bypasses the state legislature and governor. The initiative was originally promoted by late-nineteenth-century Populists as a mechanism that allows the people to govern directly. Populists saw the initiative as an antidote to interest-group influence in the legislative process.

Ironically, many studies have suggested that most initiative campaigns today are sponsored by interest groups seeking to circumvent legislative opposition to their goals. In recent years, for example, initiative campaigns have been sponsored by the insurance industry, trial lawyers' associations, and tobacco companies.[30] The role of interest groups in initiative campaigns should come as no surprise since such campaigns can cost millions of dollars.

initiative A process by which citizens may petition to place a policy proposal on the ballot for public vote.

---

[30]Elisabeth R. Gerber, *The Populist Paradox: Interest Group Influence and the Promise of Direct Legislation* (Princeton, N.J.: Princeton University Press, 1999), p. 6.

Interest Groups: Are They Effective?

Do interest groups have an effect on government and policy? The short answer is yes. One of the best academic studies of the impact of lobbying was conducted in 2001 by John de Figueiredo of the Massachusetts Institute of Technology and Brian Silverman of the University of Toronto.[31] Figueiredo and Silverman focused on a particular form of lobbying: efforts by lobbyists to obtain "earmarks" (special, often disguised congressional appropriations) for colleges and universities on whose behalf they are working. Millions of dollars in earmarks are written into law every year.

The authors discovered that lobbying had an impact. The more money schools spent on lobbying activities, the larger the total quantity of earmarked funds they received. The extent of the effect, however, varied with institutional factors. Schools in states with a senator on the Senate Appropriations Committee received $18 to $29 in earmarks for every $1 spent on lobbying. Schools in congressional districts whose representative served on the House Appropriations Committee received between $49 and $55 for every $1 spent on lobbying. On the other hand, schools lacking such representation averaged only about $1 for every $1 spent on lobbying—hardly worth the effort.

These results suggest, as is so often the case, that institutions and politics are profoundly related. Schools without access to members of Congress in positions to help them cannot gain much from lobbying. Schools with such access still need to lobby to take advantage of the potential that representation on the Senate and House Appropriations Committees can give them. But if they do so, the potential return from lobbying is substantial.

GROUPS AND INTERESTS: THE DILEMMA OF REFORM

We would like to think that policies are the products of legislators' concepts of the public interest. Yet in reality, few programs and policies ever reach the public agenda without the vigorous support of important national interest groups. In the realm of economic policy, social policy, international trade policy, and even such seemingly interest-free areas as criminal justice policy (where in fact private prison corporations lobby for longer sentences for lawbreakers), interest-group activity is a central feature of American politics and public policy. But before we throw up our hands in dismay, it is worth remembering that the untidy process and sometimes undesirable outcomes of interest-group politics are virtually inherent aspects of democratic politics. At times, our larger interest in maintaining a vigorous and democratic political system may require us to tolerate such foolish things as tax subsidies for chicken poop.

---

[31]John de Figueiredo and Brian S. Silverman, "Academic Earmarks and the Returns to Lobbying" working paper 9064, National Bureau of Economic Research, 2002; substantially rev., 2003 (web.mit.edu/jdefig/www/papers/academic_earmarks.pdf).

Interest Groups and Representation

As noted in the chapter, Americans have been attuned to the dangers of organized interests since the earliest days of the republic. James Madison, in *Federalist* 10, notes the concern of "our most considerate and virtuous citizens" regarding factions, a "dangerous vice" of "popular governments."[1] Yet Madison also writes that the "causes of faction are ... sown in the nature of man" due to our tendency to form different opinions and passions under conditions of political liberty.[2] Thus the problem of faction, or what we might term the dangers of interest groups, is a part of democratic politics. Madison proposed a two-pronged solution that included (1) representation and (2) extending the "sphere" of interests and factions by having a larger society. In this chapter, we have looked at the theory of pluralism (which corresponds to the second part of Madison's solution): this is the idea that the number and diversity of interests serves both to moderate the influence of any particular group and to make political moderation more likely. How, though, might *representation* serve to check the influence of interest groups?

On one level, we might expect that the presence and power of interest groups would hinder representation. Let us take the U.S. Congress as our example. If we view the task of the House and the Senate to be the expression of the interests of their constituents, we can see why interest groups may pose a problem. While interest groups lend financial support to candidates as part of their effort to influence them, critics of these contributions argue that interest groups distort the legislative process and that "special interest money is drowning out representation."[3] The latter criticism focuses on the concern that because members of Congress generally rely on contributions to fund their reelection campaigns, they may serve the interests of their backers rather than their constituents.

PAC type	Contributions to Candidates (in millions)		
	1999–00	2001–02	2003–04
Total	259.8	282.0	310.5
Corporate	91.5	99.6	115.6
Labor	51.6	53.9	52.1
Trade/membership/health	71.8	46.3	83.2
Nonconnected	37.3	75.1	52.5
Cooperative	2.4	2.7	2.9
Corporation without stock	5.3	4.4	4.2

[1] James Madison, *Federalist* 10, in *The Federalist Papers*, ed. Clinton Rossiter (New York: Penguin, 1961), 77.
[2] *Ibid.* 78–79.
[3] Richard Bolling, "Money in Politics," *Annals of the American Academy of Political and Social Science*, Vol. 486 (July 1986): 76–85, 80.

Yet Madison suggested that representation can "refine and enlarge the public views" in part because these views pass through a select body. Members of Congress face a particular dilemma. While Senators and Representatives "may wish to develop expert-informed legislation," their constituents are rarely experts on policy intricacies.[4] In committee hearings, some members of Congress engage in detailed policy discussion, while others "routinely engage in unscientific anecdotal discourse aimed at constituents."[5] Research by Kevin Esterling suggests that interest groups contribute more heavily to members of Congress who have "a higher analytical capacity to work on policies" because these groups want to be sure that the information they provide receives a more attentive and expert audience.

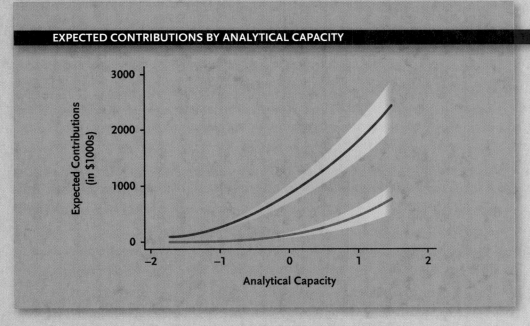

EXPECTED CONTRIBUTIONS BY ANALYTICAL CAPACITY

From this perspective, interest groups do not distort policy, but actually foster political behavior that leads to better policies. Keeping this in mind, we may note that Madison argued that representation helps to prevent the evils of faction not by ensuring that elected officials listen to and serve only their constituents, but rather because of the qualities—"wisdom ... patriotism and love of justice"—of those to whom government is delegated.[6]

[4] Kevin M. Esterling, "Buying Expertise: Campaign Contributions and Attention to Policy Analysis in Congressional Committees," *The American Political Science Review*, Vol. 101 (February 2007): 93–109, 93.
[5] *Ibid*. 93.
[6] Madison, *Federalist* 10, 82.

When Madison wrote that "liberty is to faction what air is to fire,"[32] he meant that the organization and the proliferation of interests were inevitable in a free society. To seek to place limits on the organization of interests, in Madison's view, would be to limit liberty itself. Madison believed that interests should be permitted to regulate themselves by competing with one another. As long as competition among interests was free, open, and vigorous, there would be some balance of power among them, and none would be able to dominate the political or governmental process. The Analyzing the Evidence unit in this chapter takes a closer look at Madison's solution and some related research.

There is considerable competition among organized groups in the United States. Nevertheless, interest-group politics is not as free of bias as Madisonian theory might suggest. Although the weak and the poor do occasionally become organized to assert their rights, interest-group politics is generally a form of political competition in which the wealthy and the powerful are best able to engage.

Moreover, although groups sometimes organize to promote broad public concerns, interest groups more often represent relatively narrow, selfish interests. Small, self-interested groups can be organized much more easily than large and more diffuse collectives. For one thing, the members of a relatively small group—say, bankers or hunting enthusiasts—are usually able to recognize their shared interests and the need to pursue them in the political arena. Members of large and more diffuse groups—say, consumers or potential victims of firearms—often find it difficult to recognize their shared interests or the need to engage in collective action to achieve them.[33] This is why causes presented as public interests by their proponents often turn out, upon examination, to be private interests wrapped in a public mantle.

One additional answer to the problem of interest-group power is strong political parties. A number of political scientists, including the late V. O. Key, argued that unlike interest groups, strong political parties mobilize the have-nots and offer them a voice in political affairs.[34] As we saw in Chapter 11, American political parties today lack the cohesion and the discipline of their nineteenth-century forebears. The decline of party power is indeed one of the reasons interest groups have grown in importance over the past century. For political support, contemporary politicians rely on organized interests and electoral resources that once were controlled by party leaders. Strong political parties, though, create their own problems. America's experiment with "machine politics" was often associated with governmental incompetence, public fraud, and widespread corruption. Few Americans are ready to return to the good old days of Tammany Hall.

Thus we have a dilemma to which there is no ideal answer. To regulate interest-group politics is, as Madison warned, to limit freedom and expand governmental power. Not to regulate interest-group politics, on the other hand, may be to ignore justice. Those who believe that there are simple solutions to the issues of political life would do well to ponder this problem.

ONLINE READING ○

[32]Hamilton, Madison, and Jay, *The Federalist Papers*, no. 10.

[33]Mancur Olson Jr., *The Logic of Collective Action: Public Goods and the Theory of Groups* (1965; repr., Cambridge, Mass.: Harvard University Press, 1971).

[34]V. O. Key, *Southern Politics in State and Nation*, rev. ed. (Knoxville: University of Tennessee Press, 1984).

Rationality Principle	Collective-Action Principle	Institution Principle	Policy Principle	History Principle
In a group setting, rational individuals have an incentive to free ride. Organizing collective action can provide private benefits to a political entrepreneur.	The prisoner's dilemma, an example of a collective-action problem, explains why cooperation in groups can be difficult to achieve. Selective benefits are one solution to the collective-action problem. Lobbying and cultivating access require coordination across the legislative and executive branches. One means groups use to overcome collective-action problems is to mobilize public opinion in their support.	Groups can turn to the courts if they are not successful in the legislative and executive branches.	Public policy can reveal the impact of lobbying.	The explosion of interest-group activity has its origins in the expansion of the role of government, especially since the 1960s.

SUMMARY

Efforts by organized groups to influence government and policy are becoming an increasingly important part of American politics. Such interest groups use a number of strategies to gain power.

Lobbying is the attempt to influence the policy process through the persuasion of government officials. Lobbyists—individuals who receive some form of compensation for lobbying—are required to register with the House and the Senate. In spite of an undeserved reputation for corruption, lobbyists serve a useful function, providing members of Congress and other government officials with a vital flow of information.

Access is participation in government. Most groups build up access over time through great effort. They work years to get their members into positions of influence on congressional committees.

Litigation sometimes serves interest groups when other strategies fail. Groups may bring suit on their own behalf, finance suits brought by individuals, or file *amicus curiae* briefs.

Going public is an effort to mobilize the widest and most favorable climate of opinion. Advertising is a common technique in this strategy. Others are boycotts, strikes, rallies, and marches.

Groups engage in electoral politics by embracing one of the major parties, usually through financial support but perhaps through a nonpartisan strategy. Interest groups' campaign contributions are now flowing into the coffers of candidates at a faster rate than ever before.

The group basis of politics, present since the founding, is both a curse and a blessing. In overcoming the hurdles of collective action, groups are an important means by which Americans participate in the political process and influence its outcomes. But participation in group life does not draw representatively from the population. So while it increases citizens' involvement, influence is not evenly distributed. Collective action thus remains a dilemma.

FOR FURTHER READING

Ainsworth, Scott. *Analyzing Interest Groups*. New York: Norton, 2002.

Alexander, Robert, ed. *The Classics of Interest Group Behavior*. New York: Wadsworth, 2005.

Birnbaum, Jeffrey H. *The Money Men*. New York: Crown, 2000.

Cigler, Allan J., and Burdett A. Loomis, eds. *Interest Group Politics*. 7th ed. Washington, D.C.: Congressional Quarterly Press, 2006.

ONLINE READING Esterling, Kevin. *The Political Economy of Expertise*. Ann Arbor: University of Michigan Press, 2004.

ONLINE READING Kollman, Kenneth W. *Outside Lobbying: Public Opinion and Interest Group Strategies*. Princeton, N.J.: Princeton University Press, 1998.

Lowi, Theodore J. *The End of Liberalism: The Second Republic of the United States*. 2nd ed. New York: Norton, 1979.

ONLINE READING Moe, Terry M. *The Organization of Interests: Incentives and the Internal Dynamics of Political Interest Groups*. Chicago: University of Chicago Press, 1980.

Nownes, Anthony. *Total Lobbying: What Lobbyists Want and How They Try to Get It*. New York: Cambridge University Press, 2006.

Olson, Mancur, Jr. *The Logic of Collective Action: Public Goods and the Theory of Groups*. 1965. Reprinted with new preface and appendix. Cambridge, Mass.: Harvard University Press, 1965.

Rosenthal, Alan. *The Third House: Lobbyists and Lobbying in the States*. Washington, D.C.: Congressional Quarterly Press, 2001.

Rozell, Mark, Clyde Wilcox, and David Madland. *Interest Groups in American Campaigns*. Washington, D.C.: Congressional Quarterly Press, 2005.

ONLINE READING Sheingate, Adam. *The Rise of the Agricultural Welfare State: Institutions and Interest Group Power in the United States, France, and Japan*. Princeton, N.J.: Princeton University Press, 2003.

Truman, David B. *The Governmental Process: Political Interests and Public Opinion*. New York: Knopf, 1951

Historically, lobbyists have taken a bipartisan approach. After all, they don't know which party will be in power after the next election, and most interest groups organize around narrow interests that can often be accommodated by either a Democratic or Republican majority.

After the 1994 election, however, the newly elected Republican majority in Congress decided that lobbying in Washington, DC, needed to change. Members such as Tom DeLay of Texas believed that the Republicans should cement their influence among private lobbying firms as part of the effort to transform their electoral coalition into a lasting Republican "revolution."

The K Street Project was a broad initiative to place former Republican staffers and other loyalists in the lobbying firms that congregate on K Street, one of the main thoroughfares of Washington, DC. The Republicans' logic combined two of the principles of politics—the rationality and collective action principles. By placing individuals in these firms who shared the interests of the GOP, the firms could be used to help build support coalitions.

The K Street Project succeeded for twelve years, until the elections of 2006. With a new Democratic majority and DeLay's departure from Congress, would a Democratic version of the K Street Project replace the GOP machine? As the story below shows, lobbying firms quickly became interested in working with Democrats, as the rationality principle would suggest. But Democrats claim that their historical legacy is different from the Republicans, and they will reform rather than take over the K Street Project.

The New York Times, November 14, 2007

As Guard Changes in Congress, Lobbyists Scramble to Get in Step

BY JEFF ZELENY

Republicans do not cede control of Congress for nearly two months, but money, power and influence are already beginning to change hands. The political economy, at least here in the capital, is humming for Democrats.

Democratic lobbyists are fielding calls from pharmaceutical companies, the oil and gas industry and military companies, all of which had grown accustomed to patronizing Republicans, as the environment in Washington abruptly shifts.

Take, for example, Vic Fazio, a California Democrat who rose through the ranks of Congress and reveled in the majority for all but 4 of his 20 years in office. In his second career as a lobbyist, Mr. Fazio did not experience the pleasures of Democratic rule—until now. Suddenly he is in demand.

For Mr. Fazio, who is close to Representative Nancy Pelosi, the California Democrat who is set to become House speaker, the power switch is, quite simply, good for business. Companies are scrambling to fortify lobbying teams with well-connected Democrats.

While Mr. Fazio declined to divulge his still-evolving list of prospective new clients at the law firm Akin Gump Strauss Hauer & Feld, he said he intended to bring in Democratic reinforcements to cover the load. "I'll just have more to do and have a little more help to do it," he said.

The Republican Party lost its grip on Congress and is now bracing to lose its hold over K Street, the bustling corridor that has become synonymous with the lobbying industry. The so-called K Street Project, an effort engineered by Republicans to dominate the trade, is unraveling, and Democrats say they intend to pass sweeping reforms rather than reverse the project for their benefit.

Democrats say the changing of the guard provides a raft of opportunities, second only to winning the presidency.

Former members of Congress who left Washington have placed confidential calls to headhunters, wondering whether firms are hiring. (They are.) Former staff members have fielded inquiries from lobbying shops that have an urgent need for people with current contacts and old relationships with Democratic leaders. One prominent lobbyist said a former Senate aide was offered a starting salary of $500,000.

Though this is the moment Democrats have been craving—winning a majority so they can help shape politics and policy—some senior aides are now tempted to leave Capitol Hill to become lobbyists and potentially quadruple their salaries. At the same time, some Republicans began receiving materials on unemployment benefits this week as the party sheds thousands of jobs, relinquishing staff committee assignments and leadership posts in both chambers for the first time in 12 years.

"If you're a Democrat, it's a good time to be looking for work," said David Urban, a Republican who is the managing director of American Continental Group, a bipartisan lobbying firm. "For Republicans, there is a little bit of panic that sets in when people realize they have to move out of their office into a cubicle."

* * *

Even though most firms are bipartisan, the shift in the balance of power has resulted in a shift of responsibilities between Republicans and Democrats.

"I've told my Democratic partners it's time for them to buy some suits," said Wayne Berman, a well connected Republican lobbyist. "I went out and bought two new fishing rods and looked into yoga classes."

He was joking, sort of.

Even before Election Day, the pharmaceutical industry hired Democrats to bolster its public relations efforts, hoping to ease the blow if Republicans lost their majority and Democrats followed through on pledges to let the government negotiate prescription drug prices.

"You literally have to create war games to plan for worst-case scenarios," said Ken Johnson, the vice president for government affairs at the leading trade association for drug companies. "We've got a lot of friends on the Democratic side, but clearly we need some more."

Acquiring those friends, however, may not be easy.

Steve Elmendorf, a longtime senior adviser to former Representative Richard A. Gephardt who began working as a lobbyist at Bryan Cave Strategies in 2005, said Democrats in the House and the Senate would operate differently.

"The Republicans' view of lobbying is we give people money, we buy them lunch and then go up and tell them what to do," said Mr. Elmendorf, whose client roster included Shell Oil and Ford before the election and has grown since then. "We go in and make public policy arguments. The business community is going to have to reorient their view."

As Democrats prepare for January, implications of a change in power extend across Washington.

Lawyers say they expect their business to increase if House Democrats follow through on their pledge to investigate the Bush administration. Real estate agents paid careful attention to the election results, too, sending welcome packets to newly elected Democrats.

"Because both the House and the Senate went to the Democrats, there will be a new wave and new energy,"

said Michael Rankin, managing partner of the Washington office of Sotheby's International Realty. "A lot of people from around the country will be coming to Washington."

* * *

Though the supply and demand of lobbyists is shifting, well-connected Republicans have hardly been put out of work, particularly given the narrow majority in the Senate. Many lobbying firms, recoiling from a year of controversy and scandal, sell continuity as the most valued asset.

"As we move into a new Congress, people are wiser and they learn to distrust quick fixes," said Nick Allard, a Democratic lobbyist at Patton Boggs, the city's largest firm. "That's one reason why the lobbying scandal fell apart like a political Ponzi scheme: it oversold the notion of political access."

Two days after the election, when it first became clear that the levers of power were shifting, a team of lobbyists at Patton Boggs prepared an analysis of what its clients could expect from a Democratic takeover.

To place the change of power in perspective and to lighten the mood, they opened with the timeless tale from Dr. Seuss: "If I ran the zoo."

Collective-Action Principle

Lobbying groups may have to adapt their appeals in order to build relationships and construct coalitions among the new Democratic majority.

13

The Media

IN MARCH 2003, American and British forces attacked Iraq to oust long-time Iraqi dictator Saddam Hussein. For the first time in history, reporters accompanied the troops into battle and provided real-time broadcasts from the battlefront twenty-four hours a day, seven days a week. The reporters' presence of course was no accident. Allowing journalists to accompany the troops was part of a purposeful Defense Department strategy. Military planners believed that the so-called embedded reporters would quickly identify with the troops, whose hardships they shared, and write positive accounts of their activities. Here was a case where U.S. military policies were shaped by the desire to obtain favorable news coverage rather than by the anticipation of combat effectiveness. And for the most part, this Defense Department strategy was successful. The journalists' identification with the troops was so complete that writers often used the pronoun *we* when discussing military operations.

While the embedded reporters generally provided favorable accounts of U.S. military activities, their colleagues behind the lines reporting from U.S. headquarters in Kuwait or commenting from New York and Washington were not always as kind. Before the war, there had been clear divisions within the media regarding the desirability of attacking Iraq. Generally speaking, the more liberal, Democratic-leaning press, led by *The New York Times* and several of the networks, had been sharply critical of President Bush's diplomatic efforts and his intention to oust Saddam. For the most part, the more conservative, Republican-leaning media, led by such publications as *The Washington Times* and *The Weekly Standard* and by the Fox News Channel, staunchly supported the president's policies. Some divisions on the war, to be sure, manifested themselves even within these camps. For example, the normally liberal and pro-Democratic *Washington Post* and *The New Republic* backed the war, whereas Pat Buchanan's *American Conservative* opposed American intervention in Iraq.

Policy Principle

The media do not make policy, but policy is often made in response to or anticipation of the media's reactions.

American forces had barely crossed the Iraqi border when journalists—particularly those who had been critical of President George W. Bush's policies—began questioning the conduct of the American campaign. Some journalists and commentators, including several retired military officers employed by the networks, suggested that not enough troops had been committed to the battle, that supplies were inadequate, that Iraqi resistance had been underestimated, and that the war could easily become a Vietnam-style "quagmire." Defense Secretary Donald Rumsfeld and military briefers were subjected to withering questioning from journalists, who clearly doubted the veracity of the answers they were given. Some commentators, again resorting to Vietnam-era imagery, referred to a "credibility gap."

The gap became an ever-widening chasm when Iraqi resistance to the U.S. occupation began to produce a steady stream of American casualties and nightly newscasts featuring violence and mayhem in Iraq's cities and villages. The media also gave enormous coverage to charges that U.S. forces had abused Iraqi prisoners at the Abu Ghraib detention facility near Baghdad. Night after night, images of cowering Iraqi inmates mistreated by smiling American guards dominated the news.

PREVIEWING THE PRINCIPLES

Media coverage can be analyzed in terms of the interests of members of the media, politicians, and consumers. The conflicting goals of politicians and members of the media help explain their adversarial relationship. This relationship can be analyzed as a prisoner's dilemma. Both politicians and members of the media benefit from mutual cooperation but are tempted to defect on occasion to secure even larger gains. The historical relationship between government and media in the United States differs from that in other democracies because of the freedom of the press, guaranteed by the Constitution. This guarantee has led the United States to favor regulation of the press over public ownership.

In 2006, daily media accounts of the continuing violence and chaos in Iraq persuaded many American voters that it was time for a change and helped the Democrats win control of both houses of Congress. In 2007, when President Bush announced that he planned to stabilize Iraq by sending more American troops, the media gave extensive and respectful coverage to congressional critics who asserted that the president's efforts were destined to fail. And in 2008 the media remained skeptical of Republican claims that the president's "surge" policy was leading to victory over Islamist fighters in Iraq.

One feature of American journalism highlighted by these events is the tendency of the press to criticize programs, policies, and public officials. This tendency, sometimes called adversarial journalism, has become commonplace in America. While this form of journalism sometimes irritates many Americans, it should probably be seen as a positive feature of American press coverage. A number of critics have suggested that the media have contributed to popular cynicism and the low levels of citizen participation that characterize American political processes. But before we begin to think about compelling the media to adopt a more cheerful view of politicians and political issues, we should consider that media criticism is one of the major mechanisms of political accountability in the American political process. Without aggressive media coverage, would we have known of Bill Clinton's misdeeds or of Richard Nixon's? Without aggressive media coverage, would important questions be raised about American foreign and domestic policy? In the absence of extensive reporting, how would President Bush's claims of success in Iraq have been challenged? It is easy to criticize the media for their aggressive tactics, but would our democracy function effectively without the critical role of the press? Public officials often accuse the media of presenting excessively negative coverage of political events and public affairs. But without the media's investigations and exposés, citizens would be forced to rely entirely on the information provided to them by politicians and the government. Such reliance hardly affords citizens a proper opportunity to evaluate issues and form reasoned opinions. A critical media play an essential role in a nation whose citizens hope to govern themselves.

We should also evaluate the sometimes adversarial relationship between the media and politicians in terms of the interests of each. Both media and politicians follow the first principle of politics: They engage in purposive behavior. Politicians want to sell their policy agenda to citizens and mobilize support for it, but they need the media to help communicate their message. Politicians would prefer to control the content of the news, but because the media have different goals and interests—market share, professional prestige, and in some cases political influence—journalists and elected leaders often come into conflict with each other. Finally, we should take into account the interests of citizens—the consumers of the news—and how their demands for certain types and amounts of political news influence the adversarial nature of media politics.[1]

In this chapter, we examine the role and increasing power of the media in American politics. First, we look at the media industry in relation to the government. Second, we discuss the factors that help determine what's news—that is, the factors that shape media coverage of events and personalities. Third, we examine the scope of media power in politics. Finally, we address the question of responsibility: In a democracy, to whom are the media accountable for the use of their formidable power?

 Rationality Principle

Media coverage can be analyzed in terms of the interests of members of the media, politicians, and consumers.

THE MEDIA INDUSTRY AND GOVERNMENT

The freedom to speak one's mind is one of the most cherished of American political values—one that is jealously safeguarded by the media. As we mentioned above, a wide variety of newspapers, newsmagazines, broadcast media, and Web sites regularly present information that is at odds with the government's claims and write editorial opinions that are sharply critical of high-ranking officials. Yet even though thousands of media companies exist across the United States, surprisingly little variety appears in what is reported about national events and issues.

Types of Media

Americans obtain their news from three main sources: broadcast media (radio, television), print media (newspapers and magazines), and, increasingly, the Internet. Each of these sources has distinctive institutional characteristics that help to shape the character of their coverage of political events.

Broadcast Media Television news reaches more Americans than any other single news source. Tens of millions of individuals watch national and local news programs every day. Television news, however, covers relatively few topics and provides little depth of coverage. Television news is more like a series of newspaper headlines connected to pictures. It serves the extremely important function of alerting viewers to issues and events but provides little else.

The twenty-four-hour news stations like Cable News Network (CNN) offer more detail and commentary than the networks' half-hour evening news shows. In 2003, at the start of the war in Iraq, CNN, Fox, and MSNBC provided twenty-four-hour-a-day coverage of the war, including on-the-scene reports from embedded reporters,

---

[1]John R. Zaller, "A Theory of Media Politics: How the Interests of Politicians, Journalists, and Citizens Shape the News," unpublished manuscript, 1999 (workingpapers.org/amerpol.htm).

TABLE 13.1 The Trend in Regular News Consumption, 1993–2006

	1993 (%)	1996 (%)	2000 (%)	2002 (%)	2004 (%)	2006 (%)
Local TV news	77	65	56	57	59	54
Cable TV news	—	—	—	33	38	34
Nightly network news	60	42	30	32	34	28
Radio*	47†	44	43	41	40	36
Newspaper*	58†	50	47	41	42	40
Online news‡	—	2§	23	25	29	31

SOURCE: Pew Research Center for the People and the Press, "Maturing Internet News Audience—Broader Than Deep: Online Papers Modestly Boost Newspaper Readership," 30 July 2006 (people-press.org/reports/pdf/282.pdf).

*Based on use the previous day.

†Data from 1994.

‡Viewed at least three days per week.

§Data from 1995.

expert commentary, and interviews with government officials. In this instance, these networks' depth of coverage rivaled that of the print media. Normally, however, CNN and the others offer more headlines than analysis, especially during their prime-time broadcasts. In recent years, cable has been growing in importance as a news source (Table 13.1).

Politicians generally view the local broadcast news as a friendlier venue than the national news. National reporters are often inclined to criticize and question, whereas local reporters often accept the pronouncements of national leaders at face value. For this reason, presidents often introduce new proposals in a series of short visits to a number of cities—indeed, sometimes flying from airport stop to airport stop—in addition to or instead of making a national presentation. For example, in February 2002, President Bush introduced his idea for a new national volunteer corps during his State of the Union message and then made a number of local speeches around the country promoting the theme. While national reporters questioned the president's plans, local news coverage was overwhelmingly positive.

Radio news is also essentially a headline service without pictures. In the short time—usually five minutes per hour—that they devote to news, radio stations announce the day's major events without providing much detail. In major cities, all-news stations provide a bit more coverage of major stories, but for the most part these stations fill the day with repetition rather than detail. All-news stations like WTOP (Washington, D.C.) and WCBS (New York City) assume that most listeners are in their cars and that, as a result, the people who constitute the audience change markedly throughout the day as they reach their destination. Thus, rather than use their time to flesh out a given set of stories, these stations repeat the same stories each hour to present them to new listeners. In recent years, radio talk shows have become important sources of commentary and opinion. A number of conservative radio hosts, such as Rush Limbaugh, have huge audiences and have helped mobilize support for conservative political causes and candidates. Liberals have had less success in the world of talk radio and have complained that biased coverage helped bring about Democratic defeats in 2000 and 2002. In 2003, however, a group of wealthy liberal political activists led by Anita Drobny, a major Democratic party donor, created Air America, a liberal talk-radio network designed to combat conservative dominance of this important medium. One executive of the new network said, "There are so many right-wing talk shows, we think it created a hole in the market you could drive a truck through." Liberals hoped their network would be entertaining as well as informative, specializing in parody and political satire.[2] In 2007, however, Air America filed for Chapter 11 bankruptcy protection and was later sold.

In recent years, much of the content of the news, especially local news, has shifted away from politics and public affairs toward "soft news"—coverage focusing on celebrities, health tips, advice to consumers, and other topics more likely to provide entertainment than enlightenment. Even a good deal of political coverage is soft. For example, media coverage of the 2005 presidential inauguration devoted nearly as much attention to the dresses worn by President Bush's daughters as it did to the content of the president's address.

Softer even than soft news is a category of programming sometimes called infotainment. This neologism refers to material that purports to combine information with entertainment. For example, in 2003, Arnold Schwarzenegger appeared on *The Tonight Show,* exchanged jokes and insults with the host, Jay Leno, and announced that he would be a candidate for governor of California. A currently popular infotainment program is *The Daily Show,* which presents comedic parodies of political figures and called itself America's "most trusted name in fake news." While purveyors of the "true" news often sneer at *The Daily Show* and other infotainment programs, one recent survey suggested that *Daily Show* viewers do receive a surprising quantity of correct information along with their fake news. Perhaps *The Daily Show* producers are right—we understand politicians better when we see how funny they are.

Print Media   Newspapers remain an important source of news even though they are not the primary news source for most Americans. The print media are important for two reasons. First, as we shall see later in this chapter, the broadcast media rely on leading newspapers such as *The New York Times* and *The Washington Post* to set their news agenda. The broadcast media engage in very little actual reporting; they primarily cover stories that have been "broken," or initially reported, by the print media. For example, sensational charges that President Bill Clinton had an affair with a White House intern were reported first by *The Washington Post* and *Newsweek* before being trumpeted around the world by the broadcast media. It is only a slight exaggeration to observe that if an event is not covered in *The New York Times,* it is not likely to appear on the *CBS Evening News.* One important exception, obviously, is the case of "breaking" news, which can be carried by the broadcast

[2]CNN.com/Inside Politics, "Liberal Radio Network Planned," 18 February 2003 (www.cnn.com/2003/ALLPOLITICS/02/17/radio.politics.ap).

media as it unfolds or soon after, while the print media are forced to catch up later in the day. Recall the dramatic real-time videos of the collapsing Twin Towers seen by tens of millions of Americans. Second, the print media provide more detailed and more complete information, offering a better context for analysis. Third, the print media are also important because they are the prime source of news for educated and influential individuals. The nation's economic, social, and political elites rely on the detailed coverage provided by the print media to inform and influence their views about important public matters. The print media may have a smaller audience than their cousins in broadcasting, but they have an audience that matters.

The Internet   A relatively new source of news is the Internet. Every day several million Americans, especially younger Americans, scan one of many news sites on the Internet for coverage of current events. For the most part, however, the Internet provides electronic versions of coverage offered by print sources. One great advantage of the Internet is that it allows frequent updating. It can potentially combine the depth of coverage of a newspaper with the timeliness of television and radio and probably will become a major news source in the next decade. Already most political candidates and interest groups have sites on the World Wide Web. Some of the more sensational aspects of President Clinton's relationship with Monica Lewinsky were first reported on a Web site maintained by Matt Drudge, an individual who specializes in posting sensational charges about public figures. Though many deny it, most reporters scan Drudge's site regularly, hoping to pick up a bit of salacious gossip. Many Americans relied on Web sites such as CNN.com for up-to-the-minute election news in the days after the 2000 presidential election, the dramatic post-election battle in Florida, the 2001 terrorist attacks on New York City and Washington, D.C., the war in Iraq, and Hurricane Katrina.[3] Acknowledging the growing importance of the Internet as a political communications medium, the U.S. Supreme Court posted its decisions in the Florida election cases as soon as they were issued. Online magazines such as *Slate* have a growing audience and often feature the work of major political writers such as Christopher Hitchens and Ed Finn. Also, a number of political entrepreneurs have sought to organize online advocacy groups to raise money, make their positions known through e-mail and letter campaigns, and provide support for politicians who accepted their views. One of the most successful of these enterprises is MoveOn.org, founded by two liberal Silicon Valley entrepreneurs. MoveOn seeks to build electronic advocacy groups, allowing members to propose issues and strategies and acting on behalf of those that appear to have the highest level of member support. In 2008, the Internet played a vital role in Barack Obama's presidential campaign. As discussed in Chapter 10, the Obama campaign harnessed the power of social networking as a communication, mobilization, and fund-raising device, generating hundreds of millions of dollars in small contributions that helped Obama win the Democratic nomination and the general election.

In addition, hundreds of thousands of readers turn to more informal sources of Internet news and commentary: Web logs, or blogs. Blogs are intermittently published online by thousands of individuals and generally feature personal opinion and com-

---

[3] For a discussion of the growing role of the Internet, see Leslie Wayne, "On Web, Voters Reinvent Grass-Roots Activism," *New York Times*, 21 May 2000, p. 22. See also James Fallows, "Internet Illusions," *New York Review of Books*, 16 November 2000, p. 28.

mentary on national and world events. Some bloggers occasionally achieve fame or at least notoriety among online readers for their political and social views. Many blogs invite readers to post comments and can become online discussion forums. In 2002 and 2003, Howard Dean's presidential campaign relied on hundreds of friendly bloggers to publicize the candidate's views and tout his virtues. Bloggers also helped Dean raise tens of millions of dollars in small contributions to finance his presidential bid.

In recent years, some news stories first discussed by bloggers have been picked up by mainstream journalists and have had a major impact on political events. In December 2002, for example, bloggers criticized Senator Trent Lott for praising the one-time segregationist Senator Strom Thurmond at a birthday party for Thurmond. A few days later the mainstream press focused on the story, and Lott was forced to resign his post as Senate majority leader. In 2004, after CBS aired a story claiming that George W. Bush had received preferential treatment while serving in the Air National Guard, conservative bloggers mounted a campaign charging that the documents presented by CBS had been forged. The network ultimately admitted that the documents had not been properly authenticated, and CBS anchor Dan Rather was forced to resign. In 2006, liberal bloggers attacked Democratic senator Joe Lieberman, whom they called a "cheerleader" for President Bush's policies in Iraq. Lieberman was defeated in Connecticut's Democratic primary, although he later won the general election, running as an independent. Also in 2006, bloggers and other avid Internet users, sometimes called netroot activists, helped bring about the defeat of the Virginia Republican senator and presidential hopeful, George Allen. After it was shown on the YouTube Web site, a video clip of Allen directing what appeared to be a racial slur at a Democratic campaign worker was downloaded to hundreds of thousands of computers and discussed by thousands of bloggers. The story was then featured by the television networks. Allen was defeated in his bid for reelection and saw his presidential hopes destroyed.

In 2003, Republicans sought to counter what they viewed as liberal dominance of the "blogosphere" by launching Blogs for Bush, an online community of bloggers who support the president. Calling itself "the White House of the Blogosphere," Blogs for Bush was active in the 2004 presidential election and continues to provide online support for GOP initiatives. In 2005, Blogs for Bush played an active role in the battle over the president's Supreme Court nominees, seeking to mobilize grassroots support and counter Democratic bloggers who criticized the president's efforts. In 2007, Blogs for Bush praised the president's plan to send more troops to Iraq and waged online battles with Democratic bloggers who castigated the president's policies.

Regulation of the Broadcast and Electronic Media

In some countries, the government controls media content. In other countries, the government owns the broadcast media but does not tell the media what to say (as is the case with the BBC in Great Britain). In the United States, the government neither owns nor controls the communications networks, but it does regulate the content and ownership of the broadcast media.

The print media in the United States are essentially free from government interference. The broadcast media, on the other hand, are subject to federal regulation. American radio and television are regulated by the Federal Communications Commission (FCC), an independent regulatory agency established in 1934. Radio and TV stations must renew their FCC licenses every five years. Licensing provides a mechanism for allocating radio and TV frequencies in such a way as to prevent broadcasts from interfering with and garbling one another. License renewals are almost always granted automatically by the FCC. Indeed, renewal requests are now filed by postcard.

Through regulations prohibiting obscenity, indecency, and profanity, the FCC has also sought to prohibit radio and television stations from airing explicit sexual and excretory references between 6 A.M. and 10 P.M., the hours when children are most likely to be in the audience. The FCC has enforced these rules haphazardly. Since 1990, nearly half the $5 million in fines levied by the agency have involved Howard Stern, the shock jock whose programs are built around sexually explicit material. In 2004, after another set of FCC fines, Stern's program was dropped by a major outlet, Clear Channel Communications. Stern charged that the Bush administration had singled him out for censure because of his known opposition to the president.

For more than sixty years, the FCC also sought to regulate and promote competition in the broadcast industry, but in 1996 Congress passed the Telecommunications Act, a broad effort to do away with most regulations in effect since 1934. The act loosened restrictions on media ownership and allowed for telephone companies, cable television providers, and broadcasters to compete with one another for the provision of telecommunication services. Following the passage of the act, several mergers between telephone and cable companies and between different segments of the entertainment media produced an even greater concentration of media ownership.

The Telecommunications Act of 1996 also included an attempt to regulate the content of material transmitted via the Internet. This law, known as the Communications Decency Act, made it illegal to make "indecent" sexual material on the Internet accessible to anyone under eighteen years of age. The act was immediately denounced by civil libertarians and brought to court as an infringement of free speech. The case reached the Supreme Court in 1997 and the act was ruled an unconstitutional infringement of the First Amendment's right to freedom of speech.

Although the government's ability to regulate the content of the electronic media on the Internet has been questioned, the federal government has used its licensing power to impose several regulations that can affect the political content of radio and TV broadcasts. The first of these is the **equal time rule**, under which broadcasters must provide candidates for the same political office equal opportunities to communicate their messages to the public. If, for example, a television station sells commercial time to a state's Republican gubernatorial candidate, it may not refuse to sell time to the Democratic candidate for the same position.

The second regulation affecting the content of broadcasts is the **right of rebuttal**, which requires that individuals be given the opportunity to respond to personal attacks. In the 1969 case of *Red Lion Broadcasting Company v. FCC*, for example, the U.S. Supreme Court upheld the FCC's determination that a radio station was required to provide a liberal author with an opportunity to respond to an attack by a conservative commentator that the station had aired.[4]

For many years, a third important federal regulation was the **fairness doctrine**—under which broadcasters who aired programs on controversial issues

---

[4] *Red Lion Broadcasting Company v. Federal Communications Commission*, 395 U.S. 367 (1969).

were required to provide air time for opposing views. In 1985, the FCC stopped enforcing the fairness doctrine on the grounds that there were so many radio and television stations—to say nothing of newspapers and newsmagazines—that in all likelihood many different viewpoints were being presented even without the requirement that each station present all sides of an argument. Critics of this FCC decision charge that in many media markets the number of competing viewpoints is small. Nevertheless, a congressional effort to require the FCC to enforce the fairness doctrine was blocked by the administration of President Ronald Reagan in 1987.

Freedom of the Press

Unlike the broadcast media, the print media are not subject to federal regulation. Indeed, the great principle underlying the federal government's relationship with the press is the doctrine against ***prior restraint.*** Beginning with the landmark 1931 case of *Near v. Minnesota*, the U.S. Supreme Court has held that, except under the most extraordinary circumstances, the First Amendment of the Constitution prohibits government agencies from seeking to prevent newspapers or magazines from publishing whatever they wish.[5] Indeed, in the case of *New York Times v. United States,* the so-called Pentagon Papers case, the Supreme Court ruled that the government could not even block publication of secret Defense Department documents furnished to *The New York Times* by an opponent of the Vietnam War who had obtained the documents illegally.[6] In a 1990 case, however, the Supreme Court upheld a lower-court order restraining CNN from broadcasting tapes of conversations between the former Panamanian leader Manuel Noriega and his lawyer, supposedly recorded by the U.S. government. By a vote of 7–2, the Court held that CNN could be restrained from broadcasting the tapes until the trial court in the Noriega case had listened to them and decided whether their broadcast would violate Noriega's right to a fair trial. This case would seem to weaken the "no-prior-restraint" doctrine. But whether the same standard will apply to the print media has yet to be tested in the courts. In 1994, the Supreme Court ruled that cable television systems were entitled to essentially the same First Amendment protections as the print media.[7]

Even though newspapers may not be restrained from publishing whatever they want, they may be subject to sanctions after the fact. Historically, newspapers have been subject to the law of libel, which provides that newspapers that print false and malicious stories can be compelled to pay damages to those they defame. In recent years, however, American courts have greatly narrowed the meaning of libel and made it extremely difficult, particularly for politicians and other public figures, to win a libel case against a newspaper. The most important case on this topic is the 1964 Supreme Court case of *New York Times v. Sullivan,* in which the Court held that to be deemed libelous, a story about a public official not only had to be untrue but also had to result

prior restraint An effort by a government agency to block the publication of material it deems libelous or harmful in some other way; censorship. In the United States, the courts forbid prior restraint except under the most extraordinary circumstances.

[5] *Near v. Minnesota ex rel.,* 283 U.S. 697 (1931).

[6] *New York Times v. United States,* 403 U.S. 713 (1971).

[7] *Cable News Network v. Noriega,* 498 U.S. 976 (1990); *Turner Broadcasting v. Federal Communications Commission,* 512 U.S. 622 (1994).

ONLINE READING
ONLINE READING

from "actual malice" or "reckless disregard" for the truth.[8] In other words, the newspaper had to deliberately print false and malicious material. In practice, it is nearly impossible to prove that a paper deliberately printed false and damaging information, and as conservatives discovered in the 1980s, it is very difficult for a politician or other public figure to win a libel case. Libel suits against CBS News by General William Westmoreland and against *Time* magazine by Ariel Sharon of Israel, both financed by conservative legal foundations that hoped to embarrass the media, were defeated in court because they failed to show "actual malice." In the 1991 case of *Masson v. New Yorker Magazine*, this tradition was again affirmed by the Court's opinion that fabricated quotations attributed to a public figure were libelous only if the fabricated account "materially changed" the meaning of what the person said.[9] For all intents and purposes, the print media can publish anything they want about a public figure.

Organization and Ownership of the Media

The United States boasts more than 2,000 television stations, approximately 1,400 daily newspapers, and more than 13,000 radio stations. Even though the number of TV and radio stations and daily newspapers reporting news in the United States is enormous, and local coverage varies greatly from place to place, the number of sources of national news is actually quite small: one wire service, five broadcast networks, public radio and television, three elite newspapers, three newsmagazines, and a scattering of other sources, such as the national correspondents of a few large local papers and the small independent radio networks. Most of the national news that is published by local newspapers is provided by one wire service, the Associated Press. More than 500 of the nation's TV stations are affiliated with one of the five networks and carry its evening news reports. Dozens of others carry Public Broadcasting Service (PBS) news. Several hundred local radio stations also carry network news or National Public Radio (NPR) news broadcasts. At the same time, although there are only three truly national newspapers, *The Wall Street Journal, The Christian Science Monitor*, and *USA Today*, two other papers, *The New York Times* and *The Washington Post*, are read by political leaders and other influential Americans throughout the nation. Such is the influence of these two "elite" newspapers that their news coverage, plus that of *The Wall Street Journal*, sets the standard for virtually all other news outlets. Stories carried in *The New York Times* or *The Washington Post* influence the content of many other papers as well as the network news. Note how often this text, like most others, relies on *New York Times* and *Washington Post* stories as sources for contemporary events.

National news is also carried to millions of Americans by the three major newsmagazines: *Time, Newsweek*, and *U.S. News and World Report*. Beginning in the late 1980s, CNN became another major news source. The importance of CNN increased dramatically after its spectacular coverage of the Persian Gulf War. At one point, CNN was able to provide live coverage of American bombing raids on Baghdad after the major networks' correspondents had been forced to flee to bomb shelters. By

[8]*New York Times v. Sullivan*, 376 U.S. 254 (1964).

[9]*Masson v. New Yorker Magazine, Inc.*, 501 U.S. 496 (1991).

ONLINE READING

2003, though, Fox had displaced CNN as the nation's primary cable news source. The rise of Fox had important political implications because its coverage and commentators are considerably more conservative than CNN's. The emergence of Fox also demonstrates the importance of the existence of more, rather than fewer, news sources. When there are few sources of news, each is likely to appeal to the same broad national audience and, accordingly, to maintain a middle-of-the-road stance. When there are more sources, each is likely to position itself within a discrete ideological or partisan niche, increasing the diversity of viewpoints presented to listeners and viewers.

The trend toward homogenization of national news has been hastened by dramatic changes in media ownership, which became possible in part as a result of the relaxation of government regulations since the 1980s. The enactment of the 1996 Telecommunications Act opened the way for additional consolidation in the media industry, and a wave of mergers and consolidations has further reduced the field of independent media across the country. Since that time, among the major news networks ABC was bought by the Walt Disney Company; CBS was bought by Westinghouse and later merged with Viacom, the owner of MTV and Paramount Communications; and CNN was bought by Time Warner. NBC has been owned by General Electric since 1985. The Australian press baron Rupert Murdoch owns the Fox Network plus a host of radio, television, and newspaper properties around the world. A small number of giant corporations now control a wide swath of media holdings, including television networks, movie studios, record companies, cable channels and local cable providers, book publishers, magazines, and newspapers. This development has prompted questions about whether enough competition exists among the media to produce a diverse set of views on political and corporate matters or whether the United States has become the prisoner of media monopolies (Figure 13.1 and Table 13.2).[10]

In June 2003, the FCC announced a set of new rules that seemed to pave the way for even more concentration in the media industry. It mandated that the major networks could own TV stations that collectively reached 45 percent of all viewers, up from 35 percent under the old rule. The new FCC rule also permits a single company to own the leading newspaper, as well as multiple television and radio outlets, in a single market. In the largest cities, this could include a newspaper, three television stations, and as many as eight radio stations.[11] Major media companies, which had long lobbied for the right to expand their activities, welcomed the new FCC rule. Critics, however, expressed grave concern that a decision would result in a narrowing of the range of views and issues presented to the general public. Congressional opponents of the FCC's action sought to overturn the rule but were stymied by opposition from the House Republican leadership as well as a threatened presidential veto. However, a federal appeals court placed the new regulation on hold, and in January 2005 the Bush administration decided not to appeal the case to Supreme Court.

---

[10] For a criticism of the increasing consolidation of the media, see the essays in Erik Barnouw et al., *Conglomerates and the Media* (New York: New Press, 1997).

[11] David Lieberman, "How Will FCC's Action Affect Consumers?" *USA Today*, 4 June 2003, p. 48.

FIGURE 13.1 Number of Corporations That Control the Majority of U.S. Media

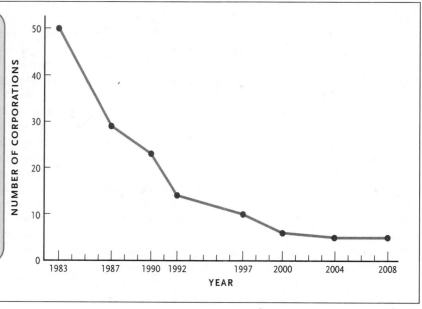

SOURCE: Media Reform Information Center (www.corporations.org/media).

NOTE: Included are newspapers, magazines, TV and radio stations, books, music, movies, videos, wire services, and photo agencies.

Nationalization of the News

In general, the national news media cover more or less the same sets of events, present similar information, and emphasize similar issues and problems. Indeed, the national news services watch one another carefully. It is unlikely that a major story carried by one will not soon find its way into the pages or programming of the others. As a result, we have developed in the United States a centralized national news through which a relatively similar picture of events, issues, and problems is presented to the entire nation.[12] The nationalization of the news was accelerated by the development of radio networks in the 1920s and 1930s and was brought to a peak by the creation of the television networks after the 1950s. This nationalization of news content has had important consequences for American politics.

Nationalization of the news has contributed greatly to the nationalization of both politics and political perspectives in the United States. Before the development of the national media and the nationalization of news coverage, the news traveled slowly. Every region and city saw national issues and problems mainly through its own local

---

[12]See Leo Bogart, "Newspapers in Transition," in "The News Media," special issue, *Wilson Quarterly* (1982); and Richard Harwood, "The Golden Age of Press Diversity," *Washington Post,* 22 July 1994, p. A23.

TABLE 13.2 Who Owns What? Viacom

Television

| • CBS stations: 17 | • UPN stations: 18 | • Other local stations: 5 |

Cable TV Stations			Cable TV Production and Distribution
• MTV • MTV2 • Nickelodeon • BET • Nick at Nite	• TV Land • NOGGIN • VH1 • Spike TV • CMT	• Comedy Central • Showtime • Movie Channel • Flix • Sundance Channel	• Spelling Television • Big Ticket Television • King World Productions

Radio

Infinity Broadcasting				Viacom Outdoor Systems
• Northeastern stations: 42	• Southern stations: 42	• Midwestern stations: 34	• Western stations: 34	• Stations: 2

Film

| • Paramount Pictures | • Paramount Home Entertainment |

Publishing: Simon & Schuster

Simon & Schuster Adult Publishing Group	Simon & Schuster Children's Publishing Group
• Atria Books • Howard Books • Pocket Books • Scribner • Simon & Schuster • Strebor • Free Press • Touchstone and Fireside Group	• Aladdin Paperbacks • Atheneum Books for Young Readers • Libros para Niños • Little Simon • Little Simon Inspirations • Margaret K. McElderry Books • Simon & Schuster Books for Young Readers • Simon Pulse • Simon Spotlight • Simon Spotlight Entertainment
Simon & Schuster Audio **Simon & Schuster Digital**	**Simon & Schuster UK** **Simon & Schuster Australia**

SOURCE: "Who Owns What?" Columbia University, Graduate School of Journalism, *Columbia Journalism Review*, 27 June 2006 (www.cjr.org/tools); and "About Simon" (www.simonsays.com).

lens. Concerns and perspectives varied greatly from region to region, city to city, and village to village. Today, in large measure as a result of the nationalization of the media, residents of all parts of the country share similar ideas and perspectives.[13] They may not agree on everything, but they at least see the world in similar ways.

WHAT AFFECTS NEWS COVERAGE?

Because of the important role the media can play in national politics, it is essential to understand the factors that affect media coverage.[14] What accounts for the media's agenda of issues and topics? What explains the character of coverage—why a politician receives good or bad press? What factors determine the interpretation, or spin, that a particular story will receive? Although a host of minor factors plays a role, there are three major factors: (1) journalists or producers of the news, (2) politicians or other sources of the news, and (3) consumers.

Journalists

First, the character of the news is shaped by the institutions that produce it. Media content and news coverage are inevitably affected by the views, ideals, and interests of the individuals and organizations that seek out, write, and produce news and other stories. At one time, newspaper publishers exercised a great deal of influence over their papers' news content. Publishers such as William Randolph Hearst and Joseph Pulitzer became political powers through their manipulation of news coverage. Hearst, for example, almost single-handedly pushed the United States into war with Spain in 1898 through his newspapers' relentless coverage of the alleged brutality employed by Spain in its efforts to suppress a rebellion in Cuba, then a Spanish colony. The sinking of the American battleship *Maine* in Havana Harbor under mysterious circumstances gave Hearst the ammunition he needed to force a reluctant president William McKinley to lead the nation into war. Today few publishers have that kind of power. Most are more concerned with the business end of the paper than its editorial content, although a few continue to impose their interests and tastes on the news.

More important than publishers, for the most part, are the reporters. The goals and incentives of journalists are varied, but they often include considerations of ratings, career success and professional prestige, and political influence. For all of these reasons, journalists seek not only to report the news but also to interpret it. Journalists' goals have a good deal of influence on what is created and reported as news.

Those journalists who cover the news for the national media generally have a lot of discretion or freedom to interpret stories and, as a result, have an opportunity

---

Rationality Principle

The goals and incentives of journalists—such as ratings, career success, and prestige—influence what is created and reported as news.

---

[13]See Benjamin Ginsberg, *The Captive Public: How Mass Opinion Promotes State Power* (New York: Basic Books, 1986).

[14]See the discussions in Michael Parenti, *Inventing Reality: The Politics of the Mass Media* (New York: St. Martin's Press, 1986); Herbert Gans, *Deciding What's News: A Study of CBS Evening News, NBC Nightly News, Newsweek, and Time* (New York: Vintage, 1980); and W. Lance Bennett, *News: The Politics of Illusion,* 5th ed. (New York: Longman, 2002).

to interject their own views and ideals into news stories. For example, some reporters' personal friendship with and respect for Franklin Roosevelt and John F. Kennedy helped generate more favorable news coverage for those presidents. On the other hand, many reporters' dislike of and distrust for Richard Nixon was also communicated to the public. In the case of Ronald Reagan, the disdain that many journalists felt for the president was communicated in stories suggesting that he was often asleep or inattentive when important decisions were made.

Conservatives have long charged that the liberal biases of reporters and journalists result in distorted news coverage. This charge was supported in a 2005 academic study by the economist Timothy Groseclose and the political scientist Jeffrey Milyo, who found a pronounced liberal bias in the news presented by many major papers and all but one broadcast network (Fox).[15] In a similar vein, a 1996 study of Washington newspaper bureau chiefs and correspondents conducted by the Roper Center and the Freedom Forum, a conservative foundation, found that 61 percent of the bureau chiefs and correspondents who were polled called themselves "liberal" or "liberal to moderate." Only 9 percent called themselves "conservative" or "conservative to moderate." And 89 percent said that they had voted for Bill Clinton in 1992, while only 7 percent indicated that they had voted for George H. W. Bush. Approximately 50 percent said they were Democrats, and only 4 percent claimed to be Republicans.[16] Another survey has indicated that even among the radio talk-show hosts lambasted by President Clinton, Democrats outnumber Republicans by a wide margin: Of 112 hosts surveyed, 39 percent had voted for Clinton in 1992, and only 23 percent had supported George H. W. Bush.[17] Generally speaking, reporters for major national news outlets tend to be more liberal than their local counterparts, who often profess moderate or even conservative views.

The link between journalists and liberal ideas is by no means absolute. While the most important national newspapers, such as *The New York Times* and *The Washington Post*, are liberal and Democratic in their orientation, many smaller papers support the Republicans. Indeed, in recent years more newspapers have endorsed GOP presidential candidates than have supported their Democratic rivals, although in 2004 Kerry received slightly more endorsements (51 percent) than Bush (Figure 13.2). In 2008, Barack Obama received endorsements from 240 metropolitan newspapers, with a combined circulation of nearly 22 million, while John McCain was supported by only 115 papers, with a combined circulation of barely 7 million.

In addition, most reporters attempt to maintain some measure of balance or objectivity, whatever their personal views. Moreover, over the past several years a conservative media complex has emerged in opposition to the liberal media. This complex includes two major newspapers, *The Wall Street Journal* and *The Washington*

---

[15]Timothy Groseclose and Tom Milyo, "A Measure of Media Bias," *Quarterly Journal of Economics* 120 (2005): 1191–1237.

[16]Rowan Scarborough, "Leftist Press? Reporters Working in Washington Acknowledge Liberal Leanings in Poll," *Washington Times*, 18 April 1996, p. 1.

[17]Michael Kinsley, "Bias and Baloney," *Washington Post*, 26 November 1992, p. A29; and John H. Fund, "Why Clinton Shouldn't Be Steamed at Talk Radio," *Wall Street Journal*, 7 July 1994, p. A12.

ONLINE READING

FIGURE 13.2 Newspaper Endorsements

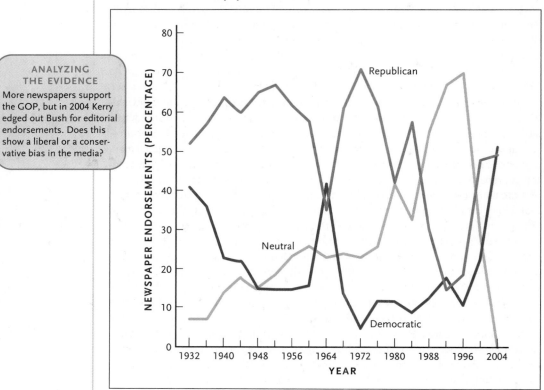

SOURCE: Harold W. Stanley and Richard G. Niemi, *Vital Statistics on American Politics, 2001–2002* (Washington, D.C.: Congressional Quarterly Press, 2001), pp. 194–95; 2004 data reported by Jacobian.org, compiled from *Editor and Publisher.*

Times; several magazines, such as *The American Spectator* and *The Weekly Standard;* and a host of conservative radio and television talk programs. Also important is the media baron Rupert Murdoch, creator of the Fox News Channel and financial force behind *The Weekly Standard.* The emergence of this conservative media complex has meant that liberal policies and politicians are virtually certain to come under attack even when the "liberal media" are sympathetic to them.

Probably more important than ideological bias is a **selection bias (in the media)** in favor of news that the media view as having a great deal of audience appeal because of its dramatic or entertainment value. In practice, this bias often results in news coverage that focuses on crimes and scandals, especially those involving prominent individuals, despite the fact that the public obviously looks to the media for information about important political debates.[18] For example, even though most journalists may be Democrats, this partisan predisposition did not prevent an enormous media frenzy in

selection bias (in the media)
The predisposition of consumers to choose particular types of stories.

────────────

[18]See Joseph N. Cappella and Kathleen Hall Jamieson, *Spiral of Cynicism: The Press and the Public Good* (New York: Oxford University Press, 1997).

January 1998 when reports surfaced that President Clinton may have had an affair with Monica Lewinsky. Once a hint of blood appeared in the water, partisanship and ideology were swept away by the piranha-like instincts often manifested by journalists.

News Sources

News coverage is also influenced by politicians, public officials, and other news sources whose interests and activities are actual or potential news topics. Politicians want to be seen by the public as trustworthy, energetic, caring, and generally able to discharge the public duties with which they have been or hope to be entrusted. Accordingly, most politicians will seize or, if necessary, create opportunities for media coverage they deem likely to contribute to the public image they wish to fashion. Presidents, for example, know that their speeches on vitally important topics will be televised throughout the nation. Thus they have an opportunity to use the media to demonstrate that they possess strong leadership qualities and fully understand the problems and issues facing the nation. President George W. Bush's speech in the wake of the September 11 terrorist attacks, for example, was designed to reassure Americans and demonstrate that he was firmly in command. In a similar vein, presidents and other politicians know that the media will give considerable coverage to floods, hurricanes, earthquakes, and other natural disasters. Thus, as a general rule, politicians are drawn to natural disasters like bees to honey. Indeed, the televised official inspection tour of a disaster site is a staple of American politics. This tour consists of the president and the affected state's governor, senator, or other politician, trailed by staff and reporters, all of whom first fly over the scene of the disaster and then land—at a safe location—so that the politicians can offer condolences to survivors and, finally, pledge to devote the resources of the government to make things right. Politicians hope that viewers will see them as compassionate problem solvers, certainly worthy of the public's trust. President Bush's failure to make a prompt visit to New Orleans and other disaster sites in the wake of Hurricane Katrina in 2005 was widely criticized and cited by the media as an example of the president's lack of empathy for common citizens—or at least his inability to give the appearance of having such empathy.

Politicians use many other techniques to develop favorable media images. President John F. Kennedy sought to develop strong relationships with influential journalists. Bill Clinton thought that appearances on soft news and entertainment programs allowed him to connect with ordinary Americans and show them that their president was not aloof or out of touch. Thus Clinton famously tooted his saxophone on a late-night entertainment program and discussed his choice of underwear with teenage reporters on MTV.

Politicians, interest groups, government officials, and other news sources employ a variety of techniques in their efforts to shape news coverage. These include news leaks, news releases, and in some instances cash payments to journalists. Although the news media are not oblivious to the efforts of sources to manipulate them, journalists and editors sometimes have a stake in allowing themselves to be manipulated. Journalists may publish leaked information in order to maintain good relations with important sources even when they know the source is pursuing his or her own political agenda. Editors and publishers have a financial stake in relying heavily on press releases even though they know the information they present is not

 Rationality Principle

News coverage is influenced by the interests of politicians.

objective. In such ways, the institutional stakes of the media may interfere with the unbiased and objective presentation of the news.

Institution Principle

The institutional stakes of the media sometimes interfere with objective and unbiased news coverage.

News Leaks A news leak is the disclosure of confidential information to the news media. Leaks may emanate from a variety of sources, including whistle-blowers, lower-level officials who hope to publicize what they view as their bosses' improper activities. In 1971, for example, a minor Defense Department staffer named Daniel Ellsberg sought to discredit official justifications for America's involvement in Vietnam by leaking top-secret documents to the press. The so-called Pentagon Papers were published by *The New York Times* and *The Washington Post* after the U.S. Supreme Court ruled that the government could not block release of the document. In a similar vein, President George W. Bush was infuriated in 2005 when he learned that a still-unidentified source, presumed to be a whistler-blower, had leaked information concerning the president's secret orders authorizing the National Security Agency to conduct clandestine surveillance of suspected terrorists without obtaining authorization from the special federal tribunal created for that purpose. Bush ordered the Justice Department to launch a probe of the leak. In 2006, a still-unidentified source leaked to the press part of a secret intelligence summary that seemed to contradict the administration's claims of progress in the war in Iraq. The president claimed the leaked portion of the report did not accurately reflect the full report. The administration proceeded to declassify other portions of the report, which seemed to support its claims about the war.

Most leaks, though, originate not with low-level whistle-blowers but, rather, with senior government officials and prominent politicians and political activists. Such persons often cultivate long-term relationships with journalists, to whom they regularly leak confidential information, knowing that it is likely to be published on a priority basis in a form acceptable to them. Their confidence is based on the fact that journalists are likely to regard high-level sources of confidential information as valuable assets whose favor must be retained. For example, I. Lewis "Scooter" Libby, former vice president Dick Cheney's former chief of staff, was apparently such a valuable source of leaks to so many prominent journalists that his name was seldom mentioned in the newspapers despite his prominence in Washington and his importance as a decision maker.[19] And the more recipients of leaked information strive to keep their sources secret, the more difficulty other journalists will have in checking the validity of the information.

Through such tacit alliances with journalists, prominent figures can manipulate news coverage and secure the publication of stories that serve their purposes. One recent case that revealed the complexities of this culture of leaks was the 2005 Valerie Plame affair. Plame was an undercover CIA analyst who happened to be married to Joseph Wilson, a prominent career diplomat. Wilson had angered the Bush White House by making a number of statements that were critical of the president's policies in Iraq. In an apparent effort to discredit Wilson, one or more administration officials informed prominent journalists that Plame had improperly used her position to help Wilson. In so doing, these officials may have violated a federal statute prohibiting the disclosure of the identities of covert intelligence operatives. The subsequent investigation revealed that the story had been leaked to several journalists, including *The Wash-*

---

[19]Michael Massing, "The Press: The Enemy Within," *New York Review of Books*, 15 December 2005, p. 36.

ington Post's Bob Woodward, who did not use it, and *The New York Times'* Judith Miller, who did. Miller spent several months in jail for contempt of court after initially refusing to testify before a federal grand jury looking into the leak. After Miller finally testified, Scooter Libby was charged and convicted of lying and obstruction for his role in the affair, although it later emerged that the information was actually leaked by a former State Department official, Richard Armitage. The leak in the Plame case came to light only because it might have been illegal. Thousands of other leaks each year are quietly and seamlessly incorporated into the news.

The Press Release   Also seamlessly incorporated into daily news reports each year are thousands of press releases. The press release, sometimes called a news release, is a story written by an advocate or publicist and distributed to the media in the hope that journalists will publish it under their own byline with little or no revision. The inventor of the press release was a New York public relations consultant named Ivy Lee. In 1906, a train operated by one of Lee's clients, the Pennsylvania Railroad, was involved in a serious wreck. Lee quickly wrote a story about the accident that presented the railroad in a favorable light and distributed the account to reporters. Many papers published Lee's slanted story as their own objective account of events, and the railroad's reputation for quality and safety remained intact.

Consistent with Lee's example, today's press release presents facts and perspectives that serve an advocate's interests but is written in a way that mimics the factual news style of the paper, periodical, or television news program to which it has been sent. It is quite difficult for the audience to distinguish a well-designed press release from a news story. For example, a recent posting by PharmaWatch, a blog monitoring the pharmaceutical industry, identified an article published in *The New York Times* Science section that rehashed a news release issued by Pfizer, the giant pharmaceutical corporation. "A lawyer in New York, has had to deal with what is politely referred to as 'bladder control' for as long as she can remember," the article began. "Even as a teenager she woke up at night feeling the urge to urinate but not always making it to the toilet in time." Fortunately, thanks to the press release it copied, the article was able to propose a solution. "Urge incontinence is often treated with drugs like tolterodine, sold as Detrol."[20] Not surprisingly, the drug touted in this helpful news story is sold by Pfizer.

To take another example, an April 2005 article sent to thousands of newspapers by the Associated Press (AP) was headlined "Fed Unveils Financial Education Website." Apparently written by an AP reporter, the article discussed the various ways in which a new Web site developed by the Federal Reserve could help consumers make informed decisions. The article did not mention that the information was basically a slight revision of a press release that could be found on the Fed's Web site.[21] Similarly, a recent *Houston Chronicle* story on teacher training claimed that students taught by teachers provided by Teach for America and other nontraditional sources performed significantly worse on standardized tests than students taught by traditionally certified instructors. The article failed to note that it was essentially a copy of a Stanford University

---

[20]Michael Lascelles, PharmaWatch, 25 October 2005 (pharmawatch.blogspot.com); and Mariticia Heaner, "Enduring Incontinence in Silence," *New York Times*, 25 October 2005.

[21]Brian Montopoli, "Press Release Journalism," *Columbia Journalism Review Daily*, 18 April 2005.

press release touting the work of a Stanford professor who directs a traditional teacher training program.[22] And what about the June 2005 *Los Angeles Times* story "County Homeless Number 90,000"? This article claimed, without offering an explanation, that the number of homeless individuals in Los Angeles County had quintupled since the previous year. In presenting this shocking news of the increase in homelessness, though, the reporter neglected to mention that the data came from a press release issued by the Los Angeles Homeless Services Authority (LAHSA), whose budget is tied to the number of clients it serves. For the LAHSA, more homelessness equals more money and more staff. Indeed, on its own Web site, it indicated that it had undertaken its new count of homeless individuals in part to "increase funding for homeless services in our community."[23] These should not be seen as isolated examples. According to some experts, more than 50 percent of the articles in a newspaper on any given day are based on press releases. Indeed, more than 75 percent of the journalists responding to a recent survey acknowledged using press releases for their stories.[24]

Journalists are certainly aware of the fact that the authors of press releases have their own agendas and are hardly unbiased reporters of the news. Nevertheless, the economics of publishing and broadcasting dictate that large numbers of stories will always be based on press releases. Newspapers and television stations are businesses, and for many the financial bottom line is more important than journalistic integrity.[25] The use of press releases allows a newspaper or a broadcast network to present more stories without paying more staff or incurring the other costs associated with investigating and writing the news. As one newspaper executive said, the public relations people who generally write news releases are our "unpaid reporters."[26]

In recent years, the simple printed press release has been joined by the video news release, which is designed especially for television stations. The video release is a taped report, usually about ninety seconds long, the typical length of a television news story, designed to look and sound like any other broadcast news segment. In exchange for airing material that serves the interests of some advocate, the television station airing the video release is relieved of the considerable expense and bother of identifying and filming its own news story. The audience is usually unaware that the "news" it is watching is someone's canned publicity footage.

One recent example of a video news release was a pair of ninety-second segments funded by the U.S. Department of Health and Human Services (HHS) in 2004. After Congress enacted legislation adding a prescription drug benefit to the Medicare program, HHS sent a video release designed to look like a news report to local TV stations around the nation. Forty television stations aired the report without indicating that it had come from the government. The segment was introduced by the local news

---

[22]Anne Linehan, "Another Example of Press Release Journalism?" BlogHouston, 18 April 2005 (bloghouston.net).

[23]"LA Times: County Homeless Population Tops Two Kazillion, No Further Reporting Required," IndependentSources, 16 June 2005 (independentsources.com).

[24]Dennis L. Wilcox and Glen T. Cameron, *Public Relations: Strategy and Tactics*, 8th ed. (Boston: Allyn & Bacon, 2006), p. 357.

[25]See, for example, Davis Merritt, *Knightfall: Knight Ridder and How the Erosion of Newspaper Journalism Is Putting Democracy at Risk* (New York: Amacom Books, 2005).

[26]Quoted in Wilcox and Cameron, *Public Relations*, p. 357.

anchor reading from a government-suggested script. Referring to the new Medicare law, the anchor read, "Reporter Karen Ryan helps sort through the details." Then, against the backdrop of film showing President Bush signing the law and the reactions of apparently grateful senior citizens, an unseen narrator, speaking like a reporter, presents the new law in a positive light: "The new law, say officials, simply offers people with Medicare ways to make their health coverage more affordable." The segment concludes with the sign off "In Washington, I'm Karen Ryan reporting." Viewers are not told that the entire story was distributed by the government. Nor are viewers informed that Karen Ryan is not a reporter at all. She was an employee of the ad agency hired by the government to create the video release. In response to criticism, an HHS spokesperson pointed out that the same sort of video news releases had often been used by the Clinton administration and was commonly used by a number of firms and interest groups. "The use of video news releases is a common, routine practice in government and the private sector," he said. "Anyone who has questions about this practice needs to do some research on modern public information tools."[27]

Hiring Reporters   From creating phony reporters to reading make-believe news stories, it is but a small step to hiring real reporters to present sham accounts. And this step has been taken frequently by both the government and private advocates. A number of cases have come to light in recent years in which the government or a private concern has paid journalists to write favorable accounts of its activities and efforts. Late in 2005, for example, the U.S. military acknowledged that contractors in its employ had regularly paid Iraqi newspapers to carry positive news about American efforts in that nation. The Washington-based Lincoln Group, a public relations firm working under contract to the federal government, says it placed more than 1,000 news stories in the Arab press over the past four years.[28] Iraqis reading the articles would have had no way of knowing that the material presented was produced at the behest of the American authorities.

In a similar vein, the U.S. military and the U.S. Agency for International Development (USAID) operate or subsidize radio stations and newspapers in Afghanistan, staffed by local journalists who write or broadcast in local dialects. Every effort is made to maintain the impression that these media outlets are autonomous Afghan-owned organizations with no connection to the United States. One USAID representative explained, "We want to maintain the perception that these [media] are in fact fully independent." Needless to say, the American-controlled media painted a rosy picture of U.S. efforts in Afghanistan. Apparently there was no bad news emanating from that impoverished and war-torn country. "We have no requirements to adhere to journalistic standards of objectivity," said a U.S. Army spokesperson.[29]

The government's practice of hiring journalists is not limited to operations abroad. In recent years, federal agencies have paid several journalists and commentators to report favorably on government initiatives and programs in the United

---

[27]Quoted in Ben Fritz, Bryan Keefer, and Brendan Nyhan, *All the President's Spin* (New York: Touchstone Books, 2004), pp. 252–53, 357.

[28]Jeff Gerth, "Military's Information War Is Vast and Often Secretive," *New York Times*, 11 December 2005, p. 1.

[29]Quoted ibid., p. 18.

States. The Department of Education, for example, paid the commentator Armstrong Williams $241,000 to promote President Bush's No Child Left Behind Act. Williams wrote favorably about the law in his newspaper column, commented positively about it during his cable television appearances, and urged other commentators to interview Education Secretary Roderick Paige.[30] Williams did not disclose his financial relationship with the agency whose programs he was touting. In a similar vein, HSS paid the syndicated columnist Maggie Gallagher $20,000 to promote the administration's views on marriage. Gallagher wrote several columns on the topic without revealing her financial relationship with the administration.

Williams and Gallagher worked for the government, but the private sector is also active in this area. Corporations, trade associations, and interest groups have been known to provide gratuities to journalists. For example, in 2005 one well-known columnist was forced to resign his position with the Cato Institute after it was revealed that he had accepted payment from a prominent Washington lobbyist in exchange for writing newspaper columns favorable to the interests of some of the lobbyist's clients. The lobbyist, Jack Abramoff, who in 2006 pleaded guilty to a number of violations of federal lobbying laws, had paid the writer, Doug Bandow, to promote the causes of the Northern Marianas Islands, the Choctaw Indians, and other Abramoff clients. In one nationally syndicated Copley News Service column, Bandow defended the Choctaws' operation of gambling casinos, asserting, "There's certainly no evidence that Indian gambling operations harm the local community." Abramoff had been arguing just that point to lawmakers. In another column, Bandow opposed federal "economic meddling" in the Marianas, precisely the position the Marianas government was paying Abramoff to advocate on Capitol Hill.[31]

There have been several other recent cases in which reporters and columnists were found to have received payment from industries and interests about which they wrote. In 2005, Indiana Wesleyan University professor Tom Lehman, published a piece in *The Hill*, a magazine read by congressional staffers and members, praising so-called payday loans. It turned out that Lehman had accepted money from the industry that provides these high-risk loans to poor people.[32] In another case, the syndicated columnist Michael Fumento praised Monsanto, a huge agribusiness enterprise, in his columns and in a recent book. Fumento, it turns out, received $60,000 from Monsanto, although he denies that the payment influenced his writing. Fumento's weekly column was canceled by the Scripps Howard News Service after the revelation.[33]

One group especially noted for paying writers and reporters for favorable coverage is the pharmaceutical industry. As the Detrol example suggests, many of the articles that appear in popular—and even scientific—journals reporting favorably on particular drugs are written by the drug companies themselves. In some cases, the writers are in the direct pay of the drug companies; in other reported instances, the writer cited in the story's byline is not the actual author of the account. Often a

---

[30]Howard Kurtz, "Administration Paid Commentator," *Washington Post*, 8 January 2005, p. 1.

[31]Anne E. Kornblut and Philip Shenon, "Columnist Resigns His Post Admitting Lobbyist Paid Him," *New York Times*, 17 December 2005, p. A15.

[32]Eamon Javers, "This Opinion Brought to You By . . .," *Business Week*, 20 January 2006, p. 35.

[33]Ibid., p. 36.

ghostwriter employed by a drug company writes the story while the nominal author is paid for the use of his or her name.[34]

But, of course, while politicians try to use the media for their purposes, reporters often have their own agenda. Often enough, hostile or merely determined journalists will break through the smoke screens thrown up by the politicians and report annoying truths. Thus, for example, despite the Bush administration's best efforts to manage the news from Iraq, journalists have filed accounts of Iraqi resistance, abuse of Iraqi prisoners, and other unpleasant facts that the administration might have preferred to keep off the table.

Consumers

The print and broadcast media are businesses that, in general, seek to show a profit. This means that like any other business they must cater to the preferences of consumers. Their doing so has very important consequences for the content and character of the news media.

Catering to the Upscale Audience   In general and especially in the political realm, the print and broadcast media and the publishing industry are not only responsive to the interests of consumers generally but are also particularly responsive to the interests and views of the better-educated and more affluent segments of the audience. The preferences of these segments have a profound effect on the content and orientation of the press, of radio and television programming, and books, especially in the areas of news and public affairs.[35]

Although affluent consumers do watch television programs and read periodicals whose content is designed simply to amuse or entertain, the one area that most directly appeals to the upscale audience is that of news and public affairs. The affluent—who are also typically well educated—are the core audience of newsmagazines, journals of opinion, books dealing with public affairs, serious newspapers like *The New York Times* and *The Washington Post,* and broadcast news and weekend and evening public-affairs programming. While other segments of the public also read newspapers and watch the television news, their level of interest in world events, national political issues, and the like is closely related to their level of education (Table 13.3). As a result, upscale Americans are overrepresented in the news and public-affairs audience. The concentration of these strata in the audience makes news, politics, and public affairs potentially very attractive topics to advertisers, publishers, radio broadcasters, and television executives.

Entire categories of events, issues, and phenomena of interest to lower-, middle-, and working-class Americans receive scant attention from the national print and broadcast media. For example, trade union news and events are discussed only in the context of major strikes or revelations of corruption. No network or national periodical

Collective-Action Principle

The relationship between media members and politicians is a prisoner's dilemma. Each participant benefits from mutual cooperation but finds himself or herself tempted to defect on occasion to secure even larger gains.

Rationality Principle

The preferences of consumers, such as the affluent or the people who watch news for its entertainment value, influence news content.

---

[34]Anna Wilde Matthews, "At Medical Journals, Writers Paid by Industry Play Big Role," *Wall Street Journal*, 13 December 2005, p. 1.

[35]See Tom Burnes, "The Organization of Public Opinion," in *Mass Communication and Society,* ed. James Curran, Michael Gurevitch, and Janet Woollacott (Beverly Hills, Calif.: Sage, 1979), pp. 44–230. See also David L. Altheide, *Creating Reality: How TV News Distorts Events* (Beverly Hills, Calif.: Sage, 1976).

TABLE 13.3 Education and Attention to the News

Level of Education	Level of Attention to Hard News *		
	High (%)	Medium (%)	Low (%)
College graduate	43	53	4
Some college	33	57	10
High school graduate	28	57	15
Not a high school graduate	16	58	26

SOURCE: Pew Research Center for the People and the Press, "Media Consumption and Believability Study," 8 June 2004 (people-press.org/reports/pdf.215.pdf).

*Persons with high levels of attention follow international, national, local, and business news closely; those with low levels do not follow the news.

routinely covers labor organizations. Religious and church affairs receive little coverage (unless scandal is involved, as was the case in 2002 and 2003 in many dioceses of the Roman Catholic Church). The activities of veterans', fraternal, ethnic, and patriotic organizations are also generally ignored.

The Media and Conflict   While the media respond most to the upscale audience, groups who cannot afford the services of media consultants and issues managers can publicize their views and interests through protest. Frequently, the media are accused of encouraging conflict and even violence in response to the fact that their audiences mostly watch news for the entertainment value that conflict can provide. Clearly, conflict can be an important vehicle for attracting the attention and interest of the media and thus may provide an opportunity for media attention to groups otherwise lacking the financial or organizational resources to broadcast their views. But while conflict and protest can succeed in drawing media attention, these methods ultimately do not allow groups from the bottom of the social ladder to compete effectively in the media.

The chief problem with protest as a media technique is that, in general, the media on which the protesters depend have considerable discretion in reporting and interpreting the events they cover. For example, should the media focus on the conflict itself, rather than on the issues or concerns created by the conflict? The answer to this question is typically determined by the media, not by the protesters. Therefore, media interpretation of protest activities is more a reflection of the views of the groups and forces to which the media are responsive—who, as we have seen, are usually segments of the upper middle class—than it is a function of the wishes of the protesters themselves. It is worth noting that civil rights protesters received their most favorable media coverage when a segment of the white upper middle class saw blacks as potential political allies in the Democratic party.

Typically, upper-middle-class protesters—student demonstrators and the like—have little difficulty securing favorable publicity for themselves and their causes. They are often more skilled than their lower-class counterparts in the techniques of media manipulation. That is, they typically have a better sense—often as a result of formal courses on the subject—of how to package messages for media consumption. For example, it is important to know what time of day a protest should occur if it is to be carried on the evening news. Similarly, the setting, definition of the issues, character of the rhetoric used, and so on all help determine whether a protest will receive favorable media coverage, unfavorable coverage, or no coverage at all. Moreover, upper-middle-class protesters can often produce their own media coverage through "underground" newspapers, college papers, student radio and television stations, and the Internet. The same resources and skills that generally allow upper-middle-class people to publicize their ideas are usually not left behind when segments of this class choose to engage in disruptive forms of political action. Note the media attention given antiwar protesters in 2003 even though polls indicated that such groups were a minor force in American politics.

SOURCES OF MEDIA POWER IN AMERICAN POLITICS

The content and character of news and public-affairs programming—what the media choose to present and how they present it—can have far-reaching political consequences. Media disclosures can greatly enhance—or fatally damage—the careers of public officials. Media coverage can rally support for—or intensify opposition to—national policies. The media can shape and modify, if not fully form, public perceptions of events, issues, and institutions.

In recent American political history, the media have played a central role in at least three major events. First, the media were critically important factors in the civil rights movement of the 1950s and 1960s. Televised photographs of peaceful civil rights marchers attacked by club-swinging police helped generate sympathy among northern whites for the civil rights struggle and greatly increased the pressure on Congress to bring an end to segregation.[36] Second, the media were instrumental in compelling the government to negotiate an end to the Vietnam War. Beginning in 1967, the national media, reacting in part to a shift in elite opinion, portrayed the war as misguided and unwinnable and, as a result, helped turn popular sentiment against continued American involvement.[37] Finally, the media were central actors in the Watergate affair, which ultimately forced President Richard Nixon, the landslide victor in the 1972 presidential election, to resign from office in disgrace. It was the relentless series of investigations launched by *The Washington Post*, *The New York Times*, and the television networks that led to the disclosures of the various abuses of which Nixon was guilty and that ultimately forced him to choose between resignation and almost certain impeachment. And now the media are emerging as a major force in the debate over American involvement in Iraq.

---

[36] David J. Garrow, *Protest at Selma: Martin Luther King, Jr., and the Voting Rights Act of 1965* (New Haven, Conn.: Yale University Press, 1978).

[37] See Todd Gitlin, *The Whole World Is Watching: Mass Media in the Making and Unmaking of the New Left* (Berkeley: University of California Press, 2003). See also William M. Hammond, *Reporting Vietnam: Media and Military at War* (Lawrence: University Press of Kansas, 1998).

Agenda Setting

The power of the media stems from several sources. The first is **agenda setting**, which means that the media help determine which political issues become part of the public debate. Groups and forces that wish to bring their ideas before the public to generate support for policy proposals or political candidacies must somehow secure media coverage. If the media are persuaded that an idea is newsworthy, then they may declare it an issue that must be resolved or a problem to be solved, thus clearing the first hurdle in the policy-making process. On the other hand, if an idea lacks or loses media appeal, its chance of resulting in new programs or policies is diminished. Some ideas seem to surface, gain media support for a time, lose media appeal, and then resurface.

In most instances, the media serve as conduits for agenda-setting efforts by competing groups and forces. Occasionally, however, journalists themselves play an important role in setting the agenda of political discussion. For example, whereas many of the scandals and investigations surrounding President Clinton were initiated by his political opponents, the Watergate scandal that destroyed Nixon's presidency was in some measure initiated and driven by *The Washington Post* and the national television networks.

Priming

A second important media power is **priming**. This occurs when media coverage affects the way the public evaluates political leaders or candidates for office. For example, nearly unanimous media praise for President Bush's speeches to the nation in the wake of the September 11 terrorist attacks prepared, or "primed," the public to view Bush's subsequent response to terrorism in an extremely positive light even though some aspects of the administration's efforts were problematic.

In the case of political candidates, the media have considerable influence over whether a particular individual will receive public attention, whether a particular individual will be taken seriously as a viable contender, and whether the public will evaluate a candidate's performance favorably. Thus if the media find a candidate interesting, they may treat him or her as a serious contender even though the facts of the matter seem to suggest otherwise. Similarly, the media may declare that a candidate has "momentum," a mythical property that the media confer on candidates, if the candidate happens to exceed the media's expectations. Momentum has no substantive meaning—it is simply a media prediction that a particular candidate will do better in the future than he or she has done in the past. Such media prophecies can become self-fulfilling as contributors and supporters jump on the bandwagon of the candidate possessing this "momentum." In the 2008 Democratic primaries, the media never seemed to think that Hillary Clinton had done as well as expected and always appeared to believe that Barack Obama had exceeded expectations. To the chagrin of the Clintons, the chief story was nearly always how well Obama had done. The Clintons frequently complained that media priming was helping Obama and hurting Clinton.

Framing

A third source of the media's power, known as **framing**, is their power to decide how political events and results are interpreted by the American people. For example,

agenda setting The process by which it is determined which issues are taken up by political actors and institutions.

priming A process of preparing the public to take a particular view of an event or a political actor.

framing The power of the media to influence how events and issues are interpreted.

during the 1995–96 struggle between President Clinton and congressional Republicans over the nation's budget—a struggle that led to several partial shutdowns of the federal government—the media's interpretation of events forced the Republicans to back down and agree to a budget on Clinton's terms. At the beginning of the crisis, congressional Republicans, led by House Speaker Newt Gingrich, were confident that they could compel Clinton to accept their budget, which called for substantial cuts in domestic social programs. Republicans calculated that Clinton would fear being blamed for lengthy government shutdowns and would quickly accede to their demands. The Republicans reasoned that once Americans saw that life went on with government agencies closed, they would support the Republicans in asserting that the United States could get along with less government.

For the most part, however, the media did not cooperate with the GOP's plans. Media coverage of the several government shutdowns during this period emphasized the hardships imposed on federal workers who were being furloughed in the weeks before Christmas. Indeed, Newt Gingrich, who was generally portrayed as the villain who caused the crisis, came to be called the Gin*grinch* who stole Christmas from the children of hundreds of thousands of federal workers. Rather than suggest that the shutdown demonstrated that America could carry on with less government, media accounts focused on the difficulties encountered by Washington tourists unable to visit the capital's monuments, museums, and galleries. The woes of American travelers whose passports were delayed were also given considerable attention. This sort of coverage eventually convinced most Americans that the government shutdown was bad for the country. In the end, Gingrich and the congressional Republicans were forced to surrender and accept a new budget reflecting many of Clinton's priorities. The Republicans' defeat in the budget showdown contributed to the unraveling of the GOP's legislative program and, ultimately, to the Republicans' poor showing in the 1996 presidential elections. The character of media coverage of an event thus had enormous repercussions on how Americans interpreted it.

In 2001, the Bush White House recognized the importance of framing when presidential aides held extensive discussions with television networks and Hollywood filmmakers about the portrayal of America's war on terrorism. The White House asked the media to sound a patriotic note and frame the "war" as a patriotic duty. By all accounts, the media responded favorably, especially after several network news anchors became the target of anthrax-laced letters that had possibly been sent by terrorists. The Analyzing the Evidence unit on page 588 takes a closer look at when and how the media are able to influence public opinion.

The Media and Elections

Because of its power to both influence the political agenda—primarily the public's perceptions of issues and candidates—and frame the political debate, the mass media can have considerable influence on national elections. In the 2004 presidential contest, the national print and broadcast media were firmly convinced that national and homeland security issues were the top items on the national political agenda. Other issues received less attention, if they got any attention at all. This media perspective served the interests of the GOP, which is generally seen by most Americans as the party best able to protect the country from its foreign foes. Indeed,

How Powerful Is the Mass Media?

The mass media are a big part of our everyday lives and provide a lot of political information. For example, on television we encounter news programs, campaign commercials, and presidential speeches. It is therefore easy to think that the media strongly affect our political attitudes. But are the media really that powerful? What affects the media's ability to influence public opinion?

For messages in the media to change our minds, two things must happen. First, we must "receive" the message—that is, we have to be reading, watching, or listening. Second, we must "accept" the message—that is, we have to understand and believe the message. Each of these steps can limit the media's ability to affect our attitudes. Let us consider some data related to television coverage of politics.

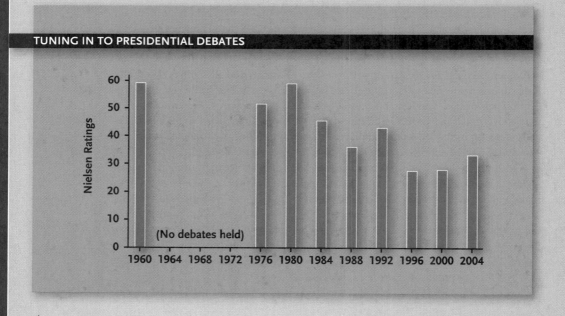

TUNING IN TO PRESIDENTIAL DEBATES

▲

Reception is often limited because people pay little attention to political news and instead consume media for sports, movies, and other types of programming. In fact, the growing number of entertainment options on cable television and elsewhere has helped shrink the audience for many political events. These are the average Nielsen ratings for the presidential debates in each year. A score of 50 would mean that an estimated 50 percent of all American households were tuned in to the event. Over time, the percentage of American homes tuning in to the debates has decreased.

Source: Martin E. Wattenberg, "Turnout in the 2004 Election," *Presidential Studies Quarterly* 35(1): 138–46.

But even if people watch an event like a presidential debate, their attitudes may not actually change. People often filter new information through their preexisting beliefs, accepting what they already agree with and rejecting anything different. Thus, media messages may only reinforce attitudes, rather than change them.

After the last presidential debate on October 13, 2004, ABC News asked a sample of registered voters which candidate, Bush or Kerry, had won the debate. Preexisting party preference strongly affected responses. The vast majority of Democrats (81 percent) thought Kerry had won. The vast majority of Republicans (73 percent) thought Bush had won.

WHO WON THE DEBATE?

	Bush	Kerry	Neither
Democrats	5%	81%	11%
Independents	35%	42%	22%
Republicans	73%	12%	11%

If the media cannot always change what we think, they may be able to change what we think *about*. Media attention to particular issues can make those issues more important to us. In this way, the media help shape the public's agenda. For example, in one study, one group of people were shown television news broadcasts that had been edited to include more coverage of nuclear weapons, while others were shown broadcasts that had been edited to include more coverage of unemployment. People were asked whether each of these issues was a serious problem both before and after they viewed these programs.

ISSUE IS A SERIOUS PROBLEM

	Before Experiment	After Experiment
Nuclear Weapons	35%	65%
Unemployment	43%	71%

In each case, watching more coverage of an issue increased the percentage of people who thought it was an important problem.

Source: Shanto Iyengar and Donald Kinder, *News That Matters* (Chicago: University of Chicago Press, 1987), 20.

President Bush had positioned himself as a strong military leader who responded to the challenge of terrorism with overwhelming military might. This agenda played an important role in the Democratic party's nominating process. Many leading Democrats were convinced that only a candidate with strong national security credentials would have any chance against Bush. Of course, Democrats eventually turned to Senator John Kerry, a decorated Vietnam War veteran whose combat record could be contrasted favorably with Bush's "stateside" service in the Air National Guard. Republicans nevertheless were delighted that security issues would be the focus of the contest as far as the national media were concerned. They were convinced that security was the GOP's strong suit, despite setbacks in Iraq and Democratic attempts to chip away at Bush's military credentials.

While the major media focused on national security, another important media segment saw the 2004 political agenda in somewhat different terms. For religious print and broadcast outlets associated with conservative religious denominations, the chief agenda items in 2004 were moral issues, particularly abortion and the question of whether same-sex unions should receive legal sanction. GOP strategists worked hard to keep these issues on the political agenda, sponsoring referendums on gay marriage in a number of hotly contested "battleground" states like Ohio. What was later called a "stealth" agenda, it also worked to the advantage of Bush and the Republicans in the general election.

Though the 2004 election was fought on issues that provided the Republicans with favorable terrain, media priming and important media frames tended to be more helpful to the Democrats. In particular, the media presented Kerry as considerably more intelligent than Bush. Bush's alleged lack of intelligence had been a media theme since the 2000 contest. The president was generally described as lacking a firm command of policy issues, depending heavily on his vice president and close advisers and generally lacking the ability to even construct a coherent sentence without the help of speech writers. Senator Kerry, on the other hand, was usually portrayed as intelligent, articulate, and cultured.

These depictions of the candidates primed Americans for the way in which the media framed many campaign events, especially the all-important presidential debates. Before the debates, Bush had led in the polls by a solid margin. The national media, however, almost unanimously declared Kerry the winner of the debates and devoted considerable air and print time to discussing the magnitude and meaning of Kerry's forensic victory. In subsequent polling, even Americans who had not seen or heard the debates asserted that Kerry had won. The media frame became a fact, Bush's commanding lead evaporated, and the election remained too close to call until the final hours of Election Day.

The Rise of Adversarial Journalism

The political power of the news media has increased greatly in recent years through the growing prominence of "adversarial journalism," a form of journalism in which the media adopt a hostile posture toward the government and public officials.

During the nineteenth century, American newspapers were completely subordinate to the political parties. Newspapers depended on official patronage—legal notice and party subsidies—for their financial survival and were controlled by party leaders.

(A vestige of that era survived into the twentieth century in such newspaper names as the *Springfield Republican* and the *St. Louis Globe-Democrat*.) At the turn of the century, with the development of commercial advertising, newspapers became financially independent, making possible the emergence of a formally nonpartisan press.

Presidents were the first national officials to see the opportunities in this development. By communicating directly with the electorate through newspapers and magazines, Theodore Roosevelt and Woodrow Wilson established political constituencies independent of party organizations and strengthened their own power relative to Congress. President Franklin D. Roosevelt used the radio, most notably in his famous fireside chats, to reach out to voters and make himself the center of American politics. FDR was also adept at developing close personal relationships with reporters, which enabled him to obtain favorable news coverage despite the fact that in his day a majority of newspaper owners and publishers were staunch conservatives. Following Roosevelt's example, subsequent presidents have sought to use the media to enhance their popularity and power. For example, through televised news conferences, President John F. Kennedy mobilized public support for his domestic- and foreign-policy initiatives.

During the 1950s and early 1960s, a few members of Congress also made successful use of the media—especially television—to mobilize national support for their causes. Senator Estes Kefauver of Tennessee became a major contender for the presidency and won a place on the 1956 Democratic national ticket as a result of his dramatic televised hearings on organized crime. Senator Joseph McCarthy of Wisconsin made himself a powerful national figure through his well-publicized investigations of alleged Communist infiltration of key American institutions. These senators, however, were more exceptional than typical. Through the mid-1960s, the executive branch continued to generate the bulk of the news coverage, and the media served as a cornerstone of presidential power.

The Vietnam War shattered this relationship between the press and the presidency. During the early stages of U.S. involvement, American officials in Vietnam who disapproved of the way the war was being conducted leaked to reporters information critical of administrative policy. Publication of this material infuriated the White House, which pressured publishers to block its release; on one occasion, President Kennedy went so far as to ask *The New York Times* to reassign its Saigon correspondent. The national print and broadcast media discovered, however, that there was an audience for critical coverage and investigative reporting among segments of the public skeptical of administration policy. As the Vietnam conflict dragged on, critical media coverage fanned antiwar sentiment. Moreover, growing opposition to the war among liberals encouraged some members of Congress, most notably Senator J. William Fulbright, chair of the Senate Foreign Relations Committee, to break with the president. In turn, these shifts in popular and congressional sentiment emboldened journalists and publishers to continue to present critical news reports. Through this process, journalists developed a commitment to adversarial journalism, while a constituency emerged that would rally to the defense of the media when it came under White House attack.

This pattern endured through the 1970s and into the present. Political forces opposed to presidential policies, many members of Congress, and the national news media began to find that their interests often overlapped. Adversarial, or "attack," journalism has become commonplace in America, and some critics have suggested that the media have contributed to popular cynicism and the low levels of citizen

History Principle

The Vietnam War shattered the favorable relationship between the news media and elected leaders.

participation that characterize contemporary American political processes. Of course in October 2001, the adversarial relationship between the government and the media was at least temporarily transformed into a much more supportive association as the media helped rally the American people for the fight against terrorism. And, indeed, some commentators have suggested that segments of the media, the more conservative media in particular, became far less adversarial in their tone during the Bush presidency than they had been in prior years.

The adversarial relationship between the government and segments of the press has resumed, however, during the war in Iraq. Such newspapers as *The Washington Post* and *The New York Times* castigated President Bush for going to war without winning the support of some of America's major allies. When American forces failed to uncover evidence that Iraq possessed weapons of mass destruction—a major reason cited by the administration for launching the war—these newspapers intimated that the war had been based on intelligence failures, if not outright deceptions by the Bush administration. The president, as noted earlier, denounced the media for distorting his record. Thus after a brief interlude of post–September 11 harmony, the customary hostilities between the government and the press seemed to manifest themselves once again.

MEDIA POWER AND RESPONSIBILITY

Free media are absolutely essential to democratic government. We depend on the media to investigate wrongdoing, publicize and explain governmental actions, evaluate programs and politicians, and bring to light matters that might otherwise be known to only a handful of governmental insiders. In short, without a free and active media, popular government would be virtually impossible. Citizens would have few means by which to know or assess the government's actions—other than the claims or pronouncements of the government itself. Moreover, without an active—indeed, aggressive—media, citizens would be hard pressed to make informed choices among competing candidates at the polls. Often enough, the media reveal discrepancies between candidates' claims and their records and between the images that candidates seek to project and the underlying realities.

History Principle

The increasing decay of party organizations over the past fifty years has made politicians more dependent on the media.

At the same time, the increasing decay of party organizations (see Chapter 11) has made politicians ever more dependent on favorable media coverage. National political leaders and journalists have had symbiotic relationships, at least since FDR's presidency, but initially politicians were the senior partners. They benefited from media publicity, but they did not totally depend on it as long as they could still rely on party organizations to mobilize votes. Journalists, on the other hand, depended on their relationships with politicians for access to information and would hesitate to report stories that might antagonize valuable sources. News reporters feared exclusion from the flow of information in retaliation. Thus, for example, reporters did not publicize potentially embarrassing information, widely known in Washington, about the personal lives of such figures as Franklin Roosevelt and John Kennedy.

With the decline of the parties, the balance of power between politicians and journalists has been reversed. Now that politicians have become heavily dependent

Rationality Principle	Collective-Action Principle	Institution Principle	Policy Principle	History Principle
Media coverage can be analyzed in terms of the interests of members of the media, politicians, and consumers.	The relationship between media members and politicians is a prisoner's dilemma. Each participant benefits from mutual co-operation but finds himself or herself tempted to defect on occasion to secure even larger gains.	The institutional stakes of the media sometimes interfere with objective and unbiased news coverage.	The media do not make policy, but policy is often made in response to or in anticipation of the media's reactions.	The Vietnam War shattered the favorable relationship between the news media and elected leaders.
The goals and incentives of journalists—such as ratings, career success, and prestige—influence what is created and reported as news.				The increasing decay of party organizations over the past fifty years has made politicians more dependent on the media.
News coverage is influenced by the interests of politicians.				
The preferences of consumers, such as the affluent or the people who watch news for its entertainment value, influence news content.				

on the media to reach their constituents, journalists no longer need fear that their access to information can be restricted in retaliation for negative coverage.

Freedom gives the media enormous power. The media can make or break reputations, help launch or destroy political careers, and build support for or rally opposition against programs and institutions.[38] Wherever there is so much power, there exists at least the potential for its abuse or overly zealous use. All things considered, free media are so critically important to the maintenance of a democratic society that we must be prepared to take the risk that the media will occasionally abuse their power. The forms of government control that would prevent the media from misusing their power would also certainly destroy our freedom.

---

[38]See Martin Linsky, *Impact: How the Press Affects Federal Policy Making* (New York: Norton, 1991).

SUMMARY

The American news media are among the world's freest. The print and broadcast media regularly present information and opinions critical of the government, political leaders, and policies. The media help determine the agenda, or focus of political debate; shape popular understanding of political events and results; and influence popular judgments of politicians and leaders.

Over the past century, the media have helped nationalize American political perspectives. Media coverage is influenced by the perspectives of journalists, politicians, and upscale audiences. The attention that the media give to protest and conflict is also a function of audience factors.

Free media are an essential ingredient of popular government.

FOR FURTHER READING

Arnold, R. Douglas. *Congress, the Press, and Political Accountability*. Princeton, N.J.: Princeton University Press, 2004.

Bagdikian, Ben. *The New Media Monopoly*. Boston: Beacon Press, 2004.

ONLINE READING ◯ Cook, Timothy. *Governing with the News: The News Media as a Political Institution*. Chicago: University of Chicago Press, 1997.

Fenton, Tom. *Bad News: The Decline of Reporting, the Business of News, and the Danger to Us All*. New York: HarperCollins, 2005.

Fritz, Ben, Bryan Keefer, and Brendan Nyhan. *All the President's Spin*. New York: Touchstone Books, 2004.

ONLINE READING ◯ Goldberg, Bernard. *Bias: A CBS Insider Exposes How the Media Distort the News*. New York: Regnery, 2002.

Hamilton, James. *All the News That's Fit to Sell*. Princeton, N.J.: Princeton University Press, 2004.

Iyengar, Shanto and Jennifer McGrady. *Media Politics: A Citizen's Guide*. New York: W. W. Norton, 2007.

ONLINE READING ◯ Kellner, Douglas. *Media Spectacle and the Crisis of Democracy: Terrorism, War, and Election Battles*. Boulder, Colo.: Paradigm, 2005.

Merritt, Davis. *Knightfall: Knight Ridder and How the Erosion of Newspaper Journalism Is Putting Democracy at Risk*. New York: Amacom Books, 2005.

ONLINE READING ◯ Norris, Pippa, Montague Kern, and Marion R. Just, eds. *Framing Terrorism: The News Media, the Government, and the Public*. New York: Routledge, 2003.

Rutherford, Paul. *Weapons of Mass Persuasion*. Toronto: University of Toronto Press, 2004.

Shogan, Robert. *Bad News: Where the Press Goes Wrong in the Making of the President*. Chicago: Dee, 2001.

Starr, Paul. *The Creation of the Media*. New York: Basic Books, 2004.

Trippi, Joe. *The Revolution Will Not Be Televised: Democracy, the Internet, and the Overthrow of Everything*. New York: Regan Books, 2004.

YouTube, like blogs, bypasses many of the traditional paths by which news is made. Instead of an institutional structure made up of journalists, editors, publishers, and politicians, each with their own interdependent set of interests, we have a bewildering cacophony of "citizen journalists." How do the principles of politics apply to a media outlet like YouTube? Do the traditional rules of media apply?

As the rationality principle teaches us, all political behavior has a purpose—even on YouTube. Some video posters are motivated by interests that are very traditional: they work for a candidate's opponent, capture an embarrassing moment on video, and post it anonymously on YouTube. Some enterprising amateur political activists even create humorous, and sometimes quite cutting, responses to advertisements in the commercial media.

At the same time, actors in the mainstream media—journalists, editors, and publishers—have a self-interest in remaining the primary source of political news. Just as citizens may be tuning in to YouTube and other citizen-driven information outlets, we can be sure that journalists tune in as well, drawing on new media but also attempting to maintain their role as the more "legitimate" source of news and information.

YouTube also provides an example of the collective-action principle. It is becoming an essential and inexpensive avenue by which politicians solve the collective-action problem inherent in political campaigns: recruiting activists, disseminating their message, and motivating voters.

Ultimately, YouTube and other citizen-driven outlets such as blogs are changing our perspective on the institution of the news media and turning us along a new historical path.

The New York Times, November 6, 2006

The Media Equation;
Online Player In the Game of Politics

BY DAVID CARR

Ken Avidor would not seem to constitute much of a threat to the Republican Party. A Minnesota graphic artist with no official political role, he is a self-described Luddite and a bit of a wonk with an interest in arcane transportation issues.

But last month, Mr. Avidor, a Democrat, managed to capture some video in which Michele Bachmann, a Republican candidate running for election from Minnesota's Sixth District, suggested that, after some fasting and praying, not only had God told her to become a tax attorney, he had called her to run for Congress. And now that the election was near, God was "focused like a laser beam, in his reasoning, on this race."

In the parlance of politics, Ms. Bachmann was "speaking to the room," in this case, a group at the Living Word Christian Center in Brooklyn Center,

Minn. The speech was Webcast live by the church group, allowing Mr. Avidor to capture the shaky but discernible video off his computer monitor. He then used a three-year-old Mac to edit the piece and then forward it to, well, the world at large.

The video on YouTube and Mr. Avidor's video blog (michelebachmann-movies.blogspot.com), was picked up by other bloggers and eventually, *The Star Tribune*, the daily newspaper in Minneapolis. Ms. Bachmann's opponents did everything they could to circulate the video and put her in a position of explaining God's unpaid consulting role in her campaign.

People in the elections business often say that the most powerful form of endorsement, next to meeting and being actually impressed by a candidate, is the recommendation of a trusted friend.

In this election, YouTube, with its extant social networks and the ability to forward a video clip and a comment with a flick of the mouse, has become a source of viral word-of-mouth. As a result, a disruptive technology that was supposed to upend a half-century-old distribution model of television is having a fairly disruptive effect on politics as well.

"In politics, there is a very high signal-to-noise ratio," said Mr. Avidor, who runs his blog in his spare time. "It gives you a megaphone and allows you to break through the clutter, and maybe capture the attention of major media. If you get the right message, it can go viral in a hurry and have a big impact."

Campaign video material, once restricted to expensive television commercials that were endlessly focus-grouped and tweaked, has performed a jailbreak.

And a growing tendency on the part of people to run to the Web for current information—an Associated Press/America Online poll found that 43 percent of likely voters get political news from the Internet—means a universe of new opportunities and hazards for candidates.

By now, everyone with a keyboard knows who Senator George Allen, Republican of Virginia, is and has at least a vague notion what macaca means. In some other instances, candidates have been fighting back—literally—creating yet more fodder for digital video. One of Mr. Allen's supporters is shown in a clip putting an impertinent questioner in a headlock, and in Colorado, United States Representative Marilyn Musgrave's supporters can be seen manhandling a video crew. It is vaguely comical, and of course, eminently forwardable.

"There have always been people from the other side shooting video," said Chuck DeFeo, manager of President Bush's online campaign in 2004. "When television came along, it was an era of one message for many. Now because YouTube functions as a network, you are seeing many messages handed from one person to another. In a way, it is a return to the past, to the grass roots, and can be a great touch point for campaigns."

The free video discourse has yet to eat into paid political advertising on television—according to Nielsen Media Research, spending on this year's midterm election is up 32 percent over 2002—but there is immense potential for a more intimate relationship with potential voters who can now program their own diet of political news.

"It is especially critical at the end of the campaign when you are looking for the marginal voter," said Jonah Seiger, managing partner at Connections Media, an Internet strategy firm. "Instead of the 500th commercial or the 15th robocall, I can get a video link from a friend. There is nothing more powerful in the sort of last-mile delivery of information than a contact with a so-called influential."

Candidates are doing extensive video outreach, from the undersheriff of Las Vegas, who is running for the sheriff's job and is showing video of himself taking down perps, to United States Senate incumbents trumpeting their records. But the phenomenon does not end there—much of the more interesting video has nothing to do with individual candidates. Instead, a growing genre of self-produced commentary is being made using cheap digital tools to create engagement of another sort.

A currently popular political spot on YouTube uses a parody of the Mac versus PC television ads to deft political effect. Written by John P. Kramer, a nighttime bartender at the Second City comedy club in Chicago, the spots are charming, a rare quality in political propaganda.

In the spot, two friendly men introduce themselves as a Republican and Democrat and suggest that they have much in common, with a few critical differences.

"You should see this guy cut taxes. It's insane!" says the Democrat in a voice filled with marvel, "And he knows I am better at things like Medicare, civil rights and Social Security."

The suite of six Web-only spots gently but powerfully suggests that Democrats generally have more on the ball.

"The reason I liked the Mac/PC ads is that the two guys are obviously friends and stay that way," said Mr. Kramer, who cast a few buddies from work to play the two sides of the political coin. "I'm a Democrat and my brother is a Republican, but I don't think that we want to [get] involved in some Shermanesque march to the sea, the concept of total war. We have to live together when it's all over."

"I just wanted to get people laughing and calm them down a bit," he added.

Another YouTube classic hits on the same topic to very different effect. A swell of music plays as a title unfolds: "The Difference between Democrats and Republicans." It is followed by five seconds of the blank screen and then the words, "The end." Silly, but like JibJab.com's Kerry-Bush mashup during the last presidential campaign, the point is surely made.

"People don't want a big, long explanation of political issues," said Mr. Avidor, who is spending the homestretch of the campaign continuing to use video to document Ms. Bachmann's every wiggle and wobble. "They want the sound bite, or even better, they want to see it. Seeing is believing."

Rationality Principle

Campaigns have been quick to take advantage of YouTube. Beyond the expense of producing an ad, YouTube costs them virtually nothing.

APPENDIX

The Declaration of Independence

In Congress, July 4, 1776

When in the course of human events, it becomes necessary for one people to dissolve the political bands which have connected them with another, and to assume among the Powers of the earth, the separate and equal station to which the Laws of Nature and of Nature's God entitle them, a decent respect to the opinions of mankind requires that they should declare the causes which impel them to the separation.

We hold these truths to be self-evident, that all men are created equal, that they are endowed by their Creator with certain unalienable rights, that among these are Life, Liberty, and the pursuit of Happiness. That to secure these rights, Governments are instituted among Men, deriving their just powers from the consent of the governed. That whenever any Form of Government becomes destructive of these ends, it is the Right of the People to alter or to abolish it, and to institute new Government, laying its foundation on such principles and organizing its powers in such form, as to them shall seem most likely to effect their Safety and Happiness. Prudence, indeed, will dictate that Governments long established should not be changed for light and transient causes; and accordingly all experience hath shown, that mankind are more disposed to suffer, while evils are sufferable, than to right themselves by abolishing the forms to which they are accustomed. But when a long train of abuses and usurpations, pursuing invariably the same Object evinces a design to reduce them under absolute Despotism, it is their right, it is their duty, to throw off such Government, and to provide new Guards for their future security.— Such has been the patient sufferance of these Colonies; and such is now the necessity which constrains them to alter their former Systems of Government. The history of the present King of Great Britain is a history of repeated injuries and usurpations, all having in direct object the establishment of an absolute Tyranny over these States. To prove this, let Facts be submitted to a candid world.

He has refused his Assent to Laws, the most wholesome and necessary for the public good.

He has forbidden his Governors to pass Laws of immediate and pressing importance, unless suspended in their operation till his Assent should be obtained; and when so suspended, he has utterly neglected to attend to them.

He has refused to pass other Laws for the accommodation of large districts of people, unless those people would relinquish the right of Representation in the Legislature, a right inestimable to them and formidable to tyrants only.

He has called together legislative bodies at places unusual, uncomfortable, and distant from the depository of their public Records, for the sole purpose of fatiguing them into compliance with his measures.

He has dissolved Representative Houses repeatedly, for opposing with manly firmness his invasions on the rights of the people.

He has refused for a long time, after such dissolutions, to cause others to be elected; whereby the Legislative powers, incapable of Annihilation, have returned to the People at large for their exercise; the State remaining in the mean time exposed to all dangers of invasion from without, and convulsions within.

He has endeavored to prevent the population of these States; for that purpose obstructing the Laws of Naturalization of Foreigners; refusing to pass others to encourage their migrations hither, and raising the conditions of new Appropriations of Lands.

He has obstructed the Administration of Justice, by refusing his Assent to Laws for establishing Judiciary powers.

He has made Judges dependent on his Will alone, for the tenure of their offices, and the amount and payment of their salaries.

He has erected a multitude of New Offices, and sent hither swarms of Officers to harass our People, and eat out their substance.

He has kept among us, in times of peace, Standing Armies without the Consent of our legislature.

He has affected to render the Military independent of and superior to the Civil Power.

He has combined with others to subject us to a jurisdiction foreign to our constitution, and unacknowledged by our laws; giving his Assent to their Acts of pretended Legislation:

For quartering large bodies of armed troops among us:

For protecting them, by a mock Trial, from Punishment for any Murders which they should commit on the Inhabitants of these States:

For cutting off our Trade with all parts of the world:

For imposing taxes on us without our Consent:

For depriving us in many cases, of the benefits of Trial by jury:

For transporting us beyond Seas to be tried for pretended offences:

For abolishing the free System of English Laws in a neighboring Province, establishing therein an Arbitrary government, and enlarging its Boundaries so as to render it at once an example and fit instrument for introducing the same absolute rule into these Colonies:

For taking away our Charters, abolishing our most valuable Laws, and altering fundamentally the Forms of our Governments:

For suspending our own Legislatures, and declaring themselves invested with Power to legislate for us in all cases whatsoever.

He has abdicated Government here, by declaring us out of his Protection and waging War against us.

He has plundered our seas, ravaged our Coasts, burnt our towns, and destroyed the lives of our people.

He is at this time transporting large armies of foreign mercenaries to compleat the works of death, desolation, and tyranny, already begun with circumstances of Cruelty & perfidy scarcely paralleled in the most barbarous ages, and totally unworthy the Head of a civilized nation.

He has constrained our fellow Citizens taken Captive on the high Seas to bear Arms against their Country, to become the executioners of their friends and Brethren, or to fall themselves by their Hands.

He has excited domestic insurrections amongst us, and has endeavored to bring on the inhabitants of our frontiers, the merciless Indian Savages, whose known rule of warfare, is an undistinguished destruction of all ages, sexes, and conditions.

In every stage of these Oppressions We have Petitioned for Redress in the most humble terms: Our repeated Petitions have been answered only by repeated injury. A Prince, whose character is thus marked by every act which may define a Tyrant, is unfit to be the ruler of a free people.

Nor have We been wanting in attention to our British brethren. We have warned them from time to time of attempts by their legislature to extend an unwarrantable jurisdiction over us. We have reminded them of the circumstances of our emigration and settlement here. We have appealed to their native justice and magnanimity, and we have conjured them by the ties of our common kindred to disavow these usurpations, which, would inevitably interrupt our connections and correspondence. They too must have been deaf to the voice of justice and of consanguinity. We must, therefore, acquiesce in the necessity, which denounces our Separation, and hold them, as we hold the rest of mankind, Enemies in War, in Peace Friends.

WE, THEREFORE, the Representatives of the UNITED STATES OF AMERICA, in General Congress, Assembled, appealing to the Supreme Judge of the world for the rectitude of our intentions, do, in the Name, and by Authority of the good People of these Colonies, solemnly publish and declare, That these United Colonies are, and of Right ought to be FREE AND INDEPENDENT STATES; that they are Absolved from all Allegiance to the British Crown, and that all political connection between them and the State of Great Britain, is and ought to be totally dissolved; and that as Free and Independent States, they have full Power to levy War, conclude Peace, contract Alliances, establish Commerce, and to do all other Acts and Things which Independent States may of right do. And for the support of this Declaration, with a firm reliance on the Protection of Divine Providence, we mutually pledge to each other our Lives, our Fortunes, and our sacred Honor.

The foregoing Declaration was, by order of Congress, engrossed, and signed by the following members:

John Hancock

NEW HAMPSHIRE
Josiah Bartlett
William Whipple
Matthew Thornton

MASSACHUSETTS BAY
Samuel Adams
John Adams
Robert Treat Paine
Elbridge Gerry

RHODE ISLAND
Stephen Hopkins
William Ellery

CONNECTICUT
Roger Sherman
Samuel Huntington
William Williams
Oliver Wolcott

NEW YORK
William Floyd
Philip Livingston
Francis Lewis
Lewis Morris

NEW JERSEY
Richard Stockton
John Witherspoon
Francis Hopkinson
John Hart
Abraham Clark

PENNSYLVANIA
Robert Morris
Benjamin Rush
Benjamin Franklin
John Morton
George Clymer
James Smith
George Taylor
James Wilson
George Ross

DELAWARE
Caesar Rodney
George Read
Thomas M'Kean

MARYLAND
Samuel Chase
William Paca
Thomas Stone
Charles Carroll,
   of Carrollton

VIRGINIA
George Wythe
Richard Henry Lee
Thomas Jefferson
Benjamin Harrison
Thomas Nelson, Jr.
Francis Lightfoot Lee
Carter Braxton

NORTH CAROLINA
William Hooper
Joseph Hewes
John Penn

SOUTH CAROLINA
Edward Rutledge
Thomas Heyward, Jr.
Thomas Lynch, Jr.
Arthur Middleton

GEORGIA
Button Gwinnett
Lyman Hall
George Walton

Resolved, That copies of the Declaration be sent to the several assemblies, conventions, and committees, or councils of safety, and to the several commanding officers of the continental troops; that it be proclaimed in each of the United States, at the head of the army.

The Articles of Confederation

Agreed to by Congress November 15, 1777; ratified and in force
March 1, 1781

To all whom these Presents shall come, we the undersigned Delegates of the States affixed to our Names send greeting. Whereas the Delegates of the United States of America in Congress assembled did on the fifteenth day of November in the Year of our Lord One Thousand Seven Hundred and Seventy seven, and in the Second Year of the Independence of America agree to certain articles of Confederation and perpetual Union between the States of Newhampshire, Massachusetts-bay, Rhodeisland and Providence Plantations, Connecticut, New-York, New-Jersey, Pennsylvania, Delaware, Maryland, Virginia, North-Carolina, South-Carolina and Georgia in the Words following, viz. "Articles of Confederation and perpetual Union between the states of Newhampshire, Massachusetts-bay, Rhodeisland and Providence Plantations, Connecticut, New-York, New-Jersey, Pennsylvania, Delaware, Maryland, Virginia, North-Carolina, South-Carolina and Georgia.

Art. I. The Stile of this confederacy shall be "The United States of America."

Art. II. Each state retains its sovereignty, freedom and independence, and every Power, Jurisdiction and right, which is not by this confederation expressly delegated to the United States, in Congress assembled.

Art. III. The said states hereby severally enter into a firm league of friendship with each other, for their common defence, the security of their Liberties, and their mutual and general welfare, binding themselves to assist each other, against all force offered to, or attacks made upon them, or any of them, on account of religion, sovereignty, trade, or any other pretence whatever.

Art. IV. The better to secure and perpetuate mutual friendship and intercourse among the people of the different states in this union, the free inhabitants of each of these states, paupers, vagabonds and fugitives from Justice excepted, shall be entitled to all privileges and immunities of free citizens in the several states; and the people of each state shall have free ingress and regress to and from any other state, and shall enjoy therein all the privileges of trade and commerce, subject to the same duties, impositions and restrictions as the inhabitants thereof respectively, provided that such restriction shall not extend so far as to prevent the removal of property imported into any state, to any other state of which the Owner is an inhabitant; provided also that no imposition, duties or restriction shall be laid by any state, on the property of the united states, or either of them.

If any Person guilty of, or charged with treason, felony, or other high misdemeanor in any state, shall flee from Justice, and be found in any of the united states, he shall upon demand of the Governor or executive power, of the state from which he fled, be delivered up and removed to the state having jurisdiction of his offence.

Full faith and credit shall be given in each of these states to the records, acts and judicial proceedings of the courts and magistrates of every other state.

Art. V. For the more convenient management of the general interests of the united states, delegates shall be annually appointed in such manner as the legislature of each state shall direct, to meet in Congress on the first Monday in November, in every year, with a power reserved to each state, to recall its delegates, or any of them, at any time within the year, and to send others in their stead, for the remainder of the Year.

No state shall be represented in Congress by less than two, nor by more than seven Members; and no person shall be capable of being a delegate for more than three years in any term of six years; nor shall any person, being a delegate, be capable of holding any office under the united states, for which he, or another for his benefit receives any salary, fees or emolument of any kind.

Each state shall maintain its own delegates in a meeting of the states, and while they act as members of the committee of the states.

In determining questions in the united states, in Congress assembled, each state shall have one vote.

Freedom of speech and debate in Congress shall not be impeached or questioned in any Court, or place out of Congress, and the members of congress shall be protected in their persons from arrests and imprisonments, during the time of their going to and from, and attendance on congress, except for treason, felony, or breach of the peace.

Art. VI. No state without the Consent of the united states in congress assembled, shall send any embassy to, or receive any embassy from, or enter into any conference, agreement, or alliance or treaty with any King, prince or state; nor shall any person holding any office or profit or trust under the united states, or any of them, accept of any present, emolument, office or title of any kind whatever from any king, prince or foreign state; nor shall the united states in congress assembled, or any of them, grant any title of nobility.

No two or more states shall enter into any treaty, confederation or alliance whatever between them, without the consent of the united states in congress assembled, specifying accurately the purposes for which the same is to be entered into, and how long it shall continue.

No state shall lay any imposts or duties, which may interfere with any stipulations in treaties, entered into by the united states in congress assembled, with any king, prince or state, in pursuance of any treaties already proposed by congress, to the courts of France and Spain.

No vessels of war shall be kept up in time of peace by any state, except such number only, as shall be deemed necessary by the united states in congress assembled, for the defence of such state, or its trade; nor shall any body of forces be kept up by any state, in time of peace, except such number only, as in the judgment of the united states, in congress assembled, shall be deemed requisite to garrison the forts necessary for the defence of such state; but every state shall always keep up a well regulated and disciplined militia, sufficiently armed and accoutred, and shall provide and constantly have ready for use, in public stores, a due number of field pieces and tents, and a proper quantity of arms, ammunition and camp equipage.

No state shall engage in any war without the consent of the united states in congress assembled, unless such state be actually invaded by enemies, or shall have received certain advice of a resolution being formed by some nation of Indians to invade such state, and the danger is so imminent as not to admit of a delay, till the united states in congress asssembled can be consulted; nor shall any state grant commissions to any ships or vessels of war, nor letters of marque or reprisal, except it be after a declaration of war by the united states in congress assembled, and then only against the kingdom or state and the subjects thereof, against which war has been so declared, and under such regulations as shall be established by the united states in congress assembled, unless such state be infested by pirates; in which case vessels of war may be fitted out for that occasion, and kept so long as the danger shall continue, or until the united states in congress assembled shall determine otherwise.

Art. VII. When land-forces are raised by any state for the common defence, all officers of or under the rank of colonel, shall be appointed by the legislature of each state respectively by whom such forces shall be raised, or in such manner as such state shall direct, and all vacancies shall be filled up by the state which first made the appointment.

Art. VIII. All charges of war, and all other expences that shall be incurred for the common defence or general welfare, and allowed by the united states in congress assembled, shall be defrayed out of a common treasury, which shall be supplied by the several states, in proportion to the value of all land within each state, granted to or surveyed for any Person, as such land and the buildings and improvements thereon shall be estimated according to such mode as the united states in congress assembled, shall from time to time direct and appoint. The taxes for paying that proportion shall be laid and levied by the authority and direction of the legislatures of the several states within the time agreed upon by the united states in congress assembled.

Art. IX. The united states in congress assembled, shall have the sole and exclusive right and power of determining on peace and war, except in the cases mentioned in the sixth article—of sending and receiving ambassadors—entering into treaties and alliances, provided that no treaty of commerce shall be made whereby the legislative power of the respective states shall be restrained from imposing such imposts and duties on foreigners, as their own people are subjected to, or from prohibiting the exportation of any species of goods or commodities whatsoever—of establishing rules for deciding in all cases, what captures on land or water shall be legal, and in what manner prizes taken by land or naval forces in the service of the united states shall be divided or appropriated—of granting letters of marque and reprisal in times of peace—appointing courts for the trial of piracies and felonies committed on the high seas and establishing courts for receiving and determining finally appeals in all cases of captures, provided that no member of congress shall be appointed a judge of any of the said courts.

The united states in congress assembled shall also be the last resort on appeal in all disputes and differences now subsisting or that hereafter may arise between two or more states concerning boundary, jurisdiction or any other cause whatever; which authority shall always be exercised in the manner following. Whenever the legislative or executive authority or lawful agent of any state in controversy with another shall present a petition to congress stating the matter in question and praying for a hearing, notice thereof shall be given by order of congress to the legislative or executive authority of the other state in controversy, and a day assigned for the appearance of the parties by their lawful agents, who shall then be directed to appoint by joint consent, commissioners or judges to constitute a court for hearing and determining the matter in question: but if they cannot agree, congress shall name three persons out of each of the united states, and from the list of such persons each party shall alternately strike out one, the petitioners beginning, until the number shall be reduced to thirteen; and from that number not less than seven, nor more than nine names as congress shall direct, shall in the presence of congress be drawn out by lot, and the persons whose names shall be so drawn or any five of them, shall be commissioners or judges, to hear and finally determine the controversy, so always as a major part of the judges who shall hear the cause shall agree in the determination: and if either party shall neglect to attend at the day appointed, without shewing reasons, which congress shall judge sufficient, or being present shall refuse to strike, the congress shall proceed to nominate three persons out of each state, and the secretary of congress shall strike in behalf of such party absent or refusing; and the judgment and sentence of the court to be appointed, in the manner before prescribed, shall be final and conclusive; and if any of the parties shall refuse to submit to the authority of such court, or to appear to defend their claim or cause, the court shall nevertheless proceed to pronounce sentence, or judgment, which shall in like manner be final and decisive, the judgment or sentence and other proceedings being in either case transmitted to congress, and lodged among the acts of congress for the security of the parties concerned: provided that every commissioner, before he sits in judgment, shall take an oath to be administered by one of the judges of the supreme or superior court of the state, where the cause shall be tried, "well and truly to hear and determine the matter in question, according to the best of his judgment, without favour, affection or hope of reward:" provided also that no state shall be deprived of territory for the benefit of the united states.

All controversies concerning the private right of soil claimed under different grants of two or more states, whose jurisdictions as they may respect such lands, and the states which passed such grants are adjusted, the said grants or either of them being at the same time claimed to have originated antecedent to such settlement of jurisdiction, shall on the petition of either party to the congress of the united states, be finally determined as near as may be in the same manner as is before prescribed for deciding disputes respecting territorial jurisdiction between different states.

The united states in congress assembled shall also have the sole and exclusive right and power of regulating the alloy and value of coin struck by their own authority, or by that of the respective states—fixing the standard of weights and measures throughout the united states—regulating the trade and managing all affairs with the Indians, not members of any of the states, provided that the legislative right of any state within its own limits be not infringed or violated—establishing and regulating post-offices from one state to another, throughout all the united states, and exacting such postage on the papers passing thro' the same as may be requisite to defray the expences of the said office—appointing all officers of the land forces, in the service of the united states, except regimental officers—appointing all the officers of the united states—making rules for the government and regulation of the said land and naval forces, and directing their operations.

The united states in congress assembled shall have the authority to appoint a committee, to sit in the recess of congress, to be denominated "A Committee of the States," and to consist of one delegate from each state; and to appoint such other committees and civil officers as may be necessary for managing the general affairs of the united states under their direction—to appoint one of their number to preside, provided that no person be allowed to serve in the office of president more than one year in any term of three years; to ascertain the necessary sums of Money to be raised for the service of the united states, and to appropriate and apply the same for defraying the public expences—to borrow money, or emit bills on the credit of the united states, transmitting every half year to the respective states an account of the sums of money so borrowed or emitted,—to build and equip a navy—to agree upon the number of land forces, and to make requisitions from each state for its quota, in proportion to the number of white inhabitants in such state; which requisition shall be binding, and thereupon the legislature of each state shall appoint the regimental officers, raise the men and cloath, arm and equip them in a soldier like manner, at the expence of the united states, and the officers and men so cloathed, armed and equipped shall march to the place appointed, and within the time agreed on by the united states in congress assembled: But if the united states in congress assembled shall, on consideration of circumstances judge proper that any state should not raise men, or should raise a smaller number than its quota, and that any other state should raise a greater number of men than the quota thereof, such extra number shall be raised, officered, cloathed, armed and equipped in the same manner as the quota of such state, unless the legislature of such state shall judge that such extra number cannot be safely spared out of the same, in which case they shall raise, officer, cloath, arm and equip as many of such extra number as they judge can be safely spared. And the officers and men so cloathed, armed and equipped, shall march to the place appointed, and within the time agreed on by the united states in congress assembled.

The united states in congress assembled shall never engage in a war, nor grant letters of marque and reprisal in time of peace, nor enter into any treaties or alliances, nor coin money, nor regulate the value thereof, nor ascertain the sums and expences necessary for the defence and welfare of the united states, or any of them, nor emit bills, nor borrow money on the credit of the united states, nor appropriate money, nor agree upon the number of vessels of war, to be built or purchased, or the number of land or sea forces to be raised, nor appoint a commander in chief of the army or navy, unless nine states assent to the same: nor shall a question on any other point, except for adjourning from day to day be determined, unless by the votes of a majority of the united states in congress assembled.

The congress of the united states shall have power to adjourn to any time within the year, and to any place within the united states, so that no period of adjournment be for a longer duration than the space of six Months, and shall publish the Journal of their proceedings monthly, except such parts thereof relating to treaties, alliances or military operations as in their judgment require secresy; and the yeas and nays of the delegates of each state on any question shall be entered on the Journal, when it is desired by any delegate; and the delegates of a state, or any of them, at his or their request shall be furnished with a transcript of the said Journal, except such parts as are above excepted to lay before the legislatures of the several states.

Art. X. The committee of the states, or any nine of them, shall be authorised to execute, in the recess of congress, such of the powers of congress as the united states in congress assembled, by the consent of nine states, shall from time to time think expedient to vest them with; provided that no power be delegated to the said committee, for the exercise of which, by the articles of confederation, the voice of nine states in the congress of the united states assembled is requisite.

Art. XI. Canada acceding to this confederation, and joining in the measures of the united states, shall be admitted into, and entitled to all the advantages of this union: but no other colony shall be admitted into the same, unless such admission be agreed to by nine states.

Art. XII. All bills of credit emitted, monies borrowed and debts contracted by, or under the authority of congress, before the assembling of the united states, in pursuance of the present confederation, shall be deemed and considered as a charge against the united states, for payment and satisfaction whereof the said united states and the public faith are hereby solemnly pledged.

Art. XIII. Every state shall abide by the determinations of the united states in congress assembled, on all questions which by this confederation are submitted to them. And the Articles of this confederation shall be inviolably observed by every state, and the union shall be perpetual; nor shall any alteration at any time hereafter be made in any of them; unless such alteration be agreed to in a congress of the united states, and be afterwards confirmed by the legislatures of every state.

AND WHEREAS it hath pleased the Great Governor of the World to incline the hearts of the legislatures we respectively represent in congress, to approve of, and to authorize us to ratify the said articles of confederation and perpetual union. KNOW YE that we the undersigned delegates, by virtue of the power and authority to us given for that purpose, do by these presents, in the name and in behalf of our respective constituents, fully and entirely ratify and confirm each and every of the said articles of confederation and perpetual union, and all and singular the matters and things therein contained: And we do further solemnly plight and engage the faith of our respective constituents, that they shall abide by the determination of the united states in congress assembled, on all questions, which by the said confederation are submitted to them. And that the articles thereof shall be inviolably observed by the states we respectively represent, and that the union shall be perpetual. In Witness whereof we have hereunto set our hands in Congress. Done at Philadelphia in the state of Pennsylvania the ninth Day of July in the Year of our Lord one Thousand seven Hundred and Seventy-eight and in the third year of the independence of America.

The Constitution of the United States of America

Annotated with references to *The Federalist Papers*

Federalist Paper
Number (Author)

[PREAMBLE]

We the People of the United States, in Order to form a more perfect Union, establish Justice, insure domestic Tranquility, provide for the common defence, promote the general Welfare, and secure the Blessings of Liberty to ourselves and our Posterity, do ordain and establish this Constitution for the United States of America.

84 (Hamilton)

ARTICLE I

Section 1
[LEGISLATIVE POWERS]

All legislative Powers herein granted shall be vested in a Congress of the United States, which shall consist of a Senate and House of Representatives.

10, 45 (Madison)

Section 2
[HOUSE OF REPRESENTATIVES, HOW CONSTITUTED, POWER OF IMPEACHMENT]

The House of Representatives shall be composed of Members chosen every second Year by the People of the several States, and the Electors in each State shall have the Qualifications requisite for Electors of the most numerous Branch of the State Legislature.

39, 45, 52–53, 57
(Madison)

No Person shall be a Representative who shall not have attained to the Age of twenty-five Years, and been seven Years a Citizen of the United States, and who shall not, when elected, be an inhabitant of that State in which he shall be chosen.

52 (Madison)

Representatives and *direct Taxes*[1] shall be apportioned among the several States which may be included within this Union, according to their respective Numbers, *which shall be determined by adding to the whole Number of free Persons, including those bound to Service for a Term of Years, and excluding Indians not taxed, three-fifths of all other Persons.*[2] The actual Enumeration shall be made within three Years after the first Meeting of the Congress of the United States, and within every subsequent Term of ten Years, in such Manner as they shall by Law direct. The Number of Representatives shall not exceed one for every thirty Thousand, but each State shall have at Least one Representative; *and until such enumeration shall be made, the State of New Hampshire shall be entitled to chuse three, Massachusetts eight, Rhode-Island and Provi-*

60 (Hamilton)
54, 58 (Madison)

55–56 (Madison)

[1]Modified by Sixteenth Amendment.
[2]Modified by Fourteenth Amendment.

dence Plantations one, Connecticut five, New-York six, New Jersey four, Pennsylvania eight, Delaware one, Maryland six, Virginia ten, North Carolina five, South Carolina five, and Georgia three.[3]

When vacancies happen in the Representation from any State, the Executive Authority thereof shall issue Writs of Election to fill such Vacancies.

The House of Representatives shall chuse their Speaker and other Officers; and shall have the sole Power of Impeachment.

Section 3
[THE SENATE, HOW CONSTITUTED, IMPEACHMENT TRIALS]

The Senate of the United States shall be composed of two Senators from each State, *chosen by the Legislature thereof*,[4] for six Years; and each Senator shall have one Vote.

Immediately after they shall be assembled in Consequence of the first Election, they shall be divided as equally as may be into three Classes. The Seats of the Senators of the first Class shall be vacated at the Expiration of the second Year, of the second Class at the Expiration of the fourth Year, and of the third Class at the Expiration of the sixth Year, so that one third may be chosen every second Year: *and if vacancies happen by Resignation, or otherwise, during the Recess of the Legislature of any State, the Executive thereof may make temporary Appointments until the next Meeting of the Legislature, which shall then fill such Vacancies.*[5]

No person shall be a Senator who shall not have attained to the Age of thirty Years, and been nine Years a Citizen of the United States, and who shall not, when elected, be an Inhabitant of that State for which he shall be chosen.

The Vice-President of the United States shall be President of the Senate, but shall have no Vote, unless they be equally divided.

The Senate shall chuse their other Officers, and also a President pro tempore, in the Absence of the Vice-President, or when he shall exercise the Office of President of the United States.

The Senate shall have the sole Power to try all Impeachments. When sitting for that Purpose, they shall be on Oath or Affirmation. When the President of the United States is tried, the Chief Justice shall preside: And no Person shall be convicted without the Concurrence of two-thirds of the Members present.

Judgment in Cases of Impeachment shall not extend further than to removal from Office, and disqualification to hold and enjoy any Office of honor, Trust or Profit under the United States: but the Party convicted shall nevertheless be liable and subject to Indictment, Trial, Judgment and Punishment, according to Law.

79 (Hamilton)

39, 45 (Madison)
60 (Hamilton)

62–63 (Madison)
59, 68 (Hamilton)

62 (Madison)
64 (Jay)

39 (Madison)
65–67, 79
(Hamilton)

84 (Hamilton)

---

[3]Temporary provision.

[4]Modified by Seventeenth Amendment.

[5]Modified by Seventeenth Amendment.

Section 4

[ELECTION OF SENATORS AND REPRESENTATIVES]

The Times, Places and Manner of holding Elections for Senators and Representatives, shall be prescribed in each State by the Legislature thereof; but the Congress may at any time by Law make or alter such Regulations, except as to the Places of chusing Senators.

59–61 (Hamilton)

The Congress shall assemble at least once in every Year, and such Meeting shall be on the first Monday in December, unless they shall by Law appoint a different Day.[6]

Section 5

[QUORUM, JOURNALS, MEETINGS, ADJOURNMENTS]

Each House shall be the Judge of the Elections, Returns and Qualifications of its own Members, and a Majority of each shall constitute a Quorum to do Business; but a smaller Number may adjourn from day to day, and may be authorized to compel the Attendance of absent Members, in such Manner, and under the Penalties as each House may provide.

Each House may determine the Rules of its Proceedings, punish its Members for disorderly Behavior, and, with the Concurrence of two-thirds, expel a Member.

Each House shall keep a Journal of its Proceedings, and from time to time publish the same, excepting such Parts as may in their Judgment require Secrecy; and the Yeas and Nays of the Members of either House on any questions shall, at the Desire of one-fifth of the present, be entered on the Journal.

Neither House, during the Session of Congress, shall, without the Consent of the other, adjourn for more than three days, nor to any other Place than that in which the two Houses shall be sitting.

Section 6

[COMPENSATION, PRIVILEGES, DISABILITIES]

The Senators and Representatives shall receive a Compensation for their Services, to be ascertained by Law, and paid out of the Treasury of the United States. They shall in all Cases, except Treason, Felony and Breach of the Peace, be privileged from Arrest during their Attendance at the Session of their respective Houses, and in going to and returning from the same; and for any Speech or Debate in either House, they shall not be questioned in any other Place.

No Senator or Representative shall, during the time for which he was elected, be appointed to any civil Office under the authority of the United States, which shall have been created, or the Emoluments whereof shall have been encreased during such time; and no Person holding any Office under the United States, shall be a Member of either House during his Continuance in Office.

55 (Madison)
76 (Hamilton)

---

[6]Modified by Twentieth Amendment.

Section 7
[PROCEDURE IN PASSING BILLS AND RESOLUTIONS]

66 (Hamilton)

All Bills for raising Revenue shall originate in the House of Representatives; but the Senate may propose or concur with Amendments as on other Bills.

69, 73 (Hamilton)

Every Bill which shall have passed the House of Representatives and the Senate, shall, before it become a Law, be presented to the President of the United States; if he approve he shall sign it, but if not he shall return it, with his Objections to that House in which it shall have originated, who shall enter the Objections at large on their Journal, and proceed to reconsider it. If after such Reconsideration two-thirds of that House shall agree to pass the Bill, it shall be sent, together with the Objections, to the other House, by which it shall likewise be reconsidered, and if approved by two-thirds of that House it shall become a Law. But in all such Cases the Votes of both Houses shall be determined by Yeas and Nays, and the Names of the Persons voting for and against the Bill shall be entered on the Journal of each House respectively. If any Bill shall not be returned by the President within ten Days (Sundays excepted) after it shall have been presented to him, the Same shall be a Law, in like Manner as if he had signed it, unless the Congress by their Adjournment prevent its Return, in which Case it shall not be a Law.

69, 73 (Hamilton)

Every Order, Resolution, or Vote to which the Concurrence of the Senate and House of Representatives may be necessary (except on a question of Adjournment) shall be presented to the President of the United States; and before the Same shall take Effect, shall be approved by him, or being disapproved by him, shall be repassed by two-thirds of the Senate and House of Representatives, according to the Rules and Limitations prescribed in the Case of a Bill.

Section 8
[POWERS OF CONGRESS]

The Congress shall have Power

30–36 (Hamilton)
41 (Madison)

To lay and collect Taxes, Duties, Imposts and Excises, to pay the Debts and provide for the common Defence and general Welfare of the United States; but all Duties, Imposts and excises shall be uniform throughout the United States;

To borrow Money on the Credit of the United States;

56 (Madison)

To regulate Commerce with foreign Nations, and among the several States, and

42, 45, 56
(Madison)

with the Indian Tribes;

32 (Hamilton)

To establish an uniform Rule of Naturalization, and uniform Laws on the subject of Bankruptcies throughout the United States;

42 (Madison)

To coin Money, regulate the Value thereof, and of foreign Coin, and fix the Standard of Weights and Measures;

42 (Madison)

To provide for the Punishment of counterfeiting the Securities and current Coin of the United States;

To establish Post Offices and post Roads;

42 (Madison)
42, 43 (Madison)

To promote the Progress of Science and useful Arts, by securing for limited Times to Authors and Inventors the exclusive Right to their respective Writings and Discoveries;

81 (Hamilton)

To constitute Tribunals inferior to the supreme Court;

To define and Punish Piracies and Felonies committed on the high Seas, and Offences against the Law of Nations;

42 (Madison)

To declare War, grant Letters of Marque and Reprisal, and make Rules concerning Captures on Land and Water;

41 (Madison)

To raise and support Armies, but no Appropriation of Money to that Use shall be for a longer Term than two Years;

23, 24, 26 (Hamilton)

To provide and maintain a Navy;

41 (Madison)

To make Rules for the Government and Regulation of the land and naval forces;

To provide for calling for the Militia to execute the Laws of the Union, suppress Insurrections and repel Invasions;

29 (Hamilton)

To provide for organizing, arming, and disciplining, the Militia, and for governing such Part of them as may be employed in the Service of the United States, reserving to the States respectively, the Appointment of the Officers, and the Authority of training the Militia according to the discipline prescribed by Congress;

29 (Hamilton)
56 (Madison)

To exercise exclusive Legislation in all Cases whatsoever, over such District (not exceeding ten Miles square) as may, by Cession of particular States, and the Acceptance of Congress, become the Seat of the Government of the United States, and to exercise like Authority over all Places purchased by the Consent of the Legislature of the State in which the Same shall be, for the Erection of Forts, Magazines, Arsenals, dock-Yards, and other needful Buildings;—And

32 (Hamilton)
43 (Madison)

To make all Laws which shall be necessary and proper for carrying into Execution the foregoing Powers, and all other Powers vested by this Constitution in the Government of the United States, or in any Department or Officer thereof.

29, 33 (Hamilton)
44 (Madison)

Section 9
[SOME RESTRICTIONS ON FEDERAL POWER]

The Migration or Importation of such Persons as any of the States now existing shall think proper to admit, shall not be prohibited by the Congress prior to the Year one thousand eight hundred and eight, but a Tax or Duty may be imposed on such Importation, not exceeding ten dollars for each Person.[7]

42 (Madison)

The privilege of the Writ of *Habeas Corpus* shall not be suspended, unless when in Cases of Rebellion or Invasion the public Safety may require it.

83, 84 (Hamilton)

No Bill of Attainder or ex post facto Law shall be passed.

84 (Hamilton)

No Capitation, or other direct, Tax shall be laid, unless in Proportion to the Census or Enumeration herein before directed to be taken.[8]

No Tax or Duty shall be laid on Articles exported from any State.

No Preference shall be given by any Regulation of Commerce or Revenue to the Ports of one State over those of another; nor shall vessels bound to, or from, one State, be obliged to enter, clear, or pay Duties in another.

32 (Hamilton)

No Money shall be drawn from the Treasury, but in Consequence of Appropriations made by Law; and a regular Statement and Account of the Receipts and Expenditures of all public Money shall be published from time to time.

---

[7]Temporary provision.

[8]Modified by Sixteenth Amendment.

No Title of Nobility shall be granted by the United States: And no Person holding any Office of Profit or Trust under them, shall, without the Consent of the Congress, accept of any present, Emolument, Office or Title, of any kind whatever, from any King, Prince, or foreign State.

Section 10
[RESTRICTIONS UPON POWERS OF STATES]

No State shall enter into any Treaty, Alliance, or Confederation; grant Letters of Marque and Reprisal; coin Money; emit Bills of Credit; make any Thing but gold and silver Coin a Tender in Payment of Debts; pass any Bill of Attainder, ex post facto Law, or Law impairing the Obligation of Contracts, or grant any Title of Nobility.

No State shall, without the Consent of the Congress, lay any Imposts or Duties on Imports or Exports, except what may be absolutely necessary for executing its inspection Laws: and the net Produce of all Duties and Imposts, laid by any State on Imports or Exports, shall be for the Use of the Treasury of the United States; and all such Laws shall be subject to the Revision and Control of the Congress.

No State shall, without the Consent of Congress, lay any Duty of Tonnage, keep Troops, or Ships of War in time of Peace, enter into any Agreement or Compact with another State, or with a foreign Power, or engage in War, unless actually invaded, or in such imminent Danger as will not admit of Delay.

ARTICLE II

Section 1
[EXECUTIVE POWER, ELECTION, QUALIFICATIONS OF THE PRESIDENT]

The executive Power shall be vested in a President of the United States of America. *He shall hold his Office during the Term of four years and, together with the Vice-President, chosen for the same Term, be elected, as follows:*[9]

Each State shall appoint, in such Manner as the Legislature thereof may direct, a Number of Electors, equal to the whole Number of Senators and Representatives to which the State may be entitled in the Congress: but no Senator or Representative, or Person holding an Office of Trust or Profit under the United States, shall be appointed an Elector.

The electors shall meet in their respective States, and vote by ballot for two Persons, of whom one at least shall not be an Inhabitant of the same State with themselves. And they shall make a List of all the Persons voted for, and of the Number of Votes for each; which List they shall sign and certify, and transmit sealed to the Seat of the Government of the United States, directed to the President of the Senate. The President of the Senate shall, in the Presence of the Senate and House of Representatives, open all the Certificates, and the Votes shall then be counted. The Person having the greatest Number of Votes shall be the President, if such Number be a Majority of the whole Number of Electors appointed; and if there be more than one who have such Majority and have an equal Number of Votes, then the House of Represen-

---

[9]Number of terms limited to two by Twenty-second Amendment.

tatives shall immediately chuse by Ballot one of them for President; and if no person have a Majority, then from the five highest on the List the said House shall in like Manner chuse the President. But in chusing the President, the Votes shall be taken by States, the Representation from each State having one Vote; A quorum for this Purpose shall consist of a Member or Members from two-thirds of the States, and a Majority of all the States shall be necessary to a Choice. In every Case, after the Choice of the President, the person having the greatest Number of Votes of the Electors shall be the Vice-President. But if there should remain two or more who have equal vote, the Senate shall chuse from them by Ballot the Vice-President.[10]

The Congress may determine the Time of chusing the Electors, and the Day on which they shall give their Votes; which Day shall be the same throughout the United States.

No Person except a natural born Citizen, or a Citizen of the United States, at the time of the Adoption of this Constitution, shall be eligible to the Office of President; neither shall any Person be eligible to that Office who shall not have attained to the Age of thirty-five Years, and been fourteen Years a Resident within the United States.

64 (Jay)

In Case of the Removal of the President from Office, or his Death, Resignation, or Inability to discharge the Powers and Duties of the said Office, the same shall devolve on the Vice-President, and the Congress may by Law provide for the Case of Removal, Death, Resignation, or Inability, both of the President and Vice-President, declaring what Officer shall then act as President, and such Officer shall act accordingly, until the Disability be removed, or a President shall be elected.

The President shall, at stated Times, receive for his Services, a Compensation, which shall neither be encreased nor diminished during the Period for which he shall have been elected, and he shall not receive within that Period any other Emolument from the United States, or any of them.

73, 79 (Hamilton)

Before he enter on the Execution of his Office, he shall take the following Oath or Affirmation:—"I do solemnly swear (or affirm) that I will faithfully execute the Office of President of the United States, and will to the best of my Ability, preserve, protect and defend the Constitution of the United States."

Section 2
[POWERS OF THE PRESIDENT]

The President shall be Commander in Chief of the Army and Navy of the United States, and of the Militia of the several States, when called into the actual Service of the United States; he may require the Opinion, in writing, of the principal Officer in each of the executive Departments, upon any Subject relating to the Duties of their respective Offices, and he shall have Power to grant Reprieves and Pardons for Offences against the United States, except in Cases of Impeachment.

69, 74 (Hamilton)

He shall have Power, by and with the Advice and Consent of the Senate, to make Treaties, provided two-thirds of the Senators present concur; and he shall nominate, and by and with the Advice and Consent of the Senate, shall appoint Ambassadors, other public Ministers and Consuls, Judges of the Supreme Court, and

42 (Madison)
64 (Jay)
66, 69, 76, 77 (Hamilton)

---

[10]Modified by Twelfth and Twentieth Amendments.

all other Officers of the United States, whose Appointments are not herein otherwise provided for, and which shall be established by Law: but the Congress may by Law vest the Appointment of such inferior Officers, as they think proper, in the President alone, in the Courts of Law, or in the Heads of Departments.

67, 76
(Hamilton)

The President shall have Power to fill up all Vacancies that may happen during the Recess of the Senate, by granting Commissions which shall expire at the End of their next Session.

Section 3
[POWERS AND DUTIES OF THE PRESIDENT]

69, 77, 78
(Hamilton)
42 (Madison)

He shall from time to time give to the Congress Information of the State of the Union, and recommend to their Consideration such Measures as he shall judge necessary and expedient; he may, on extraordinary Occasions, convene both Houses, or either of them, and in Case of Disagreement between them, with Respect to the Time of Adjournment, he may adjourn them to such Time as he shall think proper; he shall receive Ambassadors and other public Ministers; he shall take Care that the Laws be faithfully executed, and shall Commission all the Officers of the United States.

Section 4
[IMPEACHMENT]

39 (Madison)
69 (Hamilton)

The President, Vice-President and all civil Officers of the United States shall be removed from Office on Impeachment for, and Conviction of, Treason, Bribery, or other high Crimes and Misdemeanors.

ARTICLE III

Section 1
[JUDICIAL POWER, TENURE OF OFFICE]

65, 78, 79, 81, 82
(Hamilton)

The judicial Power of the United States, shall be vested in one supreme Court, and in such inferior Courts as the Congress may from time to time ordain and establish. The Judges, both of the supreme and inferior Courts, shall hold their Offices during good Behavior, and shall, at stated Times, receive for their Services, a Compensation, which shall not be diminished during their Continuance in Office.

Section 2
[JURISDICTION]

80 (Hamilton)

The judicial Power shall extend to all Cases, in Law and Equity, arising under this Constitution, the Laws of the United States, and Treaties made, or which shall be made, under their Authority;—to all Cases affecting Ambassadors, other public Ministers and Consuls;—to all Cases of admiralty and maritime Jurisdiction;—to Controversies to which the United States shall be a party;—to Controversies between two or more States;—*between a State and Citizens of another State;*—between

Citizens of different States,—between Citizens of the same State claiming Lands under Grants of different States, *and between a State,* or the Citizens thereof, *and foreign States, Citizens or Subjects.*[11]

In all Cases affecting Ambassadors, other public Ministers and Consuls, and those in which a State shall be Party, the supreme Court shall have original Jurisdiction. In all the other Cases before mentioned, the supreme Court shall have appellate Jurisdiction, both as to Law and Fact, with such Exceptions, and under such Regulations as Congress shall make.

81 (Hamilton)

The Trial of all Crimes, except in Cases of Impeachment, shall be by Jury; and such Trial shall be held in the State where the said Crimes shall have been committed; but when not committed within any State, the Trial shall be at such Place or Places as the Congress may by Law have directed.

83, 84
(Hamilton)

Section 3
[TREASON, PROOF, AND PUNISHMENT]

Treason against the United States, shall consist only in levying War against them, or in adhering to their Enemies, giving them Aid and Comfort. No Person shall be convicted of Treason unless on the Testimony of two Witnesses to the same overt Act, or on Confession in open Court.

43 (Madison)
84 (Hamilton)

The Congress shall have Power to declare the Punishment of Treason, but no Attainder of Treason shall work Corruption of Blood, or Forfeiture except during the Life of the Person attained.

43 (Madison)
84 (Hamilton)

ARTICLE IV

Section 1
[FAITH AND CREDIT AMONG STATES]

Full Faith and Credit shall be given in each State to the public Acts, Records, and judicial Proceedings of every other State. And the Congress may by general Laws prescribe the Manner in which such Acts, Records and Proceedings shall be proved, and the Effect thereof.

42 (Madison)

Section 2
[PRIVILEGES AND IMMUNITIES, FUGITIVES]

The Citizens of each State shall be entitled to all Privileges and Immunities of Citizens in the several States.

80 (Hamilton)

A person charged in any State with Treason, Felony or other Crime, who shall flee from Justice, and be found in another State, shall on Demand of the executive Authority of the State from which he fled, be delivered up to be removed to the State having Jurisdiction of the Crime.

No person held to Service or Labour in one State, under the Laws thereof, escaping into another, shall, in Consequence of any Law or Regulation therein, be discharged from

---

[11]Modified by Eleventh Amendment.

such *Service or Labour, but shall be delivered up on Claim of the Party to whom such Service or Labour may be due.*[12]

Section 3
[ADMISSION OF NEW STATES]

43 (Madison)

New States may be admitted by the Congress into this Union; but no new State shall be formed or erected within the Jurisdiction of any other State; nor any State be formed by the Junction of two or more States, or Parts of States, without the Consent of the Legislatures of the States concerned as well as of the Congress.

43 (Madison)

The Congress shall have Power to dispose of and make all needful Rules and Regulations respecting the Territory or other Property belonging to the United States; and nothing in this Constitution shall be so construed as to Prejudice any Claims of the United States, or of any particular State.

Section 4
[GUARANTEE OF REPUBLICAN GOVERNMENT]

39, 43 (Madison)

The United States shall guarantee to every State in this Union a Republican Form of Government, and shall protect each of them against Invasion; and on Application of the Legislature, or of the Executive (when the Legislature cannot be convened) against domestic Violence.

ARTICLE V

[AMENDMENT OF THE CONSTITUTION]

39, 43 (Madison)
85 (Hamilton)

The Congress, whenever two-thirds of both Houses shall deem it necessary, shall propose Amendments to this Constitution, or, on the Application of the Legislatures of two-thirds of the several States, shall call a Convention for proposing Amendments, which, in either Case, shall be valid to all Intents and Purposes, as Part of this Constitution, when ratified by the Legislatures of three-fourths of the several States, or by Conventions in three-fourths thereof, as the one or the other Mode of Ratification may be proposed by the Congress; *Provided that no Amendment which may be made prior to the Year One thousand eight hundred and eight shall in any Manner affect the first and fourth Clauses in the Ninth Section of the first Article;*[13] and that no State, without its Consent, shall be deprived of its equal Suffrage in the Senate.

ARTICLE VI

[DEBTS, SUPREMACY, OATH]

43 (Madison)

All Debts contracted and Engagements entered into, before the Adoption of this Constitution, shall be as valid against the United States under this Constitution,

---

[12]Repealed by Thirteenth Amendment.

[13]Temporary provision.

as under the Confederation.

This Constitution, and the Laws of the United States which shall be made in Pursuance thereof; and all Treaties made, or which shall be made, under the Authority of the United States, shall be the supreme Law of the Land; and the Judges in every State shall be bound thereby, any Thing in the Constitution or Laws of any State to the Contrary notwithstanding.

27, 33 (Hamilton)
39, 44 (Madison)

The Senators and Representatives before mentioned, and the Members of the several State Legislatures, and all executive and judicial Officers, both of the United States and of the several States, shall be bound by Oath or Affirmation, to support this Constitution; but no religious Test shall be required as a Qualification to any Office or public Trust under the United States.

27 (Hamilton)
44 (Madison)

ARTICLE VII

[RATIFICATION AND ESTABLISHMENT]

The Ratification of the Conventions of nine States, shall be sufficient for the Establishment of this Constitution between the States so ratifying the Same.[14]

39, 40, 43
(Madison)

Done in Convention by the Unanimous Consent of the States present the Seventeenth Day of September in the Year of our Lord one thousand seven hundred and Eighty seven and of the Independence of the United States of America the Twelfth. *In Witness* whereof We have hereunto subscribed our Names,

G:⁰ WASHINGTON—
*Presidt, and Deputy
from Virginia*

New Hampshire	JOHN LANGDON	New York	ALEXANDER HAMILTON
	NICHOLAS GILMAN	New Jersey	WIL: LIVINGSTON
Massachusetts	NATHANIEL GORHAM		DAVID BREARLEY
	RUFUS KING		WM PATERSON
Connecticut	WM SAML JOHNSON		JONA: DAYTON
	ROGER SHERMAN		

---

[14]The Constitution was submitted on September 17, 1787, by the Constitutional Convention, was ratified by the conventions of several states at various dates up to May 29, 1790, and became effective on March 4, 1789.

Pennsylvania	B Franklin	Virginia	John Blair—
	Thomas Mifflin		James Madison Jr.
	Robt Morris	North Carolina	Wm Blount
	Geo. Clymer		Richd Dobbs Spaight
	Thos. FitzSimons		Hu Williamson
	Jared Ingersoll		
	James Wilson	South Carolina	J. Rutledge
	Gouv Morris		Charles
			Cotesworth Pinckney
Delaware	Geo Read		Charles Pinckney
	Gunning Bedfor Jun		Pierce Butler
	John Dickinson		
	Richard Bassett	Georgia	William Few
	Jaco: Broom		Abr Baldwin
Maryland	James McHenry		
	Dan of St Thos. Jenifer		
	Danl Carroll		

Amendments to the Constitution

Proposed by Congress and Ratified by the Legislatures of the Several States, Pursuant to Article V of the Original Constitution.

Amendments I–X, known as the Bill of Rights, were proposed by Congress on September 25, 1789, and ratified on December 15, 1791. *The Federalist Papers* comments, mainly in opposition to a Bill of Rights, can be found in number 84 (Hamilton).

AMENDMENT I

[FREEDOM OF RELIGION, OF SPEECH, AND OF THE PRESS]

Congress shall make no law respecting an establishment of religion, or prohibiting the free exercise thereof; or abridging the freedom of speech, or of the press; or the right of the people peaceably to assemble, and to petition the Government for a redress of grievances.

AMENDMENT II

[RIGHT TO KEEP AND BEAR ARMS]

A well regulated Militia, being necessary to the security of a free State, the right of the people to keep and bear Arms, shall not be infringed.

AMENDMENT III

[QUARTERING OF SOLDIERS]

No Soldier shall, in time of peace be quartered in any house, without the consent of the Owner, nor in time of war, but in a manner to be prescribed by law.

AMENDMENT IV

[SECURITY FROM UNWARRANTABLE SEARCH AND SEIZURE]

The right of the people to be secure in their persons, houses, papers, and effects, against unreasonable searches and seizures, shall not be violated, and no Warrants shall issue, but upon probable cause, supported by Oath or affirmation, and particularly describing the place to be searched, and the persons or things to be seized.

AMENDMENT V

[RIGHTS OF ACCUSED PERSONS IN CRIMINAL PROCEEDINGS]

No person shall be held to answer for a capital, or otherwise infamous crime, unless on a presentment or indictment of a Grand Jury, except in cases arising in the land or naval forces, or in the Militia, when in actual service in time of War or in public danger; nor shall any person be subject for the same offence to be twice put in jeopardy of life or limb; nor shall be compelled in any Criminal Case to be a witness against himself, nor be deprived of life, liberty, or property, without due process of law; nor shall private property be taken for public use, without just compensation.

AMENDMENT VI

[RIGHT TO SPEEDY TRIAL, WITNESSES, ETC.]

In all criminal prosecutions, the accused shall enjoy the right to a speedy and public trial, by an impartial jury of the State and district wherein the crime shall have been committed, which district shall have been previously ascertained by law, and to be informed of the nature and cause of the accusation; to be confronted with the witnesses against him; to have compulsory process for obtaining Witnesses in his favor, and to have the Assistance of Counsel for his defence.

AMENDMENT VII

[TRIAL BY JURY IN CIVIL CASES]

In suits at common law, where the value in controversy shall exceed twenty dollars, the right of trial by jury shall be preserved, and no fact tried by a jury shall be otherwise re-examined in any Court of the United States, than according to the rules of the common law.

AMENDMENT VIII

[BAILS, FINES, PUNISHMENTS]

Excessive bail shall not be required, nor excessive fines imposed, nor cruel and unusual punishments inflicted.

AMENDMENT IX

[RESERVATION OF RIGHTS OF PEOPLE]

The enumeration in the Constitution, of certain rights, shall not be construed to deny or disparage others retained by the people.

AMENDMENT X

[POWERS RESERVED TO STATES OR PEOPLE]

The powers not delegated to the United States by the Constitution, nor prohibited by it to the States, are reserved to the States respectively, or to the people.

AMENDMENT XI

[Proposed by Congress on March 4, 1794; declared ratified on January 8, 1798.]

[RESTRICTION OF JUDICIAL POWER]

The Judicial power of the United States shall not be construed to extend to any suit in law or equity, commenced or prosecuted against one of the United States by Citizens of another State, or by Citizens or Subjects of any Foreign State.

AMENDMENT XII

[Proposed by Congress on December 9, 1803; declared ratified on September 25, 1804.]

[ELECTION OF PRESIDENT AND VICE-PRESIDENT]

The Electors shall meet in their respective states, and vote by ballot for President and Vice-President, one of whom, at least, shall not be an inhabitant of the same state with themselves; they shall name in their ballots the person voted for as President, and in distinct ballots the person voted for as Vice-President, and they shall make distinct lists of all persons voted for as President, and of all persons voted for as Vice-President, and of the number of votes for each, which lists they shall sign and certify, and transmit sealed to the seat of the government of the United States, directed to the President of the Senate;—The President of the Senate shall, in presence of the Senate and House of Representatives, open all the certificates and the votes shall then be counted;—The person having the greatest number of votes for President, shall be the President, if such number be a majority of the whole number of Electors appointed; and if no person have such majority, then from the persons having the highest numbers not exceeding three on the list of those voted for as President, the House of Representatives shall choose immediately, by ballot, the President. But in choosing the President, the votes shall be taken by states, the representation from each state having one vote; a quorum for this purpose shall consist of a member or members from two-thirds of the states, and a majority of all states shall be necessary to a choice. And if the House of Representatives shall not choose a President whenever the right of choice shall devolve upon them, before the fourth day of March next following, then the Vice-President, shall act as President, as in the case of the death or other constitutional disability of the President. The person having the greatest number of votes as Vice-President, shall be the Vice-President, if such a number be a majority of the whole number of Electors appointed, and if no person have a majority, then from the two highest numbers on the list, the Senate shall choose the Vice-President; a quorum for the purpose shall consist of two-thirds of the whole number of Senators, and a majority of the whole number shall be necessary to a choice. But no person constitutionally ineligible to the office of President shall be eligible to that of Vice-President of the United States.

AMENDMENT XIII

[Proposed by Congress on January 31, 1865; declared ratified on December 18, 1865.]

Section 1
[ABOLITION OF SLAVERY]

Neither slavery nor involuntary servitude, except as a punishment for crime whereof the party shall have been duly convicted, shall exist within the United States, or any place subject to their jurisdiction.

Section 2
[POWER TO ENFORCE THIS ARTICLE]

Congress shall have power to enforce this article by appropriate legislation.

AMENDMENT XIV

[Proposed by Congress on June 13, 1866; declared ratified on July 28, 1868.]

Section 1
[CITIZENSHIP RIGHTS NOT TO BE ABRIDGED BY STATES]

All persons born or naturalized in the United States, and subject to the jurisdiction thereof, are citizens of the United States and of the State wherein they reside. No state shall make or enforce any law which shall abridge the privileges or immunities of citizens of the United States; nor shall any State deprive any person of life, liberty, or property, without due process of law; nor deny to any person within its jurisdiction the equal protection of the laws.

Section 2
[APPORTIONMENT OF REPRESENTATIVES IN CONGRESS]

Representatives shall be apportioned among the several States according to their respective numbers, counting the whole number of persons in each State, excluding Indians not taxed. But when the right to vote at any election for the choice of electors for President and Vice-President of the United States, Representatives in Congress, the Executive and Judicial officers of a State, or the members of the Legislature thereof, is denied to any of the male inhabitants of such State, being twenty-one years of age, and citizens of the United States, or in any way abridged, except for participation in rebellion, or other crime, the basis of representation therein shall be reduced in the proportion which the number of such male citizens shall bear to the whole number of male citizens twenty-one years of age in such State.

Section 3
[PERSONS DISQUALIFIED FROM HOLDING OFFICE]

No person shall be a Senator or Representative in Congress, or elector of President and Vice-President, or hold any office, civil or military, under the United States, or under any State, who, having previously taken an oath, as a member of Congress, or as an officer of the United States, or as a member of any State legislature, or as an executive or judicial officer of any State, to support the Constitution of the United States, shall have engaged in insurrection or rebellion against the same, or given aid or comfort to the enemies thereof. But Congress may by a vote of two-thirds of each House, remove such disability.

Section 4
[WHAT PUBLIC DEBTS ARE VALID]

The validity of the public debt of the United States, authorized by law, including debts incurred for payment of pensions and bounties for services in suppressing insurrection or rebellion, shall not be questioned. But neither the United States nor any State shall assume or pay any debt or obligation incurred in aid of insurrection or rebellion against the United States, or any claim for the loss or emancipation of any slave; but all such debts, obligations and claims shall be held illegal and void.

Section 5
[POWER TO ENFORCE THIS ARTICLE]

The Congress shall have power to enforce, by appropriate legislation, the provisions of this article.

AMENDMENT XV

[Proposed by Congress on February 26, 1869; declared ratified on March 30, 1870.]

Section 1
[NEGRO SUFFRAGE]

The right of citizens of the United States to vote shall not be denied or abridged by the United States or by any State on account of race, color, or previous condition of servitude.

Section 2
[POWER TO ENFORCE THIS ARTICLE]

The Congress shall have power to enforce this article by appropriate legislation.

AMENDMENT XVI

[Proposed by Congress on July 12, 1909; declared ratified on February 25, 1913.]
[AUTHORIZING INCOME TAXES]

The Congress shall have power to lay and collect taxes on incomes, from whatever source derived, without apportionment among the several States, and without regard to any census or enumeration.

AMENDMENT XVII

[Proposed by Congress on May 13, 1912; declared ratified on May 31, 1913.]
[POPULAR ELECTION OF SENATORS]

The Senate of the United States shall be composed of two Senators from each State, elected by the people thereof, for six years; and each Senator shall have one vote. The electors in each State shall have the qualifications requisite for electors of the most numerous branch of the State Legislature.

When vacancies happen in the representation of any State in the Senate, the executive authority of such State shall issue writs of election to fill such vacancies:

Provided, That the Legislature of any State may empower the executive thereof to make temporary appointment until the people fill the vacancies by election as the Legislature may direct.

This amendment shall not be so construed as to affect the election or term of any Senator chosen before it becomes valid as part of the Constitution.

AMENDMENT XVIII

[Proposed by Congress December 18, 1917; declared ratified on January 29, 1919.]

Section 1
[NATIONAL LIQUOR PROHIBITION]

After one year from the ratification of this article the manufacture, sale, or transportation of intoxicating liquors within, the importation thereof into, or the exportation thereof from the United States and all territory subject to the jurisdiction thereof for beverage purposes is hereby prohibited.

Section 2
[POWER TO ENFORCE THIS ARTICLE]

The Congress and the several states shall have concurrent power to enforce this article by appropriate legislation.

Section 3
[RATIFICATION WITHIN SEVEN YEARS]

This article shall be inoperative unless it shall have been ratified as an amendment to the Constitution by the legislatures of the several states, as provided in the Constitution, within seven years from the date of the submission hereof to the states by the Congress.[15]

AMENDMENT XIX

[Proposed by Congress on June 4, 1919; declared ratified on August 26, 1920.]
[WOMAN SUFFRAGE]

The right of the citizens of the United States to vote shall not be denied or abridged by the United States or by any state on account of sex.

Congress shall have power to enforce this article by appropriate legislation.

AMENDMENT XX

[Proposed by Congress on March 2, 1932; declared ratified on February 6, 1933.]

Section 1
[TERMS OF OFFICE]

The terms of the President and Vice-President shall end at noon on the 20th day of January, and the terms of the Senators and Representatives at noon on the 3rd

---

[15]Repealed by Twenty-first Amendment.

day of January, of the years in which such terms would have ended if this article had not been ratified; and the terms of their successors shall then begin.

Section 2
[TIME OF CONVENING CONGRESS]

The Congress shall assemble at least once in every year, and such meeting shall begin at noon on the 3rd day of January, unless they shall by law appoint a different day.

Section 3
[DEATH OF PRESIDENT-ELECT]

If, at the time fixed for the beginning of the term of the President, the President-elect shall have died, the Vice-President-elect shall become President. If a President shall not have been chosen before the time fixed for the beginning of his term, or if the President-elect shall have failed to qualify, then the Vice-President-elect shall act as President until a President shall have qualified; and the Congress may by law provide for the case wherein neither a President-elect nor a Vice-President-elect shall have qualified, declaring who shall then act as President, or the manner in which one who is to act shall be selected, and such person shall act accordingly until a President or Vice President shall have qualified.

Section 4
[ELECTION OF THE PRESIDENT]

The Congress may by law provide for the case of the death of any of the persons from whom the House of Representatives may choose a President whenever the right of choice shall have devolved upon them, and for the case of the death of any of the persons from whom the Senate may choose a Vice-President whenever the right of choice shall have devolved upon them.

Section 5
[AMENDMENT TAKES EFFECT]

Sections 1 and 2 shall take effect on the 15th day of October following ratification of this article.

Section 6
[RATIFICATION WITHIN SEVEN YEARS]

This article shall be inoperative unless it shall have been ratified as an amendment to the Constitution by the legislatures of three-fourths of the several States within seven years from the date of its submission.

AMENDMENT XXI

[Proposed by Congress on February 20, 1933; declared ratified on December 5, 1933.]

Section 1
[NATIONAL LIQUOR PROHIBITION REPEALED]

The eighteenth article of amendment to the Constitution of the United States is hereby repealed.

Section 2
[TRANSPORTATION OF LIQUOR INTO "DRY" STATES]

The transportation or importation into any State, Territory, or Possession of the United States for delivery or use therein of intoxicating liquors, in violation of the laws thereof, is hereby prohibited.

Section 3
[RATIFICATION WITHIN SEVEN YEARS]

This article shall be inoperative unless it shall have been ratified as an amendment to the Constitution by conventions in the several States, as provided in the Constitution, within seven years from the date of the submission hereof to the States by the Congress.

AMENDMENT XXII

[Proposed by Congress on March 21, 1947; declared ratified on February 26, 1951.]

Section 1
[TENURE OF PRESIDENT LIMITED]

No person shall be elected to the office of President more than twice, and no person who has held the office of President or acted as President for more than two years of a term to which some other person was elected President shall be elected to the Office of the President more than once. But this Article shall not apply to any person holding the office of President when this Article was proposed by the Congress, and shall not prevent any person who may be holding the office of President, or acting as President, during the term within which this Article becomes operative from holding the office of President or acting as President during the remainder of such term.

Section 2
[RATIFICATION WITHIN SEVEN YEARS]

This Article shall be inoperative unless it shall have been ratified as an amendment to the Constitution by the legislatures of three-fourths of the several states within seven years from the date of its submission to the States by the Congress.

AMENDMENT XXIII

[Proposed by Congress on June 21, 1960; declared ratified on March 29, 1961.]

Section 1
[ELECTORAL COLLEGE VOTES FOR THE DISTRICT OF COLUMBIA]

The District constituting the seat of Government of the United States shall appoint in such manner as the Congress may direct:

A number of electors of President and Vice-President equal to the whole number of Senators and Representatives in Congress to which the District would be entitled if it were a State, but in no event more than the least populous State; they shall be in addition to those appointed by the States, but they shall be considered, for the purposes of the election of President and Vice-President, to be electors appointed by a State; and they shall meet in the District and perform such duties as provided by the twelfth article of amendment.

Section 2
[POWER TO ENFORCE THIS ARTICLE]

The Congress shall have power to enforce this article by appropriate legislation.

AMENDMENT XXIV

[Proposed by Congress on August 27, 1963; declared ratified on January 23, 1964.]

Section 1
[ANTI-POLL TAX]

The right of citizens of the United States to vote in any primary or other election for President or Vice-President, for electors for President or Vice-President, or for Senator or Representative of Congress, shall not be denied or abridged by the United States or any State by reasons of failure to pay any poll tax or other tax.

Section 2
[POWER TO ENFORCE THIS ARTICLE]

The Congress shall have power to enforce this article by appropriate legislation.

AMENDMENT XXV

[Proposed by Congress on July 7, 1965; declared ratified on February 10, 1967.]

Section 1
[VICE-PRESIDENT TO BECOME PRESIDENT]

In case of the removal of the President from office or his death or resignation, the Vice-President shall become President.

Section 2
[CHOICE OF A NEW VICE-PRESIDENT]

Whenever there is a vacancy in the office of the Vice-President, the President shall nominate a Vice-President who shall take the office upon confirmation by a majority vote of both houses of Congress.

Section 3
[PRESIDENT MAY DECLARE OWN DISABILITY]

Whenever the President transmits to the President pro tempore of the Senate and the Speaker of the House of Representatives his written declaration that he is unable to discharge the powers and duties of his office, and until he transmits to them a written declaration to the contrary, such powers and duties shall be discharged by the Vice-President as Acting President.

Section 4
[ALTERNATE PROCEDURES TO DECLARE AND TO END PRESIDENTIAL DISABILITY]
Whenever the Vice-President and a majority of either the principal officers of the executive departments, or of such other body as Congress may by law provide, transmit to the President pro tempore of the Senate and the Speaker of the House of Representatives their written declaration that the President is unable to discharge the powers and duties of his office, the Vice-President shall immediately assume the powers and duties of the office as Acting President.

Thereafter, when the President transmits to the President pro tempore of the Senate and the Speaker of the House of Representatives his written declaration that no inability exists, he shall resume the powers and duties of his office unless the Vice-President and a majority of either the principal officers of the executive departments, or of such other body as Congress may by law provide, transmit within four days to the President pro tempore of the Senate and the Speaker of the House of Representatives their written declaration that the President is unable to discharge the powers and duties of his office. Thereupon Congress shall decide the issue, assembling within 48 hours for that purpose if not in session. If the Congress, within 21 days after receipt of the latter written declaration, or, if Congress is not in session, within 21 days after Congress is required to assemble, determines by two-thirds vote of both houses that the President is unable to discharge the powers and duties of his office, the Vice-President shall continue to discharge the same as Acting President; otherwise, the President shall resume the powers and duties of his office.

AMENDMENT XXVI

[Proposed by Congress on March 23, 1971; declared ratified on June 30, 1971.]

Section 1
[EIGHTEEN-YEAR-OLD VOTE]
The right of citizens of the United States, who are eighteen years of age or older, to vote shall not be denied or abridged by the United States or by any State on account of age.

Section 2
[POWER TO ENFORCE THIS ARTICLE]
The Congress shall have power to enforce this article by appropriate legislation.

AMENDMENT XXVII

[Proposed by Congress on September 25, 1789; ratified on May 7, 1992.]
No law varying the compensation for the services of the Senators and Representatives shall take effect until an election of Representatives shall have intervened.

Federalist Papers

NO. 10: MADISON

Among the numerous advantages promised by a well-constructed Union, none deserves to be more accurately developed than its tendency to break and control the violence of faction. The friend of popular governments never finds himself so much alarmed for their character and fate as when he contemplates their propensity to this dangerous vice. He will not fail, therefore, to set a due value on any plan which, without violating the principles to which he is attached, provides a proper cure for it. The instability, injustice, and confusion introduced into the public councils have, in truth, been the mortal diseases under which popular governments have everywhere perished, as they continue to be the favorite and fruitful topics from which the adversaries to liberty derive their most specious declamations. The valuable improvements made by the American constitutions on the popular models, both ancient and modern, cannot certainly be too much admired; but it would be an unwarrantable partiality to contend that they have as effectually obviated the danger on this side, as was wished and expected. Complaints are everywhere heard from our most considerate and virtuous citizens, equally the friends of public and private faith and of public and personal liberty, that our governments are too unstable, that the public good is disregarded in the conflicts of rival parties, and that measures are too often decided, not according to the rules of justice and the rights of the minor party, but by the superior force of an interested and overbearing majority. However anxiously we may wish that these complaints had no foundation, the evidence of known facts will not permit us to deny that they are in some degree true. It will be found, indeed, on a candid review of our situation, that some of the distresses under which we labor have been erroneously charged on the operation of our governments; but it will be found, at the same time, that other causes will not alone account for many of our heaviest misfortunes; and, particularly, for that prevailing and increasing distrust of public engagements and alarm for private rights which are echoed from one end of the continent to the other. These must be chiefly, if not wholly, effects of the unsteadiness and injustice with which a factious spirit has tainted our public administration.

By a faction I understand a number of citizens, whether amounting to a majority or minority of the whole, who are united and actuated by some common impulse of passion, or of interest, adverse to the rights of other citizens, or to the permanent and aggregate interests of the community.

There are two methods of curing the mischiefs of faction: the one, by removing its causes; the other, by controlling its effects.

There are again two methods of removing the causes of faction: the one, by destroying the liberty which is essential to its existence; the other, by giving to every citizen the same opinions, the same passions, and the same interests.

It could never be more truly said than of the first remedy that it was worse than the disease. Liberty is to faction what air is to fire, an aliment without which it instantly expires. But it could not be a less folly to abolish liberty, which is essential to political life, because it nourishes faction than it would be to wish the annihilation of air, which is essential to animal life, because it imparts to fire its destructive agency.

The second expedient is as impracticable as the first would be unwise. As long as the reason of man continues fallible, and he is at liberty to exercise it, different opinions will be formed. As long as the connection subsists between his reason and his self-love, his opinions and his passions will have a reciprocal influence on each other; and the former will be objects to which the latter will attach themselves. The diversity in the faculties of men, from which the rights of property originate, is not less an insuperable obstacle to a uniformity of interests. The protection of these faculties is the first object of government. From the protection of different and unequal faculties of acquiring property, the possession of different degrees and kinds of property immediately results; and from the influence of these on the sentiments and views of the respective proprietors ensues a division of the society into different interests and parties.

The latent causes of faction are thus sown in the nature of man; and we see them everywhere brought into different degrees of activity, according to the different circumstances of civil society. A zeal for different opinions concerning religion, concerning government, and many other points, as well of speculation as of practice; an attachment to different leaders ambitiously contending for pre-eminence and power; or to persons of other descriptions whose fortunes have been interesting to the human passions, have, in turn, divided mankind into parties, inflamed them with mutual animosity, and rendered them much more disposed to vex and oppress each other than to co-operate for their common good. So strong is this propensity of mankind to fall into mutual animosities that where no substantial occasion presents itself the most frivolous and fanciful distinctions have been sufficient to kindle their unfriendly passions and excite their most violent conflicts. But the most common and durable source of factions has been the various and unequal distribution of property. Those who hold and those who are without property have ever formed distinct interests in society. Those who are creditors, and those who are debtors, fall under a like discrimination. A landed interest, a manufacturing interest, a mercantile interest, a moneyed interest, with many lesser interests, grow up of necessity in civilized nations, and divide them into different classes, actuated by different sentiments and views. The regulation of these various and interfering interests forms the principal task of modern legislation and involves the spirit of party and faction in the necessary and ordinary operations of government.

No man is allowed to be judge in his own cause, because his interest would certainly bias his judgment and, not improbably, corrupt his integrity. With equal, nay with greater reason, a body of men are unfit to be both judges and parties at the same time; yet what are many of the most important acts of legislation but so many judicial determinations, not indeed concerning the rights of single persons, but concerning the rights of large bodies of citizens? And what are the different classes of legislators but advocates and parties to the causes which they determine? Is a law proposed concerning private debts? It is a question to which the creditors are parties on one side and the debtors on the other. Justice ought to hold the balance between them. Yet the parties are, and must be, themselves the judges; and the most numerous party, or in other words, the most powerful faction must be expected to prevail. Shall domestic manufacturers be encouraged, and in what degree, by restrictions on foreign manufacturers? are questions which would be differently decided by the landed and the manufacturing classes, and probably by neither with a sole regard to justice and the public good. The apportionment of taxes on the various descriptions of property is an act which seems to require the most exact impartiality; yet there is, perhaps, no legislative act in which greater opportunity and temptation are given to a predominant party to trample on the rules of justice. Every shilling with which they overburden the inferior number is a shilling saved to their own pockets.

It is in vain to say that enlightened statesmen will be able to adjust these clashing interests and render them all subservient to the public good. Enlightened statesmen will not always be at the helm. Nor, in many cases, can such an adjustment be made at all without taking into view indirect and remote considerations, which will rarely prevail over the immediate interest which one party may find in disregarding the rights of another or the good of the whole.

The inference to which we are brought is that the *causes* of faction cannot be removed and that relief is only to be sought in the means of controlling its *effects*.

If a faction consists of less than a majority, relief is supplied by the republican principle, which enables the majority to defeat its sinister views by regular vote. It may clog the administration, it may convulse the society; but it will be unable to execute and mask its violence under the forms of the Constitution. When a majority is included in a faction, the form of popular government, on the other hand, enables it to sacrifice to its ruling passion or interest both the public good and the rights of other citizens. To secure the public good and private rights against the danger of such a faction, and at the same time to preserve the spirit and the form of popular government, is then the great object to which our inquiries are directed. Let me add that it is the great desideratum by which alone this form of government can be rescued from the opprobrium under which it has so long labored and be recommended to the esteem and adoption of mankind.

By what means is this object attainable? Evidently by one of two only. Either the existence of the same passion or interest in a majority at the same time must be prevented, or the majority, having such coexistent passion or interest, must be rendered, by their number and local situation, unable to concert and carry into effect schemes of oppression. If the impulse and the opportunity be suffered to coincide, we well know that neither moral nor religious motives can be relied on as an adequate control. They are not found to be such on the injustice and violence of individuals, and lose their efficacy in proportion to the number combined together, that is, in proportion as their efficacy becomes needful.

From this view of the subject it may be concluded that a pure democracy, by which I mean a society consisting of a small number of citizens, who assemble and administer the government in person, can admit of no cure for the mischiefs of faction. A common passion or interest will, in almost every case, be felt by a majority of the whole; a communication and concert results from the form of government itself; and there is nothing to check the inducements to sacrifice the weaker party or an obnoxious individual. Hence it is that such democracies have ever been spectacles of turbulence and contention; have ever been found incompatible with personal security or the rights of property; and have in general been as short in their lives as they have been violent in their deaths. Theoretic politicians, who have patronized this species of government, have erroneously supposed that by reducing mankind to a perfect equality in their political rights, they would at the same time be perfectly equalized and assimilated in their possessions, their opinions, and their passions.

A republic, by which I mean a government in which the scheme of representation takes place, opens a different prospect and promises the cure for which we are seeking. Let us examine the points in which it varies from pure democracy, and we shall comprehend both the nature of the cure and the efficacy which it must derive from the Union.

The two great points of difference between a democracy and a republic are: first, the delegation of the government, in the latter, to a small number of citizens elected by the rest; secondly, the greater number of citizens and greater sphere of country over which the latter may be extended.

The effect of the first difference is, on the one hand, to refine and enlarge the public views by passing them through the medium of a chosen body of citizens, whose wisdom may best discern the true interest of their country and whose patriotism and love of justice will be least likely to sacrifice it to temporary or partial considerations. Under such a regulation it may well happen that the public voice, pronounced by the representatives of the people, will be more consonant to the public good than if pronounced by the people themselves, convened for the purpose. On the other hand, the effect may be inverted. Men of factious tempers, of local prejudices, or of sinister designs, may, by intrigue, by corruption, or by other means, first obtain the suffrages, and then betray the interests of the people. The question resulting is, whether small or extensive republics are most favorable to the election of proper guardians of the public weal; and it is clearly decided in favor of the latter by two obvious considerations.

In the first place it is to be remarked that however small the republic may be the representatives must be raised to a certain number in order to guard against the cabals of a few; and that however large it may be they must be limited to a certain number in order to guard against the confusion of a multitude. Hence, the number of representatives in the two cases not being in proportion to that of the constituents, and being proportionally greatest in the small republic, it follows that if the proportion of fit characters be not less in the large than in the small republic, the former will present a greater option, and consequently a greater probability of a fit choice.

In the next place, as each representative will be chosen by a greater number of citizens in the large than in the small republic, it will be more difficult for unworthy candidates to practise with success the vicious arts by which elections are too often carried; and the suffrages of the people being more free, will be more likely to center on men who possess the most attractive merit and the most diffusive and established characters.

It must be confessed that in this, as in most other cases, there is a mean, on both sides of which inconveniencies will be found to lie. By enlarging too much the number of electors, you render the representative too little acquainted with all their local circumstances and lesser interests; as by reducing it too much, you render him unduly attached to these, and too little fit to comprehend and pursue great and national objects. The federal Constitution forms a happy combination in this respect; the great and aggregate interests being referred to the national, the local and particular to the State legislatures.

The other point of difference is the greater number of citizens and extent of territory which may be brought within the compass of republican than of democratic government; and it is this circumstance principally which renders factious combinations less to be dreaded in the former than in the latter. The smaller the society, the fewer probably will be the distinct parties and interests composing it; the fewer the distinct parties and interests, the more frequently will a majority be found of the same party; and the smaller the number of individuals composing a majority, and the smaller the compass within which they are placed, the more easily will they concert and execute their plans of oppression. Extend the sphere and you take in a greater variety of parties and interests; you make it less probable that a majority of the whole will have a common motive to invade the rights of other citizens; or if such a common motive exists, it will be more difficult for all who feel it to discover their own strength and to act in unison with each other. Besides other impediments, it may be remarked that, where there is a consciousness of unjust or dishonorable purposes, communication is always checked by distrust in proportion to the number whose concurrence is necessary.

Hence, it clearly appears that the same advantage which a republic has over a democracy in controlling the effects of faction is enjoyed by a large over a small republic—is enjoyed by the Union over the States composing it. Does this advantage consist in the substitution of representatives whose enlightened views and virtuous sentiments render them superior to local prejudices and to schemes of injustice? It will not be denied that the representation of the Union will be most likely to possess these requisite endowments. Does it consist in the greater security afforded by a greater variety of parties, against the event of any one party being able to outnumber and oppress the rest? In an equal degree does the increased variety of parties comprised within the Union increase this security? Does it, in fine, consist in the greater obstacles opposed to the concert and accomplishment of the secret wishes of an unjust and interested majority? Here again the extent of the Union gives it the most palpable advantage.

The influence of factious leaders may kindle a flame within their particular States but will be unable to spread a general conflagration through the other States. A religious sect may degenerate into a political faction in a part of the Confederacy; but the variety of sects dispersed over the entire face of it must secure the national councils against any danger from that source. A rage for paper money, for an abolition of debts, for an equal division of property, or for any other improper or wicked project, will be less apt to pervade the whole body of the Union than a particular member of it, in the same proportion as such a malady is more likely to taint a particular county or district than an entire State.

In the extent and proper structure of the Union, therefore, we behold a republican remedy for the diseases most incident to republican government. And according to the degree of pleasure and pride we feel in being republicans ought to be our zeal in cherishing the spirit and supporting the character of federalist.

PUBLIUS

NO. 51: MADISON

To what expedient, then, shall we finally resort, for maintaining in practice the necessary partition of power among the several departments as laid down in the Constitution? The only answer that can be given is that as all these exterior provisions are found to be inadequate the defect must be supplied, by so contriving the interior structure of the government as that its several constituent parts may, by their mutual relations, be the means of keeping each other in their proper places. Without presuming to undertake a full development of this important idea I will hazard a few general observations which may perhaps place it in a clearer light, and enable us to form a more correct judgment of the principles and structure of the government planned by the convention.

In order to lay a due foundation for that separate and distinct exercise of the different powers of government, which to a certain extent is admitted on all hands to be essential to the preservation of liberty, it is evident that each department should have a will of its own; and consequently should be so constituted that the members of each should have as little agency as possible in the appointment of the members of the others. Were this principle rigorously adhered to, it would require that all the appointments for the supreme executive, legislative, and judiciary magistracies should be drawn from the same fountain of authority, the people, through channels having no communication whatever with one another. Perhaps such a plan of constructing the several departments would be less difficult in practice than it may in contemplation appear. Some difficulties, however, and some additional expense would attend the execution of it. Some deviations, therefore, from the principle must be admitted. In the constitution of the judiciary department in particular, it might be inexpedient to insist rigorously on the principle: first, because peculiar qualifications being essential in the members, the primary consideration ought to be to select that mode of choice which best secures these qualifications; second, because the permanent tenure by which the appointments are held in that department must soon destroy all sense of dependence on the authority conferring them.

It is equally evident that the members of each department should be as little dependent as possible on those of the others for the emoluments annexed to their offices. Were the executive magistrate, or the judges, not independent of the legislature in this particular, their independence in every other would be merely nominal.

But the great security against a gradual concentration of the several powers in the same department consists in giving to those who administer each department the necessary constitutional means and personal motives to resist encroachments of the others. The provision for defense must in this, as in all other cases, be made commensurate to the danger of attack. Ambition must be made to counteract ambition. The interest of the man must be connected with the constitutional rights of the place. It may be a reflection on human nature that such devices should be necessary to control the abuses of government. But what is government itself but the greatest of all reflections on human nature? If men were angels, no government would be necessary. If angels were to govern men, neither external nor internal controls on government would be necessary. In framing a government which is to be administered by men over men, the great difficulty lies in this: you must first enable the government to control the governed; and in the next place oblige it to control itself. A dependence on the people is, no doubt, the primary control on the government; but experience has taught mankind the necessity of auxiliary precautions.

This policy of supplying, by opposite and rival interests, the defect of better motives, might be traced through the whole system of human affairs, private as well as public. We see it particularly displayed in all the subordinate distributions of power, where the constant aim is to divide and arrange the several offices in such a manner as that each may be a check on the other—that the private interest of every individual may be a sentinel over the public rights. These inventions of prudence cannot be less requisite in the distribution of the supreme powers of the State.

But it is not possible to give to each department an equal power of self-defense. In republican government, the legislative authority necessarily predominates. The remedy for this inconveniency is to divide the legislature into different branches; and to render them, by different modes of election and different principles of action, as little connected with each other as the nature of their common functions and their common dependence on the society will admit. It may even be necessary to guard against dangerous encroachments by still further precautions. As the weight of the legislative authority requires that it should be thus divided, the weakness of the executive may require, on the other hand, that it should be fortified. An absolute negative on the legislature appears, at first view, to be the natural defense with which the executive magistrate should be armed. But perhaps it would be neither altogether safe nor alone sufficient. On ordinary occasions it might not be exerted with the requisite firmness, and on extraordinary occasions it might be perfidiously abused. May not this defect of an absolute negative be supplied by some qualified connection between this weaker branch of the stronger department, by which the latter may be led to support the constitutional rights of the former, without being too much detached from the rights of its own department?

If the principles on which these observations are founded be just, as I persuade myself they are, and they be applied as a criterion to the several State constitutions, and to the federal Constitution, it will be found that if the latter does not perfectly correspond with them, the former are infinitely less able to bear such a test.

There are, moreover, two considerations particularly applicable to the federal system of America, which place that system in a very interesting point of view.

First. In a single republic, all the power surrendered by the people is submitted to the administration of a single government; and the usurpations are guarded against by a division of the government into distinct and separate departments. In the compound republic of America, the power surrendered by the people is first divided between two distinct governments, and then the portion allotted to each subdivided among distinct and separate departments. Hence a double security arises to the rights of the people. The different governments will control each other, at the same time that each will be controlled by itself.

Second. It is of great importance in a republic not only to guard the society against the oppression of its rulers, but to guard one part of the society against the injustice of the other part. Different interests necessarily exist in different classes of citizens. If a majority be united by a common interest, the rights of the minority will be insecure. There are but two methods of providing against this evil: the one by creating a will in the community independent of the majority—that is, of the society itself; the other, by comprehending in the society so many separate descriptions of citizens as will render an unjust combination of a majority of the whole very improbable, if not impracticable. The first method prevails in all governments possessing an hereditary or self-appointed authority. This, at best, is but a precarious security; because a power independent of the society may as well espouse the unjust views of the major as the rightful interests of the minor party, and may possibly be turned against both parties. The second method will be exemplified in the federal republic of the United States. Whilst all authority in it will be derived from and dependent on the society, the society itself will be broken into so many parts, interests and classes of citizens, that the rights of individuals, or of the minority, will be in little danger from interested combinations of the majority. In a free government the security for civil rights must be the same as that for religious rights. It consists in the one case in the multiplicity of interests, and in the other in the multiplicity of sects. The degree of security in both cases will depend on the number of interests and sects; and this may be presumed to depend on the extent of country and number of people comprehended under the same government. This view of the subject must particularly recommend a proper federal system to all the sincere and considerate friends of republican government, since it shows that in exact proportion as the territory of the Union may be formed into more circumscribed Confederacies, or States, oppressive combinations of a majority will be facilitated; the best security, under the republican forms, for the rights of every class of citizen, will be diminished; and consequently the stability and independence of some member of the government, the only other security, must be proportionally increased. Justice is the end of government. It is the end of civil society. It ever has been and ever will be pursued until it be obtained, or until liberty be lost in the pursuit. In a society under the forms of which the stronger faction can readily unite and oppress the weaker, anarchy may as truly be said to reign as in a state of nature, where the weaker individual is not secured against the violence of the stronger; and as, in the latter state, even the stronger individuals are prompted, by the uncertainty of their condition, to submit to a government which may protect the weak as well as themselves; so, in the former state, will the more powerful factions or parties be gradually induced, by a like motive, to wish for a government which will protect all parties, the weaker as well as the more powerful. It can be little doubted that if the State of Rhode Island was separated from the Confederacy and left to itself, the insecurity of rights under the popular form of government within such narrow limits would be displayed by such reiterated oppressions of factious majorities that some power altogether independent of the people would soon be called for by the voice of the very factions whose misrule had proved the necessity of it. In the extended republic of the United States, and among the great variety of interests, parties, and sects which it embraces, a coalition of a majority of the whole society could seldom take place on any other principles than those of justice and the general good; whilst there being thus less danger to a minor from the will of a major party, there must be less pretext, also, to provide for the security of the former, by introducing into the government a will not dependent on the latter, or, in other words, a will independent of the society itself. It is no less certain than it is important, notwithstanding the contrary opinions which have been entertained, that the larger the society, provided it lie within a practicable sphere, the more duly capable it will be of self-government. And happily for the *republican cause*, the practicable sphere may be carried to a very great extent by a judicious modification and mixture of the *federal principle*.

PUBLIUS

GLOSSARY

administrative adjudication   The application of rules and precedents to specific cases to settle disputes with regulated parties.

administrative legislation   Rules made by **regulatory agencies** and commissions.

adverse selection problem   The problem of incomplete information—of choosing alternatives without fully knowing the details of available options.

affirmative action   A policy or program designed to redress historic injustices committed against specific groups by making special efforts to provide members of these groups with access to educational and employment opportunities.

after-the-fact authority   The authority to follow up on the fate of a proposal once it has been approved by the full chamber.

agents of socialization   The social institutions, including families and schools, that help shape individuals' basic political **beliefs** and **values.**

agency loss   The difference between what a principal would like an agent to do and the agent's performance.

agency representation   The type of representation according to which representatives are held accountable to their constituents if they fail to represent them properly. That is, constituents have the power to hire and fire their representatives. This is the incentive for good representation even when the personal backgrounds, views, and interests of the representatives differ from their constituents'.

agenda power   The control over what a group will consider for discussion.

agenda setting   The process by which it is determined which issues are taken up by political actors and institutions.

amicus curiae   "Friend of the court," an individual or group who is not party to a lawsuit but seeks to assist the court in reaching a decision by presenting an additional **brief.**

appellate court   A court that hears the appeals of **trial court** decisions.

Articles of Confederation and Perpetual Union   America's first written constitution. Adopted by the Continental Congress in 1777, the Articles of Confederation and Perpetual Union were the formal basis for America's national **government** until 1789, when they were supplanted by the Constitution.

attitude (or opinion)   A specific preference on a specific issue.

Australian ballot   An electoral format that presents the names of all the candidates for any given office on the same ballot. Introduced at the end of the eighteenth century, the Australian ballot replaced the partisan ballot and facilitated split-ticket voting.

authoritarian government   A system of rule in which the **government** recognizes no formal limits but may nevertheless be restrained by the power of other social institutions.

autocracy   A form of **government** in which a single individual rules.

bandwagon effect   A shift in electoral support to the candidate whom public opinion polls report as the front-runner.

bicameralism   The division of a legislative assembly into two chambers, or houses.

bicameral legislature   A legislative assembly composed of two chambers, or houses.

Bill of Rights   The first ten amendments to the U.S. Constitution, adopted in 1791. The Bill of Rights ensures certain rights and liberties to the people.

block grants   Federal funds given to state **governments** to pay for goods, services, or programs, with relatively few restrictions on how the funds may be spent.

briefs   Written documents in which attorneys explain—using case precedents—why the Court should rule in favor of their client.

bureaucracy   The complex structure of offices, tasks, rules, and principles of organization that are employed by all large-scale institutions to coordinate the work of their personnel.

bureaucratic drift   The oft-observed phenomenon of bureaucratic implementation that produces policy more to the liking of the **bureaucracy** than to the original intention of the legislation that created it, but without triggering a political reaction from elected officials.

by-product theory   The idea that groups provide members with private benefits to attract membership. The possibility of group **collective action** emerges as a consequence.

cabinet   The secretaries, or chief administrators, of the major departments of the federal **government.** Cabinet secretaries are appointed by the president with the consent of the Senate.

casework An effort by members of Congress to gain the trust and support of constituents by providing personal service. One important type of casework consists of helping constituents obtain favorable treatment from the federal **bureaucracy.**

caucus system A normally closed meeting of a political or legislative group to select candidates, plan strategy, or make decisions regarding legislative matters.

checks and balances The mechanisms through which each branch of **government** is able to participate in and influence the activities of the other branches.

chief justice The justice on the **Supreme Court** who presides over the Court's public sessions.

civil law A system of jurisprudence, including private law and governmental actions, for settling disputes that do not involve criminal penalties.

civil liberties The protections of citizens from improper governmental action.

civil rights The legal or moral claims that citizens are entitled to make on the **government.**

class action suit A lawsuit in which a large number of persons with common interests join together under a representative party to bring or defend a lawsuit, as when hundreds of workers join together to sue a company.

clear and present danger The criterion used to determine whether speech is protected or unprotected, based on its capacity to present a "clear and present danger" to society.

clientele agencies Departments or bureaus of **government** whose mission is to promote, serve, or represent a particular interest.

closed primary A primary election in which voters can participate in the nomination of only those candidates of the party in which they have been enrolled for a period of time before primary day. Contrast with **open primary.**

closed rule The provision by the House Rules Committee that prohibits the introduction of amendments during debate.

cloture A rule allowing a supermajority of the members of a legislative body to set a time limit on debate over a given bill.

coalitional drift The prospect that enacted policy will change because the composition of the enacting coalition is temporary and provisional.

collective action The pooling of resources and the coordination of effort and activity by a group of people (often a large one) to achieve common goals.

commander in chief The power of the president as commander of the national military and the state national guard units (when called into service).

commerce clause Article I, Section 8, of the Constitution, which delegates to Congress the power "to regulate Commerce with foreign Nations, and among the several States, and with the Indian Tribes." This clause was interpreted by the **Supreme Court** to favor national power over the economy.

concurrent powers The authority possessed by *both* state and national **governments,** such as the power to levy taxes.

conference committee   A joint committee created to work out a compromise for House and Senate versions of a piece of legislation.

congressional caucus   An association of members of Congress based on party, interest, or social characteristics such as gender or race.

conscription   Compulsory military service, usually for a prescribed period or for the duration of a war; the draft.

conservative   Today this term refers to those who generally support the social and economic status quo and are suspicious of efforts to introduce new political formulas and economic arrangements. Many conservatives also believe that a large and powerful **government** poses a threat to citizens' freedoms.

constituency   The district making up the area from which an official is elected.

constitutional government   A system of rule in which formal and effective limits are placed on the power of the **government.**

cooperative federalism   A type of **federalism** existing since the New Deal era, in which **grants-in-aid** have been used strategically to encourage states and localities (without commanding them) to pursue nationally defined goals. Also known as intergovernmental cooperation.

court of appeals   A court that hears the appeals of trial-court decisions.

criminal law   The branch of law that deals with disputes or actions involving criminal penalties (as opposed to **civil law**). It regulates the conduct of individuals, defines crimes, and provides punishment for criminal acts.

de facto **segregation**   Racial segregation that is not a direct result of law or **government** policy but is, instead, a reflection of residential patterns, income distributions, or other social factors.

defendant   The individual or organization charged with a complaint in court.

de jure **segregation**   Racial segregation that is a direct result of law or official policy.

delegate   A representative who votes according to the preferences of his or her **constituency.**

delegated powers   Constitutional powers assigned to one governmental agency but exercised by another agency with the express permission of the first.

delegation   The transmission of authority to some other official or body for the latter's use (though often with the right of review and revision).

democracy   A system of rule that permits citizens to play a significant part in the governmental process, usually through the selection of key public officials.

devolution   The policy of removing a program from one level of **government** by deregulating it or passing it down to a lower level, such as from the national government to the state and local governments.

discuss list   List circulated by the chief justice of all the petitions to be discussed and voted on at the Supreme Court's conference.

dissenting opinion   A decision written by a justice who voted with the minority opinion in a particular case, in which the justice fully explains the reasoning behind his or her opinion.

distributive tendency   The tendency of Congress to spread the benefits of a policy over a wide range of members' districts.

divided government   The condition in American **government** in which the presidency is controlled by one party while the opposing party controls one or both houses of Congress.

double jeopardy   The Fifth Amendment right providing that a person cannot be tried twice for the same crime.

dual federalism   The system of **government** that prevailed in the United States from 1789 to 1937, in which most fundamental governmental powers were shared between the federal and state governments. Compare with **cooperative federalism.**

due process   The guarantee that no citizen may be subjected to arbitrary action by national or state **governments.**

electoral college   The presidential electors from each state who meet in their respective state capitals after the popular election to cast ballots for president and vice president.

equal protection clause   The provision of the Fourteenth Amendment guaranteeing citizens "the equal protection of the laws." This clause has served as the basis for the **civil rights** of African Americans, women, and other groups.

equal time rule   The requirement that broadcasters provide candidates for the same political office an equal opportunity to communicate their messages to the public.

establishment clause   The First Amendment clause that says, "Congress shall make no law respecting an establishment of religion." This law means that a wall of separation exists between church and state.

exclusionary rule   The ability of courts to exclude evidence obtained in violation of the Fourth Amendment.

Executive Office of the President (EOP)   The permanent agencies that perform defined management tasks for the president. Created in 1939, the EOP includes the Office of Management and Budget, the Council of Economic Advisers, the National Security Council, and other agencies.

executive orders   The rules or regulations issued by the president that have the effect and formal status of legislation.

executive privilege   The claim that confidential communications between the president and the president's close advisers should not be revealed without the consent of the president.

expressed powers   The notion that the Constitution grants to the federal government only those powers specifically named in its text.

fairness doctrine   An FCC requirement that broadcasters who air programs on controversial issues provide time for opposing views.

federalism The system of **government** in which a constitution divides power between a central government and regional governments.

fighting words Speech that directly incites damaging conduct.

filibuster A tactic used by members of the Senate to prevent action on legislation they oppose by continuously holding the floor and speaking until the majority backs down. Once given the floor, senators have unlimited time to speak, and it requires a **cloture** vote of three fifths of the Senate to end a filibuster.

527 committees Tax-exempt organizations that engage in political activities, often through unlimited "soft-money" contributions. The committees are not restricted by current law on campaign finance, thus exploiting a loophole in the Internal Revenue Service code.

formula grants **Grants-in-aid** in which a formula is used to determine the amount of federal funds a state or local **government** will receive.

framing The power of the media to influence how events and issues are interpreted.

free exercise clause The First Amendment clause that protects a citizen's right to believe and practice whatever religion he or she chooses.

free riding Enjoying the benefits of some good or action while letting others bear the costs. See also **public good.**

full faith and credit clause The provision in Article IV, Section I, of the Constitution requiring that the states normally honor the public acts and judicial decisions that take place in another state.

gatekeeping authority The right and power to decide if a change in policy will be considered.

gender gap A distinctive pattern of voting behavior reflecting the differences in views between women and men.

gerrymandering Apportionment of voters in districts in such a way as to give unfair advantage to one political party.

going public The act of launching a media campaign to build popular support.

government The institutions and procedures through which a land and its people are ruled.

grand jury A jury that determines whether sufficient evidence is available to justify a trial. Grand juries do not rule on the accused's guilt or innocence.

grants-in-aid A general term for funds given by Congress to state and local **governments.** See also **categorical grants-in-aid.**

Great Compromise An agreement reached at the Constitutional Convention of 1787 that gave each state an equal number of senators regardless of its population but linked representation in the House of Representatives to population.

home rule The power delegated by the state to a local unit of **government** to manage its own affairs.

illusion of salience The impression conveyed by polls that something is important to the public when it actually is not.

impeachment The charging of a governmental official (president or otherwise) with "Treason, Bribery, or other high Crimes and Misdemeanors" and bringing of him or her before Congress to determine guilt.

implementation The efforts of departments and agencies to translate laws into specific bureaucratic routines.

implied powers Powers derived from the **necessary and proper clause** (Article I, Section 8) of the Constitution. Such powers are not specifically **expressed** but are **implied** through the expansive interpretation of **delegated powers.**

incumbency Holding a political office for which one is running.

in forma pauperis **petitions** Requests to waive most rules and fees for indigent petitioners.

informational benefits Special newsletters, periodicals, training programs, conferences, and other information provided to members of groups to entice others to join.

inherent powers Powers claimed by a president that are not expressed in the Constitution but are inferred from it.

initiative A process by which citizens may petition to place a policy proposal on the ballot for public vote.

institutions The rules and procedures that provide incentives for political behavior, thereby shaping politics.

instrumental Done with purpose, sometimes with forethought, and even with calculation.

interest group An organized group of individuals or organizations that makes policy-related appeals to **government.**

intermediate scrutiny The test used by the Supreme Court in gender discrimination cases. Intermediate scrutiny places the burden of proof partially on the government and partially on the challengers to show that the law in question is constitutional.

issue advocacy Independent spending by individuals or **interest groups** that supports a campaign issue but is not directly tied to a particular candidate.

judicial activism The judicial philosophy that posits that the Court should see beyond the text of the Constitution or a statute to consider broader societal implications for its decisions.

judicial restraint The judicial philosophy whereby its adherents refuse to go beyond the text of the Constitution in interpreting its meaning.

judicial review The power of the courts to declare actions of the legislative and executive branches invalid or unconstitutional. The **Supreme Court** asserted this power in *Marbury v. Madison* (1803).

jurisdiction The sphere of a court's power and authority.

Kitchen Cabinet An informal group of advisers to whom the president turns for counsel and guidance. Members of the official **cabinet** may or may not also be members of the Kitchen Cabinet.

legislative clearance   The power given to the president to require all agencies of the executive branch to submit through the budget director all requests for new legislation along with estimates of their budgetary needs.

legislative initiative   The president's inherent power to bring a legislative agenda before Congress.

legislative supremacy   The preeminent position assigned to Congress by the Constitution.

Lemon test   Rule articulated in *Lemon v. Kurtzman* according to which governmental action in respect to religion is permissible if it is secular in purpose, does not lead to "excessive entanglement" with religion, and neither promotes nor inhibits the practice of religion.

libel   A written statement made in "reckless disregard of the truth" and considered damaging to a victim because it is "malicious, scandalous, and defamatory."

liberal   A liberal today generally supports political and social reform; extensive government intervention in the economy; the expansion of federal social services; more vigorous efforts on behalf of the poor, minorities, and women; and greater concern for consumers and the environment.

line-item veto   The power of the executive to veto specific provisions (lines) of a bill passed by the legislature.

lobbying   An attempt by a group to influence the policy process through persuasion of **government** officials.

majority leader   The elected leader of the party holding a majority of the seats in the House of Representatives or the Senate. In the House, the majority leader is subordinate in the party hierarchy to the Speaker.

majority party   The party that holds the majority of legislative seats in either the House or the Senate.

majority system   A type of electoral system in which, to win a seat in a representative body, a candidate must receive a majority (50 percent plus 1) of all the votes cast in the relevant district.

mandate   A claim by a victorious candidate that the electorate has given him or her special authority to carry out promises made during the campaign.

material benefits   Special goods, services, or money provided to members of groups to entice others to join.

measurement error   The failure to identify the true distribution of opinion within a population because of errors such as ambiguous or poorly worded questions.

minority leader   The elected leader of the party holding less than a majority of the seats in the House or Senate.

Miranda rule   The convention derived from the **Supreme Court**'s 1966 ruling in the case of *Miranda v. Arizona* whereby persons under arrest must be informed of their legal rights, including their right to counsel, before undergoing police interrogation.

mootness   A criterion used by courts to avoid hearing cases that no longer require resolution.

moral hazard Not knowing all aspects of the actions taken by an agent (nominally on behalf of the principal but potentially at the principal's expense).

multiple-member district An electorate that selects several candidates at large from an entire district, with each voter given the number of votes equivalent to the number of seats to be filled.

National Security Council (NSC) A presidential foreign policy advisory council composed of the president; the vice president; the secretaries of state, defense, and the treasury; the attorney general; and other officials invited by the president.

necessary and proper clause Article I, Section 8, of the Constitution, which enumerates the powers of Congress and provides Congress with the authority to make all laws "necessary and proper" to carry them out; also referred to as the elastic clause.

nomination The process by which political parties select their candidates for election to public office.

oligarchy A form of **government** in which a small group of landowners, military officers, or wealthy merchants controls most of the governing decisions.

open primary A primary election in which voters can choose on the day of the primary which party to enroll in to select candidates for the general election. Contrast with **closed primary**.

open rule The provision by the House Rules Committee that permits floor debate and the addition of amendments to a bill.

opinion The written explanation of the **Supreme Court**'s decision in a particular case.

oral argument The stage in **Supreme Court** proceedings in which attorneys for both sides appear before the Court to present their positions and answer questions posed by the justices.

oversight The effort by Congress, through hearings, investigations, and other techniques, to exercise control over the activities of executive agencies.

party activists Partisans who contribute time, energy, and effort to support their party and its candidates.

party caucus (party conference) A normally closed meeting of a political or legislative group to select candidates, plan strategy, or make decisions regarding legislative matters.

party identification An individual voter's psychological ties to one party or another.

party machines In the late nineteenth and early twentieth centuries, the local party organizations that controlled local politics through patronage and the nominations process.

party vote A **roll-call vote** in the House or Senate in which at least 50 percent of the members of one party take a particular position and are opposed by at least 50 percent of the members of the other party. Party votes are less common today than they were in the nineteenth century.

path dependency The idea that certain possibilities are made more or less likely because of the historical path taken.

patronage The resources available to higher officials, usually opportunities to make partisan appointments to offices and confer grants, licenses, or special favors to supporters.

per curiam A brief unsigned decision by an appellate court, usually rejecting petition to review the decision of a lower court.

permanent campaign Presidential politics in which all presidential actions are taken with reelection in mind.

petitioner's brief Document filed by the party bringing an appeal stating the facts of a case and reasons why the lower court's opinion should be overturned.

petitioner's reply brief Petitioner's answer to the respondent's brief.

plaintiff The individual or organization that brings a complaint in court.

plea bargains Negotiated agreements in criminal cases in which a **defendant** agrees to plead guilty in return for the state's agreement to reduce the severity of the criminal charge the defendant is facing.

pluralism The theory that all interests are and should be free to compete for influence in the **government**. The outcome of this competition is compromise and moderation.

plurality system A type of electoral system in which victory goes to the individual who gets the most votes in an election, but not necessarily a majority of the votes cast.

pocket veto A veto that is effected when Congress adjourns during the time a president has to approve a bill and the president takes no action on it. See also **veto.**

police power The power reserved to the **government** to regulate the health, safety, and morals of its citizens.

political action committees (PACs) Private groups that raise and distribute funds for use in election campaigns.

political caucus A normally closed meeting of a political or legislative group to select candidates, plan strategy, or make decisions regarding legislative matters.

political ideology A cohesive set of beliefs that form a general philosophy about the role of **government.**

political socialization The induction of individuals into the political culture; the process of learning the underlying **beliefs** and **values** on which the political system is based.

politics The conflicts and struggles over the leadership, structure, and policies of government.

pork-barrel legislation The appropriations made by legislative bodies for local projects that are often not needed but are created so that local representatives can carry their home district in the next election.

precedents Prior cases whose principles are used by judges as the bases for their decisions in present cases.

priming A process of preparing the public to take a particular view of an event or a political actor.

principal-agent relationship The relationship between a principal and his or her agent. This relationship may be affected by the fact that each is motivated by self-interest, yet their interests may not be well aligned.

prior restraint An effort by a government agency to block the publication of material it deems libelous or harmful in some other way; censorship. In the United States, the courts forbid prior restraint except under the most extraordinary circumstances.

privatization The act of moving all or part of a program from the public sector to the private sector.

privileges and immunities The provision from Article IV, Section 2, of the Constitution stating that a state cannot discriminate against someone from another state or give its own residents special privileges.

probability sampling A method used by pollsters to select a representative sample in which every individual in the population has an equal probability of being selected as a respondent.

professional legislature A legislature whose members serve full-time for multiple terms.

project grants Grant programs in which state and local **governments** submit proposals to federal agencies and for which funding is provided on a competitive basis.

proportional representation A multiple-member district system that allows each political party representation in proportion to its percentage of the vote.

proposal power The capacity to bring a proposal before the full legislature.

prospective voting Voting based on the imagined future performance of a candidate.

public law Cases involving the actions of public agencies or officials.

public opinion Citizens' attitudes about political issues, leaders, institutions, and events.

public opinion polls The scientific instruments for measuring public opinion.

purposive benefits **Selective benefits** of group membership that emphasize the purpose and accomplishments of the group.

push polling A polling technique in which the questions are designed to shape the respondent's opinion.

random digit dialing A poll in which respondents are selected at random from a list of ten-digit telephone numbers, with every effort made to avoid bias in the construction of the sample.

random sampling Polls in which respondents are chosen mathematically, at random, with every effort made to avoid bias in the construction of the sample.

recall The removal of a public official by popular vote.

referendum The practice of referring a measure proposed or passed by a legislature to the vote of the electorate for approval or rejection.

regular concurrence A concurring opinion that agrees with the outcome and the majority's rationale but highlights a particular legal point.

regulatory agencies Departments, bureaus, or independent agencies whose primary mission is to eliminate or restrict certain behaviors defined as negative in themselves or negative in their consequences.

reserved powers Powers, derived from the Tenth Amendment to the Constitution, that are not specifically **delegated** to the national government or denied to the states.

respondent's brief Document filed by the party that won in the lower court explaining why that court's decision should not be overturned.

retrospective voting Voting based on the past performance of a candidate.

right to privacy The right to be let alone, which has been interpreted by the Supreme Court to entail free access to birth control and abortions.

right of rebuttal An FCC regulation giving individuals the right to have the opportunity to respond to personal attacks made on a radio or TV broadcast.

roll-call votes Votes in which each legislator's yes or no vote is recorded.

rule making A quasi-legislative administrative process that produces regulations by **government** agencies.

rule of four The rule that *certiorari* will be granted only if four justices vote in favor of the petition.

salient interests Attitudes and views that are especially important to the individual holding them.

sample A small group selected by researchers to represent the most important characteristics of an entire population.

sampling error A polling error that arises on account of the small size of the sample.

selection bias A polling error in which the sample is not representative of the population being studied, so that some opinions are over- or underrepresented.

selection bias (in the media) The predisposition of consumers to choose particular types of stories.

selective benefits Benefits that do not go to everyone but, rather, are distributed selectively—only to those who contribute to the group enterprise.

senatorial courtesy The practice whereby the president, before formally nominating a person for a federal judgeship, finds out whether the senators from the candidate's state support the nomination.

seniority The priority or status ranking given to an individual on the basis of length of continuous service on a congressional committee.

"separate but equal" rule The doctrine that public accommodations could be segregated by race but still be equal.

separation of powers The division of governmental power among several institutions that must cooperate in decision making.

single-member district An electorate that is allowed to elect only one representative from each district—the typical method of representation in the United States.

slander An oral statement made in "reckless disregard of the truth" and considered damaging to a victim because it is "malicious, scandalous, and defamatory."

solidary benefits Selective benefits of group membership that emphasize friendship, networking, and consciousness-raising.

sound bites Short snippets of information aimed at dramatizing a story, rather than explaining its substantive meaning.

sovereignty Supreme and independent political authority.

Speaker of the House The chief presiding officer of the House of Representatives. The Speaker is elected at the beginning of every Congress on a straight **party vote**. He or she is the most important party and House leader and can influence the legislative agenda, the fate of individual pieces of legislation, and members' positions within the House.

special concurrence A concurring opinion that agrees with the outcome but disagrees with the rationale presented by the majority opinion.

speech plus Speech accompanied by activities such as sit-ins, picketing, and demonstrations. Protection of this form of speech under the First Amendment is conditional, and restrictions imposed by state or local authorities are acceptable if properly balanced by considerations of public order.

staff agencies The agencies responsible for providing Congress with independent expertise, administration, and **oversight** capability.

standing The right of an individual or an organization to initiate a court case.

standing committee A permanent legislative committee that considers legislation within its designated subject area; the basic unit of deliberation in the House and Senate.

stare decisis Literally "let the decision stand." The doctrine whereby a previous decision by a court applies as a precedent in similar cases until that decision is overruled.

state sovereign immunity A legal doctrine holding that states cannot be sued for violating an act of Congress.

states' rights The principle that states should oppose increases in the authority of the national **government**. This view was most popular before the Civil War.

strict scrutiny The criteria used by the Supreme Court in racial discrimination cases and other cases involving civil rights. Strict scrutiny places the burden of proof on the government, rather than on the challengers, to show that the law in question is constitutional.

supremacy clause A clause of Article VI of the Constitution, that states that all laws passed by the national **government** and all treaties are the supreme laws of the land and superior to all laws adopted by any state or any subdivision.

supreme court The highest court in a particular state or in the United States. This court primarily serves an appellate function.

third parties Parties that organize to compete against the two major American political parties.

Three-fifths Compromise An agreement reached at the Constitutional Convention of 1787 stipulating that for purposes of the apportionment of congressional seats, every slave would be counted as three fifths of a person.

totalitarian government A system of rule in which the **government** recognizes no formal limits on its power and seeks to absorb or eliminate other social institutions that might challenge it.

transaction costs The cost of clarifying each aspect of a principal-agent relationship and monitoring it to make sure arrangements are complied with.

trial court The first court to hear a criminal or civil case.

trustee A representative who votes based on what he or she thinks is best for his or her **constituency**.

tyranny Oppressive **government** that employs the cruel and unjust use of power and authority.

unfunded mandates National standards or programs imposed on state and local **governments** by the federal government without accompanying funding or reimbursement.

values (or beliefs) The basic principles that shape a person's opinions about political issues and events.

veto The president's constitutional power to turn down acts of Congress within ten days of their passage while Congress is in session. A presidential veto may be overridden by a two-thirds vote of each house of Congress.

veto power The ability to defeat something even if it has made it on to the agenda of an institution.

War Powers Resolution A resolution of Congress declaring that the president can send troops into action abroad only by authorization of Congress or if U.S. troops are already under attack or seriously threatened.

whip system A communications network in each house of Congress. Whips poll the membership to learn their intentions on specific legislative issues and assist the **majority** and **minority leaders** in various tasks.

White House staff The analysts and advisers to the president, often given the title "special assistant."

writ of appeal Writ that may be issued to accept appeals, mainly from the decision of a three-judge district court.

writ of certification Writ issued when a U.S. Court of Appeals asks the Supreme Court for instructions on a point of law that has never been decided.

writ of *certiorari* A formal request by an appellant to have the Supreme Court review a decision of a lower court. *Certiorari* is from a Latin word meaning "to make more certain."

writ of *habeas corpus* A court order demanding that an individual in custody be brought into court and shown the cause for detention. *Habeas corpus* is guaranteed by the Constitution and can be suspended only in cases of rebellion or invasion.

CREDITS

Alexei Barrionuevo: "Springtime for Ethanol," *The New York Times*, January 23, 2007. Copyright © 2007 The New York Times Company.

David Carr: "The Media Equation: Online Player in the Game of Politics," *The New York Times*, November 6, 2006. Copyright © 2006 The New York Times Company. Reprinted with permission.

Linda Greenhouse: "Case of the Dwindling Docket Mystifies the Supreme Court," *The New York Times*, December 7, 2006. Copyright © 2006 The New York Times Company. Reprinted with permission.

Carl Hulse: "Flag Amendment Narrowly Fails in Senate Vote," *The New York Times*, June 28, 2006. Copyright © 2006 The New York Times Company. Reprinted with permission. "Moderate Republicans Feeling Like Endangered Species," *The New York Times*, October 28, 2006. Copyright © 2006 The New York Times Company.

Carl Hulse, et al: "How 3 G.O.P. Veterans Stalled Bush Detainee Bill," *The New York Times*, September 17, 2006. Copyright © 2006 The New York Times Company. Reprinted with permission.

Adam Liptak: "Secrecy is at Issue in Suits Opposing Spy Program," *The New York Times*, January 28, 2007. Copyright © 2007 The New York Times Company. Reprinted with permission.

Jesse McKinley: "Immigrant Protection Rules Draw Fire," *The New York Times*, November 12, 2006, Copyright © 2006 The New York Times Company. Reprinted with permission.

Eduardo Porter: "This Time, It's Not the Economy," *The New York Times*, October 24, 2006. Copyright © 2006 The New York Times Company.

David E. Sanger & Scott Shane: "The Ruling on Tribunals: The Context," *The New York Times*, June 30, 2006. Copyright © 2006 The New York Times Company. Reprinted with permission.

INDEX

Brown v. Board of Education, 118–19, 148–50, 170, 341, 545
threat to, 154
Warren's fears about, 365
"Brutus," 57, 60
Bryan, William Jennings, 503
Buchanan, Pat, 560
Buckley v. Valeo, 127–28, 459
budget, Congress and, 178–79
Budget and Accounting Act (1921), 306
Budget and Impoundment Control Act (1974), 246*n*
bureaucracy, 284–323
appointment process and, 304–5
Congress and, 292, 307–10
control of, 301–10
credibility of, 290
efficiency of, *289*, 290, 318, 321–23
Homeland Security Department and, 284–86
motivational considerations of, 301–3
possible reduction of, 310–11, 314–18, 321–23
principle-agent problem and, 303–5
procedural control and, 305
war on terrorism and, 286
bureaucratic drift, 304, 310
Bureau of Indian Affairs, U.S., 161
Burger, Warren, 96, 139, 143, 156, 158, 375
Burnham, Walter, 427
Burr, Aaron, 439
Bush, George H. W., 24, 26, 93, 166, 306, 509
Cheney as secretary of defense for, 264
Congress and, 231
Joint Chiefs of Staff and, 263
judicial appointees of, 334, 335, 337, 355, 368
1992 election loss of, 450
NSC and, 263
Panama invasion ordered by, 242–43
partisan struggles and, 219
public appearances of, 269–70
reporters and, 575
as vice president, 264
Bush, George W., 578
abortion ban desired by, 365
appointments by, 262
approval rating of, 271, 378–79
bipartisanship requested by, 488
Bush doctrine of, 237–38
cabinet of, 262

Cheney as vice president of, 264
communication skills of, 276
as compassionate conservative, 393
Congress and, 231
domestic surveillance program of, 173–75
drug company funding of, 522–23
in election of 2000, 324–26, 422*n*, 440, 450, 459, 460, 491, 504, 530
in election of 2004, 24, 425*n*, 440, 447, 450–55, 469, 504, 590
energy policy of, 31–33, 246
executive agencies and, 273
executive orders issued by, 275–76
executive privilege claimed by, 246, 343
faith-based initiatives policy of, 530
federalism of, 93–94
filibuster threat and, 267–68
flag-burning amendment and, 72
framing and, 587
Homeland Security Department created by, 249–50, 271
hurricanes and, 244
"intelligence czar" and, 25
Internet as campaign tool of, 512
Iraq war and, 23–24, 243, 263, 378–79, 560–62, 592
judicial appointments of, 225–26, 335–36, 361
judicial nominations of, 215–16
Kuhn as friend of, 542
management strategy of, 306
media portrayal of, 402–3, 576
Medicare bill signed by, 265, 266
Miers nomination and, 336, 547
military tribunals set up by, 146, 281–83, 329
national protection and, 241
No Child Left Behind Act and, 92
partisanship and, 219–20, 445
policies of, 487
privatization increased by, 321–22
public appearances of, 270
public opinion and, 400
same sex marriage and, 81

Senate partisanship and, 184
September 11 terrorist attacks and, 284, 577
Social Security reform and, 210, 398
stem cell research bill vetoed by, 213
Supreme Court appointments of, 27, 546–47
tax policies of, 24, 398
in 2000 election, 509
and 2006 election, 455
veto and, 248, 250
war on terrorism of, 145–46, 233–35, 265, 281–83, 306, 343–44, 393
Bush, Jeb, 512
Bush, Laura, 269
Bush doctrine, 237–38
Bush v. Gore, 337
Butler, Pierce, 46
by-product theory, 15
Byrd, Robert, 223*n*

cabinet, 260, 262, 294
Cable News Network (CNN), 130, 563–64, 570–71
CACI International, 31
California, 547
gerrymandering in, 192–93
illegal alien referendum in, 443
immigration in, 159, 160
Proposition 187 in, 160–61
Proposition 209 in, 413
recall election in, 444
same sex marriage and, 81
welfare in, 93
California, University of, 165
California Civil Rights Initiative, 168
Cameron, Charles M., 265
campaign contributions, 11*n*
campaign finance, 457–60
Campbell, John, 109
Canada, 41
capital punishment, 141–42
Capuano, Mike, 191
Cardozo, Benjamin, 118, 137
Carter, Jimmy, 26, 262
draft evaders pardoned by, 244
Case Act (1972), 226
"Case of the Dwindling Docket Mystifies the Supreme Court" (Greenhouse), 373–75
casework, 187
categorical grants-in-aid, 87–89, *87, 89, 90*
caucuses, 197, 198, 210, 228, 512–15
caucus system, 240
CBS, 378
CBS Evening News, 565, 575

funding for, 92
Hurricane Katrina and, 25
war on terrorism and,
24–25
home rule, 83
Home School Legal Defense
Fund, 455
homosexuality, 144–45
Hoover, Herbert, 503
Hoover Institution, 401
Hopwood v. Texas, 166
House of Commons, British,
39, 178
House of Representatives,
U.S.:
Agriculture Committee of,
20, 199, 204–5, 207, 208
Appropriations Committee
of, 198, 199, 204, 216, 551
Armed Services Committee
of, 204
bicameralism and, 183–84
bills per session of, 206
Budget Committee of, 198
California gerrymandering
and, 192–93
campaign committees of,
514
campaign expenditures for,
190, 455, 482
Clinton's impeachment
and, 184
committee meetings in,
308
in Connecticut Plan, 44
in Constitution, 45, 47–48
Constitutional amendments
and, 61, 62
debate in, 211–12
discharge petition in, 208
elections and, 63, 435, 438
electoral college and, 439
electoral districts of, 440
electoral system and,
185–94
Energy and Commerce
Committee of, 204, 222*n,*
540
Ethics Committee of, 198*n,*
222
federal judges and, 334
flag-burning amendment
and, 72–73, 129
impeachment power of, 227
lawmaking ability of,
183–84
organization of, 183–84,
198–99
oversight and, 308
Oversight and Government
Reform Committee of,
322
partisanship in, 184
party leadership in, 183–84
presidential elections and,
239

Republican control of,
505
rulebook for, 18
Rules Committee of, 204,
211, 212, 216, 229
Senate vs., 233–35
seniority rule in, 207, 209
subcommittees in, 207
terms of, 47
Texas gerrymandering and,
193–94
turnovers in, 192
in 2004 elections, 24, 452
in 2006 election, 24
vetoes overridden by, 213,
248
Washington's refusal of re-
quest by, 245
Ways and Means Commit-
tee of, 199
whip system in, 223
see also Congress, U.S.; Sen-
ate, U.S.; Speaker of the
House
House Practice, 18
Housing and Urban Develop-
ment Department
(HUD), U.S., 297
Houston Chronicle, 579
"How 3 G.O.P. Veterans
Stalled Bush Detainee
Bill" (Hulse et al.),
233–35
Hoyer, Steny, 198
Huckabee, Mike, 456
Hughes, Charles Evans, 78
Hughes, Karen P., 269, 400
Hulse, Carl, 233–35
Human Rights Campaign
Fund, 163
Hume, David, 7
Humphrey, Hubert, 509
hurricanes, 23, 25
Hussein, Saddam, 23–24, 25,
243, 276, 378, 453, 560
Hustler magazine, 130

IBM, 527
Idaho, 316
ideology, 536
in party identity, 492
in political parties, 505
"I Have a Dream" speech, 150
illusion of saliency, 409–10
"Immigrant Protection Rules
Draw Fire" (McKinley),
108–9
immigrants, immigration,
159–61, 387, 388, 398
illegal, 108–9
public opinion and, 387,
388
Immigration and Nationality
Services Act (1965), 160
Immigration Reform and Control Act (1986), 160

impeachment, 227
see also Clinton, Bill, impeachment of; Johnson,
Andrew, impeachment of
implementation, 291–92
implied powers, 79
incumbency, 185, 186–92,
189
Indian Self-determination and
Education Assistance Act
(1975), 161
informal bargaining, 13
informational benefits, 535
infotainment, 565
inherent powers, 241
initiative, 550
initiatives, 443–44
Inouye, Daniel, 71
In Re Oliver, 119*n*
institution principle, 16–19,
23, 28, 29
Articles of Confederation
and, 41, 68
Bill of Rights and, 120, 170
Brown v. Board of Education
and, 150, 170
Budget and Accounting Act
and, 306, 319
bureaucracies and, 292,
293, 319
and checks and balances,
76, 96, 106
collective action and, 109
committee system and, 204,
208, 209, 211, 230
Congress and, 76, 180, 181,
183, 202, 204, 206, 208,
209, 211, 230, 234, 235,
260, 278, 292, 293, 305,
319, 375
constitutional amendments
and, 61, 68, 72
Constitution and, 46–47,
66, 77, 106
courts and, 76, 344, 346,
351, 370
election outcome effected
by process as, 432,
442
electoral college and, 239,
278
energy policy and, 33
federalism and, 80, 83, 106
G. W. Bush and, 25
increasing voter turnout
and, 466
interest groups use of judicial branch and, 544
legislative supremacy and,
97, 106
party rules and, 513, 517
policy inconsistent with
public opinion as, 412
political participation regulated by electoral process
as, 425

technology used by, 510–12
third parties and, 506–9
2004 election and, *508*
see also party identity; party
 systems
political socialization, 384–92
political speech, 126–28
politics:
 as collective action, 12–16
 complexity of, 10, 21, 28
 definition of, 10, 28
 five key principles of, 10–29
 purpose and, 11–12
 "retail," 12
 "wholesale," 12
polls, polling, 404–6, 415, 454
 design of, 406, 407–9
 measurement error of, 406
 probability sampling in,
  404
 push polling and, *406,* 409
 random digital dialing in,
  405
 sample size of, 406
 selection bias in, 404–5
Populist movement, 550
Populist party, 502–3, 506
pork-barrel legislation, 21, 94,
 188, 216–17, 298
pornography, 131–32
Port Authority of New York
 and New Jersey, 82
Postal Service, U.S., 296
poverty programs, 90
Powell, Colin, 23, 25, 233, 234,
 263
Powell, Lewis, 167
PRA (Personal Responsibility
 and Work Opportunity
 Reconciliation Act), 93,
 301
precedents, legal, 328, 373
precinct captains, 514
presidency, 236–83, *261*
 administrative state and,
  271–77
 budget and, 306
 Congress and, 18, 224, 231,
  236–39, *307*
 congressional powers given
  to, 180
 Congress vs., 104–5
 in Constitution, 239–51,
  254–56
 constitutional principles
  and, 21
 of 1800–1933, 256–57
 elections and, 438–39
 executive office of, 271–73
 executive orders and, 251,
  254, 274–76
 expressed powers of, 240,
  241–51, 254
 formal resources of power
  by, 260–65
 lobbying of, 542

performance ratings of,
 271, *272*
policy and, 265
post-New Deal power gain
 by, 257–58, 260
power bases of, 266–71
public and, 268–71
regulatory review and, 273
and separation of powers,
 76
Supreme Court's relation-
 ship with, 52, 360–61
veto power of, 18, 213
see also executive branch
presidential debates, in election of, 2004, 454–55
Presidential Election Campaign Fund, 460
presidential power, 146,
 258–59
press, freedom of, 129–30
see also First Amendment
press release, 579–81
primary elections, 483–85
priming, 586
principal-agent relationship,
 19
principals, 18–19
print media, 563–64, 565–66
Printz v. United States, 95
prior restraint, 129–30, 569
Prisoner's Dilemma, 533–35,
 583
privacy, right to, 120, 142–46,
 342
privatization, 317–18, 321–23
privileges and immunities
 clause, 81
professional legislature, 186
Professional Services Council,
 322
Progressive era, 502, 506, 509
Progressive Party, 508
Progressive reformers, 428,
 508
Prohibition, 61, 62, 64, 69
project grants, 89
property, 7, 55
proportional representation,
 431–32
proposal power, 206
Proposition 22, 81
Proposition 187, 160–61
Proposition 209, 168, 413
prospective voting, 448
protected speech, 126–30, *127*
PRWORA (Personal Responsibility and Work Opportu-
 nity Reconciliation Act,
 93
Pryor, William, 361
Public Affairs Council, 401
Public Broadcasting System
 (PBS), 570
public goods, 7, 10
public interest groups, 527

public law, *327,* 328
public opinion, 269, 378–80,
 396–404
 origins of, 382–96
 policy influenced by,
  410–13
 political ideology and,
  392–93, 396
 political socialization and,
  384–92
 polls of, 404–6
Public Transportation Act
 (2005), 94
"Publius," 57
Pulitzer, Joseph, 574
purposive benefits, 535
push polling, *408, 409*

Quayle, Dan, 264
Queenan, Joe, 402

race, in party identity, 490–91,
 492
racial gerrymandering, 433
racism, 385
radio, 563, 564–65, 568, 572
Radio Act (1928), 365
Randolph, Edmund, 43–44, 46
Rasul v. Bush, 103
Rather, Dan, 575
rationality principle, 11–12, 23,
 28, 29, 173
 beliefs driven by objective
  political interests, 390
 Bill of Rights and, 112, 170
 bureaucracy and, 290, 301,
  304, 319, 321
 candidates converge toward
  median voters as, 448
 Congress and, 73, 180, 182,
  185, 195, 199, 230, 259,
  278, 321
 Constitution and, 47, 66, 68,
  77
 of cost in political information gathering, 397
 court challenges and, 367,
  370
 elections and, 186, 230
 energy policy and, 33
 executive branch and, 321
 federalism and, 78, 106
 Federalists vs. Antifederalists and, 55, 68
 free-ride incentive and,
  534
 grants-in-aid and, 109
 G. W. Bush and, 24
 of ideologies as informational shortcuts, 392
 impact of a single vote and,
  468
 and Iraq War, 520
 judges and, 326, 370
 lack of voter participation
  and, 467